New York Book Festival 2016

Awarded an

'Honorable Mention'

To

Carole Jordan:

For this Autobiography; **All** Written in Rhyme of:

*"Until I Flew...
   & On The Inside;
      Became Beautiful!"*

"Until I Flew... & On The Inside... Became Beautiful!" Copyright © 2016, by Carole Jordan. All rights reserved. No part of this document may be reproduced in any manner whatsoever or transmitted in any form or by any means, electronic, mechanical, photocopying, recording, or otherwise, without prior written permission of Carole Jordan.

Until I Flew....
....& On The Inside;
Became Beautiful!

An Autobiography
By

Carole Jordan

A Conversation Of Realization, Travelling From:

Pain to Peace

Victim to Victorious

&

Rage to Rest with Riches Residing in our Heart

With: Striving Dissipated and Triumphantly Thriving Instigated

Where: In-spite of me became In-spite of them

&

When: Nourished, I Flourished!

Notes

May they Bless Your Recovery

& For 'ease' available in a TRILOGY:

Until I Flew...
PART ~ 1
À Paris   (To Paris)

Until I Flew...
PART ~ 2
Après Paris   (After Paris)

Until I Flew...
PART ~ 3
À Paris; Encore!   (To Paris; Again!)

Plus
Coming soon

Carole Jordan's much anticipated release:

"The He In Me!"

All available on:
Amazon & Kindle

Notes

May they Bless Your Recovery

MY PURPOSE:

To provoke thought, break illusions and effect change,
For inner-healing and growth
Through: Education & Empowerment.

~~~~oOo~~~~

MY MISSION STATEMENT:

To move people:
From "Where they are"
To "Where they desire and deserve to be.'

~~~~oOo~~~~

MY VISION:

For woe-men: to be women of inner strength, through love, power and protection of themselves. And enable men, to be gentle once again.

~~~~oOo~~~~

OUR INNER-POWER:

Self-respect
Self-observation
Self-determination
&
Self- choice.

Notes

May they Bless Your Recovery

Table of Contents

Purpose	Page	5
Table of Contents	Page	7
About The Author	Page	8
Introduction	Page	10
Prelude	Page	14

PART ONE ~

À Paris   (To Paris)

Chapter 1	Step On Up!	Page	23
Chapter 2	Step On In!	Page	42
Chapter 3	Step On Through…	Page	66
Chapter 4	Keep Stepping	Page	96
Chapter 5	Step On Relentlessly	Page	126
Chapter 6	Step With Consistency	Page	144
Chapter 7	Step With Persistence	Page	171
Chapter 8	Step With Resilience	Page	201
Chapter 9	Step With Intent	Page	219
Chapter 10	Step In Truth	Page	242
Chapter 11	Step, Just Step	Page	270

PART TWO ~

Après Paris   (After Paris)

Chapter 12	Step, Because We Must	Page	285
Chapter 13	One More Step	Page	308
Chapter 14	Step, Remarkably Onward	Page	330
Chapter 15	Step, Encore	Page	355
Chapter 16	Step Unconditionally	Page	388
Chapter 17	Step In One's Own Truth!	Page	410

PART THREE ~

À Paris; Encore!   (To Paris; Again!)

Conclusion		Page	447
Bonus Chapter	Step! One More Time! Because….	Page	454
Acknowledgements		Page	515

Notes

May they Bless Your Recovery

About The Author

Carole was born in a seaside town made popular by the Victorian aristocracy, on the northwest English coast, with 3 piers, a Tower and many Theaters to its credit, where in the 60's the Beatles played and the Queen visited. Though from Blackpool she departed at the age of 19 years, to study and lay claim to her nursing career, her earliest dream from yesteryear, as to it she held steadfast, through her sheer determination, she was to achieve it.

It was 15 years after her career began and following a Caribbean island vacation, Carole was to start to relinquish the boundaries of her past that had held her back, as a new beginning began to beckon her. And it across the dateline and off to Auckland on the northern island of New Zealand, where she was to live for five years, and though she settled well, her nursing career took a tumble, so it was off to Australia, Sydney in New South Wales she was to venture in continued pursuit of her nursing profession. But alas, with the weather too hot and humid for her comfort, 8 months later it was an interstate relocation down to Melbourne on the southeast coast, where a further four years were to pass, she was employed in the nursing field, though not her preferred of Occupational Health & Safety which she missed, and with work and health unsatisfactory, she departed those shores after a choice to move to France, where in Paris she attempted to learn a **nouvelle**, new language, before travelling **'dans le sud de la France'** down to the south of France, to pursue her new dream, to renovate a property and become her own boss as she was to open a **'Chambre d'Hote,'** a Bed & Breakfast retreat, or a **'Gite**,' Holiday Cottage, close by the Mediterranean Sea.

~~~ooOOoo~~~

For Carole had come from a childhood of adversity, where constant abuse was a daily encounter to face, yet through it all she had survived, and even though, 4 out of 5 decades her life had been-threatened, somehow, still she lived and pulled through, becoming determined as her experiences grew, taking a route, from survival through to recovery, where eventually, thriving became possible. For whatever evolved posing as barriers against her, somehow from somewhere, she mustered the strength to plough right on through, determined to be healed as she let her soul grow and repair, for she persisted so consecutively so; deliberately determined to discover an antidote to her poisonous past, to become the person who she believed she was able and deserved to be, thriving, enveloped by most favorable future prospects, as her heart no longer dead, but restored, with genuine love within, to be gratefully, revered and adored.

And so it was, she leant to master the art of regrouping "Me, Myself and I," as she transposed a catalogue of corrosive-errors, into an aspect, of not viewing misfortune or mistakes as overwhelming, but as an opportunity to lean and grow as she formed her personal ledger of lessons, that had served unwittingly as tools of transformation, of she who used to be on the blame, holding in her hand a first class ticket, but she was to relinquish it, as she jumped right off, onto stable ground, which no longer shuddered beneath her feet. For forgiveness, a tricky route at first, but though practice she mastered it, and it served as a friend and not a foe, as it aided to propel her forward, to a future that was beckoning her, with new-found hope, where what she had always deserved, a life in which to flourish, were awaiting her.

For low self-esteem and confidence that she lacked, became personality traits that were surpassed, as worth-less-ness was replaced by a healthier worthy-ness, as that ingrained fear, that she knew not by name, though it effected all she ever thought or did, yet all were to be eradicated and expelled, as no longer could those previously harmful days and ways from her abusive childhood, effect that future of pleasant and nurturing memories she was determined to amass.

And all this became possible that she was to escape her debilitating past, when eventually Carole recognized a missing though crucial element, to first admit and accept what was done against her, so at last with that key finally found, she was able to move on, travelling through those inviting doors widely swung open before her. Then happily, healing on the inside, onward, she was heading toward to an honest life, moving away from pain and distress, to the one she deserved of comfort, peace and a gentle warmth in which to bathe her soul, as her heart became whole, and living afresh and anew, in *freedom*, was what she was **truly worthy** and able to do!

Notes

May they Bless Your Recovery

Introduction

> "The beauty of a woman is not in the clothes she wears, the figure that she carries, or the way she combs her hair. The beauty of a woman is seen in her eyes, because that is the doorway to her heart, the place where love resides. True beauty in a woman is reflected in her soul. It's the caring that she lovingly gives, the passion that she shows & the beauty of a woman only grows with passing years."
> ~ Audrey Hepburn

From whence my journey began, to where I now am, it would be a great underestimation and gross misrepresentation to say my achievement was easy, for initially, how could I even believe goodness was possible for me to enjoy, when my mind pre-weaved, woven with threads of debilitating negative emotions, so impossible to conceive, for the hurt and the pain from the history of the traumatic life I was dealt, lingered in the present, where neglect and violence had served me so ill, where to be told and shown what was wrong was right, then to try and go through life, fighting against the current, for all truths that my parents showed and told, were complete lies, and love, caring and certainly any form of support, to a child so young were withheld, with only arrows of hate, coming my way. But was only until one day, by chance, when a revelation was to come my way, and those prolonged decades of debilitating pain, I trudged through, were of far less significance, than the destination we I chose to head toward.

And those crevices of my mind, that had bee made into deep ruts, from the inherited and debilitating curses I had endured, although science said it was a problem, and agreed, I knew it to be so, but that was of little relevance to stop me to be, for I, through self-adaptation, was determined to find a magnificent way, for I was resigned to never to give in. For I made a decision and chose to destroy those inherited lingering and debilitating curses causing damaging destruction through my life, where the only predictability of my existence, was that at any unpredicted moment, violent behavior, hovered everywhere, when a hand, hidden from view, would whip so quickly around the corner or from behind a door, delivering increasing increments of harm, to that frighten little child, who had, nowhere to run, nowhere to turn.

And they who delivered such vengeance, whose blood ran in my veins, my mother and my father, controlled me totally, through the portions of dogmatic reign, and my childhood had passed me by, and my adolescent too, indeed, a qualified nurse was I, and still I held no idea, of what harm they had done, so emotionally to me, rendering me so disturbed, that a relationship, of normality, it appeared impossible to function in, and why, for I had never once seen by example how it was done, isolated with them, without any friends, or relationships of any kind for a blueprint to work from, and so there I was, wandering around in the dark, not even aware that there was light, that I should be looking for, but thank goodness, that on that bright day on my first sole vacation in the Caribbean, "Where to from here?" became a notion for me to explore, and true, what was to unfold, was many a battle on my road to recovery I was to go through, but the good news was: one day, I was to win the war!

Yet true, many-a-trial and tribulation was yet to be uncovered, as I hiked up, many a steep learning curve, but that mattered far less, from the road to self-discovery, along my road to self-recovery, as any desire to give-in, I resisted, as I was to implement new-found courage to combat the unfamiliar, and so much easier it would have been to give-up, and end up right back where I started from. But process, that would not have been, and quite boldly for the benefit of me, my future, to those trials and lessons from errors, for my recovery to carry-on, as quite brazen I became, as "Bring it on" I beckoned, without reserve and quite enthusiastically, for I grew and knew, that each challenge I overcame, through progression, I was placing a greater distance between me and my destructive past, and that hurtful place of self-loathing, self-blame and worthlessness, I used to live, as that bitterness and rage that used to live within, were dissolved away, through a healing heart and a soothed soul, and rewards to adore, harmony, triumph and victory, were to call me by name.

For then, with progression toward my freedom, escaping those shackles of the past, was I to believe that, "Dreams are a possibility, really do come true?" And was I to find one of my own, refusing to absorb any longer the words of scorn delivered my mother, all through my childhood and beyond, "Get your head out of the clouds!" Followed relentlessly by, "When will you learn? "I've told you, you're wasting your time, dreaming your days away." Or what about my father, his mantra to me, spoken with such harsh and abrupt emotions, "You're stupid!" "You're as thick as 2 short planks and you always will be!" But his curses not done with his frequently finishing line, diminishing my self-image, designed certainly to demoralize, "I've told you before, *you'll* never amount to anything!"

"Wow! Thanks for your vote of confidence" I could have said, but of cause I dare not, as I absorbed what he told me like a sponge, not daring to disagree, for I knew that would land, further trauma to collide with me, and more obviously or absurd "Why would I?" When as that innocent child, held captive of their indoctrinating thoughts, I held none of my own, for no other examples anywhere had I seen or heard, to counteract his definition of me, to be anything except the truth. Yet just possibly, somehow, I knew of Oscar Wild's perception, that we may all be sitting in the gutter, but we may still choose, to look up at the stars, for dreaming is absolutely free, as not a penny does it cost, to hold dear and nourish our ideas we keep tucked within until the time arrives for them to flourish. And really, why would I not?" For those terrible people, who were supposed to protect me were the ones who caused me such tremendous harm, and this I knew, "They had stolen my childhood, but I refused to permit them to steel, my adulthood!"

And so invaluable my compatriots of 'resilience and persistence' along this journey proved to be aiding tremendously my recovery as I, was able to move from poisonous point A to blissful point B, as I was to take possibly the longest journey of all, to travel, that 18 inches between the heart and the head, and unite the 2, as I grew in gentle appreciation of myself, as I denounced my past of having any power over me, as daily, I pushed on through, determined, to feed my spirit, until it lived once again, and I was freely able to give and receive love, to soar like and eagle, and master my future, determining it to be, a life spent, free from pain, in peace and harmony.

And how wonderful, to rise above those barriers of adversity, as my broken wings, almost miraculously healed and learnt, how to fly, knowing that my history was only a start, no more than a geographical location, and formed little relevance to my final destination, of reaching my desires and dreams of my chosen destiny. And true, a 'job in progress,' I remained for quite a prolonged time, as rewards came my way, in snippets of wisdom, that regret reduces recovery and rest, with rapid restoration, impossible, unless forgiveness is granted, so I, relinquished the debilitating rage, and released it from deep within, casting out their sin, that they transposed onto me, for I, in-spite of them, was to be me, and live free!

And so I grew, as I dared to dream of wonderful opportunities and good and marvellous things to do, and how I could help others through the things I'd endured and been subjected to, for now my heart has healed, but for those who remain so deeply entrenched in pain, I pray you get away from that place, and believe, that when you are at the bottom of a dark and dingy place, it is possible to use counterbalance of force, as from its depths you push hard, like a springboard right back to the top. So above all, when all else seems lost, cradle the seed of hope, close to your heart, and never let it be lost, as within you nurture courage, as the day will arrive, when what you planted bears fruit and flourishes, and as the old unhelpful is replaced with the new delightful, you will discover yourself to be in a far better place, to lovingly embrace.

May each one of you, be blessed as you read this, and through this heartfelt story of sensitivity with occasional humour thrown in, may this 'bucket of hindsight,' form at least a perfect portion of your, 20/20 vision.

Prelude

From centuries past to centuries present, strewn are "Women of Valor" throughout history, where their personal commitment, made all the difference, to their own lives and others they positively impacted, where they let not their birthplace, that simple equation of geography and circumstances effect them adversely, noting it significantly, to symbolize only their 'starting position' while holding insignificant relevance to their 'finishing position.' For these women let not, race, color, creed, social-economic status or disability to form as a formidable opponents against them. For in totality, it was not what was on the outside, but what lay on the inside, from where these "Women of significance" drew their guiding and perpetuating strength.

And the dates provided of the evidence below, that from so long ago, women have pushed through societal restraints, pushing against what they were expected, nay permitted to do, yet they, refused to be held back, forging their own path, in a world, that was unwelcoming to them, yet with inner-strength, they did exactly what they must, to help themselves, and along their way, lift others up too, to a place higher, with greater safety and fulfillment, which they deserved to achieve; as step-by-step, they placed on the ground one after the other, determined to get from place A to place B, and when there was no direct path to be found, well, they simply took the higher road, and forging a way through. And what an example to you and me, for if we experience a bad day, we can reflect on these ladies lives and contemplate, "Oh my" if they can do and achieve *all* that, to 'fight the good fight' against *all* the odds, to come out of *it all* triumphantly in victory, surely, I too, am going to give *it all* a jolly good shot."

~~~o0o~~~

For it was way back in 1875 when Mary McLeod Bethune, the fifteenth child of seventeen, was born in South Carolina, and unlike the rest of her family was born free and not into slavery. And what was to serve her well, as she seized upon her talent of reading, as pioneering, she pushed and partitioned to be permitted to go to school, and so successful Mary, later to Chicago she moved, breaking free of her boundaries, as most uncommonly she attend a school for Missionaries, as it was so on her heart to travel to Africa, and to 'make a difference' there. Yet her choice was denied, as that was not 'done' in her day, but undeterred she was to contemplate, "OK. So really, what road now, can I take?" So persistence won through, of what next to achieve it was teaching that she set her goal and mind to. Then, through a 'chance meeting,' she received encouragement, and seizing her presented opportunities, took action as Mary them moved to Georgia before on to Florida, and there in 1904, she was able to establish a school, with students adding in number of 5 girls, significantly so, and 1 boy, her son, who had not seen his father since the aged 2.

And blessed for the building, but it, completely ill equipped, it was a 'make-do and-mend' attitude, that prevailed for Mary, as around the streets she searched for discarded wooden pallets for furniture, and burnt or charcoaled wood to serve as pencils. Then how wonderfully from that small acorn, a great Oak tree grew, as in just 6 years, had over a hundred students and boarders. With the school training in business matters too, and maintained by her entrepreneurial fundraising with local businesses and Church donations greatly helping.

To achieve so much and get that far, Mary's journey had not been easy, and true, her first desire was to visit Africa and be a missionary, though that prohibited in that era, but Mary undeterred by anything that faced her, and through her passion of 'inclusion of all,' girls and the poor, where she stayed benefitted from her work there. Significantly Mary an advocate for African-American youth, women's and men's 'Rights.' So much so, her commitment to propelling herself forward to new territories of roads less-traveled, as to many an organization she became, a Director or President, able to positively impact the needs of many, through her fortified efforts bearing many achievements and causing her to cross paths and enjoy a friendship with Eleanor Roosevelt, The First Lady of America. And to Mary's credits, in 1930, she was recognized and included on a journalist's list of America's greatest women, before posthumously in 1973, Mary was inducted into the National Women's Hall of Fame.

~~oOo~~

In New York in 1797 Sojourner Truth, had no control, as she was born into slavery, yet she chose a name to give herself, and speaking only Dutch, at only 7 years old, she was inherited by her 2nd master, before she was sold to her 3rd owner as still a life without her control, with her 4th final sale in 1810, for the sum of $175. But *hope*, was to meet her as she fell in love, but no, for her owner forbade it, and cruelly to have him beaten snatched, stole, her lover away, until he killed him. Yet before that was done, her lover had fathered a child, and then with an arranged marriage Truth bore 5 children more, and like Mary, the last was born into freedom, but treated, not so. So Truth mustered all her courage as she clung so tightly and cradled the child in her arms, as daringly in 1826, she escaped and fled from her brutal employer, and in a farm close by, received care and support and was able to purchase her freedom. Then, through her huge portions of inner-strength and commitment, unprecedented for that era, she, took her ex-owner to court for illegally selling her son, and her case, she won!

A willful-power was hers to harness, for strength she gained, and in 1844, with Gender Equality and Women's Rights as her motivators Truth joined an Abolitionists group, and there she met the man, who was to write and publish six years later, her memoirs in secret, significantly creating such an income, that she was able to buy an up-market house in Northampton. And Truth didn't stop there, for her commitment to making a difference saw her speak publically at the 1st, National Women's Rights Conference in the same year, where, many a-grand impromptu speech was to follow, with *"Ain't I a Woman?"* perhaps her most famous. And Truth never ceased in her goal to effect positive change, as she, bearing huge significance, forged a path on that road previously untraveled, and through her efforts she met such greats as President Lincoln and President Grant, to aid to achieve greater benefits for all. "Oh my" what a life well spent, and in 1883 shortly before her death, reaching an astonishing age way back then of 86, it was to be said of Truth, "Her body was weak, but her eyes, remained, most bright."

~~oOo~~

Jane Adams, the youngest of 9 brothers and sisters in 1860 was born in Illinois into a prosperous family, to parents of English American decent, though mother died in childbirth when she was just a toddler. Then with the passing of only a couple of years Jane contracted a serious illness, that spared her life, but left her with a severe spine curvature, that from therein, caused her emotional and physical problems. Yet, that failed to stop her pushing through them, as determined was she to follow her childhood dream to become a doctor, which in 1881 after the sudden death of her father, ironically she possessed the funds to follow her goal, so off to Pennsylvania she was to go, to attend Medical School, and wonderfully, her siblings and stepmother beside her for support and comfort, yet sadness was to prevail after just 1 year, her ill health inhibited her from being able to continue on.

Yet her passion remained constant, to help those less fortunate than herself, and her vision to 'make a difference' to achieve success she searched for something else, and through that process, for the middle-class's, Jane became a role-modal and was able to raise and fund in 1889 in Chicago, 'Hull House;' as a 'settlement-house' for the poor and multinational immigrants. Her theme consistent, that a person's circumstances should not be permitted to form a barrier, or pre-determine their destiny, inhibiting their transformation, to achieve something better or improved. And so, confidence was able to be built, as that meeting place, in safety, provided, education, recreation, and hygiene, where women and men were treated equally, and for both, a progressive business mind was encouraged and promoted, and a place where youth and children were cared for, and all purposely so, to soothe the body and the mind.

Later, Jane placed her attentions on Suffragette and Civil Rights, evolving to be an outspoken Pacifist against World War 1, and through her efforts working on international peace, in 1915 she was elected as Chairman of the Women's Peace Party and elected also as the President of the Women's International League for Peace and Freedom. Her worthy legacy includes memorials such as Hull House, which was relocated and preserved as a museum, and with Bronx High School for Academic Careers, and a Business Careers Center in Ohio being positively impacted by her efforts, with a College Residence in Connecticut named after her, perhaps no surprise, in 1931, Jane was awarded the Nobel Peace Prize.

~~oOo~~

Susan Brownell Anthony, born in 1820, and raised in Massachusetts by a Quaker family, with their business in cotton manufacturing, and they, also avid Abolitionists. And as a child, playing with toys was forbidden, yet reading encouraged, as her father supported her education, and when her school teacher refused to teach Susan long division, because she, was not a boy, it was her father's progressive thinking, to employ a Governess, so Susan could learn so much more, than those societal constraints of the day. But in 1837 disaster was to fall, when the panic of the economic depression struck, and like so many other families, her father's wealth was gone, so 2 years later her family moved to New York, where Susan became a school teacher herself, paying off her father's debts, and in 1846 through her skills and efforts, over the Female Department she was promoted to Headmistress; but then just 3 years later in 1849, she chose to leave teaching, as she learnt that as a female, with inequality rife, she earned, a staggering 75% less, performing the same job as her male counterparts.

Efforts to change such unequal situations became her goal, as she put aside her own personal insecurities of her physicality's, as Susan was to blossom into a renowned public speaker, successful, in stirring the voice of change, leading women's movements, for Women's Rights and equality through speeches and journals and the Suffrage movement, for the middle-class and the working class too. And in 1868, The Revolution journal, owned an managed by Susan was first published, with its motto, "The True Republic—Men, their rights and nothing more; Women, their rights and nothing less." In that era, succinctly profound were her statements, yet so sadly, almost from the beginning, after running at a loss financially, the journal only survived 3 years, before it was sold for just $1, and the huge debt hanging over it, was still to be paid in full by Susan.

Though her commitment and campaigning unwavering, and through doing so was arrested and the case sent to court, where her defense of the 14th Amendment was ignored, and she was charged and find, yet undeterred, refusing to be kept down, and seeing a silver lining in the cloud, notching it, not a stumbling block but a steppingstone, as Susan used that adversity of bad and turned it around for good, using that case and situation for what she believed in, to raise her profile, for her positive message pertaining to change, that she so desired to deliver. And that was so, as over 2 States of America her voice was then to be heard, reaching a far wider audience, as she was unafraid to be controversial, with her goals enforced to emancipate women, to gain Equal Rights, for labor, wages and choices, the Rights for African Americans, and for women, 'the Vote.' And the seeds planted by Susan, were not in vein, for her efforts were yet to produce fruit and bloom, as it was to be, 14 years after her death, with battles fought and overcome, that on the 26th August 1920, women were finally granted, the *right* to Vote.

~~o0o~~

Helen Keller, born 1880 in Alabama, lived until a ripe old age of 88, far surpassing the average mortality rate of that day, and how amazingly surprising, as it was against all the odds, as at 19 months old, Helen suffered a serious illness, possibly Rubella, and although it spared her life, when she recovered to some degree, it had taken her hearing and her sight. Disadvantaged, but she was not to live in despair or self-pity, as her inner-drive, her yearning spirit from somewhere within, caused her to surpass and excel all expectations in life, of what she had been predetermined by other to be able to achieve. As at the age of 7, it was not stumbling blocks in her path, when after being inspired by many a Dickens novel, her mother for her daughter, was to search out help for "Where to from here?" And so it was, through connections and introductions that a young lady, also visually impaired of 20-something years, was to be employed as Helen's companion and to help her.

And so a friendship began, which lasted 49 years, and that pivotal point in Helen's life positively turned it around, as knowledge and education were going to prove the key, where suddenly, she was able to start a learning process on the road to understanding the world that surrounded her, of the most simplest things, like how to ask, recognize or comprehend "What is a cup of tea? Then slowly, through that patiently unraveling process, Helen's tantrums and frustrations, though not instantly but eventually, subsided and ceased, as successfully, communication increased and gathering momentum a whole new world opened up to her, where all sorts of comprehensions, became complete.

Then it was school where Helen was most keen to enroll, and from 1888, she attended schools for the deaf and visually impaired, where she became accomplished at reading brail, and in 1904, and at 24 became the first deaf and blind impaired person to earn a Bachelor of Arts degree, and with her achievements and considering herself fortunate, she was keen to help others, became an advocate for people with disabilities, an author of 12 published books and international speaker added to her credits. Yet her passion grew, for the Equality of Women's Rights, and the working-class, and so in 1912, she joined the Industrial Workers of the World, and for them for 2 years, submitted written articles. And with the passing of a decade, Helen co-founded the Helen Keller International Organization, which was most valuably dedicated to researching into the fields of: vision, health and nutrition.

Whilst during her later years, tirelessly she dedicated her time to raising funds for the American Foundation for the Blind, with her vast efforts and travels she visiting 40 countries, and her personal connections the same, knowing inventors, including Alexander Graham Bell, and writers such as Mark Twain, and movie stars, and also USA Presidents who she met along her way. Then in 1965, Helen was elected into the National Women's Hall of Fame at the New York's World Fair, and then posthumously in 1971, Helen was awarded a place in the Alabama Women's Hall of Fame, 3 years after, in her sleep she had died peacefully.

~~oOo~~

Anna Eleanor Roosevelt in 1884 in New York City, was born into a family of wealth of privilege, until at the age of 8 she lost her mother, and before she turned 10, she lost her father to alcoholism, and although her Grandmother took the responsibility to raise her, and from her it is thought Eleanor received little affection, and of herself, in her appearance she lacked confidence, considering herself to be extremely unattractive. Her education lacked for nothing, as tutored privately at home, before being sent to a private finishing school, where slowly, eventually, her confidence began to blossom, as did her relationship with Franklin, who in-spite of the union being opposed by her soon to be mother-in-law, in 1905 she married him. Yet ironically, as a twist of circumstances, in 1918, when Eleanor chose to divorce her husband as he was being unfaithful, it was that same person who opposed the marriage who for the purpose to protect her son's political career, persuaded Eleanor not to do it, and Eleanor under-pressure, ignoring her own gut-instinct, she gave-in and agreed, but only under the proviso that her husband was never again to see the woman he was having an affair with, but when he conceded he lied, as so hurtfully many years later Eleanor leant after he had died, of his word, he did not keep it.

Yet she, refusing to be depressed, putting aside her personal trials, threw herself into the positive changes she could effect, for Women's Rights and the African-American Civil Rights movement, where she appointed Mary McLeod Bethune, as Head of Division of Negro Affairs, as Eleanor became a formidable 'champion for change.' Also joining and working with the Women's Trade Union League, Eleanor raised funds to lobby for; a 48hour week, a minimum wage and the abolition of child labor. And she didn't stop there as she became; a leader, a speaker, an author and a columnist for a women's magazines, before being appointed as the First Lady of New York. With numerous credits to her name, maybe it was best put by President Truman who was to refer to her, not only as the First Lady of the America, but also the First Lady of the world. His opinion dittoed by many, as Eleanor, the longest serving First Lady of America, through her influential and successful endeavors, posthumously in 1999, was included, on the top ten of Gallup's List, of Most Wildly Admired People of the 20th Century.

~~oOo~~

Sarah Breedlove, was born in Louisiana in 1867, an entrepreneur in the making, the first in her family to be born not into slavery, but into freedom. Yet sadness and more was to strike her life, as before the age of six her mother had died and her father died soon after, and in that house she was then being brought up, to escape the abuse from the hands of her brother-in-law, she married at the age of just 14, so she could escape, to a safer place. And then, just 3 years later, she had a child, but because of the death of her husband, she was forced had to bring the child up on her own, so moved to be closer to her brother in St Louis, and there, in 1906 remarried.

And then, a master at survival, it was not a stumbling block but a steppingstone that was to present itself to Sarah, as she like many other women of that day, an unpleasant skin condition of her scalp developed, with hair loss too, yet Sarah, determined to discover a cure, she began experimenting with varying substances of liquids and soaps and other produce purchased at her local stores. Then through her endeavors of trails and errors, of mixing concoctions of 'this and that' in varying quantities, eventually, success was hers, as the right-mix, she was arrived at. Then with a desire to help others with the same issues, she and her husband began selling her new hair products, as they traveled inter-state, and with good marketing, her brand began to expand, and engaging the family, a factory was started to meet the demand, and a mail-order business began.

To also to help women in a different way, Sarah opened a training school, with its culture, to express to women, that their appearance is of significant importance, whilst lecturing on economics, social and even political issues too, while teaching women, how they also could start a successful business. Then quite a philanthropist Sarah became, donating to causes and schools for African American children, Orphanages and others, and joining the National Association for the Advancement of Colored People to effect greater change.

And so successful financially was she, Sarah commissioned the building of her home in New York, in an extremely prestigious area, and there she died at the age of only 51, in 1919. Sarah was considered to be, the first self-made female American millionaire, and posthumously, Sarah's life and works have been highly notarized, as in Chicago 1992, she was inducted into the Junior Achievement Business Hall of Fame, and following on, in Seneca received the same, and admitted to the National Women's Hall of Fame, before in New York, using her married name of Madam Walker, a road was to bear *her* name. The sincere gratitude for all her life's accomplishments continued, as in 1998, Sarah was honored, by appearing on a commemorative postage stamp.

~~oOo~~

Admiration and respect, I hold hugely for the accomplishments of these women, for their strength, their determination and their resilience not to give up, and when they had saved themselves, they held not a concept that, "I'm alright now my job is complete." "No." Wonderfully, amazingly so, after they managed to survive and get through, what they needed to, drawing so magnificently, on not what lay without, but what laid somewhere within, they went on, to help others to fight for what's right. And I contemplate, should I have been faced with 'all that' in those centuries past, when life was a vastly different place to be, "Could I have survived?" And I like to believe, "Yes indeed."

For really, "What other option is there?" One more time, to roll over and take 'it,' or formulate a plan, to get the hell-out of whatever it is you are in. And what I learnt for sure, escape is our best policy, and never to be afraid to leave behind that or those, who serve us least well. For this is our life, and not theirs, and before their words or actions of accusation and condemnation tie us up in knots, rendering it so extremely difficult almost impossible to resist their taunts and curses, reaching deep into our heart or soul. But for ourselves, be not deterred, as quietly, subliminally, without even alerting anyone that we're doing it, we may seek and endeavor until we discover, *our* personal *inner-strength*, that as a tool, a weapon, for our own *protection* and self-*preservation*, "Oh my" 'this' can and will, *serve us* so very extremely well.

So lets seize the opportunity and take a leaf out of the book of these wonderful "Women of Valor," for they have shown examples, how against the odds, when everyone tells you "No" it does not make them right, but possibly most wrong. For draw upon, the lessons these ladies who have gone before us provide us, as perhaps through their stories we may meditate and contemplate, and really they may form as the catalyst for our progression, to move-on purposefully and importantly, really, "Where to from here?"

"Oh my!" To arrive somewhere, somewhere else, at destination where we choose to be, and especially, importantly become someone, who we are pleased to be, a person for whom those curses of words or worse, are all left behind in our past, as quite remarkably we are able to give and receive love, as metaphorically, we blossom into a beautiful butterfly, as on the warmth of a soft breeze with gentle delight, wonderfully we take flight, toward our new, true and prevailing,

PIECE of PEACE!

"AWARENESS"
"Is the First tool in the box of change."
~ Carole Jordan

Part One

~~~ooOoo~~~

À Paris

(To Paris)

Chapter 1

Step On Up!

"An original life is unexplored territory. You don't get there by taking a taxi – you get there by carrying a canoe"
~ Alan Adla

Around the world, a brand new day was dawning, and as the moon faded away, that darkness turned into light and the sunrays of the day came out to play, as hope and anticipation began to shine on the inside of me, for *'that day'* had arrived, that for which I had mastered a plan, I named, "P Day," 'Parisian Day,' 'Promises Day,' or dare I even think 'Perfect Day,' when my fortune was to improve, as I flew far away from that vast island of Australia, as determined was I to be on track, to achieve my next great thing, as through my pre-planned success, I was to dance for joy as "Hip-hip-hooray" were to be words I'd sing.

For surely that was to be, for were my dreams whole and healthy, or was it to transpire, that I was to relinquish those thoughts of optimism, as many a trial and tribulation were to visit me at my new destination, giving way to many a sorrowful situation, and was that place, that I visited for the first time 20 years earlier, to resolve itself as my friend or foe, as possibly, it was to eventuate that 'Problem Day,' lay ahead of me?

Yet learning curves, difficult and steep, were not a stranger to me, for so many I had trampled upon, from my youth, and even younger years, not through choice but necessity, as I needed just to survive, to trudge my way each day through life, and although I knew it not, regimented in control, was what I became, and harder on myself than anybody else, and I, a human-doing, rather than a human-being, striving endlessly, yet searching not for anything better, to improve, to alter or to change me, for in truth, I didn't know of any other way to be, for in my soul, dead, there was only a beating pulse amidst that vast nothingness, of anything positive, for only fear, shame and guilt survived, though in skill, for a life of practice, of it, so well, I learnt to hide.

For mechanisms of distraction accompanied me through life, my antidote, dipping deeply into my career, climbing its ladder, and my hobby, that thing that I enjoyed so, to purchase properties in need of renovation, and how I enjoyed doing that so, and I, became quite a dab-hand at using screw drives, and drills, and saws in tandem with mitre boards, as I was to even put up, my own dado rails, and such a pleasure it all was to do, as the mind, constantly busy with what I had to do, not giving it a nano-second to ever think about anything else, as eagerly each weekend around the countryside I would travel, traversing county lines, from Manchester to Lancashire, visiting all the Mill Stores and

Antique Warehouses, to purchase all my necessities, and exquisitely more, at most favourable prices.

And so my quest, I'd pursue for hours, those *gourmandieses*, petite & special something, a remnant of fabric here, and pieces of ribbon there, and with my expertise all were sewn together, adding fringes and tassels, all so perfectly colour coordinated, to match the little wee vase at the opposite end of the room, perfectly placed, adorning a piece of refurbished antique furniture, aside, the curtains and drapes, which I never did tier of seeing each time I walked in the room, and all hung from beautiful brass curtain rails with matching tie-backs, I placed them everywhere, and always purchased for a bargain price, most fair.

But the hurt and pain, of decades gone by, did not disappear, or even dissolve in the slightest, they were simply hidden under my business, as like a robot I ventured though life, unwittingly harbouring the weight of rejection, that had taken up residence within me, and though no physical scars could be seen outwardly, crippled inside, was life to me, where moving geographically, I had escaped their terrible ways, those of my parents which they cast on me each day, yet emotionally, I was not free, for I unwittingly remained unable to break their formidable curses upon me they had made.

And so rigid control reigned, as I deviated not from my narrow course, which was self-sufficiency and protection, the very best of which I could afford myself, as I buried the past, but one day, it was to come back to haunt me, and how grateful I grew to be, that toxins will-out eventually, for really, was that a revelation that I was so blessed to come my way? As one day, on the inside, I was to be healthy, and fly, nay soar, triumphantly like an eagle, and fly away.

For a Caribbean holiday I was to venture upon, as something kind-of-weird, happened on the beach, as in my mind, I received a notion, nay a clear message, and from where it came from I did not know, I just knew, I had to 'do something for my soul.' But where to find one, was it, Bloomingdales, Fifth Avenue, or down at the bargain-thrift stores, I had not a clue, and as I carried on walking down the beach that conundrum in my mind gave way to great contemplation, and though I knew it not then, that was the catalyst, for a chain reaction was to commence, where lessons, disguised as nightmares, were really precious pieces of wisdom, and when learnt, took my life happily in a new direction, onward, upward, forever forward, toward healing and harmony, where I had the opportunity, to learn, how to be *ME*.

"A miracle, my friend, is an event that creates faith"
~ George Bernard Shaw

"So what to do?" I could not shake that concept from my head, and the amazing thing there, normally, when a thought or concept I could not control, I permitted it not to be there, but that, continually rolling around and jumping up to say "Hello," when I thought it had gone away, but "No" it was not to let go of me, and then quite astonishingly, one morning when I awoke, with a notion I had never before contemplated, I simply said, "I know what I'll do, I'll go working abroad." And so the seed was laid, and I cracked quickly on with the work to be done, as to Bolton Library I did travel, a place of wood-clad walls, and ornate ceilings tall, located in the Exchange Building built in 1853, where I trawled through those beautifully polished wooden bookshelves, for my research, investing the best place for me, and simultaneously, investigations I made, all 'old school' of cause, because this was a time before the Internet, that my Nursing Registration overseas, would be recognized and transferrable, then suddenly it became clear, New Zealand, (NZ) was the place, to be, for me.

But my life "Was it bad?" Certainly not! Especially when viewed on-paper, for really I seemed to be doing rather well, with a career that I loved and was quite excelling in, with house renovations, such joy and accomplishment it bought me, and a financial advantage too, and I safe and secure in both, but in me, that was not to be said, for still, lingering in-between each cell, were those unseen and untouchable lies that I was worth-less, nay, worth nothing, and I held not an ounce of an idea that I was so bruised, battered and torn, that was until, I moved from that dark and caustic place, as I discovered the light at the end of the tunnel, and when, I eventually raised above my impasse, believing it was the lights of another impending disaster, of the lights of an oncoming train, with relief I was to realise, that it was hope that was illuminating on me, and then, toward it, I hurriedly ran.

And so the path I was about to plough, I was to realise, the field in which I had been fallowed, was barren of nutrients, as no sun shone upon it, and not even a glimmer of a warm breeze passed by, and the soil unfertilized, where not even a weed could grow, and the birds, never to be seen flying overhead, and the leaves from the trees, starved, fell to the floor, and disappeared as if like snowflakes, never even there, and the bark crumbled, and the roots withered and died, as within that hostile environment, only death, for nothing healthy was able to survive.

But a plan it transpired to be, as I organized the first chain of the positive reaction of "Where to from here?" Though at that time, I remained obliviously unaware of what truly laid ahead, hidden and underlying those benefits of my choices, yet of trials, twists and turns that were to reveal themselves to me, and the longest journey I was to take, was not the 11271 miles of a simple plain ride away, but the longest and most complex journey of all I had commenced upon, as courageously, or perhaps in blind belief, I placed one step before the other, along those twists and turns of the maize of roads to navigate, as I was on route not to simply dwell in another geographical location, for that proved of far less in significance, than the road I was to travel, to heal and get to know, me.

And there it was, that something, which I knew not what it was, kept niggling at me, and knowing no better of what to do, it was off to the library I was to go, located by the sea, on the northern shores of Auckland, on that northerly island of NZ, and searching for what, still a conundrum, it remained unknown, and as I flicked my fingers through those books, seated on the powder blue metal shelves, in neatly regimented rows, many a book I took in my hand, and scanned its cover with my eyes, before venturing to peruse the synapse of the book, then a paragraph I may read to see if I was intrigued to read more, yet one title perplexed me, "There's more to life than sex and money" and confused, as I thought instantly, "No. There's definitely not!" But so much more I had to learn, and so fortunately, I grew and realised, that title, happened to be true.

And then I came across it, almost hidden out of view, that tiny book, of not so many pages, with were all tattered and dog-eared, yet still, I furred to take it in my hand, my eyes keen to see, yet really, that rainbow, so faded, struck a cord directly somehow, with something inside of me, perhaps an awakening of some sort, but I recognized it not, for it was something I had not felt before, and as I fingered through its pages, as patiently I turned each one, a message was to scream at me, and I was almost to be with excitement overcome, for there I read on the pages, a revelation, that was to serve me so amazingly well, "When your climbing your career ladder, make sure, its leaning on the right wall."

There it was, 'Bamb!' a cord those words struck with me, igniting something inside of me, though still I knew not what it was, though I knew I wanted to know more, and right there an internal eagerness erupted as never before. And the first astonishing thing, having never been a big reader, in-fact true say, a pretty small one really, posed not as a barrier, as I trotted merrily along that road to self-discovery, onto recovery, as metaphorically, a beautiful and grand door swung wide-open into a perceived magical place, which previously I knew not, as the cells in my body, no longer dead, but tingling all alive, and with my mind and total being, I was so eager to investigate more.

For really, what could life possibly hold in store for me, could it be, a place where I was equal, where I quit putting everyone else's needs above mine, possibly just in hope that one-day just somebody, may like me just the way I am, and I could stop putting everyone else first, in a higher position than me, submitting to all their wants and desires, at the expense of my own, for wasn't I so consecutively taught, "That they were right and I was wrong" no matter, "Who" they happened to be. "Oh my goodness" could I dare to believe it could be true, "Was I to relinquish those septic emotions?" from that catalogue of errors from my past, strewn with troubles and strife, as I *dared to believe*, for just once, *in me.*

And so, "Seek and you will find," that's what they say, and I found for me it to be true, as I set a wheel in motion, as I considered "Where to from here?" I was determined to leave all that tricky stuff behind that tripped me up along my way, for as many times I as fell, mustering all my strength, I got up just one more time, because ultimately with no other option or possibility, I had to, for I was only able to rely on me, to survive and escape that emotional hell. But then, was that toxicity, delivered to me by my parents, only to form a part of my history, and not my legacy, for suddenly, the words so transferable, came ringing in my head, that a tutor had told the class as I a fledging nurse at 19 years, at that 'Hospital on the Hill,' "It's not quantity its, quality of life, we should pursue." And that phrase so powerfully afresh and succinct in its simplicity, stuck a cord deep for my contemplation, as I was to consider, my destination and time frame for arriving there, I knew not, but I knew for a better future, I was a willing participant in its activation.

> *"Happiness is not a goal; it is a by-product."*
> *~ Eleanor Roosevelt*

But my choice, was I formidably brave following my dream, to not Paris in Texas, for how much easier that would have been, but to that the capital of France, where the language *'je ne comprends pas,'* I did not understand and systems or protocols I knew not, and where my money was to be worth 35% less, so really, maybe, I was propelling myself forward toward a waking nightmare of great folly, where perhaps at that point I should have discarded those rose-coloured spectacles, and changed to a lens of crystal clear clarity, but "No, I did not," as I steamed on ahead, with a lens of smoky-grey, obscuring my in-sight. But really, was it simply over-sight, I was suffering from, for what was I really placing my assessments to move there on? Perhaps my reasons flimsy at best, for it was history of 20 years earlier, when a most kind boyfriend, was to take me there for an 8 day break, and then again in 2003, an amazing adventure was to accompany me on my wonderful 3 day stay, on my first round-the-world tip, of packing-in all the sights, was to ignite a flame, of how I so adored Paris, and for me, at least for a time, for me, that was the place to be.

For didn't I love so all the monuments and architecture, and the Parisians too, and how kind they were to help me when I got lost, as I raced around, filling my schedule with everything I wanted to see and do, but first of all, it had to be, that which *Monsieur Maurice Koechlin* and *Emile Nouguier* who envisioned and designed through his imaginary in-sight, that iconic structure taking 2 years to be built, using an astonishing 10 thousand tons of steel, and opened on the 31st March 1889 for the *Exposition Universelle*, World Fair, and how grateful the 6.5 million visitors must be, who ascend its height of 320 metres annually, to gleam the views, of those symmetrical boulevards stemming from the circular crescent of the *Arc de Triomphe*, and the manicured *Jargdins*, gardens with their bold and beautiful lush tree tops, full and perfectly formed, and how wonderful that way-back-then, the *Parisian 'Artisans Protest*, to prevent the *Tour d'Eiffel*, Eiffel Tower's construction, was unsuccessful yet then, almost ironically, it was only through a further Parisian outcry, that prevented the tower, as previously planned, being torn down again.

And what a sight I must have been, in my choice of dress, based purely on efficiency to prevent the cold of that winter air, drizzly and damp with a wayward wind wrapping itself around me, as a cropped black imitation leather jacket I wore, trimmed with a cream *faux*, fake fur collar, and on my heard, a wrap of brown and beige fur of the same, and my scarf and gloves, well, in grey they only managed to match with each other, and my black leather pants I adorned, really too big, yet fitting rather too snugly at the angle, and there at the bottom, as if Minnie Mouse, with boldly prominent bulky white running shoes. And true, perhaps it was not a fashion statement I made, but more a *fashion faux pas*, mistake, but at least I was on my way, happily content, as in truth, against those elements, my wardrobe designed for comfort, for really I was rugged up lovely and warm.

Then it was a treat that unexpectedly came my way, as at that time of the year, out of season, my favourite time for travel, for less tourists about, queues are few, and prices are less, and I was able to master my way around that city of love, amongst the rabbit warren of railway lines of the *Métro*, within the city boundaries of 245 stations, avoiding the fumes from those congested roads on those *rue's,'* streets above, as rapidly I was to be transported to where I needed to be, yet the ebb and flow was interrupted, and mild chaos ensued, when yet another, and I was to learn, quite regular, *grève*, strike ensued, just to put a spanner in the works of an anticipated peaceful day, but I was not to be deterred as I trampled those *petite rue's*, narrow streets and spacious boulevards, lined with imposing buildings, of *Haussmann* architecture built between 1853-1870 under the commission of Napoleon 3rd, their facades, concealing their inner opulence, built not yesteryear but yester-century. "Oh my" 'if only' they should speak, oh what secrets to share, splendid, sordid, perhaps rare, yet sparse in number, perhaps not likely.

As I meandered, down *rue Dauphine* and traversed *Pont Neuf* that oldest bridge built crossing the river *Seine* alongside its promenade wall, I let my bare hand drag across its stone wall, so old, yet somehow, seeming so alive, while I to-and-froe'd, across the other bridges, standing and admiring each one, and the statures the same, in bronze and guilt, and the lamps, artistically, architecturally and historically decorative, and all the way of the mile or so from *la Rive Gauche,* the Left Bank, as my mind whirled and marvelled, for soon I was to embrace with true captivation, with a glint and a smile in my eyes, as I was to gaze upon my favourite monument, *la Tour d'Eiffel,* I so adored, especially when bathed in soft night light, as it casts its shadow all around and "Oh how its sight, I feel in my heart, though I know not why, as I become enchanted with a warm and gentle glow."

So much joy and pleasure was to cradle me along my way, until, "Yeah!" In the 7eme *arrondissement (arr,)* suburb, I stood, beneath that structure of cold burnt red painted steel, with my *billet,* ticket secured and held tightly in my hand, so wonderfully my spirit soared, as on that Parisian day, as I wondered what was held in store, and as my imagination whirled with expected delight, as the clanging rhythm of metal on metal, made my heart do a merry dance, as up and up the elevator rose to the *premier* first, *deusième* second and *triosième* third *étage* floor, levels, and with anticipation the cells in my body tingled, as I was so eager, to hold on to those rails as I stood close to the edge, and view, the wonder of the Parisian landscape as I stood in that amazing monument to the fête of engineering, that had change the Parisian cityscape forever.

"If you are lucky enough to have lived in Paris as a young man, then wherever you go for the rest of your life, it stays with you, for Paris is a moveable feast"
~ Earnest Hemmingway

So then, how fortunate was I, as one of the attendants, in a long green uniform coat, which stretched down to the floor, with thick leather black gloves, and that quaint-essential Parisian adornment, worn casually, yet appearing pristinely placed, a woolly, *une écharpe a* scarf, and I humorously mused "What perfectly appropriate Health & Safety apparel and fit for purpose, as its designed to be." And he, who took a shine to me, permitted me a pass, to travel between floor to floor, which I do believe is not quite regular, and even to a hidden place he was to take me, and that quite thrilled me, not because he was cute and quite gorgeous, but perhaps, for that tower named *Eiffel* after the Corporation who commissioned it, right at the very top, not many people had been there before, and he who taught me words of French, as we peered over the banister rail, certainly aided to give me a spring in my step.

And so, off to my next monument I was to speedily travel, ignoring the deepening chill in the air, as dusk was falling and the lights on the monuments were shining, as their historic grandeur bathed in the shadows of light, revealing more of their magnificent glory, and on that peaceful evening, the cold biting of the wind on my face, held not a candle to the warm glow that surrounded my heart, as I, knowing my possessions were secure, and a warm clean bed was awaiting me, with nowhere else specific to be, I was open to all kinds of spontaneous possibilities.

Then out of the blue, there it was, my *prochain*, next encounter, was to visit me as I meandered down the street, as a man walking in the same direction, though I had to say, notably, as up northern England we would say, "He was not really dressed for the weather," as he with fairish hair and quite short, only wore black jeans and a cropped brown leather bomber-jacket and flimsy scarf to protect him from the mildly cruel elements, and he, started talking to me, as I carried on at my usual speed, and he began to roll out his story, perhaps prompted from a couple of my inquisitive questions, and he, turned out to be Spanish, and in France, working in the hospitality industry, and as a true local, I was so fortunate, and after observing 'safety first,' I accepted his dinner invitation, where he was to take me to a place, off the beaten tourist track, that perhaps only the locals frequented because of its obscured location.

As in plain view, it was hidden on a major *rue*, that petite and disguised doorway, where unless you knew it was there, right past you would continue, as force was needed to pull the ancient and solid wood door open, and doing so wide, my companion, beckoned me inside, and immediately onto the first step of a most narrow staircase I was to stand, as I searched for a non-existent hand rail, so my hand clung as tight as it could to the cold blocks of stone, as I placed one tentative foot before the other, upon the tapestry threadbare carpet, just hoping that on the straggly tassels I wouldn't trip, as I descended into a darkened space, with ceilings so low, that for some, it was almost difficult to stand right up, without knocking their heads on the dark wood beams.

Waiting besides the table where the double thickness of the deep red velvet curtain was once more drawn around the bottom of the stairs, to keep those howling winds out, a waiter with a step of authority was to greet us, and after a short French conversation ensued, we were shown to our table, where quite astonishingly, the traditional English reserve, held no capacity to raise its head there, as so tightly were the tables stagged together side by side, the waiter, sporting gold cufflinks on his uniform of crisply starched shirt, with his black waistcoat over the top, adorned with multiple tiny pockets, which I grew through observation to learn that each was designated for a specific coin, for ease of preparation of supplying the *client,* customer with their *petit monies,* change, yet how uncomfortable I did consider, his apron, of thick black fabric, almost wrinkling on top of his shoes it was that long, and wrapped all around his waist, each step must have required effort to take, and "Oh my" I was to think of the waiters, in France, as I believe it to be, a career of choice, and seriously, how hard they seem to work, and certainly when they choose, they deliver it with expediency and efficiency.

So it was, across the room we were shown, to a table against the wall, where the waiter, slim and tall, his hair of dark soft curls, and his eyes, the colour "Who could tell?" for the lighting too dim to see, as he placed a hand on the closest table corners, and he pulling firmly, taking care not to disturb the polished wine and water glasses, sitting closely beside the cutlery so gleaming brightly and all upon a densely starched white fabric tablecloth, which my grandma must have thought would surely have been washed with a 'dolly-blue.'

And I squeezed behind, placing my butt on the uneven padded red velvet seat, but comfortable it was most certainly not, for so narrow in width, it hardly supported even the upper part of my legs, so continually slipping forward and almost falling off, I devised a counter plan, to balance myself by leaning back, but my method for comfort not compete, as between the jaggedness of the natural stones and the chill they omitted, to do achieve such I was not permitted, but not to worry, I was so hungry, surely, I could sit up straight and forget about it, but as I perused the menu, I was to realise, that nothing suited my tricky digestive system or my tastebuds or appetite, so I, a little stuck, but as my companion, he from one European country, and I from another just over the sea, joined together by chance that evening, nothing was I going to permit to trouble me, as I simply got stuck in and *mangé,* ate the *du pain,* bread.

But in truth, I was quite fascinated to be in such a place, a place I would not have ventured into on my own, and true I felt quite privileged to observe, how the real-deal French behaved, in the privacy of their native space, and it appeared they had come up with a tick, to avoid those episodes of discomfort as they, all around, were lent forward with their elbows on the table, and cigarettes in almost everyone's hand, with the women adorning manicures with jewellery bold and glistening, while eating and smoking, and caring not for the conversation for the one to either side, which, without effort in such close proximity of maybe only six inches apart, but no one seemed to spare even the slightest notion for that concept, for they all, tied up in their own, and so flamboyant, was the delivery of each of their lines, with facial expressions aghast, for really, few seemed to smile, though nor did anyone appear angry as they possibly, rolled over the business of that day.

How refreshingly invigorating to experience all that, and the night, as we left that restaurant, quite young, and my companion, who I held no romantic notion in, was happy to continue along with our *rendezvous (rdv)* and so it was to be, up the *Champs-Élysées*, on route to the *Arc de Triumph*, and there on the vastness of the boulevard, Salsa music, of the kind I used to dance to, court my attention, so for a while in we ventured, to watch the couples on the dance floor do their thing, until once again, the winter air was to scratch at my face as we wandered on our way, and the reward, was to be quite huge, as at nearly midnight, with no traffic on the roads, we used not the underground walkway, but ran, frantically with joy and glee across the empty renowned roundabout, known so well for its congestion and colossal number of cars which engulf it each day, or maybe, that was only me, screaming with delight, for I felt, as I so rarely did, free of emotional or regimental restraints, with the lightest heart, as I truly felt somewhere deep within, I rested so comfortably, securely, safely and warmly, enchanted and wrapped in reams of, well, I really knew not quite what is was, as I nestled for the very first time, on cloud, numbered 9.

> *"Faith is taking the first step when you don't see the whole staircase"*
> *~ Martin Luther King Junior*

Yet really, all those years later, "What on earth did Paris hold in store for me and was it to be providence and possibly a pivotal part of my journey?" Yet so convinced was I that I had placed myself on the right track. But for sure, I was not aware what my journey held in store, but for the first time, life was moving me, rather than me moving it, and what a pleasure that proved to be, as from my emotional past, those septic emotional ties were about to disintegrate and split, as I became not the master, but a participator of what I was about to travel through, along my road to self-awareness and healing, though really, I may have served myself so much better, by packing extra portions of positivity, or was that wisdom to be, may have proved a most astute thing to do, rather than packing those extra pairs of shoes.

And true, of those moments, I so wished for some to last longer, and others, well I wished for them to be skipped quickly through, though such a benefit they became to be for my recovery, as my mind, no longer busy with everything, as it began a process to unwind from that tightly wound up spring, as my emotions no longer concealed by being tied up in tasks, and as it wondered, as if almost by mistake, hints of that poisonous past I was submersed in, came back to haunt me quite dramatically, but where, I had not even considered, was it to lead me next. So really, could I have aptly named it, "F Day" 'Fateful Day,' 'Folly Day,' 'Failure Day?' Yet "No."

For how fortunate I was to realise, through all the pain which was yet to rear its head, that I, like everyone else, can only walk so far into a dark dense wood, and get scared and lost, until, halfway in, we suddenly become, halfway out, and so it was not to be devastatingly, but a process of positivity, which although I was slow to embrace, it was to propel me forward, to a much brighter and better place. And though not immediately, indeed, quite tardily, yet certainly, "Was to transpire that 'P Day' was actually to be 'F Day' aka, 'Fulfilment Day?'"

Yet perhaps too late was I to contemplate, what I had based my decisions on, which was too little in reality, of a short conversation in a Parisian gift store, where the shop assistant complimented me, on the delivery of my well observed and well rehearsed phrase, as I spoke my request to purchase my goods as I paid. For he, replied to me in his native tongue, and when I said, "Oh I am so sorry, I do not understand of what you speak," his words with a gentle smile sprung back, "Aarrh, you spoke so well, I thought you spoke French fluently." And somehow, his words struck a cord with my heart, and the seed was planted and hibernated there, awaiting for a time to blossom and flourish, as I simply for the next ten years, got on with life as I knew it.

But really, "Was that it?" Just a desire, a notion, a feeling, to make such a bold decision upon, for was I to be courageous or simply a foolhardy fantasy, that I was to travel, to the other side of the world, in anticipation, nay, expectation, that I was to achieve my dreams, but really why not, for I had left the UK and then NZ, and that worked out OK, so I had no knowledge or benchmark to the contrary, that this adventure would turn out to be anything less.

And really, I was completely-over Australia, for my health had been so bad, with 'Melbourne Maladies' haunting me at every juncture, and I was quite honestly, sick of being sick, as my body experienced a weakness, as never before, with 4 day headaches crippling me, as my digestive system shut down, and not even sips of water could rest in my stomach, without my bodies rejection of them, as they were brought right back up again. And how debilitating, as my favourite, Salsa dancing I had to give up, for my energy levels so poor, I had not enough to sustain either the effort or the time of night to stay up and go to a club, and my work situation too, not really so much in Sydney, but certainly in Melbourne, where 2 female bosses, were to bully me, one at the hospital from where the helicopter would take off and land on its roof, serving major traumas, State-wide. With the other, at a multidisciplinary Health Care Service Community Centre, so really, leaving those Australian shores was to serve not as misery, but as a most welcomed relief.

> *"The boisterous sea of liberty is never without a wave"*
> *~ Thomas Jefferson*

Yet, "Was I mad to follow a dream?" No, I don't think so. "Was it easy?" No. "Was I relaxed about it?" That was also, no. "And courage?" Well, I had sufficient. "And fear?" Well, yes, I had rather more than a healthy portion of that, but I was not to let that stop me, for I was to face it, and did it anyway.

And true, there were a few hurdles to jump over and hoops to jump though, as I, unravelled the chaos in my mind, but strategically, I had made my list of pros and cons and performed all my Risk Assessments, and was quite convinced, to follow my dream, I was quite capable off, and more, of cause, be successful at it too, and as I did all that, something quite amazing came to light, as I was clearing my belongings from my 2 bedroom apartment, that on my Inspirational Wall, of all the pictures I'd put up there, quite amazingly there was only one of Canada, a surprise really, as that was the country, with my nursing career I had intended to move next, and so many more of Paris, as the *Eiffel Tower* presented quite obviously dominantly, yet why had I never noticed it before? For true, I must have been all so subliminal of what resided in my heart, and just perhaps to go there was almost majestically destiny.

My heart, it breathed such a deep sigh, as one pictures cut from a magazine, that I took down from my wall, of a lady, with blonde wavy hair, viewed from the back, in a white wedding dress, with a small train resting on the floor, with multiple layers of delicate fabric, so much like a 'rah-rah' skirts that I so like to wear, but she placed in the distance, and to see her, to see the Aga cooker, in cream, my favourite colour, and even more in the for-view, just the hint of a corner of a solid wood farmhouse table, and all placed and large slate style quarry stones, in a rich deep grey, and "Oh my" the vision of hope and dare I say anticipation, made my heart all a flurry, and of that picture, though not of any other, I safely packed and kept.

But true, I have grown to know, often the fuss that is made over a wedding, is just the tip of the iceberg of what lies below, but more so, it is not the dress I desire, or a marvellous wedding day, even though my own, so unfortunately, was the worst wedding I've ever been to, and possibly one of the worst days of my life, and believe me, for that unpleasant award or recognition, there were more than a few contenders, for I have grown to know wholeheartedly, it is not simply a wedding I want of one fine day of 'something special' but rather, a life time in harmony and compatibility, wonderfully and lovely, together. And that is why I do believe, that picture spoke o much to me, for it represents a feeling, a notion, a resonation, with all my deepest hopes and dreams, of a home, and a place, where everything emotionally healthy and wholesome is mine, truly mine to absorb and adore.

"Oh my" such an in-depth revelation I so wish I was able to arrive at earlier, before I so misguidedly trotted merrily down a road I never should have been, right before, I knew I had arrived at a dead end, but found no way out, as I with someone with a miss-matched mindset, and someone, who I recognized not was full of deceit and hiding his true character from me, and what he did reveal, I so sadly had no revelation, that he was a tricky person and further down the track he was to commit me, to suffer harm at his hands, and from his false and callus heart, his poisoned darts, were a devastating process of emotional injury was to be set in motion to so adversely, stripping me of my treasures of hope and self-protection, as it was not just money he took from me, but ripped me of my valued, priceless and all precious security.

But like a phoenix from the ashes I was to rise again, for I was higher than he in morals and capability, and ultimately, I may have been down, but most certainly, I was not out, and I was, after licking my wounds and grieving for what he had taken from me, to push through all boundaries, choosing not to believe the hospital doctors, who told me, "You will never work again." "What! No!" I had to, I simply must. For giving up was not an option, so from somewhere, I mustered the strength of the magnificent trait of durability, as robustly, I continued on, making not huge plans, but plans of baby steps, with one tiny one after the other, commenced me on the road to recovery, and "Why did this all work out well in the end?" Because I head set my overriding goal, on something much higher than me, and I held no concept in my mind, that somehow I would get there, and for really, there was no plan B, or any other option except to *achieve, success*.

> *"A man is not old until regrets take the place of his dreams"*
> *~ Oscar Wild*

"For is life a journey?" It must be, weather we accept that notion or not, for we are all born somewhere, and after passing thought time and years we all end up somewhere, and sometimes that is the place from where we began, but "Oh so hopefully" I hoped wherever it is we end up, that our hearts, will be healed and fulfilled, with a notion of a dream not to be held in captivity, but on wings of self-love, we allow it to take flight. As each of us, takes our heard out of the gravel on the ground, and stop pecking around for all or any scraps like the chicken, but choose to look up, and see what is around, and know that we too can take steps, somehow to achieve that status too, and for know other reason, that simply, everyone deserves, with healthy hearts to achieve that too.

But "Oh how sad it can be," as I was to witness as I worked in my wonderful Occupational Health & Safety Nurse job (OH&SN) in a soap manufacturing company in Salford, England, and I, on the first day of employment had several people visit my surgery, and they, complaining of 'their lot in life' how it was unfulfilling and boring and how they were so totally dissatisfied with it they were, as their moans and groans came from their mouths, but in essence, appeared to lay so heavily on their hearts. And I, making attempts to help, to give them thoughts for contemplation, a different point of view, even a strategy or 2, for how they could move themselves from "Where they were, to where they wanted to be," but regardlessly of my attempts, their default mechanism remained consistently the same, with their forever words relayed to me, "Well, I cant do that." But "Why?" I would ask, "Well its not meant to be. But "Why?" I petitioned, "Well mi-Mam did it like that, and her Mam before her, so that means I have to too." But, I inquisitively enquired, "Does it really?" while offering various alternatives, just hoping that a different concept may be gleamed or ignited inside of them, but "No," for resolutely, as if set in stone, because their mothers before them, had done it 'that way,' so without thoughts for change or something new, unquestioning or investigating, they, would too.

How sad I did contemplate, and treading carefully, even mentioned it once or twice, that perhaps, their grandmothers, or mothers, who may not voice it, for a mirage of reasons, and may just have been overwhelmed with joy, to seize upon the available opportunities, that where presented to her, in society that day. But the beliefs that were potentially limiting and confining for those ladies who visited me, as adamantly, to do anything different was met with a response, "No, that wouldn't be right." Casting other ideas out of sight. But to my "Why?" Yet a reasonable explanation escaped them, except to wander back to the realms of their past, unable from its captivity, that really, with inner turmoil they were fighting against, but or them, so unfortunately nothing did improve, for the same people who knocked on my door, the day of my arrival, were the same who knocked on it once again on the day of my departure, having done nothing, made no decisions or better choices and searched not for the key, for their escape, as they still remained, complaining of the very same.

But really, "Who gave them those notions and planted those seeds of restriction?" And of those who did, "What was their real intention, was it logic or a deceitful or misguided self-serving agenda, to not want another family member to excel more than they, so seeds of doubt, or destruction may be planted, through, quiet concealed resentment, of something that they were unable to?" Or possibly, through the excelling of ideas, it may serve to shine a light for those who, for whatever reason had been unable to, from restraints, perhaps from society, history or a legacy of circumstances that prevented them reaching their destiny, but not through a mindset of inadequacy but opportunity. Yet true, how harming it can prove to be, when another having not reached their full potential, so desires that others suffer the same fate, through perhaps selfishness to not want to be alone, when the successful one, moves up in status, with homes or finance or simply moves away. And perhaps it serves well to remember, that when a person screams, "You think you are better than me!" When in reality, it is from their heart, that they believed, that scenario to be so.

And true, we all have our own journeys to walk up on, and they can be treacherous enough, with out our families creating problems too, and true, when it seems to serve us least well, there seems little point in giving credence to the concept that, its always been done the way, so we will ask no questions and just regard-less-ly, of anything new, appealing or invigorating, something that gives us a springing our step, or joy in our heart when we thing about it, to simply carry-on getting what we always got. For really, "Can we at least consider all possibilities?" that resided deep inside, cradled by our instinct and our very-being that we resinate with, as we aspire to something different. And for sure, that doesn't make us good or bad, right or wrong, it simply means, that we are in-touch with our inner-self and desire something different to what those had before, and I so, so wholeheartedly believe, residing at different times, on both sides of the track, we need to follow our hearts desires, so on the inside, truly we give ourselves the best opportunity, to simply and magnificently, on the wings of our inner-love, we soar.

For sure, a notion for contemplation, as our dreams are adored, they take flight and come alive, as we muster the courage to take them in our hands, and through them, weave loops of abundant hope, to rest and settle deep within, and through our worthwhile exploration, rewards of transformation, to become a person, no longer steeped in misery, as successfully, we surpass the worst, and circumnavigate the complacency of mediocrity, as onward we venture toward the very best that we can be, healed, empowered and in-recovery, and how do I know all this? For what I describe, it happened for me.

> *"It's never too late to become what you might have been"*
> ~ George Elliot

Yet true, perhaps, dreams and logic are seldom form an alliance of being best buddies, as different as black is to white, only permitting shades of grey, as they try to intertwine in shades of grey, where mediocrity or boredom lay, in that all favoured comfort zone. Perhaps, where nothing goes wrong, but alternatively, perhaps for the nourishment of the soul, nothing goes particularly right either, so "Why not?" set off on a journey of self discovery, and take that longest journey of all, from beginning to end, the 18 inches, to unite our head with our heart, or our mind with our soul. And from that stable place, we can banish, deliberation and confusion, and cast out disbelief or self-doubt, as we find a way, to not delay, but work out our *own route*, for "Where to from here?"

And you see, I know this is all possible, for I escaped generational and genetic curses from dysfunctional childhood abuse, as my only goal everyday, so simple, just to try my very to keep out of harms-way, and free from violence and physical pain, though so easier said than done, as in its proximity, it hovered everywhere. Yet as I grew older, I refused to be controlled by the crushing effects of those emotional and debilitating freeloaders of, fear, guilt, and shame, that unbeknown to me, took up residence in my hurting heart, as simply I continued to push on through life, ignoring the battering I constantly got, as I, slammed from this way to that way into the jagged rocks in the white wailing torrents of water that carried me along, and my cries, of "Help! Help! Please someone help me!" Yet I, unable to be heard above the sound of those crashing debilitating waves, and that was until, simply, I learnt to help myself, for that was the only single way, I was to *set myself free*.

Yet still, those notions deep inside, for I knew not way back then, that healing and growth could be mine to win, for my simple endeavour, not to thrive, but merely survive each day, but thankfully, they who criticized and punished me, I grew and knew that they were liars, speaking only untruths, and I knew not why, for I, was only a child, and deserved not to endure their burdens of horrific harm of dysfunction they cast daily upon me. Yet a day did come, but I recall it not being accompanied by a band of trumpets or trombones, but only the softest tones, awakened me, that I was not to be controlled by the collaboration of their destruction, for I was to go on, resilient, stronger, and refute what they said about me, as willingly, I set a new course, to *achieve my own destiny*.

So I activated my own, super-efficient GPS, or that was what I expected it to be, but not in reality, as along those rickety roads, there were no signs, telling me "Where to go or what to do?" and many a pot hole I was to fall into too, and such a long while seemed to pass, before those stumbling blocks turned into steppingstones, and I ceased to be, my hardest critic of me, as those very best cousins of Resilience and Persistence, were to accompany me, as when I fell, I resiliently, regrouped that fantastic and formidable trio, "Me, Myself and I," as I dusted myself off, and perhaps true, on occasions, had a cry or a tiny tantrum or 2, through emotions of frustration or worse, as at times, it all seemed all to get just a little too much to continue, yet always, I picked myself up one more time than I fell, and carried right-on, as I, may have been a product of my past, but I refused to remain a prisoner to it, held in captivity, for I made a choice, and had a purpose, to masterfully and willingly, to seek doors of opportunity, and with great opiumism, to become, a *better* me.

"Time fly's its up to you to be the navigator"
~ Robert Orben

France, it "Was placed in my heart, or so it appeared, but was it by choice, destiny or the misery, of second best that I had arrived at, or was it the place I was to be?" For many a question had been asked from those colleagues up and down the corridor, from that World Health Organization Project, I was getting ready to leave, as they enquired, "So where to from here?" But really, first, had it not been Vancouver in Provence of British Columbia. For really, perhaps only logical, for I had spent 5 years in NZ, followed by 5 in Australia, so it stood only logical and reasonable to me, that, 5 years in Canada, as a winning tri-facto, it appeared only right in my logic that should come next.

Vancouver I chose for it ticked all those boxes congenially so, for my pastime pursuits to nourish me, physically and spiritually, for my hobbies and interests, the forests filled with fresh air, the rain I so missed while living in Melbourne, and ice-skating and rollerblading around the waterfront, well I was so excited at the prospect of that healthy hobbies, and so much more, for I would be far better placed to travel and tour frequently the USA, and event the rest of the world, which certainly, I desired to achieve for sure.

So hoops I jumped through as the timely submission of a myriad of papers needed to be submitted to gain my Canadian Nurses Registration, but how amazingly well I did it, as within 2 weeks of gaining all my necessary authenticated and certificated papers, from counties pertaining to my global working history, and to be submitted, with fees. And what great news, as I immediately received great news back, that I had been afforded the opportunity, to take further exams, and as a nurse, reside in that country, nay, that city, in that annual race, which often tied with Melbourne in First place, for the number 1 place to live in the world, yet 8202 miles apart.

And so the Internet I turned to, to search for those valued websites and jobs that were to be the next step along my journey, of what I was to do next, then there it was, a prefect job, one that would utilize all of my skills and talents, working as a Health & Safety Wellness Nurse. "Oh my" so excited I became, as 2 jobs I found fit me so perfectly, as it was so, 'right up my street,' so immediately online, my application was filled, and I was to await some anticipated good news.

Then it came one day, joy and glee were to visit me, as I was offered a telephone interview, as a dateline and substantial time differences all navigated through, and so it was one day, as I sat in my car under the blazing sun rays, I was to answer the questions delivered by the Director of Nursing, and the Nursing Manager of a major Vancouver Health Authority, and as their most innovative questions continued, I began to think, "Surely this must be the last one" as an hour on the clock ticked on by, and the sun dispensed its rising heart, and so unprepared I was for the longevity of the conversation, without even a sip of water to hand, and to put on the air-con on, was my next step to take, but the noise the engine did make, not a word I could hear of what those interviewers spoke, so as my temperature and dehydration rose, swiftly I needed to switch it off again, for on my old and outdated mobile phone, which I had resisted the urging of friends to update, for it was petite, pretty and pink, a flip top, as I had always desired, and up until hat moment had always been adequate and served me perfectly well. As really, so reluctant for change I was, for once before I had made a miscalculation, to make a top of the range purchase, which really completely exceeded my needs, as never, that VCR could I work, nor even my male friends, equally the same, and consequently, even before it became obsolete, it remained only a dormant ornament, useless, only serving, as aesthetically pleasing.

Yet the process, I was so keen was I to undergo, even though, in that sweltering heart, it was 1 hour 40 minutes before they were through, "Wow" I thought, perhaps with the logistics of it all, they had combined interviews 1 and 2, as they were quite pleased with me as a potential candidate, as I contemplated positively of my time spent with those potential Canadian bosses of mine, and what a delight, as I began to reflect and contemplate, from their personalities they presented to me, I was already looking forward to working with them, and the positive, proactive difference I could make.

Then it came, a surprise telephone call at only 8am, from one of those 2 interviewers and she posed a question to me, "Of the 2 jobs on offer, which would you prefer?" I'd never been asked that question before, a little shocked I guess, as I hadn't thought that far ahead, that I may have done so well to be asked such a question, not excitement but mild panic set in, as I wondered, is this a trick, as if I choose one, I will be immediately barred from the other possibility. And my head not thinking clearly, I opted to use 'Old School' philosophy and 'edge my bets' replying, "I do believe with my skills and experience I am equally capable of doing each one." And true, that I certainly believed, yet, clearly I knew in my heart, which I preferred and suited me best, but I was not prepared to say, for of fear of what my total honesty would deliver, as by making that choice "Would it reduce my possibility to live in Vancouver?"

Yet how generous that lady was, as 2 further opportunities she pressed me for a firm answer, and I totally failed with my lack of confidence, not in my career, but in myself, to consider, that just possibly the team of 2 who interviewed me, were so convinced, that 'yes,' they too knew I was capable of doing a good job, that they were offering me a choice. But that concept certainly even those few years ago, sprang not passed my mind, but later a thought was to spring into it, that my true passion, willingness and honesty, that must have come through so clearly during the interview, was contrary to the restriction of my commitment to be honest on that day, which in truth, may have served for them to re-evaluate and concede, to a different choice.

"Mmmm" really, "Had I actually stabbed myself in the foot?" As without a firm conclusion the telephone call ended, and as I was to check my post daily, kind of expecting a job offer in writing, yet "No" it was not to come, so I was to telephone them, only to be told, "The position was not filled, as the financial crisis adversely effected our available funding." But I took it as a rejection, and internalized 'that sort of thing' as always I had, believing, that perhaps, that was not quite the full truth, and it was something I had done wrong, again. Then, it was a mini revelation that was to come my way, as a lovely colleague down the corridor, a friend to be, knowing I was looking to move, gave me a journal, concerned with all things of nursing and careers. And how amazing it proved to be, as a light flashed on immediately, of 'New School' philosophy,' as when an interviewer asks 'which job you prefer,' you *must* give a definitive answer, for if you don't, they may view you as an employee, unprepared to stand up for what is right, for the good of the company or your department, being only a 'yes' person, lacking in strength or commitment to decisions making, and through not keeping up with trends had I misguidedly, unwittingly, proved to be, 'a case in point?'

For they say, 'those who hesitate are lost' and that certainly proved to be me on that day, as I, so disappointed and deflated, that my Vancouver ship sailed, without me on it, and my hearts desire to be unfulfilled, or really "Was it to turn out to be, a folly, fate or fortune, or simply my destiny?" or more simply, on my 'dot-to-dot' picture of life, "Was I connecting the wrong dots?" or may be, speaking metaphorically, "Was rubbing them out, whilst choosing a new direction to travel toward, as regrouping once again, Me, Myself and I?" And true, I did not necessarily have a clear view, of my journey to continue, but I had learnt what didn't work out, so by definition, as I did not waste, but learnt by those mistakes, surely they were to serve to empower me, and so I set a new route with a little more wisdom packed onboard, as "Onward toward my positive prevailing future" I gently cried. For I grew and knew, while spending too much time licking my wounds and holding onto tight, to that, which has already 'been and gone,' we can miss our opportunities to be the creator driving our own destinies, to be our own best champions, of wonderful creative change, as we discover, really, "Where to from here?"

"Acceptance of what has happened is the first step to overcoming the consequences of any misfortune"
~ William James

But of "My future, my dream, was I to relinquish it or seize upon one afresh, one anew?" And so, back to the drawing board I went, as so frequent my visits, my name was etched upon it. And Toronto in Ontario, was next for my consideration, but it, 40 below in winter, and +40 in summer, where the locals informed me they live in those spacious malls underground, just to escape it. But what of those wonderful ice-skating rings right next to the lakes, and the ancient architecture to marvel at, such a favourite thing of mine to do, and the Arts, plentiful, and the local, so close to the US for me to continue with that which pleases me so much, travel. And a more permanent idea I had of achieving my goal as 'off to Canada I was to go' but that was not to be, for my papers pristinely completed in the shortest of time, well they were missing for the longest of time, and 4 months it took for them to arrive, after the law had changed in Canada, and it transpired, I, was out of luck.

And so it began, my non-stop disparaging, for the decision I had made on that day, even though as I was to let the envelope drop out of my hand into the Post box, my mind, my gut, my inner instinct screamed at me "NO!" But what a huge folly, dismissing it merely as my imagination, I let go of what was in my hand, and as I did so, I had no idea of the huge regrets that I was to pick back up, after ignoring that fail proof warning system. And that simple action, was to create a chain reaction, where like falling dominos everything went wrong, and right there, that was the basis, "Why I couldn't let go?" for I blamed myself, that I did not listen more keenly, and act more promptly on that internal system, that *always* protects me.

Then "What if?" Became the name of the septic game, a curse down in my soul, as so negatively I mulled over the consequence of each individual link, in that chain reaction, that I, commenced, and so opposing to good or rational thinking, as I studied ever so hard my rear view vision, but not as a healthy tool for reflection, but a negative one serving only for self-disparagement and self-deprecation. But "Why was I being so dreadfully mean and unrealistic with my own emotions?" Well that was easy to answer, for so long ago, I'd been trained to do so, for so sadly its true you see, the harm that children suffer, emotionally and mentally, the trauma it leaves behind, and the way they have grown to think and believe about themselves, doesn't suddenly disappear, or even fade away, just because another birthday was surpassed, or a different geographical location was sought, as many times it leaves behind a spirit and mind of debilitating destruction.

But I was 'down and not out' and there were other choices to make in life, and I was to seize the proverbial by the horns, with "Would of + could of + should of = what if" no longer being an equation I was to consider, as my thoughts turned to what's next, what is going to warm my spirit an ignite my heart, just sufficiently to take positive action, and as I began to focus on the frivolity of the future and not the pull from the past, I experienced a conscious mind-shift, which proved to be a process that wilfully I permitted to give me time, to pass through, and then, quite suddenly, I was to relinquish my hold on 'what might have been' as so fortunately, amazingly swiftly, I was set free. And then purposely in my mind, that which I had almost tried to hide, as perhaps inwardly I tried to fight it, considering it whimsical and illogical, but no longer, for I had exhausted all other avenues of choice and they were not to be, an how *J'adore*, I adore Paris, so that was it, a decision made, I was off to follow my dream, and it was to be France for me, where I, was to enjoy the beautiful life, *'La Belle Vie!'*

"If you can dream it, you can do it"
~ Walt Disney

Chapter 2

Step On In!

"Sometimes the hardest journey we'll ever make, is to stay exactly where we are"
~ Carole Jordan

À Paris, à Paris! {Pronounced ~ Pa-ree} To Paris, to Paris! And a perfect plan in my mind, I did devise, to learn French in just 3 months and be fluent by 6, and then continue onto a 3-week business-language course, for I wanted to be so prepared as I set up my *bonne affaire*, good business, which I was convinced I would excel, but in reality, was I simply in a world of impractical and imaginary make-believe, where I was in folly casting my own spell, and as the delusion broke, it was to be, a very different tale to tell.

For time was to reveal itself to me, as the master of all, as through its passing I was to realise, that moving to France, was not to be an imaginary walk in the park' as moving to NZ, I conceived to be, and truly, it turned out that way, and onto Australia, first to Sydney in New South Wales, the trek 'across the pond' as they view it, just 2 hour 40 minutes by plain, was really rather easy, and onward, as I moved interstate to Victoria, exactly the same, and that was with the drive I had, with my car piled up with my most needed possessions, of music centre and TV, and of cause, heaps of clothes that I had packed up in my car. And so confident was I, I travelled for 4 days, here and there, enjoying the coast and countryside, and how marvellous as I looked out one day, and saw the sea, so dense in navy blue, it looked just like I could have taken a knife and sliced it right in 2.

But those previous moves, just simple logistics, but that latest move, emotionally charged, yet still I held not a notion did I ever give, that anything could possibly go wrong, for I was convinced I was right in what I did, for when 'something' in my life, is not working out for me, or the way I prefer it to be, I simply take control, educate and empower myself, and make a move, always designed for the better, so really, I obviously did consider, as I packed up one more time, not "What will go wrong?" but how wonderfully, of course, everything will be right!"

But not straight away, as one by one my employment opportunities, evolved to be rather glum, as in Victoria, on the south-east coast of Australia, my fixed-term contract was coming to an end, and "Harrah" I proclaimed, for no longer would I be required, to laboriously stand and watch health care workers, during the '5 moments for hand hygiene,' not wash their hands, and 'elbow-taps' were used by their hands, and during education sessions, I could receive a barrage of excuses could be submitted, why they did not, but for the patients best interests, surely I thought, to prevent cross-infection, at least they should give it a shot.

And my boss, how wonderful it would be, not to see her again, with critical acclaim appearing to be her perceived power-game, as she made an exhibition of me, standing centre stage in the office, criticizing and humiliating, with her daily doze of demoralizing hostility, in front my peers accusing me of inferior work, with the incapacity to follow instructions, with stupidity and insolence forming close compatriots of what she thought, and openly expressed of me, and my embarrassment appeared to deliver her, more than a degree of glee, as the harshness of her attitude echoed off the walls in that office void of windows, with the walls stark white, with shelves stacked tight, with files of red, green and blue, reaching tall, to break the glare, but not of her stare as so intently she stared as if the Prey in her sight, as she, continually disagreeing and refuting all logical reasoning I presented, only responding that I was wrong and she was right, and before she began, likely that pre-formatted conclusion in her mind, was always there by design.

So perhaps no surprise, her colleagues, her friends, as I walked in the office to greet the team, with an enthusiastic, "Good morning," not a one of them would reply, and the same in reverse as at half past 4, as "Goodnight, have a good evening." would unwaveringly be met with silence as they insisted on ignoring me, "So why did I not give up?" I often wondered as I pondered, how they excluded me from the Team, and how quite incorrectly I was told there was no "I" in team, for it appeared each one of them had found the E+M = Me, as they cast me from it.

But workplace bullying, "Really?" It seemed such a shame at 50-something, that she had not developed more in her soul, than to treat another in that manner, that if done to her, it would surely hurt, and where was the history of her misery, where meanness flowed out of her, and how sad she had not sought more, and embarked on a path of self-discovery, dispelling the inner-pain, while finding her own-self-worth. For to cast hostility externally, forms only a *faux pas*, for healing cannot be gained, while a prescription of hostility is dispensed.

Yet I, having placed a footstep and then another, and another, upon that path of trepidation, before I realised the benefit of what it had in the realms of healing growth and providing a resolution for me, where acceptance and forgiveness became my key, to set myself free of bad experiences, for through them, like a great oak tree of strength, positivity I became determined to nourish me, as I learnt to discard their nuisances and to let-go. Because my life is so much more important and valuable than what they did to me, and now to the future I look, actually, with added peace and tranquillity, resigned, always, "To thyn own-self be true."

"Great minds discuss ideas, average minds discuss events and small minds discuss people."
~ Eleanor Roosevelt

But really, was that not enough, "Oh why, was there to be more?" To have a boss as a female nurse, in that multidisciplinary office of maybe 20, so obviously had her favourites, and so obviously after starting, she revealed to me, I was not to be one of them, and I grew to ponder, "Did she have a 'to do' list, and each morning place my name at the top, then deciphering different ways she could trouble me?" For sure, it seemed like it. For so obvious her verbal assaults, as she criticized and condemned me daily, and at first, though feeling hurt and uncomfortable, but almost subliminally accepting it, as intrinsically accepting abnormal as normal on the platform of life I stood upon, for that was what I'd been taught by my parents to do, where to treat me kindly or justly, or even equally to others, was something I had not experienced, so perhaps, from her behaviour, nothing unusual at first.

But then, highlighting the uncommon situation, from my colleague's questions and comments commenced as 1st the Physiotherapist asked, "Does your boss always speak so badly in front of other colleagues in meetings and try, 'put you down'?" 2nd the Speech Therapist one day was to swing by my desk, after my boss had left, to enquire, with deep concern registered in her eyes enquiring, "Are your alright? Because if someone would have spoken to me, the way she spoke to you, I would be in floods of tears right now." And the Podiatrist, the 3rd, well she came with the same sort of concerns, all noticing the unreasonable, unacceptable bias, but what was I to do about it, at first, and for a long time nothing, as so well trained I was by my parents, I simply continued to let her do what she wanted to. But then, the time came for my awakening, as it was to eventuate that bad and substandard behaviour had an expiry date, and eventually through the encouragement of other team members, though I did hesitate, I was to take, affirmative action and hold her accountable for what she was doing, and of no surprise, served elevate her malice most vile.

And one day, my colleagues found me unconscious on the restroom floor, and took me by wheelchair around to the surgery, where from nurses and doctors, I received basic observations, and ice-pops for hydration, and there I remained for an hour or so until I was fit to go. But my boss, so vexed with the situation, and unconcerned with my health, as boldly, scornfully, plundering in, "You received care and you had not right!" And I perplexed, explaining "Sorry, I don't understand," as she continued, "You, don't live in the municipality of our catchment area, so you should have called an ambulance and gone to the hospital to be treated there." Well, that quite astonishing even for her, as I repeated my explanation, "I was unconscious so helpless, to do such a thing." But her determination eased not, as she sat on my desk, where her spiky red hair surrounded her stare, in an all too familiar pattern, with her eyes fixed and staring, through her garishly-coloured square framed spectacles, as if I were prey in the forest, while I futilely repeated the truth, with failed to appease her, so as I turned towards my computer, I offered to give her the names and numbers, of those who had intervened to help, and only then with her folded arms and tightly puckered face did she retreat, with her departing words, "Don't do it again!"

Then with my claim for 'bullying' upheld, after I refused to be sent, by those who were supposed to be there to help me, and after I was out of there, and safely away, "How so very sad" I was later to reflect, that whatever it was, that boss harboured inside of her, that at her age of over 50 still through her life, she had not dealt with it, and how much longer was she to go on, before, maybe she considered, this is not healthy, or practical to serve a happily life, so perhaps I should do something about it. For as cruel as she was, I was lucky, for from her I was able to escape and get away, but for herself, well, until she started her healing process, she was simply, to have to live with herself everyday.

Yet "Yeah!" It was true, I had made astonishingly wonderful steps forward, as from those 2 Australian bullying situations received from female bosses, again, I refused the same, for the 1st situation, I had *reacted* to, with 'putting up and shutting up' my delivered an unwavering doctrine growing up, and falsely remaining as my default status and MO, *'Modus Operandi'*, mode of operation, as I, become physically ill, with headaches commencing on Friday afternoon, and diarrhoea starting on Monday morning. Yet somehow, subliminally, I had learnt from that lesson, and gained a bigger portion of self-worth, as it was not a stumbling block that I allowed the previous incident to be, as I forged it into an emotional steppingstone, quite valuably, as to the 2nd incidence I was to *responded* to, and set in motion the appropriate process, to hold her accountable for her inappropriate behaviour.

And right there I do believe lay the *difference*, for I was no longer a victim, for I was living in victory, as inner-growth became my new companion, for I was to arise from under the cloak of the underdog, into a place of greater balance and equality, as I reeled-in strength I was to swing right back, the weight, of life's unwelcomed pendulum.

> *"The funny thing about life is that when you refuse to accept anything but the best, you very often get it"*
> ~ W. Somerset Maugham

For sure, I had made my decision and remained convinced what I was heading to was far better than the gloomy nature of my life, where I lived in boredom, and that, so often our enemy, for it poses to hold us back, as we wallow in mediocrity, going nowhere and achieving no-thing, only make-believing like a chameleon adapting to our environment, pretending that everything is all right, when really, our comfort zone has transformed to a territorial rut, where perhaps, we are simply stuck, for comfort, no longer wraps around us, as we are only restricted and harnessed in our lack of action or motivation, to change, to improve what we have, and perhaps, because we are tied sorrowfully, restrictedly so to a negative past, where someone once clipped our wings and so meanly said, "You! You'll never be able to do that!" But, just for the first time maybe, dare to consider, that they were wrong, and absolutely so, and through doing what serves you best, to stretch your way out of the boredom and its demoralizing restraints, you can spread your imagination on the wings of inspiration, and like an eagle, take flight, to soar high, to reach and spy, all those amazing opportunities awaiting you, to be filled with your life's future of inner-growth, and wonderful life-changing, empowering, fulfilment.

And how wonderful, that I was leaving behind a life unwanted, unsatisfying, where I was unable to thrive, and those employment situations on a sliding scale, descending from dismal to darn right miserable, and onto, simply sufferable. And with my health fairing worse, with Temazepam, simply needed every night, just in an to subside the pain and relax, so I may possibly get some hours sleep, and so late in the day I was to learn, that just by missing day 3 or 4, an addiction to the medicine may be avoided, and how necessary to know that. "Health as I knew it, how to regain it?" Yet I tried so hard with additional extra large portions of my monthly expenditure, exchanged with practitioners, for weekly appointments of Reflexology, Myotherapy, Physio, Chiro, Osteo, Cranial, Reiki and Acupuncture, and the list goes on, and pharmaceuticals, well, don't get me started there, and all I tried and tried, just hoping, nay believing that one might work, but still I remained incapacitated, as ill health conditions seemed to perpetuate on their own and plague me. But through it all, I was down but not out, for I remained optimistic, and mustered in my mind, that I was victorious in my recovery, as I refused to live with a mentality, of victimhood.

But *"Pourquoi pas?"* "Why not?" For surely I was not to worry, for the future was ahead of me and didn't I have a most wonderful dream inside of me, and didn't I search for that opened door, so surely, well prepared, it was impossible as I could see to 'fail to thrive,' as was documented back in the days on 'Workhouse' certificates, meaning, that the in adverse conditions and situations, flourishing was impossible, and death inevitable. But, my dreams were alive, and I was determined to make them stay that way, so I was in healthy portions, to take a pill of my own medicine, and stay not in a place where I preferred not to be, but really, "What lay ahead of me?" yet I'd already decided, "My time + commitment + availability = my perfect opportunity." So willingly, I was to fling wide open those doors in-front of me, and trot merrily on through, onto what I believed, was just the right thing to do.

For whole-heartedly, I believed in my goal and the decision I had made, and for consideration I was rapidly researching a plan, in perfect preparation to prevent any downfall, but time was to reveal, that of my certainty, to the rest of the world, 'life' had forgotten to tell. For was I on-track to learn a lesson in humility, or so much more, as so slowly, the misery that cradled around me, I was so totally unprepared for, as it proved to be, my evaluation was a great *faux pas* of a credible calculation, as time was to continue on, to demonstrate to me, that it, capable of highlighting good or bad through its passing, and time, sometimes, as much as we like, like the flow of the tide, it never can be stopped. And perhaps I had only deceived myself, for what awaited me, was it to be, prevailing good fortune, or through possible delusion, a bitter sweet equation, of, Me + France = 'A Collection of Calamities.'

"In Paris they simply stared when I spoke to them in French; I never did succeed in making those idiots understand their own language"
~ Mark Twain

Joie de vivre, the joy of life, "Oh what a precious commodity," perhaps so rare, as so seldom people retreat, from reaching for the stars, as they stay in mediocrity, dare not follow that dream that lays so deep within their heart, even embedded deep in their core, and "Why?" For so often, naysayers are the downfall of so many ideas not reaching fruition, and of those who discourage or partition "No. You cant do that," as they hasten, "Disaster lingers there and danger lay everywhere," as they choose, not to encourage but discourage, so consider most carefully of their caution, as just because they cant do it, doesn't mean that you cant, and more, "Do they have a hidden agenda?" For keeping you where you are and not wanting you to excel, for would that mean you moving away, and "Would that place a burden on them, of filling a gap, without their own inner map?" or perhaps, "There were smarting, stinging memories, of their dreams that without a trace they let slip away, only to be replaced, with memories creating inner-turmoil, because earlier in their lives, 'someone' persuaded them not to do, something, which 'Once Upon A Time,' so very much, they deeply desired to."

Though remember, there is no substitute, to seek good counsel and perform wise due diligence, to carefully investigate your plans, for fully armed is fully warned, of what twists and turns may be avoided, but mostly I have found to be, to land yourself in the right place at the right time, "Do what your gut tells you!" And "Oh my" was that what I had done, been fully prepared, for sure, I thought I had, as I found my self in Paris, and chatting with a lady, Mather May, for the US of A, while sitting in the Rocco period style lounge, of tall ceilings, expansive bold gold mirrors, and furniture, soft and welcoming, in fabrics in cream and eggshell blue, as we bathed in the warmth away from the snow-laden Parisian streets, in *Café Laurent*, on *rue Dauphine* in my favourite 6th $^{(eme)}$ *arrondissement*.

So I, enthused by an inspiring conversation with Martha-May, as with confidence of gusto her story she did relay, as she, embraced the tide of change, as she succumbed to that deep yearning in her heart, as she stood strong against the thong of naysayers of family and friends, enabling her spirit to flourish. As a decade earlier, it was a move from the East coast to the West, where in San Francisco, it was an Interior Design business she began, and nourished through to her core, "Happiness and abundance as never before are now mine" she, with gratitude enthralled, and when did that brave lady make that change? Well that was, at nearly the age of 60.

And "Her catalyst for change?" Well nothing profound, Mather-May simply preferred the vibe and the weather over in California, and sensibly she did consider, less competition and larger business opportunities, and so leaving behind her life run on autopilot, she packed up her bags and moved over 2000 miles, to embark on her new adventure, and as she entwined herself in a wholesome gratitude and splendour, as through her choices her life expanded, to where she came to be, a person who travelled the world, to fairs and conferences, all tax deductable, and to me that seemed a life, most pleasingly manageable and a seed was planted where I hoped that my new career could become comparable.

Yet, she not alone, as a different hemisphere I was to travel, and a lady I was to meet, so petite at perhaps only 4ft 3 inches, frail in stature, though on the inside holding a fortitude of great in might, and with passion she revealed her story, as we stood in the fine Hawaiian air, as the harmonious Choir sang on that Honolulu street, nearly 5000 miles from where she began, as she departed the Atlantic coast, and past over a dateline to live in a place she desired the most, to make a brand new start, to follow her heart and a dream, to live on that island in the Pacific Ocean. And yes, in a time of great influx in American history when she made this move, trials and tribulations accompanied her, but she refused to give in, or consider the quite spiteful messages from her nearest and dearest, of "You're too old! It's too far! You can't do that! Stop thinking about it, just stay right here and settle yourself down!"

But she was not to be deterred or give in to their imposing doctrine, as she fervently told me, "I knew I had one last good move in me, and I was determined to do it, I refused to let any of them put me off or talk me out of it." And as that little old lady who looked like a jolly good gust of wind could blow her over, asked me, "How old do you think I was when I did that?" "Well for sure, I don't know," then with a glint in her eyes, and a tone of self-confidence in her voice, she quite astonished me as she said, "I arrived here, 2 days after my 73rd birthday."

How wonderful that those admirably courageous ladies did not give up, as the admirably harnessed their courage, and how wonderful I met them along my way, so I could be reenergized and revitalized by their quite innovative stories, and their determined choices, and hadn't I read all those autobiographies and stories of women, who had left one country to live in another mainly, heading toward France, and hadn't they prepared me and my heart and imagination enhanced? So all of it really, along my journeys way, as in bits and pieces, it all added up to a whole, a whole where I believed, I was capable of achieving it too, so I was determined to give it my jolly best shot, as I kept on seeking, and forging ahead, to whatever was to reveal itself, either as a help or a hindrance, toward my goal, my dream, I was to keep on pushing right on through.

For their reward was clear of their personal pioneering steps, through their commitments and accomplishments, their striving and achieving, in the knowledge that through their decisions, their choices and their effort to themselves, their opportunities had been seized and their self-worth enhanced and verified, for through their lives they were to enjoy, a greater fulfilment of peace, to be emphasized.

"We meet no ordinary people in our lives"
~ C.S. Lewis

Really, could I do it to, indulge myself in the belief that I could do it too, could I add myself to that statistic, for the ones throughout my life I had already been added to the pain and suffering, saturated through to my core, where fate had propelled me into a desperate barrel of statistics, where all today's experiences, effect all tomorrows events, and so my life raged from childhood abuse, onward to that all unfavourable battered wife syndrome, before an ex-fiancé almost took my life from me, and in-between, shortly after I had left by teens, a rape victim I became, and to be a life or dead after the event, I had only a stomach of fear, for I knew not what he lay in-store for me. So after such seriousness, the rest of that statistical pile I fell into almost failed into insignificance, as my ex-husband took my house, and as a young nurse, after a back injury, I was retired from my career, that very thing that meant the world to me, and when at the age, of only about 23.

So to be plagued by bullying at work, in that country down-under, and be added to their number, seemed almost superfluous under those circumstances, but life is such, and onward it goes, propelled by its own motion, relentlessly not deviating until we take control and meaningfully change its direction, as so valuably for ourselves we deserve to do this, so life, and how wonderful it can be, we do not miss, as *pattern's* of *behaviour* we make it our purpose to recognize and identify its source, so we can work out a plan to eradiate them. For what I have learnt and gleamed our strength to be, to take the *power* of those delivered lessons forward, that were delivered without our consent, and leave the pain of their acquisition behind, as we quite rightly refuse, to live within the presence of anything they did against us, for ultimately, in-spite of them, we will win.

As higher levels of tolerance we expel to lowers of behaviour, that really, are substandard and we should not except, but so woefully do, for our training took care of that attitude, to see, or more to feel, that everyone is right, and so by definition, that must make us wrong, but that is not true, it was simply a falsehood, pre-programmed in us, by those who had no right to. So perhaps not surprising as they from our youth deceived us in believing there was no other way, so not difficult to conceive that, patterns of old, intrinsic in us, pop up and scream "Hello" interrupting our lives, preventing even a hint, of an easy flow, as relentlessly we muddle through our lives, accepting the abnormal as normal, for in truth, that is all we know, as we continue to live in the dark, where not even in our wildest imagination, do we believe there to be light, to illuminate our path, to a better place, a wonderful destination, to be treated better than ever we were, to get to know ourselves, and be illuminated with *beautiful* and *powerful insight*.

For the sad truth, until we do, our perception-deformed restriction propels forward on autopilot, as we by misfortune manufacture more of the same, until we recognize and interrupt its septic cycle, as hidden from view, that extravagant weight we may inadvertently buckle beneath, our concealed cloak of condemnation, until we take control of our life's journey, repelling those harmful misfortunes in our history, which may simply keep repeating itself, the same steps we keep stumbling on, but to work-out the route of bad behaviour patterns that we are continually subjected to, is for our very best purpose, for we will be, wiser, empowered and stronger, and then our reward, we break free of those restraints, we cast our net wider, for ourselves to encompass growth and harmony, as we take control and create an improved and better life, with a far more deserving of an; "Oh so much more," pleasant legacy.

> *"Too often we underestimate the power of touch, a smile, a kind word, a listening ear, an honest complaint, all of which have the potential to turn a life around"*
> *~ Leo Buscaglia*

"Oh what corrosive webs are cast," as innocent children we are caught and trapped within them, not knowing of escape, or daring to believe we can, and what an incompatible start to life, as such unstable ground for us to stand, with not a person around to share love, or from the heart offer an ounce of care, or to take us gently by the hand, and we by their behaviour, preconditioned to receive only bad, as sadly, desperately, continually we flounder, unknowing of that false start, that we are worthy of more, and life can hold something far better in store.

And of it all, I learnt to recognize patterns of my opportunities to learn, and seize them fervently, as I refused to simply accept my 'lot in life,' as I learnt not to waste but value experiences of adversity, of those gifts of the gaining of wisdom, wrapped up in the disguise of trails and tribulations, as slowly I began to realise, that they were there to 'school and improve' me, and to break those curses of old, as out from the past I was to escape, for something afresh, brand new as I become patiently and eventually, lovingly; bold!

So quite a petite 'smarty pants,' I became for my positive and improved future, as I placed myself in the frame, with a newly created philosophy, encompassing 'onward and upward toward success,' as I taught myself not to waste those experiences, but of them to grasp. For of battles and hurdles overcome, truly forward I did move, with a new inner-strength as my constant companion which increasingly enriched me, as of the jagged edges they were severed, disintegrated and removed, as a brighter future was mine to seek, with my new winning format and strategy, then complete.

For I had learnt, and learnt the lesson well, of the resounding truth, that, "We cannot always control what comes against us, but we can control as we choose, the way we respond to that which does." And that a most valuable lesson, it had formed apart of the structure of my personal growth, as no longer did I react needlessly, from old trapped habits hiding in the corners of my mind, but responsibly respond, for an improved outcome to serve me better, not randomly, but frequently.

As resolutely as I was to live, free, realising our trials and tribulations can teach us so much, as I tried so much to worry less, often proving as our 'school of learning,' and deepest catalyst for change, as I became determined, somehow, that I was still figuring out, to love myself and live in harmony, for by the passing through that debilitating time I had learnt of another and preferred way of being, one I so deserved, and I began to beckon and seek, not the treasures to purchase, but those priceless, those that cannot be purchased, and a job in progress, I learnt to live, with a healing heart, wonderfully and gloriously, inside of me!

"Success is not the key to happiness, happiness is the key to success.
If you love what you are doing, you will be successful."
~ Albert Schweitzer

So quite determined to be my own boss, I was to pack up my formidable trio, you may have guessed it, Me, Myself and I, and not look back, as I left behind a land, that I really did not enjoy, with the exception of only Balmain, where I lived for 8 months, to the west of Sydney's, city centre, where so fortunate had I been, to rent a little apartment, and walk just 5 minutes to the ferry, and even in the middle of winter, as we sailed for those 15 minutes across the harbour, not even a jacket was required, and then as I disembarked, another treat awaited me, as a coffee I would purchase, as up the hill I walked, past the buildings so grand, and architecture so fine, and all such a thrill, as all was to be enjoyed, and it hadn't even turned, 8 in the morning.

True, a friend or two, though more of casual acquaintances I made in Melbourne at Port Philip Bay, but only through the Thrift stores, and the best part of that city was the weather I did enjoy, for unlike the other, cooler it got, so what a thrill as I wore my winter fashions, of scarves and gloves all to match, with a hat or two to choice, just for good measure. And the choice in the stores, well that was quite fine, but so little else to positively reflect, as I mulled over my thoughts like a whirlwind in a winter storm, until with certainty like a summer breeze it flowed with ease, with my mind made up, with no second thoughts, it was onward and upward, to the northern hemisphere, where the dateline I was to cross, as I headed toward the Mediterranean Sea, to give France a jolly good old shot.

But really, "Was I to do it? To trot off, to pastures new and bright? Was it to be my dream, my destiny or perhaps hailing providence?" For surely it was the right time frame, as 5 yeas in NZ then the same in Australia, so to leave seemed for me, like the right thing to do. And Paris, "Wow!" That historic city, but of my decision eventually, was I to be happy or sad, for was I later to contemplate, misfortune, or mini-miracles, that were to jump up unexpectedly in my face, as with my baton firmly in hand, holding precociously tightly, jumping clear over those hurdles, as I continued along with life's 'meaningful' race. And "When oh when" was that race to become a dance, slowing from a Quickstep to a Foxtrot, and to slower down again?" As those unknown experiences that lay ahead, yet to be uncovered, and I 'job in progress' as I eventuated to be, along that path of potholes to healing recovery, and "Was I to grow and were they to prove, worthwhile stitches made with precision accuracy, in my 'Life's Tapestry' with colours bold and bright, perhaps subtle or dare I hope for delicate and gentle, with the finest of details, or was it to be, a rollercoaster ride, where stitches, were hurriedly put in without time or trouble, and as I prepared to meet my future, was I simply to become grateful, that anything was added at all?"

"Hope like faith is nothing if not courageous; it is nothing if it is not ridiculous"
~ Thornton Wilder

My contract complete, formalizing plans, with time on my hands, I was to again volunteer at those favourites of mine, Thrift Stores and give of my time, to help others, for that I find such a positive situation to venture into, and as I had done so in Auckland, working in a Hospice Shop, and even delivering H&S training, and then in South Melbourne, I was about to do a similar thing, giving of 4-6 hours, 3 days a week, to work in that store where previously I had spent, a pretty portion of my salary. And as one persons trash became another's treasure, I purchased another carefully chosen piece not because I needed it, but quite oddly, effectively, through scarcity, where the word scared, is hidden within, just for good measure, and as my collection grew in size, my bank account reduced, which I failed for a long while to realise, as I'd return to my flat, and all my finds were neatly stacked on shelves or attentively hung on rails.

And "Yes, I would admire them all," but only for a moment or two, as those precious items of a bygone age, most popularly, the 1980's, though the 1960's, I particularly liked them too, and known of it was to be worn, as all too big, or unpractical, suiting not my lifestyle, but its uselessness deterred me not, for it was the quality and the style and the irreplaceable nature, that drew me to them all, the tailored lines, the cut of the fabric, the quality of how it was made, as my mind wonder, of what was the life like of the person who wore these clothes, their work, their home, the medical care that surrounded them, the comparisons all served to invigorate my concepts of social medical history. Yet really, a quite profound discovery, of a simplistic notion, that enabled me to change my way of being, of spending as I kept my money, and watched my bank account grow, as I had a new Golden Rule, which was to add to the list, as beamed with a smile, succinctly I learnt wonderfully, "To admire, without having to acquire!"

So there it was in my 2 bedroom apartment that looked out over the bay, through the 4 years I lived there, the spare room became totally full, and I was unable to push open the door, to place my latest in there, and such a problem it all became emotionally, as I became so unrealistically attached to them, but there again, with such gross ill health, and no social life available, and nowhere around, 'social-connectedness,' a term I learnt while working as a Community Nurse, perhaps it was not surprising that I found an outlet of something to do, that I was able to invest time and effort on, completely unaware of the future ahead of me, of that impending move in my future was to cause such exasperating stress and overwhelming angst, as so sadly I was to have to dismantle and pick it out item by item and give it away again.

But I totally strange, for I thought I had formulated a plan, like my fathers mother, who owned very little, but all she had was of the very best quality, and my mothers mother, who had good taste, but chose quantity, and I, thought I was so clever, and found a route to combine the 2, shopping at my favourite kind of store, those known as Thrift. But perhaps I should have given a little more consideration to my grandma, who trawled the thrift stores, looking for homemade wool garments, which she purchased and washed, before pulling-back' and rewinding the wool in reusable balls, to be placed in big black bin liners, and placed in the loft, until it was time to use them, but the amazing thing abut that all, upon her death, her attic spanning the dimensions of the bungalow, were packed full of those bags, reaching into every corner, which she collected but didn't need, and too late I began to wonder, really, "Have I followed in her footsteps?" and "Why hers and not the other grandmas?"

For it transpired, my perpetuating purchasing of mild obsession, equated to a basic calculation: old + beautiful + or - unusual + quality divided by the price = perfectly mine! But "Why had I forgotten my grandad's rules, forever important rules?" "Everything in moderation" and "Always live within your means." he would say so positively," with "Watch the pennies, and the pounds/dollars will look after themselves." and then, "The 95%/5% rule." I was to learn, through learning much later, where weekly, to "Spend a maximum of 95% of your wages and put the other 5% always save it, in your Savings Account and delightfully watch it grow." and through that experience, perhaps most relevant to me, which I re-learnt and re-implemented, "To buy more than you need, equates to a waste."

But all too soon the notion was to grab a-hold of me, of "Why why why?" did I concede to "More more more?" Perhaps because, all purchased financially easily, those period clothes, which all transferred to be my valued possessions, yet not an excuse, and "Oh so valuable" it would have been to me, 'if only' I would have known previously, that children who have suffered abuse, often hold a strong propensity, to collecting or hording, and I grew and knew, that was true of me too. And so powerful that knowledge proved to be, for there seemed a reason why perhaps I had acted so predictably unwisely, as for sure, of all those purchases, other than the initial thrill of buying them, I didn't even look at them again, so really, "What use were they to me?" Through time it transpired, absolutely none.

"You can't depend on your eyes when your imagination is out of focus."
~ Mark Twain

As there, I was putting temptation in my path, while volunteering at the thrift store, and so much more pleasurable the job, than the one at the hospital I had left, and the team the same, and one of the members, who came in on a Saturday morning, James, a young gentleman in his 20's, with quite a philanthropist spirit, also building drama stages for another organization, so smart, that he had been approached to publish his Thesis, and how wonderful I was to discover, that he had already done what I was about to do, to move across to France, and so, not wishing to reinvent the wheel, "For why would ya, when you didn't have ta?" Yet to use another's Blueprint, well that only seemed astute, when it had worked so well, so asking so many questions and listening astutely to the answers to interpret and implement, for wasn't it sensible and practical, as really, "What could possibly go wrong for me?"

Yet I knew not, as I was so impressed and so eager to discover more, of his move to Paris, where he was to study, one subject he knew not, and that class, taught in *la langue française*, the French language, which at that time he *ne pouvait pas parler*, could not speak either, and so courageous was he to undertake such a thing, and so his recipe, as he helped me with information here and strategies there, and I was to be so very grateful, but I failed to calculate, his character, personality and education abilities, his enthusiasm and the way he was able to socialize easily and get involved and 'put himself out there' ready to learn and to embrace what passed his way, nor embarrassed should he trip or fall, and right there lay the difference, our individuality, resolving resolutely, that one methodology, does not fit all, as I was to discover, through errors of misguided miscalculations and mini-nightmares, as many there turned out to be.

Perhaps simplistically, "Had I thought rationally, substituting me for him, in his equation prescription?" as so much angst I could have saved myself, and not tripped or fallen, even before I got off the starting block, creating an emotionally taunting and draining, *faux pas*, as so much better to avoid that negative chain reaction I should have calmly evaluated, not just, "Where to from here?" or "What comes next?" but a far greater question would have served me best, of "How best to achieve that outcome best for my peace and harmony?" And to make a better assessment, it would not have been difficult to do, for my instinct was shouting at me so utterly loudly, as I chose to follow James's format, of only taking with me in only 4 boxes of 160kg of possessions, but "Why was I so foolish as to give everything else away, as that decision proved to hold little logic along that way." For on reflection, it made absolutely no sense to follow his plan to the letter, for he a student back then and had so little to leave behind, and his treasured items, well they were left in safe keeping, and 2 years later when his study was complete, family and friends were awaiting him back in Australia.

"Wow!" So amazingly obvious with hindsight, but not way back then, before I had the benefit of 20/20 hindsight, but not back then, when panic became my enemy, and blurred my vision as so regularly it does, and no matter which step I took, it appeared to be wrong, and as I ran around like a headless chuck, still I could not stop myself, to find a quiet place, or other counsel, that may have given me a different perspective, and put a helpful spanner in the works, to prevent me from endlessly going around and around on the endless roundabout, and I could have stopped it and got off, and taken a while to contemplate, that screeching and shrieking of my inner-gut, telling me, 'not to do what I was doing.' But you see, I misunderstood, for never before, had I felt fear, in the realms of, something I was about to do, so I had no compass to lead me to know that I was doing anything wrong, or out of place, as I only concluded of those terrible debilitating and destructive pains, it was because I was going out of my comfort zone, so I thought, I had to face the fear and do it anyway, but "No." It was not because of the decision I made, but the route I was taking to achieve my goal, for my aptitude and capabilities, so dreadfully terribly, out of sequence, and out of place, and started a disastrous, chain reaction.

So on I went with angst overtaking me, but on a mission to achieve my goal, of leaving that British Colony of old, as I commenced a struggle to empty my 2 bedroom apartment, of all my beautiful collections, of vintage clothes, apparel and accessories, in idyllic lace, to metallic leathers, and I was not done there, as my everyday clothes also had to go, and "Oh my" my pairs of shoes, and there were many, and the traditional design of handbags with fastening clasps, to be hung from the wrist, in suede or lizard skin, and all so elegantly chic or funky, as my desired style I like to aspire to, where Coco Chanel meets Audrey Hepburn, with the character's wardrobe of Carrie Bradshaw thrown in, and that superfluous collection, all added up to a more than a pretty-penny of $8000, as my monthly credit card statement gave testimony, and true although practically, I let go of those treasured items, it was to be an excess of time which was to pass, before I was able to let go of my attachments emotionally.

But worse was to come as those items that I liked perhaps even better, my collection of antique leather suitcases, practically for storage, while more importantly, aesthetically pleasing on the eye. And my chairs, "Oh my chairs" Edwardian and Victorian, in pairs, for that pleases me best, Nursing chairs, with spindled inlaid backs and cabriole legs, and bedroom chairs, so pretty in pink, and of cause the traditional fabric that pleases me best, that of Damask, then an Edwardian Carver, inlaid with rose and box wood, and as beautiful as it was, nowhere near as delightful of the bedroom chair, inlaid with pear wood, and Mother of Pearl, and the detail, it even continued to along every piece of wood, and quite unusually, decorating the legs at the back. Then there was my Victorian bedroom chair in rich mahogany displaying ornate carvings, a little more unusual than a Balloon-back where from 1 piece of wood, a bouquet of roses had been carved, and "Oh my" how exquisite and delightfully beautiful, but of all I owned, I do believe, they are the adjectives most commonly used.

For my physical and emotional habits had spurred me along that route, Little could I do with my days, except shop, and did I delude myself, to believe, that more than one or two of those assistants were my friends, when really they were simply there, doing their job, talking to me, meeting their business targets and getting the money in the shareholders accounts. Or simply was shopping an emotional release or my excuse, but exercise I never liked to take, even though to walk along the beautiful and refreshing water front was free, I decided, it was a little too much and not for me. The same so sadly can be said to stroll along the roads past the delightful and historic housing of that aged suburb with was my favourite, but no, it was excuses that I made not aloud, but subconsciously, as all I needed was my succinct refusal to take part in even the mildest of activity, which resided quietly, still and motionless, inside me.

But "Oh what a joy," that we do learn and grow, as human beings we hold the capacity within to change ourselves and metamorphosis so completely, as I used to be a 'fine weather girl' in the realms of exercise, yet how gladly I grew and developed into an 'any weather girl,' as exercise I grew to adore, as it happened so sublimely and certainly surprisingly, for my transformation, I knew not it was in process, yet that stopped me not at the outcome to rejoice with glee, at my new preferred attribute, as I experienced and learnt to enjoy taking exercise, everyday.

With that lesson packed onboard, not superficially but deeper within my soul, I grew with a desire to serve myself better and make me, whole, for more importantly, I piggy-backed on that achievement, as I began to change increasing amounts of old, outdated, ill-serving habits, for ones brand new, that towards a brighter future, were to serve me, brightly, so extremely well, as I used not excessive force, but gentle loving persuasion, as if soft waves, lapping at the awaiting shore, and with this temperate wisdom that grew to accompany me, so grateful for a greater gift, as I permitted myself to grow in health and peace, along my journey way.

"The years teach much which the days never knew"
~ Ralph Waldo Emerson

Yet my collection that resided not just in my apartment, but the emotion of it all, resinated somewhere in my heart, but true, what else was there to occupy it, well that was to be a 'whole lot of not much,' and how beautiful it was, to run my fingers across that warm and ancient wood, and imagine the skilful artisans who had crafted such a thing, and how pleasant it was to sit, and flick through one of my favourite books, for another collection, of the 1st editions, St John's Ambulance, amazed at the way conditions used to be treated before the expansion of modern science and medicine, and what of those Alice In Wonderland 1st editions and those with the pictures included and how wonderful as simultaneously I would look at them, and see the interpretational differences of illustrations.

And as I passed on the way to work, or stood and styled my hair, how wonderful it would be to look in a mirror, with a beautiful and decorative built *Rococo* frame, lavishly exquisite in detail, and pictures, of water colours or prints, back form a certain era of yesteryear, all continually, and never failed to enthral me. And my bed, how I simply loved getting in that, for the frame so femininely pretty all dainty in alabaster white, with the bits that went on top, fur in fabric or maybe silk, and high thread cotton sheets to slip right into, a pillows made of duck-down, and a heated blanket too, and all I was so going to miss, of their mellow hues, with calming and peaceful colours, of antique dusky pink and cream, and the mirror, the frame almost ornate to distraction, iridescent, in platinum, such ease at the start and end the day, and all so wonderfully, they eased my heart, and soothed my soul, and such an awe inspiring and delightful ensemble, so "Why oh why, so foolishly, did I let them all go?"

Yet the full picture I failed to consider, so it was, those treasures of mine, that had previously proved to be trash by another, I was to give them back from whence they came, and those shoes, which were always bought new, and my other clothes also, well such fun I had enjoyed buying them at the regular store, but they were to find themselves to the same place too, and my bedding, you guessed it, and although bargains, all of my pristine precious collection, had added up to a pretty-penny, but the antiques, and 3 seater leather settee, and even rug to match well they all went off to the auction along with my new fridge freezer, used only for 6 weeks, while I embarked on a healthy eating program, to try and assist with gaining better health, and true it did work, as that home-delivery program, kind of kick-started an appropriate eating routine and re-jumped my appetite, so all was not bad, but a loss $800, and all those other items, the vintage collection of clothes that took me 5 years to gather, with the antiques bought in Honiton, the antique centre of the south, in Devon, all were to fall under the hammer, and the only revenue I was to receive in return, was the measly sum of just 495 dollars in my hand.

"Oh my" could I have possibly got it any more wrong, and so pleased I had been with James's generosity, which blinded my judgment and rational in my decision-making but really, confused, tormented, in turmoil, lacking totally in clarity, where a self-misguided chain reaction what was to unfold, which transformed to cause me huge servings of trouble and strive only aiding in the smarting of opening wounds, that I still failed to realise, invisible to the human eye, but not to the feeling heart, so "Why oh why?" did I not listen to its warnings, as they establishing a route of cross-infection, multiplied and festered, as I could simply not forgive myself for what I'd done, to make so many, quickly repetitive mistakes, and through the unravelling of the foreseeable time, comfort, for such a long time, I was unable, to call mine.

Yet still, most miserably I pushed on through, not knowing what else to do, adamantly refusing to be discouraged by those pit-falls and miss-haps, as they appeared to do their best to formulate a plan to prevent me from reaching my goal, but "Oh what a folly" for I now realise, that they may have been a prescription to save me from myself, of making those competitive mistakes, causing only discontent and humongous amounts of unease, through the torrent of those white roaring waters, trying not to destroy me against the hard rocks, but just hoping in their endeavours to wash me up on safe land, yet as that fear continued to consume me, fraught with anguish, lacking in wisdom, I understood not, and that was to be a price, due to my unwitting contemplation, that as to trouble me, quite a lot.

But really, "Why was I so fearful?" that even basic maths calculations, I appeared unable to do, for surely, just half an hour spent on those, I would have realised the $3000 it was to cost me to take 4 boxes across to France, was not to be cost-effective at all, for storage for a year, for all of it, where nothing I would had to have given away, would have come to less than that amount, so "Why oh why?" I screamed and cried with utter frustration, did I, not stop myself in my tracks and pull on the breaks, and right there, given myself one too, as I meandered down the road, perhaps a little too focused, so unable was I to see the warning signs as I hurriedly went along, with only the final result, missing the journey and the benefits it can provide, and perhaps just maybe, that is why it is designed to take time, so as we pass through it, we can recalculate and make necessary adjustments along the way.

Yet "Wasn't I to feel better, when those boxes arrived at the apartment I stayed in Paris?" Well that was to be sadly "No" for although those goods had so far travelled the world by sea, those most valuable of valuables I had entrusted to an Australian company to use airfreight, well my possessions were to be delivered to me broken, and "Oh such a shame" for the first thing to find, was a large powder blue vase, embossed with flowers of white enamel, the last gift my Grandfather gave me, was so sorrowfully broken. And as I went through everything else, I pondered with perplexity at the choices I had made, and woefully, came to the conclusion, whatever I did was not right, for then, examining the few things I had left, and the drastic effect of ignoring my gut-instinct to *stop* and *examine* what I was *doing*, and as a result of my miss-actions and unfolding consequences, of 'acting in haste & repenting at leisure,' my unravelling debilitating emotions roared with fear, with nothing left to ground me, I felt so horrendously sick and tremendously so, absolutely all alone.

> *"You gain strength, courage and confidence by every experience at which you stop to look fear in the face....you must do the thing you think you cannot do"*
> *~ Eleanor Roosevelt*

But "How could I have possibly got it all so wrong? For hadn't I done the right thing?" Immersed myself in that which I wanted, for don't they say, 'Whatever you focus on will grow greater each day,' and France was my hearts desire, and I so eager for it to transpire to reality, so each evening after work, after first visiting the Avenue Food Store for my dinner, for so welcoming the staff and so good the food, and a good price too, so there I would be found when the working day was done, as I hid away from the ironically named rush-hour traffic. For really, in it, when was the last time anyone rushed anywhere, and more, just how many years have passed since it lasted for just one? But I digress, a $10 salad, I had the same every night, either chicken or smoked fish, and even at the end of the day, it was so wonderfully fresh, and always followed by a half-strength flat-white coffee, before into the evening air I would trot, my feet upon the footpath, as up the road where the tram tracks cut through, until after only 5 minutes or more, in my favourite hamlet of Albert Park, I would find myself after a short walk through the different coloured wooden historic houses, in the comfort of The Avenue Book Store.

And there, in the comfort of a lounge chair or seated on the leather ottoman, as my fingers flicked through the large and glossy books, of varied types of French properties, from Parisian loft conversions, bright, airy and funky, or a castle, standing bold at the peak of a hill, a feast of history to ponder, as its walls and turrets built from the largest blocks of grey bland stone, to the delights of *Chateaus*, elegant to the extremes, or further into the countryside, where nestled within the rolling hills, farmhouses of beautiful stone, all renovated and looking so grand, with their interiors, shabby chic or traditional regional French style, and so often for family and friends, and depicting the benefits of the sunshine, an alfresco area in where to dine.   Then the idyllic villages, separated by rambling hills, with groups of cottages, perhaps in a mews, and all painted in winter pink, with petit blue shutters aside those tiny windows, with rooves of bright red tiles, where often could be seen, a meandering brook splicing through the middle and I could almost imagine the sound as it gently flowed the crystal clear water meandered across the rocks, appearing as steppingstones, or perhaps concealed were their rough edges of stumbling blocks.

But my favourite, and go-to, a book on *Aix-en-Provence*, which really I could not get enough of, as I immersed myself so thoroughly init, as I devised a plan as my imagination enhanced and flowed, surpassing my mind, seeping into my heart, as my thoughts expanded, of just how wonderful it would be, to buy a derelict property, that no one else wanted, to renovate and have a dream come true, as I was to set up a *Chambre d'Hote*, Bed & Breakfast, amidst the fragrant roaming hills of lavender, and as I permitted my mind to frivolously frolic, in all that was possible, I failed to consider, that I was to be drenched by an attack of 'naysayers syndrome, and of my dream, "Was it to become weak or frail?" and "Was success to be mine to hail?"

For was my dream not complete, as I so constantly fuelled it, with images of me, in my little CV2 convertible Citron car, where the colour didn't matter, as with the roof rolled back, there would be me, rambling along, my hair blowing back through the French countryside with the lush green foliage bordering each side, and onto my morning coffee I'd ride, where I held images of sitting beneath the warmth of the early sun, enjoying a chat or two with the locals, while continuing to read autobiographies, of women, who had already done which I so desired to achieve, to leave one country to live in another, and start their own business, and eventually, succeed, in a way to flourish. And then off to business, as back I would travel, with *du pain* French bread, beside me on the passenger seat, and reaching up to the sky planks of wood and beside it, with a drill, screws and nails, which, soon they where to be used by me, as I was to carry-on my own home renovation, with exceptionally more than a small degree of glee.

Or was I simply being too optimistic, and should I not have remembered those curses as my mother from I such a young and impressionable child, who tried so hard to debilitate me, telling me from as early as I could remember, "You're too independent I tried so often to knock that out of you, but never could!" but how weird, for "Why would you even try?" as an independent spirit is so good to have. But her curses didn't stop there, but I hasten to say, thank goodness somewhere in my core, as she spurned me, I gave her not the power to prove them prophecy, "Get your head out of the clouds." or worse "You're a dreamer. You're foolish. You're only asking for disappointment if you carry on that way." with "You're no better than you should be" thrown at me. Well "Thanks for the vote of confidence mummy-dear." "Oh my" was it deliberate that she tried so hard to mislead me, as her own potential she did not realise, and at least in part, and at least in part she blamed me for that, or perhaps, her intentions were good, though my experience of her, I consider her attitude not accidental, but a deliberate intent to cause me harm, far more likely.

"Triumph can't be had without a struggle"
~ Wilma Rudolph

Yet somehow, thank goodness, but perhaps not through a hope for happiness, but sheer determination, to be in a better position than the one I then lingered in, that Oscar Wild's notion and insight somehow filled me, with his consideration, that "You can be in the gutter, but you can still gaze upon the stars." And perhaps how pointedly profound to the life I endured. But better his notion was to serve my imagination his words, perhaps of wisdom, "...the only thing one never regrets are one's mistakes." So I reflected and considered, "Really, why not for me too?"

My enthusiasm waned not, as my format to seek and find, to propel me on each night, until 7pm, when the bookstore closed, and the bridge was clear, to drive my 7km journey home, as then it was not to take me an hour plus, and during those hibernation hours, a young man from that store, I began to chat, as he showed me the books and CD's on the shelf, to try and enable me to get a heads-up on the language of French, and s much information was for discovery, as he enlightened me to his schooldays and Exchange Student Program, and how very useful as a teenage boy of 14 years or so, to live with a French family in their home, for their he told me, quite a startling recipe, for picking up all the idiosyncrasies of the language, and French culture simultaneously, and from what he experienced he thought, "What a good thing to do."

"Oh my" so was I to jump ship from one plan, zigzagging through the treacherous tide, darting spasmodically, with the headless chuck syndrome not relenting, as skipping from one idea to another, or was I empowering myself with another option for sturdy consideration, or was I to confuse the ruder as I became that practicing Mariner, turning it from this way to the other, increasing the uneasy movement in the water, or was I sensibly, absorbing for consideration the enlightening facts that had fallen on me, where I was to make a more balanced decision, for increasing choices available to me? For no longer need it simply be, a 3 month stint in short term accommodation, but a 3 night stay in a hotel, while I looked through the university for help, in attaining a placement to stay with a family, and there I could too benefit from what the former schoolboy had too, for that, a little more of a logistical procedure, but the benefits seemed to multiply, for that route would mean, what I so needed, a bigger saving to gleam.

And "Oh my" 'if only' I had more money to spend, and for sure I could have had several thousand, nay more, should I have not bought, that needless depreciating item, of a hard-top convertible car. True, it looked quite beautiful, a tad sporty with its deep tinted windows, and true, I had placed a picture of it up on my 'inspirational wall' and how soon I got one to come by me, perhaps aided by a friend, as he so loved all-things-cars, he made it his mission to find me the exact one I wanted, so I thought, "It's meant to be," when the exact one popped up, and being a bloke, when I asked him to negotiate, on my behalf, man to man, I thought more, "I cannot believe my luck."

But "Too quick" was to be my cry, as I was to discover, that things, situations and certainly people are not all what they seem, as with the money gone, I realised all too late, that do nothing, without personal due diligence, even if it only to check on what others have done, and just because a person is priced in the arena of which the search entails, it means nothing, when the bottom line is drawn, and the money they are negotiating for belongs not to them but another, it may not be the best price that is arrived at, but just a different one, and I was left, owning a car, that for 2 years of my ownership caused nothing but scorn, as credit in my Savings Plan, became hugely depleted, tattered and torn.

"Oh why; did I need such a car?" For really, the other suited me so perfectly, a 3 door, 4 seater car, low on petrol and insurance, and a doddle to park, and "Yes" much was going wrong with it, but surely that would desire a change only, not an investment, and oxymoron in terms, as most often, a looses not makes money, as an investment is designed to do, for that car, the engine never worked correctly, the hard pull to the left hand side of that French manufactured car was dangerous, the hydraulics broke on the roof, and what went on with the engine, that became quite repetitive, and so much more, on that was spent, not to mention, multiple times of inconvenience. And the man who helped me purchase it, to stand by and help, as the Australian Dealership people so repetitively, disrespectfully delivered their verdict, "Nothing is wrong with the car." Then that 'friend,' who did the deal, man to man, was nowhere, to be found, to intervene or maybe assist me ever again, as those salesmen in their trade, disparaged me so. But "Should I be surprised?" Maybe not, and certainly, lessons we learn, although so miserable, we must not discard them, but for or benefit, consistently learn to heard and hold them in esteem.

The cost of what I did suddenly to hit me hard, as I struggled to gain and conserve money for my Parisian leg of life's journey, heading toward my new future that needed funding ahead of me, and my little practically purposeful car, I paid $10,000 for that, and got $8000 in return, loosing $2000 straight away with trade-in. And the Peugeot, I paid, $22,000 for that vehicle that I thought suited me so much better, when in fact, the money in my account would have given me far greater pleasure. And in 2 years it was to be gone, after causing me only trouble and strive, and guzzling the gas, my fuel bill doubled and my insurance almost the same, with those figures, just for running around town, adding extra $3,400 to my annual budget of unnecessary expenditure.

Plus the price of the car, of $14,000 to pay, tallying in one year to $17,400, but the amazing thing is, there was no man around to help negotiate a sale, and all the garages I took it to, had very bad new to give to me, bewilderingly, the only revenue that car was to return me, was a measly figure of $8000, meaning in effect, just on the price of the car, I lost a staggering $14,000. But more I was to realise, "Yes, that was my loss" but in actual fact, because that was a debit and needed to be replenished and repaid for, in actual fact equated to a $32,000 deficit, from where I began to where I ended up, and what a bitter pill that was to swallow, on that one frivolous purchase, just because, I thought, quite irresponsibly, not of my future but superficial gratification, but a lesson which was well received, for never will I do that again, "As once bitten, twice; not on your life!"

For in a deep deficit, I have to replenish it, and that $32,000, out of my savings account where I first begun, formed as a barrier to property and other investing, for even at a conservative 5.99% over a 25 year mortgage, at a compounding rate, really I was to suffer decidedly so, of 100% loss, to be reimbursed only by paying greater taxes through working harder, and in doing that, really, succinctly put, all that cost I had to ingest, just so, in my imagination darting spasmodically around my head, I had a vehicle that "better represented me." Yet "How bizarre" that concept I now consider, for in reality, it caused great angst financially and caused me nothing but an elongated, proverbial, pain-in-the-neck.

Such huge and extraordinary angst that deal caused me, as such horrendous accommodation situations were to plague my stay in 'a gay Paris" as with that financial deficit, I tried so hard to evaluate, what and where I could afford, and so much of my Parisian experiences were to be totally effected by that one decision of infatuation, and instant gratification about buying a car, that in essence was only to transport me from A to B. As all proved such a hindrance for my future, where basic comfort and peace I could not afford, and luxury or beauty, for years ahead, my chain reaction continued to detangle, as I held not the capacity to afford what I could before. As my huge folly rolled effortlessly on, as self-disparagement followed me around shouting my name, as it, I could not escape, became my daily companion, twisting and tightening my spirit, as emotionally distraught, they too heavy to take flight, at what I permitted me to do to me, and the lack of consideration I gave to the consequences of such an action, as my security all around in France proved to be less, and I was to wonder really, in totality, "Did I succumb to all, solely, because of my vanity?"

For in totality, all of it aided not, to ease my fear, only doubled my confusion, for the decision I now consider simple enough, but in the midst of panic, nothing was I able to see clearly, and not once did it occur to me, as I floundered about on the white waves of those rolling seas, that really, and simply, I need to *stop*, and take a breath, and re-evaluate my situation, but that is the problem with panic it stops our minds working, in a rational format, so the clear way forward, or away out of those potential dangerous rapids I found myself in, simply unable, with the absence of good, necessary counsel, pertaining not of good intentions from other kind people, but particularly and specifically pertaining to my specific needs, from my emotions in turmoil, through to my intricate finances, for a *valid* and *appropriately correct* plan, to be made for safety, free from harm and inner-peace, for really, "Where to from here?"

And with such confusion lying everywhere, amazingly, obliviously, I still failed to consider, those obvious messages of my gut-instinct clearly shouting and screaming, trying so, so hard to impart their perfect wisdom for my protection, astonishingly not recognizing that simply, "*I must surely have been doing something wrong!*" but "No" for I continued on regard-less-ly, increasing my catalogue of errors, that was tallying up to an epic, "*As I, was not true to me,*" and a heavy price I was to have to pay, not so far away. For "Was I to reap the rewards of using another's blueprint, without reinventing the wheel?" and "Was I to double my chances and by intertwining 2 reap the rewards, or in essence was I to discover, that my ladder was leaning against the wrong wall?"

"Only a life lived for other is a life worthwhile"
~ Albert Einstein

Australian society did not suit me, as un-nurturing, unfulfilling I found it to be, and certainly not with me, a good fit, and a successful period of my life, certainly it was not, and I began to wonder, "Do places or relationships people have an expiry date attached to them?" So perhaps no surprise, it was not to be a sweet sorrow but a "Wahoo, here I go!" As I was to reel with delight, thank goodness that's over as I was preparing to take flight, yet a waste of time, that I cannot say it was, for on one Saturday morning, not my history, but a new legacy was to eventuate, and what a pleasure arose, to leave Australia on a high, as those previous 5 years of calamity, I was to leave behind.

Yet before I was to leave on that jet plane, not knowing when I would be back again, my routine continued, working the 4 or 5 hours each Saturday at the Thrift Store, giving of my time, to 'give-back' to help others less fortunate than me, but one particular morning, one of 'those headaches' came on, and instead of pushing through it, that so often I would, when only I could, that day for some reason, I had little resolution to do just that, so decided unusually to leave, and drove the kilometre or 2, returning for another half-strength flat-white, at my tremendously favourite coffee store.

With a change in routine, my table in my preferred spot, where I always sat was unavailable most unusually, so not at the back, but the front of the café, I was to sit, where in front of me through the vista of the windows, not normally, a view across the tram tracks I was clearly able to see. Then after nipping to the restroom, and retuning to sit at the square table by the wall, on those not quite so comfy wooden chairs, I peered through the large pain of glass, that covered the wall, trying to comprehend exactly what it was, that fell in my vision.

Then, I, able to decipher what was going on at the other side of the roundabout, jumped quickly from my chair ready to take action, pushing open the heavy brass framed door, and dashing across the road, to make sense of the commotion, and there in the midst, a man, tall, with grey hair led on the pavement, in physical distress, unresponsive, unconscious on the floor, with his skin passing from white to crimson red. And quick as a flash, I remembered my refresher course, First Aid at Work Training, I enquired who else was present at the scene, and there I was told, the lady holding the patients head said, "I'm a GP" {general practitioner} and the young gentleman of 30-something, explained to me, "I took a First Aid course just last week, as a requirement that I had to do, before out of an aeroplane, they'd let me jump."

He was doing a good job, but he realised not, to be better effective, on a mature male, he needed compressions of about 2 inches, and them, seeing no results for his efforts and perceiving no patient improvement, exhausted, he ceased the CPR compressions. But I, with a fresh eyes on the scene, I knew what to do, so as I knelt down at the opposite side of the patient, in front of that 30 something year old man, I began clapping my hands to the speed and rhythm of the Nursery Rhyme, "Bar bar black sheep" with simple and precise instructions, "Go deeper, go quicker, go harder." and as I continued to clap to the tempo, singing the song out loud, and as the words were sung, and after a few well-placed compressions, "Yes sir yes sir, three bags full," and *success* was to be had, as for that 50-something year old man, who had a 7 year old son, with his refreshed beating heart, his life once again, had begun.

And as that man, whose life was saved, his heart beat re-started, pumped blood to replenish his cells with oxygen, and his skin wonderfully changed, from a very poor prognosis of blue, retuning upward to a deep red, though crimson and returning to pallor, certain progress, and one of the best outcomes right then, we were able to hope, to possess.

What an amazing trio joined together, all by chance, or happy circumstance, on that Saturday morning early in Spring, for so powerful to contemplate, that in life, perhaps there are no coincidences, but often perfect missions delivered from a higher vision, as on that day, the GP only at that café, because her friends had just been successful t secure a house at auction around the corner, and that café, so rare to sell champagne, so they decided to idle a while and partaking of a salad. And the other young gent, well he was there, only because he was having such a bad day, and needed to stop and get out of his car, so his mind from stress, could recuperate. And only because he decided to give himself a treat to fulfil a desire on his heart, decided to jump out of a plain with a parachute the previous week, and only there, was the reason that he had learnt the skills, First Aid provides and CPR and how to save, another's life.

Than I, working with a history of Health & Safety Nursing, learnt only more recently such a rhythm and speed to use, and that is the interesting situation of progress, as we keep up with it, it is not only ourselves who may benefit. And I reflected and was quite proud of us, as our skills marinated instantly in a melting pot, as so gladly our services we volunteered, to save a stranger on the street, with a recipe of skills to bring a life back from the grips of death. And for sure into the bargain of good fortune, a passing off-duty Paramedic, pulled up, and by good fortune, his 'tools of his trade' in his car, the blood pressure metre, and most importantly, an Airway, to be used to keep the tongue from falling into the back into the throat, so therefore, securing an open airway to permit the air to guaranteed to pass more freely with greater efficiency into the patients lungs, and secure in the Recovery Position, his safety restored.

For that man with a wife and a young son, they were able still to move forward in a life together, and for sure it was not guaranteed, as after the ambulance arrived, the Paramedics placed the patient on heart-trace monitor, and confirmed that indeed, he had flat-lined, clinically died. And "Oh my" what an honour, or maybe a mini-miracle, to know that I had taken part in our trio, and were able to cheat death and save for him, so with his family, he could continue to live a life, hopefully, in the fullest of joy, with peace and harmony.

And we, a 'team of coincidence,' brought together in synchronicity, strangers, in that moment, gelling effortlessly together, each possessing a piece of knowledge to contribute, to give gloriously to serve another, and what a blessing I found that to be. And from my Australian adventure, in that land down under, which really was a less than good experience, though, ultimately, I was "Oh so happy" to be there, for the legacy I was to leave, 'was to have save a life, and his family, and of that, with me, I must say, I was pretty pleased!"

..........*And then*

"Paris is always a good idea"

~ Audrey Hepburn

Chapter 3

Step on Through....

> *"Courage is not the absence of fear, but rather the judgment that something else is more important than fear."*
> ~ Ambrose Redmoon

So there it was, "P Day," had arrived, as I walked unsure as was it with angst or anticipation, as I ventured into that brightly lit atrium, where my mind needed to remain alert, and my heart in check not permitting it to flounder or fly, with the precarious troffs or triumphs that may lay ahead, I packed in my suitcase, rather larger than average portions of courage, and perhaps too late to wonder, of the uncertainties that awaited me, really, for making such a bold decision and move perhaps precariously, "Was I sensible, brave or foolhardy?"

As I unaware, that 'odd' situations lay ahead, with debilitating echoes from childhood, and of life's longevity, as unwittingly, weapons of destruction, tried their best to form adversaries against me, yet, ultimately, standing strong, I permitted them not forever to inhibit my future, for I was to keep searching for something to nurture me, to escape those invisible ties, until I discovered that place within, where from its harness of despair, I no-longer needed hide.

"Was France to prove to be, an area which was put in my path, to aid my journey toward my destiny?" And 'Oh my' was my spirit at such a prospect, to ruffle its feathers with pure delight, to enhance that slow track to recovery, where such inner-growth, through made or presented opportunities were possible, or so unpredictable?" For 'what came next' I was so ill prepared, for my impending journey, I was so unaware it held a far greater number of stumbling blocks than steppingstones within it, and so as I contemplated my forthcoming adventure positively, of "What did it have in store for me?" I had no idea misfortune was to descend over my choices, even before I'd even departed the Australian shores. And indeed what for others too, for as I stood and looked about the queue, of the expressions adorned on peoples faces, for was it for business or pleasure which they were to travel, and of meet their expectations, was it to do so or was it to fall short, and of a stitch in their tapestry of life, "Was it to be nasty, harsh or warming and nice?"

So there it was, as I stood patiently awaiting, and a comfort zone or two I was about to pass on through, and as Charles Dickens talked of his 'great expectations,' I wondered, "Was I to receive trouble and strive, or possibly attain happiness to some greater degree of less or more, along this journey of life?" For really of note, I hoped and planned so that it would be the latter, for in effect, perhaps quite recklessly, I had burnt my bridges and of plan B there was not, as effectively there was no other, so it was to be plan A all the way.

But the first trial, there it appeared knocking at my door, as I was told of my business class seat that had been awarded me in exchange of the masses of money I had spent to earn air points, was a little shabby I did conclude, for of luggage allowance, it did not permit me the extra 6kg. But "What?" I persisted, as I looked down the line, and of me, 47kg soaking wet, any of those people beside me, their body weight in comparison to mine, was in differential, greater that. For the seat business class seat I was to relish for the first leg of my journey of 7 hours and 35 minutes from Melbourne to Singapore, but really I considered, surely, there should be the full entitlement. So I persisted with that national Australian airline of how it appeared so unacceptable, that I had spend sufficient funds, not be given but to earn and earn well, an upgraded ticket, so "Why oh why was I not to receive the benefit in full?" "Oh, it would be funny, 'if only,' it most certainly, was not."

So I persisted over the discrepancy, the supervisor be called, and a collaboration took place where I was effectively informed, "You may have the business class seat and your entitled, you can even use the Business Class Lounge, but of the extra 6kg weight between business and economy class, well, you're not entitled to that." Perplexed at the irony, my persistence failing to achieve a different outcome, as there I stood in the ticketing line, with excess baggage equating to 13 lb's in totality. For sure, I could have chosen to pay $397.00 for such, but that was not in my plan or my budget, so of another way there had to be found, and then the assistant told me, "Go purchase a carry-on cabin back and swap over that 6kg."

As a plan I thought to work, for as much I had given away of my vintage clothes collection, and more of clothes I so liked so very much which were highly serviceable, for really, I desired not as panic as desperation within my heart rapidly arose and a cold chill encompassed me in that airport, for really was I to sit on that floor, and from what was left of what were my dear collection and life's possessions, and in front of those strangers, all looking, in that big bright loft and unfriendly hall, decide in an instance, tragically torn on the inside as I contemplated, really, "What else, from me, was to depart and be mine, no more?" sadly, "Yes." So piece by piece I contemplated what to swap and what not, trying to judge desperately the weight which was the extreme sticking point easily, and when the job was complete I was free to go, but what I did consider, as the weights had evolved to work evenly, what of the scales, for no account was afforded the weight of the additional case, so "Were they even calibrated evenly?"

Quickly as I could, it was off to the business lounge for me, but to enjoy a relax and the great food available, well that was to be slim pickings for me, as the check in baggage I had to rearrange, while unfortunately so many did peer, but that was the least of my problems, as I was soon to realise, as I approached the aircraft door, as yet, I was not on a clear run, home and free, as by an Australian male airliner staff member I was abruptly stopped, and in the absence of any polite "Hello," or "Excuse me," nor did he make an enquiry, but rather a challenge as his prickly words he jutted directly, his command, "You can't bring that onboard!" which he seemed to deliver with a little too much degradation and glee.

That hurdle, had I got safely over it, for after that initial stumbling block I considered it had transformed into a steppingstone, but it appeared I had wooed myself into a mistaken sense of security, for in a very short while, it was to appear I was back at square 1. For there it was once again, a demand for that $397 fee, to place a piece of hand luggage in the aircraft hold. But fortuitously for me it turned out to be, for the machine to take money for that flight had already 'shut,' so of me, he checked my back into the 'hold' but of a dime he could not charge. And pleased I was for a reason more than one, I would have paid it on my credit card, and of points for that airline at that time, I preferred not a one to add.

Yet, unrelentingly that Australian airline employee, as from around that back of his counter he did venture, and a much taller man that I, far too close to me he stood, overpowering my personal space, as he commenced to deliver his lecture of condescension, as he broached my personal space, but "Why?" Perhaps through ignorance, or perhaps, he believed it his given right. Yet certainly, I consider most fervently, of that most arrogant and condescending manner in which he spoke to me, "Would he have done the same to a passenger of the male gender?" "I think not." and for further consideration, should I have been a full fee paying business class passenger and attained my spot through the air point loyalty scheme program, again I do question, "Would he have behaved the same disparaging manner toward me?" and again, strongly I surmise, "I think not!"

At that time I was far less inclined to listen to his lecture, which appeared to be both personal and unprofessional, on how "You had no right to attempt to take such an amount of hand luggage up to the cabin." Quickly I reflected on how absolutely blessed I had been with the outcome, so I chose a strategy of listening and saying nothing. For as they say, and I remember this well, "When you have achieved what you wanted simply shut up and be quiet." I seized that thought. For I had ultimately achieved my goal, the 6kg in weight transferred at no extra charge, so, holding tightly to my personal thoughts as 'not to rock the boat,' not a word did I say, as my thoughts in my mind were sufficient for me, and was a sweetish smile and a nod of the head that deal was sealed, and I perhaps quite deservedly achieved the right outcome and effectively won the day!

For sure, I do believe, not a good representation of that airline, or that country really for that matter, for that was the last of my encounters with it, and as a sideline I did consider of those air-points gained, of that Program I have payed to belong to, and of the loyalty I showed to them to choose their airline on which to travel above another, and of a specific credit card to use to achieve their allotted air-points, in comparison or perhaps contradiction, of the loyalty they demonstrated to me their supposed, valued clientele, of note it was not obvious, but obscure, and a disappointment for sure.

"Oh deary deary me," not a good vibe at all from that airline, and of their apparent 'penny-pinching' ways at their disloyalty of how they treat their clientele, I was to ponder, really, "Do they deserve loyalty?" Well in my opinion for consideration, that is most certainly "No." For my experience was sufficient to persuade me to peruse an alternative airline in future, as surely, there are many to choose from. Plus I do believe of good note, though I discovered it far too late, that their airline competition appears significantly cheaper by comparison, so really I wondered, whose loyalty does it serve, for it appeared to me not to be reciprocated. So there you have it, a gleam of reality, a lesson overcome, with that experience never to be repeated as that job is sealed and well done.

Yet a twinkle for consideration, as thoughts, like magnets attracts one to another, and so it began my tale of perplex-tion, of the money the airline collected for its passengers, inviting them to add to the fund they reported as the staff over the intercom, gathered millions of dollars each year, and the sum, we were invited for their charitable donations to add to, but it occurred to me, "Who exactly receives tax benefits on the money given freely to that Australian airline? Is it them, for they simply submitted it?" and if so, "I'm not sure I agree," for a company who has treated me so shabbily, to gain tax saving through mine and other passenger's generosity, I suggest is a little vexing.

"Disgruntled?" Certainly; and wiser too that had made me, for no longer do I blindly spend on a credit card for what it can give me, for I consider much more astutely what does it give them? and in return, "Will they be courteous giving back to me?" or "What, or where am I loosing out elsewhere?" For sure, it is dollars that I have saved for shopping around on different airlines, and in my experience, they have all embraced me with greater appreciation for my patronage than that which was supposed to be, the loyalty one. "Well oh my" of a lesson learnt, I'd learnt it well indeed, as my purchasing patterns changed, no longer blindly paying a higher fee for that airline, when no good favour was appearing to be reciprocated, of those identified lessons, for my financial protection and advancement, I was to astutely transfer them to other areas too.

From Singapore to France, was to be the second leg of my journey, an 11 hour flight, of which, "Mmmm," it is fare to say I was not looking forward to with even a tad of glee, and of my notions for the sleep I was hoping to get, of my travel companion on the seat beside me, I wondered, hoping sincerely, a person not nasty but nice it was to be. But with joy initially, as on that national airline of France I was to find, the passenger to sit beside me, or sleep hopefully, as I planned to do, was not intrusive of my space, but perfectly peaceful in her 'vibe.' A relief I may say for sure, and not one to be underestimated, for on a flight once before, coupled through air-points affiliation of that native Australian, as upon a native airline of American, the same could not be said, as I was on route to a vacation in the Caribbean.

For on that so un-preferable flight, of request to change my ticket from the back to the front of the plane for ease of aggress, it was not of fortune to be, but interestingly, just before the ground crew employee pressed his button to deliver the new boarding pass, my gut instinct resisted it and announced to me, so quickly and quietly, "No don't do it," but of its instruction, I did pause, but then, let it pass, and of that, the price I was about to pay. As there I was, I boarded the flight to discover who in row 12 was to be sat next to me, and it was man and his wife, she appearing quite timid and quiet, but of his 'vibe' quite huge, imposing and appearing intimidating. He had portrayed by his body language his position most clear, as it was the armrest, and indeed a portion of my seat, which he claimed for himself, deliberately imposing and I believe, encroaching domineeringly.

For even the space at my feet wasn't mine to have, as he oppressed me as he occupied it so, and to my requests, move his feet, so I could comfortable place mine where on the aircraft they were designed to be, it only met with an aggressive verbal response. And so the seen was set, for me so unfortunately, as that 5 and a half hour journey was to be fraught with his overpowering abuse, physically and verbally as he sat next to me, and through the ordeal as I tried ultimately to defend myself from that situation, his wife remained, so still and significantly, quietly.

Trapped I had been on that flight, with apparently no place to go or any place to escape to as packed tightly in economy class on that plane, but then, 'the final straw' was to be delivered to me, and of course, it will always come, when of ourselves, of such trouble and strife we succumb, as he rose from his seat so quickly and pushed so hard to push past me, that my body was physically flung, not to face forward, but to face the man on the other side of the isle, to the left of me.

Suddenly, trembling, I got up, and scared I walked to the rear of the aeroplane, and of his personality I had made a fare and accurate assessment, for I deduced history had served as a formidable teacher you see, and of what mood or violence he was to escalate into, I knew not exactly the specifics, but what I knew for my safety, from him I needed to separate, for punished in innocence, tormented no more, of his actions, I was determined to close the door.

In shock, to some degree certainly, as I reached the rear of the second class cabin where 3 air stewards, with their beverage cart put away, were standing, as the service had been completed for that flight, and shaking so scared I could hardly speak loud enough for them to hear, as I unfolded the tale and explained to them of my plight, and supporting words and empathy they did give to me, but of another seat it was difficult, for the plane was full to capacity. But the chief air-stewardess who was called, perhaps in age 20 years younger than I, held a difference of opinion to those who around were empathetic of the situation, as with her arms folded, her body language cold, in abstract and mild hostility, poised, with an air of contempt displayed upon her face, in complete opinion and contrast to what her colleagues believed to be true and worthy of me, of the police to be 'standing by' for the plane landing, she, unremorseful as delivering her stinging line, "Well there really isn't any point of having the police meet you, to tell them of such a tale, for it will simply be a battle, for it will be your word against his, for there are no witnesses." And upon that, as she turned sharply and walked away, she dismissed me, literally, out of sight.

"Oh my!" Her colleagues appeared perplexed at her, as so did I, for such trouble had taken place in the air, of an environment, certainly post 9/11, "Should it on any account not be taken so lightly?" and "What of the effect of the violence of a man against a woman, and what of he, being twice the size and the strength of she? Did that woman not care, or was she not aware, or was it possibly the paper-work which she cared not to trouble herself with or implement, or was it something in her personal history, that was causing her to behave cavalier and callously toward me?" As in totality, I do believe, that could have been the case for me.

Thankfully on that aircraft an off duty air-steward, who was sought and agreed for the last half hour of that journey, to swap her seat with me, and with great relief I did so most gratefully, and of "What else to do?" I knew not, for it was not those who had been so kind and so caring of me, whose attitude I was grateful for and of my own to unite. "No." So unfortunately, it was to be her of a more aggressive and unhelpful, may I say certainly obstructive nature, the more forceful, that one who spoke the loudest, as who from days of old, a poor and ill-serving legacy indoctrinated in me, "Who was I of my needs, or others actions against me, to ever receive help or care or respond to positively?"

I was not to see the chief air-steward again until I was to disembark the plane, and with her cold attitude and persona remaining steadfast, of a comment she made to me, "A witness came forward and approached me, confirming of your story of what that passenger next to you did." "Oh my" stunned, surprised, still in a little shock, but hang on, "Wasn't that what she told me I needed to make the formal and justified complaint?" Yes indeed it was, so I asked of her, what was his name or in which seat did he sit, so I was able of the police on the ground to approach and hold that passenger of his actions accountable. Appearing to look at me with mild distain, but why of that I could not comprehend her hostility toward me, as her dark eyes pierced through her dark skin and painted lips poised at me, as she replied with implied deliberant nonchalant, "I cant remember." "But you must remember, its important," I replied, but in her fortitude, with an air of contempt, "Its too late now!" Was all she replied.

"The supreme happiness in life is the conviction know that we are loved"
~ Victor Hugo

"Yet his wife, what of she?" She sat most silently, and as a side-glance I noted that of her apparent submissive response, I gained and air of a notion that her perception my well have been, 'this time, thank goodness this time it isn't me.' As that chief air-stewardess, how missgivingly that the authority invested in her, appeared to be so misplaced, as an opportunity she held, to do some good, so much in fact, not only may it have helped me achieve justice and closure, such a powerful knock-on effect, may have provided for his wife, and other females that came around him in his life, that of violence or abuse it is not to be tolerated.

For the confidence portrayed therein, a different way, a better way, may have provided that man's wife, the commencement of another way, of hope, to alert her senses, to enable her to travel, out of the darkness to a place where there is light, where faded away would be her ill-gotten plight, as no longer to stay emotionally or physically afloat in that needless flight. But such opportunities, all lost surrounding that circumstance, to aid to spread women's inner-power, as that 'one' proved not as an advocate but the opposite for her fellow women, and failed to instigate a potential positive chain-reaction, that in the small and large affairs of life, held power-within, but not realised, for she gave up, simply without a fight.

My voice, "Why did I not make it be heard?" and "Oh why, had I permitted her, to so easily dissuade me?" Because, of it all, that was what previously for decades I had been pre-programmed to do. But a new day was yet to dawn, where I was to wallow in the bright morning sunlight, the mourning of my past was to be over and done as I was determined that my history was to unravel, and I was became adamantly convicted to create something new and ultimately, precious and wonderful.

Yet there was a delay in achieving that great expectation, for in truth, in logic of the former I knew intellectually I deserved, and was working toward it, but at that time in reality, I knew not in my emotions that I was worthy of it, but that little equation of inequality, never ever prohibited me from pushing on through. But 'too early was my cry' on that day, as a petite fellow passenger much shorter in stature and older in age, stood beside me, at the end of the baggage carousel, where I with anxiety filling my stomach, I was trying to obscure myself from he, who had armed me on the plane, "Are you all right?" she enquired, "For I saw everything that went on." Then, as I listened to that lady delivering sympathy, I listened relieved, and gratefully. But 'too late was the cry,' as I too exhausted, perhaps too slow, to seize of the moment and think, "Oh my, this is my whiteness right here." As there it was, of that opportunity I let it slip away, and of remorse, of not asking for her seat number, her name, telephone number or address, by some means or other the contact her, encore, "I let it slip away," and with it, my opened door.

How supremely sadly, our past training can prove to be, when decades later it still holds such a wealth of capacity, to cause us harm. "Oh why, did I not hold him accountable, for his odious assault or crime?" As justice received, was not going to be mine. But really, seriously, "Why was I so easily swayed and passively gave in, to something that for the good of me and the good of other women I should most certainly not have done so?" Because that was what my brain had been trained to do and accept. Yet; I was on my way joyfully, for at least my growth was sufficient at that point to thankfully note and recognise, to seek help, as I then knew it to be wrong!

"Oh!" Of that ultimately inspiring and healing journey I remained upon to recognizing my self-worth and standing firmly and adamantly up for me. Yet on note perhaps sadly, I had a few miles or more left to travel, and upon reaching its end, and gladly, I firmly grew and knew that as I continued along it, towards its end, ultimately, triumphantly, I will be loudly singing a victory song!

*"Courage doesn't always roar,
sometimes it's the quiet voice at the end of the day saying, 'I will try again tomorrow.'"
~ Mary Anne Radmacher*

So you see, of my concerns of "Who was travelling companion next to me?" was not of any faint or flimsy enquiry, and for such a petite and quiet girl I was sincerely most grateful in my fortune, for not a short spans of time was to pass, for it was an 11 hour flight which we were to sit upon, but one I did desire, that I was to sleep for two parts of it, or better, even three. As a little habit I have now established for myself on long-haul flights, is to eat the dinner that is provided, while an in-air movie, hopefully a best seller will on the entertainment menu be there, then, teeth cleaned with anti-inflammatory medicine taken for my lower back, it will be off to sleep for a good portion of the journey for me.

Yet two little hiccups were to pose a wee problem to me upon that flight, of the cuisine, it was not palatable for me, as a 'tricky' digestive system I sometimes was subject to, and of count my blessings on that flight, I was not to partake in that which held the potential to upset it, and of the second, "Oh my" of my back that I so sought to rest, by that 3 or 4 inches of my seat to recline, for the ease and comfort of the spine, so crucial for achieving that bit of improved sleep, well, it was not to be, as the seat broken, it was not to be.

But wait a minute, I was to call over the dashing and tall French man, a steward by another name, and of tell him of my mild plight, he looked at the button and pressed the arm, declaring in his accent appearing fine, "It is broken, there is nothing that can be done." Not helpful for sure, and of the *Gallic* shrug, which I was soon to discover, in that land I was on route to, all to commonly and widely utilized, inferring effectively, unhidden of their true intent, 'there is nothing more I can or care to say or do,' so he swiftly turned and down the aircraft walked away.

"Oh my" not a good outcome to my endeavour of resolution, for there I remained on that 11 hour flight, particularly hungry, most uncomfortable and extremely cold, but I had little alternative left, other than to utilize a colloquialism of my own, which was to 'shut up and put up,' for nothing it appeared on that 11 hour flight was to alter or improve, so of my future I had time to ponder, was such to be the fruit of the future, was it to be, *très bon*, very good, or possibly, *Ce n'est pas bon!* It is not good!

> "A woman is like a T bag, you can't tell how strong she is until you put her in hot water."
> ~ Eleanor Roosevelt

A crowded airport it was for sure on the occasion of "P Day" as I stood inline to pass Passport Control. I feel so blessed to be the proud owner of two passports, so really I need not have stood for over one hour and a half, I kid you not, patiently waiting to have my European passport checked, though not stamped as I recall as I passed through to my destination of choice, and preferred 'gay Paris.'

It was a decidedly chilly autumn day in late September, as I arrived at *Charles de Gaulle Airport,* named after a French past President, on that my official 'P Day.' And the rain was to be viewed through the large planes of glass as like cattle we were herded into the passport lounge, and of the brightness, warmth and sun, which in the southern hemisphere adorn each day, but in Paris of such, right then, it didn't bode well for there being too much.

But of 'lounge,' in that passport control line there was to be none, as perhaps half a kilometre long, it weaved in and out, as we were all huddled together to wind our way, so painfully slowly to the front of the queue. Then I turned around as I heard a kafuffle behind, in one of those long lines that weaved in and out, until in that great lofty atrium it spread out into the narrow corridors to its rear, and there a group of local French people, two couples in there 50 or 60 something years, took it upon themselves to storm, not that Bastille, where actually, on the 14th July 1789 when they did so, there were only 7 or 8 inmates in it, they charged the business class passport control line masterfully, mindfully with staunch determination, dragging their suitcases behind them.

Then those 'rebels' from their native country, who had broken the ranks and slipped under the canvas barriers, were swiftly charged at and 'put back' where they came from, though perhaps their actions unsurprising as who could blame them, for an hour or more we had already spent stood in-line, and still reaching nowhere close to the front it, and true, in just *75* minutes, an aeroplane could have taken off from London and arrived on the tarmac in Paris in the same time-frame.

True their method was un-conservative, though thankfully it did promote activity, as in that team of 2 'business class' passport control officers who were sat in their booths as the business class station, appearing to do nothing, started to do something, perhaps through shame or harassment by their country-folk, perhaps an embarrassment, but of cause I hugely-joke and speculate, as the checking of us, the economy class began, as their time and availability they for whatever reason decided at that point but not before to share, and for sure, economic with my time they had not been, for it was to be in excess of 1 hour and 40 minutes before I was to get out of there, and back into fresh air.

So perhaps not a smooth initiation into France, and I so hoped that was not to prove as an omen for what was to follow, but some peace was to come, as in the midst of that busy Parisian International Airport, I believe renowned for its hectic chaos and designed in the shape of a spider, I searched for my pre-booked shuttle bus, where I was to find a group of Americans already seated upon it, who thankfully, patiently awaited my arrival, and almost ironically, had surpassed the passport control line a full 40 minutes ahead of me.

"Oh my! Was it all too soon to consider, hiccups or stumbling blocks?" Or was I simply to relax and consider, "Oh jolly me, I'm in France, in Paris, a place I have elected to be?" So really in that city of love, that is quite beautiful, though I was soon to note, quite dirty; "Were there ever to be for me, steppingstones on which to place my feet sturdily, steadily, upon or was it all to prove a little bit precarious as I moved from A to B?" But indeed, I need not have pondered too long, for soon enough, my realization of such, was soon to come along.

So comfortably we sat, those temporary travelling companions and me up that mini coach, as in turn they began discussing each others reasons for their trip to France, and of there hopes and expectations there, perhaps what they hoped as they, those two couples compared it with others, as their excitement spilled forth from within and intertwined their stories of what they had left behind and of joyful tales they were sharing of what they were to do and who they were to see at familiar and happy places and in their spirits and minds of being assured of the same, they were truly, expectful, as their delight was portrayed so freely.

Though they had no idea of what their conversation triggered in me, of it, "Was I to be a little bit jealousy or was I simply feeling hopeless?" As their happiness reached out and encroached into my space dropping into my soul, shining an unwelcomed light on that area in my life where insecurity reigned, as unlike them, I had no friends or family awaiting me, or even a home for that matter with any kind of stability, for they had so much and I appeared to have so little, and as I listened, so sincerely pleased for their good fortune, a heavy sadness nestled upon me, wrongly so, though I couldn't help in those moments, I felt less than them, and deprived of something valuable and great, as regret of my unfulfilled life seemed to constrict and encompass me, tightening my brain and swelling oddly in my heat, for I, so sorrowfully, had no-home and on-one to go back to.

"Oh my" as we drove away from the larger of the 2 Parisian international *aéroports*, airports, the smaller being colloquially known as *Roissy*, and as it faded into the distance, my stomach felt increasingly substantially sick, and I was to wonder, what lay ahead of me and of those forever resited 'Once upon a time stories' my mother frequently told me, rambling in my head and deep my inner-core, "Could they ever be recanted, and how much more effort did I need to put in and what else could I possibly do, and when was I ever going to leave 'it' all behind, to clear myself further away from my past history of what my parents did to me, and 'when oh when,' were *they* to get out of my psyche, so I too, would have such wonderful tales to share as in a foreign country on a shuttle bus with strangers I would sit, to tell of stories true, soft and sublime, that I too, had accumulated over time?"

"The happiest life is that which constantly exercises and educates what is best in us"
~ Hamerton

Spiralling out from the city centre of Paris, there are 20 *arrondissements*, and I was on my way to the 18th, for that was where my budget hotel was situated, but as we drove closer to it, and the toots of the horns became more frequent, an people walking the street, well, not those I would care to meet at certain parts of the day, and even the vibe from outside the shuttle bus I could sense and quickly surmising, that the price I had paid, was cheap yes, but of cheerful, I felt that of my booking I had missed the mark, and "A wise choice to choose that hotel and commence my Parisian experience?" Possibly; or possibly not.

For sure that *arrondissement* is most fine, or so I was to believe, that was until more information came to light and all to late as a local was to inform me, the 18th is effectively divided into 2, of the fine part located between Paris centre and the Mount of *Sacré-Cœur*, Sacred Heart, and on the opposite side stretching to the outskirts of Paris, well, apparently according to him that's not so good, and no prizes for guessing, within my budget, the side, the location of where my hotel was situated in.

"Oh my" emotional regret rapidly rolled in, pouring over me with the harshness of the chilly winter waves that in Blackpool in northern England bring in the icy cold sea that stretches far over the promenade, as so severely I began to commence a whirlwind of chastising myself, apparently unable to give up, not forgiving myself for the error of my decisions, and the folly of my ways and how they left me in Paris strapped for cash, "For really where had all my money gone?" And really, I had earned it but had nothing to show for it, of purchasing that hardtop convertible, black with tinted windows; my obsession with shopping never seemed to cease, though "To use what I bought?" That would be "No!" As I'd simply hang it on a rail, or neatly place it on a shelf, was my format, as effectively, so un-sensibly of enjoyment or pleasure from many of my purchases, well really, there was non, for seriously, superfluous to my requirements was pretty much all that I bought; and so it prevailed as there in Paris I was paying the price, of a life's hardened lesson, of what not to do, for really, "You never know what's ahead of you," though I was given plenty of time to make that old adage come a true reality, in the school of, "Act in haste, and repent at leisure."

For squandered it needlessly, for far more importantly I was in deed of it then to follow my dream, and through it have security, but of it I did not, for in deficit of where I should have been and what I should have had, geographically and more, it was disparagement and distain of me, which I appeared unable or incapable of its overpowering weight, to shake from my metaphoric door. And there was the result, evidentially, surrounding and stretching out before me, where I had ended up, as of those particularly poor choices and thousands of dollars effectively squandered, to bring me comfort or even a morsel of such, I had them no longer available to spend, and with only fear of my financial future so repetitively welling up inside my mind, with sickness in the pit of my stomach exacerbated, of peace, for me, I held absolutely non of the kind.

Yet: *J'adore,* I adore Paris, for in my mind, the vibe strikes a cord with me, "What's not to love?" OK, they be one or two things, but moving on, which is what I did, meandering through *'la Rive Gauche,'* the Left Bank, up and down the petite rues I went, then, always, finding myself to be at the end, or is that the beginning, depending on your perspective, at one of the 37 bridges traversing the river *Seine*, which effectively meanders through the centre of Paris splitting the city in 2 halves, and from any point, a awe-inspiring vision to behold, of a legacy of wealth that through the centuries has adorned that city, of *la Louvre,* the Louvre Museum, or perhaps the famous *Champs-Élysées* in the 8eme *arr,* yet of more modern occurrence, lit by dainty night lights the festive Christmas market may be enjoyed, or a quite pleasant but mildly intense *marcher,* walk up to where the magnificent *Arc de Triumph,* Arc of Triumph. Though my personal favourite most definitely speeding out ahead of the rest, in *première,* first position, without exception, that of the *magnifique,* magnificent monument that I tire not of feasting my eyes upon, situated in the 7eme *arr,* and built specifically for the *Expostion Universal de 1889,* World Fair, and perhaps the most famous Parisian landmarks, that awe inspiring, at least to me, *la Tour Eiffel,* the Eiffel Tower.

> *"When you get into a tight place and everything goes against you, till it seems*
> *as though you could not hang on a minute longer, never give up then,*
> *for this is just the place and time that the tide will change."*
> ~ Harriet Beecher Stowe

As it turned out, though I am still not sure why, of the people in that French nation I was often described of *très fort,* very strong *et* and *très courageux,* very courageous, but perhaps undeservedly so, for perhaps foolishly or not, it was a bold a desire I held to run toward something rather than run away, or simply stay-put mindlessly, as with purpose, I refused to quite my search until I had discovered whatever it was I was searching to uncover, and simply, I refused to give up, until for me, of its glory I was to gleam and see. And blissfully, a mild note I do make, that all who wander are certainly not lost.

Yet an added concept for contemplation as indeed with sincerity I was to ponder pensively, yet not until I had departed those shores, "Was I simply doing what came naturally, or was I complexly doing what was necessary?" Perhaps of the exact answer I was uncertain, but of life and of its trials and tribulations and more that had gone, before I grew to be, extremely grateful that "I had made it, thus far."

And with such profound thoughts upon my heart, as I squeezed my 2 suitcases into that tiny, not so clean, yet cramped hotel room, of walls stained from nicotine from when in hotel rooms it was safe to smoke, with the terribly shoddy bed draped in blue, and curtains of orange at the window, from which held no view, of the pillows uncomfy, yet 'hurray' the sheets appeared clean, most thankfully.

Off to climb the 130 metres to the top of *Montmartre*, I was to go, where on a pew I was to perch, in that magnificent, Church, *Sacré-Cœur*, designed by *Paul Abadie* and completed in 1914 after 39 years, that imposing place of Worship, where in regularity, Services are held for locals and tourists alike, where in the vast awe inspiring space, beneath its opulent domed roof, I also with gratitude was to give Praise, not for what I didn't have, but for what I did. For all my blessings, and of their true value retrospectively, in truth, I had begun to recognize their disguise, of something less pleasant. For it appeared to be so, that each one transpired to be a gift, to take me from A to B, from where I was, in my mind, in my emotions, in my soul, to where truly, I wanted and deserved to be.

And so with map in hand I navigated my way through the picturesque and narrow streets, imagining the humungous hoards of people from many a century earlier who had trampled them before, and of their lives, really, "Through those harsh times, what must have they been like?" And of my contemplation, my progress slow as mesmerised I malingered and marvelled at all of what Paris had been and what it to offer and of my *nouvelle aventure,* new adventure, what it was to be and mean to me.

I was absorbed, the sights, the sounds, the architecture, the people, the pavement café's even the smells, enthralled me, as all my senses were alight, as all a saw as if as a soaring eagle in magnificent flight. I had to pinch myself, in awe, it seemed incredible that I, I was actually there, in the living breathing flesh, that I had achieved my goal, my dream, I was to live it, I was excited, nothing was to stop me, except....'If only' I would have picked up a map or the address for my hotel, it would have helped my return journey immensely! "Mmmm," as quite lost I became, yet fortunately in the centre of Paris, its not possible to be lost for long, for every *rue*, street leads somewhere, and the lyrics of Bonnie Tyler's hit pop song, "Lost in France in Love," from 1977, which according to one particular TV advertisement for one particular perfume is, 'That one perfect thing.' "Did I disagree?" Perhaps, or perhaps not!

I wandered, yet not 'as lonely as a cloud' but on direct route to *la Sorbonne University* to register, on route to my consecutive step to achieving my goal of, *parler et comprendre la langue française,* speaking and understanding the French language. "Oh my" really, I was oblivious to exactly how many steps I was to make, and 'then some.' Yet, ultimately lost, and terribly so, geographically, but it was to be in the realms of *l'apprentissage de la langue française*, leaning the French language I was to become also, metaphorically. "Oh my" "What a folly" I did consider, and how could I have possibly got that far along that particular metaphoric road, without realising that of that university class which I had been searching, was to be taught in a language I failed to understand, and in my mind continuing on with that theme, "How on earth I ponder, was I ever of an ounce of comprehension to gleam?"

I mean, "How can anyone do that?" OK, I knew James had, but in my mind he was an exceptional young man, but then I did consider, not to be unkind to me but to consider realistically, "Was I really capable to do that?" For to enter into such a circumstance appeared simply foolhardy to me, so why was it, that I succumbed to that Professor of such young years of only twenty something, as she talked to me inside those tall and blank walls that bare and cold auditorium, where, I had waited inline to talk with her, to be ultimately dissuaded from my deep concerns which I relayed to her, "Well I don't think I can do that." To be effectively swayed into the arena of, "Well, you know submersion is the best thing to do, when of knowledge you want to learn, and of this route, it may be the best way forward for you."

And so the conversation went on, I felt persuaded, not convicted that I should continue along the process, as that professor who may have been able to gleam a job as a sales person in another field, continued in her persuasion of, "It is normal to be a little bit scared at first, but of the *debutants*, beginners, who sit in the classroom looking nervous at initially, their anxiety passes away, as at the end of the 12 week course, of just 25 hours per week of which you seek, they hold, a new welcomed and founded clarity.

"Oh why did I listen, to something that in my soul as it gently shouted out, it was so fundamentally wrong for me?" But to late was my cry to be, with a *faux pas* missed by my calculation of its spiralling preparation, as off to join another queue I did go, to pay that quite exorbitant tuition fee. And there she sat at a desk to my right, a lady who spoke English in an accent quaint essentially French, who effectively gave me a get out clause, as she posed the question to me, "Are you sure you want to do this?" Of the reason for her question I knew not, but of it, "Oh my" I wish so I had of it pondered and poured, as effectively, willingly I added the sum of 2400euros(E) to the sum of the 300euros already payed as a deposit online, and there it was, aquatinting to a figure of $4000AUD, as I ignored her portion of wisdom which perhaps she attempted to divulge to me, an opportunity in disguise, to reduce my risk as she shot my way a 'get out safely key,' but too retarded I was to respond, as my credit card it was swiped, and the deal, good or bad was sealed and done.

But "Oh my" 2 years were to pass, before of a new concept I was to grasp, of schools and colleges around France, of live-in situations they provide, and more, of private schools also, even situated amongst that favourite portion of Paris which I adore, that *St. Germaine arrondissement,* "Oh why oh why?" Transferred to be a monotonous debilitating cry of some disparaging magnitude, for I considered of another's blueprint I had grasped, of further due diligence of that I had done none, and as I had not talked to another than one, and he who had not mentioned those live-in schools or private institutions, I was oblivious of such, but of the price I was to pay for my ignorance, I believed that it was not to be a little, but quite a portion of significance, certainly in the unfolding realms emotionally, under the heading of 'Quite, too much.'

And so it was to be, as that cost had provided for me a place to belong to, in that huge and dirty city I may say, but so pleased I was to be a card carrying holder on that day, of un *étudiant de l'Université de la Sorbonne,* a student of the Sorbonne University, so it was merrily I did trot, off to yet another queue, to wait inline, for information, nay opportunity, to obtain, as it was for *mon habituation domicile,* my home, abode, but of the time and effort spent in it, as it "Was to transpire, to be a friend or a foe?"

It was off to the *douzième,* 12eme *arr* I was to travel, on the *Métro* line blue, where I was to meet the *propriétaire,* landlady, after I had climbed just a small stairwell of three flights of stairs, and as I knocked at the door, it was a petite lady who stood before me, of smiles gentile and friendly, as she invited me in, and of around her apartment she did show, and of the room I would be taking for the 500E per month, should I choose to take it, and really, of her amenable nature, and clean and pleasant surroundings, I thought, "Well, why not?" and so it was, the deal was struck and the date and time was agreed and set for me to move it.

But things were afoot, that I did not know of, and of signs perhaps I wondered through, as the first was to transpire, to arrange transportation from the *arrondissement* of 18 and my hotel to that of the 12th, with my 2 suitcases, became a terribly difficult job to overcome. And more so on that very morning of my hotel departure, a telephone call I did receive, from she who was to be my new landlady, and in a voice she spoke, "It is impossible to receive you at 11 o'clock as pre-arranged, as I have tennis, so you will have to wait, as it will have to be half past 3, before I can accommodate you."

"Mmmm;" with due scepticism, I should have made more profound note of that as a sign received of things to come, and accordingly replied, "No thank you, lets consider our business deal, as unfulfilled, over and done." And as it turned out, a knee-jerk reaction it would not have proved to be, for of that clean and neat apartment which I did see on my visit that interview day, well that was the only time it was to be seen, for the norm as my 2 suitcases and I moved in on that Monday, there was a stench that greeted me as that little lady opened the door, it was not with a smile but intolerance she appeared to show, with fangs almost ablaze, as the disguise dropped away, apparently the wolf had come out to play as she gave *'Little Miss Red Riding Hoods'* cloak away.

"I believe in being strong when everything seems to be going wrong. I believe that happy girls are the prettiest girls. I believe that tomorrow is another day, and I believe in miracles"
~ *Audrey Hepburn*

And before I had walked to the end of the corridor to little room I was to rent, my instructions were bellowed and barked at me, "You pay me in cash and you must not tell anyone you are a student at the *Sorbonne*, and you must tell everyone who asks, that you are niece of a friend of my family." "Oh my" a web of deceit and my coat was not yet taken off, now what did that remind me off, and of things to come, the obnoxiously mild web was weaved most certainly, and of that women whose roof I was to live under, she transpired to be, not a nice woman but one, who was quite nasty.

Perhaps I should have 'run for the hills,' say with tongue in cheek, but then in fairness, time was to portray, that it may have proved a most astute decision to make. For unravel before me, a tale of errors that perhaps quite rightly would amuse the onlookers of a good sitcom, only it was not funny in reality, as the onset of rules begun, in sharp contradiction to those which were agreed upon. And so first it was, of a wardrobe I was to prohibit to use, and maybe not a huge-biggy, it was a role of counsellor to her I did become, most unwillingly. As one day her reply to me, as I gave what I thought a quite generalised and non-specific response, of gentle but non-committal support to her specific and multiple questions, only hear her say, "Well now you have told me to do that I will." What! Hold up! Swiftly back peddling, to a distance of safety and a mission I was to accomplish, of my thoughts and suggestions shared with that landlady, which untoward were not to be mistaken or open untoward misinterpretation. For really, I was only the lodger you see, and of pressure or trouble I desired none, so when requested from there on, of my opinion, perhaps wisely, uncommitted, I provided non.

And try to study with all my might, or did I really, but at the table I was to sit, as it was only the place where I was able to hook up with wifi, but study I could not, for as early evening began, the ritual of preparing and cooking her food went underway, then at 8 o'clock on the dot, the Formica and aluminium, T-trolley, circa 1970's was wheeled across from the kitchen to where I sat and the rattle did commence of metal serving spoons being thrown into each pot and pan, the high pitched tones echoing into those towering high ceilings, quite Parisian, the banging and crashing of dishes and crockery onto the table were to follow, as almost deliberate in dominance it appeared, her napkin of aged food solids was thrown over her knee of her stained matching nightgown, before finally, the tea towel of quite a pungent aroma as if weaved between its thread, was to obscure my text books as it flung over towards me.

Really, of the loud TV was I really making excuses as why I was not excelling more at the subject I was there to learn, or was it rational full and appropriate or even partial, of those circumstances to hold concern. And complain needlessly is not my intent, for in my room I could and did go, to study in silence, where in peace I did try to achieve, hidden behind that closed door with the brisk Parisian autumn breeze, blowing through my window slightly ajar, as I studied merrily.

But that proved not to be a perfect plan, for flimsy were the boundaries that *propriétaire* held at best, for of privacy deserving to me, she recognized not, as flinging open the door to my room, without knocking or invitation she did burst, not on one occasion, but ignoring my requests that she did not, in excess of one more time than three. Then, with the dawning of another beautiful day outside, inside, the bizarre concept of normality continued inside that Parisian *maison*, house, where I lived, as follow me around that aged French women did peering from behind doors at her failed attempt to conceal herself, and of her actions, I did my best to ignore.

Yet "What are you doing?" Became her demand as she crept up behind me one morning as my habitual breakfast routine was underway, "Organizing my muesli and *croissant au chocolate,* chocolate croissant," I replied. "Liar!" was her response, as hastily she demanded, "What are you looking for?" I remained her while secretly contemplating, "What!" "Excuse me?" Her tale continued, "I heard you, opening draws and cupboards I want to know what I was looking for." As I relayed the tale, but without humour to my university *comarades*, I was so glad that they were able to see the funny side of it, as they joked, "What could you have possibly have been looking for, perhaps crockery and cutlery?" I was pleased for their light-hearted approach, but I was becoming weary, as rest transposed to stress.

Yet all seemed so mild in comparison to the prohibition of me using *la machine à laver,* the washing machine, as she demanded all I was permitted to do, once weekly, was simultaneously place my clothes for washing in amongst hers. But "What?" Perhaps in disagreement I should have declared, "Are you serious?" For of her laundry it was not mildly dirty, but worse, stained with multiple types bodily fluids, and of my most adamant conclusion, "No no no; I won't do that." So then, negotiations began, as I was to reiterate to that lady of old, to whom I had specifically enquired of when I first visited her home to check it out and assess "Would this house be a contender for me?" "Are there any restrictions to me using the washing machine?" With her adamant reply, "Oh no, absolutely none."

"Mmmm," and worse was yet to come, the proverbial 'straw that broke the camel's back' came right along, for it always will, when of time, you give it quite enough. For it transpired that as one morning I did arise, and thank goodness on that day, the sun had already risen, for I would not have seen in the dark, that faecal matter on the door, on the handle and the door seat, and the same on that toilet flushing mechanism. "Oh deary me" this was not a senile lady whose house I was to stay in, so astonished, astounded I went to find her, to enquire, of what she'd done did she know, and of clean it up safely, well "When was that action to begin?"

So into the galley kitchen I went, where I did stand in the morning to enjoy the quiet vista of the garden at the beginning of each day before off to the *Métro* I did go, to speak to the lady who had left those bacteria laden parcels around her house, to cause harm her and to me as well. But what a surprise I received when I told her of the problem, when to me I heard the resounding reply with the hint of a *Gallic* shrug, "That is *no* problem!" What! I persisted most definitely, that of 'the problem' she was to come and see, but no, reluctant, adamant, that lady remained, refusing to do so.

"Oh my" of that training I'd received whilst working under the umbrella of Infection Control in Victoria, I wondered momentarily, what those peers would have made of that, but back to the job at hand, it was a managerial insistence I did make, and there down the *couloir*, corridor, together we walked. "There is nothing wrong with this," she said, as of her bear hand of the toilet seat, she began to wipe the faeces away, "No." I expressed exuberantly loudly, as I waved my arms up in the air and turned around in full circle, in astonishment and disbelief. "Please wash your hands," I wanted to cry, but quietly insisted instead, of her persistence, accompanied by that never failing *Gallic* shrug, but "I have not reason to do that," and eventually, to do such she did not concede or agree.

In disbelief, as it had been several months earlier, during my audit as a Hand Hygiene Officer, where I had observed a student nurse, strip a patients bed, and of those covers, permit them to fall onto the floor. And instead of picking them up and taking them away to be washed and replacing them with clean, she was not to do, as step over them repeatedly was her action to peruse. And there it was of, the 16 full minutes which she took to remake that bed, and her seniors of qualified staff members who observed her actions and nothing they did or said, of hand hygiene and the risk-full hazards that they are to health, and the overwhelmingly easy way they can cause infection to be transported effectively easy and free of charge, it is sad to consider of that generation old and new, of different hemispheres in which they grew, that with 'training' or not, appearing ultimately, that one knew no better than the other.

My Risk Assessment had completed in a nano-second of harm to be done, but even after several minutes, of that lady who left her risk-full faeces there she seriously appeared to see non, but I wonder, was it conveniently so, that she held that regard? Superfluous I guess the answer to that question now to be, but what I do know, is that I did succumb to quite severe gastric infection just 2 or so days later, and I think I know the cause, for I am sure it did not happen miraculously.

"Oh my oh my," of that young man's experience at the book store in Albert Park, a Melbourne suburb, when he told of his childhood of a French school exchange program, so good was his experience, yet of the concept I attempted to replicate, to effectively, 'kill two birds with one stone,' by saving money and learning French 'at home,' yet in my case, clearly, neither were derived at all, to be anywhere near so positively fine, or even close, but not to worry I guess, for of it all, it was only to be for a period of time, until the strange and bizarre 'goings-on' in that residence domicile, were to almost in the middle of the night, see me, flee as to a safer place I took flight.

> *"Don't wait until everything is just right. It will never be perfect. There will always be challenges, obstacles and less than perfect conditions. So What. Get started now. With each step you take you will grow stronger and stronger, more and more skilled, more and more self-confident and more and more successful."*
> *~ Mark Victor Hansen*

But alone I was not in those situations forlorn, for in that great capital of France, hidden behind the façades quite ostentatious, the same could not be said for the single women, perhaps f a certain age, or indeed married, who were to rent a room, those young ladies of a nationality different, who perhaps quite falsely believed that they would receive a 'fair-go' in exchange for their buck, but of it almost likely, they were to find, the accommodation was to fall short and they were to be out of luck.

So unfortunately with regular occurrence, of lodgers on the ground floor being prohibited from opening the metal shutters and being informed they must live in the dark, and a room in the basement of a house, covered with not much more than dirt, and a pipe coming out of the wall, where almost into a tin bath the water was to fall to be drained away, and of the toilet for such accommodation to be to trample carefully up an old wooden and rickety staircase covered with half empty paint cans, and tools of over the edges they did jut, to ascend into the 'masters' house, next to the front door, then across the main family dining room it was required that they traverse, until to a door, directly *'enface,'* facing the meal table, was where, night or day, the only place where 'personal ablutions' were permitted to be dispersed, and perhaps amazingly or not, my total fee for that per month, was 600euros.

So many there were, another I heard, of a girl who lodged for three months or more, come the day she was due to leave, after a counsellor to the *propriétaire*, through her out of the door at 11a.m. even though her ride was not due until half past two, and where it appeared she had been an unpaid counsellor, but only on those days when she was told to 'get out of the house and not come back until late,' for of a dinner party, or entertaining a gentleman caller there may be, where the landlady's word was doctrine and reined absolutely, and of the monthly payment parted with, on occasions such as those, where unfortunately not even 'Maslow's Hierarchy of Needs' were to be succumb to.

So as luck would have it, of a friend of a friend, I was to encounter as a new place to live I was seeking, so fortuitously I was to stumble upon, as she was to 'fill me in' with the true details and not those as portrayed by that perhaps "Oh so mean" and may I say, dishonest, dishonest, *propriétaire*. Then her story unravelled of her living circumstance, of how when she rocked up with her 2 suitcases, while not shown to her room, but made to wait in the *salon*, lounge where she was not permitted to sit, as a demand was placed on her, to pay the 3 months rent 2100euros in advance and in cash, then, quickly to turn and walk away was the students first choice, but so aware was that *propriétaire*, that Parisian hotel prices were high, plus the majority of *domicile placements* were already taken, so effectively only the crabby-crumbs were left in that situation as the landlord knowing most placements were already taken for that season or term.

Then unravelling the threads were to begin, for that new washing machine in the mid-sized and modern kitchen she was forbidden from using, as her laundry she had to pack up in bags and with detergent to, to traverse a couple of major *rues* streets and roundabouts, until at the laundry mat she found herself to sit and guard her clothes so in that Parisian *arr*, to prevent the theft of them.

Then that Parisian landlady, a second room she did have for rent, where all her possessions in it were to remained in place, piled high on the floor to ceiling bookcases, of the apparent ugly clutter of ornaments and magazines, effectively to 'doss' in the spare room. But what, of the room I was told it was quiet, but of that fortuitous reencounter, of that information it was not true, for that room was wedged effectively over a nightclub, with music pounding loudly, it was heard until the morning of half past 3.

Bad its true, but worse was to come, as cats that friend of a friend had an allergy to, yet as she was about to get in bed one night she found one between her sheets, but how could that be, for the bed was smooth and there were no apparent wrinkles in it where the cat would have snuck in, and wrongly or rightly, of a vibe of a notion she got, that of that landlady, she had done such most deliberately. That cat at 4 in the morn continually it woke her up scratching at her bedroom door, and although the lady who owned that property, refused to anything about that, quite often in the morning, after the student then being unable to sleep, and a little unsafe of her safety in the house in which she stayed, was to place the side light on, which from that landlady in the morning, did always receive, for the extra electricity she used, complaint and chastisement.

"My oh my" 'intrusion' was her last tactic of attack in her armoury, in that place where really, perhaps she no-longer wanted her to stay, as that Parisian property, had been on the market for sometime and remained unsold, when a potential buyer was to rock up, there was not preplanning or warning, or knock on the door, as boldly and rudely, barging right in, to the privacy of her room, prepaid in cash, a party of 3 or more, unapologetically, inward, they'd dash.

How sad, how bad, that she had to succumb to so much unpleasantness and inconvenience, and having paid for that privilege, yet what a relief, that through such happenstance of good fortune, she later in secret was to share her unfortunate experiences with me, yet unaware was the *propriétaire*, as a potential candidate as *une colocataire*, a flatmate, I was being shown around that apartment. And so I continued my search, as out of the 'frying pan into the fire' was not on my list of 'things to do' so for those consecutive 2 months of my Parisian study, I needed to rest at a better residence, but "Was I to find it?" and when I did, "Was it to be perfect, or minimally, even an improvement?"

> *"You can tell more about a person by what he says about others than you can by what others say about him."*
> ~ Audrey Hepburn

But first, I had circumnavigate, what turned out to be a rather complex system, of receiving my few remaining processions in the world, *par avion*, by air, eventually delivered, "Oh my, how I had missed them and anticipated their arrival, and what a great relief, with complicated telephone calls here and there, as in my room rented in that house, at last, they sat before me.

Though that short, sharp-featured Parisian landlady, held not the same concept, as upon seeing them, she demanded, "Have you got drugs inside of them?" "Oh!" Surely, I was rather surprised at that one, and a little perplexed, as never would such a concept have occurred to me, asking, "Why on earth would you possibly think such a thing?" With intense, staunch vigour she spoke, "Well I don't know where you get your money, you're always well dressed and in such good quality; you're not married, so really, what else could it be?" Really! "Where do you get your money?" Placing aside her archaic narrow-minded opinion of women's positive independent progression throughout the years, replying, "Excuse me!" "All you need to know is, there are definitely no drugs in those boxes," and as to the rest of my personal business, you have not right to be so intrusive, or to demand to know." Unequivocally, that was so!

"Wow" for real, she had no idea of what those few processions meant to me, of the regret that was wrapped and packaged up in them and of the weight of it, surely if calculated, of afford the airfare transit fee, I would not have been possible for a payment to be made. "Oh my" I had so many questions starting to rise their ugly heads of self-disparagement, as pre-parting Australia decisions were starting to bombard and emotionally arrest me, and of them all and of that pit in my stomach of major discomfort, I was yet to conclude, that in the lyrics to a song co-written and sung that Frank Sinatra in 1969, "Regrets I have a few, but then again to few to mention," was not to be of me, for quite some time, with portions of sadness oversized, my regrets most unfortunately were not yet few.

> *"The knowledge of the past stays with us. To let go is to release the images and emotions, the grudges and fears, clinging and disappointing of the past that bind our spirit"*
> ~ Jack Kornfield

I had to create a more peaceful me, but how? For poor choices made haunting me, and of all those decisions it transpired I had made so badly, before from that last Continent I did part, "Oh my" within me, as a downward spin I appeared to be in, they imposed and weighed so heavily upon my heart. For what had really gone before, and simply gone, for my choices, they were apparently, 'oh so poor' as they seemed to be troubling me deep to my core.

Self-pity was to forge as a strong companion to me, not a friend but a foe, and so much, I so wanted, so desired to shake it off, but it did not leave, diminish or go anywhere. As 'woe was me,' became the title of my song which I was to whine and wail so inwardly so relentlessly, as I felt so sad to my core, as I fell head first into despair, where a life of helplessness was beginning with my memory to play a game, and hopelessness was to join it there.

And what of my French, unable I appeared to leant that, distraught, and of those physical ailments I had sustained throughout the years, of 'oh so poor' choices again made, "Oh my" I could not stop beating myself up, from the scars of old of what my patents, fiancé's or others did unto me, until I became wise and able, to *accept*, *open-up* and *let go*, of all that compounding and rising issues, developed from a life lived in pain and fury, as developed was my capacity, no longer to permit it, to dispatch a severe blow.

From times of old, comparisons of me and my *comarades de classe*, classmates, I commenced to make, and in Paris, their security they enjoyed of husbands, fiancés, siblings and friends, with health insurance too and all without financial concerns, and back home more of the same awaited them, a *home* they held dear, a place to return void of physical or emotional sacrifice, for theirs was a place of safety and sanctuary, a place where their loved ones relished their safe return.

Their communication included Skype, they used everyday, just to keep in such close contact with those they loved, and within me, it only enhanced a concept of remorse and sadness through my own negligence, of friends I'd let slip-away, and as I reflected of their sacrifice to achieve the same as me, there appeared to be little to non, and my comparison only made me increasingly sorrowful and indeed a little bitter, because I think in essence in the deepest part of my heart, it was not that I begrudged them having the love they did, it was more simply, that I knew-not how to get it, but I think I knew, that I desired to cherish it too.

Comparisons negatively and rapidly grew, not only on the outside but on the inside of the classroom too, as of *la langue française,* I did not learn as quickly as them, and yes I know, fighting for my life through an assault sustained, really had a negative impact on my cognition, but that I permitted not to support my case, as continue in the hugely disparaging stakes against me, of that circumstance, I failed not to take head hold warmth toward myself, as that was really not my fault, and give myself a break, but of it no I did not, for I continued on with my folly and mistake.

For it was much later you see, a month or two to be precise, as the truth of the matter as it so often does unravels and is plane to see and behold, that of the Australian who I most compared myself to, well, it was to transpire that she had

6 other languages under her belt, and had excelled at Ancient Greek and Latin, at university. And the girl from Eastern Europe, well she was just off the educational train of studying English for the last 6 years, so was in the swing of it quite finely, and more, she had studied French before.

Of the Spanish girl who found it so *facile,* easy, well she was married to a Frenchman, and also had a kiddie you see, and of the girls from Scandinavia, well they had study and were most fluid already in English, studied for forever it appeared, and of the values and pronunciation of French that I found so terribly difficult, well they were to reveal, they were almost identical to their own native language. There was more, the other Spanish in the class and the Italians too, well I was to discover, that the reason they found it so terribly easy, was because their languages were classed as cousins, of words, sentence construction, and pronunciation.

"Oh my" what a waist of time and emotional energy I had spent, comparing their best strengths with my weakest, as my heart, flailing unable to cease the reflection of such comparisons of discrepancies began, and from so young, as it was my mother who I reverted to and of what she told me so repetitively, "You know your grandma prefers your cousins to you! So I wouldn't think too highly of her if I were you!" "Oh my" she missed not an opportunity, or so it appeared, that the only comfort she brought herself in her own life was to make every attempt to emotionally stab and destroy me.

> *"We only become what we are by the radical and deep-seated refusal*
> *of that which others have made of us"*
> *~ Jean-Paul Sartre*

What of my father, well he was blatantly clear, how 'everyone was better than me,' as he did criticize, "You're thick as too short planks, don't deserve to be in that class, and you'll never amount to anything." And so with that said and so much more, so often, as a girl so little, a curse was born, and I scorned, and perhaps there it was, the initiation where I became a fully paid up member of 'Comparison City,' as I purchased my life membership ticket and jumped right onboard.

"Oh really" 'if only' I had one person to love and support me, or a mentor, what a difference to my life it may have made, but I didn't, and in truth, others have been through greater adversity. And as my insular reflection of 'pity-party' continued, I recalled a movie staring Will Smith, 'The Pursuit of Happiness,' which jump-started me somewhat as it inspired me to my core. For the lead character of that true story, through his trails and tribulations gave up not, for his son and himself he forged a way through all adversity which he needed to. But there, once again, it struck a nerve, that they had each other, they had love to behold, and of that nature and knowledge unconditionally, I was just beginning to be aware, and for me, of its purity, I grew to desire it so.

Perhaps I thought of my past favourite TV show, of four friends tied so tightly together of those portrayed in 'Sex And The City,' and of their interwoven and valuable relationships transcending decades, it was with new found hope created and established in my heart, that I began to ponder, of such companionship of joy, of security, "Was that mine to win?"

Yet I was not to be, 'out of the woods' for a while, as through the process I was to note, perceivably drowning in condemnation, with questions swirling around my head and colliding with my soul, as I searched and searched trying to bypass the sharp, unrelenting pain, but until I surrendered and realised I needed to give-in and go-through it and not around it, was really, when the real and nurturing benefits of those healing trials and tribulations did begin.

But so unaware and slow to catch-on was I as those contemplations struck a cord with me, of that process which had begun to unravel, yet of its admission to my life I remained oblivious, though surely a blessing it was in disguise, as formidable trials and tribulations were to unfold, and of those stories of old, first to hurt and smart- severely from their habitation inside of me.

Yet through the pain as I relived then released each one so thankfully with magnitude, a change had begun in me, where, with courage I was to hide from no-longer, for perhaps rightly so, just maybe, that was the 'right time,' when most deservedly, I was to earn the wings of my inner-strength and inner-growth, as in-spite of my past, I was to excel and overcome, and as an assured asset, proved to be mine.

> *"To conquer oneself I the best and noblest victory;*
> *to be vanquished by one's own nature is the worst and most ignoble defeat"*
> *~ Plato*

Yet of such unfolding inner glory, I had not quiet arrived, with comparisons looming certainly so, I held not meanness or contention toward those classmates who enjoyed such good fortune to be married to a native French men, and one to be engaged to another, another to live with her sister, and yet another to be with friends from her own country, and sharing a magnificent apartment off the *Champs-Élysées,* and of her loving parents, they visited frequently. With no financial worries either, with their accommodation costs paid for by their parents or government, and they held security of ownership of European health card, where I held non.

Of course I was pleased for them, but within my soul, it left a great big hole, to realise of what they had, I had not, in fact not once, not ever, and the deepness which began to swirl violently inside of me as I was to consider at such an age as I, and have never amounting to achieving such a basic and necessary thing as love I was to discover, "Was I always to be alone, unloved and sad, was the curse set on me? Was it a limiting belief I had taken and board and in stone considered set," or "Was I to be free, and of the most important person on earth for me to begin to love, was that not me?"

"Oh my" that served as only one portion as I tried so hard but failed so miserably, as of that sum of several thousand dollars and more which I squandered so unnecessarily on that motor car, for sure, of that money, it would easily have bought me, accommodation so fine in any *arrondissement*. "Oh my" hate, was welling up, and night and day I seemed not able to hold it back, but what I knew not at that time, really, it was all a process I needed to go through, to get from where I was, in my heart and my spirit safely to the other side.

> *"Never smother your regrets; never smother your sorrow, but tend and cherish it till it comes to have a separate and integral interest. To regret deeply is to live afresh"*
> ~ Henry David Thoreau

I was on a rollercoaster asking "Why not me?" For my *comarades* all had homes to return to in the country from which they came, and had not given away their entire valuable or adored processions, but kept them free of charge at their parent's homes. They need not miss them or disparage themselves at the decisions they had made, for in fullness they had sacrificed nothing in their leaving. And most surely, I was pleased for them, but of my continued comparisons, they only aided to fuel masses of negative and mental conditioning absorbed from an inadequate and basically faulty and wrong childhood training, resulting in compounding septic issues arising from that life spent in pain and fury. And of the chain-reaction with resulted from such, I had arrived inside of me, at a cold, dreary and derelict place inside of me. Yet fortune was suddenly to unfold and be my friend, as ultimately to release and let-go, and that was to become my increasing goal, onward to the end.

> *"Reassess: as so easily; Negative thoughts hold tight, while positive thoughts, take flight"*
> ~ Carole Jordan

"Arrhah" New Zealand, the name I used to say with glee, with it diverse terrain and its magnificent sands on which to bathe, its mountains to climb and its Fiords to sale upon, how wonderfully diverse, and it was there in the largest city of greatest population, on the northern island of Auckland, yet that is not NZ capital for that is on the southern coast, named Wellington. As so fortunate I was to buy there, a house so magnificent, and of a vista from my wrap around deck from that elevated property located at the top of a hill, Rangitioto could be seen, an island of only 5.5 km in length, and from the other side of the deck, tall and straight at 328 meters high, the tower of Sky City, with its revolving restaurant deck and colourful changeable lights shining each night, so ornate, where New Year fireworks display can be seen so bold and bright.

Of that house, as those I had owned in England, so large where inside I appeared some may say to rattle around, but of it, I loved it so, and of those who suggested a lodger I may take, to supplement income and have company too, in an instant, my reply, "No way," this is my huge space in which I am to revel and excel in the enjoyment of it, as at my core for me, it created a magnificent spell. Nor damage did I choose to risk to sustain, to those carpets of 100% fine wool and the fine fabrics of my drapes, or the little wee vase that in the corner of the room I placed so precisely, to match the ensemble of the chaise lounge upholstered in fabric and fringes all to match with petite cushions of silk too, all forming together perfectly in my minds eye, a notion which bounced downward to my soul, to please me, utterly so beautifully.

But a bigger problem I did have, thanks to my mother, "Thankyou mum," as a habit that should be so natural, so simple, but of my habit toilet training I had been taught in a fury, that they were dirty and bad. And of comparisons I had there too, for I was too noisy, too smelly or I took to long, and shouts of "What are you doing in there?" she would almost burst out in song. With instructions to follow of how, "Never sit on a public convenience seat," but of my friends or relatives too, my grandma included, I was prohibited to doing so, and to never ever, use anyone else's toilet at all to do a number two.

And there it was, a theme was set, and when visiting at a friends or relatives house, as soon as I stepped into the toilet room, I would mildly panic and be so utterly conscious of the time I took, and concerned, were they waiting and listening to me? Then interestingly, a bit of a problem was to plague me before it turned out to be a mild obsession, for even of a boyfriend, a partner who I was with, I remained unable to use the toilet when they were in the house, and over the decades it was a mild panic of such that situation transpired to be, before of determined action I did consciously take, of it poor function to eradicate.

Likely a mistake of what my mother did, of her induction and the onward flowing ramifications, perhaps misguided, perhaps unaware, a web she did weave within that child so inadvertently, likely by the age of 3, and of the social and physical restraints they did contribute to, ultimately, through mindful practice perhaps bizarrely I must say, the peace to pass what I 'must' from that basic bodily function, was to eventually, visit and stay with me.

'Protection' became my mantra, of pieces of peace I aimed to gain in greater portions consecutively, as self-preservation transposed to be my ultimate game, and the only one I was to take part in, though remained resolute and determined to win. For a format I developed for living, or was that survival? But poignantly it was isolation of my own creation which inadvertently, as I was to surround myself, for those bigger and greater metaphoric castles I did build, so determined to keep those who were bad, or mad {angry} or would harm me, out.

Yet those impervious walls of steel six foot deep, the drawbridge of iron metres tall, and the moat most deep, deliberately infested with aquatic species dangerous, still failed to protect me. And worse, as I tried so drastically to keep 'them' out and my space not to share to keep me safe, inadvertently, it was a prisoner within which I made of me. For I was to risk nothing else, yet it was all-else, that fell into oblivion of which I held no real interest, as I could see not past my Risk Assessment for self-preservation and safety, free from all harm. "Thank goodness" I declare that through my trials and growth I am a more healed human being, a person who today, having gained that of what I needed, I now need not protect my domain with such viscous fortitude.

Yet was all that behind me? "Oh my" I so desired and aimed so, for I had truly grown through some adversity and a new chapter in my life I had ordained, and of optimism for what it could afford me, I was optimistic for it in advance. And so in Paris, I wandered the streets, not wanting to go back to that place where I rented a room, perhaps quite understandably, so it was down the *rue étroite*, narrow streets I did walk enjoying the ambiance, where an unexpected turn in the road, sublimely created a new opportunity to get lost, and although historically doing such a thing would provoke anger at myself, or panic to set in, in Paris I was cool, collected, safely knowing, loosing myself afforded me the opportunity to marvel at more architecture of substance, often hidden in a nook or cranny down somewhere down a tiny street, or in a hidden courtyard, yet soon, I would find myself somewhere which was familiar to me.

How I longed for that peace to immerse into other areas of my Parisian experience. I was not "Lost in France in Love," not quite, there was loss for sure, but no love in sight. Yet true, sometimes, too many to count of the prevailing sadness in my heart at what I gave away, and of the peace, even in Australia that I left behind.

Loss of those comforts of privacy and space, rejuvenating long hot showers, oh how I missed those. My music and educational CD's which fed me so while stuck in traffic jams, of driving around the tree-laden roads visiting my favourite book store, of reaching my favourite café where to linger, to relax and enjoy a good read, and guaranteed to be served the best half-strength latté in town. I missed my comfy bed and pillows too of natural fibres of such pleasing colour schemes easy on the eye, to relax the spirit and the mind.

Familiarity gone, and a good coffee so hard to find, so strong and unpleasant I did find, it was to a glass of *Bordeaux* that I turned my attentions to, for when chosen to partake at the right place, even when seated at a bistro enface the river *Seine* only half the price was to be charged and of the taste, so much more palatable. But that being said, at the hour of *ce soir*, the evening, though really, as many times as I posed that question, "Of what hour is that?" no one could quantify, or even agree, and it appeared a perplexing mystery, or maybe that was quite *Gallic* and on purpose, undefined, so as 'they' determined what that was to be, the glass of wine which was on the *carte de menu*, menu, not another customer was able to disagree when of their prices at the fall of the evening, perhaps as early as half past four, the fee did rise 30% or more.

And of tips too, they are so slightly undefined, as an Irishman of some mature years educated in France, did tell of me, "Don't tip them, for they are already given 5.5% of the total *l'addition*, bill/check, price." So "Why did I too late consider, of a French waiter who did lean over me at the end of his shift, take all the money from my change tray, to place it in his *purses du monnaie*, purse for change, effectively as a tip?" As so rudely leaned over me as I was doing my study, "Oh my" of his actions, "Why did I not stop him, and why had he done that?" and "Why did I not challenge him?"

I believe it was from my training of the past, and what judging from my persona he knew he could get away with, and he did, a tidy few Euros it did seem. And temporarily annoyed at myself of my non actions, but a notion I was to gleam, which I believe was to form as testimony to my growth of notes times two. First I noted what he did, and not hold a grudge against me of 'how stupid I was.' Yet the second was to examine me, and consider, really what was I portraying to him that of his behaviour it was to be accepted, and how I was for the future of my internal Barometer I was to reset, so ultimately it was to be eradicated.

It was with a saddened and heavy heart I was to realised so slowly, what had ultimately gone, disappeared, and what I really missed was my freedom and ability to make, my 'choices.' Those preferred and familiar for wrapped up within them, lay the ability to relax and unwind. "Oh my" and perhaps testimony to my inner-growth, how I identified with the theme tune from the 1982 American comedy show, running for 11 years, for I so longed to be in a place, "Where everyone knows my name." "Olalla!" Indeed I did.

A sanctuary and solitude I held non, so perhaps, of no surprise that I would wonder the streets of Paris in the evening when the university class had closed for the day in avoidance of the ever-deteriorating living arrangement I would wander frequently around my preferred location, the Left Bank, situated along the river *Seine* which meanders through the extravagant city of Paris until it exits at the mouth of the estuary, Northern France, in the English channel, a place I felt greater nourishment in my soul than any other *arrondissement*.

And so synonymous with many an artist, philosopher or writer it was, such as Ernest Hemingway, Jean-Paul Sartre, Henri Matisse, Scott Fitzgerald and Simone de Beauvoir and more, who sat for hours under the coloured canopies on the pavement terraces, inspiring or being inspired, idling away the hours, in chatter or contemplation and in totality, soaking up all of what was and probably is the quaint-essential Parisian population. And of such I did consider, with delight in my heart I wondered with eagerness, "In their literary footsteps, was I to follow?"

So "Where to sit and read?" It is said 'seek and ye shall find,' and so I did, ever hoping to discover that elusive good cup of coffee in Paris, yet a discovery I made along the way, of the quality it was precarious at best, yet of a glass of *Bordeaux*, a fine and palatable tipple was to be gained every time. "Why?" It was half the price of coffee, even when sat at a Bistro with the pleasant sight *enface*, facing the river *Seine*, a slight calculation of my beverage habits were to be reviewed and I, of them, re-enthused.

Then full to over-flowing, of study not wine, I commenced my final walk of the night toward *la Métro* station, a quick step I had not, for I was not keen to return to my lodgings, yet more, in the Parisian ambiance I was pleased to meander. And slowly I paused as a I caught sight through the corner of my eye, a little black dress, that was so, Audrey Hepburn, and also just the same as one I had given away prior to my recent departure.

"Oh my" those comparisons septic inside of me, quickly darted in my mind, of the valuables so regrettable as I mulled over it at leisure and locked myself up in its memory of misadventure of what I'd given them away and left behind. And of my *comarades* not having done the same, indeed I was so pleased for them and their situation, but of my action, toward me I held desolate shame, of my self-imposed perceived unwise stupidity.

But, my fortune was suddenly to change, as on my arm I felt a tug, then surprisingly, but not threateningly, a man had his arms around me, not my choice from a stranger, so I quickly turned to see. He Spoke, "You like that dress, it's yours free," my immediate thought was "Yes please," for on that tight budget I had not the finance to buy it. But my question, "Why, do you own the shop?" In his French accent he continued, "No. But for you its free." Confused, "Yes," and a cheap and cheesy pickup line, that would be another "Yes." And later I was to take note, of that dress, if exact, it was to be half the price on *Boulevard du Montparnasse*.

I turned around to see a man of slightly unusual in Parisian appearance, tall, with dark hair, mildly greying at the temple bones, nestled beneath a golf cap of one colour and a tweed tailored jacket of another, which casually lay over a V-neck jumper of green wool, with blue jeans and brown dress shoes his ensemble was complete. It was a short conversation, which ensued *avec l'homme*, with the man, who enquired as to my preference for jazz music, well for sure, it is, I like it a lot, and there it was *il a posé la question*, he asked the question, "Would you like to join me at a venue playing jazz this very evening?"

"Arrhah!" First and foremost, my safety, enquiring of its exact location and walking distance and time taken to get there, establishing my own 'safe egress' should I need one, with my Risk Assessment complete, I answered, with a motto that had evolved during my short time in that land of the French, of, *"Oui. pourquoi pas"* "Yes. Why not?" "Ahhh yes," it evolved also that a further 2 motto's I commenced to live my life by, though perhaps wisely or not, "What can you do?" {about it} and "It is, what it is!" Perhaps precarious motto' to live by, perhaps wise or not, as emotionally supportive to me somehow, as they enabled me as smoothly as possible transverse each day.

So, speedily I was whisked away trampling along the large and dirty paving stones, for only five minutes or less, before the biting chill of the night air could get us no more, as there before us, our destination, and as the grandiose of the French pained glass doors drew apart, and a tall Bellboy dressed in a uniform of finery, of green adorned with buttons of gold with matching cap, greeted us into that establishment, a hotel dating back to the 17th century.

Instantly, I felt at home, so it turned out to be my first visit and not my last, indeed on that fine establishment I was certainly to pass many a good and fine time, at *Café Laurent*, a bar of some quite refinement, on *rue Dauphine*. It is the people who make the place and the vibe it holds, it is not the four walls that confine it, which of all will send me away or cause me to stay. And emphatically an intrinsic decision was made, I felt good, I felt, at ease yet stimulated simultaneously and I was emphatically, staying.

As I was directed gently passed the rail of winter coats and many of fur, scarfs and quaint-essential Frenchman's hats, it was at the pristine and polished bar where I was to sit, and upon were petite plates of canapés for all to eat, as the soft music tones rang out from the jazz quartet, across the room in the diagonal corner, with a grand piano of deep black and high gloss, posed centre stage, and tucked around were other musicians of string and wind.

The spirit in place, "Oh what joy" filled that space, with a hum in the air of congenial chatter, as *clientele*, patrons most valued, sipped on champagne most fine, while other watched intently to the feast of the jazz quartet and the elegance of the well-dressed four. The ambiance, most jovial and chic, a gentle bustle, to be experienced and absorbed, and I was, so pleased to be amidst it.

Paris, a vibe and a beauty to behold, yet of noise and congestion it holds its fair share, and a place to escape to, perhaps not daily but I suggest a place is necessary, and I had found my refuge, at *Café Laurent*, hidden within the *Hotel d'Aubusson*. And where for me, a most pleasurable experience was most unexpectedly to bloom and blossom. And so it was, a marvellous world opened up before me, as on many a blustery and chilly Parisian evening, or indeed after the university day was done there I could be found to be studying there, where rest and peace could accompany me, escaping the hustle and bustle, and the noise of *'a gay Paris.'*

The staff I met it's true, all amenable, unrelenting in their courteous and friendly manner, from the kind and young hotel shift manager and his team of receptionists, to the entertaining and handsome barman, yet better was to come, for yet it was he, who I liked in an instant, wonderfully flamboyant, with an effervescent personality and delightful and exuberant character, he who I understood not of all what he spoke, but all of what he meant, and gladly and proudly I say, he who was to become, my good and dear friend, Flavien.

"The best thing about the future is that it comes only one day at a time."
~ Abraham Lincoln

Chapter 4

Keep Stepping

"No trumpets sound when the important decisions of our life are made.
Destiny is made known silently"
~ Agnes de Mille

"Paris oh Paris," a city of such beauty, yet such problems as yet another arduous day had passed at that place of study, opened in 1257 by that Parisian theologian, *Monsieur Robert de Sorbonne,* followed what was to be a delayed return to that place where I had not yet escaped from the 'old-duck,' a northern English expression for someone of a 'certain age' and disposition. For the only comfort I could afford myself not to return to that, her abode, was not to go 'home. So there it was I found myself, in that favourite *arrondissement* till way after dark, where even tourists were able to stop me and ask for directions to here or there, I was able to assist as through my own wanderings I had grown to know *St. Germain,* so absolutely well.

And there one evening I was to have a *rencontra,* meeting, with that Frenchman I had met, who teased me about buying me that petite evening dress, who in reality turned out to be, not French at all, as Tunisia born, he emigrated to France with his family as a toddler, and when his parents returned to their country of origin, well he preferred to stay. And there before me, in the disguise of he, a steep leaning curve lay, of a gradient quite excessive, practically and emotionally to its peak, as perhaps they so often are, and to it was the passing of time, and of circumstances I was to gleam that was with clarity to reveal to me, of him, "Was he to be a friend or a foe?"

Enchanted, perhaps I was initially to some degree, by that man from a far away land, who appeared somewhat eclectic and interesting, particularly of his, *je ne sais pas,* I know not what, yet quite rapidly warning signs began to reveal themselves to me. For I believe it to be said, a good memory is a prerequisite to be a good liar, and with his inconsistencies of what he spoke with his ever changing format of portrays of his chosen repeated subjects, time and an astute mindfulness of mine, appeared to reveal, that the second he maybe, but the former, absolutely not.

"Arrhah, did I alert him of what I had observed?" "Oh definitely not!" For that was my purposeful power in my wise and well serving consciousness to protect me, for should I have done such a thing, his guard of deceit would have been raised, to possibly a level to where I would unaware, then his dark-game would have remained concealed, and ultimately, of a victory song of inspired and personal growth, would have alluded me, to sing.

It was patience and time that gave me the prospective, while my eyes remained opened with a willingness to see, of that charade of his personality, and of his cloak as it began to fall to reveal his true character which lay below, open brightly, as unbeknown, he did show. Perhaps in the past, I should have used a far greater tool for calculation, for should a beau be morally and ethically suitable, nay compatible, rather than, "Does he have bright shiny shoes?" For sure, it appeared I'd been foolish, I checked the shoes, checked the style, but I had not checked the character. That was to be an unresounding, "No."

And there it was, a concept that also suddenly shone brightly, as to why it is said 'people change' post marriage ceremony, perhaps they do not, but perhaps the married-ones succumb to two points, one, that pr-marriage with rose-coloured glasses firmly placed on, all looks good, and tied up in hope are the expectations of what is to come, but really, perhaps it is the escalated joy of the wedding ceremony. And the second perhaps, of the personality which is put on display, as peoples 'best behaviour prevails, well the effort to do so, becomes tiering, and the façade it fails, as the true cracks appear as behind that outer exterior, to the core, the true character of each of the married couple, is revealed. "Buyer be aware," is of mine in that arena a message to share!

Yet blissfully aware I was of my surroundings at least, as I seated comfortably at the bar, on raised seats of deep chocolate brown leather, with the glass of a fine wine resting on the polished marbled bar top, the sophisticated ambience listening to the musing of that music of jazz, *concert jazz*, momentarily, reminiscing of the wonderful midweekly evenings spent at Ponsonby jazz night in Auckland, in the land of the 'long white cloud' according to Maori folk law heritage. So keen to replicate and enjoy more, I enquired, "How often do you have this concert?" Wonderful was the concept in my brain as a menu was accounted, for Thursday through Saturday of the quartet with varying instruments and artists played, while Wednesday nights given to the genre of traditional French flare, singing and percussion performed by a duo or solo artist. "Oh what joy," for sure, that was music to my ears, if you forgive the pun. At last, a place of familiarity to visit, a place I could feel comfortable, myself, and it was myself who I was eventually able to be in Paris, *tranquile et calme*, quiet and peaceful.

With my new companion exchanging not a hearty but palatable conversation as we underwent the process of getting to know each other, exchanging pieces of information, I revealed the unpleasantness of the situation of which I lived, and surprising, he expressed with ease, "I might have a solution for you." I did find it quirkily amusing that within the language of French and its gender orientations, that *un problem*, is masculine and *une solution*, is feminine. "Arrhah," a solution. Was there a light at the end of the tunnel or was I to jump out of the frying pan into the fire in the vision on an oncoming train? For through its advancement of that frequent master of time a 'the bitter sweet pill,' was to revealed, that it may be mine to swallow.

I was to be informed that he owned 15 apartments city wide, and as one was to be vacated that month, I could take it over if I chose to, for the sum of, 850E per month. A tidy sum for sure, and a higher one than what I had budgeted for. Continuing, I was given a second option, that of taking a room in his large Parisian apartment for 650E. Choices are good, right? Though I contemplated silently, 650E what a high fee, to share an apartment, the kitchen, the bathroom and toilet, with him and a Russian girl, with only a bedroom to call my own, "Errrmm, I don't think so!" Zero intention I held of taking the latter option, predominantly due to my, oh so negative experiences of renting rooms in NZ, so in response I questioned not the extremely high price for the latter, "Not likely."

And, "Not really," was my concept of he who, may or may not soon to become my new landlord, where from the onset of our initial encounter he was to say repeatedly to me, "You're my girlfriend." An odd notion of premature advancement, and, "Doesn't a girl like to be asked," but perhaps I should have paid more attention to the accompanying strangely odd expression on his face as he spoke. Yet true, progress had been made, for at the notion, I did not go running for the hills, as in days of yesteryear, such a phrase would, and did, render any 'relationship' underway, over, finished, completed, done and dusted, and I may say, in an instant. For no such title was to be mine, nor was such associated actions or notions of commitment were to be either. Point: 1) For my only associations with relationships inferred unequivocally, persecution and pain in life and in extreme. 2) My male friends made me aware that having sex for six weeks doesn't constitute a relationship. "Seriously," I didn't used to know that, for that was the only type, that *used* to work for me.

The duties of that man, of which one of his tales included "I own many shops," and on several accounts of relaying such a story, of businesses he owned, in their number fluctuated, but of one right then, he was required to leave the bar, to cash and close up, and invited me to wait for his return. Well, of that place of *Café Laurent*, once found I was in no hurry to leave, so of his suggestion and invitation, I did concede. Then upon his arrival past 10pm, when in Australia I would have been in bed, he my *nouveau,* new companion, returned to escort me for a meal.

And as I waited patiently, absorbing and enjoying so of what was around me, for dare I say for the first time since I had arrived in Paris, and "Minding my own business," as so often joked, as really the most amazing coincidences happened to me while doing so, an American man was to speak, and for sure, he must have taken me for another, as into a conversation on the topic of sex he pounced immediately. A finish line I placed in the midst of his conversation, of his uncouth and rude attitude, and of his invitation to travel to a different bar with him and his friends I did decline, but then it was out of the blue, on another matter, which his friend did butt in.

His topic, I had no idea from whence it came, yet in earnest while the jazz played and pleasant patrons mingled all around, he began to share personal details of how through unforseen circumstances, he and his lady began a personal relationship, with its base of trust and mutual respect, and where ultimately he became 'the one.' Continuing, he explained that he never expected to achieve such healthy emotions as he enjoys in that relationship, and then seamlessly transferring to me, he expressed gently but fervently, "Although many a Miss Wrong may be encountered Mr Right, is out there?"

How bizarre, "Why did he choose that topic?" For sure, although he was not privy to his colleagues, it was from a different, and even out of left field. What profoundly struck me about the whole situation, was that was a man I did not know, who talked of a topic that I had hardly permitted myself know was important to me.

I had not at that time, yet dared to dream that I could have 'love' as those classmates at uni had, it was as though he had looked deep down into my soul, I mean, "Could I? Would I? Was it even possible for me?" It was as though by some most strange coincidence, he had given me an answer to a question that I had thought or dared to ask myself. But perhaps a more deep-seated question he was to brightly ignite was "Was I worthy?"

I was never to see that man or his lady whom he introduced me to, after only 5 minutes or more, they disappeared out of the door into the cold Parisian air, and although they had gone from my eyes, a seed they left behind most definitely lingered and did not depart, as it was to be nourishingly germinated. Yet a little perplexed and with tentative reservation, I was to consider, of a healthy relationship, I did not know how to behave or to behold such? For of positive example I held not much, but of the message of hope he delivered I was to remember.

Complex in totality was my knowledge, nay experience of relationships, at home, at work, at play, uneasy to define, difficult to navigate through, with potholes and landmines it appeared at every stage or turn to trip up or of my notions to confuse and confine. Yet a lifeline I may have just been thrown, with my concept that, I didn't have to avoid everyone, or put up with just anyone, but indeed expect and believe that I was worthy, "I also could have the one, the right one."

After all, it stands to reason, if we are with the wrong one, would that by definition mean that we were in the wrong place? Do we not have to let-go of what serves us ill, to afford ourselves the best opportunity to be in the right place, at the right time, to meet the right one? I contemplated on the transferable concept, 'Perfect preparation prevents poor performance' "Oh my" it may just be true. I chose to begin my preparations, for what we do today affects our tomorrow, so I choose to prepare, I choose to hope and I choose to change myself, and my circumstances, for me.

I began to imagine so, that life is like a 'dot-to-dot' picture; we need to join all the right dots in the right order to achieve the right picture, or outcome. And when we make a small mishap or as I like to say miss-happening, or mistakes, or as I like to say, miss-taking appropriate action necessary; wrong or as I like to say, incorrect dots maybe joined, where upon an incorrect picture we may stumble or effectively create; so it may eventuate that at the right place and the right time, possibly, no we are not.

But the great news is here to follow, as we can easily put the picture right, by erasing those lines of error, as we erase not the lessons from our consciousness but the pain of learning them from our mind, as we view the picture and consider of stumbling blocks or steppingstones, really, "Where to from here?"

The errors I'd made seemed all to easy to count up, and of an eraser, "Oh my" I preferred I would have invested in one of those, metaphorically speaking, so long ago. For in that adopted city I chose, relentlessly I counted up the cost of money I'd spent, the decisions made in gross error, of which I could not accept what foolish things I'd done, forgive myself, or let-go.

Circles in my mind manifested as a pit of blame, as I was to regret, not what had inadvertently come against me, but what I had brought against myself, and at the most low-ebb of which I was feeling, seemingly without interruption the list catapulted around my head. I had bought a first class ticket and was on 'the blame train,' and of all my scorn, it was directed like sharp arrows directly toward me, of my heavy burden of financial restraints of my circumstances I found myself in, charged heavily with emotional regret, of choices, decisions and actions made and taken, of partners chosen, and in those relationships 'accepting unacceptable abuse as acceptable,' where sitting in that classroom of strangers, of 23 international students, so rapidly were they brought home to me, as difficult it was to learn because of an injury sustained during a life threatening assault, at the hands of one fiancé, who was supposed to love me.

"Oh why, had I remained a captive so long?" and "Why was I not wiser, more empowered, thinking more greatly of me?" For the chain reaction had been set in motion from that child so long ago, and the burden of blame and shame, it had not dissipated but multiplied, and as the unravelling, unpleasant chain reaction unfolded in 'A Paris,' and of the strain, was I to give in and remain captive as its cold metal wrapped itself around me, or was I to refrain from scumming to its captive trick, as an unwilling participant I was to be, recognizing gladly how to escape, as renewed empowered, and retrospectively I was to be a 'job in progress, yet, magnificently, I was to break free.

"Blame, only succeeds in building walls to exclude change"
~ Carole Jordan

As the hour rolled around, my new host to that fair city returned true to his word, from his shop-closing duties and whisked off to the *brassier*, restaurant of his preference, yet as I walked in, I knew it not to be the same for me, for the ambiance, staff and later I was to realise food, unpalatable it emerged and most definitely, not for me.

Yet 'when in Rome,' dare I say, a concept I resorted to, as I was to succumb to what seemed perhaps so reasonable, as food off his fork I chose to eat, perhaps considering, when repeatedly presented with it, but of my choice not to partake, "Oh why, did I permit that to take second place?" Yet perhaps my first notion was more superficial as I merrily contemplated, of a quaint essential Parisian romantic movie, 'oh how cute, oh how sweet.'

Yet persistently, I have never tolerated well the smell of the shellfish in which he chose to feed me, yet that was a choice of food I had always resisted previously, and the reason for that was to become clear, as my bodies inner mechanism, guarding me from what innately it knew, of that food source, it did not serve me so, for intolerant and allergic I appeared to be, as those incrustations I was to be seeing them twice, past the hour in the morning of half past three.

Yet how bizarre, a stranger before me, so why did I not persist, in my choice, my decision in such a simple matter and overrule his as "Try it, try it," he proclaimed and insisted, as his cutlery he waved before my face? For I was able and capable and worthy of such, yet sucked in to give in on such a simple matter as that, I was to wonder, was that by his design, as he tested me, to see, how easily I would fall to his desires, his demands and how easily he was able to infiltrate my domain and manipulate me?

For really, when and were of those origins of their plans of manipulation begin, and surely, they do indeed though our way a prototype of what is to come, to see, just how easily, we submit and succumb. For so sublimely are the seeping infestations of their deceit, that we can be surrounded in its mist and knee deep, before of all the warning signs, we realise, only retrospectively, we missed.

Then it was to be shortly before 2a.m. when my host was to drop me off at the *Métro* station at *Hotel de ville*, in the 4eme arr, where following a 20 min journey underground, and a further 20 minute walk before I was to arrive at that place, where so I dearly desired, to depart.

Perhaps past the hour of 5a.m before I was eventually able to ease myself and fall asleep, only to rise quite early requiring hot water to drink in plentiful amounts, and oh, with that a serving of peace. But the latter was not to be, as jump, is what I did, as around the corner the lady came creeping from along the corridor, though of small dimensions in her stature, with her shoulders pushed way back, and hands grasped in front of her, her head stiff, her lips pinched and pert, with her eyes piercing, as arrows darting directly to disarm, presenting a demur and posture much more suited to yesteryear.

Accusingly and demandingly domineering her perceived jurisdiction over me, she demanded, "Tell me why you're were sick!" A quick note to self, of her 'little red riding cloak' it had been completely discarded and put to bed, or perhaps put in storage until her 'pretence' needed to arise its hiding place, for the next innocent and foreign university student who was to come her way.

"It was the faecal matter from the toilet door handle and the bacteria which laid within, passed by you to me" is the way I may have accurately began my retort, but of that matter I did not, as pretty sure of the answer I knew, "It's the seafood I ate." Yet the answer only served as irritation, as ignoring my response the question flew, "Have you been drinking too much alcohol?" "Not at all," proved insufficient in calming her mind, as the Spanish Inquisition sprang to mine, but oh how nice it would have been should she have just asked, with care or consideration, "Are you feeling much better?" And I may have pleasingly replied, "Thanks for asking."

"The road ahead may be a little difficult, uncharted, unplanned, unprepared for, we must forge our own path, falling as least as possible, navigating through the stumbling blocks until they transpose into steppingstones."
~ Carole Jordan

Yet thank goodness, like a little homing pigeon, in that unsettled and unpleasant habitation with the on the outskirts of Paris, and only 1 *Métro* and almost 25 minute ride to take me there, and so far away, but then whatever I am, I guess I quickly search out a place to rest, with good company and coffee the same, and the closest to resinate with my heart, was a niche I calved out for myself on the Left Bank, as I sat upon a Bistro wicker chair at the café's street terrace to, *boire un café*, drink a coffee. Yet in small proportions I did miss that petite Melbourne suburb by the bay, of its wide and tree lined streets and of its inhabitants of mild manner, and most importantly *pas de fumées de voitures* no car fumes in contrast to Paris, where finding an outdoor space of quiet or solitude or certainly free from car emissions, remained elusive to me.

And peace, was I to find it? For sure I was to look for it, as I remembered gladly, a ladies autobiography who wrote, Paris which she had made her new home, where she found difficulty in finding solace, off she would wander to *Jardin Luxemburg*, Luxemburg Gardens, that great public park located in the 6eme arr, where to rest and recuperate, yet sadly for me, it didn't work, and "Why?" I was much later to reflect, for I never ventured further than the entrance where it was safe, and the masses of tourist 'hung-out' and the buzz, still very much alive, where in the middle of mediocrity, I risked nothing and searched for no more, as I sat or promenaded, only around its busy circumference, adventuring not into the midst of its greatness, the joyous peaceful sound I had hoped to ring in my heart, remained a distance apart.

"Oh my" I was to too lately gather, how sadly I missed that opportunity, as further I failed to investigate, and so never discovered, the other vast space of 22.5 hectares, as there, hidden amongst it all, may have been, my preferred and secret little place, where solitude and I may have become friends once more, for such an opportunity I missed, as I reached out, no further, than what I was able to see right in front of me, receiving not the greater reward, by going out on a limb, reaching for the ripest and most nourishing fruit, yet the risk I took was none, so my prize, only to be unable to distribute, the solace to feed my soul, with peace and harmony.

> *"The only thing that will stand between a person and what they want in life, are the will to try it and the faith to believe its possible."*
> *~ Rich Devos*

But, surely things had to get better right, by he, that landlord who was possibly to be, was to throw me a lifeline, and "Yeah," I jollied myself along with glee, as the apartment, only a hop skip and a jump to the centre of the city, and he, that man, informed me, he would telephone me upon his return from the coast of Spain, and whilst still at *Charles de Gaulle,* airport he did just that and was true to his word, as waiting to view was a vacant apartment, which I was told he owned, so "Hurrah," as jumped with delight, as our *rendezvous* was arranged, as a welcomed calmness fell upon me, but it proved to be, a tad prematurely.

Along *la ligne de Métro sept,* Metro line 7, exiting at stop *Poissonnière, dans l'arrondissement neuvième,* in the 9eme arr I travelled and was greeted by he, with my initial response was, "Oh what a stagnant smell?" first arriving at my nostrils, where taking a deep breath was highly not recommended, and the noise dense, and the population mass the same, rattling around me ears, with not passing past the tulips which was required but the bypassing of the broken liquor bottles, the crushed beer cans, and the doggy-do-do in copious amounts, all adorning the dirty and freshly urine-stained footpaths, yet to judge too early I refused to do, and remained perhaps mildly desperately, with eager anticipation and hope.

Only a few hundred yards to walk before we arrived at our destination, and standing before the awe-inspiring doors of great grandeur and dimensions, of natural wood, lacquered to a glossy sheen, with brass trimmings gleamingly polished, not an attribute of a street scene viewed so much more commonly in days of old, and there, almost intrusively into yesteryear my imagination flooded, of its construction and those who would have taken such strength to push that door open, and the walls concealed behind and the steps trampled progressively upon. For of those centuries passed, really, how did they live? The lady of the house and the fine fabrics she did wear, the servants, the infants, the elderly, the sick, the infirm, the healthy, the poor and the wealthy, and the man of the house, who used to be the forever bearing matriarch, and of all succumbing to cultural, medical and economic restraints of their 'class' "How did their lives collide, tumble or excel?"

Then there it was, my imagination interrupted as the old met with the new, as to the right of that imposing door, a small computer box, in which to key a number into, released a lock, and the door, was opened for us to walk through. An ordinary, traditional key was then used to unlock a further door of far less inspiring dimensions, almost disappointing in comparison, as behind it lay that which was in appearance dark and dingy, absent of fresh air, nothing to please the eye with the exception of what is one of my favourite worldly architectural objects, a spiral staircase, which I so adore, yet the smallest I'd seen with its dimensions wide, no greater than 24 inches or more.

And up that *escalier*, staircase, to the 6eme *etage*, level we were to ascend, precarious it was underfoot, as the extreme indentations of those steps were a classic visual clue history flooded, *encore*, again my imagination ran, to where I believed the servants quarters would have been, as perhaps as with so much of life, not so glorious hidden behind the outward façade.

But independence, escape, were notions still haunting me, as logically, I failed to consider the logistics and restraints of what I was almost blindly to walk into and commence, a constriction to be, where awakened to that situation I was, by the forth or more speaking of that potential landlord, of *faire du sport*, exercise, as it was he who against his desire, which he tried to detract me from, alerted me to issues with holding potentially high, ramifications. And of accommodation calamities, to escape, I suddenly became mindful of, the adage of the frying pan and fire, of which a fare paying passenger I was resolute not to become.

"Oh my" yet another door was unlocked, so tremendously narrow in width, and of tall, no it was not, and what lay behind, as an Occupational Health & Safety Nurse, took me no time at all to complete my Risk Assessment, as I deemed it dangerous in which of a place as such, with a safe egress from danger of fire there was non, and of consider the idea, of a notion I was not to give it much. For in addition to the glaringly obvious, were other door rooms so closely packed together in proximity, posed an additional personal safety risk, and in the event of an emergency, or more seriously the unsecured electrical cables hanging from the ceiling and traversing the door wells, or lying on the floor, to stumble or trip upon. "The score of hazards?" Multiples of many! and a "Safe Egress?" No, there weren't any! Yet still, so quaint, I was yearning to succumb.

Another key turned, and into a quaint apartment, where immediately I felt at home, and how instantly I imagined myself living there, studying while soft music played after a day spent at, *l'ecole*, the school, eventually excelling as expected, at what I had chosen to do, within the area so light and bright and yeah importantly self-contained, the best thing of course was that it was private and to be all mine. But was I falsely seducing myself as bypassing the dirty and beshrivelled furniture, I was to stand at one of the three tiny windows in the apartment, standing on tippy-toes to peer through them, but "Oh my" more seduction, as the feast that awaited my eyes was a vista clear across, the Parisian aged terracotta and grey chimney tops, as the lyrics sung by Julie Garland, 'Some where over the Rainbow' a song I was to have joy for my ears to here at every turn that Christmas in Paris, I contemplated, "Was it a sign?"

"Trust instinct to the end, even though you can give no reason."
~ Ralph Waldo Emerson

Quickly pinching myself, I was to consider the downturns in the equation. The apartment, most dirty, but then he did say, "I'll get it all cleaned up." The hot water cylinder, broken and rendering, no heating, yet more, no hot shower, but he did say, "I'll get that fixed." "Mmmm," perhaps the progression of the lullaby, with lyrics, 'problems melting like lemon drops' were not necessarily to be an unfolding progression of events. I wondered of that occurrence, was it all destiny or of the princely sum to be charged for that perhaps 'dodgy' accommodation, was it deliberate deflection or distraction, that as he who had that place to rent, placed his arm around my waist pulling me romantically toward him, before we kissed above those chimney tops, our first 'real kiss?'

Yet, shouldn't I have considered that as normal, for after all, he did keep up his vein of concept, or was that to unravel to be, a vein of pretence, as he continued to declare me, as his girlfriend. Really, "Was it passion or manipulation?" The answer, as it so often is, was soon to be, that giver and taker away, of *'time.'*

My tour of that magnificent building was not yet complete as with insistence, yet on my part, not consideration, he persistence my guide persuaded me to cast an eye over his personal apartment in view to renting a room within it, but really I was resistance, as repeat bad history or have that ticket purchase for a kettle frying pan scenario, it appealed to me in any portion of measure, absolutely none.

Then descending the stairwell, slowly, uncertainty prevailed, as so much more precarious my footing was to be than on the ascent, triggering a reality check, of how the logistics would prevail of getting my 'stuff' up it and perhaps more importantly in the event of a quick exit, getting it sown and out again.

With all my concerns raised, it was put to me as not a problem, as that landlord to be or not to be, was to provide a solution, as he concluded a staff member of his would do the trick of accessing all I need in the reals of lugging my bags up there, and all for the sum of only 20euros. "Mmmm, was he being nice or too amenable?" And how, when leaving was I to get them all down again, for when he had no rent or nothing to gain, was he to be so obliging in extreme, or was there a hidden trick, which was looming to trap me, which as yet I had not worked out or a notion gleamed.

Reaching the bottom, "Yeah," breaking through that almost mouldy door into the brightness of the hallway, my soon 'to be landlord' or not to be, produced yet another key to enter into a stairwell obviously so much grandiose, as viewed through the big and clear open expanse of the tempered safety glass doors with a basic white and bold metal framed, with its circumference appearing glued to the circumference of the original cornice stone, of such an installation appeared not only uninspiring, but blatant injustice.

And there to my secret joy, displayed was another spiral staircase of splendour, larger in size, for within its winding circumference, encased an elevator, of perfect proportion, of its metal concertina doors, and underfoot to step upon, plush carpet of pale greens and creams, while to hold on to, a banister rail of old weathered and polished oak, where observed were dents and chips which had been accomplished from life from over the years, and as wistfully mind absorbed my contemplative thoughts, of yesteryear, or yester century, and really, of them all, "Who had trodden that path before?"

How quaint, and how absolutely practical designed, I was enthralled its fare to say, and as I cast my eye on something I believed to be unique, I was to find I was wrong, for of the format and design, most common in Paris, as banging, clattering and ringing were the sounds as the brass doors collided with the metal frame, as in the elevator, yet not at a swift but dormant speed we rose to the 3rd floor, and there I was shown to a pair of eggshell painted floor to ceiling doors, the entrance to his apartment. "Oh how wonderful" I thought it must be, of what lay behind, of the lofts and interiors as I gleamed so with glee as I fingered through those glossy books way-back-when in the book shop in Albert Park.

But I need not have got excited or anticipate such, for as he unlocked the door, it was darkness which was to greet me, and as he beckoned me in, it was no Parisian design I did feast my eyes upon, but a style quite Moroccan. "Oh my" in the vastness of an excessively spacious duel living room, appearing as two rooms had been joined together, where the walls were clad with dark wood from floor to ceiling, and sited in the middle of that room, sucking further portions of unaffordable daylight from the space, a pair of rather under-embellished black wrought iron gates, of a meter or so tall, more suitable for the garden than where they stood, perched almost precariously, and of their purpose a perplexing curiosity to me, as left ajar, and attached to nothing except themselves at either end, bizarre, but of all, "Why not attach it to a post or perhaps a wall?"

With the lounge area to the left, where a huge TV screen could be seen, and sofa's of square angles, upholstered in deep brown leather, and a fireplace, oh yeah, but ultimately, "Oh no" as appearing to be a 1960's renovation decision, not at all, quaint Parisian. And to the right, was a table extra large in size, wooden it appeared but with an over imposing high gloss sheen of yacht varnish, with chairs chunky and dare I say ugly, well at least to me, and of comfortable, well I was to be happy if I was never to sit upon them. And on the sideboard that stood boldly adjacent, it appeared to be a trio of swords that of its service it adorned, and "Were they real? Were they sharp?" Questions I chose not to trouble myself with, as I wanted not to discover.

Forming the last-bastion of defence on the exterior wall, 5 French windows, by any other name, cried out to be seen and recognized, but there was to be non of it, as the small pains of glass were not seen, as the 1960's flowered nylon curtains and pelmets from the eye did conceal and not till at the side I stood, through the dirty pains of glass was I able to see the traditional and petite Juliet balconies situated beyond. Peculiar, such a dismal vision, so disappointing, so not Parisian, and that classic and historic building, did it not deserve better? But then by definition, that phase, that period of time, though possibly not on-purpose or by-design, but accident-ly yet regard-less-ly, was perhaps forming, a significant part of its own evolving and entwining history.

The odour oozing from the apartment like the décor, most unappealing, as heavily it hovered in the atmosphere of each room I was shown on that ensuing tour. The stench depicted grubby and the kitchen which was to lay before my eyes, with small white cupboards appearing too high on the wall for comfort or accessibility, with doors of sky blue, and handles that may have been chrome back in the day, but with layers of dirt, quite then, it was difficult to tell, and grimy with pans and crockery, dirty and unwashed laying everywhere, and even the petite Formica table squashed unceremoniously into the corner, was not spared of the disarray it shared.

The Lino old as tattered and torn, and where in the corners it was crinkled and cracked, where the shapes of square in yellow and blue of age and wearing were hard to define, and where all may have been designed or last cleaned in that decade when everything became, swinging. Yet my eyes were to bypass all that perceived debris, as it was through the window I stared, past those white nylon net curtains of swags and the broken pains of glass, where enface, the apartment block of architecture most fine, enlightened my imagination, as it appealed to me so.

A reaction to all of that man, was he that landlord or boyfriend to be or perhaps to be another defining 'something' else, as he launched with ease his defence, his typical MO, method of attack, with the blame game being his tactic, as waving his hands around in the air, he was to declare, "It's the Russian girl, who does all this and I will speak with her to clean it all up." Right there you see I should have been more aware, of his speed of response to abdicate responsibility, was a foundation of a pattern, and not, a one off affair as he spoke of she who was or not to become my new *colocataire*, flatmate.

A master at disguise he turned out to be, as quite masterfully on his tour he steered me away from the shower and toilet cubicle, and of telling me they were to be shared with just one other turned out not to be quite true, but "Why should I care?" For I was to leave and flee, without a second glance, a second glare "Right?" "Arrhah yes;" although… as I unravelled the idiosyncrasy's which were to become the not quite so enamoured of the 'tea-towel-trot,' and the 'shower shuffle,' that was to be a firm and resounding, unfortunate, "No."

For really, "Was there any good thing about that property?" "Arrhah," there was just one, but one of significance, for its proximity to my favourite place, presented with ease, as a swift 15 minute ride on pink line on the *Métro* map, and there I was to be exiting at the bridge of *Pont Neuf*, first bridge, enface the river

Seine, "Oh my! Oh yeah!" Such pleasure, which would always permit my heart, my spirit to rise, then only 5 minutes more, before at my favourite haunt of *Café Laurent*, well I would be standing at its door.

That place of study too proved for easier access, for only 35 minutes it took and only one swift line change before a brisk walk or run on those extra cold days, did see me at that place of learning, a place where I am to confess, it proved increasingly harder to attend each day. Yet "Oh my" so much to gain, as how all would aid for me a far greater Parisian social life, and all for the monthly price of 65euros, for the electronic pass, of the *Navigo*.

"Seek not good from without: seek it within yourselves, or you will never find it."
~ Bertha von Suttner

Develop, blossom and bloom was what I evolved to be able to achieve, at that unforgettable *Café Laurent* as my arrival at any time of day did rendered a piece of peace to come my way, as the Parisian odours, the dirt and grime were outside, and calm and tranquillity abound behind the walls which it was cradled within, and with the many conversations I was to enjoy with the tourists and French who frequented that pristine venue, and all for the price of an amazingly good, hot and creamy *choclate au chaude*, hot chocolate, peace and joy of solitude were mine to wallow in and adore. And there seated on chairs of mahogany, gazing out onto the Parisian *rue*, I pondered peacefully as possible, with anticipated excitement, of my future "Where to next?"

For the progression of those Parisian weeks had sped along so rapidly and 'university as I knew it' and its daily grind were gladly I have to say approaching their nearing end, and increasingly with intensity, "What stretching out before me and laying ahead, and how good was it going to be?" as my options were many, "For didn't I not have a whole country to choose from, and really, "Was I not on my way to that I had absorbed myself in of glossy photographs, and wasn't I on my way to *Aix en Provence*?"

For was I not connecting my 'dots' in the correct order, and sewing the thread of my life's tapestry of subtle and vibrant colours with extreme precision, from my choices, sadly or expertly made, so by definition "Was I not further ahead than where I began on my journey, of the evolution me?" And as I contemplated such, of that uncharted territory which lay ahead of me, was I not prepared, prepared to follow a dream, and of those naysayers, assure them, of the world, like Columbus, "I was not to fall off the edge?"

And with my evenings in number drawing to a close in Paris, it was *Saint Michel* I wandered, buzzing with the usual horde of malingering tourists seizing opportunities to cast an eye upon the street entertainers, and where that particular evening it was a band, not typically traditional but one of an eclectic mixture of other street entertainers who 'banded' together had taken centre spot in front of the *Fountain Saint-Michel enface* the river *Seine*. Interestingly I paused for a while, until I went to my favourite *crêperie*, before onward to a place to be seated on the street to absorb the atmosphere of the bussing streets, of nice to choose to rest for a while but not b forced to stay as a matter of permanency, as I partook in a fine *vin rouge*, red wine, I rested there, until the late evening light began to decline.

Yet so much time I was still to pass by myself, often by choice and design. But it was the passing of time which was to reveal to me, as increasingly healed I became, that of that format of being alone, in isolation which was the place I had carved my name upon so no one could be cruel again to me. And of those Parisian blessings I counted and "Oh so I did," it was a bitter sweet pill of reality, that of all those circumstances gone before me, to get me to that point of time and place in life, really, of all the fear and the insecurities, I so preferred that I had not had to go through them all.

For some were of my own making and some were not, some were because of the residue of unpleasantness which was left behind, as an unwanted waist product of toxicity in my soul or mind, after the aggressor had abandoned me, or those who viciously assaulted me, regardless of financial cost, for my physical and emotional safety, I cast them out.

Yet at that time surprisingly, of my actions taken I knew not of their strength or purpose, how in my survival they proved so valuable, as I grew to rebuke their sin from me, and learnt to forgive them, eventually. For that tapestry of life, no longer were random colours to end up there, but colours of my choice, and stiches arranged as suited and served me best, but not from a place of the negative ego, but a place of wonderful positive love. And along this road to recovery, of a 'job in progress' I remained, yet I had commenced my journey, I was on my way, and "Where ever was to be next?" and of that destination, I was to continue my momentum of moving forward, for when I arrive, I know I will see a sign, and on it will be written my name and under a welcoming message, with letters delicate and pristine, of which I am worthy and deserve, with peace in my heat and a song in *my soul,* I will read, *"I am free."*

"Failure is only postponed success as long as courage 'coaches' ambition.
The habit of persistence is the habit of victory."
~ Herbert Kaufman

Wandering and wondering, "Why did those 'mother type' personalities keep coming against me?" For sure, I wasn't even free when I was working as an OH&SN in Sydney for the chief nurse there, replicated exactly the relationship between her, a male nurse and me, as my mother did between her my brother and I. I mean really, what was that all about? And I hasten to point out, of what I speak is of my mother and not generally of that general and accepted notion of one who is loving, caring, supportive and kind mother, for mine was non of the above, only critical and ultimately, damn right mean, and I pondered, "How was I to escape?"

Yet no time to dwell for I was nearing the shop of my, query to be landlord; yet of personality types, of a certain type of genre, well I had no idea, one was to come against me once again. For was it to be to move I was to move away from she whom had placed her red cloak in the closet until *la prochaine fois*, the next time an unsuspecting female student came to reside with her, "Oh my" such joy it was to be, as I perceived hopefully, my solution lay just a few feet away. Yet unbeknown to me, an arduous task lie in wait, really, "Could I not get a break?"

Through the tourist shop he led me, to a slender staircase of unsteady and crumbling steps, and as we arose to the top, the inner sanctuary of a one roomed space, with two petite windows opening over the bustling street below, I bypassed the boxes strewn over the floor, and the untidy piles of papers and files everywhere which appeared to be dumped unceremoniously, as I was beckoned upon a chair to sit as he cleared the debris from it, and at last I signed a relief, as I was to have by the weekend a new lodging place.

Seating himself with his arms folded he leaned forward onto the desk, and wearing his unusual attire only this time an added addition, on his face he wore a shivering smirk, *il a posé une question*, he asked the question, "Which solution did you choose?" Of what he referred was the 850E sum per month for the unsafe apartment, or the 650E for the room in his odour-full and grimy house. "Oh my own space," my mind cried out to me, and so "The apartment" I replied.

"*Bon!* Good!" Was his response, "You give me the 850E now and move in at the weekend." "What about the *domocilerie*, domiciliary?" I enquired, that very important legal document which was required to open a bank account or purchase a mobile telephone. "No no no" he said shaking his head, "There will be no pieces of paper which I give to you." "Arrhah" I thought, and peddling quickly I asked, well what about a written receipt for the 850E, that's $1150USD, and the exchange of the keys. "Oh no, not so," he said, there will be not a thing put in writing, this is 'on trust,' he said as his smirk became bigger, then moving forward leaning learning further onto his arms, with a spooky glare in his eyes, trying to convince me, "This is on trust, for we're friends aren't we?"

"*Faire attention,*" *be careful, watch out,* is what those bells and sirens quietly at first almost unnoticeable, but then inside my head shouting loudly warning me. For I knew him not to be true from his own mouth he condemned himself, for on any given day of what he owned of properties and shops varied immensely in number, from 3 to 15 to 25. And it's true, as through experience I do believe as a notion of no doubt, that when a person speaks the words, "You can trust me," usually and without reserve it translates to, "At your own risk or peril proceed."

Another question I posed, "Well what about a contract for the apartment?" And perhaps of no surprise it met with the same response, only slightly modified. For after the initial and adamant "No!" He relented saying, "Yes I can give you a contract, but it will be for one year, and you have to give me, a 1000E in cash in advance in addition to a months rent upfront." "OK," I remarked, before I thought, paused then asked, "Just who is that holds the money, an association or perhaps a government body, for the duration of that contract period?" "I do!" "You do?!?!" "Oops! I was suddenly thinking."

Then as he leaned forward on to his desk, his hands clasped resting upon it, his smirk grew sickeningly so, as perhaps he mentally calculated the extra ordinary cash flow he perceived to receive from me, perhaps a pushover he thought me to be, but my inner-logic and strength rang alarm bells inside my head, as I thought in the realms of survival and bite me once, never get to do it twice, I recalled how many-a-man had taken from me financially, and right then and there I was to close that door on him, so of that list, preventing him from joining its queue, which what best for me, I chose to do.

So, I was to stop immediately and consider this, "He has 1000E in cash in his bank account which I have no legal way to recover, he wants to tie me up in a 12 month contract, to which 'his word says because I can trust him,' noting "I will let you out of it after just 3 months with nothing extra to pay." Yet then in a flash, I considered such, of him 'stitching me up' and the likelihood I considered sincerely real, of legal recourse, of student in a foreign land, nay France, of a legal document to sign, in a language I didn't understand, and to go for help in that instance, really, "Where would that be?" Rationally, I thought, "OK," you've pretty much have, 'bucklies' of that, a quaint northern English expression meaning, of that scenario happening, there's absolutely; 'No chance!' 'None at all!'

Then hills and running; rope and old; creeks and paddles; all sprang to my mind, and more, "When did I get demoted from girlfriend to friend, for was that a minor he was casually to dump at my door?" "My-oh-my," that chappie, as he blatantly displayed his wolf-like characteristics, so sure, was he of he, he saw no need to disguise himself in a cloak of red, he may have already taken, from Little Red Riding hood.

"Wow!" In the absence of not a scrap of paper to prove my rights, of he of no disguise, so easily could change the locks while I was out, and stolen all my stuff, and I, "What prove to the contrary was I to have?" Well absolutely none, as I am sure, was by his purposeful design. So I concluded, "Here's the deal, I really don't gamble, I avoid taking risks, I don't go looking for trouble, so "Why would I ever consider, buying some?" For surely, that's what I would have evolved should I have gone along with his plan, his rules in his jurisdiction? For without speaking the language and absent of proof, where would I have gone for help, "Who'd listen to me?" And of my reservations, as I ventured sometime later, to a *ville*, idyllic supposedly, closer to the Mediterranean, *dans le sud de la France*, down the south of France, how right they turned out to be.

> "I have been and still am a seeker, but I have ceased to question stars and books; I have begun to listen to the teaching my blood whispers to me."
> ~ Hermann Hesse, Demain

Yet so keen I was to get out of the 12eme *arr* and my unsettled habitation but, "Oh what to do?" I thought a lifeline I had been granted, yet that tugging on my arm, "Was it to be pulled away from me?" Those legal matters and legal wrangling of constraint with the potential to harm severely, seemed oh so difficult to navigate, as through treacherous wasters they seemed to flow, for I had to ensure, of safety first and to stay afloat, I was to find myself a most suitable, OK, in the midst of that storm, any old lifeboat.

So it evolved, a conversation or two with my *camarades de classe*, of what to do and what not, what was safe and not, what was best for me, for study and safety, financially and emotionally, and a slow and quite unexpected and arduous decision was made, as I chose not as my first choice, but as in Health & Safety as the last resort, I was to wear my 'PPE,' Personal Protective Equipment, or in that adversity, form my own Personal Protective Reduction, as though I had only won the consolation prize, yet I did the best I could out of that bad bunch of choices, so I moved into that place, perhaps overpriced, over-dirty and over-smelly, yet with privacy, or so I thought that would be mine, and certainly in a location I noted, as quite prime, so it was, I was to take a room and move into his dark and dingy place, and he, 'ppp' was to be, my new landlord.

Of his nature forewarned is forearmed, only not quite so, I what was to occur was to throw a mildly severe blow. For of the self-professed boyfriend after choosing to spend *beaucoup*, many a *rendezvous*, drinking a wine, a coffee, or even dancing at the club of salsa, it all faded into instant obscurity, with a notion portrayed from he, my new landlord as it had never happened, the moment he had collected my processions from that last place of abode. And more was to come, as the slippers I saw at the side of the sofa on my moving in day, I presumed to belonged to my new *colocataire*, a teaching university student, Anastasia from Russia, but "Oh no" as it was another's feet they adorned, as she sat with he in a blatant early morning liaison as in the corner of the kitchen to be nestled in the corner of his kitchen, perched on stools with yellow plastic coverings with design depicting vegetables, surrounding a *très petite table*, tiny table of a blue Formica top, typically circa 1960's, and there an intimate view lay before my eyes, for she who was not his mother or sister were sharing a meal from the same platter.

"Oh my" what whiff of treachery and deceit," thank goodness I never bought into his whole "You're my girlfriend" tactic, for then that's what I understood and believed it to be, as I had thought he was trying to help me, but perhaps his personal agenda was his perpetuating priority he was simply helping himself, as I recalled our conversations surrounding money, and of "A single woman all alone in a city, did he believe, "He could mater or cajole me, while making more than a buck or two for himself,?" and on reflection, I'm thinking, "Yes indeedy."

His behaviours, his concepts, his nonsense, that's no-sense, by any other name, I was officially over it and over him, and as in all good Westerns of yesteryear, I instantly regrouped, me, myself and I and relinquished all curiosity.

> *"Instinct is a marvellous thing. It can neither be explained or ignored."*
> ~ Agatha Christie; The Mysterious Affair at Styles

"If common sense is so common, then why do so few people have it?" A concept I find to be of a quaint irony, and of another, in my life, "Why is it that people do not say what they mean and mean what they say?" For a deception was underway, for the room I was shown upon my tour and agreed, confirmed and guaranteed prior to money exchanged and suitcases moved in, unbeknownst to me, it was secretly changed by he, along the way.

The room in expanse of 5 x 5 meters almost a box, painted bland and so long ago, even dust settle upon those walls, and of opposite or prime colours I dislike, but there in contrast, the paint piled on, was the deep royal blue disguising the glory of the wooden natural grain, and plaster trims too, the door the same, except excluding its portions of bobbled glass, with the curtains the matching, though their fabric thread bare, as they reached the amazing 5 meters tall from the floor to the ceiling, until the edge tipped the ceiling, which was nice in a way, as it cast my eye across to the pretty and perhaps original ceiling rose, yet how sad it was as a paper spherical shade was to hang from there.

But what best to covert, was what lay outside the room, of the shower and the WC in such close proximity, of just 3 feet away, and such an advantage when in the middle of the night, you have to get up to pee. But serving precedence over all was the adjacent boiler standing 6 feet tall, performing a function indeed, for while the severe Parisian winter of that year blew a gale outside, and penetrate its true, through the glass of only one millimetre thick or two, it was comforting warmth that was to prevail as it radiated through that inner dividing wall.

Yet on the day of my arrival, the room that he showed me and I'd agreed upon was not the same as previously, and not a smile of conviction but of persuasion to convince me, as he spoke, "Here, I'll put you in this room, it will give you greater privacy." "Great!" was my response until in an instant, reality with more than a little force jutted right in, as he was simply changing goal posts to suit him at my expense and expected me to concede. For of first note the electric did not work in that room, and of the light switch, "Hello!" It was hanging off the wall. "Was he mad?" Or perhaps he thought that's what I was, as he persisted, just how good that room would be for me. Not with a critical eye as quite plain to see, firstly there was not bed, only a bed-settee and curtains somewhat falling off the rails and fitting poorly. Of wardrobe there wasn't any or closet or draws ether, but he told me not to worry, as the floor height cupboards around the room were good enough for me, according to him, yet funnily, I did not agree.

True, the room of grandeur or yesteryear was quite a feast on the eye with guilt strewn everywhere, yet of its colour of yellow of drapes and incredibly padded walls, I could not agree. The room felt cold and damp in extreme, such a shame the white marble *Louis the XVI* fireplace that stood so regal in that place had not been lit for many a year, and of the heat how could it be retained, for the astonishing amount of 6 French windows all standing tall, admittedly sporting petite and pretty Juliet balconies, proved insufficient as a seduction call, as many were shattered glass, and of half were ajar for their wood frames bowed or broken where the cold Parisian night air blew through.

And as I peered past the dirty panes, instantly I realised it was not rest or study that I was to enjoy, for outside lay a feast of that of all to cause noise, at the converging of 3 streets, as to the left lay a late night pizzeria with alfresco dining, and *à côté de*, next to an all night grocery shop, to the right a pelican-crossing and the noises echoed around that triangular room, of passers-by stood chattering awaiting to cross, as the electronic system bleeped furiously, as across to the bank they may have gone, where the neon lights blazed 24/7, and at the traffic lights located to its apex, car horns where were to be heard tooting loudly from those who grew inpatient.

"Oh my" was I really to get up in the middle of the night, to meander through no mans land and navigate past the free standing iron railings in the middle of the room, thought the doors and down a corridor, in the dark for there were no lights, and more, have his TV blaring until all hours outside my bedroom door? "No." In varying effects, frying pan and fire sprang to mind, and what I knew for certain; of that room, I was not to pay a dime.

> *"Success is not measured by income but by influence,*
> *not by power but by personality, not by capital but by character."*
> *~ Stephen W. Gilman*

Circumstances reviewed, options considering, against that new landlord's best efforts, I rebuked the concept of taking that room, insisting on the previously agreed upon one, the one that was smaller, located over the side street, which was near the kitchen and importantly as snow lay all around, was next to the firness and where I didn't need to take a hike to get to the bathroom. But then a series of events unfolded, as his supercilious grin of persuasion slipped from his face, which he was to replace with blubbering crocodile tears which I was supposed to believe, "But this is my daughters room," he implored, as his eyes saddened as though overcome with remorse, well, I wasn't falling for that one.

"Oh my" I was not to worry or hesitate, for history had served me well, as a lesson I had been given and learnt it well, of my ex-fiancé and how he cried so intensely, not of a repentance but of remorse, for the former a person is concerned not to repeat the act which caused harm to another, as the latter concerns only for the harm or inconvenience of penalty to pay that they cause to themselves, and of experience, for I had fallen prey to the harmful deception once, and repeat my miscalculation, I was to ensure, it was not to occur twice.

The English Channel and different continents of birth did not inhibit the similarities between the two, appearing to have attended the same school of drama, for either would have deserved an Oscar nomination for the performance they displayed, but I was stronger, I was wiser that time, and although the risk of giving in may likely have held not such a high consequence of almost loosing my life, forewarned was forearmed, and succumb to such an error of judgement again, "No," I was not to submit myself to that, or any other, trouble or strife.

That man of such insincere intent, was unable to tell me of the last time he saw his daughter or when he would see her again, and of pink ponies, butterflies, fairies or ribbons and bows there were non that may adorn a little girls room, there were non, so of his pursuit of sympathy, of a shield I protected myself with, as I gave none.

I was tired of emotional blackmail tactics, I was tired of him and his negative and manipulative MO and his last line of defence, I had learnt and leant well, and I refused to fall under his perceived and calculated spell. For I had recognised a pattern, which evidently meant, I had grown and was more whole, and empowered with the benefit of hindsight, at that very moment I was to put it to good use as I declared boldly, "The room to rent was agreed upon, that is the room I will take, or I will leave, and I will not look back, or hesitate!"

As he listened to the concise words I spoke, a change occurred in him, as he viewed my persona and body language of compete and adamant commitment to what I spoke, and glancing to my suitcases remaining packed close to where we stood, and perhaps seeing the euro's following behind me, he relented and conceded on the pre-agreed room. Yet it was not relief I felt, but indifference as I considered, within that habitation experience to unfold, "Was that to be the last or the start of the gloom?"

But true to form as it may be fare to say, quaint Parisian, of the closet tucked in the corner, it was full to overflowing with his stuff, and of the beautiful reproduction *Rococo* style *armoire*, wardrobe the same of bedding and more, yet of give me a better opportunity to find sheets that were clean and fresh, there was to be non, and search and discover, not what was good, but only the best of a very bad bunch. Grimy and stained most of it, and I chose only just what would do, until into the washing machine I was to put all of it, so at least a little comfort I may have, on that bed where so many people had rested before that there was a deep crevice in the middle of it, where, a pillow I required to the front and the back of me for support as I slept, but, not so easy in that single and tiny bed.

"Oh my" what a distant memory of those expansive and delightful properties I owned in Bolton northern England and Auckland, of my choice of Victorian in interior design, so restful, even my drapes brought me pleasure look upon. And with more than a tad of a little remorse I had rising up inside of me, for I so missed it all, my bedding of preferred quality and choice of harmonious colours and fabrics, of 250 thread cotton sheets in ducky pink, and throws of silk and others of *faux fur*, with thick fluffy towels fresh from the airing cupboard, following a long, warm and steamy shower, while my choice of tunes hummed in the background, all to feed and caress my soul and senses of the mind and body, before I danced with abandonment around my living room while sipping on a fine red wine, or off to bed, to drift-off to slumber and restful sleep.

"Olalla" such sweet memories, I so longed for again, of the security both practically and in my heart. "Was I ever to have my goodness back, my liberty of yesteryear, in the vastness of space, which was mine to embrace, or was it to be, liberty lost?" Of all those aspects familiarity, of what was in essence, was me, I missed the lot. For emotional pangs welled up inside of me, unable to be pacified, soothed or comforted, for realistically, of those attributes toward myself, I knew not how to demonstrate them, and I was to contemplate of that unpleasant predicament, "Was I ever again to feel comfy or cosy?"

As weren't they imperative, for "Who was I without it?" For didn't I define myself by the job I did, and the house I owned or by who I was personally, on the inside. For "Was it possible to achieve growth by any other name, without stepping outside the comfort zone, into a tad of unpleasantness or unpredictable adversity?" as really without risk, "How was I ever to move from where I was to where I desired and wanted to be?"

For it seemed that I had sacrificed so much to follow my dream, and of a delightful outcome, "Was I ever to gleam one?" For my castles had gone and so had my disposable income, my sanctuary and the comfort that comes with predictability. But "What of mediocrity, did I want to be there?" I thought not, for that is in the middle, where really, void of any stimulating forces, nothing much happens, of pain or pleasure or incentives, to push us, to enable us to grow, so "Did I desire a life that was ordinary and bland, or a life where I was to do my very best, to live, seeking harmony, joy and peace, to the fullest of my completion?"

As at that moment, stead fast is what I needed to remain, and committed to my own decisions, to follow where my dream was to lead me, for it appeared not an upward yet downward slope I was on, but then should I not have contemplated that, "Hard always comes before easy, and what is worth having is worth fighting for?" I had so many more questions than answers, and more it appeared were adding to the list, but was I to give up, for I was on a journey at the minimum to learn about me, so "Was I to turn back, or was I to go onward, toward something to somewhere, at least to follow for longer, and commit me, to try my blessed and best luck?" with soft and humble conviction I say, "Yes, yes and yes!"

> *"Be courteous to all, but intimate with few,*
> *and let those be well tried before you give them your confidence."*
> *~ George Washington*

The residence was not to prove to be perfect, for of 'the best laid plans of mice and men,' as really, "When are they ever guaranteed?" For rest or recovery, they were to be limited in their petite portions, as those healing showers for rejuvenation, and to feed my soul, and discover within, a piece of peace from where to begin each day, disappeared most rapidly, as most unpleasantly instead, became a system I implemented, I say with satire and perhaps a tad of contempt, to name those trials with quaint names, of the T-Towel Trot and Shower Shuffle.

"Oh my" as my eyes awoke, I was to prepare me for the task at hand, for as the title implies it took effort, and as I grabbed my towel to walk across the hall, as to open the first door to the cubicle, sideways I needed to turn to squeeze myself in, into that space not purposeful but makeshift, as previously, so small, it may have been a pantry in a previous life, then the other door was upon me, and a contortionist to some degree I needed manoeuvre myself sideways, precariously past the bi- fold opaque and knobbly glass door, with fungus filled metal trim, that was excessively large for the space only able to be pushed back ever so slightly, and when behind it, only two tiny triangles were created within that space in which confinement to choose to bathe, as neither did the door fit back again.

Of a hook there was non, so in the hand the showerhead needed to be held and swapped from one to the other, but then at the prospect of washing my long wavy hair, quite damaged by my choice of shampoo and under the Australian sunrays, but not to worry for I had decided to have it all cut off, for I knew healthier it would grow again. Yet that of cleaning it not simple but posed a little difficult, as try to tie the nozzles metal tubing around the taps on the wall was the best that I could do, but kneel or relax easily on the shower fall while bent beneath it was quite impossible, as 5 or 6 inches of waste water from the drain, always flooded back and in the base pan did sit.

But what of my feet, for I had to clean them, so of that shower a burden not a benefit, trying to squeeze out in reverse, as not to touch the grimy stained walls, while precariously placing my foot on the slippy white tiles, and having found a nonslip bath mat and placed right there, to reduce the high risk when wet as it as of a slip or a fall, but he who was the landlord, did move it away. The cleaning of the feet, more skill was required for such a feat, if you forgive the pun, as only upon a that tiny frayed and tattered T-towel I had to balance so tentatively, engaging even maximum of muscle power, precariously balancing on one foot while leaning inward to grab the showerhead and soap, to wash one before masterfully swapping to repeating, to wash away 'who knew what' from tat regurgitated pipe debris.

"Tricky?" Certainly so! "Relaxing?" Absolutely not! For by the time that job was complete, consistently I felt tired and dirty like I needed, a really good shower, but alas it wasn't to be so, as not for a while was I to enjoy a really good shower for relaxing and recovery. I'd laugh, but it really wasn't funny. And "Oh my" how low had I sunk and how long was I, could I, put up with all that?"

For it transpired of my constitution, it was to become even further robust, but of the adversity, perhaps I would be making excuses, 'if' I were to say, they negatively impacted the way I learning, or not, *la langue française*.

> *"The worst prison would be a closed heart."*
> *~ John Paul 2nd*

But all was not to be bad, for there was an exception of my *colocataire*, flatmate of ease, and how we got on well, walking and window shopping through the opulent and vibrant *Opera district*, and enjoying a coffee on the roof terraces of those department stores of grandiose spectacular of *Les Galleries Lafayette, et Au Printemps*, holding a historic niche there. And a brisk walk along the river *Seine* when it was so flooded, that the water and the rats, flooded over the right and the left banks. Yet generally, of peace and relaxation "Oh what a joy; errmm, that was to be No!" For there were only multiple system failures which became the name of the game during my time at number 10 *Poissonnière*, as a catalogue of unpleasant events suitable for many a comedy sketch did commence, but in humor at times they surpassed me, as just get through one day at a time, until that time came to leave was for myself what I was to gleam.

For Laundry Liable popped up in the show. And yes prior to moving in, I was asked, "Am I free to use it?" And with joy I received and answer of "Yes of course." "Oh my a good job done," or was that to be, as the dial was missing so of what cycle I was to wash on, clearly it was not known, so I sensibly came up with a plan to ask 'he who would know' where to find the working manual so I'd be to correlate the numbers on the dial masterfully to estimate and deduce, but his angry response, "No, you cannot have it." Disgruntled, continuing, "To me it seems you are dissatisfied, so one more complaint from you and I refuse to let you use it at all and it will be the end, I'll forbid you to use it again. You will have to take your clothes to the *laverie*, laundrette, down the road!"

"Olalla" what a response to receive, I may have used that quaint English colloquialism, "Don't spit your dummy out" was my inner-response, yet to let it out, definitely "No" as that comment may have deemed quite substantial high consequences, of his propensity, to a most irritated or stroppy defence. So a tactic, a stance for preservation and reduction of potential unpleasant situations, so quickly from my gentle opening question of *"S'il vous plait,"* please, equating to, "No worries, thank you anyway," as I did not hesitate to retreat rapidly, as I cared not to replicate, those experiences of those other French student flatmates.

And so it was, to the next step of the game, I was to reach up on top of the washer, standing tall on the drier which I was not permitted to use, and grasp a hold of the grubby and grimy orange handled pliers, and with that I was to grab tight hold that prong of metal protruding from the *machine laver*, to effectively twist the dial, and hey-presto, was it to be a quiet and educational guess or a clever calculation or fair intuition in mind and kind, where my delicates, silks and woollens, were to be dispensed from the washing machine not in a mess or exceedingly well. "Arrh;" *"Voila!"* As in-spite of his endeavours, I *achieved success*.

In my growing catalogue it was the Knuckle Knocker, implemented in quick succession, for of that dirt to be seen, and that dirt that can only be felt, it lingered invisibly everywhere without pretence or preference. For door handles, light switches, cupboards, and "Oh my" the fridge-door too, all held those bacterium, and undiscerning they are not, as those free travelers, by finger tips and hands may be transported, effortlessly everywhere. So wisdom prevailed, as I was not to permit them to take a free ride on me, and used my knuckles which went not near, or even close to my face or mouth, so of their transference they could do me wrong, and of infections, colds, infections, and more, I was for myself, and my health, adamant to remain clear.

But clear of the kitchen well that was not quite possible to do, for hot water to drink well that was a priority for which I must enter, but the work benches were rampant it appeared and the sink not shiny and clear, but stained and dull with an apparent year of grease and grime tipped down it, and of pots and pans and cutlery too, "Oh my" of use them I was certainly not going to do, and of clean them up, no, they who used that space never did, and of the dirty tea towels, well actually I took one and kept it in my room and would take it in with me when I needed to, for a plate, a dish a knife fork and spoon, one of each, sterilized, I kept in my room. And I tried to make light of it all, though quite exasperatingly so I was to declare at, Kitchen Catastrophe at *Poissonnière* was to join my growing repertoire.

"Oh my oh my," cleaning my teeth amidst the years of dirt and grime scratched into the plastic, of that deep old laundry basin, designed for the washing of clothes, disappear by comparison, as the cracked and tearing linoleum inhibited my way, with careful footing not to trip me up, and *faire attention*, as the soft and rotten floorboards beneath them, gave way underfoot in each direction, so joke, more than a miniscule of a Risk Assessments and calculations thereof were required, but seriously, in that apartment of hazards and harm, visibly or not, they appeared to be most everywhere, and was without taking into account the unpredicted and unfolding actions of 'ppp' aka, that *propriétaire*, landlord.

I had sunk to yet another level or so it appeared as I pondered, for really what had happened to all the cleanliness and quality in which I lived the everyday recurrences so responsible and reasonable to which I called normal, "Oh where did they go?" Yet I cast such thoughts aside, though perhaps quite slowly, for in common with the food which resided in that unfavourable space, as I was to consider my expiry date, and "How many sleeps to go, before my exit date and when I could get the heck out of there?"

The *piece de la résistance* was about to unfortunately and mildly formidably commence where the manoeuvrer I so jollily named the Toilet Twister' of pulling on the tarnished knob centred between the two large panes of bubbled glass that almost filled the heavily black lacquered door, void of net curtain or other to preserve privacy, a sideways slither was called upon to squeeze through as the minute gap into a common predicament of arriving in a tiny triangular space, where the door hitting the green toilet pan, and a lean forward over the same was required so it could be shut once again.

Of the use of its odd shape of its purpose before it was given the job of toilet I knew not, but my mind was curious and of the grabby cracking linoleum dating back a decade or 2 that matched that in the kitchen, the facing door not two feet away, I considered, perhaps it was a pantry. But of my logic it was to prove unnecessary, as that mild and gentle term in comparison was to be transferred with that of Toilet Tragic and darn right dangerous, as Heb B the by-product of passively provocateur, aka *propriétaire* procured the harm to adversely affect us.

That landlord taking a vacation to his land of birth, with the toilet flush mechanism, remaining broken, I enquired of a contingency plan, or "When will you be getting it fixed?" Then true to form a grumble and a grown, as he blamed the problem on a 'ladies matter,' caused by my *colocataire*, and not therefore his responsibility, he implemented that adeptly renowned Parisian landlord system toward female student and abstain from fair action. And there dismissively with a *Gallic* shrug, his words spouted, "My house, my choice!" continuing, he barked, "Perhaps 2 weeks, 2 months or 3 or 4!" Before he finalized our conversation, by abruptly turning away.

"Mmmm, not any time soon then," may have been my retort, but to vex that man, long ago was a task I had learnt to put effort-in to avoid. So it was Anastasia who became my 'right hand man,' who I called as a precision trick she had, removing the toilet system lid, and pulling with her hand just a sufficient amount for the toilet to flush perfectly. But not for I, for when of the same knack I tried to perfect, each time, that contaminated toilet water came within a millimetre of overflowing the lip of that toilet pan, it testily tested me.

Unresolved, unsurprisingly the problem escalated with tricky toilet flushing mechanism becoming unmanageable as even Anastasia's masterful technique failing to work, and it was then that faecal matter began to rise up in that toilet pan. Possibly, "Was it "Hepatitis B or other side effects gravely adverse, to grow and multiply, of our bodily systems to infect, that were to effect, Anastasia and I?" But he who we needed to be responsible to put it right was absent, and only a telephone number for texting, so needing a plumber and quickly that landlord was informed of our plight, and his response in return, of a plumber, "You call him, you pay for him."

Our landlord leaving us in the lurch and sewerage as he took off from France for a week or two vacation to his homeland, leaving not a contingency plan, a plumber, an electrician or other, and in his absence, the problem intensified and deteriorated, and that toilet bowl became unusable, filled with festering and stagnant faecal matter. The Russian did send a text asking "What do we do?" but a reply of assistance forthcoming was not to be, and I tried so masterfully not to use that toilet pan, so when out at night, I'd 'go,' just before I'd leave, and in the morning, I'd rise and wait till I was at uni, before I'd pee.

But we appeared not to be alone in that mans absence from accountability, prove bad, for the family who lived below, as a knock on the door one evening was to reveal, through the best English that they could muster infused with the best French available to me, regarding a problem, a request was accepted to visit their property. And of help I knew not of, but of try I certainly would.

"Wow!" was my thought as I walked through their doors, and oh what a joy to see, as their apartment had been sympathetically restored, of ornate guilt and grandeur, with the times of 'A Dangerous Liaison' springing to my mind. It was bright and brilliant, pristine in all its fine detail, crisp and clean, in significant contrast and magnitude, a far cry from that above. And as I feasted my eyes on that vision I felt a physiological excitement manoeuvre through me of enthralling excitement, as my spirit of optimism for what I can do, and so adore of the same, compounding in effect as my immense desire to renovate. How innate that system must be in me, for so pleasing to contemplate, of my next project and how eager of it I was to find and my inspiring and evolving thoughts as they within each cell in my body did escalate.

Leading us through the *couloir*, corridor, to their petite but perfectly normally proportioned and formed toilet cubical, where toilet water had sped through the ceiling as it trickled down and stained their wall, and they wanted an answer as I empathised completely, while a note-to-self, "Be extremely cautions of which apartment to purchase." After an explanation in my best French, and at the risk of being unkind to myself, an oxymoron in terms, I expressed that there were plumbing problems underway upstairs, and at that Anastasia and I could do no more except agree to *envoyée*, send a further text to our landlord, informing him of the situation and requesting assistance, yet as I paraphrase his response, 'shut up and put up,' or it will be a case of giving you the 'old heave ho.'

"Oh my" it was how I felt on my inside, which caused greater amazement than what I viewed, yet the same was not to be said, as Anastasia, my dear *colocataire*, and I, turned the key in the lock, to walk past the large earns at either side of the entrance door, filled with dusty forlorn rushes, while trying not to notice the blackened and decaying net curtain, such a shame over those classic and vast French panes of glass, yet too they had not escaped decay, as the paint pealed and only the first appeared to be holding the broken glass in place. Then, my heart remained not escalated, but once again, sank.

> *"The boisterous sea of liberty is never without a wave."*
> *~ Thomas Jefferson*

"How was your holiday," I would have liked politely to enquire, but superfluous to requirements as he butted in with his accusatory, "What have you done?" "Errmm!" "What had I done?" That would be nothing, nothing wrong at least.

I'd long since got an angle of my landlord's temperate and delicate moods, as on any given day any different mood to be witnessed, all varying shades of grey, depicting storms of wind or torrential rain caught up in his prevailing sail; and all to be avoided. And to do just that while studying in my room, hearing his vibrating footsteps on the staircase, quickly I'd turn off my bedroom light, knowing that I'd pre-prepared by cleaning my teeth and used the bathroom before hand, so no further need to venture out while he was in the house.

The toilet was shown to him, and quite blatantly needing professional intervention, yet he remained steadfast and complaining, how it was a problem for him, which he rejected to be accountable for, and adamant of such he continued in the same, as out of the door he slammed it shut. Returning, he brought a bottle or two of 'this and that,' all of which appeared to be detracting from the problem while refusing to provide a solution.

The bottles he returned with he pored down the pan as he strutted and stropped about, waiving his hands in the air, with a persona of irritated intolerance and for what we had risked and suffered he held, no care, as a plunger he used erratically, and I, I stayed well away from there. And as his efforts proved to no avail he protested and grumbled, and as he was unable to make it better, I stayed out of his way, hiding in my room, getting ready in silence before on that Saturday morning out of the door I was to escape as his bad mood as louder it rumbled.

Politeness struck me like an old curse, as I was to be nice to someone who was not so to me, and as his temper was escalating to full throttle, I enquired of his task being accomplished and "It will do, you try it." And at that, try it I did, but Oh my" not good at all, but only bad, as rapidly the pan did overflow as a rapid spill prevailed, and of that space I could not escape, for unprepared and not positioned well, I unable I was to tuck myself in that tiny triangular shape to squeeze out of the door, as all that fluid of 'who knew what' came tumbling over the toilet rim, all over my winter white Spanish made leather boots, my favourite boots drenched and damaged, and two inches or more lapped over the floor.

So a mop and bucket I did reach for to clear it up, as I heard that man, that so unpleasant landlord, complained to me, "You have done something wrong" "Oh would that be flush the toilet handle as normal people do," I may have said, or "It was upon your countenance I did do so." But of either I did not, for throw fuel on the fire is not a game in which I partake, for dangerous and explosive it can be, so perhaps deliberate by name, as its designed to be. But "Oh my" utilizing a 1980's phrase from an English friend, I was beginning to wonder had he 'gone clear?' But calmly, I bypassed his toxic and caustic mass, which lay inside his head, as I'd accomplished such an achievement, I concluded quite rightly so, that maybe, as I was able to recognize, understand and unemotionally move along, I was progressing extremely well on my recovery route, from A - B.

And of that experience I grew to be appreciative, for 'they' could no longer lay under a cloud of non-discovery, for I showed to me, that I had learnt, to recognize particular 'personalities' that would prove difficult or erratic to harm or curtail me, physically, emotionally or spiritually, by his personality domineering and overbearing, dogmatic invasive to achieve their accomplishments and childish, not in presentation but in required outcomes, perhaps to sum up in one word, 'abusive.'

For how far I had come along my journey and "Oh how I gave praise for that." And of that mini road tip, and yes, it wasn't complete, but a glorious stitch in the bright and exuberant colour of 'accomplishment,' it gave to me for my life's tapestry, and of that I was to ponder, contemplate and wholeheartedly enjoy.

"To reach a port, we must sail - sail, not tie at anchor – sail, not drift."
~ Franklin Roosevelt

From the need for clean hands I never could escape, though in truth, who would really want to? For as a wee girl after sitting and eating coal in the coalbunker eating coal, a sign of malnutrition I have grown to know, into the house I would go, and as was my mothers retort I stood at the kitchen door, covered in dirt, but only my hands of concern, as holding them up high I'd say, "Dirty hands mummy, dirty hands." Yet in Paris I wondered of clean hands was there any concept? For I had noticed so frequently, in public facilities, of café's, restaurants and bars, the urinal was placed just outside the woman's cubicle, and 'he' could be peeing while the woman was exiting, a strange notion for one brought up in Britain with such reserve of privacy, yet of greater importance, of *l'homme*, the man or *la femme*, the woman of wash their hands following their task, void of perceived class or wealth, little to non was mostly done. Perhaps a pattern of French life, or certainly within that apartment I lived.

For as I departed that day, lingering substances awaited to be transferred effortlessly, for as usual it was the fading brass door knob I used to open the 2 large double doors and the U-shaped door knocker on the opposite side to close once again, and no change there. And as I juggled and wiggled as I placed my keys safely in the zipped-up compartment of my shoulder bag, the hat and scarf, exactly where they should be, my folding umbrella to was to accompany me, before lastly for purposes of dexterity, I was to place my leather gloves over those digits to keep them warm away from the dampness of the day.

But something happened along the way, for my mouth, it began to have a terrible feeling and a taste most unappealing, and instantly I recognized that of those bottles emptied down the toilet, so caustic and toxic were those solutions, they displayed a scull and crossbones was printed its side, and all else he, that landlord had touched of consequence of bacterium too, for he had failed to wash his hands before he left his abode of residence. How appalling for such a risk, as all that laid on his hands transferred to those ornamental door handles, before onto my mouth, and should I have failed to be alert, and quickly return to wash it out, and clean those door ornaments too, those germs and more would have freely lingered in dormancy awaiting to complete a cycle of transference.

"Oh my" such adversity I was to contemplate, and really, "How did I end up in that place?" For sure, I had ascended a learning curve with a gift, *gratuit*, free, of wisdom and discernment and a good lesson well learnt. For "Why, how did I end up there?" As I did not recognize or contemplate, with that sickened felling in my stomach were reminiscent, of those created by my unwise choices as I prepared to leave Melbourne in the southern hemisphere, as lacking consideration for direction, of what truly lay ahead of me, and was the same not true of all those items I gave away, creating not a void, yet had not yet transposed into wisdom, as "My oh my," those items, so valuable for my future, I could have used so many of those items that eventually I gave away, and of those items I chose, treasured and adored, I only gave myself huge portions of inconsolable angst, as I beat myself up for my choices, always looking behind, and I had not yet learnt the 2 part lesson, buy everything you need and nothing that you don't, and admire without having to acquire, and more, as a hungry person should not go food shopping for it is likely to be high sugar foods that they will chose to buy, a person without money or in transit as I, should avoid clothes, shoe, accessories, soft furnishing, shopping, or buy anything at all that is less good than something already in your wardrobe that you are not yet using.

"Oh my!" Those debilitating notions of 'loss' at what I'd done were still rattling around in my brain, as to forgive myself and let-go of the torment I was feeling, or the guilt and shame of my unwise decisions, for performing such actions hunting and gathering, where my disposable income, well so sadly, wrongly, certainly most unwisely, with no good investments to show for it, or events I had attended to surge on my spirit, or adventures I had taken to enhance my life's experiences, or ploughed into help someone who *needed* it, I was trying hard, but not quite there, was yet to comply.

As really in my mind, the good disposable income I earned, with no accumulation of 'assets,' aka, those things that will make us money, as purchased as no-thing to show for it, for my hard work of getting up in the early mornings to spend time working with people whom I was most uncomfortable and incompatible, and bills to pay just to get there each day, it seemed all so superfluous for a good job done, as all my purchase of depreciating-assets had only lost me money, all of my disposable income, well, I disposed of that, as I had no-thing of value to show for all that money I earned, squandered and spent and worse, of those items, no-longer did I have them, and emotionally, I was unable to move beyond the huge emotional loss I felt, as with those items gone, really, in the world, to have and to hold, I had nothing else left .

So clearly as I repented at leisure, I recalled what a very rich man once told me, as he gravelled to save even 10 pence (5c), "You don't get rich by spending money." "Oh my" I had never forgotten it, but somehow of its succinct value of its huge lesson, with no-thing to ground me, of what I was doing or where I was going, as it had slipped away from my astute awareness, as I travelled through the torrent torment as I scurried and scrutinized all in life, for just something, anything to comfort me or protect me, and of it all, "Were they merely a substitute for something else I didn't have?" *'LOVE!'* that illusive *'something precious,'* and "Did I dare to *hope*, that one day, *love*, would bear my name also?"

Though of unwelcomed companions of folly "Was too late to be my cry?" "Oh certainly not." For I was actually able, through acceptance of what I did, to metaphorically open up my hands and let-go, yet in reality it was from much deeper place inside where I needed, where I must, let-go from, from my heart and mind and reaching down into my soul. So with those valuable lessons compounded and firmly learnt, in my imagination I saw that which enabled my spirit to soar, a luxurious, quite small box, its cover white and glistening as the iridescent lustre of dragonflies wings, with a deep rose pink velvet lining, all wrapped up in a delicately extravagant bow of shimmering silver and trimmed with soft antique pink, and there init, I place all my lessons I received over time so gratefully, and quite beautifully and magically, as I place the lid back on, those lessons they transfer to become the most astonishingly, amazingly, nurturing, and each one I gently and wonderfully place in there, they transform into jewels of wisdom, and each one I treasure, as it all a *piece*, or *peace*, of *me*.

For the fullness of time, was wasted not, as ultimately I was creating my 'How-To-Map,' and of equal or greater importance, my 'How-Not-To Map.' It appeared that there were no short cuts, not getting around it, I simply and unpleasantly in the absence of a magic wand, I was to go through the eye of the storm and not around it, equally, with a route above, under or around, it was to gorge a way through the mountain that needed to be achieved. And whether a willing participants on our journey or not, life it appears propels forward regardless, and when we fail to master it, debilitating cycles of adverse events may unfold. So *choose*; you become the master, you *dictate* to life, of what you will accept, of what is *good* for you, and *embrace* with dogmatic due diligence, refuse to accept anything less. "And my prize?" *Abundant* and precious peace!

"Remember, if you ever need a helping hand, it's at the end of your arm, as you get older, remember you have another hand: The first is to help yourself, the second is to help others."
~ Audrey Hepburn

Chapter 5

Step On Relentlessly

"Ordinary riches can be stolen, real riches cannot. In your soul are infinitely precious things that cannot be taken from you."
~ Oscar Wilde

As I sat all cosy, my gaze passed above that grand piano in black polished to a high sheen and out through the window located just behind it, landing on the passersby in *rue Dauphine*, where on many an evening, as the mellow sound of the soft jazz sped out, passersby could be spied, spying in, as huddled they were beneath their hats of fur, and rugged up tight in their scarves of colours bright, with temperatures that plummeted, they rushed as quickly as they might, with attention not to slip on the slush that cradled their feet, as day or night I grew to gratefully recognise, how treasured was my spot and the warmth that surrounded and caressed me.

Another day another opportunity to visit that wonderful oasis, which was the *Café Laurent*, the environment of bourgeoisie and luxury, offering a pristine side-effect to gain a piece of peace and quiet tranquillity from the hustle and bustle everywhere from that world at its polished marble doorstep. And a better way I knew not to meet an array of wonderful 'globe-trotting' people predominately hailing from a country far younger by centuries than France, which essentially grew following the landing of the 'Mayflower' ship in that bygone year of 1620, carrying those who cast British democracy aside, with the number of brave Pilgrims amounting to just 102.

And everywhere as I looked around that historic establishment visitors maybe seen sipping on fine champagne, relaxed and as I, soaking up the ambiance, where frequently it was spoken, "You seam to know everyone here, do you come here often?" With an ease of response, and a smile on my face, "Well yes indeed I do" was forever my response. And so it was, the same to be asked by a gentleman one blustery and ordinary Saturday afternoon, but of my experience of him, sadly I am to say nothing was ordinary, and too retarded I was, and doubtful of my own inner convictions to deflect him and permit me to easily from his presence pass far away.

As he spoke, looking down towards me from his lofty height of 6 feet plus tall, debonair in his sense of dress, sporting a long beige trench coat which almost touched the floor, topped by the sophistication of a trilby hat, reminiscent of any a Hollywood 1940's movie in design, certainly a garment to sport for the Parisian winter of that year, and as he removed his hat and rested it on the bar, he revealed his thick dark curls which fell and lapped about his face, of which perhaps, many a man of his age of 60 years or more would be glad to have. And as he removed his overcoat, his choice of apparel immaculate, with a crisply ironed shirt of fine pink and white stripes, sitting neatly below his deep blue tailored woollen jacket, with smart jeans modern in design and highly polished laced up shoes, it appeared an ensemble of refinement.

Our conversation initially congruent, as he presented himself as a well-travelled man, but it grew to on of intrigue, transferring onward to one of perplexing, for those clothes that he chose to wear, as a disguise perhaps as to hind behind, as he deliberately displayed a carefree attitude, yet what was his purpose? To detract possibly from pent-up anger or rage or an emotion of low self-worth lingering below the cloak of disguise to all who viewed him, he did deliberately disperse.

Do not judge the book by its cover, so often said for it is right, as that is merely the outside view for the world to gaze upon and from those of great disseat or possibly illness, of a true representation of their character it may not be. And personalities so often displayed, like the painted façade of a building, looking fine on the outside but crumbing on the inner, while clutching the capacity to conceal the real-deal, of values and behaviours, perhaps inadvertently by limiting beliefs they hold or possibly by design and deliberate intent aim to deceive or manipulate.

"Oh my" how oblivious I was, as I sincerely did not contemplate hard enough, and I should for I had sufficient experience tucked under my belt from yesteryear and more recently, to the deception and danger that lay concealed his demur of that mask he portrayed to the world as I, was about to ascend a most unpleasant and steep learning curve.

Albert, spoke English so well, with colloquialisms understood and void of a striking Parisian accent, difficult it was to detect that he was indeed French born, and the credit he gave for his in high accomplishment was a foreign education from a young age his parents insisted upon. And so interesting to absorb of what he knew of those differences explained so well of what separated our two nations in concept as they spaned the English Channel, yet as the afternoon progressed, it was question marks that I placed invisibly above his head.

For the cracks had began to show, and I have since learnt, that how a person may present to one and to behave to them the same, to another, they may present and behave, completely differently. For it is our past history you see, which draws one to another, and of what we hold inside, of what we will accept or not, which attracts them or sends them, to find and easier target, running clear.

Jingle jangle became the noise I heard ringing in my mind, so as the hour of *ce soir* this evening fell, I enquired of the Café staff who appeared to know him so well, "Is he OK or is he not? As I, have accepted an invitation from Albert to *la Louvre* restaurant, to dine and meet with his friends, but I'm wondering of my acceptance if it was a little bit premature?" They assured me "It is fine, he is fine, you will be safe," but if that was really true, "Why inside of me, was there a little voice, gently dishing out, portions of hesitations?"

> *"Learning is not compulsory and neither is survival."*
> *~ W. Edwards Deming*

So there I was, walking into the night, leaving the safety and sanctuary behind, as I departed to where I was to wish I had not, through those hotel doors. But why did I not reflect longer, and what was my real purpose for wishing to go to *la Louvre,* for sure it wasn't to pass anymore time with he, but was it to do what I thought could benefit me, to network, that system of functionality, who so many enjoy and are good at, but of either aspect, both eluded me. And why should I try for tiresome I found it to be, and superfluous to requirements, as I knew by history, follow up with them I would not, for I preferred to opt for time spent by myself, considering it most enjoyable and good for my health.

But then, in Paris, "Had a new day not dawned in my life?" and "Should I not go that extra mile to achieve more, and make a greater number of acquaintances?" for who knew who I'd meet and if they, "Would be the one to help me in transition along my Parisian and French way?" Possibly I'd gain an introduction of significance. But what I have learnt, and learnt well, when I do something, anything without commitment of true intention and a pure heart, of hidden karma to somehow bite me, it is on its way.

"You're too fussy; you want to lower your standards," my mother had always told me, in the realms of men and other opportunities which she saw as non-existent. Perhaps her hidden covert intent, to express to me, that I wasn't 'good enough' and any old thing or any-body I should be grateful for and would do. "Had I not always cast her opinion aside?" or "Had it infused into me, at a level so invasive it had formed a natural part of me? Well, did I not try to follow her counsel?" as "Was I not lowering my expectations? Was I not trying to go with the flow?" or "Was I to learn a lesson, that was first presented, so long ago?"

"And of her other advice, was that too to serve me badly?" You see a newly qualified nurse in the early 1980's, it was a man who was chasing me, for a date the was, but I held little interest in he, so upon his requests repeatedly said "No." But board I became with life, so in the absence of nothing better to do, I said "Yes," and of that mistake, for a while, backwards, I was to regress.

In those distant days of "Half a larger please and a packet of crisps please," my usual order and that night no exception, which was unpleasant all through, and how I longed for my bed, but he, that uninteresting man, wanted to come up for coffee, and being of a well taught 'people-please' and doing the bidding of their requests and not mine, reluctantly, as natural and innate within my psyche as the sunrays arising the next day, I gave in. But precautions I did take, to not join him on the sofa, as on the single chair I did sit, upon that oyster coloured fabric settee suite which I had purchased at auction at the base of the valley just across from that previously named, 'hospital on the hill.'

And safe I presumed myself to be, but of such, he, had other ideas than me. For suddenly, without warning, and "Why?" still to this day I do not know, standing, he took a few steps forward toward me, and of his right hand, of my face he did hit, and so hard, it smart and stung as my head with the force it faced the other way.

Suddenly, appearing to be frozen in that space and time, I knew not what to do, for shocked and unarmed, for I saw not warning signs so was so ill prepared to predict his next move, and history, it had taught me, as in that early childhood I so wished had only been imaginary in nightmares, for I remembered well, of when the violence began, I held no notion or control, of when it would cease again.

As malfunctioning pathways were developed in my young brain, yet I held not the concept to consider way back then, of their intent to cause severe harm from their destructive doctrine, would they had been pleased of their continuing side-effect it held as violence through life was to follow me, would they have considered such, or concerned them with such a fact as that, or likely, they may have considered in their dismissive naivety, 'yeah, over her, we did master and win.'

Seeds of evil and neglect distorting that developing child's brain of innocence and purity and a disjointed 'dot-to-dot' dysfunctional picture formalized, void of any training tools to wipe the errors out, eradicate and recrate, with no instructions given of significance or help, wrapped up in even a sprinkling of love, for me to navigate through life. Yet of it all, she who was me, was I eventually to rise through it, and in-spite of them, not because of them, be in victory, all-in-all?

"The secret of getting ahead is getting started"
~ Mark Twain

Hovering over me, with his hands loosely by his side as if posed ready to strike, "You're not so in control now are you?" Came his confusing words, as his face contorted and scornful. Perplexed, I did not speak as my mind was rapidly searching within all its crevices to find a 'how to' to surmise why and formulate a plan to get him out of my home while I remained safe. I knew to of the route, but I tried desperately to tiptoe around his personality, so of it a minefield I did not step upon, for I held no concept of what, or the severity of what next he was likely to do. And safely I exhaled, with such a sigh of relief as I heard the click of the safety switch, as on the other side of the dor was he, and I was free to breath once again.

Panic, then set in, and distraught and shaking I could not comprehend what had just gone on, "Was that not an unprovoked attack, or had I done something wrong to deserve it?" were thoughts crowding my head as I phoned my flatmates mum at the early hour of half past two, what peace she did try to cradle upon me with sympathetic and encouraging words, as I telephoned her in such distress, and of my own mother, I would not have dared do, I heard her comforting words of, "Just get in a taxi and come over."

"Oh my" a person in my life not to shout at me, to care of my distress, and that was my fortune of Mather of whom I had met whilst nurse training at that general hospital in north Manchester, a former 'Workhouse,' and she, she amazingly shared her family with me, and was the very first person, who appeared to want to help me, through my defaulting and malfunctioning life predicaments, administering time and effort, in her goal to achieve such a feat, but so sadly, so emotionally injured and destroyed on the inside, I was neither capable of accepting or receiving, for I knew not how to venture out from that protective place which behind my fortress I did hide.

As we continued to talk and he continued to calm me, more questions flooded my mind as if an erupting volcano spilled over; "What had I done to vex him? Had I deserved his actions? Who would do it next time?" and "When would that next time be? Would there be warning signs? Would I be able to predict it, and escape it?" Pervasive, that boiling laver as a ravage of thoughts trapped, crashing mutating in my mind, "Did he know my father? Did my father send him? How did my father know where I was? Will my father send other men the same way? How will I recognize them? Who do I know, who my father knows? Who else will my father send to hit me, to punish me?" and "How serve was it going to be?" My mind chaotic, trying desperately to work it out, for on the inside, imploding, I was screaming, "Was he paying those men to search me out, and be cruel to me? What wrong thing had I done? Who else was there going to be; and when?" and really, "What was he telling them to do to me?"

For when I knew not the answer to these questions, "Would I be free from 'he'?" As then, my history for examination and validation, held crystal clear clarity, evidential proof, that my fathers apparent hate of me held not boundaries, so sure, he could do that, I was so *wounded* and *scared*, *timid* and *vulnerable* extreme in emotions, that jumped within me everywhere. So strongly I'd believed that such violence and fear I had left behind, but *I was wrong, suddenly*, I couldn't even trust myself, "So how could I protect myself? How could I hide from them? How could I prevent them from doing whatever they wanted, to hurt me, to harm me?" and "Was 'he' *always* to send them?" or maybe, one day, incredibly, "Might they stop?"

The theme was relentless running through my core with the trail pain of punishment oozing from my every pore, for out of physical proximity away from he I had become, but absent of his emotional residue torment, so drastically, I was unable to succumb, for that fear was real and tangible as if he was stood right there with me in that room, and my feet formed as concrete blocks, frozen unable to move, and the pain in my heart too deep to bare as I could all but feel it being torn into tiny pieces, as I failed to wonder for how damaged I was, would I ever be free, and of those septic portions forever present reinfecting me, of it all one day, "Would it only serve as my past history?"

"You gain strength, courage and confidence by every experience at which you stop to look fear in the face...you must do the thing that you think you cannot do."
~ Eleanor Roosevelt

"Shocked?" Yes. "Confused?" Certainly! "Desperate?" Absolutely so! as *needed* to understand, but at that time, I understood, nothing. For were all men always to be cruel to me or was it a set of limiting or fixed beliefs that I had created, for what was done so incessantly and so wrongly to me, and void of any other, notion or concept, unchallenged, simply, they cemented themselves in that domain where only fear resided with twisted ideas of what was true and in my mind and grew. Scared, for normality held no place, as I lived a perpetual cycle of constant distress, terrified, unable to sidestep the blows, blow to the body, blows to the mind, blows to the spirit, in that place where hope was banished long ago and all that was left from me to perceive, so young, not yet wise, was thankfully, a *will* to SURVIVE!

"But of that process of contemplation, was it not positive?" For never before that day had I ever held a thought, that there was another way, so maybe, progress was being made, and one day, just maybe, a little hope may reside, previously where there was non, and I may be able to stand tall. For dared, I hoped, to dream of a life free from physical harm, "Had I grown sufficiently to venture upon a new path, to true growth and recovery?"

Yet "Why did my mind consistently play those damaging and distasteful tapes, on a never-ending loop like a merry-go-round, in rapid movement pausing not at all, affording me an opportunity, to get the heck-off, as his curses of hostile words sped around, "You're never good enough for anything and you never will be!" "Be a nurse, you?" belittling, "You're too thick for that." snarling "You will never amount to anything!" "Success?" "You?" *"Don't make me laugh!"*

But more was to come, for even my release of hate he was to take from me, as he scornfully appearing with pleasure did cast his spell that I remember so well, and "Did he practice it, or did it ooze from him so naturally?" His poisoned words cast: "You think you hate me, and I know you want to, but remember this, there is only a hair's width between love and hate, for they are opposite sides of the very same coin." And with a scorn of superior satisfaction, designed to goad, cripple and hurt, "So really, that means you love me!"

Deliberately, he left me nothing! His wheedling wrath, endless, he knew exactly what he was doing, and he did it with sincere intent as he stole my last-bastion gone, he took it all, stripped naked, my last defence, gone, he was purposefully managing that situation of what he did, in his evilness, he took everything from me. And so it was, deeper and deeper those emotions slipped inside of me, caustic, corrosive was the environment within my tissue cells, with my soul, another casualty, nowhere to survive, and I having no use for it, not reluctantly, but unawares, it departed from me, as daily I lived in mild terror, unable to breath, yet still, the years rolled on, and as an adult, of his actions, and so sorrowfully, I believe he knew exactly the pain he was causing and so much worse, it was pleasure, he derived from doing so.

I understood of my father's cruelty, but of my mothers, I had not succumbed to know, the relevance of how she treated me so, or the words she spoke to me, "You're just like your father!" Her curse; "Don't think you can get away with hating him, for blood is thicker than water, and his blood runs through your veins!" Really, "What had I ever done to be so bad, that having blonde hair and blue eyes as that child was to render her to caste hate, in abundance upon me?" And truly to this day, and she, possibly dead and gone, still, of her reasoning, I have absolutely no idea. "Meek?" She was not, as her words fixed and mean, throughout everyday, whipped and lashed out at me, yet it never occurred to me "Why should she say such things, to be so mean when she knew it did wound me so?" True, I was to be a slow learner, to recognize 2 decades for more later, that her purpose, to deliberately, maim and destroy.

But really, "Was I as bad as they both did say?" Surely that could not be, and to be like him as accused so often, was a crime I could almost not bare, and so without escape upon myself I turned their hate and internalised it within me, confused, believing wrong was right, and wrong was right, for those teachers called parents, had always told and shown me that. And so, oblivious to what was real in the world, of what was good or bad, void of any twinkle from a beacon of light to guide me through the oncoming storms, I set out on my voyage, to navigate to a place, anywhere, where I was to be surrounded by less destruction and hate.

Yet, wasn't I already growing to 'one step' ahead of their game, for didn't I recognize their cruelty, of the burden so huge they gave me to bare, I knew with intent, to another should I pass it along would only cause me despair, but of "How?" It was to be huge proportions of exploration and navigation, over mountains high and valleys deep, through tuff uncharted territory, before I was to arrive at that place where as yet, I knew not, that I wanted or deserved to be.

Fervently, I propelled myself forward only achieving the basics of the 'Maslow's Higher Archie of Needs.' For I had survived, "Phew!" For that was of no easy feat, and swiftly I continued securing the next step of security, achieving that which I was always told I was incapable of, that of a nursing career, and following on, came my house, aka my castle by any other name and financial security. But alas, that was where my 'needs' no longer progressed. For that in which I held little to no emotional stake, and indeed knew not how to nurture or belong, those illusive relationships of love and friendships completely eluded me.

Yet at that time remaining in a land of self-distain and self-flagellation, having not yet commenced my journey into self-discovery and empowerment, I had previously done the best that I was able with the information open to me, as I had charted my precise course, my true intent to banish those imposed limitations. But a shock lay in store for me, as I was to realise so sadly, that distance of time and space separated them and me, of trials ad tribulations to pass through, not quite so quick or easy as I had hoped was my recovery to be. Yet, perhaps perfectly in their purpose to grow me, particularly on the inside, minor battles to be fought, won and lost, before one unobtrusive and favourable day, blossoming through adversity, in the realms of love and peace, I was to not suffer perpetual defeats, but ultimately, in victory, I was to win my war!

"You have to fight the battle more than once to win it."
~ Margaret Thatcher

So it was on that blustery Parisian night, listening to the counsel of *pas problem*, no problem, I walked but with an increased portion of trepidation, from the safety which lay behind those doors with that Frenchman with his trench- coat sweeping the floor, and onto *rue Dauphine*. Though already, unravelling discrepancies in his web continued as only a few feet through the ice we did tread, before a *coiffeurs*, hair dressers window in a bizarre fashion how he relaunched the product on view there, and although I do believe that all people are capable of all things, I knew of that product, and knew he spoke was unlikely true. The sirens now screaming in my head, for really it was not so much of what he spoke, but more of his 'nature' surrounding that he did, but unawares he had caught me in his web, and not wanting to appear to him rude, with our *rendezvous* I continued.

Greater credence I should have afforded my reservations, and upon my feet placed wings of fight, for increasing in his bizarre concepts, with UFO's and ultra beings in his confused cognition arose, and safety or there lack of I was suddenly aware, as in a dark street lit only by the moonlight and cars parked everywhere, and of the ancient Church with a wall around it, all posing a hazard should his concept of the mind, transfer to action of the real kind. Panicking not, but walking on the other side of the street and placing those parked cars between he and me, I focused my eyes on where the bright lights shone and hurriedly rushed to the bright lights of *rue de Rivoli*.

"Phew!" Relieved I was in a safe on a safe place filled with traffic yet "Why did I not make hast my escape?" For I rationalised "I'll be safe, for *la Louvre* is only just around the corner. Yet what a folly it is when of our instinct no matter how small we ignore, for trouble of the disastrous kind can come a knocking or even breaking in our personal, not mythical door.

So along the boulevard as the *voitures*, cars, passed with headlights blaring bright, in greater comfort and safe, I perceived myself to be, as they surrounded us on that blustery night, and as the rain did fall and suddenly we were getting extremely wet, I enquired where was his umbrella, and there it was, blowing in the path of those oncoming vehicles, so quickly I fetched it to prevent potential harm, still ignoring the same for me, or how, right then, I should flee!

I enquired as to "Why he had done such a thing?" he told me because "The hotel has entrusted me with this green and gilt umbrella, so I can." A poor rational certainly, but of an explanation it did not suffice, as quite unnerved and wanting from his company to leave I was keen, then quite suddenly the openness of that path diminished, and the few people that walked upon it vanished, as my unwanted companions behaviour became even more erratic, and as I wondered "Should I leave to escape his mildly increasingly threatening behaviour, would I be safe, or would he follow me, or disturbed, lay in wait somewhere and 'get me'?" Then at the back of my mind, I, repeatedly remembering, those people at my beloved hotel, vouched for this man, so really, "Is 'all this' me, and not he?"

"But what of my gut-instinct?" *Again* "Why was I ignoring that?" Then logically concluding not to vex him, and it was all my imagination, and importantly, the restaurant was quite-ish close by, "Now that will be a safe place," so I continued down the wide open boulevard convincing myself with all my might, that "*Surely*, I must be safe." But then with his voice in the distance disappearing in the gales of wind, it was down on one knee his did go, with his arms outstretched, demanding that I accept his marriage proposal of "Marry me!" "Oh my" how romantic those women may have thought as they passed by from their advantaged positions inside their warmly heated cars. "Spooky," it was for me, not natural at all, for of his words once again, depicting some creation of an extra-planetary craft.

"Almost there," I reassured myself, as the restaurant was in my sights, its lights displaying the magnificence of its architecture, that which was to be my sanctuary. Yet as we approached the door, that forever increasing bizarre man was to stop me, and as he hovered over me more that a foot taller, he stood, bowed his head and commanded, "Remove my Trilby!" Then I, quickly taking 2 steps backwards regained my personal space, and hesitated not in replying "No!" Yet undeterred, his demand came twice more, and the of his oddness I understood not and cared for it even less, but at that moment what I knew, was that I could almost feel the warming heat from inside that building, and where behind the protection of those inviting doors, I perceived myself to be safe there.

> *"The doors of wisdom are never shut."*
> ~ *Benjamin Franklin*

Yet, a 'job in progress' it appeared I remained, for I found myself to be a recognizer of 'bad, strange, or potentially threatening behaviour,' though true, the ladder of success of identifying such I had definitely ascended, but a student and not a scholar I remained, as I knew not, sufficiently in advance to remove myself from hovering, potentially troublesome situations, and quickly move into a place of safety away from strife; and although in such matters I was not yet a

T-shirt bearing fully flying fledgling, certainly my wisdom was expanding, and for my wings of life, strength, admirably I was gaining.

Certainly, an observer of people, is what I've grown to be, of behaviours, situations and interactions too, and most pleasing I am for such, and indeed the words we speak are only responsible for 7% of communication, and as such I gleamed from insight, and of the 'polite reserve,' portrayed by the young female *maître d'hôtel,* head waiter, who greeted he, with more than a morsel or caution I thought, and although I stood some distance away from daringly stark odd companion, still, the red flags had obviously not wafted strongly enough in the wind, for still, I failed to flee.

For her facial expression her demeanour, her body language, slightly but surely demonstrating, something, that was not 'quite right,' it appeared to be a heightened her persona depicted a healthy caution, relaxed she was not as in front of her he stood, as if an animal in the jungle astute for predators, slightly but noticeably 'wary' she appeared, unusual I perceived and not conducive with what would have been expected from a greeting of a guest at such a prestigious establishment. "Oh my" of her reluctant presentation, 'time' lingering just around the corner, was to gleam to me the reasons for her concerns, those that she did not speak, but easy to read, and never would I have suspected, against me they were all to become true.

Escorted, into such an overtly impressive room, depicting and over indulgence of opulence and wealth from yesteryear, with grandeur and opulence, flowing drapes with their folds of curves, from the ceiling to the floor, perhaps the height of a house, demure they were not as they cradled the suitably intrusive windows, the shades of guilt in extreme on the cornice of depth and character, the mirrors of massive and impressive proportions, the marble fireplace simply ostentatious, with original and obviously obligatory antique details, preserved in pristine condition, and from its overly *grande* proportions it exuded elegance and charm.

Yet even all that, with my interior-design eye, in an ambiance that normally I'd relish, rest and soak within that environment most fine, yet that night it proved most insufficient as too wary was I to 'let my guard down' I posed the question as we were shown to our seat, "Where are your other guests that you told me you'd like to introduce me to?" His flippant reply, "There aren't any," continuing, "I ordered a table for 4, because I didn't want to be seen, to be on my own."

Then before I had time to digest the implications of exactly what all that meant, he bid me to stand, as he began leading me around the room, explaining the history of the marble, paintings and more, as though proudly providing a non-discreet tour of his personal palace and not a place frequented by the public, intrusively, disregarding those patrons who seated around ate with elegance partaking of the finest of cuisine and likely the same in champagne.

Then to another room on that tour, and to another level of 'gobble-de- gook' of what he spoke, with topics transferring from the sublime to the ridiculous with topics that I understood not of what he spoke and emotive too, so "Why oh why, at that juncture, did I not listen to that 'quandary' in my gut and run away?" Perhaps I seduced or was a foolish as I took onboard a notion to see the opulence of a balcony up on the top level, accessed by a stairwell just a couple of feet wide the same distance from where we stood, then expressing wistfully how the views to be seen stretched across to *la Louvre Museum*, lit beautifully by the accent lighting and the moon, insisting, beckoning me, not to miss such an opportunity.

True, I had grave concerns and increasing decibels of caution and 'jingle jangle' sirens they transferred to, so "Why oh why, did I override them?" Because my natural-self reasoned, "What could possibly be wrong?" So falsely persuaded, I permitted logic to perceive me as safe, for he explained there was a bar up there, and "That meant people, right?" "Oh no" that was to prove a total *faux pas*. And to me, my instinct for of protection, as yours is to you, I ignored it, that 'inner-me,' that faint quiet voice, that nudging-notion whispering, "Do it at your peril!"

But a mistruth of what he told, for arising to the top of the narrow wooden clad stairwell, fenced in by two tall brick walls, as it was only into a small space of only 7 X 4 metres wide, we arrived, where patrons there were non, but only one upholstered settee to the left to seat just two, and to the right, the bathrooms for *l'homme et la femme* too, but of a bar, a balcony or a view, absent or invisible.

"Oh my" instantly I appeared trapped for Albert his mood and character, for contemplation, suddenly transposed, and my instinct shouting, foretelling of danger, so I turned quickly to bid a hasty retreat. But fraught was my escape, as quickly as a flash, he made a dash, as my safe egress he did barricade, and in that slim width of my only exit leaving that room, leading to people and safety, and of his large structure belittle that space he stood firmly in my way.

My temperature surged, as sweat on my palms I felt, as rubbed them intensely I did, perhaps wishing that it was a Genie in a lamp to come and rescue me, as I be-quested of him frightened and almost weeping, my posture weakening, "Please let me go." But he ignored my recurrent plight and barred the same of my exit attempts, and spoke more of what I could not comprehend, except for that twice spoken "You have to help me!" No I could not, he had made me a prisoner and I was quite terrified, for I knew not what his 'trigger' had been to set him off on such a rampage and I knew not would 'trigger' it to become worse, so to the only recourse of action and position of safety I tried as not to vex him without weakness, angst or malice and in a neutral tone, and as he demanded again, "You have to help me!" But weak, all I could muster in reply, "I don't believe I can help, I believe you need to go to hospital for proper help."

Then, he squat on the floor, I saw my opportunity and seized it as I raced to pass him at "Yes, my exit" but my plan tumbled as he rising in a flash as I retreated at warp-speed, walking backward as he walked forward toward me once again, his arms outstretched his voice pleading yet dominant as he directed me, "Sit on the sofa with me, we must talk." In fear I pleaded with tears cascading across my cheekbones, "No. No. I want to leave, let me go!"

He cared not for what I spoke and in response, insisting more fervently, that sit beside him on the settee, but refuting each of his attempts to coerce me in that manner, for of such close proximity, his possibilities to perform harm increased dramatically, for greater may his entrapment have been only serving me greater portions of helpless, and my exit, then proved totally unavailing, so sidestepped I did around that room so tentatively to prohibit his proposed action and further my exit to ever inhibit.

My unwelcomed companion commenced walking rapidly toward me, and I instantly, took several steps backwards into that room void of any other exit opportunity, and of he, to touch me, I was afraid, for I knew not, would it be physical violence or sexually that he was to be the format of his damage.

"Oh why, did I not use a tone of voice of greater authority?" or "Shout?" or "Why did I not put into practice my training from the days working in the mental health field of nursing, for did I not know them?" But my mind, my brain, free from logic to call upon, inert, appearing free from functioning, with no rational flow, not working at all, my body limp I was giving in, but "Were my actions caused by a the severity of a memory, being triggered within me from so long ago, and in that moment the innate trauma of it all, after all those years, like laver from an erupting volcano, was flooding out from my inner-core?"

"Hope!" I heard footsteps; a lady ascending the stairwell, a lady to use the bathroom and my captor stepped aside to allow her access. Walking from the cubical and standing before the mirror, looking at her, unable to verbalise, hoping so that the 93% of non-verbal communication would be sufficient, as with eyes filled with desperation, screaming silently, pleading with her, "Please, please help me!" I wondered, I hoped, "Would she understand English and of what I spoke, would she know that I was pleading with that assailant before me, that destabilised man, that potential loaded cannon, or was it beyond the realms of possibility?"

As I stood in the centre of that cold and barren space, peering at her, though speaking nothing, except with my eyes, I was to seize my opportunity, I followed her so closely, as I walked calmly and calculatedly heading toward the staircase exit, but after letting her pass, his outstretched arm quickly jutted, and the tallness of his frame and the width of his body, I was unable to pass as his specific intention, once again, posed as a formidable barrier for me to cross.

Trapped, again I retreated, but the lady did not, speaking in French what I did not comprehend, she addressed he, by the title "*Monsieur,*" and I recognised she was petitioning for an answer, and for him to let me pass, but Albert responded not to her. And as I heard her footsteps disappear into silence, so too my hope disappeared with them, as alone I stood, feeling so cold, emotions like a whirlpool within spinning frantically, I began to sob like a child and uncontrollably trembling, as for the unravelling outcome, I became immensely afraid for what he could possibly do next.

Weeping, my face fell in my hands, then, seeming almost in an instant that the lady had sent the men of that fine restaurant to rescue me, for in rhythm with my pounding heart came the pounding of footsteps up the wooden staircase, and as I raised my head, there rising up into the room I did see, a shining silver grey suit, of a most fine fit, a *maître d'hotel*, with fine dark well-kept hair, and fixing his eyes, they looked directly at me, and as our eyes locked, I knew I was safe and for the first time in my life, I felt, an all encompassing, and immediate ease of relief.

But my rescuers were not complete as racing behind came another bowling-in his suit just as fine in a darker shade of and the two of them, in rapid succession were joined by a third and in a spontaneous moved across toward my captor, heading him off to the corner of the room, with an unwavering fortified gusto and although non equalled his size, there was no deterrent or hesitation in their actions, their persona active and clear, as they made a barrier between he and me, so I could be led away to safety.

"Oh the relief!" Hyperventilating with hands shaking, my cry louder in decibels as the tension overflowed out, and as I glanced up momentarily I saw the young female *maître d'hotel*, whose body language I observed when first arriving, with her long blonde hair framing her face cradling an expression of nurture and comfort, she walked in a deliberate direction, her persona of care and proficiency with her intent, to comfort and care for me.

Gently, firmly placing a hand over my shoulder and another on my arm, she led me out of that environment to safety, as her gentle tones and affirmations reassured me, the words of which she spoke I understood not, but what I did know, not once before had I remember being cared for in such a manner, feeling absolutely so secure, not by my husband, certainly not by my mother, not even when I told her of the vicious rape I suffered, not when returning from my honeymoon I was told of my Grandmother's sudden death. And never before when I have been sad or upset, or certainly when of treatments or behaviours or worse I received at the hands of others, of aid, help or reassurance there was non, not as a child, nor a teenager, and as a young woman, certainly not, as never before had received such selfless giving, of such kindness and gentleness, what an astounding revelation, the security of the emotion that it gave, that I received, never, never before in my whole life had I experienced it, but "Oh my" *FIRMLY I KNEW*, that my *HEART DESIRED*, as my *SOUL CRIED OUT*, that 'if' I ever needed it again, it would be there and waiting and given to me! "Please!"

"For me?" Almost so incomprehensible that she would do that for me, and suddenly I had a window to look through to experience what others who are fortunate and perhaps it is their norm to be so been blessed that they travel though life with such security as that whenever they need to call upon it. And my heart, my mind, they were truly mesmerised, as I had only been able to live my life with turbulent torrents of sorrow only interjected with unhealthy portions of malicious of solitary storms. Yet in that moment of that disaster of sorts, at that restaurant of opulence in Paris, I received a glimpse into a world that belonged to people, other people than me, a world where it may not be normal to be afraid and to receive comfort, reassurance and even rescuing from harm when necessary and hold a sublime trust that through adversity, that receiving caring, and security, emotionally and physically, will always be so.

"Wow!" Of that glimpse into 'their' world, those who had 'love' that I just had, as just in that moment, to experience those treasures so regal, of compassion, it had awakened a gentle resonance, normally reserved for others, was for my grandest fortune, even for those moments within me, interestingly never before had I been able to fathom or contemplate, it's enormous beauty or majesty, so gentle, so perfect, it resinated within my very soul, I wanted to cling to it and never let it go, I wanted to claim it as my own, with the deepest desire to intimately know it, to have it, to bequeath it as a gift to me, forever more, for it was mine to keep, as wholeheartedly I'd know, that never ever, was I to let it go!

"Let your hopes, not your hurts, shape your future."
~ Dr Robert H Schuller

Calming myself, composing my posture in preparation for walking through that space where *la Louvre's* customers were enjoying the fine cuisine served on the finest of china with utensils of highly polished silver, laid upon a white, stark crisp tablecloth of linen, all while seated on plushly cushioned seats, most refined, and all while I tried to be discreet, nay invisible as I was led from the stairwell across that large opulent room, light and bright of lofty ceilings with cornices of opulence around the light fittings, where at the other side, seamlessly concealed within the wall, a door, and behind it, as different as night is to day, a treasure befell my sight, as that petite space where I stood was clad from floor to ceiling in magnificently polished, not lacquered, stunning dark wood panelling of mahogany or walnut, absorbing all the light and a little unsure I was to consider, "Was that the reason for the particular aroma that I could not exactly decipher?"

Such a sad situation as to why I found myself there, but at the vision before me I could not help but stare, at the almost overpowering and beautiful structure to the staircase, too beautiful to be hidden in that inner-sanctum out of sight, in that building from yesteryear served the Parisian aristocracy, my eyes could not help but pause for a while, at that piece of architecture in its own right, that rambling structure with one step unsupported on top of the other, curving around and rising up before it was to apparently disappearing through that low ceiling, and as my eyes paused on the way back down, I observed and admired the skills of the artisans who built it in centuries past, obvious was the craftsmanship they possessed, as the joints seamless, perfectly portioned those steps as one nestled on top of the other as with precision balance, as I the air it appeared to be floating, with its edges gliding, effortlessly blending into the adjacent wall.

Then looking across that private office room, a quite huge desk, almost in proportionate to the rest of that quite small space, where sitting were papers piled high with a traditional office light located to the right, and peering over to the other side, discreet at floor level, a petite window, seeming only a couple of feet wide, and at first imagination, I would not have thought out of it, there would be much to see. But "Oh my" the effort of stooping to look through it was so worth it, as stretching afar, a most beautiful, though untypical, yet awe inspiring, picturesque Parisian view.

Then worthy of note; that memory of description, over and above everything of bad that happened on that evening, still holds the power to make me smile and my heart flutter and to be grateful that through the bad, I was blessed with such a privilege, to see such a secret treasure of a hidden place, and for me, from here on in, of my cloud that formed, I choose this memory, as my cloud's silver lining.

The height low, in that room I bowed beneath the low beams to reach the tiny stool, which I was bid to sit upon, and with a cup of warm to tea in sip, it was in the privacy of that space, all alone, that I broke down, not sobbing but crying, without restraint, almost uncontrollably. Yet "Where were those emotions coming from?" Perplexed, I was not sure, "Was I crying for what had just occurred or, indeed crying for what happened so very long ago?" That rape, where I was held captive for some five and a half hours, there was no help, no escape, and very my life, it held in the balance, for of those circumstances, I held no assurance, that by the end it all, "Would I survive, to be 'alive'?" But of that question, it was to difficult to answer, as through his intent and purpose, it appeared, to be, a severely dwindling, guaranteed.

Yet perhaps then, since its occurrence some 25 years earlier, quite absurdly never, not once had I ever cried of what I went through or what I'd lost, nor ever released any ounce of pent up anguish, anger or rage of that debilitating, freezing fear, "No! I hadn't done that once," it all stayed inside me, from on that night when I nearly had the breath of my life, clutched, stolen from the very inside of me. Then sometime later I was to wonder, what occurred in that finest of Parisian restaurants, "Was that the catalyst that proved a step too much to trigger the out-pour of so much from deep in me?"

Unbeknownst to me, the Parisian police had been contacted, and also ducking their heads below the beam, while still adorned, all rugged up in their winter woolly uniforms, with notebook in hand they began to ask me what had unfolded with that man Albert. Still shaken, cognition a little uncertain, perhaps making little sense or not quite comprehensible, taking too long in the officers mind for me to relay events of the evening, as he was quite quick to reefer back to his repeated, pointed question, mildly running out of patience maybe, "Yes; but did that man *touch* you or not?" My answer, definitively, "No."

The officers, appearing completely disinterested, in any middle-ground, turning on their toes, turning around and leaving as suddenly as they came. Yet I, was suitably content, for then, that man's name, was to be on record, and of that I felt most satisfied, as I considered it balanced the system a little, for never had I ever taken such an action previously, not ever, regardless of what to m e those men had done, not for the rape, nor my father's abuse, or my ex-husband or after my ex-fiancé, nor the passenger on the plane, for all of what they did I failed to report, not to the police, a doctor or any legal or medical person for any accountability toward them to be appropriately forthcoming. But "Why?" Because of overwhelming portions of fear, shame and guilt, burdens that were so heavy to carry, but still I failed to rest them down, as I internalised each emotion and sadly to say, miss-placed love and pity, also reasons for perhaps wrongly, not reporting them! So no justice was done, for any one.

For time so sadly repeated misfortune portioned my life, in a catalogue of catastrophic events, and "Through my silence of those who harmed and injured me, did I inadvertently protect them?" Of their destructive and violent actions, were they able to go along their chosen way, unimpeded from what they did, disappearing under the radar, free when they chose, to cause more harm? I needed to revise that error, and now I say to aggressors, "Your behaviours are wrong, unacceptable and I will hold you accountable!"

Another truth I found along the way, as I was sat 'pulling myself together' in that restaurant so fine, with a glass of wine they gave to me, and of cause put distance in between that man who the police had spoken to and released, was that a few days earlier, Albert had visited that restaurant, and behaved most bizarrely, inappropriately and scaring the female staff, and that is why of the police constabulary they telephoned, for the future their staff would not suffer again. But their intent I did not mind, for I was glad to play my part, having added my statement to theirs, and of suffering in the future, unlike I, there would be no need, to take part. And of he, his health condition then noted, he may be in a better position to receive the help that maybe perceived he needed.

"Failure is simply an opportunity to begin again more intelligently."
~ Henry Ford

The crime of rape, is not over when the man who performed such a heinous crime leaves, for the victim, she carries a daily burden of rage from that barbaric act, and of my personal experience, 30 years on, I was to learn, that of the 5 and a half hour ordeal that I was subjected to, it was Post Traumatic Stress Disorder, (PTSD) unknown, undiagnosed that I had been suffering and living with since. The pain the shame of that brutal rape internalized, with no avenue for escape, never spoken of, no action for help ever sought, until one day, completely out of the blue, following terrible 3 days of emotional flashbacks, 15 years after that brutal assault, caused me to telephone the Rape Crisis Helpline.

How alone I felt, and how my life was forever changed, and not even my favourite pastime of shopping in the Arndale Centre did I escape with out an adverse effect, for even in that brightly lit place, when footsteps I heard behind me, quickly I moved to the wall, and trying to protect myself from perceived danger, I stood frozen, my temperature souring and my palms sweating, panic set in, and as I saw who it was, sometimes a lady, I waited for them to pass, and as I rationally knew I was safe, of those physiological response to that horror relived, I breathed again and rested, but of the rest of my physiological reactions, the same was not regained.

Walking down the streets fearful emotions flooded me, as panic plagued me, at the sight of an oncoming man, I hurriedly crossed the street, dashing between the cars to secure my escape, and late, no, no more did I go out, not to dancing lessons, for I needed to park the car, a couple of blocks away, and nor did I join the OH&S Association, for too feared was I, to get out of my locked car, to walk to the venue, alone across that well lit car park.

Disturbed sleeping patterns ensued, for "How was I supposed to sleep, when the rape took place in my own home, in my own bedroom, in my own bed, and I heard from a man at the hospital where that rapist worked, that he was looking for me?" My dress code changed radically, the movies I watched, the TV programs, humour and jokes, they never were the same, and conversations too, all changed and all while silently I was drowning beneath an iron casket of blame, and directed, all internally. And "What of he?" He who did that to me, he held no responsibility, there to do it again, to cause devastation like vile seeds of devastating destruction of evil, and I know it not by any other name.

Albert was history, and shaken but not stirred I did conceive, but luckily a fortuitous rendezvous was scheduled with a friend from New south Wales, and over coffee the next day on *Champs-Élysées*, a debrief did unfold, and how pleased I was to release those emotions and queries of resolute concerns, of severe self-disparagement were underway, as I relayed my story, major being, "Why did I not activate my mental nurse training and bid a better escape?" Her reassurance most welcome, as she, a Prosecution Lawyer soothed my misery, recalling a case she worked on, with the moral of the story being, my benign actions may have been best, for I knew not his 'breaking point' or what could possibly in him, 'trigger' something extra. Plus to my worry, that I should have shouted or 'done something' her note was that, should I have done such a thing, the French lady who instigated my rescue party, may never have known she needed to, then worse could have happened. "What about trying to push him out of the way?" Then she pointed out, I could have fallen and injured myself, or worse case scenario, he could have taken a tumble and been injured, then I could have been lavishing in a French prison rather than sipping coffee on the most prestigious boulevard in Paris.

"Oh dear" it appeared I may have been quite lucky in my escape, effectively unharmed, some years later I was to consider, really "Of my reactions, of my past misfortune of trauma and suffering, on that day, would they have produced 'triggers of their own?" And really, were they dormant and, "Ready and waiting to be activated?" Without checking out research I held no firm knowledge, but it seemed significantly rational that would be so, so I ceased blaming myself, for my apparent non-actions, as with a new perspective and confidence, I was able to breath a huge sigh of relief that unharmed I did escape, and from there-on-in, without delay, I was always to listen to and take notice of, those smallest of messages, those queries, those notions, that doubt, almost a bizarre 'knowing' sometimes, that I receive innately from my gut, to keep me safe and free from harm.

I placed that lesson in my toolbox of tests, as I had ascended that steep learning curve and vowed that I wouldn't need to re-do that one, so better choices, of my actions and omissions I actively pursued, though gladly on route, I learnt to be kinder, gentler and more patient with me, for I was and remained a 'job in progress,' so taking a portion of my own medicine, I delivered a measure of praise to me, for my achievements were growing and my accomplishments more, and for the 'value of me,' as I was just growing to believe, that I was in my life, deserving of so many more good things of comfort and love, and so those hills I was to climb, of steep gradients where needs-be, because 'I was worthy,' to do all that, just for me.

For I had set upon my road-trip, my destination, to discover 'who I am' and not who they made me, resolutely, I place one foot in front of the other, empowered with choices, by knowledge from free tools from the library, of, journals, magazines, audio-books DVD's and courses, all available to experience and use, to learn and teach, and to borrow all, it was to a café I would wander, to relax over a latté as I read and listened of all, to enlighten and propel myself along my road, as wonderfully, it was *me*, who I got to know.

Enhanced, my spirit and mind, my reward, those mistakes and mishaps from that past became less, because I made a commitment to me, to not get mad or upset, but learn from every little thing that tripped me up, because I bypassed they potholes and sidestepped the ditches, and climbing my way up to the top of the hills to admire the view, of how far I'd come, but that made me not afraid to travel down, to ascend a new one, to gain clearer and enlightening perspectives, for I was on a quest, to *FIND ME* and to myself, give the generosity, of my life, with *LOVE* and *LIBERTY*.

"Set your light by the stars and not by the passing ship."
~ Gen Omar Bradley

Chapter 6

Step With Consistency

> *"Courage: the most important of all the virtues because without courage, you can't practice any other virtue consistently."*
> *~ Maya Angelou*

Such comfort can be gleamed from life, of where we live and where we go, where we travel to, the restaurants we prefer, and even 'our usual' table we sit at the same, so perhaps in Paris no wonder that I tried to replicate the same. And on *rue Dauphine*, I'd certainly found one, but of the price, as the ambiance, a little supreme, so on that budding writers salary, who was then a university student, there had to be a cheaper place to find, to rest and hang out. So out of *Café Laurent's* extreme comfort it was off down the road I did go, to the junction where several of them did meet, and leaving luxury behind, but it was price that I had in mind and savings for me to greet.

Initially and remaining the same, the bar staff, medico at best and untrustworthy of particular note, not a patch on my favourites, and of trust worthy I think not, for over charge me I knew they had, and when I queried them of it, blindly, rudely they insisted of English they understood not, and what a disappointment, or was that 'quite French' to think or conclude that a rapport has been built, when it was calculated and one sided and only specifically for their convenience.

But there was one possible thing I could do, worthy for me, was to sit and gaze through the window while I drank *un verre de vin rouge* a glass of red wine or, *une café crème*, a white coffee, and did so, in prime position perched high seat at the bar, for the price tag, half of that to be seated at a table, a little bizarre but I'm sure, not quite mad? And when not studying, there I watched the world go around and soaked up every morsel, every crumb, as my eyes gazed with joy, observing something interesting, something unusual, a habit that I had let go so long ago.

From my advantage point I had to smile, for there were two men, English maybe, as identifiable by their supporting football jerseys of Arsenal and West Ham, amazing really, for there I was sat in a Parisian café having left the UK, yet instantly, my mind in a flash travelled back in time, and anxiety and discord arose of that life left behind over a decade ago, odd, how it conjured emotions so real, so discouraging, so negative, then slowly, my mind came to its senses, of where I was, where I had been, and most importantly, what I had accomplished, and then with relief, it settled down once again.

My attentions back to the street, and I had to smile, as quaint essential

Frenchman, puckering his lips so, fighting the wind, yet still, his huge cigar waivered not in the blustery wind, as he continued walking briskly by, with his hands in his pockets. Yet I was guessing a couple for the American continent as identified by their style, whose teeth so brilliantly white, dazzled from a distance far away across the busy boulevard, a little strange amongst the mist of all the drizzle and the grey but perhaps not so glaring beneath the Californian sun.

And to their right, a Frenchman easily identified by his flair, of casual clothes with a certain understated air of chic, adorned as if with a careless paleaceous splendour of a scarf of the boldest pink, placed with precision it appeared, but in reality, a seemingly simplistic style achieved with a sweeping action of one swift movement, and *'Voila'* the job is done. Yet fair to say the *'pièce de résistance,'* copious coats of fur in colours and designs adorning those generations young and old and restricted not to exclusive use by the *'femmes,'* women, and *'dames,'* ladies, certainly not, for they frequently adorn the men as well.

> *"The quality to a person's life is in direct proportion to their commitment to excellence, regardless of their chosen field of endeavour."*
> *~ Wince Lombardi*

It was an unforgiving and terribly uncomfortable stool of wood on which I sat to study, and a barman was to take a shine to me, as he stood tall, yet not quite so fine, as he held onto the beer pumps and started to relay a casual interest in a conversation increasingly over time. And eventually, when his work was complete, around to sit and the patron's side of the bar he did come, with pen and paper in hand, to practice verb conjunctions with me. Then spontaneously one day, though why he said it I knew not, "I don't want anything from you." A little surprised but noncommittal, with a mild Manchester shrug, I commented unremarkably, "I never assumed you did."

"Was I blind, oblivious, should I have thought more or that? For why would he proclaim such a thing, without cause or provocation?" But I did not, but the web was to be woven, as it was to be in a distant time and at a different location, when all was to unravel and become crystal clear.

The days passed the routine the same of impromptu verb conjunction lessons of *travail à la maison français,* French homework, where we were interrupted, quite intrusively so, by a lady of taller than average height, her blonde hair backcombed in a style of yesteryear and almost bleached white. Fifty-something in years, but dressing much younger than that, with her tight fitting deep blue velvet dress, plunged down at the breast and up at the thigh, and although, true, she had a figure that could pull it off, I believe that be it that the style council to be believed, for a lady to reveal both, is a major *faux pas,* mistake.

After talking quite rapidly for a while, I became perplexed of why her French companion, seated just to her side she did not introduce, for herself she boldly declared, "I'm Patsy from San Francisco." "Hi. Pleased to meet you I'm sure." Then after jettisoning herself into our conversation, where my companion and I were effectively voyeurs as she talked of who knew what, for who knew how long, absent of an attempt to introduce her so obviously French companion, who sat alone at the adjacent window, which really, isn't the 'French way,' at all.

Then enquiring of my frequency I visited that bar, the crescendo of her mystery unravelling, as abruptly announcing, "I'm going to go now. Is that all right?" Surprised, "Go for your life" I could have said, but politely replying instead, "Sure, do exactly as you like," and with that, her and her French companion who looked a tad detached, walled out of the door. Yet leaving physically her question puzzled was inquisitive to me, for as her coming or going held no importance or consequence to me, but really, "Why did she ask my permission?" as I held zero authority to say "No!"

Our paths crossed once again, as into that bar on the corner she returned one evening, and gladly we chatted as I learnt of her job, as a Registered Nurse, but working in movies and such, pretending to be the hands of those actors performing medical procedures, to be filmed and inserted into the TV programs or the likes, and from that, for rest from work and life it turned out, it was a sabbatical she was to take, and such good fortune was hers to gain, as she knew a friend, she was careful not to name, who amazingly wonderfully at least to me, was able to rent her his apartment at such little cost, in my beloved, *St. Germain*.

Interest, normally surrounds my notions when I meet a fellow traveller, for I so like to learn of the good, the bad and the ugly, of helpful and interesting tips arising from their experiences and travelling exploits, of countries visited, their culture, prices, ease of transport, likes, dislikes and also that of their homeland. For so powerful is mutual knowledge we learn along the way, and how to prevent mishaps of any sort, and more I must say, for on such occasions as those, I have been noted to add a thing or two to my bucket list which firmly I intend to peruse.

And during such, she enquired of me, would I like to live in USA, and when I replied "No" as I stated my reasons, a full blown verbal attack she directed at me. Prolonged was her rant and rave, and ignoring those onlookers who may have wondered, what on earth had I done to warrant such, I but I permitted her to finish, before I calmly responded in a clear and concise, "I did not invite you here. You have no need to stay. You are most welcome to leave."

Suddenly, surprised, she retracted her body posture, which she had set forth hovering over me, and said "Sorry" while shyly, immediately, enquiring, "Have I upset you?" "Absolutely not." I replied, "For your actions hold no power to do such." And although I did not explain then, of the concept, 'behaviour breeds behaviour' I hold full credence, and whatever that retched thing inside her personal concept was, the result in such an action as that, I simply refused to take any part.

An onslaught of excuses then out-spilled from Patsy of why she'd done such a thing, of her family history dynamics and an unfair childhood, she claimed as the instigator of her outburst. "Get inline!" I could have retort so sarcastically, but instead chose the route of forgiveness and large portion of kindness, not to be mistaken for weakness, or meekness, where harnessing inner strength over it, maintaining control.

Through blessing and trial and error I have learnt to do just that, and so, to listen, support, understand and encourage others is now what I do, evidentially so for people who I knew not well, as they trample upon their precarious journeys, at junctions undefined, somehow our life lives became intertwined, and at that unperceived point when perhaps they needed help or direction the most, before simply slipping away as inadvertently as they'd come, there I'd be, to give a free to give it, practically and emotionally to relieve their misery.

Ce soir, that evening, had passed onto to such a late hour it almost belonged to the next day, once again I was to have the opportunity to do just that, for as the temperature dropped and amidst the softly falling snow flakes, huddled beneath the umbrella on that Parisian pedestrian walkway, with tears filling her eyes and desperation consuming her voice, Patsy spoke those words to me, "This evening I sat on my bed and all alone screamed out the words, God please help me!"

Suddenly, ignoring the throngs of tourists still hurriedly doing their thing, and in temperatures unusually low for that time of year, their impromptu purchases of those commonplace scarves and hats, though perhaps not in a deliberate attempt to copy French style, but huddled under what they bought, *à vendre*, for sale at those tourist souvenir gift shops, their only aim, to afford themselves a preferable portion of warm.

The quaint essential Parisians, passing by without a care, in beige duffle coat barely sweeping across the cobbled floor, with leather gloves brazen in theme, and a scarf in a colour most vibrant, that in another country only a women would wear, raced not down the street, but carried on as usual, for the weather likely meant nothing to them for in their lives were too interesting and precious to be interrupted for they held far greater concerns, with a *Gallic* shrug sufficing as they raced to, 'what was next,' a favoured sharing of an *apéritif*, a late night rendezvous or perhaps an elicit liaison, perhaps 'ranking of higher importance and far higher consequence.'

And as we continued to stand, as I listened intently and tried to help her, yet time was passing and I really needed to be leaving, absent she was of my repeated plight, that really, I have to leave now, for I need sleep in preparation *à apprendre le français langue*, to learn French early at university the next day. Yet how fortunate she was, that a few steps away she was able to lie her head, as I, a brisk walk through the biting cold, as I awaited my ride in the odour-full *Métro* station, then beckoning me a further few strides through the sludge and across the ice, all before I was able to reach my bed, and I did contemplate,

"Perhaps she's too upset to consider my logistical late night predicaments," but unfortunately "No" as self-absorbed without consideration or recognition, proved to be her reoccurring MO.

> *"If you try to fail, and succeed, which have you done?"*
> ~ George Carlin

Yet I believed I had entered into Patsy's life for a reason, a season, or lifetime, but unlike the multiple other occasions, this was a more difficult job to handle, for an easy lady she was not, nor did her behaviour, ethics or values resinate with mine, but large portions of patience was to be required a ruthless in her disregard for others, or was that just me, as I did my best to assist her in relieving those chaotic patterns of cognition and emotions to which over the years she had succumb.

Sibling rivalry and parental comparisons from her childhood vexed her, with portions of emotions, appearing trapped and pent up, with the blame and shame she attributed to her strict Catholic up bringing. "Its hell and damnation that I think will fall on me if I have sex" she told to me, though perhaps that formed apart of her issues, for never did stop her, and no one would have guessed from the sexual-being she portrayed to be, to the outside world, of her dresses snug and short, her flirting, body posture with her landmark provocative stance of, leaning on one leg, while placing her hand on hip and tilting her pelvis backwards and her bosoms forward, with her deep cleavage, blatant unable to be missed; true her preference, her choice, but definitely men in general, a passive message misconstrued, as they may not understand that beneath that façade, hides a woman in disguise, with contrary tightly held believes what she portrays, and a woman of inner, downward spiralling discord.

So many occasions as she spoke to me, I so wanted for her sake to approach this subject and shine a light on the matter for her, but, I had already had her fly off the handle at me before, and I came to realise it was because, as for so many of us, it was 'her past' that caused her to be that way, but still really, I never could discover a route that I felt confident or safe enough to approach that subject, without her flying off the handle, again; so unfortunately, her lesson opportunity slipped by, and perhaps she will just have to let it take time, until it flows around to her way again.

Yet as the weeks at university flowed on, so did the acquaintanceship between Patsy and I, but unlike other occasions where I have been able to add to and help others evolve out of the minor pit where they may be, for Patsy the same could not be said, for there was never a path of facilitation made, for a forward, onward, upward motion, more of a circular moving in ever decreasing circles. And difficult it was too much to bear, as 'crutch to lean on,' was subsequently substituted by a 'bridge to build' that she designated as my task, then of repetition obstinately protesting, and of that metaphorical bridge, she refused to put a foot on it, to take her from where she was to where she wanted to be.

I was worn out, I was tired of her telephoning me at one in the morning, waking me up from my slumber to tell me of 'who knew what' and when I turned off my phone so she could not, in the morning at 6.30 a.m. I'd turn on my phone to find texts galore from her, followed by a further telephone call incessantly questioning, "Why weren't you available when I wanted to speak to you?" "Errmm!" Demanding to know, "Well what do you think?" "Are you kidding me?" may have been a worthy response, but instead I opted for "I'm getting ready for uni, "I haven't had time to read them," which only caused her greater emotional provocation.

With rendezvous arranged, where I placed my schedule to fit with hers, only she didn't have one, yet still, she would be late, and why, "I've been shopping?" then maybe after just 10 minutes proclaim, "Oh I've arranged to meet someone else" and then be on her way. "What; was I going mad, or was she?" A perpetual merry-go-round, I arrived at the conclusion I could help her no further, for I appeared in her presentation to have only assumed the position of 'scapegoat.'

"Finish there?" Sadly no, for Patsy's imposing persona was void of social norms or etiquette as rudely, she pushed her way into conversations of privacy, between my companion and I, blurting out a rendition of her latest sexual or not encounter, demanding, "Tell me what to do and I'll do it!" Brazenly, hurriedly, "Listen, I'll speak normally so he won't have a chance of understanding." No pause was afforded, as quickly upon my non-committal response, she turned to my French companion, demanding, "You tell me; is he wrong?"

There it was, a Frenchman before me, whose comprehension of English was pretty poor, being coerced by an American insisting he tell her that other Frenchman, her lover-non-lover was wrong. "Oh my" as I heard her adamant words, "Yes, now you've told me that, I will go and tell him what you said!" "Oops!" With the guillotine gone, my mind conjured up pistols at dawn. "Hold-up, hold-up" was my cry, and having previously switched off to what she spoke, I switched myself back on, to ensure of all, that no harm was done.

It was on a fine Parisian night as into the bar Patsy bounced, jutting her way between me and the barman who invited me to dinner where he insisted I *manger des cuisses de grenouilles*, eat frogs legs, incidentally, to be my first and only time, as we practiced French verbs, a most provocative Patsy in her usual attire and provocative stance did demand of he, "Well, you help her with French so why won't you help me?" He declined, and I resigned, that the complexity of our intertwined paths had come to an end, as had, the friendship of she and me.

So weary, as Patsy sucked life's energy from me, I tried to help her, repetitively so, yet I was unable so I chose to move myself way, for a horse can be led to water but it does not mean it will chose to drink. "Is this a consideration for all I contemplate, should we all recognize, when our doing is done?" On that occasion a rapid rate of personal recovery was not to be her prize. But equally, with hope, reflection and a lesson learnt, when the next door of opportunity opens, she might be wiser and stronger, and walk right on through it. Then of course there is the concept of the straw that broke the camels back, and I do believe that maybe she placed the last one on me and of the duration of time and my efforts afforded to her needs had well-passed their expiry date, so a decision, I was to cut her loose and from her, set myself free.

"After the verb 'to love,' 'to help' is the most beautiful verb in the world."
~ Bertha von Suttner

The countries I visited mounted as did the years I progressed through life, France, Jersey, Jamaica, Portgigal, Lancerottee, Tenerrife, Crete, Australia, New Zealand, New Caledonia, Canada, Hawaii, USA, but was I in search of something, wandering aimlessly, or believing that all who wander are not lost, and was it true, through all that discovery, in the lyrics of that well known song, "I had never been to me?"

My family having disappeared so long ago, and that was their choice, one by one, to reject and abandon, before disowning me. So nothing and no one was a steadying block in my life of which to cling to, with no one to hold me back, my future opened wide, it was inadvertently an adventure I began, perhaps, to discover me. For what else was I to do, as with dismay my realisation rose and simultaneously my heart sank to have been cast out and disowned by my family, to stand alone, but was reality over the coming years not to highlight that their cruelty inadvertently, as I sped from their darkness toward the awaiting, *light* of *liberty*.

And so it was, as I sat on my sofa, which I had bought for so little from a neighbour, of Regency reproduction in style, and upholstered in fabric of green and gold damask, and their I rested as I 'plucked' up my courage to telephone my brother who I had not seen for years mounting up to 10. He, brother by name but not by nature, and 15 months my senior, barely tolerated me, unsupportive at best, utterly, blatantly, dissatisfiedly dismissive at worst. And how did he learn such a strategy of contempt of how to treat me, well, he had 3 teachers, his farther, his mother, and his Grandfather, who was also his special mentor, who treated my grandma, quite abominably.

Yet on that day, it was I who was to be designated as a 'crutch' for him to lean on by he, quite undeservedly so, his presumption was misplaced in what he deserved, yet what he wanted was what I gave into be, he cast his wide opened his net, as he launched into his normal collaboration of self-pity and blame, but just once look inside himself, reviewing responsibility for those circumstances of criteria which he had played part in any scenarios, "No," of those, he never met.

So it was, my $5 for a global telephone call was to afford him something he never afforded me, free, the time of day. "Was he to pick up the phone or would I leave a message, would his telephone number have changed, I knew not and more, would he be pleased to hear from me?" "Hi sis, pleased to hear from you" he responded quite quickly, but of the same vein, I was to believe that was not quite true, for following the preliminary bouts of 'small talk' we entered into, a bizarre concept, for siblings, as never when reuniting with friends after many or just a few years, has such a superficial process, ever been needed to go through.

Launching into a conversation, a one sided I must say, of 'woe is me' as he relayed all of his wife's 'going on' and how 'stressed was he' of how she cleared off with his mate and clearing the money from their bank account on route, but my only thought though of my opinion I voiced it not, "What took her so long?" A kind husband, I witnessed not, and in front of her children he would refer to her as a 'reptile' and during one such occasion while standing proud centre stage parading himself in front of the open coal fire, in the living room, he proclaimed with a sincerity of arrogance, "I come first, second and third," then gesturing his hand toward his two young boys, "They're fourth" then gesturing across to his wife, "And she, comes somewhere else!" "Oh my goodness!" Of love, I had not in my life, or could I recall receiving respect, but categorically I knew, whatever I had, being on my own, well, it was definitely better than being in that.

Not so good I do declare, but worse was to come, as unusual day, my sister-in-law had me take her around the factory shops which I so adored, and my nephew's, of maybe eight and ten, were left at home with their father, to play or do some such thing, and upon our return, we enquired of the boys, and my brother, who so proclaims what a good father is he, for, "I've never hit my children!" was to again stand centre stage, in-front of the open coal fire, with again cigarette in hand, perhaps a pattern I should have noticed, but so rarely was I welcomed in, as he scorned those little ones, saying "He's a big girls blouse! A 'puffta.' He's in the kitchen, bloody blubbering about something or other."

Down the corridor their mother and I walked, and what was before me, took me amazingly be surprise, there was my eldest nephew having an asthma attack and quite rightly in much distress and it was his little brother of two or three years younger who was so close beside him, trying so hard to take such good care of him. Quickly I insisted to call the ambulance, but with the hospital only 10 minutes away, I drove the tree in the car, for my brother still complaining "He's just soft" refusing to come along, it for a nebulizer and to hospital and A&E where we hurried along.

Parking the car, I went to find them in the cubicle, and there was my nephew safe, with his tubes in his lungs returning back to a safe dilation, and what a joy, when I saw, the exact moment of recovery, and like a light switch, I knew by all my nephew portrayed when the job was done, and his little petite face and little body, relaxing they gave up that anxiety.

My sister-in-law then referring back to 'type,' asking me, "What does this machine do?" Well for sure, I had not seen it before and wasn't quite sure, for following my back injury and specializing in OH&S, I had not worked on the wards for 15 years, a long time in the medical field, missing significant equipment advancements, then ignoring all else, she forever relentless with such disdainful disparagement, sneering with the corners of her mouth distorted, turning down, as boldly in front of her 2 sons, my nephews, and at an age, so impressionable, "You! You call yourself a nurse, and you don't even know that is!" Spouted as a demoralizing statement, and not a question. "Well I knew enough to bring him here, when you, were going to send him to bed." And only later I was to learn, that machine was registering the blood oxygen levels, and of that poor little boy, when I arrived in that treatment room, had minus, 72%.

Of she who was false, for she only wanted a chauffer, a teacher and petrol paid for in the running around of 'all things of factory shopping,' and I helped so happily, obligingly, but I was to discover, she was only using me, for more than once we did that for several hours around the northwest, and when completed she informed me, how the frozen pizza for tea was going in the oven, so I, I had to leave. My brother stood there deliberately silent only to say, "Well yeah, see you next time," whenever I'd hoped that would be, would be too soon for she or he, and all I wanted, desired, from the bottom of my heart, was to be accepted and dare I say, feel love.

> *"Do what you can with what you have, where you are."*
> *~ Theodore Roosevelt*

My brother, who forever declared himself to be a good farther, for "I have never hit my kids." But really I did contemplate, should there not be a sliding scale between good and bad or good and evil, and exactly what benchmark was he using for his decision did he succumb.

So why should I worry? For it cast into insignificance his treatment of me? Yet over the years of one who pushed his little sister down, while simultaneously rising others up who were harming me, sorrowful emotions pushed hard against my ribcage, remaining unwanted, inadequate, lost, and unloved. Yet validation one day was to come my way, and "Oh what a 'relief' of such great enormity," when at the age of thirty-something, one of his friends asked of me, "Why does you brother dislike you so much and treat you so terribly?" The external force of the outcome failed to alter, but of the calibration of the internal force of reassurance and comfort was immeasurable.

He held neither certainty or concern to please me, for when a new house I had purchased, to escape the presence of my ex-fiancé, for never did I trust he wouldn't come back to do what he had threaten, and a telephone call I made to my brother, with pleasure and proudly, as to my new home him I did invite. But the reception I received was not that bright, for his response, "I'm busy right now, I can't come yet, you'll have to wait till then end of June of July," and when we spoke, that was the month before May.

"Oh my" the 35 minute journey away he did not consider I was worth the time or the travel, and yet for his friends, he would travel to the worlds end, but then why should I have been surprised, for he always was committed to dismissing me as an inconvenient nuisance, placing me at the bottom of the barrel and letting me know, in his world I held no place. And so, as I turned the key in my lock of that dear bungalow three years later for the final time, the number of occasions he visited my home, equalled, not one.

The hurt of that hostile rejection still smarted but there I was on that day, with that same brother, bombarding my ears for the next two hours, and as I had moved positions leaning on the sofa, gazing upon that truly wonderful view I was afforded daily through the floor to ceiling windows surrounding my lounge room, I saw the sunlight all aglow and the leaves of the native trees mildly blowing in the breeze, and did "He pause to ask of me?" "Oh yes" he did momentarily, when with joy and excitement I told him of my dreams and my aspirations of what I was going to do, only to be met by his certified account of contradiction in an instant as he cast them down, "No. You can't do that." Which in fact, actually translated to, 'No; *he* couldn't do that!'

Then I wondered, "How did he mean that? Was it caringly or begrudgingly? Would my success and achievements trigger something in him, perhaps anxiety or sorrow, that he never put himself out on a limb, not even a hint of discovering the ripest and sweetest fruit?" and really "Who is he to tell me 'no,' when you have tried nothing and moved no further away than a 45 minute journey from where you were born 43 years ago, travelled not, been cosseted by an array of friends, had a wife who was the bread winner, and risked little if anything. So who are you to recommend anything to me, your sister who you know not?" As he hold no capability, power or impact to 'yes' to me, so I refuted, *his* consideration and condemnation of 'No.' "Absolutely, categorically and wisely!"

Yet his mind was made up, and it was opposed to mine, perhaps narrow in his conception, for I had grown through adversity, pushing and propelling myself forward, doing all that it took, holding staunchly tight to determination, facing the steep gradient of the mountain to climb before me, for single minded was I in my commitment to move to something better, of "My plans, little did he fear, interfere. For he was my family, and we were talking, so "Should I not have been pleased for that?" Yet again, "Did he deserve my compassion I showed so freely? or "Was I to judge him, as he had judged me, as completely unworthy? And was he right or wrong in his choices, in condemning and cruelly dismissing me, as he deemed me to be, significantly less in value, than the other people in his life?" Yet in exchange for his badness, I was giving goodness, as I had substituted, mercy for justice. And of his treatment of me, "Was it right or wrong, or simply a reaction, through his observational learning process, of how his mother and his father behaved toward me?" But either way, really, to try and do no better, when he could for others, really, there are no valid excuses!

I had sought a better, a higher path than the one I first trod upon, that precariously treacherous and dangerous one, the one that I so desired and needed to get away from, but as for he, my brother, "Had he chosen not to seek, to not walk on an other?" But perhaps he knew not that he may benefit from such one, "Was he lost?" or "Maybe on his inside, a little torn and worn?" But "Why would that be so, when he, held daily warmth and security from his Grandparents sanctuary, receiving affection, devotion and substantial camaraderie from his friends and acquaintances, that always he appeared to have so many of, it hurt, a lot, that he cast me aside so, dismissing me from his life as superfluous to requirements, yet still, of that olive branch, I was to extend it out to him.

"Love doesn't make the world go around, Love is what makes the ride worthwhile."
~ Franklin P. Jones

True, brotherly love, I had not, of what it looked like or felt like, I knew not, as that was a mystery to me, and certainly when a friend mentioned, that he little brother was 'looking out for her,' at the clubs, making sure she was alright, ready to intervene at any moment, 'surprise' was my first reaction, for mine was a 'big brother,' but certainly he never did any of that, and by his own confession, never would, and it felt like such an enormous hole inside, perhaps that place which was supposed to be filled with love and compassion, yet a perplexing note, as I contemplated, how utterly bizarre, "Why would her brother be even talking to her when he was out, instead of ignoring her as mine ignored me, with his instructions to go away, and not even caring if I was in trouble, for that he considered was non of his business, and true, on one such evening he proved that point, to be absolutely so?"

Certainly its fair to say, to have a good angle on love and the dynamics of it, or comprehending emotions, attitudes or behaviours within a family unit, well truly I held non or rational or good value, which proved as just part of the problem in just about all my relationships that I mistakenly entered into, and there included, the marrying of my 'first love' 10 years later, how romantic it may be thought, but not exactly so, as I was persuaded in my thoughts, and not convicted in my heart of hearts, to marry that man, as huge reservations were rising, and how true that innate GPS system proved to be, as we'd only been married for 3 months, 90 days, before the 1st time, he 'knocked me around.'

How idyllic, that supposed coveted first love, yet it was not to be a match in heaven, but verging on hell, as the dust erupted and the foundations crumbled, as rapidly within that marriage the cracks began to show, yet 'how funny' not until 'everything' was legal and binding, where he had managed to persuade me to sell my castle, and plough the proceeds and everything init, that I had bought, and transferee them to deeds with his name on, for which he had *NOT* paid a penny toward, and *ONLY THEN, DID HE SHOW HIS TRUE COLOURS* and *VIOLENCE PURSUE. Funny that!!!* And "Yes" I do believe, it was his plan all along, to take what I owned, that I had worked so very hard for, to transferred it, and make it, his, undeserved, very own.

Staunchly rapidly, he sliced through those wedding vows, and what a humongous *faux pas* for surely I was to pay a hefty price for walking down that isle and muttering those words, "I do." For truly my instinct had been yelling at me, "Stop! Don't! Save yourself! To the alter, don't go!" As shaking, almost vomiting in that wedding car, that brightly polished silver and burgundy Roles Royce, adorned with white ribbons, as I was driven to the Church amidst its plush splendour, yet as I sat beside my wonderful and dear stepfather, my nausea was so severe, so easily I could have yelled to the Chauffeur, "Stop the car, now, I'm going to be sick."

My hands were trembling uncontrollably, in a manner never that they'd done before, and as the vehicle pulled up to the pavement, outside St Johns Church, that place where my fate did await, in those moments before the door was opened, and a hand was offered to help me out, to disembark from that sanctuary, of my stepdad, did he enquire tenderly, "Are you sure you're doing the right thing, as it doesn't really appear you are, then excitedly continuing, we have the car, we can stay in it, we can keep driving, we'll go somewhere safe, safely away from him?" Yet sadly, so sadly, 'No!' That was not the scenario.

Of that notion I wonder, to protect me from a great folly, "Had he thought to enquire, recommend or propose such for me to contemplate, for my instinct to inspire, or ignite, to take wonderful and safe flight?" What a joy that would have been and how it would have served me, incomparably well. 'If only' he would hugged me tight, and with gentle-certainty in his voice of conviction, "Go, make speed, run for the hills; run for all your might!" But in his gentle-demeanour, and wising not to impose, wouldn't have afforded such a proposal, as he likely would have viewed it as overstepping his boundaries, but he had no fear, for he had non. And I had no hope as I stepped out onto the footpath, my legs so weak they were buckling under me, literally, yet still, they were to carry me, down that isle to seal my fate, as so misguidedly I was to marry that man, where unravelling and impending doom, of me, were to await.

And my reward for all, what a mockery, as at the alter we knelt, as oblivious was, to what he'd written on the soles of his shoes for all the congregation to see, written on his left 'H E and L P' on the right. How tremendously sad and embarrassing, his fortified persuasion of the previous night, supercilious, as really, HELP, he thought funny, yet evidentially, I was the one who NEEDED it.

*"Our words reveal our thoughts, our manners mirror our self-esteem,
our actions reflect our character, our habits predict the future."*
~ William Arthur Ward

For the darkest bleak place, even as an adult where in my heart I resided, I knew not of an instinct, for the concept of it, I had never been alerted to such as a child, and if I had, as the survivor I needed to be, "Would I have considered I had any need for it, or that 'instinct-thing,' that magical majestic magnet element that when we listen to it serves us enormously well, would I have considered that was for me, or only for someone else more less weak or more worthy?" So perhaps no surprise then, trying to save me it stormed those barricades of unforeboding logic on that eve of my weeding day, as 'rat-a-tat-tatting' attempting to grab my attention, alerting me that something was wrong because of its presence, still didn't get through to me. For I so unaware, was to ignore its cry even as it shouted my name increasingly loudly, for those were nudging and notions it was trying to give me, saving me, from making the mistake from walking down full and long length of the Church, where *he* and *me*, were to become *we*.

How sad, that I held not a concept that *instinct; free* and available and "Yes" worthy to serve me. But way back then, in my mind, it invisible, non-tangible, unable to be touched, unable to be held in the hand, and without clear evidence of how it could serve me, so to add to my survival kit or toolbox of control, I did not, not figuring anyway it could serve me, so superfluous my requirements, for it would not have fit in with what I knew, what I'd been used to, so I gravitated not toward it, but away from it. But what a great folly, as that opportunity to seize it and thank it for saving me, as desperately I missed on that day, as it screamed at me, "Over Here! I can help you!" I could have broken free, free from the restraints my husband was making me, 'if only' I had contemplated something new, something outside that box of 'abuse and control' as they used to, forged the confines of my everyday life.

So there I was, throwing caution to the wind, and risking bad luck, seeing the groom the night before the wedding, down by the river that evening, funny now, as at no point did I realize what an irony, that was to be, as I telephoned his hotel, one on the Blackpool prom, where the wedding reception was to be, explaining that "I need to talk with you." But "What?" Extreme reluctance, was his response, to meet the lady, who he was to marry, the very next day, sighting all sorts of reasons, yet it was all too late in the day to consider how my request seemed to pose a threat to the great plan of frivolity he had planned out before him that night, where in it, I was posing as a great and unwelcomed inconvenience.

Yet I persisted, I insisted, that "I'm not sure that I'm dong the right thing, I think we should reconsider," that got him thinking, as then he came to meet me, down by the river Wyre. Though, "Hello!" Really, "Why was I so slow of his intentions?" as that was a massive giant clue right there that I missed along my way, of how I should have been putting on my running shoes. "If only" I mused I had taken a leaf out of 'Private Benjamin's" book, a movie staring Goldie Hawn, who with recognition and confidence, walked triumphantly away from the altar, before the ring was put on her finger.

For it was not of "I love you please do this," or "I want to spend the rest of my life with you" or other such reassurances followed by kisses, cuddles or hugs. "No!" It was he, next to me sat on the bench, leaning forward with his elbows leaning on his thighs, his hands clasped in front yet moving about, as the words he spoke, void of love or compassion, as "No. You can't do that!" Was his retort, continuing, his concern not me, but, "It will upset my mum and dad." "What?" I should have screamed, but not so, and more was to come, which all included "I" and "Them," but nothing of "Us," or "We," and certainly nothing of "You." "Hey!" I should have shouted, and proclaimed boldly, Remember me? "I am the bride!" "What about including me in all this talking you're doing?"

His rational weak, yet "See right through it?" Blooming heck, "No, I did not." For I had been taught so well how to be coerced and do as others beckoned and not concern myself with my cares, for apparently, in the world according to my father, mother or indeed brother, they were superfluous to requirements and in life, were never to be considered, and should I make a mistake and do just that, well in an instance, I was expected of them to retract, and to another's wishes immediately give in.

And so it was, merrily on his way my fiancé continued; "My parents will never forgive me." "You know they thought nothing of me until I went in the army, if *you* do this to me now *you'll* make it worse all over again!" "Joking?" "No, he was absolutely serious." The only joke, and it was a 'corker' and was to be played against me! Apparently so, the responsibility fell to me, for his family not to reject him! What pressure to place on me then, for "What was I, a bandaid, or something else, to keep them together?" And I agreed! *INSTINCT Please!!!!*

Unbelievable, still I did not wake, consumed under his blanket coercion and subterfuge, his selfishness dishonest personal agenda to be completed and see fruition, for "I had heard him, but I did not listen!" "They'll never forgive me, if *you* do that" so loudly those words should have rang 'jingle jangle' in my head and my heart, my retort may have been at best "They're your parents, that's between you and them," but I thought too little of myself to question, "Why was it to be about his family's needs and not about me, me who in less than 24 hours was to be his bride, his wife? And his role as a husband to have, to hold, to cherish, to be a couple in unison?" "Oh why, of why did he not think about those?" But nay, they appeared far from his concepts or consideration.

Yet, he was to be the victor, as that training from childhood, preparing me least well as it followed me into adulthood, of the doctrine to always give-in to other peoples wants and needs over and above my own, and so it, with the light that had faded from the day, with foreboding, I permitted my desires to be overrun, as to his unloving, uncaring, selfish requests, distraughtly I was to succumb.

For way back then, oblivious I remained in my late twenties, and for a decade or more, as I had not yet grown to know what love looked like, its voice, its appearance, its ambiance, or words from the heart it imparts, I mean "Did it have a colour or a smell?" and most importantly, "Could I touch it?" For sure, I knew them not at all. "Oh my" with those questions unanswered it was misfortune which fast and hard was to strike, as mismatched, misunderstood, joining the wrong dots, my life as I knew it, was to change again.

Yet how strange, for10 years we had know each other previously, a whole decade of moving from friends to intimacy then back to friends and a relationship of such, transferred over time significantly, and evidentially, for I held not a morsel of consideration for any other way it should be, never would I have believed he was capable of such behaviour, and certainly not toward me. For demonstrate even a smidges of what was the fait awaiting me, he most certainly had not, but later when in a place safe from him, I was to consider, "Seriously, was that really all along, part of his master plan?"

Because, for good or bad:-

"Energy and persistence conquer all things."
~ Benjamin Franklin

For he, knew my history well of the abuse I received from my father, and of a tale I dogmatically told to he, "If you ever hit me, that will be it, it will be divorce courts for you and me." But right there I do contemplate, quite reasonably, and as greater time passes the more credence it does gleam, "Had I inadvertently given him that idea to establish his perfect plan?" For he had achieved nothing into the later years of his twenty-something years, which displeased his parents he parents immensely was his concept of that, as he drank his money away at the pub and bought motorbikes. And statements he would make, "My mum and dad are proud of my brother but they are disappointed in me, I am not a teacher, and only comi-chef as a career they take not seriously."

So he joined the army, and after such apparently they thought a little more highly of he, yet still he owned not a house and held no assets suitable for his age, and so perhaps of me, he saw a way to get them, and I, inadvertently, had already informed him inadvertently, that I would be gone, if harm he subjected me to, so perhaps he, even a conspiracy with his parents did hatch a plan, to falsely declare his love for me, to trick me and take, that which he had never earned, but stole deliberately.

For my house, my very first castle, I could afford that, and even following my lower back injury at work, to be placed on half pay, then early retirement at the age of only 25 was my fate, and to be told by the doctors, because of my condition, not another day would I work. So invalidity benefit I was placed, and so, through the process my income reduced significantly, and with a mortgage to pay, of rates and bills too, but I was not to give in to that risk of travesty.

It was not a case in that of Shakespeare, "A horse, a horse, a kingdom for my horse," it was, "My castle, may castle, save my castle," and so it was, as I stood outside in the tiny grassed yard, with a narrow paving stones bisecting the space, and edged by a 6 feet tall brick wall, with a wooded gate of the same height painted deep cherry red to one end, and as I turned to the other, there, I feasted my eyes on my deeply treasured piece of protection, as I viewed it, my 'two-up two-down' property, built in abundance to house those workers of the mill-processing era, and there I stood, wistfully, yet with paramount determination, loudly and boldly declaring with such clear intention and cascading rivers of devout emotion, "This is my house, I'm saving it, I'm keeping it, it's mine!"

And so I did, yet then there it was, conquering my castle of fortitude, cohesion and subterfuge of personal intent by that fiancé, to sell my house of which I did not want, for it I held financial security, yet he wanted a better location, and perhaps more significantly, my 25% profit, so with his persistence of persuasion complete, he found himself with his name on the deeds to a semi-detached property, and what was by his purpose I do believe of his malicious intent to deceive, to attain that, which I deserved not, to have taken wickedly from me.

But what of: my castle, what of my security, my financial independence? For I had ploughed into that home, through blood, sweat and tears, and the reward, my harvest was mine, to protect me, as and render me safe, as per my design. Yet so inadvertently, I had been tricked into another way, as the jingle jangle of warning bells I did not hear, "Oh my" as I then without a secure income, retired from my nursing career on ill health grounds, unable to get a mortgage, and destined to become a 'rentee,' so disdainful and emotionally difficult to bear while he, manipulated, captured and stole my castle from me.

Screaming emotions almost unbearable, of loss independence, insecurity, financial stability, all then outside my personal power to procure them for me, and lost, void of gravity, yet I had let down the drawbridge, drained the moat of man-eating sharks of good appetite, for I had trusted, I had believed, that that man of whom I married, was to be the man's arm I was be linking tottering down to the Post Office each Thursday morning matching walking sticks, to draw our old age pensions.

Previously in life, never had I felt more alone, for never before had I permitted myself to trust another, that man I married, the only one, and really, what a folly, never was I going to make that same mistake again. Devastated, distraught, all my protection gone, my distrust reunited with fervent passion, and peace, no, there was non. For images raged around my head, of my newly raised anxieties, that of trust another in the world it certainly cannot be done, as a limiting belief I set in my mind, that all who come into contact with me, in the realms of men, will let me down, leaving me tattered and torn, but more, only after beating and harming me.

Compounded immeasurably so, as everything, I had fought for, in my world since being a little girl, and there it was torn away from me, and so what to do, as the doctors delivered their verdict, "We can't operate on you and there is nothing else we can do. You'll never work anther day in your life." "What!?" I heard myself scream. "Help me!" I begged, "Please, relive this pain," I had survived my childhood, but I was not strong enough to survive that emotionally debilitating strike. Un-comprehensively I heard what he spoken, but was it not a joke, was I not on Candid Camera to myself I proposed, and in an instant the host of the show was to jump out from where he hid and shout "Got ya!" But "No!"

With the diagnosis giving way to a severe prognosis with no relief of symptoms then projected or expected, a blanket burden of blackness engulfed me to my deepest core. For really, what of children what of their safety, how was I to protect them, how could we escape harmful men, when I was not in possession or control of, career or financial independence? Furiously panic set in, for those who were not yet born, for how could I protect them without a career to rely upon, where was our hope and security to be? I knew not, but for the outcome, hope, on a cycle of revolving history, dissipated and disappeared from me.

My career had totally woven in throughout my life, as the most intricate and important portion of it, for those very reasons of survival and self-preservation, and then, in the passing of a minute's consultation with a Registrar, it appeared as if a magician, snuffed away in a puff of smoke, that which had been hard fought to earn. Initially, what to do? Distraught, removing the white gown which tied at the back and redressing within that cold and white and empty hospital cubical my mind in controversy, for sure as I began to walk along the main corridor of such length where I had stepped on night and day duty, at the hospital where I passed my nurse training exams, for should the doctor's prediction be true, I would never again work there or any other hospital.

Yet, in spite of all, I was not through, I did have 'me,' and surely I was more than enough, for my past life had provided empirical evidence that it was true, I was more than enough to see me through. Sure I may have been a poor good friend to myself, but I was an excellent advisor, my own best resource and tool. Emotionally broken, yet somewhere deep within I was to reset the Barometer and become stronger than 10,000 men, and like Custer's Last Stand, I was to regroup the honourable and dependable trio, me, myself and I, and push on through. And like the phoenix I was to rise from the flames, immeasurably stronger than ever before with my secret weapon; of 'me.' It was not to be soon, it was not to be easy, but it was to be!

"No Scrubs"
~ TLC, R&B Girl Group; Grammy Award Winning Song

Such a sorrowful a story of my wedding day, as it was only a shallow sum of 3 hours post our wedding ceremony, when that new husband of mine, lost his shiny as a new pin status. Not exactly, it was to turn out, his soul, black and dirty as coal, and that of 'forsaking all others to be true only unto you,' tumbled and capsized. Yet I, so naïve to concede, understanding so little and putting up with so much as standing up for myself I did not, but how could I when I knew no better, that I could or I should, for all my life, as I'd falsely been told black was white, and with no evidence to the contrary, indoctrinated exactly and precisely into what they told me, as if by osmosis, I believed it all, to be true.

My new husband disappeared nowhere to be found, I searched that large hotel up and down but still I could not find him or any other in our wedding party, all had disappeared, not a notion of where the man I had committed my life to had gone, I just knew he wasn't with me, and how a tad embarrassing as it was around and around the hotel I walked, before time of mobile phones, and the bar staff, wait staff and reception staff too, politely speaking, "Please tell me, have you seen my husband, he's wearing a grey suit and a flower in his lapel, he's my groom?" With a shade of pity portrayed on their face as I asked the 2nd time around, they did declare, "Sorry, can't remember seeing him in this room."

Thirty minutes or more, passed before he returned and came to launch an assault of surrender onto me, and there I was, stood in my big white dress with layers of tulle floating everywhere, a train behind sweeping across the floor, a headdress of a delicate loop of leaves and petals encrusted with shimmering pink crystals, nestling above my shoulder length ringlets of light brown hair, matching in harmony with a ring of embroidered roses of Chantilly lace, draped across the décolletage, and there I stood in my little white satin shoes, on that plush deep red Westminster carpet of squares encasing pink and cream entwined roses, as the staircase was to my left, wide and bold and most masculine, from the right I could hear the gentle clatter of the silver platers and the crockery clanging as it was being cleared away from our wedding breakfast.

The ceiling decoration overhead, with a cornice most ornate and deep and designed in yesteryear, in a manner to show off that fine chandelier, large and grand, of guilt and high proportions with crystal teardrops, large and small but most of all, so beautiful as the light fragmented and shone through, but there was nothing beautiful, bright or right, of what my new husband was to declare to me, and of the multiple layers of tulle that made those mutton sleeves on my weeding dress of splendour, by him, I was about to be made, a superfluous sacrificial lamb.

And so it was through that elegant hotel I was led, while people all around revelled on that May Bank Holiday where we actually enjoyed some sun, I was to enjoy nothing, as that bad day, it was not yet done, but had only just begun, and thank goodness I was too slow at that time to consider, of the funny irony, that I was once told how pearls were bad luck for me, so on my wedding day I deliberately chose to not have them anywhere on me, and my dress, messed-up during its alterations and my husband to be, his trousers to his suit the same, and how tardily so, retrospectively to realise, that the only pennies he had, upon them had written my name and so it was the same of those paid in total for the honey-moon, where nothing sweet, or to be wished upon was to be found.

Astonishingly, amazing, a blow was about to knock me sideways, for his steadfast phrase, "You've got to apologise to my mother of or she and all my family are going to walk out on *my* wedding day." "But isn't it my wedding day too?" Me in my big white dress and he, void of compassion for me continued, "And you know how my brother has always been favoured against me, *you'll* only make it worse if *you* let them leave?" "They'll never let me forget it or live it down." "Kidding me, was he?" So sadly, unfortunately "Not!" And until his agenda achieved, I heard his persistent whining pleas, but what I heard louder, it was a cracking sound, but what was it, it was the sound of my heart breaking, and the wind whistling past my ears as tumbling to the bottom of the cavern I was pushed, a place that with he, I never believed I'd be.

Fighting in his mother's corner, he simultaneously, of his new wife, in a fury knocked down. Yet I was too slow to recognise, as quickly forward went his petition and his belatedness he did not disguise to me, that women whom I had heard him criticize for the 10 years previously of my earliest recollection since he, I had known.

Although a bridge I was unable to build and get over it, I wondered of his mother's actions on that wedding day, and his subsequent actions, telling me, "You have to apologise to my mother." But "Why?" I asked, "I haven't done anything wrong." His hurried reply, "I know, but if *you* don't say sorry, she's going to leave my wedding, and then I'll be back to being nothing in their eyes and dismissed by them all over again." "*You* can't let them do that to me!" No pressure on me then! To make the marriage succeed, what a weighty burden unfounded, unfair, and the relationship between his parents and him, falsely designated as one for me to bear.

A pattern to succumb, established the previous night, he pushed against the boundaries until his objective achieved and I, gave in. But no credence needs to be given for his accomplishment in that field, for in truth, the president had been set in many a far off day, when just a child, and a 'how to' manual so inadvertently I gave, so he knew well what to say and what to do, for not mine, but his system to win. And yes I surrendered under duress, a habit serving him most well but destructive to me, and yes I could whine, 'woe is me,' and yes I did, but not forever, nor longevity.

My control had inadvertently gone. I did not even have the love, friendship or support of that man, who I had loved and believed, loved me, according to his testimony for the past ten years. But was it a lie, for actions speak louder than words, and they did not correlate, the only man I had ever trusted in the world had lied to me, again and again, deliberately, and reject, abandon me, to take another's side over mine and expect me to give in, and continue until I do, "What, was he my mother, my father, just who had I married, and what to me was he to do?" My control = zero. My panic + distress + terror = expediential in calculation.

My stomach whirled and reeled in pain and anguish, I was out of control, unwanted and abandoned by that man I had just legally sacrificed myself to, I was trapped in dismay, no way out, no career because of my back injury, no house because he persuaded me to sell, married, also because of his persuasion. And where was I, I looked inside, I looked outside, I had no-thing and no-where, not even my name to call my own. Uncertainly everywhere, anxiety and discomfort, not felt not since childhood, consuming my body and mind of the fearful and scary for the outcome ahead.

"Oh my! Why did I get on that plane the next morning to travel to the destination of our honeymoon?" all paid for by me incidentally, when really, as he had refused to consummate the marriage, as it was of to the lawyers I should have rapidly gone, to legally have that marriage annulled.

As his MO was so quickly established, as he kicked those wedding vows to the curb drastically, as no dust had time to settle on my veil, before that fateful wedding day, when he knocking me all around the dinning-kitchen, breaking the cooker handle with my hip, and that was before pinning me up against the fridge freezer door, in a rage shouting, his teeth snarling as his face almost touching mine screeching, *"I'm* getting a knife and *killing YOU!"*

Bewildered, my mind numb, not moving a muscle, frozen to the spot, unable to comprehend, to conceive what he had done, for only replaying in it was, "This is my best friend, the one I've loved all along, he would never do this to me." But there it was, my ears unravelled the noise as he rattled loudly the knifes around the draw, searching for the perfect one, then in a flash out he came with his hand stretched high above my head, and in a downward swing jabbed it forcefully onto my shoulder, but, so fortunately, a knife, was not held there within.

And there was I, emotionally in a flash, more tattered and torn than ever before, as that man I trusted, the only one I ever had, and that's what he'd done to me, but "Why?" I thought he loved me. Yet "Divorce, divorce" I shouted as I moved across to the sink to carry on washing his lunch dinner pots, "I always told you it would be, and it is, were getting a divorce." But that was not a one off incident, as there commenced a catalogue of domestic violence and I, I was to loose the security of my home, as mortgage I was unable to pay in that era, as I was on invalidity benefit, and the mass destruction of my life, 2nd time around had just begun. But I began to wonder, "Was that all apart of his master plan all along?" Definitely, I think so.

But was it, possibly his perfect plan contrived, concealed and conducted, was it beyond the realms of possibility, or likely to be true? As he got in his car and started driving to work, perhaps he concluded, 'not a bad days work done,' with his desired outcome achieve, as he was laughing all the way to the bank. Transporting himself up a steep gradient from zero assets, to a fully equipped and furnished semi-detached house, while I simultaneously was knocked right back down.

A life time, all I'd ever needed, wanted, desired and worked so hard for, through sacrifice, blood, sweat and tears, hard study and substantial deprivation, when at 17 years and older, I was not going out clubbing it, I was saving all my money so a house I'd be able to afford to buy for safety and sanctuary, I even had to give up food to afford to pay my bills after suffering my back injury. Yet against all the odds, not because of them, practically, physically and emotionally, I-saved-it! And suddenly, it dawned on me, he who had nothing, that man who manipulated, beat me, and took the lot of what I had, my property my emotional and physical independence, knowing exactly what he was doing, I believe now deliberately so and "How long did it take him to strip me of all that?" Staggeringly so; less-than, 2 years.

Really "Where to from there?" I was to take a leaf out of my grandma's book, the lady who never could remember the name, of he I was to marry, yet always remembered the name of a gentleman I did date sometime earlier, and perhaps right there, that was a subliminal sign that I recognised not. And I was to take a leaf out of her book, to "Pick myself up by my bootstraps and keep on going." For really, what else was there to do? So there it was, a tentative step-by-step process, I placed one before the other with persistence and resiliency, those cousins of companionship, as I strode on and forged a path ahead, from the blackness and harsh chill of the past, onto a brighter future, resolute, to where a new chapter was to begin, *most* thankfully.

"One should always play fairly when one has the winning cards."
~ Oscar Wild

I remember not the divorce date, but I do remember it was the season of autumn when I made good my escape, yet as a fugitive, with nothing to call my own, with my castle gone, I was all alone, and true, a concept that had never given me a thought for concern before, but this was different for all my hopes, and my security and independence had been torn. My career, my castle, my health, my solace, my love, my lifeline, my rock who was my best friend, gone, as with my hope, and worse inside of me, no dreams left to protect, in despair, and desperate times need desperate measures, so I was to do that which I had never been welcomed, I was to request a visit just for the day, to join my family around the Christmas table.

So I plucked up the courage to telephone my brother, but what reception I would receive was never guaranteed, and after a morsel or more of superficial chit-chat, I inhaled a deep breath, and with an apology in my voice gave my first ever plea, "I feel really bad right now and so alone, I wonder, if you don't mind, may I please join you for Christmas dinner?"

The response perhaps predetermined with his actions and concept of me, yet he did not say "No" right away, which was a little surprising, so at first gave me hope, but quickly it was whisked away, as his manner, his tone, his words all demoralizing, as he replied, "I don't know, there's not enough room, and I'll have to ask, 'her indoors,' his wife." I always knew my place where my brother was concerned but I thought just once he could, maybe would afford me a break, but that was not going to be.

A sickness fell in my stomach as I dared to ask, "When do you think you'll know?" with smarting words of irritation in his response, "I don't know maybe next week or the one after that, you'll just have to wait." OK, my status confirmed, as little sister, annoying and surplus to requirements. Yet really, I felt so uncertain about everything at that time as never before, and of just a gleam of acceptance from my family, "Oh my" how sublime that would have been, but no, for my brother once again was to clip my wings.

My big brother not responding to me, a telephone call I did propose to make, some two weeks later, just with a glimmer of hope that I was to deem an answer positive, "Did you manage to ask your wife if its alright if I can join you on Christmas day?" and in a flash, the abrupt answer right back, "Yes I did and *you* can't, there's not enough space!" Space! His house a detached 3 bedroom property, downstairs with a large open-plan living space where seated at the front, a suite of cream leather, and of where to eat, a Jacobean style dark wooden table, and how many to seat, from 8 to 10, so of their number of 6, "Couldn't they just fit me in?" Well evidentially, that was to be "No." "Surprised?" No. Not really. True, being alone on Christmas day had never been a problem for me, in fact from those I endured growing-up, they were a welcomed rest-bite and sanctuary, a relief from that bitter painful, past history.

It was my mother who then I telephoned for she was the one who told me, "Oh yes your stepfather and I are going to your brothers on Christmas day, its going to be a family affair," so really I perplexingly pondered, "Shouldn't that include me?" But that was to be a negative, for her words and my request of "Mum, will you please have a word and intervene?" with "No!" she hollered back, "It's nothing to do with me!" was her abdication; "Now wasn't that a familiar story?"

For those were the exact words my brother used to me, when I was trying to explain to him, perhaps recruit empathy, to share a burden of the terrible and faulty substandard work completed in my house, my castle, my fortress, by his builder friend who I had employed and already paid, yet to listen, to support, help me in anyway, help me? "No." With his returning words, "Don't tell me! It's nought to do with me and I don't want to know about it! You deal with it!"

His words not open for discussion. So imagine my surprise, when some significant time had passed and he's telling me about that very situation and his friend, and taking a moment to catch up, for "Didn't he tell me he would have no-part of it?" So perplexed I asked, "How do you know that, and why do you hold an opinion, in opposition to my welfare I may add, when you wouldn't discuss it, or hear of its name mentioned by me?" Well of course it was for it was his friend and not me, and at my enquiry, realising his slip-up of letting me know he was understanding and giving to others on the exact same thing he restricted and refused for me, angrily he said, "Yeah; well; that's it and that's the end of it, I'm not saying any more!" And right there, that epitomizes my big brothers concept toward me, so sad, but so true.

"But its Christmas," my heart broken more than usual, unashamed, I begged, "I've never asked before, and seriously, I won't do it again, but please, just this year, please let me be join you. For I would so love to enjoy a family Christmas, and of my nephews too, for I hardly ever see them." But her mind made up, ignoring my emotional petition and plight, and truly, not caring in any regard, the answer remained, categorically, irritatingly so, "No!" How naïve I was, for firmly I knew my place as they had determined it to be, and "Oh silly me," to think that just maybe, just once to contemplate to step out of it!

Her mind closed, but perhaps not beyond the realms of possibility when her love for me, was never open. And so it was, her decision, as my brother, identified the topic was not up for discussion and was not to be talked of again. The concept cast out, I was to shut up and go away, and not trouble them with such nuisances of my emotions or needs ever again.

For that's the way it had always been through my childhood, them verses me, that was until my father's car pulled up in the driveway, then a new instruction given by my mum, "Right, its not just me and your brother together anymore, we have to stick together and pull against him, and put up a united front." "Are you listening to me?" she would shout, and of cause my reply, "Yes I know you tell me every night." There was a pattern, me rejected totally, but when the command was given I had to obey, physically, emotionally, even though inside I knew, for she showed and demonstrated it so easily, it was not me she wanted, it was just that she wanted to presume, to he who she wanted less, to isolate, hinder and hurt him, my father more. Ironically, though I realised not at that time, that was exactly the role she thrust upon me, when he was not there.

Unknown to me at that time was that my self-esteem or my self-worth could get much lower, but a splash they were to make to the depth of the deepest pool, as in the pool of optimism they waned and flailed, as they desperately tried to stay afloat. "Was I hurt?" Most definitely! But I had never tested those waters before, specifically asking for help, probably because I knew the question would likely render a response of "No." And with rejection all about and my name on speed dial, really, there was no need to seek any more, of that which would cause me, so much more, so I guessed there it was, my subliminal notion, 'too scared to confront the truth,' to be confirmed but not rectified, not then or since.

Perhaps, I was no-less and no-more than 'foolhardy' to believe or hold a romantic notion in an idyllic fairy tale day, and some may say normal, and of which I speak is not a wedding day, but a Christmas day of cheer with a family dear, near. But of no surprise it was not to be, for a familiar story, I was shut out of 'their' family to survive, alone. And with a loud bang the door slammed shut, and displayed for all to see was a clear sign of declaration: battered wife, subject of domestic violence, new divorcee, distraught damsel in distress, sister-in-law, auntie, daughter, little sister, yet survivor of all, the result the same, yet I was to survive all on that day, as that designated sign they placed on the door of their home that day, not wanted, not welcome, unloved, 'go away!' "For this Christmas Day, for you, *'there is NO room at the inn!'*

"Forgiveness doesn't change the past but it does enlarge the future"
~ Paul Boese

For sure, a far superior start in life my brother held above me, for he was subject not to maternal deprivation or neglect as I, by my mother, who made it quite clear, I was unwanted and for the reasons she gave, eventually her hatred rendered resolute, as simultaneously she cosseted my brother while rejecting me, and sending him out of harms way, away from my father, to my grandparent's home at the weekends, to enjoy nourishing food, learn of normal socialization, as both grandparents were popular, to learn of the world, trades useful around the house, to enjoy the outdoors, but mostly to receive love and safety. Yet I, enjoying no such luxury as trapped in the house with her, void of a safe egress, by she who scorned me so actively and her destructive spite whirled around me like a howling wind, as with my mind she did mess.

Yet there it was a decade later, from the other side of the world, a telephone call that I was paying for, that so significant in my family, the one who pays, presides over the call, then to he, who had withheld help, comfort, support and encouragement from me, and "An advocate for me?" No, most definitely not, as only spite was his address to me. And as his story promptly spilt out, perhaps I should have re-payed like with like, disparaged him and withheld validation, or was I to turn the other cheek so he could hit that one too, or perhaps Kama was to play a card. "Was I to repay like for like, which he deserved = justice?" or "Was I to give him that which he never gave to me, that which cannot be earned only freely given, a precious portion of emotion = that of mercy?"

Always he was a tell-tale, telling on me, if I did something wrong, which was rarely for I was so scared to, but what of all those times he begged and coaxed me, "Don't tell on me, for I'll get in trouble, and I'll do the same for you." "Oh my" you think I would have woken up to his deception of untruths, and yes I did, but somehow, he always persuaded me to give into his desires, but never once, did he fail to going running to mum, to dish the dirt and get me in strive, with the minimal of opportunity to do.

And I never did stop protecting him from my omissions, and there it was it was my actions, which was to take a stance of a proactive, supportive and educational nursing approach that I was to extend to him on that day from New Zealand to Wigan. So with my listening ear, I patiently and caringly permitted him time and space while he off-loaded to me, but really, nastily I could have said, "I don't want to know, nought to do with me." But no, I did not, suggesting and explaining coping mechanisms, for emotional issues, suggesting practical measures too, so for a solution to his situations he may formulate a plan and onward to empowerment, see himself through.

Yet for each positive I suggested, a negative was his quick response, expressing how he couldn't move away from where he lived, for "My sons need me." "What, as adults, at 22 or 23, I may have asked, for you to place a roof over there head, when they both have jobs?" But a point I did not, for not my place, and nor did I ask, "Actually, didn't they need you more when just a boy your eldest was suffering an asthma attack?" But to create friction was not my intention, and perhaps a worthy question, yet of his capacity to cope I'm not sure he would, for he had created an apparent new role as 'martyr as his new occupation.

And as if transported back in time, to a concept, a behaviour, a rational so tightly held by she who loved him so, his mum, yet of reciprocate the feeling, I never was convinced he did, for way back then, and as he who was old enough to have grandchildren, he did refer to her as "Your mother," somehow forgetting or choosing, to ignore that in fact, she was his mother too. I had to smile for like her too, he cast his net wide to attach blame, and as he complained and criticize, and not on occasion during that 2 hour conversation, did he hold not an ounce of perception, that in just even a smatter or tiny way that he was to share responsibility.

"Oh my" I was the one cast out from their den, yet somehow, so much further on along my journey I perceived myself to be, for from that childhood of malignancy and from my expulsion from them, rejected and torn, but I reflected as that adult how each family member fervently down cast me, until they cast me out. Yet to be moved away from their dysfunction I was to become so thankful, for that formed a part of my saving grace, and by doing that, inadvertently they had set me free, and I was a *'VICTOR'* reigning in splendour.

Our concurrent journeys not always congruent, and as each of us step, slowly, precariously, eagerly, but at least participating, and of our journeys of discovery, with my journey enticing me, drawing me closer to recovery, and the deeper along the path I search and tread, I become ever more willing to continue for through any storms that blow, I know, that ultimately I will stand strong, and when it is gone, I will readjust my hair and clothes, straighten up and merrily carry-on.

I held sadness for that little boy, my brother who grew to be a man, of an age sufficient to be a grandad who remained shackled by the chains of childhood. Having been committed in my persistence to help him, I placed down the phone and walked into that open space which was my beautiful green and orchard filled back garden, where I was so fortunate, because within it, "I felt free."

So in the back yard, beneath the beauty of the New Zealand sky I fell to my knees to pray for him, for physically he was no-longer in that environment, but as is so common the emotional pain, and those emotions causing distress, so unfortunately does not immediately dissipate simply because, the physical and geographical environment had changed.

For sure, he had received love and compassion as that child he had many friends, and he received comfort, pleasure, security all absent from my childhood, yet it was I, who was far further along that journey which I was walking toward that of my upmost healing, I was stronger, wiser, more determined, but then I knew there was something I was searching for, something to help, improve. I knew little of what was deeply trapped, deformed within my brother's mind, of the adverse experiences he received, only by my father's hand and how they effected or injured him. For his *personal-path*, I did not, his mechanisms of coping skills or their lack of, but what I had grown to know, for my experience, rattled loudly to astutely alert me, that of judge another, we should not, until we have walked a mile in their shoes.

And so kindly for me, and for he too, I afforded him the power of forgiveness, for when we apply ourselves we can achieve this, tough if like me, it is rarely a one off commitment and the job is done, for repeatedly I need to commit to the same, effectively, removing their emotional hold over me, whoever they may be, and in doing so, I give a gift to *me*, a *gift* of *freedom*, for empty the pain and hurt that they cast on me, as I cast it away meaningfully, as I magnificently, amazingly and quite rightly rewardingly, *for I am worth it,* set myself free!

"He who cannot forgive others breaks the bridge over which he, himself must pass."
~ Lord Herbert

History holds a habit of perpetual reputation, and just possibly until we learn from our mistakes we will keep repeating them until we do. Oh what joy, to learn from our past to create, an improved future. The precious lessons our price for overcoming the adversity, enduringly uncomfortable, destructive emotionally or sometimes dangerous situations, or maybe that was just I. As should situations come against me now, in a flash I assess and try to establish "Just what exactly am I supposed to be learning from this?" I work it out, and through reflection I fast track the situation of which is within my power, quick smart; and of what I need to know next, I say, "Bring it on!"

For I have learnt to appreciate those things that 'come against me' and embrace the lessons as an opportunity to grow, to be reshaped, to improve myself, from that which did not suit me, that which was unworthy of me to behold, and to flourish into something that I deserve to hold for myself, of self-value and self-worth, enough for me, and enough to share. It is not within our power to consistently prevent or pre-determine what or who comes against us, but what is within our power is how we choose to respond or react. A powerful tool for this and more, to aid us to move forward, to guide our steps onto footings of stability, gently and firmly, simply but surely, just one step at a time.

I have created a habit of positivity, establishing self-motivation, a strategy of early intervention, recognising and responding with speed to necessary lessons to benefit my quality of life. Am I perfect in my performance of this? Not yet, but cheerfully I say, "I believe I'm on my way," yet presently, I remain gleefully 'a job in progress,' a willing participant, for he alternative I prefer not. And "Why, when the going gets tough, do I, keep on going?" Absolutely! Because I must! For in the lyrics of the fabulously sung song by Whitney Houston, in 1986, and *true* for us *all*, today: "The *greatest love* of all *is inside* of *me!*"

"The most essential factor is persistence - the determination never to allow your energy or enthusiasm to be dampened by the discouragement that must inevitably come"
~ James Whitcomb Riley

Chapter 7

Step With Persistence

"You educate a man; you educate a man. You educate a woman; you educate a generation."
~ Brigham Young

With my one dish and spoon in hand, having undergone the process of the shower-shuffle, the tea-towel trot and the toilet-twister, it was into the kitchen-catastrophe with my one bowl and spoon in hand, neatly sterilized by me and kept safe in my *chamber,* bedroom, and it want even 8a.m. I was about to partake in that what each day would start my day right, that of my muesli, with natural yoghurt and frozen berries, before off down the road I did trot, but not to tiptoe through the tulips that strewn the footpaths to the *Métro,* but the doggy-do-do. *Arh oui,* "Arh yes," an aroma of summer flowers to please the senses it was not, as the stench of stale urine and beer the same, from broken bottles and squashed cans abandoned amidst the narrow ginnels and doorways, and to stand in nothing which was to cause me harm, daily, with my all rugged up and my back pack containing quite a few books, I gave it my best shot.

Having arrived at the pink *Métro* line, descending the stairs to wait for the train, "My oh my," filth everywhere, hugged with others on the platform, just seeking a small space to call my own, I waited patiently as I observed the sign to tell me, how long until the next one, and the funny thing was, although on certain platforms at certain times of the day, it may only be less than one minute until the next one arrives, when the alarm sounds alerting all that the doors to the carriage close in just 3 seconds, most everybody coming down the stairs will make a mad dash and for it run.

Alighting, and changing just once to navigate through those odor filled underground tunnels, just a five-minute walk to the next line, to continue my journey, to take me to that place, where I had been so excited to enroll, yet disheartened I grew to be, at the prospect of another day in that classroom, where difficulties were becoming my growing companions, and from them, I knew not how to set myself free.

The wooden and metal chairs, so tiny for children not adults I do surmise, and so hard to sit upon, and as I discovered on the first day, not contusive to it with tights, fishnet in design on, and the trestle-like tables narrow and short with difficulties needing so many books to open and absorb sometimes simultaneously, and in that square bare room of maybe several metres tall, where in summer, the sun may pose a problem shining through that wall of glass with no air-conditioning and only two small windows, high up the wall on the opposite side, only there to be opened to gain, maybe just a whiff of fresh air.

What a surprise I received when at *la Sorbonne* I attended to discover there was no, softly softly approach to learning but a hard and fast, jump right in. I always surmised, that as a *débutants*, beginners class, we may commence with the alphabet, numbers and time of day, but no, no time for such, and it was not even a methodical manner in which we did work, commencing at the start of the book and working on through, for really, isn't that the design and purpose of them, but opposed to that simple and predesigned format, to the back, to the front, to the middle and all over again, was the route our *professor* took.

Was it normal, for France, for *la Sorbonne*, well I figured it must be, but I, was not to be quite right. For I was to learn, of the *débutant* class across the othersider of the corridor, that their professor indeed had taken a different stance, that of the approach that I assumed would be so, slow. "Oh why, could I not have been put in that class? Would it not have given me a better start, a least a clue, or at least an inkling I may have gained, to lighten the load bearing down on my heart?"

So 'warp speed,' ahead was the acceleration of the 12 week course of 25 hours per week and as it rolled on my, my language or knowledge of the *langue française* did not, as slowly slowly was my ascension, but not of my frustration, as it was not the alphabet and numbers that we learnt first, but grammar and more, and by week four, it was almost onto COD & COI, and those, something about grammar, I cannot even remember what those letters stand for, except to know, through the attempt to learn of their process, an insight I did not gleam.

Yet a little surprised, I was to learn of the *débutants* course equal to the class I was in, located just on the other side of the corridor, with a different professor, indeed was starting with that soft format of learning progression, so approaching the professor of the class I was in, "Why are we using such a different format to learn?" and the response I must confess proved rather surprising, and one for concern. *"Alor,"* came the response, and phonetically I write, pausing and continuing which is the French way when such a word is spoken, then, "There was a student in the class that believed her French skills of vocabulary and grammar superior to the level of the class she was placed in, so I set out 'hard and fast' to prove her wrong."

Well that was a surprise, for sure, to sacrifice many for the sake of the one, appears the incorrect way around, and surely, "Should that not have been down to an administration issue and something to be determined at a higher or more independent level than she?" But then, independence really didn't appear to be that professors 'thing' as so repetitively she was to call into question and speak boldly to stop the talking by two girls from an eastern European country, yet, when she who was from a country bordering France, married to a Frenchman, who believed her accomplishments too high for that class she was in, of disruption through talking, it was to me, obviously ignored.

As my best soon, became not good enough to grasp that which I so wanted to learn, and a trick learnt from old, to beat myself up I took out a great big stick, but really was there a more practical reason, for really as it my health that proved to be such a barrier or was it something else? So I had to catch myself from making a catalogue of excuses.   For true, my muscular skeletal system were proving to be a little difficult to bare, from that lower back industrial injury from 1986, and of a later occurrence, it was anther poor choice of relationships that I entered in, where another I was engaged to, was to cause me grievous bodily harm and injure me too, and in such a way, that my scalp did feel that it was being pulled back off my face so continually, so sleep, it was not so easy, and learning the same, for when it was at its most severe, it was my cognition it did effect, or "Was I, just looking for something to blame?"

Keen to study, keen to learn, keen to improve my health, keen to be free from those aches and pains, as keen to make good use of those precious commodities of time and money already spent, so enquires I did undertake, and there at my beloved haunt, someone knew someone, and an appointment was made on my behalf, and there it was, I was off to meet it, in a previously unvisited *arrondissement*.

How funny, when that little niggle nips in, into 'you don't know where or how, or what it is, but it just makes you question, well you don't really know what.' And such occurred as I waited 30 minutes past my appointment time in a cold and uninviting waiting room, with something inside me saying, "Right, my patience is done, its time to leave this room."   True, for since I have noticed it to be, that I may wait and make all excuses of why I should not be impatient, and true, I take each individual situation on its own merits for I discovered there is no set time-limit format, but as soon as impatience sets in, I have come to realise, that my time there is done, for consistently experience has taught me, whatever happens after that point, will fail to be even satisfactory.

But, not tuned in as now, I waited more until in to the tiny chaotic and cluttered clinical room I was called, where a game of charades unfolded as communication was unable to take place verbally, regarding my symptoms, and as she in that white coat beckoned me to get on the treatment couch, so unremarkably her treatment began, and in time for less than half the time span I was informed was allotted, and more, quite curiously, her skills appeared absent in any regard of healing properties, as the way she rubbed my neck, absent of cream, I could have received the same, from just about anybody, stood at any bar at any time.

With relief of 30euros, but not relief of muscular tension or pain, so it was a new avenue I was to peruse, as seduced by a gold embossed plaque outside the grand doorway of a *Haussmann* building, painted in the darkest of green, perhaps to conceal the dirt from the copious vehicles and the fumes which ensued from that tremendously busy street junction, where the entrance once designed to fit the horses and carriages from those bygone days would have trotted in, and the sound it must have been amazing as they clipperty-clopped upon those finely laid cobblestones, and once entered they would be once again closed, affording greater safety and privacy, and possibly free prove the diseases outside, caused by poverty, and there concealed within the pair of doors, today forever shut, a much smaller doorway, permitting only access for the human kind, and there it was, after the rendezvous was arranged it was through it I also walked and toward the secrets that concealed behind.

The courtyard first to behold, yet onward through the door, original in grandeur and refurbished, but then, they all do appear to be in Paris, I commenced to ascend that all-inspiring staircase, though dark its true, for inside the building no light shone through, and there on the top floor, I was to ring a bell, to await the 'Kene' coming to answer the huge, heavy, and quaintly typical Parisian door.

After the preliminary introductions were done, into a room of dimensions large, but little light, with only arched windows that were not that bright, where the walls were concealed by medical diagrams and charts from the Eastern world, and more comfortable I grew, believing that my health may well be in good hands. And so a less challenging game of charades ensued, and my issues I understood had been conveyed, before I was left alone to undress, then of comfort I felt less. For there was no towel or robe to conceal my dignity, and there I appeared in my ill considered, translucent skin-tone lingerie, almost naked, embarrassed, feeling vulnerable, it was my under-slip I grabbed to serve me best I was able.

For since days of old, since an adult I became, it is not underwear that I simply ware, but lingerie, and for a certain rhyme and reason, for this added more to my self-worth, as almost as a defence mechanism I leant and earned from myself, for underdeveloped in the bosom, and still echoing in my head, those teenage taunts of 'titless' shouted around the school yard, so a strategy I developed to overcome such, for surgery to improve their size was never an option, was to purchase the most luxurious bath and shower foam affordable to me, and after the smooth lather had nurtured my skin, within that 5 minute time frame when the skin is primed and not quite dry, I'd rub in the moisturiser of the same, and complete my confidence layer, with a layer of sheer lingerie, sealed by with a sprinkling of perfume, and hey-presto, just for me, I provide my very best start daily, an accomplished increase of inner-confidence, and from that system, I never found a reason to sway.

And true, of lingerie and bikinis I would always pay my best money for, and of top clothes, well a far second place did they take, for that was for the outside world to see, and I was more concerned, though of my route at that time I understood not, I was more concerned with what was going on within me.

As he re-entered the room the 'Kene's,' process commenced, rubbing my neck and shoulders came first, nothing unusual there, and then he went down to my feet, and a little surprise came my way, as initially he began to flicked them with his fingertips, then slowly and firmly commenced rubbing his hands up and down the full length of each leg, high up my thigh, before individually, raising each one, and shaking it about. Continuing, pulling each out to the side to the largest angle available, bend it he then did, tilt it, and then move it in toward me, and although my discomfort levels had risen immensely, I considered, at least my under-slip is preventing him seeing tomorrows washing and only that which my gynaecological physicians see. Yet I was to be wrong on that account, for I had not realised until later, with the slip draped over, and not tucked between, all would have been available for him to have a jolly good vision to, if he chose, gleam.

"Oh my" I wondered why he had repeated that action so repetitively, but so late was I to do so, by several weeks, as I misguidedly betrayed myself, and why, for better health. But more was to come, as it was my stomach were his hands then went to, and too close for comfort to my abdomen for sure, yet, as a compliant patient, I said nought, but really, in reality, I should have let go a real big shout, and proclaimed, "Right that's enough, stop that right now!"

"It is choice not chance that determines your destiny."
~ Jean Nidetch

Quite amazingly I have to say, some degree of recovery experienced from that initial treatment, so a second appointment I thought I'd give it a go, to try and claw back even more good health, but thinking far better of my undergarment choices, I prepared better than the first, as I concealed well my privacy of my private parts. And the treatment I have to say, a little different from the first, but perhaps no astonishment there, as often they are, but what was to astonishment me, was the question posed by that medical practitioner upon my leaving, was the usual, "Would you like to make another appointment?" but rather, "Is it possible, will you have dinner with me?"

Looking at him quite strangely, a little bewildered indeed, as he the practitioner and me the patient, I was not quite sure where he may have seen, or not, his ethical accountability, I paused, and then continuing, he explained his rational to me. "Well it is practical, for I can help you with French as you may in turn help me with English, and we may both learn more." Well I did see his point, and help I certainly needed, and as I knew somewhere in me, that as a patient I would not see him again, I explained I "Will think on your proposition and return the answer via a telephone call."

Reservation, as the day arrived when my acceptance was to bear fruit, and there I entered into his surgery, his home where his office was situated, but as I rang the bell, so easily I could have turned and run away. For something 'just didn't feel right,' "Was it my imagination? or "Should I turn and take flight?" As he opened the door and beckoned me in, 'Nope,' no relief from my opinion, yet in I went regardlessly, but what a fool really, for as I did so, noting he, locks and bolted the door behind me, barring a quick escape or a safe egress to make.

Showing me into a room, appearing to serve duel purpose of medical and leisure, cluttered and dark the same as the other, with a couch looking oh so comfortable, with a 'throw' upon it, and I was sincerely hoping upon it he was not to ask me it sit. Yeah, he did not, as around a treatment table of green leather, and sturdy adjustable legs, manufactured in decades past, perched on tiny upholstered yet most uncomfortable stools we sat around its edge, and placed upon it, an array of children's books, and true to his word, drinking cups of warm herbal tea, we sat to read.

So much came to light though those conversations that he did not understand, and continually beckoned that him, I explain in depth in English that he may learn and understand, and gladly I did, but of a large chunk out of that hour it took, so what I learnt, was certainly not as much as I had hoped or anticipated, yet that deal struck, so I, to return the opposite end of the bargain, and accompany him, so of *la langue anglaise*, the English language he could rise in his capacity.

The *rðv* arranged, and so when the snow had been falling for yet another day in that city of love, a quite unusual occurrence I was later to learn, and as that cold damp air masked the day, I was to ring the old brass bell sighted to the right of those exterior doors, which fed my imagination of the harsh, but retrospectively wonderful world of the crinoline dresses and bonnets so fine, yet by contrast likely the heavy and soiled cloths worn by the servants and stable hands, as I waited in that modern 21st century to be buzzed in. Winding, walking up the staircase, on less than plush carpet underfoot, I contemplated, "My oh my, how I really don't want to do this," but I felt, integrity would not permit me, from holding up my end of the bargain, and so it was, the heavy door was opened and before me stood a sight certainly not seen, in any country I had visited before.

For he, a man of sixty-something years, tall, quite handsome in and elderly sort of way, with neatly cropped grey hair and quite debonair in and unusual way, wearing slacks in pale coral of heavy cotton and laundered most well, a tailored jacket, neutral in tone and beneath, revealing only slightly, a pristinely pressed shirt of cornflour yellow and gentle green stripes. "Gordy?" You may think so, and a style suiting a man much younger years, perhaps the same, yet somehow not at all, for impressively smart, elegant and his chosen colour palette, blended seemingly effortlessly in harmony, and perhaps maybe, only in France.

And declining to share an *apéritif* it was his heavy camel coloured duffel coat he reached for next, adjacent to the front door where we stood, with accent detailed fastenings, and with accent fastenings quite easy it appeared to perceive the quality of his item, and all normal, until he added that 'quaint essential' item, the scarf, in summer or winter, male or female, children too, a stable of almost every day, reaching for his scarf, in the brightest colour of coral, which in one swoop effortlessly it was wrapped around and around before just the tip was tucked inside his coat, and transformed, before me stood an 'oh so typically, unmistakably, Parisian.

A true Parisian, born and bread, his land, surely he'd be prepared with an umbrella, yet it was not to be, as into the cold damp air we walked, and as momentarily loosing balance upon the ice that lay below, of our bodies, from side to side, preventing a fall they did sway, and thank goodness onto the ground I did not fall, for that doggy-do-do, frozen then thawing in slush, to miss it, was a definite must. So ill prepared for the uncharacteristic snow storm that was to share it deluge of snow flakes on us that day, "Oh why, had I not learnt that skill of my grandad, to look at the sky and predict what it was to do for the rest of the day?" for surely then, my umbrella given to me by the hotel, I would not have left all alone, led against the door of my wardrobe.

Riding the *Métro* crossing the city underground to a different *Quartier*, petite suburb, we were to eat, *déjeuner*, lunch at a restaurant of Italian cuisine that my host that day had firmly recommended, though the last time he was there was a little unclear, as upon our arrival, everyone was gone, and boards were up at the windows. A lengthy walk ensued as treading the treacherous footpaths bombarded by the chilling wind to mask my face, throwing the snow to matt my hair and the fur of my antique coat, that only came to the length of my knees, so warm, not that I was not, nor was I taking time to embrace that new *arrondissement*, for my mind was not on yesteryear, perhaps for the *première*, first occasion, for its much greater concern was for my stomach moaning vigorously to be fed and warm, my chilling fingers and toes instead.

"Oh my" "What a sight!" As when I eventually did get inside, the wait was so worth it, as what a delight, as we entered a restaurant, traditional and frequented not by tourists, but by the local French, we were shown to the *salon salle à manger*, eating lounge, at the top of the angled staircase. The décor of sophistication was that of a long-gone era of *Louis XIV*, an intrusive elegance, with the ambiance so magnificent, it was hovering in the air, almost tangible it felt so real. The windows original, half domed in shape and diminished not from the lustre of the lavish drapes of self-patterned damask fabrics in rich greens and deep reds, and edged with a most ornate trim of colours and magnitude designed to impress, and at there circumference, the heavy guilt plaster trim, they nestled themselves within.

Seated, I remained in awe where I was sitting, my eyes darting everywhere, eager to take it all in, and "Oh" the *carte de menu*, menu, 'if only' that could have inspired the same, but alas not, the food as is the French cuisine, appears not to do it for me, and as I looked, read, had its contents translated to me, it was only a steak, most well done, the French consider it cremated apparently, the way the English have their meat cooked. And I would not normally order a dish with the ticket of the price of a steak, but having viewed all other menu options, only that was palatable to me.

And what was he, seated adjacent to me, to eat, well that was to be a dish of, 'lamb with carrots.' "Oh my" intrigue, as I could not imagine what such an unappealing dish would look like, and as it transpired at least to me, I was right.

Though in size I could not contemplate, as that oval shaped bowl, large and deep, was to be placed before he, not to serve the whole table, but just him to eat, and to one side lay a large rack of lamb and to the other, a huge portion of carrots, quite unappealing, sliced in cross-section which releases not, the sugar from its core, and absent sauces or garnish to jolly-it-up and make it more appealing, and amazingly, that man, healthily proportionate in weight, 'tucked in' and wolfed the whole lot down, resting only to sip on the fine wine which accompanied our meal, a sophisticated tradition I could live with and so quaint essentially, *français*, French. Yet moderately perplexed, as I observed more, for what my companion had just eaten, for an English food budget where I grew up, would be sufficient and expected at Sunday lunch, to feed a family of 4.

"It's never too late to become what you might have been"
~ George Elliot

From where my interest in architecture came I know not, but of old, *Rococo*, Georgian, Victorian, *Art Nouveau*, Art Deco, pre or post war, or maybe up to the 1970's all hold their own charm, but more of those of a century or two, grand in design, hold copious interest and much joy to my concepts. The lines, the curves, imagining who had lived in the building, my imagination runs to the industrial, economic, social and medical status and conditions of those who lived, worked or wondered the corridors in those by-gone days. The architecture of Paris, daily was a feast to behold, ceasing not to ignite, something in me that I knew not, a true dream to inspire or capture as in amazement I gazed in awe.

How fortuitous on that day to be accompanied by a true Parisian, who took me on a tour, those tiny nooks and crannies of those bygone streets, that today would not hold the width of one motor car, and doorways so low, they would only permit a child access without a necessary stoop, and the windows so tiny how on earth did they let in the light, and the wood and the brick, I wondered, twisted and warped, how were they still standing. And perhaps those lanes tucked away, amidst what seemed so normal and common place in that 11th year of the 21century, and where perhaps only the true locals know, and more, as he practiced his English with my interventions of correction and explanation, and he enlightening me of the aristocracy, kings, queens and historical dynamics, surrounding France and Paris, we were both able to learn, and learn and enjoy the day.

The snow, stopped falling for a while, a rest-bite as the pleasure was unravelling further of that days wonderful adventure, we had strolled nonchalantly across the open boulevards seeking the hidden gems of Pairs, of unknown spaces, through Paris's ancient quarters, of the narrow cobbled streets, so tangible as I stroked the walls, I could almost feel 'history' seeping out of the bricks, and rocks of those buildings as they almost fell into the streets below, as beckoning me to 'come hear our tales.' I felt a sense of privilege, as almost entering in what seemed, another person's life, a hidden treasure, an era of history, and I permitted myself to revel in such marvellous magnificence, a moment in time to be treasured, and to quote French, it was most, *très agreeable,* very agreeable.

My imagination was running wild, the ladies gowns, the flamboyance of *les hommes,* the men's breaches and frilly shirts in colours bright, and wigs long and curly, and should what I read be right, full of vermin, and poisons they put on their face, all in the name of fashion, of the social splendour and its constraint, its hypocrisy, and scandalous elicit liaisons, but likely all were better than the alternative, of starvation through the up most poverty.

It was such systematic demolishing of those *petites rues,* tiny streets and laneways between 1668 -1705 by *King Louis XII.* Yet what happened to all his subjects, homeless, displaced by such, or perhaps out of that squaller and those poor living conditions void of sanitation, perhaps serving of benefit, for others no need to succumb to the same in later generations, and effective to dissipate and kill disease, maybe they benefitted by being replaced in a healthier environment of greater probability and profitability, affording new options and choices that they had never dreamed or anticipated maybe theirs to share had further adversity first not come knocking at their door. And more, without such a job to be done, the wonderful impressive creation and outlay of the linier boulevards from a central location, crystal clear to see from a height above the city, and the regal parks that are held within, "Would it be possible to enjoy so much in Paris today, should that king, of the cities transformation, not begin?"

Our exploration and *promenade,* walk along the banks of the river *Seine,* with the disintegrating lining, to my antique fur coat, almost soaked, appearing more of a shaggy dog or stranded stray cat, than a piece of protective clothing, and still, no protective brolly, trying to huddled beneath any available canopy as that cafes we passed by, as the falling snow fell heavy and fast, clumps solidifying to the curls of my long blonde hair, hanging firm from my fringe to my shoulders, and when I tried to release it, defiantly it held, refusing to give up its position and fall to the ground, absolutely drenched, and as I fought the shivers I mused, "What a wonderful scene in a movie, perhaps a comedy, it would be"

The crisp white snow gave-way to sleet my muscles receiving an extra workout as I struggled to stay balanced, my feet soaking as my black boots of patent leather Spanish-made heeled boots, perhaps not suitable for the terrane cast beneath a thickened layer of greying slush we trod, had long since soaked through and my feet cold and soaking wet. My companion not so, as his, comfortable and his footing effortlessly secure as each step he took on the ever-increasing treacherous footpaths, with formidable boots in dark tan, with a thick and sturdy sole, most suitable for the snow, and those sleet filled puddles, on occasions unavoidable, yet held not that water to his leather boots as it melted and rolled off right away as if by magic. Coveting, I could have so easily done, "What's your secret?" I enquired, "Arhah," revealed, that elbow grease and boot polish was the way to go, "Mmmm," quickly I was to place that in my armoury for next time. Yet so cold and wet my feet had been for so long, and certainly the conditions in another time or place may dampened my spirit, but I was to permit nothing to stop me, as my emotions soared, nothing was to stop me, enjoying all of that Parisian day.

Lunch extending in extreme, more than anticipated or perhaps happy with, yet off to a museum of type, free to enjoy, and as I rounded the corner, "Oh my" I gasped, as a beautiful vista caught my eyes, as we walked across the small-boxed hedges uniformed in design of an 'Elizabethan-ish' styled garden, with views across to the grand maison and my imagination ran with apparent salivation, of whom and how people past used and frequented such a building. Along the path we happened upon a stone bench, carved but over the centuries, its sharp edges of design worn away, perhaps a place where courting couples may have rested under the watchful eye of their Chaperone, or perhaps not so fine, practicing on that garden, in duels, less sublime.

Yet to learn more was to be reserved for another day, for an interruption came upon me, with my senses all aglow, for the purest of snow underfoot, crunching, squeaking with every step, as init our footprints, the first to be left. And that white fluffy stuff that laid 5 inches or more on top of that bench, and never as a child had I shown such abandonment, nor ever been shown how, for I was not permitted to perform perceived childish acts, yet quickly, so spontaneously, outstretched my arms scooping it up in my eager hands, I made ball of it, then spontaneity escaped me as unsure what to do, yet excitement still in full throw, I did so, as hard as I could muster, into those bushes not so far away. OK, the distance wasn't that great, a real girly throw, but what was great was the sudden elation I held encompassed by joy, and permitted myself, unreserved to explore it, and as my heart smiled to join the one that lightened my face, I knew, of more, I truly desired of it.

Perhaps had a mini-miracle occurred by happen-stance magical moment, and an agreement with me I made in that moment of elation, that I was to be open to more joy and abandonment, where I was to permit my spirit to rise, casting aside those restraints of the past, which only, perhaps as my parents design were to aid to my demise. "No more" was I to be closed, for I was to be kind to me, I was to be a 'change-agent' not of geography, but internally, as I was vowed to become my own best friend, for I determined, a firm choice in that, so I may have the ability to hold freedom, joy, peace and the profit each of us may gain, from leaving the past behind and living in the present, for tomorrow is not guaranteed, and of groundhog day, it may not serve us well, for the bad we can learn from and the good we may excel in, and perhaps called the present for a gift it may provide to you and me.

The bad, of course, we try and escape, but the human brain is such, that it may be beaten down, or mislead or fooled, or neuropaths created, difficult without knowledge of them a better an improved way to be cultivated to serve us best. And true, research demonstrates the same, but here a little tale to enlighten to that which is significant, and a tiny ignition may strike a cord of recognition:

The elephant trapped in captivity, shackled to a tree, unable to break free, from the restrictions of a debilitating heavy and cumbersome chain, for as many times as the elephant tried, its strength and power, in its attempts to escape, rendered useless. Remaining a prisoner, it gave up trying to, as disheartened, downhearted as all amounted to nothing, then, an agreement it falsely decided to believe, that of which it was told, it was shown, that there was no alternative for he or she, and what they had, they had to suffer, for that was there 'lot in life,' to live in emotional pain and strife.

Loosing hope and looking only within, sadly submitting to and giving-in, its perceived fate halting future progress, as it failed to observe what was outside, that its situation and circumstances had changed, for its captor requiring it for another, had removed that chain and replaced it with only a piece of string, yet the elephant noticed not for it was dwelling only on what had been, and looking to the past and not the present for an opportunity for its freedom to be gleamed.

"Oh the possibility," as such little strength it would have taken to break that thin twine, yet the seeking wasn't sought, and the favourable coincidence was missed and the reward of freedom remained unclaimed. But of that real phenomenon of the elephant, refuse, categorically, to let it be you. For wisdom is power, and for your freedom, push on through all adversity today, so ground-hog day may go away as you grow, for tomorrow, you're life maybe your own, and your heart maybe free.

"The truth is rarely pure and never simple."
~ Oscar Wilde

Within the entrance of that magnificent ancient abode, a modern quite delightful and beautiful all the same and looking surprisingly smart surrounded by the old with which it sat in harmony, where my companion pointed out, how in French the step is female gender and the staircase, male, likewise a fruit tree, female, yet the orchard, male, amusing to him, but a conundrum to me, and although I *compris*, understood, little I still held onto hope that of the penny drop, or by osmosis, I would do so perfectly one day. For hope, we all need that.

Busyness of décor surrounded me, and such normally a sight would enthral, yet a little too tired at that point to muster up much enthusiasm, as the day was growing to be long, for so many hours had passed since our 'lunch' and I was done, over it, for spending what amounted to a days work in hours, talking broken English, trying to understand what was being spoken, then asking, explaining, restructuring sentences several times, choosing verbs, nouns and adjectives, in hope that my companion might just comprehend one. As evidentially at the luncheon table, his perceived proficiency in his surgery, when outside it, demonstrated to be excessively sim, and void of vast accomplishment.

Weary, I was most ready to call it a day, and to get home, well that was not to be difficult, for the *Métro* was never far away, and the surprise that of French for that day, to learn, I wanted to take no more part, or to teach English the same, but a much larger surprise was about to come my way. Perhaps I should have not mentioned to my companion that I was ready to call and end to our *rendezvous*, for that may have been why he gleamed his opportunity, as in a room of that museum of a kind we walked, while standing in one of the smaller rooms clad with darkened wood, absorbing the limited winter light, drafts of plans for the bridges and island of the *Seine*, city plans to enthral of a bygone century, I was absorbing it all and considering the equivalent in today's society of proposals, drafts and funding, for the reasons why's and why not's of how the result eventuates.

Suddenly, my concentration was thwart as I felt a hand gently but firmly pressed onto my butt, not by a swift mistake but purposefully and provocatively, dare I say seductively, proceeding toward my hip one smooth movement as if practiced many times. And with speed lightening I rapidly moved away from he, who was to be my non-companion, yet of his unprovoked touch, he remained steadfastly by my side, as though, nothing had happened.

It was one of those bizarre moments where I caught myself, "What! Did that really just happen or was it my imagination?" Perplexed, shocked, for I had no idea what that man must have been thinking of to do such a think, yet of course, at a instinctive level I knew what must be on his mind, but then I knew not why, for certainly I had given him not an ounce of a notion that I was available for any situation romantic, certainly not sexual. Yet it opened a door for me to consider, what was 'troubling me' of those gentle nudges, niggles and notions were for a specific reason, all about warning me, regarding being with he, to save me had just popped up and said hello.

Calling an end to the day, and retuning to the 9eme *arr* it was a hop, skip and a jump to that traditional *bâtiment,* building with its fine façade and even finer impressive solid pair of wooded entrance doors, reaching some nine feet tall, adorned by polished brass finery and boasting proudly the exuberance of Paris past and Paris present, and as I waited politely as he that soon to be ex-companion of increasing speed, punched in his code onto the contrasting modern silver keypad, pushing open the door and beckoning me to go on in, and as I viewed inside, and considered those bygone days where the horse drawn carriages would have rested as its occupants of wealth and finery disembarked, secure from the dirt of the streets, pathways, riffraff and even sunshine, but "What of I? Was I simply a piece of riffraff, which he considered in his refined establishment he was to concur?" What! "Was he kidding?" I don't think so.

I was not as impressed with me, as I believe, he was in he, so rejecting his proposed invitation I took a step back and when verbally being pushed to accept, I took a stance that really I had no need to do, which was make an excuse, rather than firmly saying, "No thank you, I absolutely choose not." And although the experience of Albert was not far in the rear view mirror for a quick recollection and regrouping of 'what not to do,' remaining a slow to catch on 'people pleaser', I harnessed not the strength of commitment for the good of me that I owed and deserved of the same, as reluctantly, he cajoled and persuaded and I gave-in, as days of old, surrendered and did his beckoning and not mine, against what I sincerely desired and wanted to.

Discomfort I felt in the extreme as I ascend that stairwell, taking little note of that which surrounded me, but only the torment that was rising up inside of me, with questions and reservations of, "What the heck are you doing, run! Do it now and do it fast." But "No," as mindlessly I ascended the Parisian spiralling staircase, with threading carpet, conscious of every step I took, with my senses heightened and aware. The scale of discomfort rose, tipping off the scale, praying for God to protect me, yet amazingly, still I trod upward to his apartment, perhaps simultaneously, as he hailed his anticipated, achieved goal.

I understood not my actions. "Was I brain washed forever, always to do someone else's bidding?" or "Was there a time when I was to be free, and when was that really going to be?" and of that unwise, unfortunate unpleasant, pre-programming, provoking unwelcomed and debilitating re-occurrences, by any other name, a curse, "How many lessons did I have to experience, before I was to sever those connections and render it null-and-void, for the absolute good and love for and of me, to break free?"

Those reflective thoughts too slow, me, too slow to respond, as into his apartment I so reluctantly walked, my stomach feeling increasingly twisted with angst, as he took me in the surgery portion of his apartment, before disrobing from his chunky winter clothing, as he beckoned me to do the same. My comfort zone gone-clear, the boundaries had been pushed to their limits as I wondered why it had taken so long for me to work out, I was not in the wrong place at the wrong time. At last, the mind engaged and comprehended the present with the past, a revelation took place in my brain as I boldly but carefully declaring, "I am going to leave now." The surprise, not concealed on his face, "But I thought we will spend the evening together." "No." I succinctly replied.

'Bla-bla-bla' then spilled from his mouth, as if not wanting to give up his prize or persuasion, yet my antenna fully alert, I remained stood, ready leave, in a safe stance, ensuring nothing barred me from my exit, as I precisionaly backed toward it. Then, as if by magic his intention revealed, the key to my subliminal discomfort, as he like a young stallion, his stance strong, his persona proposing to be provocative, as he portrayed that aptitude displayed of a man far less in years than those on the cusp of twilight, perched himself in position to the edge of the treatment couch, posed, supporting his weight on his right leg with the other provocatively cast across its corner, his hands clasped across his crutch, as if a stallion taming a young filly. The stop-press breaking news, well it would have been to him, that would have rapidly wiped that suspecting grin of success from his face, and the sway and tilt of his head, it would have rectified, as he was to reveal, of what he perceived to show, he was neither.

But still, he was not deterred as in propelled motion he tried to entice me, "Perhaps a drink, water, tea, wine, you'd like to sit?" Refusing all, confirming, "No I'm just fine, I'm leaving." He persistent, "Why are you not staying?" fixing his gaze, as if a rabbit caught in the headlights, looking intently so, as if pre-determining a positive response, his imposing eyes, raised eyebrows and fixed grin of expectancy he spoke with proficiency, "Massage?" He delivered the question with a tilt of his head, and the leer adolescent, as he beckoned me toward that medical couch, from my distant position, at the opposite side of that large room.

My persistent staunch refusal received a reply, spoken in a quiet voice of condescension, "That's a shame." Perhaps his action in a perceived attempt for me to change my mind and say, "Oh yeah all right then!" Striking though, amazingly so, his expertise and apparent comprehension of exactly how well he knew, how to execute and pronounce *that* specific phrase. Certainly, of equal competency of the English language, I had not witnessed from him that day, when I not in his environment and completely free on neutral territory, with my mind switched on and my own eyebrows raised, I considered with humour, "Just how many times had he practised that one?"

> *"Believing in yourself is an endless destination.*
> *Believing you have failed is the end of your journey."*
> *~ Sarah Meredith*

Physical harm perpetuating in my life, progress appearing illusive and so difficult to make, lessons so difficult to learn, as history repeated itself in a procession, forever parading past and including me. With ever expanding queries arising of, "Why me, why again? What did I do this time to cause that this time?" and "Why did I not recognise it and end it?" or more "Prevent it?" Though maybe, that's just me. Relieved, I was to get-out of that Kene's house, safe, free from harm, but was that threat perceived potential or real? But more importantly, "Why did it take me so long to listen to my instinct, when I was at so much potential risk of that answer being inadvertently imposed upon me?"

I know I am a 'job in progress,' but of 'having a clue,' 'if only' that format for me had always been true forthright and wise, with strength and self-worth, but no, for I knew not of any of those attributes, self-serving and quite rightly so, so there, 'once upon a time' I was enter into an agreement with anther which was to cost me heavily, for longevity.

As so many moons ago, and 'if only' there were more, sufficiently so, that I was able to forget that gross error of my judgment, ignorant of my instinct, only added to the force to aid another's perpetuating plan, unravelled and executed, well, that was almost me, as my emotions were to be effectively destitute and forever alter the pathway of my life, where of the same, nothing was to be again.

+It was at the hospital where I worked, the one mounted on the hill, where I had few friends, went few places and really, did little of anything. But in that scenario, I believe I did not suffer too much unrest, for I was safe, no father to harm me, and that in my life, provided sufficient comfort and grace.

+Then it was a kitchen porter, a young man, who took a shine to me, and each time I passed the door, he would leave his post, and down the corridor with me he would walk, asking that I go out with him, but my answer always the same, no thankyou, without a boyfriend, I'm just fine as I am.

+Was it my genuine disinterest in him, or my instinct by any other name, that subconsciously persisted in my refusal of the same? And the answer from so many decades ago, amounting to three, I remember not, but either way my attitude was saving me from harm, though I did not know it way back then.

+So eventually an acceptance was made and an agreement of a date and place agreed, and my fate right there sealed, as 'clubbing' I went with him, and wayback then, streetwise, I could never be accused, but even I was able to recognise, of his friends he introduced me to, are bad people I quietly mused.

+It was not late but it was time to leave, of whose idea I do not recall, we returned to my apartment where, blindly perhaps, but I saw no reason not to invite him in for coffee and a chat, a bit of kissing may have likely ensued, but of more, on a first day, nothing else I designed to eventuate.

+So far so good, all normal as perceived to be, but definitely I should have given more credence to how 'birds of a feather flock together' or 'lay with dogs and you'll catch flees,' and so it was to be, of that badness in that club I saw and felt, of his evil capacity, at his vicious hand, I was a to be dealt.

+As we kissed, he called me by a name of another, and as I stopped and enquired who she was, most angry he became, and of the man who chased me for weeks for a date, he disappeared, as before me stood, a man I did not recognise, of persona of the same, calculating, raging he was about to start his sickening game.

+In that split-second on that day *everything* changed, and my life was no longer ever to be the same, as a five and a half hour ordeal unfolded before me that night, as he teased, taunted, and tormented as if I, a helpless animal and he, instigating its crippling plight, with his cruel and callus nature erupting in sight.

+I knew I was in trouble of a huge kind, yet still after he had stripped me down, I tried to escape and run for safety, yet only as far as the bathroom did I get, before he caught up with me, and as the green wallpaper of bamboo leaves faded to grey, he explained what he would do to me if I failed to cooperate.

+Disturbed, I shivered with cold, as I looked up to his height of a foot or more taller than I, and I felt his grip from his over developed muscles tighten on my upper arms, pulling them up uncomfortably high, as my toes barely touched the floor, and speaking, his lips pert in defiance and disgust, with his rage out of control and about to explode.

+I could have almost been sick but no time for that, as he dragged me back to my bedroom, he threw me on my bed, was I limp or ridged, or angry or scared, perhaps all of the above throughout those ordeal hours where he captured me, refusing to leave, refusing to let me go, then as the real trouble began, it was my conscious mind that from my body did leave, as he did what he did to me.

+ Helpless, I remained; I knew it had begun, but I knew not, when it would end.

+My mind shutdown as I lay pushed down on my back, and with each thrust the pain shooting past my navel, as the tears fell effortlessly rolling down my face and falling onto my pillow, as he, shrieked, "Put your arms around me!" Yet exempt from muscle tone, too weak, my mind un-penetration-able to his command as they fell harshly all around me, so he shouted more ferociously.

+Fearing for my life, for I thought, it more likely I be dead than alive when he was to leave, then my mind, as if giving information to a hollow vessel, it reminded me that not a soul knew I'd gone out with him that night, and my murder, I perceived he was to get away with, and so oddly I thought of Z-Cars, and Dixon of Dock Green, of 2 decades ago, then for DNA and his conviction, I dragged my finger nails across his back.

+Quickly; he raised the weight of his body off me, angrily he spat demanding to know what I was doing, my life, all I could think, I want to live, to preserve my life, 'life' is what I chose, so I replied that, which I have never since been able to reconcile myself with, the words I spoke, I'm enjoying it that's why I did it.

+Eventually! He was done! He withdrew and removed his body weight off me, and then, I was limp, wasted, not a cell in my body worked or responded, my soul had gone somewhere else, as had every other substance that would normally hold a working functional body together, had shut down, my life intact, but lifeless was my body, and he, he was still not gone.

+I still remember what he was wearing and as he put his clothes back on, I stared really, nowhere eventually he walked down my corridor to the front door, and I heard it shut behind him, and lifeless, I just laid there, then suddenly, a note of recognition, of what he had done hours before, pretended to leave when he had not, then jumped out from behind the hall wall, so quickly I flew up, or as I perceived, and of the safety catch turned it completely on.

+Another flash of concern quickly struck like a ton of bricks falling on me, was he just pretending, was he hiding again, was he to jump out and push me backwards down the length of the corridor, as he wore clothes and me non, and he also wore, or was it war, a large smile, sickly smirk of superiority of depicting his dominance.

+Was he lying in wait to do it again, I needed to know, so bravely I took what courage I could muster, I checked behind the living room door and inside the pantry too, to make sure he had gone, for primed, out of the front door I was to run. All appeared to be clear absent from him, but was I safe, and would I ever be safe again.

+And with all doors secured, realizing not, that my life had forever changed, work, morning, my waking up response, with my work ethic at its height, with perhaps I, in shock, or totally numb, yet feeling nothing inside, I set my alarm for an hour later, as I crawled beneath the sheets of that bed, my bed, where I had just been raped, before and early shift to try and get some sleep.

My clothes, "What of them?" Still I remember exactly what I was wearing, the colours the style, the height of my heals and the delicate details on my shoes, but "Burn my clothes?" That was to be "No." For "How?" I do not know, but I wore them again, and a shower, to cleanse oneself, crying, screaming or scared and silent, all seen on TV shows, there was none, not ever, as the scars muted hidden from view, as I mutated to form a newer model of me, not perfect, not even improved, only transmuted you see.

And in that Manchester hospital, located in the north of the city, all else remained the same, yet on occasions of nursing situations when the need arise, and I requested to collect lab results, requiring to walk past that doorway which was to haunt me of the association that lay behind, that of the rapist or lingered and worked there, for there was no escape, as so perpetually life went on. As still, no one I did tell, of "Why I'd rather not go, across the breadth of the hospital." And for sure, a great advocate for my patients I may be, but to ask for something for myself, still, I believed I should not, for unworthy was I, and they may shout and scorn at me, as was my father's ever command as he spoke trough gritted teeth, "Don't you dare ask questions just do as your told! And do it NOW!" Shouting furiously, "Or else, you will suffer the consequences!"

In my life, at the age of less than a quarter of a century, already weary having suffered more than enough, I may have made a decision with myself and chosen, 'too shut up, put up and be quiet and just get on with it,' whatever anyone else wanted, perhaps for peace, or just simply to *preserve*, my *life*!

"When you haven't forgiven those who have hurt you, you turn back against your future.
When you do forgive you start walking forward"
~ Tyler Perry

"Are you alright?" "What's wrong with you?" Came colleagues resounding yet cold questions, and strangely odd, as never so much an enquiry before form that team where normally I was banished to its outskirts and ignored. And then the Charge Nurse, he commences the same questioning, though I did not relent, refuting raising their accusations that there was anything wrong with me, off to the Occupational Health (OH) department he sent pointedly sent me, and for true, I was so used to trauma, and perhaps still suffering a proportionate degree of amnesiac-shock, I had no idea, my hear my mind my body, had shut-down.

Yet my colleagues of that day, never ever did speak of it again, so I have no idea what it was about my persona that troubled them so, but I, do remember, I was so utterly bitterly, so very icy cold, and there was no way I was able to warm myself up, and my head it hurt so much, and my posture, bent over, so weak I could hardly stand, and mild painkillers I was given in OH, but promptly they were vomited up. Invited to lie down on the bed in that prefab building, to rest, to settle. Really? "No! Not possible!" I simply couldn't do that, I couldn't stay still, I couldn't close my mind, it was wide open, bear to the world, or "Was that my soul, that had almost been killed?" as from somewhere inside of me, I think I wanted to escape, but my energy depleted, my body, unable to participate.

My speech became slower, until a mumble I think was my only response, at refuting that there was "Something wrong?" yet eventually I gave in, to a notion that something bad had happened, but of say the word, and call it by name, not caught in my throat, not even my chest, but somewhere already buried deep within of the rage and the pain, the phrase, the term, the heinous term, well deserved, 'rape' my vocal cords unable to muster the sound, and unable to pass my lips.

Nothing more the nurse could do, to the male OH Physician she sent me, and there I sat, so freezing cold, I recall my body, beginning to fall and form a ball, as he stood so aloof and tall, mean and harsh in his persona, with his pale skin and grey hair matching his grey suit, delivered testy question "Do you want to speak to the Police?" and with my answer "No," for "Why would I?" I knew what that man had done to me for no reason, so to give him a reason to attack me again, well that was to be negative, and I was going to give him non. And with my reasons, the physician he sat down, and coldly without feeling said to me, "Well go home, get some rest, get some sleep." "Yeah! Cos that was to be easy," in my-own-bed! Where the rape took place! "Oh my" as though that was to be on my agenda, for "How could that make me feel any better, to try and rest in that place where the attack was conducted?" not at all conducive with sleep, rest or recovery. Though a life spent all alone, I had no friends or family to call upon, no one to share my burden, nowhere else to go; so his instructions completed and done.

My skirt lengths grew and nothing again would ever be the same, and colours worn became more dreary, the garments greater size than needed to be as my body shape to disguise, so much that sufficed as any amount of joy in my world declined, and only hate and distain that I felt for myself in significance rose, as I felt shame, and disgust, and of seek help, no, for I knew to that I should, plus this was back in 1982, and not much was considered way back them other than, "Oh, you went out with him willingly, you were wearing a short skirt, well you must have been asking for it."

And of that I could not, would not face, and more, I felt disgrace towards, that's right, me. And psychiatry, well I didn't know of any of that in-spite of being a nurse, helping, benefitting the emotional deprivation as I had suffered, I knew not that it could be utilised for such, so I sought it not, internalising all that pain, the shame, that it was my fault, where for decades it laid, concealed in secret, undisturbed, unspoken, only viewing myself as guilty, and condemning myself for the same, as there only festering, trapped, unwavering, it all remained.

The emotions, a burden to bare, as it was to be in Auckland in my 3rd year of living there, when that trauma suddenly one day, out of that proverbial blue, came tapping at me and shouting my name, as a dormant volcano beginning to erupt, it was to cause one heck of a hullabaloo. Wiser, stronger, and more aware of what in the public domain was able to help me, I sat in distress on the end of the telephone line while I spoke to a young lady with great empathy at the Rape Crisis Centre, in New Zealand, where I was able to openly seek advice on that which for 2 decades had been buried deep within me.

"Oh my" 'I spilt the beans' as we say around Blackpool in England, not reliving the scenario chapter and verse, but asking "Why, I don't understand, why is it effecting me now?" And so interested and relieved in her responses, as a gentle but informative tone she did respond, "Between 15-30 years is a frequent time frame for recognizing abuse, and seeking help for the same, when the mind is able of its pain, to contemplate, to recognise and begin dealing with such." "Oh my, could 'release' be added to that?" I was to consider much later, that perhaps then, leaving trauma behind, I had commenced my first steps along my path to recovery. But so much more, my mind began to settle, for what a relief, as seriously, *at last,* I was living within the realms of possibility, of *normality!*

"Freedom is what you do with what has been done to you."
~ Jean-Paul Sartre

"Distractions? "No." "Perfections?" "Yes." Of all what I was able to control, became my daily-deal, my prescription for life, blinkered, I submerged myself in my career, wandering up its ladder, and my accomplishment, and how proud I was of me, I hadn't paused to recognize, for true, I didn't even know I should, until that day, when a person from my work for something I had done or achieved, and I'm not sure it was even work related, but clear as I heard it right now, he spoke, that in truth, at that bygone age of my 30-something years, never did I remember another to say, to me… "I'm proud of you!" "Wow!" Stopping momentarily with total surprise I asked, of he, "Why do you say such a thing?"

Perplexed he quickly explained, and rhymed-off as I listened surprise, of the positive difference I had made within the factory where I worked, but how amazing that he had noticed my accomplishments, when I thought I didn't have any, and certainly not expecting to receive praise or basic acknowledgement for anything, as my norm, well simply, it didn't happen. Yet how humongously grateful I am to he, of that seed that he planted that day in me, "I thank him," for it travelled an amazingly long and wonderful way.

A particular portion of my work remit, were Risk Assessments where 'designing problems out,' were a major function of my working life, and those I transposed to my personal one, and other nips and snippets of work knowledge too, with a notion reinforcement from my youth, 'I did what I could with what I had,' and more kudos, when the price tag, was zero. So money I was to save on not going to the gym, as a new routine I set upon to add my previous one, of never using elevators but always utilizing the stairs, of walking instead of catching the bus or *Métro* where I was able, to park at the furthest spot away in the car park, where possibly my car was safer away from those supermarket trolleys, and walk just that little bit further to where I wanted to be. An 'incidental' exercise, it is termed as a phrase, but best of all, what I like about it, its easy to achieve, and completely free, while becoming a better *connaisseur* of my personal safety.

So the *Métro* became my new source of exercise, up and down the copious stairs, as escalators rarely sited there, as on the train, never sitting but always standing, for cleaner I believed for sure, yet most importantly by not holding on to the rail, but steadying myself by creating an 'A' frame for my posture, that which gives us strength with my knees gently bent, and our feet apart, free muscle building exercise, almost passively so I was able to enjoy free, as they had to work so masterfully to hold me up as the train jeered and jerked around the corners and in and out of the stations, and "Where I got the idea from?" Well, shortly before my departure and sweeping Melbourne, that latest craze, 'vibration boards' available in bespoke exercise boutiques that were popping up everywhere, yet for me in Paris, it was every night and every morning, that as the carriage rattled and cajoled from left to right beneath my feet and "Yeah, fun;" a challenge and a happy distraction of *gratis*, free exercise, before I was to face another daunting demoralizing day, at that Parisian university, *la Sorbonne*.

Another day, another opportunity for the same, then as I alighted at station *Raspail* just a short jaunt until at my habitual haunt I arrived that wonderful respite Exyi, a café of healthy cuisine, with most pleasant staff, and where to rest, before cutting through the snow, new levels of exercise arose, as my umbrella precisely positioned to the side of my wardrobe door, most useful there with it snowing heavily outside, it was running the best I could, with the muscles of my legs primed, to prevent me, slipping upon that terribly slushy laden ground, that perhaps underneath, concealed, ice. Determined to stay strong on feet, with my pace accelerated as my black canvas backpack bounced up and down, more fitness was achieved, my, *faire du sport*, making sport. And with positive affirmations, "I am staying safely on my feet," "Yeah!" I thought way to go to reverse the thinning of my bones, a diagnosed condition prior to leaving Australia, and all for free and all void of pharmaceuticals.

"Lack of activity destroys the good condition of every human being, while movement and methodical physical exercise save it and preserve it."
~ Plato

I can walk all day long, I can cycle half of any day, and through each day I may dance endlessly, and ice-skating with unbridled zest the same, though of ice hocky, a sport, really I would have none. How fortunate I believe I am, to have discovered what works for me in the realms of exercise, for my mind, my body type and its natural capabilities, through contemplation and observation of what feels right, in short discovery, and when doing it, creates not, severe effort but resounding joy, so thankfully I, through trial and error I have learnt to recognize what suits me best, and of it, I refuse to push in any direction and not push against it. True, not a participator but a voyeur I tend to be, but in the realms of dance and ice-skating I make an exception, so what thrill, as I was to see, a ring full of ice, imported in, an annual event alongside the river *Seine*, enface *Hotel de Ville*, and beneath the huge Christmas tree, draped with baubles and lights all around, as that Parisian town welcomed Christmas once again.

Music played all around, with one of my favourite eras, the 1970's sounding out, such joy, and those French voices, they murmured and buzzed but did not shout, as happiness, so tangible, it could almost be touched, as those children, both young and old in their rented ice-skating boots, raced around and around, their glee depicted on their cheerful faces. "Oh what a joy," for although I did not venture onto the ice, of the ambiance I absorbed it all, and true enjoyed a good little shuffle with my feet as I placed myself in prime position to hear the best from that sound system, and as I looked all around, it was behind me that I was enthralled, for there was more, the accent lighting shining on the finery of the historic architecture behind me.

How idyllic, an euphoric moment, for all my senses integrated and ignited, and as I chose to linger for more than a while, in not much of a hurry to go anywhere else, the colours bright of scarves and hats flying quickly around the circumference and those little girls and boys, and some of teenage years, giving not up the fight, to stay on their feet, as so often they fell to the ground, and soaked up the water into their clothing now sodden from the melting ice, and of all the apparel they wore to keep them warm, of most use and most obvious, was the smile they wore across each petite face.

With peaceful observation of those who were in front of me, for quite easy to see, when just the time is taken to look, the ones who excelled were not the greatest skaters on the ice, yet, they were the most fearless, I'm guessing most optimistic, and believed in their own ability for success, or the very least in their commitment to themselves, that they were not to waste their time but maximize the most of it and have a jolly good one. And true, as I smiled all the way through, those who were most wet, fell down the most, and one little girl, she was so determined, so gutsy and forthright, with her little boots, at her age of nine or ten she did not realise, they were totally on the slant and really not working at all well, but she appeared to care not, and certainly feared not, for racing past those boys, with a spirit of eagerness and joy that could move mountains, every time she fell down, eagerly, in a flash, she got up one more time, and again, began.

What a great and forthright spirit I contemplated to see her through life, I hope she travels far, completely far as she desires to do, and of those others who were not quite as courageous or fortified, I hope for them too, for skills they learn well of facing fear and pushing right on through, then, the best life they can possibly have, will be afforded to, every-one.

Such a fortunate happenstance, of meeting a man one afternoon walking through the hotel lobby, as I enquired of him to assist me with directions, and somehow through our conversation and invitation, with, a deal was struck, for mutual satisfaction, as I go ice-skating with he, and he comes salsa dancing with me, and hay-presto, there I found myself that very evening, on the banks of the lake in Toronto, on an outdoor skating-ring, lit by lights of huge illumination, such stark contrast to the darkness of the surrounding nights sky, and there I asked for my instructions, where to place my weight and how to bend my knees, and how far my stride should be, to ensure my best opportunity to stay on my feet, and 'oh what joy' was my reward, with a good job done, and "How do I know?" As quite surprised at my accomplishments, my companion told me so.

"Wow" it made my spirit soar so instantly to be back on that ice, for short of 4 decades since I was last at the ice-skating ring at Blackpool, to participate as a teenager in a six-week school course. "Oh my" I had not imagined how I enjoyed it so, and how I seamed to have missed it the same, and I began to wonder, when working Manchester, why did I not travel from north to south to enjoy the same at Altringham, but then again, on public transport, of hours taken to arrive maybe many, and of buses the same, so perhaps, not an excuse, but a little bit of a valid reason.

Then, life, it just keeps on going, with habits often by default evolving or forming, void of conscious decision making, and when we don't check ourselves, so quickly the years can pass, and it can be gone. But "Was I to let that happen to me again, or was I to make effort to rewrite the book, the story of my life, to edit, and of that story make changes, deleting what serves me ill, fails to fill my desires or enables me to move on to a brighter future to be?"

So "Was age a barrier to conform to?" or a "Catalyst to create from?" and really, "Is it possible to teach and old dog new tricks?" For I was to discover, for even though I didn't know it, in Paris, huge changes were taking place inside of me, of energy to make seize or muster, of the possibility to change what I'd always done, as on the *Boulevard Montparnasse*, I watched almost in awe groups of Frenchmen, on their rollerblades, neat attire matching their metallic grey hair, that remained perfectly in place, as in a fury with a certain panache, exuberating their energy as they flew past, with their expert trickeries and balance precision, as curving and weaving they nipped in and out between the thongs of tourists and shoppers, often in those peek hours. I so enjoyed the vision, it inspired me to do more, but with an injured knee from a fall, and before I departed Melbourne, thinning bones was my diagnosis, so maybe I wasn't going to take it up that day, but, still I remember how that vision as they rushed by as my eye down the street followed them, with an influx of emotion, "I want to do that," perhaps I can find some common ground: I could get the old-fashioned kind with 4 wheels, and get a couple of those sticks they use for power-walking, then with my skateboard protective gear on, *"Voila!"* surly, "I will have a valid prescription for a most excellent job done?"

> *"Those who think they have not time for bodily exercise*
> *will sooner or later have to find time for illness."*
> *~ Edward Stanley*

The *Métro*, unless there was a *grève*, strike, true, there were a few of those, all ran pretty easily, but not the same to be said for my escalation accomplishing *la langue française*, for I understood nothing of what the professor spoke, but prevent my enjoyment and positivity of holding high hopes of learning French well and easily, well, that appeared of no substance, as dream to come to fruition, time was running out with increasing anxiety, too quickly. My happy thoughts of how like a jigsaw each piece of my perceive perfect puzzle was to add to the next, and build into a beautiful elaborate picture of all that I desired to accomplish, though as one day rolled into another, it appeared not anytime soon that such a hope, a dream, a desire was not to come to fruition. Dare I give-in, dare I give-up?" Even though all the odds and evidence and my health was stacked against me, "Absolutely not!" But then, my musculoskeletal system, complex in its injuries and affecting my cognition, "Was I to accept that as a true barrier to learning or was it a 'cop-out' making excuses?"

Yet I hung onto my memory of that French lady I met in Melbourne, how she complimented me on my pronunciation, and the man when I holidayed in France, he did the same thing, so really, of my plan of A, it never even occurred to me anything could go wrong. But "Was I unwise not to have a contingency plan?" To have burnt my bridges behind me, that would, I guess be possible to build up again, but on my heart for my future, that was not in my mind, on my cards. I mean really, "Was I so easily fooled or perhaps foolish to placed my whole future upon so little, with the words of just a couple of people?" Well, it appeared actually, that evolved as, "Yes."

Soon my joy of "Oh Paris" was to be overrun by concern of my simply, not getting the job of the learning the French language done, as I slipping behind, so I approached the professor post-class, where I apologized for asking so many questions during lessons, and she to me replied, "That is normal, it is part of the process." Such Relief! Continuing she explain, that through my questions, she could see by the facial expression of the other *camarades de classe*, that they were glad for clarity, "Phew!" Reassurance! *"Pas de problem,"* "No problem."

More so, she told me of a tale of a lady from USA, who moved to Paris, 'to start a new life' who apparently like me, had concerns, as she neither was able to speak the language, who had no home, no job, yet her story had a happy ending, as just 3 years on, she successfully accomplished all 3. Wow! So then, reassured I reasoned, "Well why not me?" Her story gave hope and reignited, a flicker of that flame that everything was to be alright, "It was just an adjustment, a hiccup I was in, and I would come out of it, "Right?" Arrh, well that answer didn't scream "Yes," though sadly that hope appeared not long lived, as my anticipated happy ending was not arriving, and that reassurance I was given, slipping fast through my fingers, and the light at then end of the tunnel, "Was it to be a beacon, or the lights of an oncoming and racing train?"

"Faith is putting something to the test.
It is better to try to do something and fail, than try to do nothing and succeed."
~ Dr Robert H Schuller

Competency I struggled with day on day as I battled to learn *la langue française*. I found myself contemplating the initial *la Sorbonne* professor I met, who against my genuine and turns out to realistic concerns of "Oh don't worry, its funny, to take a photo, at the course beginning, the students faces anxious, then at the end, its all gone." "My oh my," I wondered, "Why did I listen to her and not stick to my own guns? Why was I swayed?" and really, "Does she get taught to say such things to increase the universities coffers?" For really, my deposit was only taken at that time, and I could have just walked away loosing only a few hundred dollars and not the thousands that were to follow.

My determination extending through those 12 weeks, where I sat determined to excel at least to some degree, where I presumed shut I sit before that green-board, for those 5 hours per day, I rationalised that something I would learn, but my conception, it appeared thwart. My resolution high, but my ability low, yet unless I had committed to those 25 hours per week of submersion in that learning opportunity, "How was I ever to know?" Condemningly, I compared myself, to those who appeared to speak French with a pronunciation most fine, and a comprehension the same, all of what was being said and taught; while lost, me, loosing the thread, falling behind and loosing the perceived, language battle.

Only retrospectively was I to realise, of those comparisons so unjust, for I was comparing my worst with their best, ignoring any fields of expertise or specialities that I may have excelled, and any good I may have done, not least of all surviving, a childhood where in enormous quantities I was placed in deprivation with no place to run, no place to turn. Yet somehow, of all of that past history, I got through, my emotions in Paris, a catalyst to confront of painful change.

As onto a slippery slope I stumbled, and "What was that noise I heard?" It was the whistling wind that flew right past me, as I slide to the depths of the bottom of that ditch, where no light survived, only the density of that darkened place, where everyone who entered my life had resigned me to that place, as I believed *their* words and behaviours of condemnations about who I was and only be who *they* told me I could be, of how I should stay where I slipped to, and not dare to presume to get-up, or try to get-out of that place, because in they told me of only that I was only worthy. Their curses spoken against me, became corrosive over years, seeping extra harm and although I fought it everyday, what they said formed a deadly silent weapon which on the inside, I must fight everyday.

Alone, deprived and isolated is where they put me, just as everyone of *them* perceived I should be, and to muster the strength to dispel and fight *their* perceptions, *they* daily cast upon me by all *their* words and deeds, crated false beliefs of which I didn't recognise *them* by name, as over the years, I'd absorbed *their* curses as my truths. It was not easy, for a while under the pressure I was to buckle, almost breaking under the strain, as in Paris that most beautiful city where I was so pleased to be, yet so much was not right, *they* who were supposed to love me, *their* critical and contrary curses of love, were curtailing my progression as what I thought about myself was relapsing, as I reverted to that of old but active default mechanism of all they told me. "Oh my" I found it is it true, "You can travel anywhere in the world, but, you'll never get away from you!"

I grew in sadness at the cavernous separation between my *camarade de classe*, an and as they had husbands, fiancé's to help, friends and relations, only an electronic moment away, and I felt more alone, more isolated in comparison each day. Nor did they have issues and worries surrounding health insurance, accommodation, financial issues, a history of compounding regrets or more, with no worries to knock at their door, as comfort love and stability was theirs still to adore. And my gladness for them was tarred, as illuminating that dark place, my sad awareness, that my in my life never had such fortune prevailed Though too late, for a concept to consider, amidst all that treachery of torment worrying me, of exactly, 'who we hang-around with is who we will become in 5 years from now,' so really, was I to worry, or say, "Bring it on," for was I not then ready, for all that they enjoyed, of prosperity of love and peace, and in both, to behold?"

I was standing against 'all the odds,' in-spite of them, and on my own and under my own strength, I had achieved as much as I had, but really, I was so weary, of always finding myself in a battle of forced self-preservation, for I so desired to cease fight, for growing in capacity I knew I was worthy of more, to live a life, not consumed, by the replacing of copious bandaids, but of the past to refute, and their requirement to eradicate, I was never to give-in, but I was to accelerate my capacity for so much more, as I skated towards a life of hope and pleasure to be absorbed.

Another day, another dollop of free exercise, yet as the *Métro*, carriage trundled along, I was not singing a song, as desperately persuading myself, to stay on that carriage and not get off, "Yes," that became my daily mantra, as stations I passed of *St. Michelle* and *St. Germain*, my haunts of favour, for how amazingly *facile*, easy it would have been to do, if not for consideration of that huge waste of money posing not the opposite of good value, but a case of throwing good money after bad, would have eventuated that scenario, so determined was I, that at the very least, surely osmosis would kick-in and sometime soon, surely I would learn something.

"Oh my" what a new and great insight was to evolve, of why children play truancy, for sure, emotionally daunting and spiritually demoralizing in excess, to daily visit the same place, void of hope of acceleration in that which is placed in front of you that which you are supposed to learn, but for some reason or other, it proves absolutely impossible to do. And dare I say, I held a new respect, for those who believed truancy as a last resort, when all else had failed and their spirit crushed, or perhaps criticism from teachers or taunts in the playground, unsupported, they could bare no more, so truancy was seemingly all that was left for them to do.

A concept I believe to be true, money spent on education, contrives real value, but what I was to learn, amongst so much it was to transpire, that huge portions of discernment are required, when you're about to invest of time and money, we need to most certainly consider, not only our true resources but our personalities and capabilities too. And of this concept I was too late to learn, as the money invested in that which was to service me, but in fact, my investment, which it evolved, was not, only serviced me, as I appeared increasingly to fail, with an added portion of misery. As I contemplated of how many battles I had lost and wondered the number of those that lay ahead of me, before 'reward' and 'success' transfer to my future companions? And I, I *'win the war!'*

"The habit of persistence is the habit of victory"
~ Herbert Kaufman

For self-sabotaging thoughts commenced to consume my days, of the five hours I spent in that classroom and those, prior and after, equally the same, yet increasing in shrieks of decibels rolling around my head, ricer-shading from side to side and continuing in an unforgiving cycle, for all my actions, decisions and good intentions, eventuated to disharmony and loss, and all from my own choices and responsibility, so I set about, beating up on myself, for I perceived my mistakes and failures, and of good attributes, I counted none. Yet to be revealed of the physical emotions, of those imploding pains in my head, warped, twisted, mangled, deformed in my abdomen too, belonged not to me, but were planted there without my permission, by he who condemned me as stupid and useless, a dunce and so much more for as long as I can remember, by, my father.

My father condemning me, as "Too thick to go to university," and perhaps he was to be proved right, for after all, the first months exams which quite surprisingly I passed, yet the second months where I thought, I had an angle on those exam questions and was to achieve a pass mark but, failed miserably, but "How could that be?" For never before, had I failed to achieve anything I had set my mind to, so "Why was I failing at that?" My fight, simply to stay in my own race and take part as I began to contemplate, "Was he right through all those years, was I stupid and useless, thick as two short planks and worth-less?" For sure, evidence right there appeared to back up his condemnation, and I felt nauseas and weak at the thought how he would laugh with sanctimonious delight, to know, my inability in *la langue française*, proved him right.

The green board and I became not best friends, and as that concept of osmosis, passed me by, my exam results declining and my self-worth the same, as simultaneously, the Polish *camarade* sitting besides me achieving 98%, laughing, joking with others, how foolish she was to have got that 1 question wrong and lost the 2%. I felt more than a little vexed and wondered, "Was she doing that deliberately?" Man; I only felt increasingly worse and demoralized as the Professor spoke with me of my failure, in class, for all to hear, how embarrassing and how rude of those two young Scandinavian girls, who affording me no privacy, watching and listening to all she said. Still, I continued along my Parisian journey, with new though heavy companions, of 'mild shame' by any other name, 'debilitating comparison' and 'lingering regret.'

Greater disabling thoughts emerged, so worried I was that my friends would stop being my friends because I was 'so stupid,' perhaps of my greater number of years on this earth I should have been wiser to verbalise that to them, but fear, for some reason was rolling all around my head, as if a black veil encased on the outside, and only to speak of such, I thought my relieve me of the same. "Wise?" Likely no! For I knew I did not want to as soon as I commenced to speak, but of that bright white snow all around, I perhaps, hoped against hope, by taking such an action, of that dark hole I found myself in, perhaps I could climb out.

My fears evolved as justified, as a study group that was talked of so often, and I invited to, but it never quite did eventuate, nor did that, of an invitation to join a pristine group of 3, to join the Australian to visit her French Grandmother-in-law, to enjoy conversations in that language we proposed to learn, to be corrected in pronunciation, and enquire of information to fill in those gaps that from the Professor we did not gleam, and of course, I gratefully agreed. And my eager follow-up enquiries resulted in "Oh, its not been arranged yet," but not quite so, for as I waited with 2 classmates to cross a boulevard, a cryptic message between them ensued, where they inadvertently eluded, that actually that evening at 8pm provided the *rendezvous* time, concealing it from me, as I was excluded from the previously offered and accepted meeting, deliberately.

Squelched, tossed to the curb, denied, lied to, exiled, cast as worth-less, "Hurt?" "Certainly Yes," for I thought she who told me she was a friend, but she turned out to be something else, and the result did not harm her in her comfy life, but it did make me think thrice, of added convictions of my fathers comparisons about me were racing violently around on the inside of my head, that I was unwanted and unlovable, a person to be only tolerated best and despised at worst, and right there her actions, she a popular girl, and that perceived rejection I internalized with the saddest of pain, adding to the increasing weight of the argument, that my father's accusations had been right along. But "How could that be true?" As for decades I had fought with every ounce within me, to harness and muster what I could, to refute his concepts, yet seemingly although I hadn't recognized them, the still scars remained, ready and waiting to cause me pain, and as it multiplied, with every ounce of energy I had, I dared not permit myself to believe he was right, but "Was not everything pointing to the contrary, and his beliefs of me, completely justified?"

.....And I was to wonder, "Was it a case of self-fulfilling prophecy, or perhaps, a case of 'a survivor' knowing her 'turf,' recognising, of that vibe, of what was not spoken, but being so acutely, astutely aware that something deeper, more sinister, in greater or lesser degrees, lingered beneath the surface?"

"I will prepare and some day my chance will come."
~ Abraham Lincoln

Like a record that would cease playing not of "You're bloody stupid," "You're less than useless." "Thick as two short planks and always will be." "Go to university, you?" "Don't make me laugh!" "You'll never amount to anything, certainly not a nurse!" "You *dunce!*" With sneers and jeers, it was as though he was right before me, in the same room, so great was that anguish and reliving what I heard. Unable to escape, around and around my head those words wildly swirled, violently bounding off each side off my skull like a ping-pong ball made of iron in ever increasing decibels, relentless in their reputation, the pain of the emotions radiating through my body.

My father's attitude haunting me, of what I thought I'd buried so deep, that never again would it see the light of day, but in that city of love, they erupted, and worse, I felt captured, accused, convicted, guilty as charged all over again. I was to consider, for real, "Did his accusations and condemnations hold merit, and had I only ever deluded myself into believing that I was something else?" For sure, I was out of the geographical proximity of my accuser, but the pain stretched far outside his reach, surpassing distance and time as within the crevices of my mind, they remained my companions, but I needed to find a way to banish them, forever.

The exam result, the latest, my failure all too much to bear, unable to control the tears as they overspilled from the casing of the sadness from my eyes, and as I kept wiping them away, the salt, smarted my cheek bones. So fortunately I was in the Phonetics lesson, where personal cubicles were used to void the visual communication with others, so no one able to see, displaced from my heart, the distress across my face, except the professor, a young lady with a kind soul, her expression and through the two-way electric speaking system, spoke consoling words depicting concern, and as I reassured her I was 'fine,' that was not to be as uncontrollable the tears of a life of pent-up emotion began to flow, quickly turning I placed my books and pencils in my *sac à dos*, backpack and before any of my *camarades* could see, before my heart broke into a million little pieces, I got the heck out of there.

Walking, avoiding the *Métro* as a captive audience for the sobbing foreigner I cared not to be, so holding in what sobs I could as I continued walking, searching for a private place in Paris for me. Leaving that busy boulevard behind, I found myself almost at *Jardin Luxemburg*, and unable to hold onto the sobs any longer, it was in the confines of a tiny stone doorway, centuries old in age, in front of the solid wooden painted door, the pain of the age of my life was about was about to erupt, the pain of pent-up sobs grew as limitless appeared to be the destruction they caused, releasing almost 5 decades of filth oozing out that were spoken over me, where I lived in a shadow, consumed by its cold heavy burden, wrongly accepting them as my own, and falsely agreeing to live beneath their doctrine, "Oh my" the damn was breaking, the magnitude of pressure released, "Relief Oh Relief!" for me, "Was safety & peace to prevail?"

Really, I had not recognised that so many people filled Paris, and so many came, seemingly from every nook and cranny as I tried in private to hide, the eclipse of my tormented anguish and grief. I needed to find a quieter spot, so stepping out of my hiding-hole, crossing the circle as I passed the bare trees, as I stepped tentatively so not to slip on the ice underfoot, as from the passing pedestrians, carefully concealing my face stricken with tears, so quickly desiring to reach Luxemburg gardens. Gasping for a breath, "I did it," "Relief!" I pushed open those ice cold ornate iron gates and let myself in, passing the fountain, where even the streams of the water flowing from the swans mouths, were frozen.

Hurrying I found a private seat, yet in the open air, where I did not sit, but exhausted, weakly flopped down, and there with no one around to hear my cries, the wounds that tore at my mind, I let-them-go, uncontrollably, 'all were to flow,' and the pain, so physical, ripping through my chest and bursting out of the folds of my mind, refusing to be captive anymore, my limbs were weak and my head flopped, I without the strength to hold it up, as 'evil' by any other name relinquished its grasp.

Tears relentlessly flooded from the depths of my soul, from my body I heard the sounds-of-release, so much pain, pain that had been so subliminal, so much a large part of who I was and what I did, as I so unaware of it was even there, so unaware of its existence that it had planted its stake and taken up residence on a free-loading journey in my life, I made a quick pact with me, I was to face those demons of longevity, that I was to see that process though as I was to relinquish *its* hold, to dissipate *its* strength and finally, thankfully through grace, I was capable, and *it* was incapable to reside there anymore, as I *was* to be *set free*.

Funny! Failure, it was, that catalyst for so much of that process, really, it was the instigator of it all, spilling up, over and out so much of which I deserved not to be within me, for it had been buried forever, yet, it had risen to the surface inadvertently, through my stamina committed to personal growth and inner-healing, and through strength and courage, released it, for I refused to permit myself to bury it again, so adamantly allowing myself to seize that presented opportunity, not by mistake but purpose, for my absolute reward, of *"Victory!"*

…Not even my father's scorn upon the tears of a child response of, "You're ugly when you cry!" "Shut-up and get out of sight *now*!" "No." To the past I was not to succumb, as I rendered on that crisp cold Parisian day, all insufficient to delay, that which was rightly mine to be, released, whole and living in worthy *"Freedom."*

The cleansing done, as my facial skin stung and tight from that reservoir of salty tears that poured over it, and as there I sat, weak, from 2 *camarades* who had observed me slipping out of class and absent from the next, had sent text, of words of concern and concepts of caring all wrapped up in reassurance; sorrow was sweet in that instance, for in times of trouble or upset, of such I was never used to receiving, yet, *joy*, I received as the warmth of their messages landed on fertile ground, and instantly as never before, accentuating, *me*, accelerating acceptance of such, as it soothed my soul and so compatible enabling my new and beautiful self-worth began to soar.

A 'lighter-heart,' my new companion as I walked with a lighter load, feeling a little 'weird' it might be said, for something different was then most positively apart of me, and through the length of that park close-ish to the Left Bank I continued heading toward that which feeds me so, where in moments of contemplation I always head for, that open space of moving water with its creation of ions somehow calming for me, and with no ocean available, it was the river *Seine* which was to serve as a substitute so remarkably well, feeling the life from its stone walls, I meandered along its banks, with no real direction in mind, more simply an absence of mind, a mind of release, a *mind*, of *peace*.

> "The credit belongs to those who are actually in the arena, who strive valiantly; who know the great enthusiasms, the great devotions, and spend themselves in a worthy cause; who at best know the triumph of high achievement; and who, at worst, if they fail, fail while daring greatly, so that their place shall never be with those cold and timid souls who know neither victory nor defeat."
> ~ *Theodore Roosevelt*

Chapter 8

Step With Resilience

"Happiness is not a goal; it is a by-product."
~ Eleanor Roosevelt

Birthday wishes were to come my way, as a special birthday I spent in Paris, tough in reality, it was not that time of year that made it special, but the geographical locality. And "What to do? Was it to take a trip up my beloved *Eiffel Tower* and partake of fine food? or "Perhaps a cruise upon the same for more of the same, to sip fine Champagne" or "Cracking open the finest bottle of *vin rouge*, while nibbling on crackers and cheese after ascending the stairwell of the *Arc de Triumph* enjoying the vista of the encompassing city and the *Champs-Élysées?*" or "Why not, a trip to the famously historic, *Moulin Rouge?*"

Yet not quite, did I fill my own resounding philosophy of, the older we get and the less birthdays are left for delight, so the greater the celebration for us to enjoy. Yet in that year not wishing to spend it by myself, as I so often did, so enquiring of my *camarades*, "Would you like to celebrate something with me, perhaps just a coffee or a glass of wine when the university day is through?" And as "Yes" was their response, we thought to choose a venue to visit, to us brand new.

Holidays were my preferred preference, so I didn't feel like 'Billy-no-mates,' all-alone, so often I did travel at that time of year, and of benefit too, the costs were cheaper and the tourists the same, so from my perspective, so much more did I gain. And on a couple such years it was Jamaica for me, to Negril on the west coast, where magnificent sunsets may be enjoyed. And as fortune was to have it, a girl from Canada at the bar I was introduced to, as at the hotel I arrived, she, much younger than I, with magnificent curls of long locks, of the brightest carrot red hair, and how wonderful it was, as she enthusiastically explained, "Hey, have you heard about MEX tonight, the reggae party, with lots of stars and 'Beeny Man' are going on to celebrate Bob Marley's birthday, are you going to come and join me there?" Well, "My oh my," rapidly I made my decision, as a plan formulated for the evening, as in her friends car we were to travel to the West End to, 'mash it up' with Reggae artists in real Jamaican styli.

She, from Kingston, Ontario, somehow scored us a pass into the VIP section, and "Wow what fun!" Dancing and 'skanking' all the night long, feeling great, my energy levels high, such a pleasant rest-bit, from those immense lows and fatigue I suffered in Melbourne. My joy, it kept on rolling, as I chatted and danced a lot, and "Wooow!" I was to gasp, as I looked up at the sky and saw its sheen so intense, indigo in colour, and as I turned to my companion, a local boy to share the beauty of that night sky, surprised when he replied, "No mon, that's not the night sky, it's the morning, it's 20 minutes past six, and a new day is dawning." "Was he kidding me?" "No." "Wow!" Never would I have imagined that my health was good enough to last that, now that, was the icing on the cake to what was, a 'real birthday treat!'

But 2 days before my Parisian birthday, a strange phenomenon started to happen, as a phrase persisted to roll around my head, and escaping through my mouth, all day and evening long delivering a message, "I've made it, I've made it this far!" Initially, my concept of amazement, gave way to total astonishment, as really, "Why was it there?" and "What did it mean?" and "Was it to unravel into pure desperation or was that to be elation?" but difficult to decipher, as the emotions appeared entwined, yet the master of the message clearly resounding, "I had made it! Against all the odds, and all those people, perhaps when I wasn't expected to; I had made it thus far!"

Illogically buzzing around my mind, yet it seemed structured in someway, as if with a clear purpose of intent, and I tried to conceive what that might be, to alert me, of that childhood from so long ago, from my adulthood too, all too consumed by people who tried too much to conceivably harm me, in those bygone years, all at best hideous and peculiar, at worst heinous and dangerous, where my 'flight and fight' mechanism was over used until, like for so many others, it began causing me harm. Yet those spinning notions and resulting emotions, confusing, perplexing, for I understood not from where the message came or "Why it was delivering itself to me, and, what impact could, should or would it have, and more why now, was it knocking at my door?" "Chaotic?" "Yes." But somehow peaceful and cathartic, as that message after the two days, slowly slipped away, leaving the resounding knowledge, that, "I'm here now!" because *amazingly* so, "I was still alive!" and true, *"I made it, thus far!"*

For history had proved a difficult journey to travel through each day, wondering of harm, "What was to hold my name that day?" And not even a break did I get on my birthday, for my mother was always there, delivering nastily her piece of scorn, "Yes, well, I lost my figure because of you all these years ago!" But what could I do, I was only a baby, born without asking, so I suffered saying nothing, just accepting her accusations and complaints of me, because experience the teacher, like my father's violence toward me, when it began, I never did know or have any control of when it would cease.

Even my birthday parties posed a problem to her, for "Oh moan," she could have won prizes in that, sighing at her inconvenience, begrudgingly "Well! I suppose I'll have to bake you a birthday cake!" And with unwavering regularity of her annoyance that she had to organize a birthday party in the house, as tones of dissatisfaction and complaints sprang forth, accompanied by accusations how my father didn't love me, because, "Your father doesn't gives me any extra money for housekeeping?" and "Where do you think I'm going to get the money from to pay for it?" Huh! "Have you thought about what I'm going to have to give up to do it?" and "The time it's going to take, what about that then?" Really, of all her questions, before the age of 10; I so wanted to, but still, "I had no way, of answering them."

Birthday presents, of them I soon grew to not look forward to, as so disappointed I always was to be, but one year, I just hoped against hope, that really, a Tiny Tears doll I may have, I as so excited at the prospect, for all the girls at school had one, and spoke of what fun playing with them, for they were like real babies, when you laid them down, they'd cried tears, after feeding them a bottle, and that sounded like so much fun, and please, "Could I not be the same as those girls in my class; just once?" So I placed my request, and I asked, "*May* I please have a Tiny Tears doll mum?" "You'll have to wait and see." came her sharp reply and of my future requests, "Stop bothering me all the time with what you want, I'm sick of hearing about it." with her favourite, "You're really getting on my nerves" and with continuing with intolerance, "Besides that, *you* know the rules. You'll get what *you're* given. *You'll* like or lump it!" Then in her voice, with increasing hate erupting, and "Woe-be-tied *you* girl, if *you're* not grateful. Because *you, know you'll*-never-be-getting-anything else again!" Yep, all that, spoken on so many days, kind of took all my *hope* and any pleasure away.

Her other doctrine I knew well. "I want never gets!" But, my birthday had arrived, and all her annual grumbles did subside, as they made a home inside of me, and there it was, a square box, and I began to feel some happiness, for was this it, the Tiny Tears I requested, really had she bought it and was it to be mine? With joy and glee of one so young I decided, "Yes, yes, it must be," with a smile upon my face, and remembering my mother's instructions, "Be careful! With that wrapping paper, don't tare it now so I can use it again." And there, carefully unpeeling the Sellotape and pulling the box out, I saw the feet of a doll, "Oh my!" "Was it really, really to be?" I allowed myself to get so terribly excited, and then, "Yes?" NO. "No?" "No!" No Tiny Tears, instead, it was a Rose Bud doll, of brown hair, and it didn't cry real tears. Disappointed! Fool on me I thought for daring to believe, I could get something I wanted, but I remembered *her rules* about gratefulness, wanting and getting, so thanked her very much before with the doll, sadly walking away.

But "Oh so slow," and perhaps thankfully, as that child so young, or even as a teenager to realise or ask, "Why did my brother have all he desired, carriages and Pullman for his treasured Hornby train set?" And I don't mean to be bitter but am trying to understand, as more, even a reproduction of a Steam Roller that he so liked, which he saw at Leven's Hall where with Grandma and Granddad we visited, he was given a miniature one of those, so grand, it ran on mentholated spirit, and that item to purchase, surely, must have cost a 'pretty penny.' And really, "Who bought it him and why?" As of note, there was no special occasion. Then decades later I was to wonder, "The budget my father gave to my mother for presents for his 2 children, of my allotted portion, did she deliberately and unfairly transfer to the other?"

My birthday frock didn't fair any better, with my wardrobe bear, her jeers and jibe of how, "Now I suppose I'll have to make you a dress, though I don't know when I'm going to find time!" Spoke the housewife who didn't work. And the dress she did make, one year I particular remember, for it was not with love as those dresses that for me my grandma did make, for the sides were uneven, with one protruding out far away from my body in that ribbed fabric of the brightest of yellow, but when I wore it bight and loved was not what I felt, as she placed it on me, and said, "That's good enough for you!" "See, something else I've given up for *you*, and when are *you* ever going to do something for me?" "What?" I was 6 or 7, "What could I possibly do?" But apparently that was my problem not hers, as my given task, everyday, to contemplate and make it all right, of *what she gave up* and all her *sacrifices* for me. Really! "If only, I'd been able to please her, even in the most minimal way," but a lifetime was to prove, for me, that was impossible to do, and in my history, the problem was not poverty, it was 'neglect' and Maternal Deprivation.

Yet of that sunlight yellow dress that fit so baldy, that true, caused me embarrassment as into the school I walked and saw the joy upon the faces of my classmates as they twirled around showing each other their latest party frocks, sharing happily how their mummy's had bought them for them. Surely, should I even have hazard a notion that mine was made with love or care, I may have tried to join in, but of my dress, dejectedly, I felt not the same as them and with discarded glances, their eyes portraying 'nothing to talk about here,' I was cast to the outer perimeters, disinterested they moved on.

Yet for sure, skills my mother had, she was brilliant at knitting with the capacity to knit almost anything, pictures and toys most amazingly and all with ease, sew too but she chose not to, as it was my grandma who crocheted me the most beautiful dresses, just in essence so I had something to wear and I so adored what my grandma's gifts of garments. For my prize of learning how to knit coat-hanger covers, she crocheted for me two dresses, one of white trimmed with turquoise, one of yellow trimmed with white, both with long sleeves, round necks and elasticised separate belts. Gentile, ladylike and perhaps, almost special were my emotions as I treasured what I held as mine. Then as a teenager the same when a patchwork waistcoat she made me of small multicoloured crocheted squares, with a knit-one pearl-one yellow back, feeling so proud to wear it, and hoped there'd be more of it, but sadly, nope!

You may think, after so many years I'd be used to all mother's jibes of how inconvenient I was to her, but somehow they still hurt, for although I knew many were not the truth, though as comparisons I had no idea of the harm of sadness and desperation they inflicted as they accompanied me, nestling and staying, spurned with vengeance, out of my mother's mouth, "You're an accident!" "You're a mistake!" "You weren't wanted!" So innocent so young, but by her tried and found guilty, and worse was to come as to her personal vendetta I was to succumb, as she took regular trips to her martyr-wonderland, where, not my ears but my heart she bombard with her revered tales, the type I came to know and name, as her "Once upon a time stories," and word perfect was able to rhyme them off the same.

Shakespeare, my mother could have given him a run for his money, with her repertoire, as I grew-up never ending with "They all lived happily ever after." Her plots delivered with gusto, sinister and true, significantly with purpose to maim and harm and they did, should have held a PG certificate, as vivid a path to destruction, of that little girl's spirit, she who was me, creating a vacuum of emptiness, of helplessness and hopelessness, as each rendition with emotions of fortification, where perhaps with deliberate intent, she placed me where she expected me to stay, where she dictated I was only worthy of, beneath her heavy blanket of repugnance and loathing, so dark the depth so low, to see the light of day or even know of its existence. "No!" Leaving behind in its wake, only a legacy of self-hate.

"Safety, security at home?" Were not attributes I was able to enjoy, as in that house where I lived, I was recurrently told, "This is not a home. It's just four walls!" and "Soft words, cuddles or smiles?" "If only!" but "No," there were non, and bedtime stories the same, that place, a harsh environment to be, absent of love, joy or comfort, but my mothers stories were rampant there, flowing so easily, and her favourites she did have, in which she wrote and nitrated stared as the lead. "So are you ready, are you sitting comfortably?" Now I shall begin.

With a nod and a shake of her head to commence the unfoldment of the drama, her discontentment of fortitude she spoke her words, "Your brother was in his cot crying, he wouldn't stop, he was already covered in bruises *your* father had given him." A dramatic pause for effect, "He wouldn't stop crying and *your* father was really angry and going to beat him again." Then, picking-up tempo, her facial expression of utter loathing continuing, "So I stood in-front of the cot and said to *your* father, 'Don't hit the baby hit me instead,' and he did." Her tempo racing in full throttle pausing only for intakes of breath, her repugnance irrefutable, "Then *he* did, then *he* told me; Get on the bed and open my legs."

Continuing, always the same way, holding an expression that I never did quite understand, her eyes rapidly darting, vibrating in the sockets as she stood fixed and leered at me her eyes penetrating mine, as if, poisoned arrows were being stabbed directly in to my chest cavity, with vengeance seeping from her every pore, she delivered her last line of her 'oh so frequent story,' to tell, with a forceful blow with intent designed with every rendition to cause destructive harm and destroy, as she spat out those final words every time with utter disgust and contempt, "And *YOU! YOU!* came out nine months later!"

At her suffering, I mean not to be flippant, for her suffering and that of my brother were obvious, yet from my youngest age it was unjust, that it evolved, of that event, that she made it her life time goal, that for the rest of my life, she was to love-up on my brother, while making me, pay the price, forever.

"Oh lucky me!" I say sarcastically, the history of my birth, a legacy of loathing, a curse, inherited from my conception. Of what she spoke it was not make-believe, according to the record of my mother, it was empirical data. The emphasis consistently portioned, how he was my father, but never a consideration how he was her husband, or, how she chose him. How I was innocent as unborn. But no, not in her eyes, for she had a set division of blame, it was her and my brother who were innocent victims, and I, and my father, who were pronounced guilty. And so it was in my formative and forever world according to my mother, I was forbidden to be presumed innocent when I was born, for she found me guilty, as *she, charged* me, to take on those sins, belonging to my father. And in her eyes certainly, for never did she fail to show it, I was to bare the burden of his guilt and blame, as forever and always, did that doctrine of hers remain, from a mother to her daughter who always withheld her love.

> *"Darkness cannot drive out darkness: only light can do that.*
> *Hate cannot drive out hate: only love can do that."*
> *~ Martin Luther King Jr*

How unpleasant, how bitter she was and how unwanted and rejected was I. My education, on all things of 'my family' really what I could have done without, growing up in the knowledge that likely she would have 'got rid of me' if she could for more than once I was to here her emphasize emphatically with unrest, "Yes, well, there was no abortion in my day!" I did not ask the question, but I did receive the implication, for why would I not, as a new mantra she stumbled upon, after watching a TV documentary, "Yes. Well I know all about rape within marriage!" she would viciously spout.

Admittedly, at only 13 years of age, when that latest tale she began to wail, perhaps a happy coincidence or a deliberate calculation, that I may add the two 'not happy ever after stories' together of 'my conception' and the 'rape within marriage' together, through of deliberate intent, ignorance or perhaps a happy side-effect, of her game to maim, the result the same. As 3 years before my sweet-sixteen birthday, I was to conclude, that "Yes, I must the result of rape within marriage, by he, that man I want to hate, whose blood runs through my veins, and by she, my mother, who would have aborted me 'if only' she could, who kind of, almost told me!" Such burdens to bear, and in years I wasn't even reached anywhere near adulthood.

> *"Alas, I am dying beyond my means."*
> *~ Oscar Wilde*

The history of my birth, a legacy of loathing, a curse inherited from my conception, only gave my mother fortification for her relentless renditions of casting aspersions and blame, not of least how inconvenient I was to her, when as a baby I threw myself out of the pram, and how "I would have to come outside and put you back in." I hasten to assume, I hope though I never enquired, "Was I wearing reins that prevented me from hitting the ground?"

never even pausing to contemplate, "Why would a baby do such a thing?" That was until I got older and getting a tan became my thing, and then I began to notice multiple unusual scars, ridged uneven edges, that had stretched and split over time, spreading from my knees up my inner thighs and even seen on my most delicate of parts. Their origin, "Nappy rash?" possibly, though as I considered my treatment from my mother, I started feeling quite nauseous that they could be something far more sinister, and never have I dared to check out on the internet what else I think it can possibly be.

"Oh my" that poor little baby who was me "How much pain must I have been in from urine stinging into those open wounds?" I wonder, is that what I did, "Throw myself out of the pram to try and relieve the pressure of that urine laden flannel nappy from pressing on my delicate skin?" "Wow!" Her complaints so frequent at her inconvenience, "Yes, well, you were so fat as a baby, I had to pull those ugly rolls of fat apart to clean in-between them!" What happened I wondered, her disgust that even when I was the age of 30-something, still she displayed it so keenly on her face, and for possibility, "Was that a job that displeased her so immensely, quite simply, she chose not to do it?"

Though I'm pretty sure it whatever the cause of those scars, she had a hand in it, for if she had not, for gripe and concern to pass them onto me, surely, to demonstrate over again how I wasn't perfect, that is something that would have given her satisfaction to do. And even my white blonde curls posed so vexingly so as a problem for her, "As soon as I'd combed one strand straight, the other curled right back up!" "Oh my" I was a baby, an infant, and of her multiple-dissatisfactions of me, to help her, really, there was nothing I was able do.

"Caring?" "No" there was non of that gong on, sometimes it appeared she go out of her way, 'to have a go at me,' but never my big brother because, she cosseted and loved him so obviously. But I, "As a young child not even in double digits, really, was I to be responsible, for her death?" As her complaints were copious as was her victim mentality, as her words sped like missiles from her laser lips, assisted by her cutting tongue, "You better stop annoying me and do as you're told, or you'll come home and find me on the floor with my head in the oven!"

So recurrently she said that to me, and really, I never did understand "Why, for what was it that I ever did so wrong?" But I just knew *I must behave,* or I was to be the reason, she was to kill herself, and as she pointed out so venomously so, "And then, you'll be left with your father, and you know how badly he'll treat you. And your brother will get it worse, and it will *all* be *your* fault!" Her wickedness, there seemed to be nothing less. Then out of the door and off to school off I would walk, knowing I had to do well and get a good report, in just an attempt that my father would have one less reason to knock me around again. But sat in that classroom and trying to learn was not that easy, with no one to tell my worries or concerns, alone, I was only left to wonder in just a few hours, as decreed by her, because of "'Me and my selfishness,' was I to return after school and find my mother, laying on the kitchen floor, Dead?"

"Who, being loved, is poor?"
~ Oscar Wilde

Nightly, like a damn bursting its banks, uncontrollably, until I could sob no more, with my eyes stinging and tender to the touch, my head ready to explode from congestion outwardly bursting, yet emotionally exhausted, eventually I would sob myself to sleep. But my crying kept it quiet, for I knew the rules, make no-trouble and give my father no reason, to come to my bedroom, for at his convenience, to tell me "Be quiet" would only make him so terribly angry, and I cared not for the consequences that would come from that.

The intensity of that sadness and desperation, almost too much to bear, but bear it I must, as there languishing in hopelessness and helplessness was no rooftop for me to scream, "Help me! Help me! Please, please somebody help me!" But, no, there was nowhere to go and no-one to rescue me, and my heart remembered a movie I once saw, of a young girl not that different to me, and there in an attic she was put, pretty much trapped and treated badly, then a friend she made from that tiny upstairs window as she looked out, who dad turned out was a kind and rich and tenderly at the request of his daughter, rescued her. And I wondered with weeping in my soul, that had not quite yet died; "When, please when, will that ever happen for me?" and "Why did everyone so hate me?"

For there was no one to listen, no one to hear my silent screeches of pain, no one to come to my aid as alone and isolated, sinking fast and furiously, weak unable to rise up again, and somewhere along the way, all hope gone, my soul, dead, disappeared, while I survived, and from each morning when my eyes opened, it was only to be in saddened grief of angst, pain, hurt, harm and open wounds stinging and smart, until that cycle began again, and I'd sob my, way into sleep.

Within me lay nothing, only the vastness of a large hollow vessel where a little girl's heart and soul used to reside, where the capacity to-love must have once lived, but no longer for she, that little girl was dead, on the inside. No proclamation preceded that resounding traitorous situation, "Your heart has left the building!" at least to give me a heads-up, that my capacity to give or receive love dissolved, disintegrated, demolished. A slippery slope I was on, my descent complete, I had arrived at the bottom, lost, forlorn, helpless, my new status, void of contradiction, officially, was I, a "Dead girl walking!"

With the heavy velvet curtains partly drawn to keep the heat in, it was mid morning as the flickering flames of the gas fire danced beneath that antiqued-aged brass canopy, my mother and I crouched in front of it to keep warm, for we had central heating, but because, "It costs money" we were not allowed to put it on, and there the clock could have been set by rhythm of my mother's performance of regularity, of her perpetual groaning of most everything, as with the her hands full, a cigarette in one and a cup of coffee in the other, her makeup pristine and her hair the same, incessantly talking as usual, insistently professing to be an authority on great or minor subjects, yet really she rarely ventured outside that house, going nowhere and doing nothing, but hardly pausing for a break, that posed not a problem to her opinionated self.

Such a pleasant room the dining room, the wallpaper of damask pattern with a pale lustre of ivory with an accent of beautiful pale aqua, where centre stage did sit a brand new classic 8 seater G-Plan dining set, so bold, so beautiful such soft curved shapes and smooth edges, the warmth of the teak a glow, adoringly handcrafted, upholstered cushioned chairs of 4 chairs + 2 carvers, the traditional accomplishment, [my father's preference,] with their high backs of gently bowed wood, warm to the touch, where comfort was almost guaranteed, but a hiccup, as not practical, but a great ornament it proved to be, as its purpose to only demonstrate the status achieved by my father, for forbidden we were to use it, as his persistent statements of complaint, "Don't you go near it. *You're* clumsy. Stay away from it or *you'll* only ruin it." Were his forever far-flung accusations.

So sad, perhaps as I wonder, would such a great feat, and of all his others other achievements at his age of only 30-something, on his 2nd detached property purpose with a 3rd of an acre land, trips to Norway and Denmark for his family, new cars bi-annually and all on only his salary, and other than the mortgage, all paid for in cash. Somehow, for his sake, as he tried so hard to escape those 'slums' of Manchester, and to coin an old English phrase had, 'dragged himself out of the gutter,' to a place that he believed he deserved to be, and absolutely for him, of that success, I truly hope that he was able to enjoy amazingly so.

Absorbed by the flames, I thought not of much, perhaps little of anything, as my thoughts were only those belonging to my parents, and those *they* told me I could have not a mind to think for myself, for that I was told I was too stupid and irresponsible to do, infected with the lies which only served to make me captive and imprison me, yet still, when something needed to be done, I would not be shown how, but only shouted at, "get on with it." But not knowing how, and never being schooled in how to 'think for myself,' suddenly that was *my* problem again as "Use your initiative!" was hollered out with discuss force in my direction, but he never did tell me what it was or where I found it. And never dare I ask, "Excuse me father, please can you tell me what do you mean?" Certainly not, for I knew better than that, for never was I permitted or dared to ask "Why?" for in my father's eye, that a step too far and almost proved as a 'hittable offence,' as his mantra from old, "If you want to know something, go and ask your teachers; that's what I pay my taxes for!" His Victorian doctrine absolute, 'children were to be seen and not heard' and certainly not to dare, to cause him, not even, a miniscule of inconvenience.

Alive in body but dead in spirit, as just my breathing appeared to irritate my parents, void of harmony, that 13 year old girl, spontaneously arose from that fireplace and without ceremony or song, calmly commenced to walk though the kitchen space, past that 15 year old low yellow Formica top table, with the 4 tiny uncomfortable seats by its side, covered in old and cracked PVC of a colour popular back in the day, and that little girl, drenched, drowning in anxiety, the pain was a constant stream, a deluge afresh everyday, and I had no way to stop what came my way, she who was me, paused momentarily to pick up one of those little stools, with hollow framed legs so light, but of her burden, she withering, collapsing, under the weight too heavy to bear, and almost automated, not particularly aware of what she was doing, and certainly there was no plan, she passed through the utility room out into the yard and pushing open an old wooden slat gate I found myself walking into the expanse of the large lush tree bearing garden.

My body cold, my hands the same, unable to warm them up, but the cold temperatures that I felt inside, departed from me as only lovely fresh air that felt a warm, and the birds singing as and still holding the stool I began to step onto the rich colour of the deep green grass. I felt a kind of peace, a calmness that I wasn't used to, it was as though 'everything was as it should be,' and I was so glad to be there. So pleased to be outside, I twirled around admiring all the empty out-buildings that used to form as the residence for the 'Cattery,' that by the previous owners was run from that beautiful and traditional 1930's bungalow, those dwellings numbering 5, each having electricity fed through thick black cables that were strewn through the air from the main house then zigzagging across the garden from one to another, and so clearly I remembered my fathers instructions, "Don't ever touch those cables, they're 'live' and they'll kill you." and I've wondered since, with satire I'm sure, "Was he giving me an idea?"

I tramped across that uneven terrain, yet not so far from as outside my bedroom window and where those cables passed overhead, I paused and placed my stool down on which to stand. So clearly I remember what I wore, my favourite ribbed crew neck green sweater, with a cord running up through the brass islets to tie at the neck in a bow, though really that particular fashion had seen its day, the skirt the same of A-line design and emerald in colour, not a fashionable style, until that was, I went out to a remnant shop and bought a square piece of orange floral fabric, and there I cut and gathered it after fashioning it into long strip then using my mother's sewing machine I sewed it to the hem, and there reusing the 'wospy' belt, I do believe I did quite a good job, and certainly didn't look out of place.

So bright outside, it seemed as a dawn of peace had settled over me, and then I climbed onto the top, my petite feet hardly fitting on that flimsy stool, and with nothing to hold onto for balance, a little precarious but I did it, I stood there, and then, my little hand tentatively at first, though not for long my little hand reached up, as I mustered my courage, to try and touch that thick black wire, and as my brain could not quite give in to do what I was trying to, a thought trickled in, really, "Were those cables even live or not, and just because he could, was my father scaring us again, in some oddly bizarre way?"

Over and over, my opened hand precariously stretched up willing myself to touch it, but slowly it came back down again, closer and closer I got and just to give myself a better shot, I stood on my tippy-toes being careful not to fall, then up and down it went, multiple times, as I tried and attempted to succeed in my mission, and please understand, it was *not* because 'I wanted to die,' it was that, I *NEEDED, not* live, in what I was living in, anymore!'

So very long I seemed to be in that garden, trying to accomplish my deed, then my mind wondering with sorrow, "Without a word, I've been gone for such along time, 'oh why' did my mum not to come to look for me?" But I wondered not too much, for I knew of cause that she was never there for caring or support, so really, 'same old' there. Prolonged-ly I waited for my courage to meet me, my grasp, my stretch, my balance, all need to correlate, and then, persistence paid off; I did it! I touched, the cable! But "What????" "Why was I still alive????" "No, No, No!!!!!" Inwardly screaming, protesting with disappointment. That cannot be! For those out-buildings have electricity; so "Why would 'he' shout at me so persistently to keep me away from those cables when not a danger they posed?"

Despondent, getting of that tiny stool, "Why did it seem so heavy as I picked it up and why was walking back in so much harder to do than walking out sometime before?" And as if not a beat I missed to the fireplace side I returned to sit, there once again opposite my mother, who enquired not of where I'd been or what I'd been doing, her, who normally liked to know everything.

In the brass canopy, motionless, I gazed at the reflection of the flickering flames, as so loudly I wanted to cry, yet not a murmur did I make and of a sound, right there, I doubt that my mother would have heard anyway. My heart destroyed entirely, ripped again as I screamed silently, "Would anything ever except evil flow within me?" For all flickers of hope, vanquished, vanished, extinguished, as I knew so deep within, in that place where sorrow causes physical pain, that I had failed to secure a release from all that strangulating hurt and agony, and so sorrowfully it only became worse, for then I accepted to be true, *his*, my fathers false accusations delivered with rage, "You're incapable of doing anything right! You'll only ever be good for nothing!" The pit in my stomach, the pain in my head, condemned as a failure; and feeling so very much worse in everyway, for "What I had just done, inadvertently, had I made *his* prophecy come true?"

But 'she,' my mother, with my lengthy disappearance, really, "Did she even think to come and find me? Did she not wonder through the silence of my departure, where I was, or what I was up to? Could she not see the trouble that was erupting just below the surface?" or simply, "Did she care not to? Did she even bother to get up and see where I'd got to, to trouble herself to go as far as the bedroom window only a few steps away and look out in the garden where the trees were barely in leaf, to gaze in mesmerized astonishment at what her youngest child, her little girl, was in the process doing?" Though perhaps, as I say with a saddened heart, and realism for sure, maybe she did come to see 'what was going on' and saw me stood on that stool raising my hand up, to touch the cables and 'end it all' before she, taking another drag on her cigarette, not even pausing to raise her eyebrows, ignoring my plight or the impending outcome, "Did she calmly turn, and walk away?"

True, those notions I contemplate not lightly, though certainly that scenario not beyond the realms of possibility, as she was willing to put me out with 'yesterdays trash, as she, who wanted to know everything never did demand of me, for so long, "Where have you been?" And that, *most* unlike her, and "Why did she not?" Perhaps because, from that window, she'd already seen! Yet "Oh how grateful" I am today, that I was so unsuccessful in my endeavours on that day, for no-longer am I burden laden, as I have survived their crippling, manipulative and destructive spells, as now, with an independent spirit, I can see clearly, knowing my good fortunate that I am still here, to tell this story, as their rambling progression of hate of what they did to me was to be dis-spelled, as one day, I made a choice to overcome, to accept it, let-it-go and move-on, and of that process, as it served me so absolutely well, hugely, I appreciate it daily.

> *"Come away, O human child!*
> *To the waters and the wild*
> *With a fairy, hand in hand,*
> *For the world's more full of weeping than you can understand."*
> ~ William Butler Yeats; A Piece of: The Stolen Child, written 1886

For so long, so dreadfully difficult it had been to travel through life, to pass through everyday, no peace, no help, no hope, only forever living in that which is designed to save us, our 'fight or flight' syndrome, but can cause the body harm when living in it for years, scared, terrified, only pain, fear as constant companions with panic predictable in its regularity. The abuse from my father overt, and my mother covert, or by other names, aggressive or passive, but of my plight, "Did anyone see?" "Why did no one help me?" "Was I invisible?" "Was I not seen?" In the 60's, perhaps it is worthy for consideration, abuse was kept behind close doors, cloaked in the dark and not discussed in the light, as it is today, and certainly not looked for in a 'nice' village in a white upwardly mobile white middle class family, with all the 'outside' trimmings, so my teachers or significant other adults may not have noticed, any 'tell tale symptoms,' I portrayed, and if they had, as is the quaint British way, would they have chosen to, "'Not to interfere with things that don't concern you?"

Church is where I was sent on Sundays, but within the confines of those 4 walls in which I lived, through lingering daily torment, God's presence to me appeared not apparent. "Did the Vicar, did he not notice? Did he not look, did he not see?" for really, surely, "Wouldn't there have been some outwardly signs of abuse to see; hidden not too far beneath the service?" That little girl, she who was me, desperate in deepest despair of sadness inside, who soon, was to no-longer have a heart there to reside. No escape, only the threat of violence forever present, never pausing, never taking a day off, not even for a moment, not before church, nor after.

But what of those Church people, "Weren't they supposed to help those in need, to protect those who suffered, so why didn't they, why didn't they help me?" Why didn't they cry out, "Hey little girl, are you OK?" "Invisible!" No one saw my fear, no one saw my agony, no one saw, me! "Oh why, could I not have been so 'invisible' when violence was to descend upon me?" My concept as that little girl I knew even though in years I had so few, I was obedient to my father's doctrine, for too fearful not to be, to "Be quiet!" and "Not to speak unless I was spoken to." to his mantra, I was always true. I had no voice, forced to be silent, so "Why I could never comprehend, would he hide in corners, like an animal in the jungle, just ready to pounce and find fault with me, then punish me accordingly?"

Mother, my dearest mother; I could have only hoped to be draped me in a cloak of invisibility away from her, able to avoid her fortified comments of her constant irritation, "Get out from under my feet. Go somewhere else and play." "You're annoying me now! Get out of my sight!" Void of maternal love, I only wish the same could have been said of her spite she splurged out over me daily. "Please, could someone help me? Please, anyone?" Lost, alone, his cruelty obvious and overt, hers largely concealed and covert. How strange, to deflect the harm she inflicted, recurrently was her way to point the finger of complaints at my father, with unfailing aggressive retorts of, "He is so bad, he is... this and that..." ignoring the fact that 3 fingers, were pointing right back, at her.

Though not hers for concern as systematically, turning her knife with unrelenting regularity, deliberated delivering maximum emotional destruction, as she demonstrated that my emotions were unworthy of protection only annihilation, though still rarely that appeared to sufficiently appease her, as she making it abundantly clear, though true it took me a decade or 2 to work it out, that she did not desire to have me separated from my father to protect me, but greater to ostracise him, or to secure a deep and meaningful family of 3, for time was to reveal, willingly she was to relinquish me as superfluous to requirements, for a family, consisting of, just her and my 15 month older brother.

"By 'guts' I mean grace under pressure"
~ Earnest Hemmingway

Never did I ask my father "How high must I jump this time?" when he commanded me to, I simply hazard a guess and ensuring to goodness I darn well got it right, as to accomplish such a mission made it less likely a penalty of pain and punishment would follow, for really, how counter-productive to success that he demanded I should rise to, when as a human being or any other living animal, unable to function or flourish in such an environment of continual distress. For my fathers high intelligence equated not to his emotional intellect, where through the absence of commitment or even possibly trying to comprehend, for how foolish was he to attack one so young and defenceless that he had fathered, and patience, from him, "I laugh, sorry;" certainly, there was none of that, only his calculations for accusations of his supremacy, and his forever portrayed an over indulgence and a lingering presence, of irritability, anger and such rancid rage, all posing as an irrefutable lasting mess, of adverse conditions, for his abilities or there lack of, in parenthood.

Uninterrupted, deafening silence resided, from where 'comfort' should have shouted my name, but I, only to succumb to an inheritance to be subservient to *his* blame, that which was unrelieved by my death, 'guilty' I was rendered by all his charges, as I carried his shame he'd transferred to me, and as his exuberant and exacerbated emotional and physical crimes against me continued, me on the inside, abused, destroyed, "Was I only ever destined to be? "Dead girl walking!"

"Survivor" became my middle name, as resilience and fortitude became my skilful game, as I was to achieve success, and I was to achieve it well, to dispel *his* doctrine as wrong, determination to break *his* imposed burdens of bondage he laid on me and shatter *his* shackles of condemnation he encased around my feet, my aim, to disrupt *his* crippling confinements of what I was supposed to get out of life, true, perhaps I faced a bit of an uphill battle, with only, 'monkey see monkey do' as my teachers, my only clue, of how I was to conduct myself and travel through life, so a firm resolution I was to make to me, to prove *his* prophecy wrong and endeavour to prove mine correct. As resilience and persistence I took-up for my formidable companions, as step-by-step, I was ready for my journey to set out upon, for 'I had failed at death,' thank goodness, so there was only one plan left, to live, and of that, to put it right, as I was prepared, for me, for a good life, to fight.

True, life didn't improve instantly, it simply continued as 'life as I knew it!' Relentless in its daily flow of a septic caustic format, yet I calculated a plan, and imposed a mission to set me free, to strive for excellence, not in love, for I knew not of that, or even how to hazard a guess to behave within such a flimsy, whimsical, fanciful notion as that. "No!" It was my career ladder I was to march upon, as it became my primary focus to accelerate, so all men, who I had grown to distrust with every bodily tissue, for when harm they caused, and it was a 'given' that they would, for the sake of me and my, as yet, unborn children, for self-protection and self-preservation of me and them, with security of finance I considered, surely from them then, I could calculate our safe escape.

So my mission to reach my goal, of my endeavours to be swayed from them, I permitted no-thing to unbalance my finally tuned equilibrium, prohibiting anything to penetrate that delicate balance that evolved as my life, from uncertainty or veering over into oblivion. Such was my commitment, that friends came and friends went, few friends stayed for I would always find fault with them, rejecting them accordingly, though, subconsciously perhaps by design, my aim for survival, was to do it to them, before they had the opportunity to do it to me, so no further could fall, my diminished self-esteem.

Yet I remained strong with the fortitude of an ox, but not through self-love, for that notion eluded me thus far, but through a refusal of permitting self-doubt to call my name or in me make a home, as those steep learning curves of exceptional gradients came against me, for unamicable were they to me, as without exception, my only notion, that eventually, I was to soar like an eagle, for I made a pact with myself, that as I was alive, "I was to choose life, and I was to choose it more abundantly."

"Never give up on your dream... because you never know what the Lord can bless you with."
~ Kelly Rowland

Thrilled when the suggestion from a *camarade* to partake in a celebratory drink, to venture up to the lavish restaurant on the top tier of the *Tower* on *Boulevard Montparnasse*, where to be enjoyed from its high and magnificently extensive vista, a 180 degrees of the Parisian cityscape, with floor to ceiling windows, their height, of maybe a building or more, and on that early November evening, as dusk rolled in, before them we sat, chatting quite elegantly, though joviality, there was none of that, but still, "Pleased to be there?" I was most certainly.

The clock turned around, and dusk gave away to night, and there in supreme formation on the iconic Parisian skyline, that structure so fine, a picture I placed on my wardrobe to always see, was to suddenly shine bright, with an array of glistening and twinkling lights, posing no fright but a stunning sight of elation to treasure, as in my heart and my mind, wallowed in such a magnificent pleasure. Yet of insight, that profound message again came beckoning to me, not quietly or softly, but with intensity in my soul, for against all the odds and not because of them, quite opposite incredibly so; "I've made it, I've really made it this far!"

Then on the *Métro* toward my next *rdv*, as I relived the exhilaration of the *Eiffel Tower*, my mind slipped to recollection, of my inspirational wall in Melbourne, for specifically, what I viewed that night, exactly the same as a card I placed on it some 2 years ago. "Wow!" What I meditated on truly did come to fruition.

But a note of good-caution, a tale to relay, as song I so loved the melody of Akon's, "So lonely" that I so gladly sang along to, until one day I realised I was, "So lonely." "Oh what a *faux pas*, but lesson for sincere consideration, for fact, as I sang I felt real emotion, for I so liked it, yet failing inadvertently to recognize, with heightened emotion comes heightened absorption, so quickly so it was, that process captured me negatively. So astute I quickly became of that notion, and harnessed it too, to choose most carefully what to meditate on, turning it away from negativity, to utilizing it marvellously positivity. And to use a popular French colloquialism, *Faire attention!* Be careful!

Alighting at station *Opera* it was only a hop skip and a jump to find myself walking the tiny *rue's* of *St Michel* to meet a French friend, with his friend who I also knew from *Café Laurent*, where always they were to be found sat at the bar, sipping on the finest champagne, and sharing a 'yarn.' And that night saw the down of the *Boulanger Nouvelle*, the new seasons wine, and to enjoy such it was off to theirs and mine, favourite haunt, where always a pleasure to go, and a surprise awaited me, as Marceau, Luc and I, walked in on that fine evening of fine wine and jazz, where a warm welcome was received and Flavien, he had bought for me, that which I so adored but could not afford, a big-plate-selection of that delightful delicacy, with sweetness that melts in the mouth, those quite exquisite, macaroons.

And of his kindness, not once did he ask, expect or hint, for gratitude for what he'd done that night for me, and "Wow," what an amazing surprise, for from my mother or others, never had I experienced such kindness before, unbridled, unbegrudged. Yet quite amazingly, it rendered me a tad uncomfortable, for I knew not how to behave in such an unprecedented circumstance, where I needed not to profusely show my gratitude and "Was there something else I was missing, strings attached perhaps?" Though, "No!" His gift, a kindness, he, relaxed expected none, and that, "A true and most beautiful birthday gift of all!"

More macaroons were on there way, as Marceau also gave me a gift of a large prettily wrapped box, and their cost, a 'pretty penny,' and of all I expected none. And of my joy, I joke, 'anyone could have been forgiven for thinking it was my birthday.' And he bought me all chocolate, deliberately, for when I sat at the bar, partaking of wine so fine, it was not the traditional savoury *petit canopies* I would nibble upon, with not *canapés* but a petite plate of chocolate finger biscuits. How wonderful I thought, that he thought not of what he wanted to give, but he thought more of what I wanted to receive, 'the gift, the thought,' and especially more, as it was gift, I sought not to indulge or afford for myself, and another "Truest pleasure of that birthday gift to me!"

……… "Wow!" Incredibly, retrospectively I realised somewhat irrationally, that those people who knew me not hugely well, could be so kind as they were, and I was think, 'thank goodness,' that my mother they didn't know them, for surely of her scornful spite to injure me, from her to them, she was unable to influence their minds or worn them against me…. With satire: "Yeah for Paris."

I so enjoyed their company and the humour we shared that night, but then I guess it was a given, so the night, could it get much better? But those limiting beliefs, jumped up and grabbed a-hold of me, where I was to wonder of Marceau and his previous generous words, "On your birthday we can do anything you want," and as I explained that I would just love to nip to another venue for jazz, just to check it out, before returning tour favourite, *Cafe Laurent*, to rest, relax and soak up the atmosphere and all that jazz, he gladly agreed.

But the evening got, topsy-turvy in that regard, and "What to do?" I knew not, for I was still amidst my growth of increasing self-worth, and as we agreed and I wanted to go, to stay put, "Was that spontaneity? or Simply giving in?" or Did that mean, to me, needlessly he lied, and evidentially with that vein running through me, as he had begun, when would he stop? What was his purpose, and how would he try and what was his agenda to manipulate me?" So many questions, and I was unsure how to solve with them. And in a mildly rising panic, as through my growth, of embellished healing notions, I was mindful to 'stand up for me,' but equally, refute the possibility of those negative responses of the past replicating, not those of instinct to protect me, but those knee-jerk ones of relevance from those who harmed me. And on that Parisian birthday I was desperate in my search, for I was refusing to permit my past to dictate my present, as fraught, I so very much desired, to get 'it' *all* right.

Spending a moment in the ladies restroom to reflect, I decided to go middle ground explaining to Marceau that I was to visit the other jazz venue and return in a short while. "No," he said, insisting "I will come with you," but really I wanted him not for guilty I then felt, for he, having just ordered a fresh flute of Champagne, another 'pretty penny' I insisted I was good to go on my own, and supping it far too quickly to appreciate it, he pulled on his overcoat, he was ready with insistence to accompany me, as my pleas to "Stay, please, stay, I don't mean to break up your party," or indeed the vibe nor did I desire a reputation, cast of a manipulating woman who delights in spoiling friends fun, and there wrapped encompassing me, was an uncomfortable blanket of guilt.

Out into the cold we ventured, wrapping up warm, and en-route to a place so close we found ourselves lost, yet persisting we found ourselves there, and what a disappointment, as the band, was basically bad, and the venue the same, and I beckoned that we should return straight away, to the exquisite and peaceful *Café Laurent*, but perhaps my companion misunderstood, lost in translation or ignored my plea in reverse, as there we took a seat, in that most unrefined and unpleasant venue of a wine we ordered but unlike the *Saint-Émilion*, it was not fine, and petit canopies there were non, only dirty horrible nuts, all rather revolting, but the company and conversation faired far better, but still, as the seats wood uncushioned and uncomfortable, the spark was missing from all, left wondering, as I was where I really didn't want to be, had I been ignored, had I lacked fairness, had I stood up for myself, when really, "I had nothing to stand up for?" but then equally, "Should I have not insisted when it was so bad and unsuitable, that we went right back?" or "Was that a different scenario?" Really, I had ventured into completely new and uncharted territory and I didn't know!

Yet somehow, I believed that a milestone was achieved, for I had stood up for myself, a new experience for me to encounter such a thing, and accomplished through self-love and fairness, and not from fear avoiding the captivity of fear, or being trampled on. And really, of all that, for a Parisian or any other as a forty-something year had just began, and with joy and delight I considered what a wonderful birthday gift, for confirmation it gave me, that a healthy process to full recovery, had begun.

Marceau and I braved the cooling night temperatures waled our way through pat the *l'Hotel d'Aubusson*, but alas, our timing out, all had gone, and my spirit had lost a bit of panache, so we ventured not back in, and there an opportunity missed where the quartet for me was to ring out a rendition of "Happy Birthday." But perhaps the best one I had already receive in Paris on that day as upon my arrival, before that macaroons were given, my dear friend Flavien in his grey fine suit, always a crisp white shirt with exquisite gold cuffs that shone from his starched white cuffs and with his fine voice, sang that tune to me, and the best thing, how lovely to see his pleasure in doing such, and his smile, his charisma, his congeniality, he so was pleasing me, and I was so ecstatic, I smiled so heartily like a little girl, I was transported I think for the first time, to a place I deserved to be, free from pain, free from guilt, only filled with pleasure, and I, I *so loved* it all!

I treasured my evening walks to the *Métro traversing le pont*, passing over the bridge where the congestion and pollution of the *voitures*, cars fell into insignificance, as my gaze forever fixed upon that stature of splendour, *la Tour d'Eiffel*, *la Louvre* and other monuments princely lining the banks of the *Seine*. The lashings of Parisian rain, through the uncharacteristic snow and treacherous ice from freezing temperatures; nothing was able to daunt me in my task of doing so as pausing, breathing refreshingly, deeply, instigating an emotion of awe and rapture. Though that evening as the clock approached midnight and it was to be my birthday no-more, I was to do no such thing, as my companion who offered me a ride home, whom before I had refused repeated offers, that night I was grateful to accept as my spirit on balance, was warmed, through to my deepest core.

I had enjoyed his company and that of 'a gay Paris.' I had pushed through the fear to follow my dream, my reward, there in one of those many magical moments of life, all wrapped up in a beautiful bow of a most exuberant glorious colour, taking its rightful place within the restoration of my rich illustrious tapestry of a glorious life was to unfold, with treasures to behold, for lessons learnt and those yet to transpire, my persistence and resilience rewarded of those precious gifts to flourish, fortify and magnify.

For a new day was dawning, I knew each and every step was to reward me with 'recovery' to gain, and I know it not by any other name, but to say "Thank you God," for I can proclaim, for against the odds for which I was truly and amazingly grateful, I will undoubtedly soar like an eagle for I never will cease my progress, for "I have made it this far!" And with love in my heart, "I am, at last, *free* to be *me*!"

"The most beautiful things in life cannot be seen, not touched but are felt in the heart."
~ Helen Keller

Chapter 9

Step With Intent

"Your success and happiness lies in you. Resolve to keep happy, and your joy and you shall form an invincible host against difficulties."
~ Helen Keller

"Jingle bells jingle bells jingle all the way," my birthday done, Christmas just hanging around waiting to begin, as 'streams of joy' anticipated by many, effortlessly, softly tumbling buoyantly over others as they swam in a pool of anticipation, yet to me, as every year, a mini-battle to be overcome. Those *camarades de classe*, all busy in excitedness, participating with full force in family plans, for such a time to be thoroughly enjoyed, whilst visiting their homelands, parents, or distant relatives alike, yet for me, in that city of love, great Paris, "Was it to be the same?" Or inevitably, as so often as was true, more in common with those lyrics sang by the 1970's pop group, Mud, "I'm going to be lonely this Christmas without you to hold." Yet, of recent years I'd gained new deep seated flourishing hope, a desire to fulfil, a solution one day, and as one day is not a day of the week, I elect a Tuesday, for my own happy traditions to create, complete with those I love, for the Festive Season and Christmas Day.

True, heartstrings tugged, as I considered each year of my age, and less years available for my dream of such to come true, but I held onto that silver lining in the cloud, that no longer was I that helpless little girl, trapped, in a house in closer proximity to my father, where portions of his cruelty he effortlessly added into the mix, as extremely grateful and thankful was I, for the mercy for my safe exit form that, so consequently, a cloak of loneliness, subtle, subdued that was transferred beneath a veil of unpleasantness, became favoured by default in comparison, as much lighter to wear, and as I counted my blessing, as I vowed to look back no more, the only exception to glance back in that rear view mirror to emphasise the positive distance I had travelled as I ventured forever forward to something far better to greet me, awaiting on the horizon.

Arriving early on the *rive gauche*, my host that evening, he of the verb conjunction already bedded in to all that was going on, on that Christmas Eve to which I had accepted an invitation to join him, and as I sipped on the *vin rouge*, as was my tipple, an introduction he gave, to a couple who were in Paris on a Christmas break, and to my frequently asked question of travellers, "So why this destination and why now?" They declared resolutely, as though they had to make an excuse for such a thing, "We've earned it and we deserve it." "Quite right," I did believe, so gladly informed them so. For I wonder sometimes, "Is life what passes us by, while we're busy doing something else?" and worse, "Does our life come to an end, while we're postponing, that, which we want to do, so much more?"

They from the south, and me from the north of England, and there, may lay a big divide, but when travelling the differences all become few, and to sit and chat, as strangers coming together exploring each others lives and rationales for choices made, unusual yet most interesting career paths, and all, to be divulged in such ease of common colloquialisms, well that, was a Christmas gift right there, for no concentration was needed, of conjecture being misunderstood, as so effortlessly, we enjoyed humour and spoke in sentences, where words and prefixes missed out, yet nothing was missed of our intent, and successful communication was resolutely all about.

Exploring so much, for how healthy to do, and secrets spoken, no harm done, for neither were we to see each other again, and a question explored, "What do you think, where do you see yourself in 5 years from now?" And true, when this question I posed of that Parisian companion, nothing was he able to say of his future, of hopes or dreams, contemplations or aspirations, he held non, for his eyes fixated on a larger than life rear view mirror, living each day through the window of his past, expressing only negative occurrences, as each morning he awoke and greeted, and of each defining him, misguided, gladly he wallowed, resolute his past served a greater purpose than his future, refusing to move on.

Certainly, of that night a difference of huge clarity, with my English companions, had fought greater adversity through culture ad society than he, and "Bravo," the very thought of such an undercurrent of determination, places a smile of hope and a future for all, upon my face, remembering their notions and such interesting possibilities being spoken of, and reasons and considerations for such, so inspirational, and of a cultural and age divide it did interrupt, as insight to another's perspective was perceived, and their options and decisions which were not my choice, for them I did rejoice, for such possibilities they were to expand into, and quite eager, yet resolute that something positive and good was definitely designed by they to happen.

French, and the colloquialisms in that we could have touched, but rather, the nitty-gritty we mused over, of how in that language, the exceptions to the rule, on-flow to further of the same, and how it cannot be guaranteed that a firm translation of the words will depict the appropriate result. *Par example*, by example: translated from English or American, Midwife becomes *sage-femme* yet in reality in French midwife equals the words of *wise-woman*, as explained by *la Sorbonne* Uni Professor. And all a little distracting in my logic based thinking, of grabbing at straws through my pain of trying to remember, so such relief to speak to others who like me, who were not learning as quickly as they'd very much like to.

"Come, gentlemen, I hope we shall drink down all unkindness."
~ William Shakespeare

The night was passing in pure joviality and harmony, but the same was not to be said for my stomach, for so hungry was I, for the meal that I was told was to be eaten, never did arrive, so it was popcorn I ate, and a pastry from the nearby *boulangerie,* bakery to purchase carbohydrates, to get me through the night, and a bit more energy it was to suffice, as I an my new companions talked and laughed so much, and danced a little too, and of one of the guys of the other, he commented as I was to beckon him to the dance floor, a makeshift, from where the tables had been moved away, that his partner does not like to dance, so it was two years since he'd had the chance, "Oh my" I did contemplate, "Is life what happens and passes us by, as we put off doing what we love, while placing our efforts, by default, into something else?"

My companion, hovered everywhere, joining us, the English group, then mingling elsewhere, and true, I believe he may have been a little disappointed, for he congratulated himself quite generously, on how well he comprehended English, yet his personal concept was to be flawed, as when our native language we spoke, prickly emotions in him it did provoke, for his realisation, of his interpretation of his English provision, was not as high as his own recognition, it had tainted his self-imposed grandiose cloak.

And there, may be not the initial incline, that of 'he' was not completely 'right' in his perception and representation of, well, so many things really, yet my companions of that night, for some reason, though why they spoke of it, I failed in my question to ask, that they declared him, a 'good bloke.' But hold on just one minute, when my antenna once before had been on the way up, had the same scenario not happened before, so "Why did I not trust in my own gut, and to it for guidance, look?"

So I failed to trust myself, and permit that niggling trepidation to unfold, as a question mark I placed not over his head, yet a resinating notion, of "Oh no I was right?" Deservedly followed by delight, for I, progressed in recovery, for I held insight to recognize subliminal signs, so my personal antenna establishing its presence, as a previously inevitable, disdainful disaster was rebuffed and alleviated.

> *"Dripping water hollows out stone, not through force but through persistence."*
> *~ Ovid*

The bar transformed into a banquet hall, of trestles to one side of the quirky shaped area filled with platers of Christmas cuisine, and to the opposite, an eclectic selection of tables placed together, in a row, with odd chairs to either side all decked out, not with halls of holly, but with all needed for a French Noel feast. Friends and staff seated of maybe a dozen or more, it was as if, a family affair, with a sense of normality dominant in the air, of no one having a job to do, but everyone having a role to perform, all doing it effortlessly well.

Then, beckoned to be seated beside my companion, by she who was of an age suitable to be his daughter, it was picture painting a thousand words, as deliberately by design for me to see and not misinterpret, as she looked me up and down disapprovingly, at my presence, her passive aggressive expression, of disgust and disappointment, fell upon her face, as her eyeballs rolled backwards in her head, as clearly defining her emotional and territorial position, with he who was my companion, that I to her, was most unwelcomed.

But really, there was no surprise in that, for I knew of old of her concept of me, and the attention her friend gave to me, well, I believed vexed her to the core immensely, for theirs was a relationship, that through my observation, provided a mutual dependency, a crutch of the self-serving kind, for each to lean. Yet that I may say, I refuse to judge, for I, have not walked a mile in her shoes, and have not a clue, of the harm she sustained at the hands of others, along her way.

Yet, perhaps a little necessary for sustainability, for one who suffered a poor relationship with her father and had been an alcoholic, and my host, portrayed himself rather un-magnanimously in the role of her saviour, retorting effectively, that she would be in the gutter, if it weren't for he. And for the other, it fuelled his need of self-importance, and to feel superior and in anthers life, and judging by his portrayals, important and necessary, and true, his intention came to fruition each time she greeted him, for her arms, flung tightly around his neck, of hugs and kisses to suffice, worthy of a loved on who has not been seen for 4 months, not only in reality, 4 hours. I judge not, but worthy of consideration was it interdependency or a crutch to lean on, which provided their mutual support, or "Possibly potentially harming, something mildly destructive or unhealthy?"

For what I had learnt, of a conundrum in life, a concept almost mean and bizarre, that as many geographical locations we may change outwardly, repetitively within, not an ounce it is likely to change until of our journey of life, 'within' is where we look and examine deliberately so. For true it is, we can never leave the past behind while we carry it around, yet so we will, until, actively, through strength of mind we choose to put it down. For progress we need to choose to make, for when this we do not do, we stand still, moving no where, and learning no-thing, particularly of what we need to do, to grow, to forgive and take our greatest leap, to dare to commence our longest journey, of all, that 18 inches between our head and our heart for them to unite, as our soul to beckon by name, as a whole, happy and peaceful life, may be ours to claim.

"I will prepare and some day my chance will come."
~ Abraham Lincoln

The meals dished up, I sighed as my salivary glands flowed in anticipation, but not to be, for she who did not like me, in-spite of my previous efforts to befriend her, because of I'd been told of her past life troubles and I thought in someway I maybe able to help her, but I backed away when I realised that was not to be, for banking my head against a brick wall, has never been an attribute for me. And my Christmas companion, before him a plate piled up high, a mound of lush white turkey meat, and "Oh my" should politeness not have prevailed I may have shouted, "Please, give some of that" and still perhaps I should have as how disappointed as upon my plate rested in the corner, morsels of meat of the grey variety at least in appearance with the constitution of gristle. Yet of her actions, I refused to be impacted, and from her I concealed my disappointment determined to eat wonderfully and with those around me, be joyfully merry.

"Man!" My taste buds ceased, but still in Paris I was grateful to be there, and hungry I tucked in to multiple helpings of *'du pain,'* bread, veggies and roasted potatoes, and all I enjoyed, so their sustenance, they were to see me through. The serving tables cleared, dancing was to resumed, with joviality passing on to greet-in the early morning hours, where at half past three, beneath the blaring outdoor heaters we sat, where the thick plastic foldaway doors, held together by thick Velcro, kept the blistering wind out, but held all the fumes of smoke in, and still a steady stream of clientele trampled to an fro, in sobriety never the less, as though it was the middle of the day.

What a joyous night, and a great way to spend and evening, and the time I was able to afford to it, my health permitting, quite surprised me, for it appeared the maladies of Melbourne were far behind me that evening, as my energy levels were recovering, and as a Christmas gift worthy of mention, as toward the new year was beckoning, how wonderfully to take forward with me.

The evening surpassed and drawing to a close, as Christmas Day was dawning and I meandered so peacefully up *rue Dauphine*, my energy waned as the light of the moon gave way to the rising of the sun. "Arrh in Paris," no one to hug, in that city of love, but not a barrier did that pose, to the elation of all I could hold, as that truly marvellous night, filled with fun and cheer, and optimism reigned, while I continued along my habitual walk to cross the river *Seine*, encompassed in pleasure as I feasted my eyes on the glory of the *Tour Eiffel* under the days rays, and really, with a melancholy heart, I was to sigh with relief, "Christmas in Paris, a pure delight!"

> *Ring out the old, ring in the new,*
> *Ring, happy bells, across the snow:*
> *The year is going, let him go;*
> *Ring out the false, ring in the true.*
> ~ *Alfred Lord Tennyson; A Piece of a Poem; 'Ring Out, Wild Bells,' Published 1850*

Christmas was through, "Phew!" I sighed, but a new potential enemy on the horizon of what to do on New Years eve, and how could I bring joy into it, and comfort too, for really I had non of that to enjoy in the apartment where I stayed, no access to the internet, music or videos, only quietly alone, even the bed was uncomfortable, hence, out I stayed to wheedle and wangle my time away and how anxious I became of what to do and where to go, through those uncertain times of uncertainty and such a relief when a friend asked of me, to join him to pass a Parisian *soirée*, with his friends and he, and oh how grateful and relieved was I, so like 'Billy no-mates' I no longer needed to feel, and I longed to be apart of something French, so quaint essentially typical. And so it was to be, as so happily I accepted an invitation from he, who had imparted the same for Christmas in the decade that was fast becoming to be know as 'the previous.'

The impact of the dawning of a *nouveau*, new decade was wasted on me not. As my expectations high, for hopes of the same, for it was to be greater and better than *le dernier* the last one, which I had passed living, minus 1 month, 1 week, in the southern hemisphere, with debilitating aspects of maladies in Melbourne and of bullying events the same, and of that rollercoaster ride, I wanted to hitch myself off, avoiding those pit-falls and pit-stops, where tribulations extreme and steep learning curves I was resolute to eradicate, but really, is that possible, when one such as I, with adversity, still effecting all my thoughts and actions mostly adversely, as giving up never was an option to concede, so perhaps I needed the assents of those learning curves and what they provided, as up the mountain I could climb, for from its apex I was ready and waiting, for the prospect of a vista sublime, through those formidable companions on my side of resistance and persistence as my fortifying agents of pure resilience, and through my evolution to jubilation, *triumphant* freedom was to freely flow.

"Every block of stone has a statue inside it and it is the task of the sculptor to discover it."
~ Michelangelo

The night was young and 6pm was the *rendezvous* time, in which was to became a bustling bar, as before me he stood, in an unremarkable ill-fitting brown, appearing new but remaining a shabby suit, and under it lay, a shirt of off-white in colour, his shoes of the same colour, unpolished since their purchase it appeared, where his curls of darkened brown met his greying temples of his longer loose French hair style fell around his face, and his long down-turned moustache so reminiscent of the 1970's covered a large portion of his face, where with eyebrows raised he formed a smile as the bar I walked in, and greeted I was by as he opened his jacket and through it aside, to show what was underneath, a question he posed of, "What do you think?"

Remarkably, I was not able to tell the truth of what I really thought, for to be unkind, I think not one person to another should be, so I opted for the truth politely, which was, "It looks like you've put a lot of effort in," and that comment, it appeased him, as he interpreted into it as was his will, and believed he looked pretty marvellous, but really, "Who was I to disagree?"

A red wine, in a 14centremil measure accepted and sipped, as we awaited for the group to grow, from to 2 to 3 to more, until we became a minor eclectic mix of apparel most certainly, but fur coats, in France, consistently worn. Some waring jewels of pearls or beady, or magnificent hair pieces of bows of satin ribbon, while others chose *'chapeaux,'* hats, and gloves of the finest leather and boots, trendy or elite for *'les dames,'* the ladies, upon their feet, all refined yet quite sombre in colour, yet perfect in design to set aside that damp chill of that inhospitable, Parisian winter air.

The *soirée*, originally set for a distant and obscure *arrondissement*, one, causing logistical *Métro* issues for returning in the early hours after the celebration was through, yet good fortune was to be as a friend, as at the 11th hour it was transferred to a venue much closer, safer and with relief, so much more serviceable, so relaxing became my affordable forte, as I, was able to do that night, with the dawn of history upon us all, as the end of one decade approached and another before us refrained, but there just in sight, and with ease, all to be enjoyed, in my most favourable and easily accessible 6eme *arrondissement*.

A people watcher I used to be, but in some countries I've visited, quite boring the process seeming quite redundant, yet in 'Paris' no-way could that be said, as I soaked up it's ambiance with glee. Yet he who stood beside me, was to return me to the past, as a commonality he, shared with my mother, of his 'once upon a time' stories, pleased him so much to tell, but to hear for the umpteen time, well, for me they did not sit so well.

And so it came about, that I was to recap on that evening the story how his wife, she did leave him and in secret did run off with his children, when they were only about 9 or 10, and how a Russian married lady he had an affair with, had captured his heart, and of the joy they spent in his apartment before France she did part, and of the special meal he prepared for her, and the rose petals he did sprinkle upon the parquet floor, and so was he engrossed in such of a photo of the latter, he held as the screensaver to his portable phone, and too late perhaps I was to realise, of his resolutely spoken words, "You look just like her, you even sit on the same stool at the bar, and it is true for everyone says so."

He said he would and indeed he did, bring a photo album that I was told, she sent him after returning to her eastern European country of origin, her figure, far more curvaceous, and in youth, some 20 years younger than I and true she and I both with long blonde waves, hers beautiful and lush, hers healthier as not damaged by the Melbourne sun like mine. But really that was where the similarity stopped, yet undeterred he was not, and as I pointed out another lady at the end of the bar, "Look over there, that lady looks much more like your ex than me," "No!" His fast retort and disgustful frown, "She is nothing alike, she is a junkie."

So painstakingly slowly he passed through that album, explaining the history pertaining to each, as so tightly was his grip, his knuckles appearing to whiten with each rendition, and too slow was I to contemplate, was his precarious intention to secure a foothold in my life, for his implications evolved, that it was not 'looks alone' that was to matter the most, but his perceived notion of the personality that perhaps with another foreigner he was trying to reciprocate, yet so slowly was I of his interpretations, to coin an English phrase, a 'spot of bother' was to beckon, and I toward it I was to slip.

"Many people look forward to the New Year for a new start on old habits."
~ Author Unknown

On that historic night, from that bar on the corner, in my favourite *arrondissement*, people came and went and more introductions given until that one arrived, of the *vieille*, old lady {*vieil*, old man} stood before me, appearing so serene and so elegant, her rich lashings of deep brown fur enveloping her figure so petite, as it almost draped across the barroom floor, where her gentile hands were still to be seen just peeping out of the sleeves, showing hands gentile and her face, so tiny, appearing as though it needed to be caressed, and her eyes so tender, as sharing a smile simultaneously we announced, *"Enchanté,"* "Pleased to meet you."

But my companion, Stephen, introduced her by name, quite unceremoniously he pointed his finger at her, turning to me and telling me, "She's the one I told you about, she whose husband cheated on her and gave her AIDS." And more he continued, telling again how she as suffering society isolation, for this was back in the days before perceptions were changed, so he put his arm around her shoulder and said, "Now you come work for me," and put her to work in his restaurant kitchen cleaning his pots and pans, and through it all, her acceptance in society flourished and away dissolved her depression.

What quite a wonderful story it maybe conceived, should his purpose been magnanimous, but not quite so, as he banded his inappropriate story around as a flag to his major sailing ship, spreading the format of distain and trust and the possibility to cause such destructive harm, as caustic gossip holds the possibility to do, and surely I question how much was for her, and not forming a backbone of importance to his own self-worth. For should that scenario have been without self induced over-inflation, he would have no cause to band such information of such sensitivity and privacy of her life, around the bar, and maybe further afar, for he would respect it so, and know from he to her, he had from his heart performed a 'good' dead. Yet so sad I perceived, his true intention unfolded, to provide himself a proverbial pat on the back and raise his self-inflated, self-praise opinion of himself on which to feed.

And that dame, did look and stare quite perplexingly, knowing that she was being spoken about, but with her English as good as my French, of a notion of what, a guess was not hazard, and I with caring aptitude in my eyes attempted to appease her, as I tried to halt the tale of longitude that yet again my companion of the French verbs did again monotonously transmit, but of notion I did believe, to divulge such notions of another's secrets incognito, is most different to brazenly dispelling them, so intently and quite sanctimoniously, so void of a miniscule of deserved decorum.

"Oh my" my heart went out to her, and as I detracted the best I could from the presentation of my companion, a conversation ensued between her and I, and of each understanding much of what the other said, perhaps it was not so, but most enjoyable I discovered it to be, as our intent to converse collided and oh what fun was to be shared, as we racked our brains, of verbs in their correct tense, so of communication of resolve as the clock turned around, and the sips of *vin rouge* slowly consumed, resolute, we were to jump over the fence onto accommodating and enjoyable common ground.

And the time clocked around, and regroup our few from across the bar, as we set off for that destination not so far, to an apartment, so tiny and so surreal, for it was portioned in its entirety between the rafters of the attic space on the 5th floor, of a building many centuries old, and truth be told it was a treasure I was to see, as at the top of the staircase, most traditional by design, that our '*soirée,*' party wound ourselves up, as the panelled door before us, huddled in a corner so minutely stood, bizarrely, a large key was to open it, to release its secret and majesty.

Yet first, the creek and crack of the door as it was pushed open revealed a most precarious staircase to navigate, of each step a different depth, and at its undefined width, less than 18 inches at its widest point, yet impossible it was to take care exclusively to where to step, for so low were the rafters, of beams dense and dark of wonderfully natural wood, that a collision to the head could easily succumb, and just a gentle dip for one even of my height would not suffice as it was a deep lunge which was required to exclude that plight.

Like a rambling rose, I twisted around the consecutive corners, until into a *très petit salon,* very small living room, truly splendid I was to tread, with its low ceiling somehow comforting, as there to the left, a '*la cuisine,*' the kitchen, next a bedroom, with its dimensions and proportions representative of a triangular tent, and in each, a door absent and a petite window barely there, and to the right, positioned above the fireplace, deigned to reflect the light, permitted to pass through those small windowpanes, and "Oh my oh my," how bold, how beautiful, forming a vision most wonderful, my most favourite monument, the *Eiffel Tower* came in to crystal clear view, accompanied with joy, magnificently into my sight.

"Oh how it echoed so marvellously" that Parisian accent like fireflies bouncing across the room, as an *apéritif,* was offered with speed, as were an array of exquisite bite-size '*canapés,*' as around a round table squeezed in by the sofa, to the edge of the room we mingled, where bottles of fine wine and champagne waited to be opened by us, as finger food from plates round and large, adorning a tablecloth of crisp linen, on a circular table, to the edge of the room, yet even I, with a little bit of a tricky tummy, tried to partake in that French cuisine, pristine. And in that kitchen so immensely petite, in America likely complaints should their water closet be double that size, but his job commenced with a request for an apron designed, as the lady of the petite attic apartment cooked not, so it was a floral tea-towel was improvised, and stunningly, so surely it served a purpose of keeping the *cuisiniers,* attire of blue denim shirt and jeans, not looking new, though he striking quite the pose, as I wondered "Was that *typiquement français?* typically French?" as he busily prepared nourishment of fine-fare, for guests to enjoy at that *soirée*, drawing to close the old decade, and welcoming, the *la nouvelle année*, the New Year to begin.

A 'wonder,' it was to me as that evening of all I observed, was not a group of colleagues getting together, which with an exception of only 2 in fact they were, of whom, for which my companion far less than magnanimously so took all the credit, that indeed they had all become firmly-fast-friends, his account, that several years, while they walking their dogs in the park, bumped into him who introduced them, so as they remained friends until that day he gives to himself, full credence, yet in truth, the whole group formed a tightly-knit party, who gelled together effortlessly, for sure, so much closer than many families I've witnessed, and although I enjoyed my observation and was so immensely pleased for them of what they enjoyed and achieved, and for others who are so fortunate to have the same, though with a heaviness in that too familiar place within, I did wonder, really, to be a-part of something like that, "Could it, can it, will it, ever be for me?" and "When? When was it that time to begin?"

With eagerness from the table tucked to the side of the room, but quaintly, still seeming central somehow, shouting, "Who's next?" But not in English of course, as plates were dished here and there and of what I saw, I was not sure I was able to eat, for I still quite uprightly so, ate with my eyes, for if I liked not the look, I could not take it to my tongue, but with some persuasion, I was to manage it, and those roasted and mashed chestnuts that looked, a little like doggy-do, and taking a risk with my digestion, I partook as it tasted so exceedingly fine.

And our pleasant *rdv* most amenable, sustained a changed ambiance with a knock on the door, as in walked a handsome gentleman, moderate in years, tall in stature, curly dark locks, clean shaven, a look quite debonair, and a persona precisely, quite unidentifiable, wearing smartly tailored jeans, a jacket in pale grey, a smartly ironed shirt in pastel pink, and extremely attractive dress shoes, I wondered who he was, for of all my travels and deciphering 'who's who,' he posed a little conundrum, he, speaking French perfectly, through observation I'd come to know quite well and in persona he appeared not to be, and intrigued for I was unable to place the country he hailed from.

Time was to pose as a friend to me, as I somehow become in conversation with that unboxed man, and "Arhah," I was right you see, as Parisian by birth, though for a decade or 2, acquainting to half his age he had lived in the USA, and there, he had absorbed, more of how 'they' are, as he left, as we who travel the world possibly do, leave a little behind and seize a little more in front, and as we perched on tiny three legged painted stools of upholstered fabric in zebra design, a conversation ensued, and captivated I became by his story, true that not unusual, but he held an extra portion of interest to me, for what was his plan and his success. For he had renovated houses across in the USA and in Toulouse too, that an area of investment near the middle-ish of France recommended to me too. So right there, "Should that not have been a good reason to stop him in his tracts and ask for a business card?" "Yes." I do believe, but with later regrets at a missed opportunity and door close behind me, I failed to do so.

His strategy, to diverse, and refine his plan, buying cheap and changing purpose to those properties, accelerate their highest potential, to aid a favourable financial return. And "Oh my" that property investment format so on my list of desires of what I so wanted to do, so it was not so much a conversation that did ensue, but more of an interrogation of his format, his plans, his team, his structure, which professionals, connections and business team members surrounded him and what was his criteria for choosing certain properties while eliminating others, his rational I so wished to explore, eager to examine the reasons behind his mindset, and what set him apart from the others, what he got right and what mistakes he had learnt from, what worked and didn't in that business field, in each those 2 countries and so the barrage of questions went on.

Certainly, what a networking opportunity foregone, as perhaps through a lack if confidence, for I want the woman back then that I am today, and he successful in the field I preferred, and me not even off the starting block, his business card was not asked for, which I was unable to forgive myself, for my lack of sensibility, or simple courage to muster, with an extensive list of far too many items to mention of why I did not request that business card, and disparaging myself deeply, that I allowed those other people at that New Years eve party who were looking on rather intently, to intimidate and sway me from doing that most menial of tasks, that would have relieved my angst and really would have served me so, very well.

For a notion did came to light, from that group though not blood related, nepotism appeared to reign steadfast, sure they appeared kind, yet a subtle vibe most definitely there, felt and not seen, lingering in the air, perhaps prior to and a little testy and certainly a little hostile, since I was to take that 15 minutes to have a chat with that friend of the *soirée*, hostess, who she had not seen for a while, for it transpired that really I was not welcomed to do such a thing, and it evolved that really in that group of French people 'I really was to know my place' which was echoed by my companion, a friend, nothing more, though I had not yet guessed, held more of an intention toward me, than our previous conversations or his spoken word did suggest, where hidden his true vibe, and I was too slow to realise, but as *le jour de l'An*, New Years day crept in, in a blaze his character became clear.

> *"An optimist stays up until midnight to see the New Year in.*
> *A pessimist stays up to make sure the old year leaves."*
> *~ Bill Vaughan*

Peering expectedly out of the petite window, that really gave a far greater view then ever I would have thought it could, there in the distance stood that statue of iron, looking so fine, as I looked so eagerly at the clock, so keen, willing it to turn around to midnight, and how lovely I was able, for should my companion have hosted the *soirée*, at his home in a distant *arrondissement*, as was the first plan, never would I have been so fortunate to view that spectacular sight, that so happily befell me, and other than that delight, well in consideration, "Yes" I was happy to be there, though the vibe at that party had so changed ever so slightly, suitably, but sufficiently to render me feeling uncomfortable, and so feeling ever so lightly ostracized, I began, to focus on not what lay around me, but what lay ahead of me, out into the great yonder at the other side of that picturesque window.

"Oh joy" the clock was about to strike, the countdown had begun, ringing-in midnight, and *Mr Eiffel,* as with admiration I quaintly refer to the Tower, shining brightly against the blanket of blackened sky, the lights bold bright and beautiful daunted not in its capacity to overshadow the fireworks that were so high, in red white and blue, visible, with the excitement of a little girl, my heart soared in pure delight. With chatters and cheers, kisses and hugs spiralled out around the room, and Champagne corks were heard a-popping, and that Frenchman who seemed not French at all, perhaps he was a recipient of that 'vibe' too, as across the room he and I cast a glance, unsure, for New Year celebrations, should we greet each other the same, then with some hesitation, as if in unison, we commenced to move toward each other, and I was pleased that was the case, for it would almost of wrong to have done anything else, though that did not prevent me from being anxious of what the other party-goers in that room were to think of it.

As I reflected slightly as I was engrossed what was going on outside the window, and cast my eyes down to the street where people continued walking and doing there thing, unaffected what was taking place high in the air, and perhaps a melancholy feeling descended on me, were they happier on their own, than I was surrounded by those people, and how true it can be, to feel so alone when people who know, who may call your name are situated all around; and what of that decade I was so enormously happy to leave behind, and the new one I had so longed to arrive, the cusp, I was on it, no more hope only the realization of, starting from 'today' "Was my life, my hopes my dreams, what was going on, on the inside of me, going to turn out as honestly-great as I so desired with every ounce of me?"

And through my contemplations of huge and great possibilities of events, the rest in the room had made a decision that the party should continue at the bar where they, the group of 8 or 10 or more all worked across the street. Coats were sought from off the bed from where they'd all been laid upon, hats and scarfs grasped for necessary measure, but quite a surprise at that witching hour, as when we trudged down those tiny and precarious stairs and onto the street we waited for us all to arrive, the air was remarkably warm, and I was suitably tired, so of that group of 30-something in age were to wander the streets and see where it was to lead them I was to wander off to my bed, "But the night is still young" the re-paraphrased words of my companion, and a jazz bar for the longest time he wanted to take me, for some reason, perhaps it was the decade dawning Parisian air, but I succumbed to his repeated requests of persuasion, perhaps wrongly grateful that I 'felt I should' and so reluctantly gave-in, do something for him, for after all, he had invited me to that New Years party, although later I was really to wish I'd made a different decision.

Only a little down the street, that jazz club we ventured to, though on that evening had no such music to listen to, and split on 2 levels, the lower of some kind of modern stuff, that really wasn't my thing, but on the upper, well that was playing a little bit of disco, that took me back to the Illawalla, a night club I used to frequent back in the days of my youth, with its claim to fame, the largest bungalow in England, and what wonderful hours I spent there, and decades for recently, at Mondo's, a nightclub in Bolton where a friend and I, often, 2 nights weekly may go dancing, and her with a good baby sitter, her mother, meant we could stay and enjoy breakfast upstairs in the restaurant until 3 in the morning.

Then another club that popped up before I was to depart that northern English town, though its name I don't recall, I remember clearly of its open expanse of hugeness, that would on most nights of the week be filled with people and there the music type good everywhere, but I preferred the upper room, I think with a big curved bay window looking over the dance floor below, and there I would give a bit of a sway in move to the rhythm of the excellent RnB tunes that they played there. "Oh my" from back in the days I gladly remember, my preferred music and how I used to play it so loudly as around my living room floor, on plush wool carpets with surrounding décor that I adored, with a glass of wine in one hand I would shout out the words, where the volume concealed all the notes I failed to reach. Soul, Funk, Reggae and Town of Motown all my favourites, as later it was before my repertoire expanded where Classical and Jazz were to be added to my list of preferences.

"Wow!" how I missed music, it warmed my heart when I heard it, yet in the life I was living, I had not electronic devices or Internet access to 'get me some of that' and how wonderful it was to hear music again, you think it may have elated me, "Oh" it did for a while, then pangs that pulled on my heartstrings started multiplying, before melodic tunes of yesteryear provided unwanted pangs to my heartstrings for a yearning for the life I used to call mine, a job I adored, a house I liked more, a hobby that made me money, wonderful neighbours in my desired neighbourhood, my adorable kitten, and music, music, music, that I hadn't realized how much I missed it, my own home, my privacy, my rules, and all the enjoyment I was able to afford myself from an income wisely spent; peace and comfort were emotions overwhelming, as wonderfully my soul reared upwards, and of them all, right then and there, I made a commitment, a decision, thoroughly determined was I, again, to have them all.

"A New Year's resolution is something that goes in one year and out the other."
~ Author Unknown

The piano, covered up, no more jazz ringing out that New Years night that was racing into New Years morning, but perhaps better, as that variety that sung within my heart, and what a joy, and there was so much of it about that night, striking out between that which was it's opposite, as I ignored the latter smiling as I watched the young folk having such a great time and dancing all around to those tunes I had so missed, and there encouraged by a young local, I was to join her on the dance floor, where a young man was then to dance salsa with me, such fun of recollection of such up the Sky City Tower, to be spied from my Auckland living room, and then, the tempo changed, and from a wall to the side of the bar, my companion sped out his head, to peer at me across the dance floor, to propose, that he dances with me, "Well *"Pourquoi pas?" Encore,* again, I contemplated; "For we were friends, weren't we? So that was acceptable, wasn't it?" or "Was that complete naivety, for admittedly, to smooch with male friends before?" Never!

Immediately, uncomfortably, far too tight he held me, immobilizing me as he wrapped his arms completely around my whole body, "Normal?" I don't think so. Suddenly uneasy with a severe distrust of his intent as 'something' felt really wrong, I pulled away rapidly, yet he with overpowering force pulled back to him, and all just before, right bang on my lips he was to plant a grossly horrible sloppy nasty kiss. "What!" My eyes must have exclaimed opening as wide as they'd ever been, as away I pushed him firmly, he caught me off guard, he caught me by surprise, maybe that's why he wanted to dance for he figured they'd be no other chance for his, well what "Was it perhaps his plan all along?"

Mistakenly, "Had I wondered past precocious red flags I'd meandered past, not recognizing or looking for them, as I was relying on his words that he offered to me upon our first meeting," of "I don't want anything from you." "Was I fooled? Unbeknown to me, had he changed the goal posts? Was his phrase disguised, deliberately sucking me in under a false blanket of security, as his aim all along to achieve a different outcome? Was that, his agenda from the start, deceit?" Either way, to arrive at such unpleasantness, surely minimally, to throw me off the scent, it must have been a smokescreen he was to employ while he camouflaged himself in Little Miss Riding Hood cloak.

Force, real force was required to push him off, to eventually loosen his tight grip encompassing my body, for sure, I didn't even know how to flirt so I know I didn't no-thing to lead him on, I had, taken him at his word, that word he lied about, and he, in a non-parallel universe to this one, in not being 'my type,' and I was sure of my actions or omissions there was no-thing I did or said that would, even with the most inventive of imagination ever construed that I had encouraged him in any way.

Or really, "Did I need to level a degree of responsibility to me?" or "Had I over reacted?" more, "Why was I double guessing myself?" then again, "Was it all because my self-worth was that low, and my inner-resilience wearing thin within those unfolding, mildly tormenting Parisian situations?" While I still, was indoctrinated in my parents, colleagues, husbands, fiancés, beliefs and many more, that everyone else must be right, and I, "Must be always wrong?"

So "Why?" After I'd left England, I lived in New Zealand before moving to Australia and onto Europe, surely that made me capable and worthy, of something, anything, everything, better and more than ever I was told I was, and didn't that mean, I was a survivor and, right?" or "Was I to be doomed to be in that internally-emotionally-restrictive-place, for another decade more?" Certainly, that idea made my body brace and tremble with anxiety. Yet true, wherever I travelled in the world, different places, quiet or busy, great or small, cheap or expensive, those situations irrelevant, as relentlessly and always remaining, I was still, 'my own companion to me!'

Politely, quick-smart, I left that club but of that unwanted companion, still in tow, unable to shake him "Oh my" I checked the clock it was 6a.m. and sleep is what I needed, I wanted leave, wasting not time to begin to revel in the light beginning to illuminate *la première année de la décennie,* the first of a new decade; my decade, where everything was to be more harmonious, but first I needed to rid myself of that person with a new status of non-companion, as I walking increasingly rapidly toward the *Métro* and in dong so it was necessary to pass that bar where he worked, where nepotism ran rife, he beckoning me in with his repeated persuasions, "Its just for one."

"Oh why! Did 'old school' rear its ugly head?" Perhaps because with energy low and resolve of the same, I reverted to my 'default' status,' of placing other peoples needs first, 'so I gave-in' once again. But a trick he played on me, as so gingerly I sipped on that wine, not really engaged with what was going on, or realizing that actually that glass never got empty, that was until I turned around unexpectedly and there to see behind me, the barman filling it back up discreetly. "The last straw right?" Unfortunately not, for on my internal outwardly voiced command, "I really must leave now." His retort, "No, you must finish your drink before you go." "What!" Why, oh why! "Did I give in?"

Perhaps those old ways of doing things as unwittingly those 'old time' beliefs and behaviour, as I remained that 'job in progress,' that true, I was pleased to be, for I hasten to add I cared not to revert back to what I was in the realms of 'understanding men' or picking up on their MO before I commenced it. True, I hadn't been quite 'on the ball' for seeing through that Parisian mans intent, but I refused to be disheartened at my missing the 'flags,' or giving-in to his wants, for I, I was determined to use those experiences to form 'valuable practice,' only adding to my resilience and jumpstarting the next lap of my race, with a keen notion, that I will practice and improve until I get it right, for I know, "I can do better next time." Then how marvellously, to this commitment of refusing to give-up, my aspirations soared, as it evolved that for surely, *indeed,* "*NO!*" became *a full sentence,* as I freely used it as situations determined it, and there my progress speeded up, as I moved onto refined decision making and a life, safer more secure and complete with self-love.

"The difference between a successful person and others is not a lack of strength, not a lack of knowledge, but rather a lack in will."
~ Vince Lombardi Jr

Relief! From that boredom "Yeah," A smile snuck upon my face, at the sight of he, who walked through the door, and although I have not named many, this young gentlemen I choice to do so, it was Jaque from that elite establishment where I was known to pass many to frequent, and judging by his uniform, of that evening, he had passed it there working. He was so agreeably handsome, a quite toned build, of 6 foot tall or more with fair hair, not so wavy, not too short, but one of his features that attracted me the most, his eyes, they glistened crystal blue, as the inviting ocean in which to swim, his voice of decibels most agreeable, and his age far less than mine, but that failed to procure a barrier to he and I, perhaps for the sake of experience, or dare I declare delinquency as a wistful game of cat and mouse ensued between he and I, that was before its ultimate decline.

Telephone numbers exchanged, and so it began; I received texts from him, on the *Métro* or in my room, along the airwaves, little messages would filter though, though I must say, of respect or gayety they did not portray, but a nature far more risqué and perhaps their lay his full intent, unconcealed and on show to easily comprehend. Yet though as I sat at the bar, sipping a beverage of a choice of three that I ever chose from, perhaps a red wine, or on occasion a cold beer or likely on those colder days, a hot chocolate, so dense, it was possible to stand up my spoon in it, on each of those visits, a joke or 2 came through, and as if covert after reading them, smiling most often, taking care for no one at that sophisticated bar to know what was the diddly-oh, cautions not to share, in secret right in front of them, to him who stood just 2 foot away, while not a word to each other we'd mutter, I would *envoyer*, send a remarkably less risqué response.

Fun, for weeks we had, harmless flirting at best, yet such a welcomed break it was to all that which seemed so bad in my life, as a welcome distraction it made, transporting me away from all my strife. That was until, one fine evening, early, before the others we knew had arrived, and the texts substantially fast with a suggestion or 2 a little bit racy, with the stakes were apparently raised, that cat, was ready to capture the mouse. Surprised! And as his large round silver server tray, so quaint essentially used for carrying his drinks to the customers high above his head, loudly, he placed it down on the bar edge, its decibels highly ringing, as it rattled, collided and echoed before settling back on the black marbled top, then spearing a glance in my direction, not so much with a gleam or any such thing in his eye, but rather just and intent of 'knowing' that his message had been sent, took a few extra steps as he headed toward those exquisite Restrooms of cream and gold by design for the *l'homme, et la femme*, which shared a petite corridor and adjoining sink, situated just behind one primary door, and as the handle he took, pausing, deliberately serving, as an invitation for me to meet him in there.

Poised in my seat, not as a mouse but as a fellow tomcat weighing up its prey, ready to take that last leap, for that morsel of value, {or was it} that had been lying in wait its sight, and was prepared to wait for. But wait; "What was the deal? Why was I unable to move off that seat, and of an adventure, meet?" As in my imagination, what of the fury of passion, what of the kisses, what of he kissing me most romantically, his hands gently caressing my face as against this wall he leans into me, encased in a coil of delicate passion, twisting and turning like a feather taken up on a summer breeze, but oops, it ceased as quickly as it began, for really it may be no more than a dangerous liaison, so rapid so succinct, it would be business as usual as soon as it was done. So "No," I did not rise from my stool, and my poised position rested back down, for even in that tiny space where we would be, I was guessing I would be able to read the writing on the wall, so I permitted myself creative thoughts, but that was all.

But "What stopped me? Perhaps dignity? Perhaps insecurity, as just maybe I had gotten it wrong, and then really, how foolish would I have looked?" And not a word was said as he came out, and in reverse picked up his large silver tray, which never again, was thrown down in that way, or by either of us was that incident discussed, yet interpreted correctly was the flirting by he and me the willing recipient, his intent perhaps not so benign, as one day, quite out of the blue a *rendezvous*, was suggested, but not for dinner or a drink but only that liaison, which 'dash-it' still I did not expect to be elicit, as *passé la cheminée*, past the chimney, was its suggested location, my heart ever so mildly fluttering as there stood before me, my item of desire, and how I thought of that passionate kiss, and "Oh my!" "What was to come?"

As per the text, my seat I chose to leave, walking in front of the aged stone chimney the warmth from its burning logs layered the heat through the expanse to that elite *salon*, the theme pale blue and cream in French *Rococo* style, made popular at the *Palace of Versailles*, and passing all those who sat blissfully chattering, out into the courtyard I was to gracefully walk, though of my intention once there, I believe not quite so graceful at all. I waited and waited some more, resisting the temptation to think 'he isn't coming,' as I relaxed and observed such a peaceful place of raised trellises of painted wood and wrought iron, where plants from raised stone flower beds had threaded their way through, and the moon light dripped gently in to shine a soft glow on the French doors, draped at that time of the year, with heavy winter curtains designed to keep out the winter chill, then there he was, walking toward me quite rapidly, quite a striking vision with he stature tall and straight, his traditional Parisian servers attire of black fitted waistcoat adorned on top of a white neatly pressed shirt, his trousers not quite so pristine, and the polish on his shoes, no, don't remember, for my major thoughts after all that time spent 'cat and mousing,' I thought with a concoction, of trepidation and elation, "Oh my! Here we go…"

But a "Surprise!" was to greet me, for his lips only barely touched mine, before, he placed his hands on my shoulders and applied pressure, pushing me down to my knees, and it was not his lips but another appendage that he had in mind for me to place my lips upon. "What! Was he kidding?" Apparently not! True, I was against a wall, but that formed the beginning and end of where my imagination of how that *rendezvous* was to come to fruition, for there was not passion, no face caressing, no, sadly, unfortunately, his interest lay not in me, but only in that which lay a few interest below his waist. But "Was I going to do it? Was I going to give him what he wanted, clearly was his primary and overwhelming focus?" I was not persuaded, my parents had not trained me to give-in in such matters as the situation never occurred, so no default mechanism to revert to, no emotional preconceptions, no submitting to his desiring persuasions, as I rose up off the ground where he had pushed me, the answer had to be a resounding "No!" Yet, I as a willing participant and he, not a mind reader and of my petite fantasy he-held no insight, for he was concentrating on his own agenda, to which I-held no insight, and so it was, once and for all, the anticipation of the flame of passion snuffed out in a puff of smoke past the chimney.

> *"Each player must accept the cards life deals him or her: but once they are in hand, he or she alone must decide how to play the cards in order to win the game."*
> *~ Voltaire*

So it was, my responsibly for that even taken onboard, and moved on from, "Oh what a smile" and how pleased I was on the *le premier jour de janvier*, the first day of January, Jacques walked into that bar, perhaps he was happy or perhaps he was high, but either way my heart it raised a beat to meet it, raising up from that low ebb where I found myself unhappily, as from the other side of the room I observe him and the pleasure he was having, and then as a moment or two passed, I must have moved into his peripheral view, over to me he came, and hugged me while he delivered the traditional French kiss, one to each cheek, and brief words we exchanged before off to the bar he went back to his friends once again.

Contentedly with an inner-smile I continued to watch his actions, considering how, he must have worked perhaps all the night through, as his waistcoat I could see, peeping through his over-jacket, and wondered, "Oh my." What joy would have greeted me there, should a different choice I had made on that Parisian New Years evening and gone to my favourite haunt, of *Hotel d'Aubusson*. But then I would have missed the opportunity to gain that, which was about to come and serve me remarkable, immensely well, of great value to comprehend, so mistakes to make, venturing any further down that track to a cul-de-sac, which likely only held, a bad and festering end.

It was quietly pleasing and reassuring to me, that after everything that had passed between us and really since the fireplace incident never had we talked about it, that Jacques, pleased to see me, venturing across the room to kiss me another 2 or 3 more times, and with it dissolving an unspoken, and invisible barrier, his intention I was pretty sure, no more of less than to be friendly and perhaps who knows, with some weeks passing, holding a little of the same notion. Then an intrusive, inappropriate interruption, as my non-companion, demoted rapidly to ex-companion, ex-friend gaining zero status in quick succession with what I was about to witness, as leaving my side, appearing angry, briskly he walked over to Jacques, and though a foot shorter in height, that detracted not from his fortified domination, as within Jacks personal-space he stood, as it was his body language that spoke most loudly, and difficult it was to hear their conversation, until that phrase uttered for translation, "You have kissed her four times!" And with that confrontation, it appeared I was a voyeur and not a participator in my own life.

"What business was it of his?" and "Why didn't I say something appropriate about it to he who had rendered status of 'no-thing' in my life?" and "Who was I, by doing nothing to the contrary, to permit it?" But I was a little mesmerised and became more so, as I fixed my eyes carefully on them through the duration of that conversation that I was not privy to, as Jacques, listened silently, was he intimidated or threatened, as afterwards quite hectically he wander around the whole bar, kissing people and hugging, those of both genders, yet of me, he never came anywhere near. "What went on?" I was uncertain, but I knew one thing all my red flags had been hoisted to the very top of the masts, but not yet blowing in the wind, but that was not too long last, as before I went to bed on that day, a tornado force wind was to tare those flags from their poles.

Bemused, bewildered, astonished at his behaviour and attitudes of dominancy over me, his thoughts his will imposed above mine, all a little bizarre at best, and at worst, an over indulgence of his dominancy of his thoughts and more where they had no right to be, for he a person who in essence, was only and truly of zero significance or importance in it, and with no grounding or basis to give him, any idea to the contrary. Yet I had been too slow to calculate the supremacy he supposed to exude in my life, but I had to learn quickly, as quickly as he revealed it to me, for else, there could have been some real-istic issues arising against my safety. But no need to worry as thank goodness, the lessons were coming thick and fast, as I rapidly grew and knew, such harm, that he could subject, me, anyone to.

The scenario unending as more was unravelling, as another Frenchman, a customer at that establishment that was then to be subjected to 'he who was nothing to me,' anger and possible pitfalls of visiting that nepotistic bar, as that customer, unsuspecting of mild persona, absent of malice, harmless, appearing gentle wandered in, as in his long and loose pale green Gabardine coat, quietly waited at the end of the bar, to what appeared to be, query his bill. Perhaps such an occurrence not so uncommon in nature, as I encountered an issue there of the same, quite surprisingly too as I believed I'd established a rapport with the staff to not be 'taken advantage of,' yet it transpired that was not so, as on one occasion, I was charged a full 100% more for my order, and of those people I knew quite well I queried their calculation, it was complete dismissal and a blank response I received in return, ignoring me, appearing to be deaf, and suddenly, unable to speak English at all.

"Oh my" likely, that late night customer had no idea and "Why would he?" of "What badness was going to befall him next?" Perhaps revealing that Jacques appeared to get off, ever so lightly. As that poor man on that night, politely with a bar staff member, tried to explain the errors in his bill, but they appeared obstinate, unwilling to show concern or form a correction, then 1 barman became 2, then 3 to 4, as they huddled around that short statured, darked hair, non-imposing man, who appeared increasingly perplexed at what was unfolding and wondering what was going on. Cajoling, intimidating him with gestures of hostility as they waved their hands around in the air, and as they towered in height over him, pushing him everywhere, as he desperately looked around for a means to escape. "Why would they do such a thing?" I was trying to work out, as all everyone else in the bar ignored what was going on, and I, I question myself for too late, "Why did I not intervene?"

Like a wild pack toying with their prey they carried on, then after a few minutes when they seemed to have 'had their fun,' eventually, letting him pass, and like a rabbit caught in the headlamps of a car, the man appeared stunned, yet quickly seized the moment to make good his escape, but, not quite so, for it was not over yet over for he, for that non-companion stood beside me, who had observed all as I, took 3 powerful steps forward, where unprovoked, unsolicited, unwarranted yet so strong and purposeful were his actions, as with extreme force outstretching his arm, pushed that gently mannered, already shell-shocked customer forcefully, the man who received that blow to his back, he did not see it coming, as he was already on his way to the door, shocked once more, perhaps wondering what had happened, as he was knocked clearly off his balance and his body twisting and turning as desperately trying to stop himself from falling, but his long raincoat caught underfoot, and stumbling backwards onto the floor, hurriedly scurrying he picked himself up, and got himself, out of there.

Again, I stood there and did nothing, "What was wrong with me?" I didn't know, but then knew I had woken up, I was aware and able to see clearly, the flags masterfully blowing briskly like a feather in a hurricane wind and I was to leave, no persuasions were to suffice this time and not look back. The deal was done, on my tippy-toes I was off, so grateful to leave, to know I was free, and grateful that I was aware and unable to be sucked in any deeper for what 'he' have held for me, hidden in store, I too was to make my escape for from that man, I believed it the only sensible and safe action to take.

I was on my way out, but "What?" for really "When in his mind would he determine that sort of treatment was to fall upon me?" As for sure, in his 'targets' he seemed quite erratic. *Encore*, another elongated conversation arose, 'stall tactics' by any other name by he, who did not want me to stay, who insisted on accompanying me to the *Métro* some 3 blocks away, but "Really!" I now declare, "Should my insistence have been louder?" as in response, a loud, categorically and resounding, "No!" I should have replied. Yet a bad habit from way back when, as again I was to gave in to him, for it seemed so much easier to do and perhaps in that instant a strategy to employ, for at least then 'I was permitted' to leave the bar, and "Phew!" what a *relief*, be free, outside on the street. Slowly slowly went the pace, as he talked incessantly, in his English that previously I had been so grateful to hear, transposed to driving me to detraction.

His conversation I was blocking from my ears, only relieved walking up *rue Dauphine*, I was heading to the station, then my mind able to find the space to question, "Did I not think more of myself than to put-up and effectively shut-up with such?" for really, "Was I not a greater way through and further along with the 'job in progress' that I believed myself to be? Didn't I deserve to do what I wanted to do, over and above the desires of, effectively a stranger?" and "When was the day to come, when I was to put my needs, my ethics, morals and *safety* above those who in opposition, came up against them? To stand up for what I believed was right?" In short, *"to stand up for me?"*

"Oh my oh my," what a way to start 'my' new decade, for wasn't it supposed to that way, and it certainly wasn't supposed to have any bearing on it relating to the last, but progress thus far just a few hours in, really, it appeared I had already fallen behind on my own expectations for me, for my ensuing life, for my future, that would be the present, a gift, and as is the way, proceed until it automatically it transforms to the past. So, I had to be mindful, I could not give in, and I refused to do so, indications at first glance may have indicated that noting in that new decade had change, undeterred, but keenly I refuted that 'indication,' vowing of that decade I had 9 years, 11 months, 364 days and 17.5 hours available to me, to make it right.

So with resolution I bid a firm farewell, as I picked up my pace, hastily walking down the road, then a scuffle I heard brake out, so I turned to see what was going, "Oh my" not again, that customer in the long rain Mac who had been pushed out of that bar, in the street was being attacked again, by he, that zero-to-me-non-companion. Twice in one night from the same assailant, that bar customer from his plight was taking flight, as just from a few yards away I was able to see the look of astonishment with an ounce of fright written his face, that he better get the heck-out of there, then quickly as he could, struggling to stand up, into the warren of narrow laneways he swiftly scurried, as the tails of his Mac flowed behind.

"What?" Of that man that I agreed to go out with that night, I was adamant, I was to have no part of any lingering problems that were harboured in his mind, he who from his stance of stature and facial expressions appeared to relish the weapon of vengeance he wheeled around and with ease inflict on who ever he chose. Quickly to, I headed away as fast as my legs would take me, as I rushed toward *Pont Neuf*, very first bridge, placing as much space as I could between that he and me, and in doing so, something seemed in my mind, one of his, boringly resited martyr stories, how so frequently he would tell me how, "I arrived home one day to find everything gone, my wife the children, and hiding for 3 months and not her mother or anyone would tell me where they were." As always I thought it an odd story though never did question the reasons as "Why would anyone do that?" But after those few short hours, perhaps too long for him to maintain his 'best behaviour' status, his walls of camouflage broke down, and the 'real him' I was able to see, and there, in a nutshell, in one evening, abundantly, I had my answer.

My eyes wide opened, for true I pretty well sure I received the vibe from him, that should I not have given-in to his requests to stay, there may not have been hell to pay that time, but a bit further down the track, I surmise quite easily that in his mind, there would be cause to be and a penalty to pay, for not doing what he wanted when he wanted it, and of cause, violence, I believe he would not be, evidentially, unprovoked, behind the door in dishing out that and I reflected on my good fortune of 'forewarned is forearmed,' even though a tad delayed.

I was through, I distanced myself from him, where he transformed his old status into new-nuisance, as he commenced a barrage trickery, twisted text of messages of reversed psychology delivered daily, yet a master at deciphering that sort of behaviour I had long since become an expert in, with lessons lavished on me from my husband and fiancé, so easily it was to ignore and it dismiss them, that was until he upped the anti of intensity regarding his birthday, guilt, "Arrh," that emotion he manipulated it so well, twisted in his trap, doing exactly as he bid, so foolishly I succumbed to his 'woe is me,' of 'what he had done for me' and how it was then my turn to return his favours, again emotional blackmail, for talking me through my French verbs and a party or 2 inviting me, I would not have thought the price to be paid, as I gave-in again, and felt within that I was about to sell my soul, as to the restaurant I was to go, to join him and his son in a celebrated of his milestone birthday, and perhaps worse as through obligation, instigated by his messages of implication, that I stopped on route and purchased a bottle of wine to take with me on that dreaded occasion.

Of it all I knew, certainly a folly was underway, as my feet as I walked down the street the closer I got to the restaurant felt like they were sticking like glue to the tarmac, I felt nauseous as an overwhelming sensation, ripped and tore deep down in my core, as my actions were far out of alignment and the realms of sensibility and growth that I had gained thus far. "Oh the pitfalls," I knew better than to be doing what I was, but still I continued, as if on autopilot for a collision coarse with the past and not my destiny of "I am worth something so much more exceedingly better than this!" And more, with a heavy heart I felt a notion that I was betraying and dishonouring, all those women who have suffered abuse and retribution, subjected to, by the hands and the minds, perhaps so similar in nature, to he who I was walking to.
'Madness,' for by default, my actions were sanctifying his as satisfactory, when clearly they were not, and unwittingly I had permitted 'old-school' behaviours and submission to creep back in, but only momentarily I determined so no need to disparage myself too much, for of most importance I was to *give myself grace* for the tiny trip, onto that pathway that belonged to my past, so I worried not, but for my future awarded a note of encouragement, for *worthy* was I, not to be

discouraged but to gain heart, as in this process of gaining progress, along that journey of mine,' of that *faux pas* I clearly recognized, so there it formed a valuable lesson, and of it, *I knew,* I could and would, do better next time.

Yet still I sat in that restaurant, and felt shame, after being introduced to his son, as 'someone quite special' as resolute was I, that was *jamais* never to be my fate, or was I to ever permit such an occurrence of error of that again. For he, emotionally disjointed, who, true, once may have been able to reigned his power over me, but that old habit that served me ill, was cast-out and organized and resigned to a sealed box labelled, null and void, and perhaps, there that commitment and accomplishment rendered it great treasure to behold.

For progression, admirably for sure, for there as I left that restaurant, of what I experienced and witnessed from my self-healing and open heart, clearly, I was able to see his plans, of what he held in store to eventuate for me, but on his endeavours, caught-out, out of the dark and into the light, as on it, in the door pained that dismal shade of deceit I was firmly to turn the key and walk with self-confidence, self-esteem and self-absurdity, as along my road to recovery I progressed, heading towards, 'a job complete,' as my lessons I learnt increasing quickly, and quite marvellously I viewed that situation no longer as a failure but a steppingstone, to where I arrived at my destination, "I got it right this time!"

"Oh my" such empowerment was to accompany me that evening, as to a brighter future, it was beckoning me to tread upon its path, for dysfunctional habits were dissolving and those shackles from my mother and father, "Wait, what was that I could hear?" "Oh my!" "I could hear the *chains breaking* and *falling at my feet!"*

As quite deservedly, as with all women who suffer such adversity, I stepped forward with fortitude and vigour, resolute that *their* doctrines destitute, no-longer to reside in me, for so many learning curves I had climbed, nay, hiked, not up hills but mountains, to behold such amazing views from their peaks, to see outstretched, crystal clear clarity of all sorts of things, to pause, stand and admire. And on that Parisian street that evening, I walked no-longer with hesitation or 'old school' behaviours, as 'new school' had jumped right in and in it I was determined to achieve commendations of 'Honours', for no longer was I to look in my rear view mirror of where I had been, determined to look ahead, learning from history, and refusing to accept *their* worn-out legacies, as I was to continue my 'good fight' until my job was overcome and won! And to life I was to say, "Bring it on!" and "Who knew?" Me, so absolute and resolute, as 'needs must,' I became a master, and was grateful to be able, to carry my own canoe.

"You gain strength, courage and confidence by every experience in which you really stop to look fear in the face. You are able to say to yourself, 'I have lived through this horror. I can take the next thing that comes along.' You must do the thing you think you cannot do."
~ Eleanor Roosevelt

Chapter 10

Step In Truth

> *"I've missed more than 9000 shots in my career. I've lost almost 300 games. 26 times I've been trusted to take the game winning shot and missed. I've failed over and over and over again in my life. And this is why I succeed."*
> *~ Michael Jordan*

'Greatness' is not born from mediocrity; it is born from effort, by taking any given situation and working at it consistently, to perform an action sufficiently repetitively, to produce increasing capacity for its proficiency.

For ~

Mediocrity, may only serve to hold us in the middle, or the misery of the crevices we fall within when we refuse to participate with persistence, toward a direction to achieve our desires, as we resist to give in, for that will only halt our progression, becoming for ourselves, a 'Winner' of recognition.

And ~

When we master our own minds, we master with precision all that we choose to do.

True, I could have worked harder at French, I could have worked on my mindset, I could have taken additional medical appointments prior to leaving Australia, I could have chosen not to get mixed up with a man who gambled, a man, who told me he had strung his wife up by the throat while her feet dangled, I could have chosen previously to consider "Why did bad people keep coming to me?" and "Why friends did not stay so long?" But I chose not, as in oblivion I remained, not even reaching the realms of mediocrity in the service of helping myself to a higher plane of healing, wallowing in the mire, with lack of trust of everyone, yet not putting, strength in to commitment to discover what was behind it all, but merrily in ignorance going along, through the rough water rapids of life, perpetually falling off the precipice where sanity forebears to early onset senility, for so late in that game, or dance of life, or whatever your perspective may be, like Queen Boadicea, I was riding my chariot wild, and taking no prisoners. Yet, inevitably, the prisoner, she turned out to be me.

For really, as the athlete gets up each morning before the light of the day begins, to stretch their body before often their working day begins, to jump those hurdles and beat their best time, in the frost or snow if they must, to achieve their goal, to take part in the championships, of whatever it is they esteem to, and of the logistics of the same, and complicated administrative process of hoops also to jump through, that is just apart of their sporting ordeal that they must real to. So really, "Could I not have learnt, just one verb per day and its conditions the same, for how difficult would that have been?" But somehow, it seemed to surpass me in the realms of productivity to do the same, for it was not the mountain top that I was seeing in my minds eye, but the climb up to the top, where so frequently, through thoughts from the past, rocking me, making me effectively unstable, I was failing to commence my accent, as the snow and ice appeared to pose no problem, it was discussions, regrets and mistakes were encompassing me.

How shallow perhaps, for had I not made for myself, through necessity of a place to direct the fury, I felt from so long ago, and why then, were they making themselves known, when I believed they were buried and gone, and indeed they were, but most thankfully, to the surface they were to seep and rise, and through the discoloring, of what they gave, yet the color attributed to the violence of brutality and cruelty, of toxic and caustic emotional neglect and maltreatment, I still know not, perhaps, most gorgeously, most thankfully.

But "Had I not learnt to master my mind, to survive, so why suddenly was it, mastering me?" For is it not true, "When we succeed in such a thing, all things are truly possible?" and "Should we not set our direction based on the desires of our heart, then formulate a plan for its fruition?" For sure, I have learnt, that is what the wise people do, to take a job, in a place where they aspire to be, so perhaps foolhardy to work in a shoe shop to see my way through college.

"Oh my" how wise to better serve myself, to work as an Auxiliary nurse at a hospital, with invaluable insider information mine to gleam as I positioned myself well, to steer clear of those mistakes, which I took onboard at the age of 17, void of sensible parental guidance, and compounded by poor advice from the counselors and tutors at the Career Open Day at the local Secondary Education College. As an unfavorable *faux pas* of consequences unfolded, as a road commenced could have been avoided, obliterating that unraveling steady stream of stumbling blocks, expelling energy and time to reposition and navigate around, until logistical troubles and time lapsed, I joined the right dots, and found my place near still waters and stable steppingstones.

Cilla Black, so much wiser than I, for she, from those bygone days and Beatle era, a renowned singer from the 1960's and successful and adored TV hostess from a decade or so later, and expanding until this time, strategic planning her purpose, moving toward the direction she so wanted to be, as specifically she sought-out a job as a cloak attendant in a club, entertaining bands who made it great in the years of the same, for she understood of her positioning in that preferred neighborhood, to meet those who she needed to know, 'in the know,' as she watched and learnt, networking in its industry, with those who played gigs in that establishment, in her chosen field to pursue. And all without even to getting up early in the morning, perhaps more likely a rest while in bed, not to be lazy but for recovery, as she placed both feet firmly on her ladder, leading against the right wall, to begin formidably again that evening, to achieve her determined and desired successful fruition.

Her commitment propelling her forward, as she continued to join the dots, and "Put off?" "No" she was not, when her first audition for her first gig, due to insufficient rehearsal or understanding, failed to achieve her aim, as she sang in one key and the band played in another, a petite disaster ensued as after the gig a refusal remained, yet deterred not, as a learning curve she took onboard, for the next in succession, preparation proved valuable, "Yeah!" her efforts produced her residing reward.

Yet a little more was to come, her name written up in the paper, recognition, publicity, perfect for her goal but maybe not a necessity, but a mild *faux pas*, as they spelt her name wrong, indeed the concept they misplaced, writing not her surname as White but as Black, where some may have been disheartened seeing it as adversity or decline, not Cilla, disgruntled she not, as effectively seizing upon it, and 'hey-presto' her stage name, marvelously, was born. And that ladder so wonderfully placed against the right wall as she reached the top, accruing much success and adoration from the public, almost half a century later, she was bestowed with the accolade of OBE, Order of the British Empire. "Well done Cilla!"

> *"Even if you are on the right track you will get run over if you just sit there."*
> *~ Will Rogers*

One of Cilla Black's renowned TV shows, running for an amazing 17 years and called "Surprise Surprise," she also enjoyed with a single from the theme track, the lyrics from the 1985 song, re-sounding Parisian listening ears, the lyrics, "Surprise, surprise, the unexpected hits you between the eyes," could well have formed as prophecy, for my Parisian experience, was ever increasing in ferocity, as apparently, at every turn I took, I received my own and ever unravelling journey, of 'surprise surprise.'

My plan of learning French so very quickly, followed by a 3-week course of business-lingo French, hailed not, but what of my plan to be self-employed and free from bullying bosses, was that still to eventuate, or was I in the end, of my planned desire, to detract my attention or hesitate? But was my aim not the same, to achieve something more, something better than I held before, to be the master of my own plan, as I was to grow and flourish, and of it all, myself, on the inside where my good intentions tried to rise and continue to be heard, as I deserved, for of that, was I not worthy to receive? For sure, most definitely I was, but was I to be side-tracked, or singularly focused, or was I to have a great opportunity fall into my lap, but of it so disastrously missed, for I grew to be too focused on the result, to fail to recognize and avenue of bliss to help me get there, and of it all, a wonderful elderly French gentleman of maturing years, who offered me a place to stay in *Aix en Provence*, I declined, for of his 'true' intentions I was not sure, and too afraid to ask, and there, as I let the naysayers increase their grasp over me, and I, hesitant, misgivingly joined the wrong dot, and the price, it was to dearly cost.

"The world is full of magic things, patiently waiting for our senses to grow sharper."
~ William Butler Yeats

Yet life as I knew it prevailed, and time proving not to be a friend but a foe, propelled me through uni, too slow, as my proficiency and grades, failed to glow, as revealed, that institution was not to serve me the best. And how slow had I been to learn, of those other private teaching establishments on *la rive gauche*, a far favoured location than *la Sorbonne*, to me, of comparable prices yet of ability to *apprendre la langue française*, I grew to believe held far greater proficiency to do so, but what could I do? For I had paid the price, as I ignored my tiny almost unnoticeable, inaudible notion in that auditorium when that Professor assured me, that all so easy to learn a language I did not understand in another of the same, and "Oh what a folly" I made on that day, for the price paid, un-reclaimable, and the money spent, in haste, enabling me, surplus of time to repent at leisure, but really, of regrets and "Oh woe is me" yet realistically how long could I do that for, before to myself, becoming a complete bore, for I was not in a Shakespeare play, but real life, where my own determined pace, inevitably, resolute, I was to win.

Yet "Ahoy there!" Hope was on the horizon, for amongst those *camarades de classe*, were those who were prepared to help me, as I slipped behind, and one such young lady, of nationality decent from two Asian countries, with her long dark and straightened hair, and eyeliner most bold, and her dress attire, may conservatively been termed provocative, and she, Annie, befriending me and inviting me to lunch was determined to dispel they myth, that COD and COI of French grammar, was perplexing or complicated, and "No" I don't remember what they were, and true, while she sat in front of me, it could be said that she explained it well, but for I, as I commenced to put into practice her teachings, I was to fall again by the wayside, and of her question the next day of "How did you do it?" Was not the most uplifting or positive reply, as to my disappointing dismay, all she imparted, had slipped away.

"Had my father been right all along?" While College mildly obligatory, university obviously unobtainable, 'empty nesters syndrome,' never going to be as the deal of, 'a roof over my head' displayed clearly, a two-year expiry-date, as my fathers relentless disabling mantra's, the word of "Duty," but not of love or care, snarled through gritted teeth had sunk deep, "You're too thick to go to university" and "You're just as thick as two short planks." and "Questioning his viewpoint?" "Not really," accepting it sublimely, as normal, it surpassing my consciousness those taunts bedded and secured for themselves a comfortable position in my subconscious mind, bedding themselves in the deep crevices of my mind, festering and multiplying, lingering stubbornly, ready to jump up on a day such as that to remind me though notions of self-doubt and hostility, that as he cursed and condemned me to be, by those words he spoke over me, I was guilty as charged.

Yet, "Hold up one minute!" "Had I not since, carved out the crevices of, my own life?" In the real world of my reality, from where in it, decades earlier 'he' chose not to be, was I not to continue my good fight and carry that heavy canoe, for really, I had muddled my way through thus far, and continued resolutely to do, for my survival instinct remained intact, for that for-ever resoundingly imperative to ward off, his or her destructive intents, and true, it was not love, but desperate fear that had proved as the provocateur to get me that far. And indeed I was already a success, for I had gained my independence and nursing career, serviceable for me and to protect my unborn off-spring, so simply and realistically, could I not also master French, for long since, I had chosen to give up nothing that was important or imperative to me without a fight, or "Was I to conclude, that learning French, was really not worth the fighting for?"

For sure, "You're useless," "You're good for nothing and you never will be!" Condemned and convicted in full by his words, the painful wounds raw and real, and worse, appearing true, certainly made an impact on me, as at times I had stumbled and dragged myself over the rocky ground in necessity just to keep moving, battered and bruised, but quite certainly, with commitment to me, through resiliency, still forging my own path, for better or for worse, as I had already proved them to be false and unworthy, through my hard fought self-empowering growth, I transformed to stronger and wiser, then most importantly, on the inside, moving myself from "Where I was, to where I wanted, deserved and desired to be." And magnificently, I was to continue with that great fight, for that, was most certainly, *worth fighting for!*

"Triumph can't be had without struggle."
~ Wilma Rudolph

Annie, quite determined to do well on that French course, her goal enhanced by the knowledge, should she achieve such, that her employer as for the *debutants* class, was to pay for the consecutive course, covering accommodation and health insurance costs too, nice deal if you can get it is what I say. How wonderfully sensibly she was, logistically preparing in advance, arranging her Student Rail Card, for her return from Germany to France was all set, she was ready to go. "Oh comparison" it proved as a foe to me, but I did consider as I reflected on her good fortune, that who I hang around with I will become in that pre-determined 5 year time frame, so as I contemplated the love and security of those in my class, I figured, I also have a lot of good fortune to amass.

Quite eager with invitations including me, in a lunch at her friend's place of work with 2 free tickets she had, and "Grateful?" "Yes," though I chose not to accept, knowing that her time-keeping wasn't the best, and the phonetics class that came after lunch, well evidently, I was unwise to miss a moment, as I needed to enhance every possibility to improve that I could. Yet with multiple refusals accruing, I thought I best accept just one, so there it was, to meet with her flatmate after uni at a traditional Chinese market, and then, the job done.

For the mode of transport to get over there Annie opted for the bus, really I knew not why, a bus, such a slow form of transport in rush hour, and really, when was the last time anyone managed any kind of speed at that time of day, yet as the bus went along, I sang out a sad song of my woes of my living conditions and the bizarre and quite finally unbalanced persona of my landlord, and how grateful I was to have my concerns validated with affirmations for considerations of deliberation, all conceived, as poignant and relevant.

And so it was in that distant *arrondissement*, to greet us was a most congenial young French lady, and after the pleasantries of *"Enchanté"* we commenced our walk to the food hall, where observation proved as a key, that these were not friends, but appearing as lovers, and my estimation only enlightened as Annie, caressed her arm and staring lovingly into her eyes, and sharing jokes which were not to include me, and me feeling like a bit of a gooseberry and as we wandered around the supermarket I was left to consider, really, how interesting can this lot be, before I was able to make my excuses and leave but after some considerable amount of time, yet not to worry said the friend, I am leaving too, I will accompany you so you to the bus stop, which sent Annie, almost into a miniscule rage.

"That's ok, thank you, just point me in the direction of the *Métro* and I'll be fine" detracted not from Annie's onslaught of questions, of "Where are you going, who with, how long will you be and I want to come too?" All which received a non-committal response, from her 'roommate' as she was not hesitant to provide the info, but completely refusing to. Then of a stance of a little girl, cajoling her father, begging for something that was forbidden, became the next onset of mild slaughter, of with equally received the same response, as her French friend dressed so opposite to Annie, so casually, remained with her hands in her pocket, calmly refusing with a certified stare. And how quickly the concept came to my mind, that the person who cares least in a relationship hold the power within it, as equally as quickly I determined, "Oh my" certainly, it was my time to be out of there.

But suddenly, everything started to make so much sense, as my hunches proved relevant and true, as it was on a few *rendezvous*, with she who befriended me, and our conversations at various café's, where she told me of tales of her flatmate, how she had made advances to her, explaining, "My flatmate tried to kiss me last night," as she peered intently for my response, as I asked, "What did you say?" And fumbling slightly replied, "Oh, I told her I needed to clean my teeth."

And over those evenings chatting over coffee, and my neutrality, a voyeur I became, as I trod most carefully as that genera specific tale escalated and elaborated, often appearing to await my response, until she spoke, "She tried to get in bed with me last night!" my reply, "And what did you do?" "I told her to get off me, and pushed her out onto the floor." With the corners of her mouth down turning as if in disgust, continuing she said, "She made me feel sick." True, I did not wish to doubt her, but really, all the way through her tales, something did not seem quite right and so inquisitive in a kind of unusual way,

Annie beckoned me to tell her, what I felt" about it all and what I would do, if a person was to do the same thing to me.

Innocent, I considered her most certainly not to be, but a game player, most definitely. She portrayed herself as a person, as a woman scorned and perhaps when she failed to achieve my sympathy, it was the entire conglomerate of our *camarades*, she chose to tell, portraying herself as a particular victim, and dancing firmly around the edges of what was likely to be, her story but not in its entirety, as she a willing participant, but then as a woman scorned, as she was reaping what she had sewn and what lying in what she had made for herself, her own bed. Of all she coerced, her biased and unequal tale, and I knowing more, but choosing to say less, for it was her life, not mine, and non-judging, non-participating I chose to take a strictly neutral stance and said, nought.

Of cause, of that niggle of a notion, I had no evidence, only a gut feeling, of her perception of what she told was quite untrue, and there, "Was that growth I was noticing it and permitting it to float, alive on the inside me?" And true retrospectively, I had grown for sure, and I was more intuitive than I was before, because evidentially so, it appeared of my concerns for consideration to be absolutely right. "Arrhah!" And maybe for comment at this juncture, on a minor topic for exploration, as success worthy of note, the score: Deceitful Intention = 0. Listening to my Gut = 1. Progress = Experientially.

"Most of us can read the writing on the wall; we just assume it's addressed to someone else."
~ Ivern Ball

"If only" I had always been so intuitive in the line of recognizing indiscretions and idiosyncrasies in the realms of survival, I had excelled receiving a self-noted grade achieving 'Honours,' and in the realm of reading 'writing on the wall,' unfortunately for me not much excelling was done. And "Why?" For really I always did consider, coming from the legacy of harm as I had, should any person be well equipped to read such, to the repeat of negative caustic debilitating history it was to be me, but I alas, was to be so mistakenly, wrong! And worse, of that misguided notion, I was almost to pay the highest price of all, not of strife or money taken but that, of my life, as I merrily bold past warning signs in neon lights, refuting the possibility, that although my ex-fiancé, repeatedly told me, how because his ex-wife had annoyed him, he held her up against the wall by her neck, while her feet dangled underneath, but as a tale I thought it simply tall, and what's more, "Of course he wouldn't do that to me." "Oh misery," it new my name, and as I remained oblivious, it was on its way to capture me.

And I aiding and abetting its formidable destruction as I merrily trotted along, wearing glasses of the rose coloured tint, not even gleaming a hint, of the danger that lay ahead, yet *faire attention*, be-careful, a safety sign should have hung, with valued safety instructions to have sung, with its message of protection, "Wrong Way!" "Turn Back!" "Run for the hills and run as fast as you can!"

"Oh be careful what you wish for" may have become my mantra, as he wearing a suit for work and a crisp white shirt and tie, so smart, was to take my heart, but really "How could I have been so misguided, of sensibility, and so shallow?" And that was to be an affirmative, as for my poor assessment of what love really was, unknowing there I lay and wallow, festering in that dark septic, toxic place where I resided, for a time, excessively equating to, so absolutely, far too long.

"Oh my" should I have only considered something deeper than his looks, his appearance of his neatly positioned slicked back hair and unusually so, eyes of deep blue, a moustache, usually not my thing, but he had, so that would do, and so I metaphorically threw my glove into the ring, but how badly I was to serve myself in doing such a thing, a mistake in the making, as from there on in, gently but surely, it was his song I was to sing, and his tune, I was forever to dance to.

"Oh how I believed he loved me," though unawares in reality I may have just been deceiving myself, as on-flowing his traitorous nature and true intent was to do the same, as he consecrated his first piece of warfare, dividing and conquering as he separate me from the few friends I had, his MO, that initial portion of his battle plan commenced, as his determination, his purpose to enhance, to exude far greater influence than I, and hold excessively higher authority in my life than me, and there it was his mission complete, and there on his self-imposed superior footing started the descent, of my demise.

Deceived, by his true intention and misguided tales, I too easily believed his freely flowing accusations, "They're not really your friends," "They don't even like you." Yet of those falsehoods, "Why oh why, did I listen to him and not them?" "Oh my" for sure he had chosen his target carefully, one who he could see harboured 'trust issues' a target he could hit a bullseye and 'get it all' really without much effort at all. As so naively I sank into his game, succumbing to his presentation of facts, though in reality, not even facts at all, as too quickly I succumbed to his professed notions, "I'm only telling you the truth because I have your best interests at heart."

He twisted and tugged half-truths into wholes, just to suit him, as down the hole my notions of sensibility drastically fell, as my friends, who too embarrassed I was to tell them of the condemnations of his remarks, and true, perhaps I didn't trust them anymore because of the words he swore to be true. Yet they trying to help, on the outside looking in, wearing clear not tinted lenses as I, intently tried to warn me, but that saving, wake-up call, I ignored, believing him to be 'the-one' for me, because that's what he told me, and I held no reason, or chose no reason, to disagree. And so with my fate decreed, I willingly yet blindly, obliviously of the fate that awaited me trotted along that path of his hidden agenda, toward unforseen, foreboding and disastrous misery I was to absorb.

And life continued, 'as I knew it,' grateful at last to have someone it who loved me,' not realizing how I was submitting to his reign, as eggshells in increasing number I was to walk on each day, but I tried my best to avoid breaking more, with harm perceived equating to punishment received, until one fateful day following my grandad's death, he not yet buried, and the news of his passing I received from my auntie at work. While quite distraught, the instructions from my boss, "Go home and rest," but that I was not keen to do, for how could I rest, when likely I would walk through the door, and anger would face me, sex to be demanded, or yet another emotional battle, to give in to, again, yet I held not the heart and I so desired not, for on that day, I could take no more strain.

The week deteriorated as my exhaustion exacerbated, and I so chose to pass a quite weekend, for the funeral, the following week, and worse it may seem strange to say, but it was not the passing of my grandfather that weakened my resolve, but the highlight it shone on my grandma's death from a year or two before, those emotions remained raw, for that fine lady, the only person that I believed I received, true love from.

But I knew my place, he who I used to call Grumpy when we first started to date, "Oh my!" "How did I ever conceive to permit his cajoling for that notion to go-awry and how did I let it slip and forget it so easily?" Perhaps through oodles of his charm as his introduction, or reflectively seduction, where everything was wonderful, in the realms of romance or reflectively lust, either way his aim complete, as by his design I became putty in his hands, and to do his beckoning calls, whenever he wanted, that is what I did. True, I was far from stupid and I mean not to abdicate responsibility for the choices, my actions and omissions of what I did, but I hasten for myself to point out, that I was blind to his deceptions for I was not yet upon my own path, for I was only trampling upon that one my mother and father gave me and with the absence of not yet recognizing a pattern of problems, on it, not knowing there were others to look for, obliviously I remained.

Tentatively so, while he, who was soon to be my ex-fiancé was chopping vegetables, I quietly practiced my speech, of those carefully chosen words of what to say and how I was to say them, my pitch, my projection, importantly my tone aiming for perfectly delivery, before I did my very best to choose my moment well and ventured into the kitchen to ask my question. First preparing the ground, "I am so absolutely exhausted." I said and continuing, clasping my hands tightly in front of me while trying to lean nonchalantly against the wall by the window, as gently I petitioned, of his 19 yr old son who visited so frequently and from a distance only a few miles away, "Please, please, lets not have him visit this weekend." But alas my quest, my best efforts missed the mark, as loudly in that room echoed the sound as he slammed the knife down, punctuated by his retort of instant and raised irritation; "No! He's coming!" Not unexpected for my wishes were never considered and my requests, well generally I didn't dare to make them, but desperate for rest I begged, but "He was here last week and he'll be here the next, just this weekend, can he not come?"

By this time at my insistence to pursue, and my absurdity to question his decision, his vexation shot right up, I dared to continue, "I've had to go to work everyday, I have no energy reserves left to expel, I need to be quiet. Please let me have quietness." And then it was, even though he only turned half way around, as though I was too low-ranking to warrant such effort, still visible his facial expression of turning living things into stone, as he blitz my ears by jeers and jabs of hostility and rage, as he to me dogmatically, un-refutably announcing, "If my son wants to come; and I want him to come, then, he, is, coming!" The air filled with his tension and my desperation, then picking up the knife again with his annoyance deliberately displayed, reminding me who reigned and who was to be obeyed in that house, there was no negotiation only his command, "That is the end of it! And don't *you ever*, ask it again!"

"How foolish of me, to try and get something I needed or wanted, as long ago had my voice had stopped being heard," and certainly any point view, for then I was in the dark, where he put me, and so closely he drew those curtains just a fraction at a time, until it was my spirit, my life as I knew it that was fractured, cracked into little pieces, as I remained oblivious and unaware of that long path I did not tiptoe down but was coaxed beneath his veil of romance and 'love' with promises of 'this and that,' and the other side of it, I held no concept, it was pitch black or that an increasingly steep gradient, landing at the bottom with a loud thud, where those injuries, harming unseen, unperceived deep within, that was until one day, when also, on the outside they were to show.

That Friday arrived when my then fiancé's son was to visit and of course, as regular as clockwork it was off to the pub for those 2, and normally, I would gladly go too, but that night, my grandad not even buried, still exhausted I needed to rest, I was physically weary, through work and living with him, so excessively so, but I had grown to know, that was my life as I knew it, remarkably bad, but then so similar to my childhood, shouting, control and threatened harm, normal and nothing out of the ordinary for me, that was until that night, when on the outside, extreme harm was to visit me.

> *"Conformity is the jailer of freedom and the enemy of growth."*
> *~ John F. Kennedy*

"Why aren't you getting ready?" "Because I really need to stay in this evening, I'm so exhausted, really, I need to rest." "No! You're coming with me." Then, almost fumbling for the words as, emotionally and physically exhausted was I, my reply, pushing the point, "Really, I need to rest." "No!" he snarled, "Not good enough! Go get ready now. I've told you, you're coming with us." Unceasing, belligerently his teeth almost gritted taking no messing, "Get ready. NOW!"

So sadly; I never saw, or heard it, it was silent, as it crept up and overpowered me, that of his regime, governing my subserviency and obedience, and so I sat alone for such prolonged times while he and his son left me while they played on the gambling machines, they getting merrily drunk, while I, always the designated driver, from early-doors to closing time, usually 5.5 hours, unable to partake in drinks conducive to my palate or aiding a good nights sleep, and "Oh my goodness!" I was so silly as for the longest time I believed they wanted me there for my awesome company, but what a fraud, as all those years it took me, before I was to realize, their only aim as to secure a free taxi driver.

The night, tormenting, difficult to bear, and of course, they would not leave until, 'last orders' had passed and kicking-out-time, had arrived so it was midnight before walked again through our house door, and then, after walking in the direction of the stairs I was asked, "Where do you think you're going? Come here and make my son's bed!" Pleading, "Please let me go to bed, I can hardly walk I am so weary?" "No" was his angry response, for he had told me to help him make it, so that I had to do, so pulling all the tight fitting cushions from off both couches and laying them in a snug pattern on the floor before leaning this way and that then to twist and tuck to secure them with blankets before placing the sheets and other bedding over the top. And "Why did his son not do it himself?" Well, "Because he wants to go and clean his teeth." Yet too blind was I to register a pattern, that his son got what he wanted, and my fiancé the same, but "What of my opinions, wants, desires, or needs, were they ever to be warranted, or heard ever again?"

At last! The job was done, and I could go to sleep, but not quite so fast, for my fiancé or was soon to be my ex, had another plan, as he pulled me down, getting-fresh, wanting sex, but for his drunken jokes and foolery, that evening, simply I had no energy, my mind not thinking clearly, and there in that moment, by complete mistake I broke his first and forever Golden Rule, *I, was never allowed to say "No."* And although I said it pleadingly, it appeased him not. Yet what was he to do, for there was no past-president, for never in the 5 years and counting had I ever before forgotten 'my place' or dared to say such a thing, and for a few moments I knew it not, but I was in so-much-trouble and he was about to start to really make me suffer.

Trying to get up, I crawled to my feet, loudly he screeched in my ear, and fro the first time ever almost in a trance, I took no notice of him, continuing to walk away, but for him that was not good enough, as he caught hold of me, and within the confines of that doorway joining the lounge to the kitchen, standing opposite me, his anger escalating, forcibly flowing, fuelled by criticisms and accusations, but I rose not to his bait, how could I, my tank empty, nothing left to give or fight with, but my neutrality was insufficient to ease his temper as it erupted like a volcano, his hot laver of pain about to pour out all over me.

And what a huge *faux pas* of great magnitude I was later to consider, to not have listen to those words he, quite regularly spoke, as how he picked his ex-wife up by the thought, and while holding her in the air, her legs were left dangling. "Oh my" my absolute foolishness, as I believed, 'he loved me more than she,' and that he, would never lavish such harm upon me, there me and to me never would he do such a thing to me, and more wrong I could not have been, as his horrendous harm, through my self-cultivated false beliefs were just about to come crashing down most heavily.

A few steps more, I was heading toward my bed, but he had other plans as he barred my way using his body, way, in an aggressive stance he pushed his chest and his shoulders back as his neck jutted forward and refuted my repeated requests "Please please, let me pass." As his response to push and prod me holding me captive in that place, then suddenly out of nowhere in a flash, I felt a sensation like glass had sliced me across my face, as my head swung to the side, stunned, shocked, trying to process, that hard sharp pain 'where did it come from and why did it not subside.' Motionless, like a rabbit in the headlights, wondering what had he done, not thinking as far ahead of what he was to do next, but I need not wonder too long, as he knocked me to the ground then grabbing fist-full of my hair, began to drag me across the kitchen floor, as the pain ripped at my scalp, and crawling on all fours, I raced along, trying to keep up with his pace.

"Oh my!" When he stopped I scrambled to my feet, but he would not let me leave, shouting so viciously, so closely while pointing his finger wildly in my face, pushing me furiously, failing to keep my balance, stumbling backwards, as in the corner of the room, with the bottom stair my heels collided, and as my knees gave way, my head bouncing back and ricocheted off the large round cumbersome stone protruding out of the wall in that cottage centuries old. Consciousness, I did not loose and stars I did not see, but something very weird happened to me, like snowflakes and flashing lights darting everywhere blocking my vision, shocked, unsteady, almost too weak to pick myself up as I scrambled to my feet, with my only thought, "At least he'll stop now." Now, he'll realize he's made this mistake." But "No!" Unfortunately on that day, the only mistake was my perception of him.

Numb! He permitted to stand up and he barricaded not my access to climb the narrow carpeted staircase, as I hesitated not as I passed the small bright shower room to clean my teeth, most unusual, I, only heading for my bed, in a quaint room with small leaded windows of dark wood and floral fabrics, then suddenly, silently from behind, his hand cupped like a shepherds hook, caught my neck, jolting my whole body entirely backwards, before calmly delivering with vicious intent of extreme malice scorns of retribution to harm me and please him. Mild at first, unable to elicit a response with "Your father hates you." Who was I to disagree for likely he was right, and without a reaction forthcoming he upped the anti, "Your mother hates you too." Well, fair call, no argument there, but then receiving no reaction and gaining momentum, he descended to cut and slice like he had my face, for he knew the love I held so intrinsically for my grandma, then pausing before lighting a cigarette, he spoke his words with sincerest hate, "And your Grandma! Don't think for one minute that she loved you, because she, she hated you too!" Then there it was, the response he'd been waiting for, he achieved his desired goal, as those words pierced hard into my heart as my expression of sadness spilled-out, and his of gayety for a 'job well done,' he clearly displayed with pride, yet he not satisfied, as much worse was still to come.

For then, walking back around the bed, his real work destruction was to begin, as violently he threw me backwards onto the bed, trapping me beneath his body weight as he sat astride my torso each of his legs bent at the knees, pinning my arms in place, and leverage I tried to gain, to push my feet against the floor or against the side of the bed to tip him off, but of the position he had thrown me, both impossible to do, overpowered, I pleaded with him, "Please stop. Please let me go!" But my cries unanswered, nay ignored, as his mood, ice cold, he took another drag on his cigarette, then with his other hand, he placed it over my nose and my mouth, held it tight, and prevented air from getting in, impossible to breath and through my screaming there was no oxygen in them, my head, I pushed further and further back in the mattress, just in an attempt to release his grip but failed in my goal as he only exerted greater pressure and his grasp got tighter, desperate, no air, I began to thrashing my head around from side to side as rapidly as I was able, somehow, trying so hard to dislodge his hand just trying to escape, but no, as more securely he held it in place.

Remaining on top of me, he released his hand from over my face, gasping for breath, I breathed in quickly, still not sure what was going on, for my brain I think had not quite begun to process it, not a miniscule did he move, dis-belief engulfed me. Shock, despair or non-belief, my mind not functioning so well, as I stared-up and saw what I used to perceive as handsome looks, as his eyes, cold and empty with cruel contempt stared-down at me, his bare chest prominent, as his dressing gown lay open, that with a rolled-neck of deep blue and burgundy stripes cotton with accents of gold to break the harsh lines, and with warmth in mind, a special one lined with towelling, and a thick solid gold bangle on his sporting wrist, with diamonds to see in his thick gold wedding band, then on his right hand, a quite unusual signet ring, square in design and you may have guessed it, more diamonds encrusted in it, and there around his neck, that bulky linked gold chain, that one I bought for him instead of buying one for me, then one Christmas amongst others, I parcelled up and placed in the pocket of that gown he was wearing, and what joy I received in all that giving, and that price of love came easy to me. But "What of he, where had his love gone and really was there ever any?" and more, "Why wasn't he getting off me, had he not finished the harm that he'd started to do?" Well, the answer to that, was soon to become, very clear.

"Oh why, did I never once consider if our values or ethics matched, especially so our characters?" True, not even our personalities or interests intertwined, yet of such contemplations hardly in mind, as before I had a moment to think as he was grasping my throat once again, placing his thumb on my trachea, {Adam's apple} in the throat, brutally pushing hard, exuding force, no air could get through and that it really hurt too, my eyes bulging, staring directly up at his face, his intent seemed so cold, calculated and not misplaced, almost appearing he was revelling in what he was doing, and as I continued with all my might to escape, his weight resting on me, my arms becoming numb as his weight pressing on them was restricting all the blood flow to them, trapped, helpless a hostage, at the mercy of his decisions, floundering, my efforts futile, I had no fight left, I simply had to wait, wait until he stopped, or until I need wait for nothing ever at all any more. Time, passed, he stopped, and I was still alive, at last, I was able to breath as I could inhale and air could get into my lungs once again, climbing off me, still remaining chillingly calm, he walked back around to the other side of the bed, to put his cigarette out. But still, a little more to give, he wasn't quite through, with his comment deliberately cast to cause maximum and total disruption, "Don't you think of going to sleep tonight, because if you do you'll never wake up in the morning." and of his comment, "I had no reason, to doubt him."

Instantly, he got in bed and fell fast asleep, me, throwing back the covers, got straight out again, and my tan boots at the side of the dresser, managed to pull them on, then opened the top draw, where neatly I saw, piles of lingerie all colour coded, and picking them up to pack I was so used to, to travel away bi-monthly as he and I regularly used to do, but that night, my mind, completely absent of cognition, not a miniscule of movement flowing through, only the stark blankness of an artist bare canvas, as if leaning against the edge of a damp and exposed jagged edged wall, isolated, lifeless, in the cold darkened distance.

Motionless, I stood still, glued to the spot, trying so hard to think of what to do, but not a notion, absolutely nothing passed through my mind, not a cell was stirring, nothing was working, only inertia stirred, I persisted staring into the draw willing myself to do something that I needed to, but "No!" Numb, passive, nothing, was I able to think of or do, my brain, it had shut down, so unable to get out of there, and although, true, I believed his words, his threats, still, with nothing else left, I closed the draw, and removing my boots, with the energy from I don't know where, then replacing them alongside the dresser, I turned around, almost stumbling, aimlessly walking toward the bed, freezing cold and too shocked to be in distressed, as back in bed beside him, I laid my head down, hollow, on the inside, I was alive, but once again I was, a "Dead girl walking?"

Sleep, I did not get any that night, and up to the bathroom so many times, I believe for sure I must have emptied that 33 foot of digestive tract, but still I do not clearly remember my then ex-fiancé getting out of bed, but when I became aware of him, there he was fully showered and dressed, and "Yes" he had been drunk and "Had he remembered what he'd done?" "Oh yes" a clear indication, he was so nice to me, kissing and cajoling his attempts for me to be nice to him too, but I lay unresponsive, lifeless on the bed, and his persuasion tactics yet again placed him on top of me, his, a typical format of domestic violence battered wife syndrome, and true to form, that was until, business as usual after he had achieved his desired goal, which was for me to go out with him, to keep up appearances, the pretences of a loving couple, yet no one knew the real story, that before we walked in a venue, a shop or visited anybody or entered a room, I was given my instructions and told, what I was to say and to whom I was to say it, when to hold his hand and when not to, when to stroke his thigh in public and when he didn't like it, by his methods, I so indoctrinated, tainted, trained, so obedient I became, as so long ago I'd got used to, my voice superfluous to requirements, with my wishes, desires or needs were never heard never met, as his intolerance ran rife in his domain, where immovably, firmly he reigned. Where that doctrine of violence and harm: Proposed by my father, Seconded by my husband and Carried Out Unanimously by my fiancé. It all had to change!

Life as I knew it carried-on with grandad's funeral came within a few days, 56 miles to drive to Blackpool to where the service was being held, and the so sad and distraught as I felt the pain of loosing my grandma all over again, then at the wake, as we sat around a petite round table in a Reception room in a near by pub, my mother, she seated at the far side of the room appeared to be ignored by everyone, my brother as usual ignoring me, while playing best-buddies with my then ex-fiancé, but "Yes," his manipulation of persuasion complete, we were still 'together,' he who had knocked me around, and threatened my very life, yet still, so foolishly, I was sleeping beside him, still obedient, still caught up in the whirlwind of his destruction, and as the day wore on, "You're bruise is showing through. Go to the bathroom and put more makeup on!" So off I tottered, as forever I was always doing as I was told, and in that room full of people I, felt, so utterly, all alone.

Days passed, and of that haematoma displayed so clearly on my cheek, and even though of an inventive response I thought of, no one asked me about it, so my guard went down and so much going on, I forgot about it, and perhaps that was a mild mistake, as my boss 'out of the blue' visited me one day, and talking about 'this and that,' of the conversation, really I was taking not much notice, that was until quite suddenly, "What happened to your face? How did you sustain that injury?" "What?" That wasn't supposed to happen, not so long after, for surely, I thought by then the discolouration was slowly fading,

Caught off guard, as previously, in that factory full of people and a pub I visited daily, not a dicky-bird, not a soul had mentioned it, so "Why did she nearly a weak later?" My prepared, prefabricated and well-rehearsed answer, I no longer remembered it, so put on the spot, fumbling quickly, jagged and spilt words stumbled out of my mouth, "The kitchen cupboard was open and I walked right into it." But I think she may not have believed me, yet of that moment it was years before I made the connection, for then she approached the topic of Domestic Violence, and with blinkers in my professional workplace capacity, oblivious that she was talking about me, fervently replied, "Oh don't worry about that, let me assure you, in the waiting room I have all the appropriate leaflets available, I have all the phone numbers written in my diary, as I have been informed that a couple of people on the shopfloor are suffering from it, so prepared, easily I am able to intervene making appointments and lead them to the correct organizations and government bodies who can help them."

Because, "She wasn't talking about me, for how could that be, because nothing was wrong or awry in the household I lived within!" My father had inducted me so well, in those realms of accepting violence as the norm, and for his vicious mistakes, the price I was to pay, was almost my life. So deep in it, and still, I could not see it!

From a child, indoctrinated from birth into domestic violence, for in truth was the story of my conception, pre-disposed with susceptibility secured, of ill-perceived harm as an injustice in my life, in larger and more dangerous portions it kept being served, as those men appeared to help themselves to anything they could, my love, of what I had to give, my finances, my security, my independence, my emotions, my safety and on the list could go on, at the misery, that kept on coming and as that haematoma displayed outwardly, it was inwardly, where the real harm had reaped its greatest destruction.

"Oh my!" Why did I not run out of that relationship the very next morning, as should the shock not have been disappearing, or go to the police as my friends I went back to, so urged me to, but my weak stance, I only broke of the engagement and gave-in, not easily as an inner-fight pursued, but the result was the same, nothing changed, except I ceased wearing my solitaire engagement ring.

And "Oh how very much I wanted to leave," but he wanted me to stay, but of cause he did, for that served his best-interest and not mine, for he had a lifestyle to maintain off my salary, for I held a good job and received a good income and from it, where all 'our' outgoings left from it, as he, of his free-loading lifestyle, I paid the rent, the bills, I bought the clothes on his back and his shoes in his closet, of pairs he had in excess of mine, and each colour had a matching belts of leather, with shirts of silk and ties the same, with even the same fabric for his underwear, all-in-ones to keep him warm, all of the finest brands, and more gits galore, though for myself, seeing not the value, I bought little so little.

True, I gave it all willingly, pleased to do so, but for "Why?" I had not yet grown sufficiently to examine my reasons. Yet he my then fiancé, with his money, smoking, drinking and gambling in the pub on the slot machines nightly, continuing to shirk responsibilities as I even paid his Insurance dividends on the camcorder he bought, an expensive gadget in those days, also obligatory for him, to paying a substantial sum for his 21-year-old son to purchase a puppy, while to pay his portions of the accumulated and necessary household costs, he ignored, and carefully timed and poised requests, did noting to relieve his vexation at the very fact that I dared to approach him and his deflections of what I asked for transferred to his absolute annoyance as I begged for him to pay what was his, while he adamantly declined, and with a battle ensuing most every time, to keep the peace, increasingly it was solely me, who withstood the cost. Then before the relationship was through, that which he refused to do, pay a portion of the annual TV licence, his deviousness his deceit, his lies, as it transpired by direct debit, he was still paying his ex-girlfriends bill in full!

His treachery, "At last I was to wake up?" but "No!" True, my emotions on such subject were expressed, of his betrayal an misplaced responsibilities, but my rational squashed, my concerns ignored, with an expression how incompatible it was to he, that I dared venture out of my boundary, not relating at all to my then given job descriptions, of chauffeur, provider, private shopper, unpaid housekeeper, where starching his shirts were a must, where lust was disguised as love, comfort didn't exist, nothing to cherish, emotional security nowhere in the vicinity, and of fun or joy present in many a relationship, well there was absolutely non of that, and still in my world, expecting no better and receiving no more, life rolled on just the same, as in the pit of oblivion, stumbling, I remained.

Reliving those habits from childhood, put-up and shut-up as everything anything remained the same, with the exception of being an adult as then I was able to escape, 'if only' I knew that, that should have been my overwhelming aim, as like a never stopping roundabout, impossible to jump from, as all around the ground topsy-turvy, twisted and turning, upside down and inside out, or really, "Was that what was going-on, on the inside of me?" And so astonishingly, amazingly, I can hardly believe it myself, that as the bruise on my face subsided, yet the pain on my skull, which lasted for months, and when to touched, in an instant, would initiate a severe bout of nausea, it was not escape that I sought, it was more a ridiculous and irrational thought wayback then.

"Oh my desperate heart!" Perhaps, 'just a little head injury I could sustain, just to take my memory of that almost fateful night away, then I could love him all over again. "What!" Was I kidding?" or "Insane?" as "What on earth was I thinking of?" Obviously nothing any good, right or sensible, as certainly, it was not a thought, originating from a place of self-love or self-worth! A ridiculous concept, and "How absolutely injured, nay damaged I must have been on the inside, even in my 30 something years to have even minimally considered such a hideous notion. But there again, to put-up and shut-up were my go-to's, so surely my usual default position I was used to, passed from my father, freely onto every other man in the world, as any I was to meet, was to treat me accordingly to his doctrine, that I was; worth-less = less than = inferior-ority! But really of their ever-rampant creative punishments inflicted on me, from them, at last "Didn't I deserve to be free?"

"Did I really think that I was worth that little?" In brief, "Yes!" When the complex history all accumulated and delivered the answer to my soul; though, when viewed intellectually, obviously, absolutely "No!" But of that 'emotional intellect,' that proves to be quite a different story, as from an infant, as a child, through crucial and pivotal points in my life, always I had been instructed, that black was white, and that north was south, so cruelly was mixing with my equilibrium, everything was so unbalanced, topsy-turvy, with no steady ground to stand upon for good or realistic decision making, specifically in the realms of relationships, of what was acceptable or not, good or bad, I knew not what I was worthy of, and in parameters of these, too early to grow, I held *no* expertise.

Of course, I was looking the wrong side of the coin, for really, I should have been examining and devising a plan for my self-empowerment to enhance, to alter, to change my perception of men, my antenna to be modified to enlightened and see clearly those who would commit violence against me, and become a great scrutineer as to read the writing was on the wall most clearly, for if those men who coming into my vicinity were not going to change, to protect and keep me safe and free from dangerous people such as he, then on the inside, I needed to change myself.

As a 'job in progress' I had not yet become, so, so certainly in it, not picked up momentum, as poor choices were mine to recreate, with poor observations with great ramification, with a chain-reaction to unravel, and so it was, back in the day, to ignore, nay not recognise all those bouts of increasing violence, to he whom I got engaged to, but thank God I did not marry, as through the expanse of distance and time, 20 years later in France, paying good money to study at *la Sorbonne,* the choices, the mistakes I made back in those days, haunted me immensely, as the injury sustained to my neck on that almost fateful night when he trapped me on the bed, caused a neck injury that effected my cognition greatly, so as a much as tried, it appeared that in more ways than one, not just in Australian dollars, pain and suffering or copious expensive medical appointments, but in many other ways, I was still, paying the price.

Though a key component of my success, was to be an observer of me, thoughts and attitudes, for they create our actions and behaviours, so I tried, day by day, not to regress but place on my body-armour, vowing, that I refused my past to dictate my future, that those circumstances I was brought up in, I will do everything I can to leave it behind, determined was I to read learn and study, to do all I was able to create for me and any of my offspring, a better and improved environment where they may live, so they grow up untarnished by my history, as I create for them a new shiny legacy, as I aim to give them good grounding and teach them, as then I was so committed to do, asking, "What can I get right on this day?"

And for all those mistakes that had so adversely affected me, "Was I ever to forgive myself?" I didn't know, but I knew, I deserved to try.

> *"There are things known and there are things unknown, and in between are the doors of perception."*
> *~ Aldous Huxley*

The dentist, not a favourite place of mine to visit, but it had to be done, I had to go, and as I sat in the waiting room with adrenaline unwelcomingly pumping through my veins, for some odd reason, it was not a 'housey' magazine which I picked up, which was always my way, to view pictures of colours and furniture, design and décor, to include as options for my own house renovations. But surprisingly on that day it was to be, one of sport or nutrition that jumped out at me, and as I started to flick through, so unusual it do, for really their pictures were few, I stumbled upon a title, impossible to pass, so in that chair ignoring my anxiety, I sat back and rested, as I was so fortuitously to gather information, through someone else's experience that I so desperately needed, but didn't yet know it.

The title of the article had attracted my attention, only a small piece, not taking up much of the page, my eyes scanned each line, eager to absorb what the story to me was imparting, to rest deeply in my mind. A woman not unlike me, caught-up, trapped within a relationship, for she knew of no other way to be, that there was light in another place, on the other side of the darkness where she did reside, yet thankfully she found it, yet of my contemplation, "Was I really so totally oblivious to my fate?" For really, she could have been talking about me.

Wasting not the opportunity, I seized upon her experience, recognizing mine within hers, so similar, and the message to be held within it, how grateful I was for such ' a life as mine' having come into light, for it was to shine upon me brightly, for previously, after everything was done and said, wayback then, still I held no such knowledge in my sight, not a notion I needed to escape from that deprivation, yet then, quite instantaneously I began to hatch a plan, and then, suddenly I had it all, afresh in my mind, "In secret I will buy a house, and get out of there, away from him, as fast as I possibly can."

"E-Day" as I began to call it, 'Escape Day, Elation Day,' all prospects for my new future days was on the horizon, as I began to work through the process of securing the purchase of the bungalow I had chosen, yet how embarrassing it became, to be forced to explain to all involved, the Lawyers, Banks, Real Estate Agents and more, why the legalities of documentation, which must be sent to the purchasers home, *must* be bypassed on this occasion, for seriously in that instance, it was required to be sent to my workplace, and such anxiety for several weeks as I was trusting that all secretaries and receptionist and everyone involved would remember this golden rule, as for sure, my life, certainly my safety, evidentially depend on it.

The job done, the deal sealed, at last, I to move-on in just 2 days, but "Was I to tell he, my ex-fiancé that I was leaving, or disappear without such as a note, effectively to run away?" A choice of 'yeah' or 'nay' and after speaking about it with boss who by then I'd trusted to tell what was going on, and a friend who held an opposite opinion, ultimately I was to make the wrong choice, for when I told him the removal van was booked, "Oh my" how he began to cry, like a baby in so much distress, telling me how much he loved and so on and so forth, but you may have guessed, that was no less than an Oscar Winning performance, an emotional ploy to tug at my heart strings to a achieve his acquired goal, to keep a roof over his head and his foot in the door, of *my house*.

"Just one night." He begged, so keen to accompany me, his falsehoods portrayed as true, and eventually to his petitions aka, his master-plan, manipulated and coerced once again, I so foolishly caved-in and only to that the agreement, conceded, but how ironic and foolhardy it turned out to be, that I have bought that house in secret to escape for my safety, to leave that perpetrator of harm behind, and against my Solicitors strongest suggestion, persuaded, I let him come with me, and there, my greatest folly, as perhaps unsurprisingly, I was only to encounter only more of his unbridled sin.

For like a composer he deliberately orchestrated his events, and as I and just like a tambourine, to be tapped, possibly for a roof over his head, for money or simply a lifestyle he couldn't afford without another fulfilling his everyday bills, and in an area her preferred to live. Yet then mainly doing what I was told was the way I spent most of my days, so I failed to pause to recognize, that obviously he was using me, for the only thing other he ever gave me other than domestic violence, was an STD. Seriously, an RN and knowing much far better, still he tried to tell me, even though I don't sit on any but my own, that I must have caught it through sitting on a toilet seat, and so I had to go, to that special clinic.

Still unravelling his plan purposefully by design I now propose, as he continued to execute his deceitful and disturbing methods, as 1 night turned into 2 and 2 nights turned into 4 weeks with multiplications transposed into several months, where frequently I resited dates where he must leave by, and he refusing, but the truth, he had his feet had accrued time under my table, the one like the roof over his head and the TV with his preferred shows on, not mine that he watched and the machine that washed his clothes, you get the picture, all bought and paid for by me, and he contributing nothing, as his well-rehearsed excuses recycled, crashing through boundaries and like wild horses, galloping over deadlines he was refusing to go, and with each occurrence, my spirit was becoming more blue, as multiple battles did ensue, and "Oh my" 'Act in haste repent at leisure,' a notion to pursue, as I recalled so clearly the words of my Solicitor, "On no account whatsoever, permit that man, to enter your house."

"Oh my" at least one piece of advice I did follow, was to get it in writing via a Solicitor he engaged, a letter forming, legal documentation of intent, with the intent being most significant to the outcome, that, 'He held no interest whatsoever, of finance or any other to my, collaterally bought home.' "Thank goodness I did!" and more, "Thank goodness I stored it in a place that was not my home, but a place where he had no right or capacity to access, so of that letter, impossible for him to steal, destroy or possess." Retrospectively I do believe, that action I chose to take, formed my only and permitted, saving grace.

"It is never too late to be what you might have been."
~ George Eliot

Another day, another deadline of that effective squatter surpassed, another plead from me, "I keep giving you dates to leave and you keep ignoring them, a year and more has passed, will you please leave my house? I want you to leave now." And normally, such a plea from me, he would choose to spout, pacifying portrayals of his falsehood, but for some reason on that day, whatever was going on privately in his head, was to serve me most exceedingly well, as he made attempts to railroad me, as his true response was suddenly without, and oh what a brighter future it was to deliver me, as I observed his body language arched with anger, as his face so close to mine, almost impossible of his eyes to define, and as his finger ridged, poised pushing into the side of my head, as he uttered his words, oblivious to the power within their intent, were effectively to set me Free; "This is my house, I'm staying! I'm not leaving, until I'm good and ready to. So you shut up! Stop asking! Because you're really starting to annoy me!"

"WHAT? WHAT!" NOT AGAIN! NOT ANOTHER MAN TAKING ANOTHER HOUSE FROM ME! Not happening! He told me all I needed to know his true intent revealed, fear raged up inside and overspilled, as I was almost ready to vomit. My father for some reason sprang into my head, how he had held me prisoner in his captivity of cruelty, how this man had already attempted to kill me, and how through that last year or so, his control over me, he refusing to sleep in the spare room or without holding onto my 'most private part of my body.' His violence toward me had been forever escalating steadily.

"What of me? Where was my life?" and "What, was it ever to come to?" I had to stop this, my ex-husband, the layabout, had already taken one house, "Was I to loose another; to another?" Terror encompassed me! Like a flea caught up in a tornado. Danger lingering everywhere! Trapped forever! "No! No!" My soul cried out. I needed to declare. Yet it was not my soul, for long ago, that had disintegrated, unable, unprepared to live or survive in what I was to encounter throughout everyday, as through my existence and constant failing and compromise, of life as I knew it, at times it transpired, I was barely able to get through it. "Was forever I doomed, destined to be, "Dead Girl Walking?"

Concluding his intimidation he turned and walked away, but quite rapidly he returned to seal his deal of destruction, as I shocked, terrified at the future I saw unravelling before me, had not moved from my spot. His aggression paramount, his conceit the same, with the weight displayed in a 'cocky' stance, of superior authority, and with a cigarette in one had and waving his arm waving it about in the air, when he stopped, his finger was pointing in my face, as with cold sincerity, "And don't you even think about changing the locks, for I'll be in through the window, and don't think the police will be able to save you, because, by the time they get here, it will be too late for you!"

"What? Did he mean it? Would he do it?" Absolutely, quite assuredly, emphatically, as empirical evidence in copious quantities, encompassed and propelled my notions, I held no doubt, as from the first time he almost killed me, and those events in between until that moment, he left me in no doubt, that of his threat, he most definitely could make good-on. How black my heart was on that day, cradled and cursed, though most oddly, was that what I needed to hear, for as he walked away from me, quite certain he had achieved his goal of inducing mild terror and everything that would bring him, or better for me, "Did he go a bridge too far?" and "Inadvertently, give me an idea?"

Within 2 swift days I'd hatched a plan, I made an appointment for a locksmith to come, on a certain day, at a *specific* hour, I trotted along to the police station to tell them what I was about to do, and how he had threatened to harm me if I dared to, providing them with my telephone number and petitioned them to take notice, "Please, if a 999 call comes through from this address on this day, please make haste without delay, for my life, certainly, realistically may depend on it."

My plan continuing, I prepared in my head, further timeframes, of him leaving for work and me sneaking back in, and packing all his clothes, tailored wool jackets and brand named shoes, silk socks that snugly fit so within, and a matching luggage set I gave him so on his trips he worked away, so fine would be his appearance, but 'if only' I had been more concerned about what was going on in the inside of him.

Then it was upon me, "TG Day" 'Thank Goodness day,' "AL Day" 'At Last day,' as I hailed all the way, but before any celebration could begin, I had to get all my jobs done, his stuff out and neatly piled in the garage, the external doors sealed, the curtains drawn, and all alone, I waited with baited breath of sever disturbing anticipation, of that harm that could befall on me, around 3 in the afternoon, his usual time for returning, "Oh my" as I tried to cast out those thoughts, "Was I to be alive or dead, when he was to leave?" For I knew what he was capable of when I was obedient, "So what was he capable of when he perceived I was not?"

My heartbeats pounding out of my chest, feeling nauseous, light headed, as I crouched in the corner of the kitchen, I tucked myself into that a tiny space, as I heard the rattling at the front door, as his key he had failed to open it, then jumping over the high locked gated fence, loudly rattling and banging on the backdoor, where just 6 feet away I was barely breathing and daring to say nothing as a friend from work hung on the other end of the line, with her instructions that she was ready to fulfil, "If I drop the phone or start screaming, please in the same second hang up and call the police."

I heard him climb back over the fence, though relieved, I realized I was still a sitting duck and trying not to worry that through the window he was still to get in, then I easily heard the opening of the garage door where he stored his black circa mid 1900's car was stored, and then a kafuffle began, and soon, very soon, though I don't know how long, another vehicle and voices someone was there to help him, though my safety my main concern, so in a ball crouched I remained in the corner next to the telephone, scared, unable to move or rest, for I knew that man quite well by them in the stakes of his violent temper, he was spasmodic at best, and was unpredictable at worst, so on high alert with safety first, I was poised and ready by the receiver for help to hail.

Eventually, it all went silent, but venture outside I did not, or put the TV on to alert him I was in, for I knew through long-suffering he was the master of surprise and disguise, so an hour or more I must have waited, till I believed by then his patience would have worn thin, and most definitely he would have left, as I ventured out, to take a look and initially noticed, the cheque that in a white envelope addressed to him stuck to the garage door had gone, and money, perhaps one of his main motivators for so much, with mild contemplation, I sighed a miniscule of relief, then as I went to pull down and lock-up the garage door as surprised to see it was totally empty, it was not only his own belongings that he took but also mine too, though certainly, that did fit in with his personality, all my electrical tools, my paints, woods, hammers, nails, screws ladders, all needed for DIY renovations, and all piled high on multiple shelves, but what hurt, was he took my granddad's antique tools, those irreplaceable things of purpose and sentimental value, sad, disheartened, thinking not of the cost of what he took, but what he left behind, *me*, and from him, I was then *free?*

Rapidly, I returned indoors and locked the house backup tightly and to cover the parameters, turned the alarm on as soon as I got in, as more deeply of his ramifications contemplated for my actions, I knew them not, but feared a lot, so a good nights sleep I did not get, fearing more that he was to trying to break in, for true, of his words, I had no reason to believe them only as a threat, and in the morning, leaving for work as I unlocked the door anxiety consumed me, for he was an very-early-bird in his habits and I was so worried that he was lurking behind the bushes, ready to deliver, more than, hostile words or mild punches.

And such fears failed to subside, and relaxing or resting no longer possible for me in my beautiful bungalow, for I feared so he would return, wheedling his bitter sword of revenge at me, and my only saving grace I do believe, that he likely living 15 miles away, a drinker and unable to travel back, to 'get me.' So for safety, my house that I so adored I chose to put on the market, and purchase a new one, in a location, where he knew not where I was or knew where to find me, for indeed from him then, I was to be, certainly, *free*.

But "Oh how mad" my then most congenial neighbours must have thought me to be, for of their pleasant enquiries, "So where are you to move to?" Yet hesitant I was to tell, as to their questions I jumped around quite, for really I was too scared and felt too vulnerability and examining the risks, I cared not to place myself in that position of worry, and submit to a possibility that my ex-fiancé could find me again, for I knew his MO and a master at disguise and from another had a knack of getting 'just what he wanted' and just in-case he returned to wheedled his-way in to their-confidence, to discover where I had relocated to, for my future security and safety to keep me free from harm, in case he I hastened not to break my devised spell, to them I simply could not say.

My safety radar increasing with acuity, I became more able to pick up on those almost hidden glitches and correctly interpret them, for no longer did I obliviously, missing those import pieces of empowerment and education, or, accept wrong as right, where acceptance was my fallback and default position, callas and cruel behaviour was accepted as normal of weapons formed against me, for new days were dawning and greater knowledge and sensibility I was waking up to, with understanding and growing clarity, that shame and blame only served to hold me back, and true, those who did bad things against me, undeniably were responsible, but I chose a new strategy, not to look too closely in the rear-view mirror as it served me quite unwisely, so from that habit and away from its vision, I was to masterfully break myself free.

For, I made a decision, I chose something new, until I was better healed, and more capable to recognize warning signs, and installed my latest radar update in my mind, I was only going to reflect on past-treachery as a tool for moving me forward, for *they* may have won a battle or two, in decades gone by, but in this one, unmistakable I was determined unequivocally that I, I was to win the war. And further more, of their emotional legacies that they presumed to infest me with, I chose to eradicate them, as I dissipated their power as I transferred it in fullness back to me where it rightfully belonged, and "How did I achieve this?" Through forgiveness! And "Easy?" "No!" But "Worth it?" "Absolutely so!"

Such an easy word banded-about, but in truth, forgiveness, I found needs practice and due diligence, and so I did, as needs-must, in everyday in everyway, until *their* hate, rancid and putrid, was disintegrated and disappeared from the inside of me, *their* septic spells dispelled, as a brand new day was dawning, afresh and anew and in it, and with grace and empowerment, magnificently I was, *set free!* And of it, I was, *truly truly worthy!*

> *"No trumpets sound when the important decisions of your life are made.*
> *Destiny is made known silently"*
> *~ Agnes de Mille*

Decisions, "Was I ever start to make them better?" As I chose to go to *la Sorbonne*, to apparently be miserable at best and lonely at worst, for had I not simply placed myself in another poor position, void of sensible evaluation of institution or empowerment, I chose it not because I particularly wanted it, but by default, because back then, I knew not of greater options, and true it was bad, but "Was much harm to fall on me?" I think not, for learning French, surely, it could be postponed to another time, indeed another country if necessary, but for then, I was a student there and got to pass, some wonderful months in Paris.

Then after sitting on those tiny and uncomfortable wooden chairs, and risking not life but definitely limb or at least the comfort of my butt, ascending and descending that staircase to the 3rd floor classroom, so narrow and hazardous, with the floor covering, ripped, torn, curling up in some places, difficult side by side to squeeze past, and certainly more than 1 or 2 students took a tumble, then clumped together on the tiny spaced landings one serving 2 classrooms, outside the students waited for one class to come out before they could to go in, with congestion most certainly, and Health & Safety regulations, "Mmmm," unlikely.

Strolling along the boulevards, Annie and I in the busyness of the traffic and copious fumes, somehow a rest-bite we enjoyed, in-spite of all the noise, for it was Paris, and long ago, the Hemmingway's departed, and other new artists got started, but there were we just taking a break, as we talked, of her past and future expectations, and my Parisian tribulations, while she enlightened me to the concept of the 'elephant in the room' and all of it, helped to relieve my petite portions of gloom.

Sharing with her, how my experiences had evolved in Paris gave me a new and bright understanding, of really, how, 'small town girls' or those who have previously enjoyed a quiet life, or been 'sheltered' from much that the world has to offer, who travel to 'the big city,' then can find themselves lost, in all sorts of bad-stuff, caught-up, in adverse environments potentially lingering everywhere, with people who are skilled in trickery or the art of reversed psychology, prospecting or waiting to pounce, on the vulnerable through their uncertainties, rising from emotions or compromises, like a whirlwind, holding the potential and capacity to cause harm, they lay waiting, hiding with dormant disaster potentially lingering everywhere, with unprovoked, unperceived circumstances resulting, not because of what we chose to do, but because of what another choose to do to against us.

Yet be perturbed not, from follow our dreams, to pursue the desires of our hearts, for as we do, we can hold astute awareness for self-protection, so as we go to gather our experiences, we are *très prudent*, most careful, for this will likely serve us so exceptionally much *mieux*, better!

> *"Self-pity is our worst enemy and if we yield to it,*
> *we can never do anything wise in this world."*
> *~ Helen Keller*

And "Yes," I was following my dream, though perhaps not in the format I had chosen to, as it turned out not to serve me well as I intended to do, and somehow, to 'build a bridge and get over it,' was a task that escaped me, as the flow of regret relentless and self-disparagement raged so fast, of lingering effects of comparison with those in my *debutant* class, of what they had, what they had left behind in the realms of love, not to mention, their possessions in safe storage with their relatives, and all of them had homes that could easily, and wanted go back to.

Their security, that emotionally kept them out of harms way, they enjoyed and took for granted, I never with such joyous thoughts to play, and certainly, their stability and comfort, served only to expose, my greater adversity. Yet my mind, "Was it tricking me to take far too many trips down memory lane?" To a place filled with potholes and treachery and really a place where never again I want to go, but as a whirlwind of emotions reeled up within, and just maybe that was how it was meant to be, because as they came to the surface, to release them I was able, so longer inside would they fester, re-creating or self-propelling trouble or strife.

"Oh of peace!" "How could I achieve any amount of that precious commodity?" But really, "Why could I not, for wasn't I to be set free from that cesspool of regret and a catalogue of perceived inferior choices, although I didn't know it at the time, I was to pass through a ravaging revenge of deeply buried emotions, buried for a reason, too difficult too deal with, too painful to place anywhere else, yet there in Paris, situations and circumstances, unravelling a web, as a light shone into those deepest darkness crevices of my mind, where previously me, so staunchly in control reburied their sin I would have done, resolute, as too, painful, too disturbing to experience on any given day, but then erupting, bumbling to the surface, in Paris those emotions so vulnerable in my mind, as I seeming powerless to prevent such an occurrence, and although I didn't know it then, how thankfully marvellously, my upward progression, was about to begin.

Having trampled up that hazardous staircase, bustling young ladies all keen to learn as we entered our respective classrooms, I spoke with Annie about my anxiety of learning, or not, *la langue francaise*, and with my emotions remaining tentatively unbalanced at best, while wavering on a precipice at worst, so susceptible was I to criticism, and her ringing words, "Don't stress yourself, all the time you stress to much" caused more than a twinge of disparagement as they rang loudly in my head, for "What did she mean?" "Did she mean I was stupid and how many others *cammerades* thought the same way?"

In mild panic, at such an accusation as I perceived those to be, I question quickly "Why did you say that, is that how you see me?" "Not really, its just that you get stressed where others would not, but it was just a comment, I didn't mean anything by it." And then the professor about to begin, sit we must, but my mind in a fury, "What is wrong with me and were my father's daily accusations true, that I was nothing and incapable of the same?" And more, decades later, echoing around my head, "Was I no-better and unimproved, and had he over me, with his crippling condemnations, mastered and won his vile noxious game?"

My self-esteem having taken a mild battering, I was keen to know more, for reassured not but hold greater anxiety of her reply, so gently outwardly but eagerly internally, I asked, "Do you have time after class so we can talk?" Replying, "Sure." Followed with concern, of "Are you alright?" Helped to ease my immediate distraught induced emotional dilemmas, for really, what I was searching for was validation that I was not wrong, that he, my father was not right, and that I may posses in this world, hope within my sight.

Leaving class, she I so wanted to speak and I met up outside, and we, belittled as we stood on the wide expanse of Montparnasse boulevard, with me, all wrapped up in fur, knee-high boots with *chapeau et écharpe*, hat and scarf, and her with a short jacket, bare legs and tartan miniskirt. So anxious filled with woeful remorse, at really I knew not, but kind of everything, I begged the question

"Can we go for a coffee and chat?" For why not I thought, for when she wished to talk of her previous flatmates tribulations, I was there to listen, but in return I was not to receive, as the comment came back, "Well tell me the problem here."

So, uncomfortably I did, enquiring quite negatively and subdued, "If you think I'm stressed and that is part of my innate nature, does that also mean you think I'm not sensible but stupid?" "No." Came her reply, appearing a little intolerant of I, "It was just a comment," she continued, "I meant nothing buy it, you're looking too deeply into it." And there it was, another perceived criticism of me. But really, my only purpose through it all, was to establish of what she said, to please confirm of my most sincerest thought for consideration, the I was not, "STUPID" as we my fathers forever favoured acquisition, so validation, I so desperately desired and wished for, so I was not to be, guilty as he charged me.

Logically, intellectually, long since, I knew my father's words were wrong, for my life's experiences and accomplishments had proved so, but that knowledge in isolation was insufficient to break his curse of corrosive criticism. "Was I being tested? Was I to be wiser and stronger because of it through gaining insight, sufficiently so, to remove those dirty grey and opaque lenses distorting my view?" as "Was there any hope for me that those shackles I would break?" "Yes there was," for the job had already begun, and maybe the battle of being so far-out of my comfort zone proved as the catalyst for such to unfold, and though I knew it not then, I was to grow to be so pleased, so grateful to go through it.

For was I in the middle of a battle, with the perpetuating painful past returning to haunt me, to debilitate me, to trap me in a hole of harmfulness, and had I inadvertently succumbed to its action? I may have waned, I may have faltered, but in truth, the result, I went through a battle facing demons of dark, negative energy from the past, which had robbed me of my peace and tried to destroy me. Yet their failure formed my success as slowly but surely, eventually, I developed strength, I fought back, I fought for better, I fought for more and I was to continue the fight until I was free and won the war.

Annie, appearing increasingly intolerant, disinterested in extreme of the distress I was displaying, insisting she had somewhere else to be, and how my 'old school' reasoning in a flash, whipped back in, as rightly or wrongly I took as a rejection and unfair friendship, of how I had supported her emotionally, but she was not to repay the same to me, so quickly I twisted on my heels, with my closing words, "Sorry to have troubled you. See you." Admittedly, perhaps not spoken sweetly, but then again, caressed in stress, aggravated not relieved, inspite of my petition, for inside I was stinging and smarting, and as I walked away, as I did quite rapidly, I could feel her eyes piercing me, though I did not turn around, but continued heading off down the street, for my contemplation, I thought her intent to be, "You're annoying me now, get out of my face!"

Yet I knew not at that time, but that was the last time we were to speak, even when in a group with our *camarades de classe*, greeting others but staunchly ignoring me, while talking and chatting in a group, she averting her gaze deliberately the same, from the communication within that loop, and reinforced, by our phonetics exam that coincided, as she sat at the top of the stairs, I was to walk, unencumbered squeezing past young ladies as usually the norm, with heavy bulky bags of which to bang into, and with chaos occasionally ensuing, they would trip and tumble to the floor, as Annie obstinately she turned and looked away, quite bizarrely I did consider, for I thought we held a friendship tighter than, to say "Sorry" and walk away was to hold the capacity for offence.

But I troubled not, of her quite extreme response, but contemplated her actions, how full-on and then the opposite, was she treating me more than a friend in the hidden concepts of her mind, as she did her last flatmate, but of cause, simply she may just not have liked me. Or possibly, she may have suffered or had something untoward happened to her at a young age, and as science demonstrates, whenever age that particular occurrence to place, that is the age when you halt, your emotional development to trace. And for sure, I hoped it was not the latter, for I understood of all that first hand, and wished it not on another, and I said nothing, but for her secretly wished her well, for one day, she may have her own healing story to tell.

"My father used to say that it's never too late to do anything you wanted to do. And he said, You never know what you can accomplish until you try"
~ Michael Jordan

Chapter 11

Step, Just Step

"Selfishness is not living as one wishes to live; it is asking others to live as one-wishes to live. And unselfishness is letting other people's lives alone; not interfering with them."
~ Oscar Wilde

"BUT I LOVE YOU." Those words so usually welcomed, but as with so many situations, on occasions exceptions are born of the rule, and that was the way it was to be, but why, was I such an unwilling receiver of those words he spoke to me?

"Arrhah; comfort!" It was my latest Parisian daytime refuge, a café on the corner across from *Métro Odeon*, an advantage point from which to see so much, while watching the world go by and so I did, as waiters hummed around the tables in regimented format, adorned with crisp white starched table linen where polished cutlery lay on top, stark against the dark polished wood furniture where in regimented form the waiters all hummed around, in fine white shirts with fitting for purpose, loose sleeves, with waistcoats of black, fitted with tiny pockets, numerous in number, perfectly designed to fit independently each coin of currency delivering accessibility of ease to deliver change to those they served rapidly and efficiently, yet a little mesmerized I used to be, of those long heavy cotton aprons tied around the waist, most cumbersome, as in length they almost dragged across the floor as around their legs they held taught, and how uncomfortable I did contemplate, to have been continually worn.

Wait patiently I would to be served, as I took my computer out of my back and as the waiter spoke to me, in my very best French I was able to muster, *"Je voudrais un café crème avec un petit pot au lait chaud côté, s'il vous plaît,"* "A coffee please with small jug of hot milk at the side." Perhaps, not too difficult to order, but not so, for my accent improved not, and all who served would bring me what I needed, until a new waiter was to happen on me, then of cause, the perplexed look would fall on his face as it use to on the others too, until that was, they just knew what it was I was trying to say, and bring it, anyway. And with wifi included, for 4.5euros, quite the best value in town, as a petite piece of dark chocolate and not a bad way to while away, and hour or two, on some student work or a bit of writing of my own to pursue.

One fine day, as the winter sun shone past the beautiful *Haussmann* architect buildings onto the spot where I sat, my relaxation was disturbed momentarily as my phone rang, and always the first, to check caller ID, and as I did I toiled with the idea, do I answer it or not, for who it was not a person I really wanted not to speak, but there it was, the wrong button pressed and my ears were bombarded, with his miserable and whining tones of his nature where his disillusionment sped along the telephone wires, as my peaceful spirit, disappeared with a hefty thud.

Posing his statements he launched his purpose for calling, "It has been so very long since you have phoned me. I wanted to speak with you. I have missed you." Taking a solitary breath forming the question, "Why have you not telephoned me?" His tone, not gentle or enveloping, but accusatory in his presentation. My immediate thought, well if you wanted to speak to me, "Why did you not choose and take action to telephone me?" For I, have not mastered the art of telepathy. But of it, of cause I did not, for I thought it may be quite cruel, but since I have concluded, "No, quite reasonable."

Yet explaining not the full truth I made an excuse, "I have been very busy with all things French," but that explanation did not include the reality, "Really, I refuse to suffer your induced subliminal power-dominance struggle and reverse psychology non-sense any longer." His tone and spirit declining further as he continued his likely well rehearsed presentation, "I haven't telephoned you because I didn't think you wanted to see me." "Arrhah," he had assessed well and a true account resided in his mind, but what was I to say, tell him 'affirmative' and "Risk hurting his feelings?" or "Be kind and sidestep the issue," or really, "Was it a generosity of spirit to spare, his feelings?" or more significantly, simply, "Was I just not putting him out of his misery, whilst simultaneously, abdicating, failing to hold onto, my own personal-power?"

But quite a surprise of that Parisian born man, quite a rare breed it appeared, for often as is the case in many big cities, everyone comes from somewhere else, and he, sent somewhere else for his education, to the east coast of USA, but of social etiquette of either country he held non, as his persona overflowing with boundless social awkwardness. He continued, his decibels drowning down the telephone as s reluctantly I kept it close to my ear, "I will do anything for you, I am your Knight in shining armour." Were the words that tumbled, as he spoke.

Yet really the former certainly was simply his fixed imagination and running away with him, as after being extremely slow start, of a recognizer of the 'writing on the wall,' I had begun to very well be a 'reader of the signs,' observing peoples hidden agendas, and of his, he had a least one or two, that served him and certainly not me best, yet I had learnt well and those perceptions that were to unravel with others I was to eventuate to excel, but until that time came to pass, I withdrew from potential danger as I heeded warning signs, as from past strife, I learnt, and chose from it, to rest.

Yet his plan different to mine as he was not for letting me do so, continuing, "I was praying for someone like you to come, and here you are, you're who I've been looking for, you are the answer to my prayers!" "Wow! No pressure there then!" For sure, I believe in prayers coming true, really I do, but should I have been praying for my Knight in shining armour, I knew unequivocally, it would look or sound anything like he.

And I, an unwilling recipient of all he spoke, yet to reveal that startling truth, I considered cruel and unnecessarily harsh, as ultimately fragile I believed him to be, yet in reality, though wisely or possibly dangerously, protecting his emotions, "Was I not being a little cruel-ish to me?" For *fair attention*, be careful, most careful, as "Should I not have nipped it in the bud, before it nipped at me, or somehow formed something bad from his twisted, unfounded perceptions, may have caused me to land somewhere, with an unpleasing emotional thud?"

Yet such an unsuitable man for me, how did I stumble upon him, well quite simply you see, as many of my life stories do unfold, "There I was minding my own business when" I was in that wonderful city Paris, but not for long, and establishments, routines and a niche for me I was trying for ease and comfort formalize, a local to call, 'my local' to replicate that so often enjoyed in my favourite petite suburb in Melbourne.

So there I was, trudging the streets with the winter Parisian sun shining through the greying clouds, in search of maybe something that my tricky digestive system could tolerate, and my pocket could produce the funds to pay, where I paused on those cobblestones, where the damp penetrated through the soles of my boots, as along the rue I was to pursue, outside the restaurant, the *carte de menu*, menu board, where English was written under French for the copious tourists that passed that way, and so it was, I tried to persuade me, to take a weight off my feet, and eat something other than a *crêpe* de *sucre*, sugar crêpe only, 2.50euros, yet I so enjoyed them on every occasion, but indeedy, they should not posed as a treat, a preferred delicacy to tantalize my palate and such an integral part of my everyday diet.

And then by surprise and English voice spoke from between the boards, do you see something you like? For sure, it was not a waiter, for the accent, so obviously not the same, but please I was I did not need to reply, as so often said, I did master, *"Désolé, je ne comprends pas,"* excuse me, I do not understand, so bizarrely I stood for a while working out the answer, as a conversation whimsically ensued, with perhaps 5 minutes passing when another question was posed, "Would you like to come and join us?" Then utilizing my Parisian default mechanism, I replied *"Pourquoi pas?"* "Why not?" So down at the table I sat with those 2 men, where on balance, an interesting conversation did ensue.

An engrossing tale I was to learn, the Englishman, privately educated, who spoke French so well, in Paris for only the day, twenty years younger than the other and a son of the Frenchman's father and his purpose I found most intriguing, for it was for an interview, perhaps not worthy of that much note, until considered it was for, a position of 'diamond buyer.' I so adore diamonds, they're one of my very favourite stone, but of course they need to be those that are humanely mined. And sat beneath the outdoor heater, his friend Gilbert, lived in France all his life, bar the years spent being educated overseas, and of the two, with totally different personalities emerging, I was so grateful to enjoy a rest-bite from the misinterpretations and difficulties in communications, from the French insulting me quite regularly, for my pronunciation and more, and they of the vernacular and verb meaning, unable to communicate what they thought they were, as painstakingly we both repeated ourselves, and "Oh my how lovely it was to relax with strangers and just simply *comprendre*, understand.

Seating myself beneath the royal blue canopy, with the usual gold writing, I was offered a glass of red, "Well OK, if you twist my arm," as we may say up in northern England, but in that *petite rue* in Paris, I replied instead, *merci beaucoup*, thank you very much, and poured afresh from the decanter, a large glass of red, and as I took it in hand and rolled the liquid around, it's *parfum*, aroma I did smell, "Aarrh" so pleasant, and then for my tastebuds to excel, I sipped it willingly into my mouth. For sure, not too long I had spent in Paris, but already an added appreciation for fine red wine I had become, knowing what I liked, and equally of what I didn't, and of my progression, I was enjoying getting to recognize the difference.

And then onto food, and how willing was I to participate, but the cuisine at that establishment grabbed me not, and perhaps nor at any other particularly, and just maybe, that is why those *crêpe* inadvertently had indeed become apart of my regular diet, for I knew always good, always hit the spot, and left lacking, no, never I was not. So there it was a question posed, would you like to partake in *du pain* bread, the best of kind that accompanied each Parisian meal, and after initially postponing my affirmation of "Yes please," it was quite quickly to come, as to hunger pains I did succumb.

As I nibbled, the conversation, most congenial, bright and breezy, with many laughs along the way, until difficult to divert one of those hosts who got stuck in a groove on a trial to tales of woe, of global politics and violence in war, of dates resited and events unfolded, all of which gladly came to an end, as his fathers friend suggested they pay *l'addition*, the bill and to the desert parlour, serving the very best of ice cream, apparently renowned around those parts and only just around the corner, it was enquired, "Would you like to accompany us?" Well deserts of the cold variety normally I do not enjoy, but I was enjoying their company, it was the middle of the day, I had nothing to loose, so I chose to say, "Thankyou, OK."

As walking down the cobbled street something unavoidable to see struck me, of the English man, appearing dressed quite refined, well he would, as an important interview he'd had, but such a contrast of Gilbert, of pasty skin and dark eyes with hair to match, all slicked back, but not with gel but with grease as it appeared so long since it had been washed, his crumpled shirt appearing as though the same for time washing appearing grubby, and his jumper on top, acrylic and not tattered or torn, but certainly well washed and spun out of shape, all ill fitting as was the deep tan leather bomber-jacket that lay on top, which he would need with such flimsy fabrics to fight of the blistering wind, and his polyester trousers in pale fawn, "Oh my" crumpled and creased as though in the corner of the room they had been thrown for more than a week, and they fell all wrinkled onto his clumpy shoes in light tan leather, all dirty and worn, so loose they were all but slipping off with each step he took, but worse the sight, for he, only 12 years older than me, all hunched over you see, and why I thought no need, for a job he had would not cause such a thing, nor the musical instrument he played, but perhaps the trouble was not physical but the poor self-image, or confidence he held within, and of my assessment, time was to reveal that it could be true, but of help himself to get over it, basically, I think not, that was what he was to do.

Gilbert lived with his father I was told, in the family house they'd always seemed town, so of what he demonstrated, it was not financial issues which were the problem, and true, I have suffered adversity, previously in the financial department, but never have I presented myself so badly, and true also, it is not necessarily and emotional cause when you do, for my mother of cause, always done-up within an inch of her life, although in the house she stayed all day, and even though her was tall and straight, of what she concealed on the inside, it appeared to conceal, not love but bitterness and hate.

> *"Ambition is the path to success, persistence is the vehicle you arrive in."*
> *~ William Eardley IV*

Trampling over the cobblestones, it was only a few minutes before we arrived at our destination, which I had passed many times, but knew not it was famous, well at least to some, and there having chosen just a small pot we sat, ate and continued on a topic of chat, of far greater relief than that focused upon by Gilbert, as attention was grabbed, by the diamond interviewee as he was to explain, of suitable places to travel to or settle in my camper van, post my time at *la Sorbonne*, and "Oh my" so rapidly I took from my back my exquisite notebook and matching pen, to jot down that priceless information, that he as an Englishmen, having holidayed in France with his family, and knew English who held holiday homes there, was so willing to share with me.

Enthralled, what a wonderful happen-stance I did conclude, as eagerly I listened for my knowledge to enhance, as I considered wonderfully in my mind of 'where to next,' and our spontaneous *rendezvous*, it appeared not over, for then I was invited to join them, to travel on the *Métro* to a further *arrondissement*, where previously I had not visited, and with our stimulating conversation, I gladly anticipated more, so gladly did accept, as merrily I tagged along to a consecutive venue. But what a disappointment for Gilbert when we got there, for the establishment on that busy intersection had changed, no longer iconic of traditional Paris, but modern and global, quite horrid to me, but they, less interested with the décor, but more, "Does it sell a nice red?" so up we walked to the top floor, and an order was made, but of cause, after pursuing the 'carte,' menu for such, the bottled corked, it was aloud to breath, before for the three a glass was poured, and there we sat, with the same view afforded pre and post renovation, and deeper topics, of life, and the meaning of, with those intelligent men, were deeper explored.

And so it was to be, as the day drew to a close and dusk was falling, to the airport one of us needed to go, returning to the UK, while Gilbert and me, well we lived in Paris, well I so magnificently for at least a portion of time, so magically, and the diamond interviewee suggested Gilbert and I trade information, so perhaps helpful to me he could be. "Oh my" what a good idea and thank you for that I could have said, for of that topic without appearing pushy I knew not how to ask or say, and of learn by my mistakes and 'networking' the 'how to' of all that, it was coming, but slowly on its way.

Through the emerging friendship I held, gratitude for the Parisian companion, as so good it was to hold a conversation, in regular English with all the phonetics understood, as he schooled on the east coast of America, rather than listening so carefully to what was said, to try to fill in the blanks, to speak back what you thought it was, maybe incorrect, and have to start all over again, for what the English words mean, and translated to French, or visa-versa they often in format in purpose used, do not mean the same. But that of cause the worst of two evils, for when I tried to speck in French, often it was not a compliment I received but a stark criticism, with one Frenchman telling me, "You speak French so badly, you insult me when you try." Well, "Thanks very much" I could have said and brushed it aside, but unfortunately not, for I was so susceptible to criticism, for really it was all I was doing to myself of the same inside.

"Learning is not compulsory and neither is survival"
~ W Edwards Deming

Only a little time had passed, when a telephone call I did receive, by he who was to transpire to be, a *professor*, French teacher for me, and an invitation that he did extend, as his words rang out, "I want to take you to *Sacré Cœur*, for coffee and crêpe." Well, indeed, remembering our last spontaneous *rendezvous*, I had no reason to say "No," so *"Pourquoi pas?"* and so it was I agreed. So onto the *Métro* I did go and met him at the 18eme *arrondissement* and as we trudged the streets and his conversation, filled me not with glee but a mild hesitancy, and as my dwindling spirit became heavy and I was becoming more unwell, as one of those headaches that plagued me through those Melbourne maladies was popping up to say 'hello' and so on, I chose not to go, suggesting, "Here, lets *manger une crêpe*, eat a crepe, on the corner, and enjoy looking up at the magnificent *Montmartre* view."

But no, not good enough for he insisted as his mind was set, it was up the hill and a *crêpe* he was to purchase for me, and true, I was still an itsy-bitsy job in progress re the 'not being a people-pleaser' thing, as merrily with a hollow sound in my voice, to his tune I was to sing. So up to the top we trotted, really, when unwell, no easy feet, and once up there, we looked around for where to sit and eat, and walking from here to there trying to decide, really I was getting over-it, for really by then, feeling under pressure, cold and uncomfortable because with just us two, I really wanted to race back down the hill.

A stark courtyard, a place bare and unwelcoming, unable to shelter from the blustery Parisian wind, and sat perched on little wrought iron chairs, with the backrest perfectly unsuitable for me, inducing more strain on my posture, as the wind whisked around the corner and nipped at me, what a totally unpleasant place, and too unwell was I to concede to why I placed not his need but his preference higher than mine, and as the waiter came to take our order, with a cup of hot water to be 4.00euros, then add 35% conversion minimum for $-USD or £-GBP, but really, that was the only thing to help me reduce the risk of a severe headache, but although my companion had said, overly so, "This is my treat," taking advantage of him, was something that I would not do.

"Oh my" how I wanted to get away, our conversation, suitably boring and wearing very thin, giving me the realisation of the two hosts the previous week, it was the conversation of the other, that was to hold together the group of three, for on that day the group of two, was so painfully annoying, absent of glee, and to do it again, most unwise I considered I'd be. Yet, wait, there was to be more, for his repeated affirmations of "I want to do this for you" suddenly, was it to be a mystery or mild intent, as I offered, would you like me to get this meal, where he ate and in the end feeling sick I did not, where not hesitantly, but with haste, gladly did he agree. "Wow," so much more did that tell me about his character, and more about mine, and of that job in progress, I was to consider, quick-smart was I to catch up and my job to refine.

For really, tales of one-sided notions and convenience I really should have learnt by then, and withdrew, for I had previous forerunners of good teachers to recognize manipulative behaviour even of the mildest kind, from my ex-husband, my ex-fiancé, even the to be ex-*propriétaire*, for had I not learnt, did I not deserve, to eradicate such behaviours quickly, so stress and strain of the heart, financially or in the realms of career, of adversity to my life, in any small or greater amount, they held not the ability to play a part.

How much I wanted to leave that place and he, my guest, but no, for on the way down the hill he wanted me to wait, while he went into the large white Church, to light a candle for someone he knew, ok, fair enough, but please I thought inside, could this *rendezvous* not be through? And so it was, across to the candles we made our way, and not a cheep affair, with a night light type being 2E and a larger one at 10E, and in his pocket his hand did go, jingling and jangling his change, but when his hand came out again, not a cent lay within it, as he pretended with the absence of mind like a child, so obvious it was to tell, and there he lit the most expensive candle, but I wondered of his intention of paying for such behaviour, "Did that not obliterate the prayer?" really I did not know, but for whom he prayed, for the outcome, I'd risk and give, no absurdities away.

His visible deception, his apparent rouse impressed me not, for the cracks of his character, so clearly so early of his personality, his values were rapidly becoming evidentially translucent, started to illuminate through, but that is a good thing right, so time we do not waste, until our youth or simply weeks or days has passed away, while we, being involved with those who so wisely we ought not, yet his full agenda, I remained un-a-where.

> *"Experience teaches us that it is much easier to prevent an enemy from posting themselves than it is to dislodge them after they have got possession."*
> ~ George Washington

Yet that episode having slipped-by it was *'travail de la maison,'* homework which Gilbert was to help me with and how fortunate one night I was able to telephone him at 10 o'clock, so late as nothing was to interrupt that Parisians tradition of his late eating hour, and there we sat as he was to explain that which I needed to learn, so hopefully, I was to get at least something right on the next university day.

And so it was, he who became active in my *apprendre le français*, learning French, appointing himself as my 'private personal professor' ('ppp') and for sure, I needed all the help I could get, with French, opposite to my way of learning or formatting, to decipher and find a discernable spot, where a complex web of *verbes de la premier, deuxième, troisième groupes*, verbs of the 1st, 2nd and 3rd groups, with instruction from the university professor to, *mémoriser, mémoriser* before, memorizing some more. And with irregular verbs, and multiple exceptions to the rule, flying as obstacles everywhere, and all requiring a minimum of 6 conjugations to be learnt for each, it suited not my learning style, for my nature, to place everything into a metaphorical box, to be dealt with in-turn in a methodical manner, but with French I found that format impossible to do, as I, setting aside the physical limitations, perhaps unable to adapt my mind or my patience, for that new, appearing chaotic format to unfold.

So really, what a joy it was to be as Gilbert was to help me, or so I believed at first, as another *rendezvous* was to be set, in a quite a grandiose establishment, a restaurant most fine and modern, but really far from my choice of design, and with the price tag rising, the waiters dress code the same, so not a long black apron they wore, but tailored suits most refined, and as he spoke to *'ppp'* to take our order, so astutely obvious it became that Gilbert, unable to converse with he, portraying a stance of lack of confidence or demonstrating and irritable aggression, and of both routes he took, never once as he enquired of so much, did he look up. Such a sad place to be, and such a far cry from the man I appeared to meet, of intelligence and absurdity as he portrayed on that day, from being the menu board on that narrow cobbled street.

Yet the night continued but I felt a little ill at ease, as he commenced to teach me what he pleased, but stop him, I found a place to interrupt, but pleased he was not for he appeared on a roll, and I explained, "Please, don't teach me this as my tutor explained, it is far too advanced for what I need." But intent on listening not, intent, on a track and on his way, and as I found a place to interrupt once more, he became agitated that I was unable to 'get his drift' but "Please explain it more" I did insist. And then a scenario unfolded, an example he chose to gave, as right then in Paris, an earthquake was striking and buildings were tumbling, people were screaming with fear and chaotically running everywhere, being killed as electrical cables, breaking and flying through the air, with cavernous holes erupting and people falling in, drowned by the crushing pressure of the hemorrhaging water pipes, unable to escape, trapped, awaiting their fate.

"Oh my" so graphic was his explanation I realized it was not a rouse, as I stared out of the window, expecting to see all the same, ready to grab my bag, and run as fast as I could, but no, it was simply a scenario, but I wondered where on earth must his mind be, to explain with such horror the meaning of the use of one simple verb. But "Was that in isolation?" "No" there was to be more, and quite disturbing really, as he began, "There was a very young girl, soft, vulnerable, alone in the woods, it was getting dark, she was crying and afraid, unable to find her way out, and then before her stood and old lady in a long cape and a hood, who offered to help her, and as she led the little one through the trees it was not to the exit she was to go but deeper into the wood instead, and there, she was to open her cloak and reveal to the child the heinous beast lurking beneath, ready to harm and kill that little child." Really; that was his explanation! I grew to consider, I did not know what was in Gilbert's mind, but the more I knew, the more caution I held, and the more I wanted to know him less.

"Oh my" what a lucky escape I had, when to my dilemma of my Parisian accommodation I had, and Gilbert through his gauntlet in to the ring, and offered a solution, as his brother-in-law's apartment he said I could rent, and that he, would do a great thing for me, and clean it op, for it had been quite dirty and disgusting. Kind I initially thought, well "Why would I not?" That was until, to it he took me, and there it was, isolated to the end of a *Métro* line, and of that line, even that was split into two, so for frequency of accessibility to university and the city, there was to be timing and schedules to be calculated and into my daily routine, begun. And more, as we sat on the *Métro*, as he was to take me there, the people on the train I closely observed, to see, should their values, morals or likely predicaments resinate with me, for surely, should they not, located in the wrong place I was likely to be.

Then as we arose from underground and I felt the 'vibe' above, quite certainly, I felt, I believed, my gut reaction activated and I considered almost immediately, "No, this isn't right," yet likewise, hasty I preferred not to be, for the situation remained at the furthest point in reverse on the *Métro* form there, that petite French lady, with a persona quite rare, and I needed to leave, so remembering my mothers words, so to look that gift horse in the mouth,' until it was, after a most unpleasant 10 minute walk and climbing the stairs in a bare and bland 1970's building, with the atmosphere, oh so bad, my hesitation was unable to lag as Gilbert opened the door, and to a dark and dingy place we walked, hostility appearing to be tangible lingering in the air, and as he showed me around, he was quite proud of the work he'd done to clean it up, but for me there was only darkness, absent of light or sun.

To say no more, than the mattress should have been on the tip, but what was that, a brand new table pushed up against the wall next door, "Oh what is that for?" I did enquire, "Oh that will be my desk, I will be working here," he said quite confidently. "Arrhah," and with my facial expression I refused to give the game away of my true interpretation of what he said, for that would place him immediately on guard and would curve what he did say, and maybe tell a lie, so casually, I asked, "And how often do you think you'll be doing that?" "Oh all the time" he said, and completely in an instance any safety or security sprung into oblivion right away as I gave him enough line and his words spouted out quite boldly, "Oh yes, I will have the other key." "Oh No" I quickly thought, as such unpleasant scenarios rolled around in my head, where he appeasing me, "I will be here after you leave and gone before you return" did nothing to cease those raging alarm bells vibrating in my head, "Oh at last" 'progress' was to know my name.

I appeared not alarmed as I refused to give him a pre-warning and be forearmed, as he continued to talk of the rent and moving in, as I listened closely, as with his lies he tripped himself up, for previously he had told me the rent would be free, yet that having learnt from my experience in NZ, as I paid for food, petrol and more, and spring cleaned the house, still there was no such thing as a free lunch, as he, that man who had an undesirable interest in me, staged a robbery and stole my jewellery as apart of his plan, the same mistake I was to make not twice, and then from Gilbert there came a price, as his cloak once and for all, was about to tumble to the floor, for me to see absolutely clearly.

Well, "I can borrow a car and move your things in at the weekend, but we will have to do it at night when the caretaker is not longer about, for he must not know you're here." But "Why" I asked, "For people can let properties to relatives all the time, so while yours is overseas looking after his sick father, why can he not do the same." "Well I haven't asked him if you can be here, "Really?" "Wasn't he the reason why, the price for the apartment went to 500E per month, as maybe he, wanted something back?" Then tripped up, stumbling on his words, tripping himself up more each time he said something else, had I seen it, and closed down his plan?" As I, already feeling most aware, and uncertain of my companion, a little trapped even by the 'tentative' way we ascended the stairs, so until I got myself safely out of there, my priority for my safety, I was to risk nothing, to ensure my smooth and easy egress, for that apartment, my minimal response, that I felt compelled to make, constructed to be most non-committal, whilst delivered, precisely, calmly, yet simply, "OK. I'll think about it."

> *"When you get into a tight place and everything goes against you, till it seems as though you could not hand on a minute longer, never give up then, for that is just the place and time that the tide will turn."*
> *~ Harriet Beecher Stowe*

Time passed by as that potential disaster averted, I permitted it to slip by, as he remained my *'ppp'* I did, but quite unwisely, but I had learnt more, as I refused to go too far, accepting only a hotel, quite grand, yet so stark and modern, white and bold, quite garish, more in common with an empty football stadium rather than a hotel, but perhaps its popularity with business men served it well, but for my tastes too hollow, with the only exception the grand piano, where only once or twice I was to hear a pianist twinkle of the ebony and ivory, but not to worry, as my mind all a flurry, for it was not music I was there to enjoy, but my anxieties surrounding French I was there to try to appease.

With another *rendezvous*, with notebook out and several exercise books strewn about, Gilbert was to invest his time in me, or was he really, for gifts he would but, of a flat baked cake, from his region of origin and wine, and onetime I turned up, to find him wearing a suit, quite remarkably, though he was to tell me he had been nowhere special and stand up when I walked in, he came to hug me and so uncomfortably prolonged as he did let go. And then we sat a while as he talked to me, a different format for sure, and he may have been enjoying himself, but as for me, it was not to be.

Manipulated, being taught the topic he wanted to teach and not those I needed to learn, when confused, I wanted to shout, "Please stop, my head feel like it's about to explode!" Ignoring me, I wanted to scream more, "Enough already, please stop!" But he did not. And I pondered, was his purpose subliminal, by ignoring my repeated requests was he potentially making me feel worse about my abilities, or myself while through it, aiding himself to feel better, or "Dare I say superior?" or "Was it a trick to try and make me feel that I needed him more?" or in reality, "Did my realisation became, that indeed, I needed him less?" or possibly, "Was he trying to confuse me, or was it mindless selfishness, pure indulgence, or a capacity to serve only himself, to the exclusion of everyone else?" Of the answer, I was unaware, but of all aspects I considered unhealthy, and it was time, that Gilbert's and mine communication, was to be through.

For really, I had learnt my lesson, as scenarios unfolded since our communication began, how he chose, insisted to attend a service at *Notre Dame Cathedral* with me, "Oh why, did I give in, placing his needs his wants before my own?" Perhaps for on the telephone my patience with he was running thin, and "Oh what a folly" to have let that cat out of the proverbial bag, for I was unable to get it back in, so feeling pressurized under his whining, complaining presentation, "Oh my, why did I portray hesitation, to insist?" "No you're not coming with me." Opposed to arranging a *rendezvous*, set to meet at 10.30 in the morning, half an hour before the service began, and then, more socializing was to continue, "Oh my" I have no idea how I got sucked in again, and when weary and my energy depleted for he had drawn it all from me, I drew it to a close at that place it had started but not till an astonishing 4.30 in the afternoon, which when calculated in hours, equated to almost a days work I had passed with him, and still he was not satisfied, as I said, right, "I must go now," as he turned his face all distorted in one childlike response to the next, but for me, right then, I was insistent and resisted all his barracking for really, I was really over-it, over-him, and truly done.

Yet of his notions of him accompanying me, wherever and everywhere I chose, for upon telling him of a Christmas Carol Service I was with *camarades* to attend, quite tetchy did he become, demanding, "You should have told me about that, for I would have come too, and in future make sure you do." "Oh my" a lesson learnt there, so when I was to purchase a ticket to attend a Gospel singers concert in a Church off *Champs-Élysées*, "Do you think I was to tell?" Now that was to be a definite "No." A bit of a slippery slope I was to ponder, for it was not a huge leap to consider, soon he would pose the question, "Where have you been, and what were you doing?" Really! "Was I moseying down a road to where I desired, and deserved, not to be? As without being extremely careful right then, it was certainly a possibility."

As I grew to wonder, the cake from the countryside and bottles of red, were they gifts of generosity or tactics to entice, for perhaps his perpetuating purpose of a self-serving agenda, wooing-me, to have his own way, but he failed miserably, for impossible for me to succumb for I recognized his values so opposite mine in most everything, and of a as chameleon changing their appearance to conceal themselves in a changed environment, yet too far apart were Gilbert and I, so impossible it was for he adapt.

Sure, I had been grateful for the help I had received, for sure I had, but on balance and fairness, realistically, perhaps he, not caring but calculating, as each telephone call transpired to a min-battle, where he told me what he wanted and moaned groaned when I did disagree. And I totally weary of his nature, no more could I, would I, tolerate, and chose to not postpone that which I must do, to draw that lesson in that hotel to a close, and informed Gilbert, that I was not to see him again, not for a lesson or anything other.

But my requests futile, and as actions speak louder than words, his agenda appearing clear, so I, was to clear-out, for a pleasure it was not, but pitifully painful it was, as I was as I refused to masquerade through, his pleas for me to stay, for I was most weary, *I made a choice*, I was determined to leave all his passive-aggressive manipulation behind, irrespective from then on in, of him wanting me to stay.

Yet one final time of that man's whines was I to give in and permit him to accompany me for the last time to the *Métro ligne*, line, well, that was to be an affirmative, and the direction I intended to travel was the same as his, so quickly I chose to travel in the opposite direction so next to him no longer did I need to be, for really, where I was heading, held far less importance than who I was leaving behind.

And there, standing on the dirty platform the carriages rumbled in drawing to a halt, the doors opened and I was to make good my escape, and as I dutifully turned to succumb to that French departing tradition, of a kiss to each side of the face, first the left, then the right, but it was blatant cheek I was to receive, as that man, moved his head, and deliberately placed his puckered lips onto mine, big and wet and most disturbing. "Oh my" not good, not good at all.

Turning quickly away, unable to look at him, it was almost more than I could bear not to wipe my mouth right in front of him. What was he thinking to steel a kiss in such away, was it a French trick or just one he invented, and why had he done such an impertinent, unsolicited thing, perhaps simply because he could, and chose to do so for he knew he was not to see me again so took a chance, well for sure, after that certainly, from him with boundaries having been over-trampled, his cloak of concealment dropping to the floor, once and for all, not for what he did perse, but the intent behind, I would not be seeing him again.

"Oh my" such a valuable lesson learnt, for it appeared amazingly obvious retrospectively, not only 'charmers' we need to be astutely aware to take care, but also weak, the self-pitying types too, all hold the potential to trick and misled and cause us harm, and perhaps of the latter groups, they use that persona to manipulate, and calculate, some heading toward a woman of strength for they thrive on the challenge of the chaise, while others the vulnerable, yet each can twist or trap us to do that which is their bidding and not ours, as the hold and develop a cunning plan, as so inadvertently we can get tricked and sucked into their web of deceit, to benefit only themselves and no one else.

Perhaps I had been tested, and passed the exam, as greater proficiency was mine to enjoy, as next time should there be one, less tardily but more quickly, as the outcome I will clearly have come to recognize and estimate, and move myself out of harms-way, long before it has an opportunity to fall or captivate me. But gladly, not from a place of fear, but fortune, for I am wiser now and that is inner-power indeed, for never again will I be able to be pacified, by those sometimes empty words, "I love you," only spilling out, in a practiced format to get what *they want*, regardless if it is good for us or not, for remember, of those who hold hidden agendas, it is only themselves they serve, so pay heed and let not, your guard down, so no one before you will hold the possibility, of their cloak of concealment from falling to the ground.

And so often, my power was stripped away, by *they* who stole and destroyed, rendering them, tragically harmful, and me drastically helpless, but "No more," for that was only my history, in the past where only hopelessness survived, yet triumphantly their doctrine I have surpassed, as behind I left the weight of the pain, as forward I carried the light load of victory, as deliberately I cast-out their evil, refusing to submit to those ill-serving, out-dated ways any longer, to permeate through to my present, free from the septic negativity, and "How do I know quite marvellously, through this way a women can heal and grow?" "Because, I used to be, that woman."

Relinquishing the need for SOS's I was to leave behind those wailing rapids, of those fast and furious wisping white waters, as I set my course for calmer coves and bays of tranquillity, for I had learnt so much and become a skilled Mariner and of life, a proficient navigator, as the tide was a-changing, as dissipated, did those turbulent trials and tribulations, where confusion dissolved along with those whirlpools of uncertainties, as no longer was I squeamish or afraid, as I grew into the woman that I deserved to be, one of strength and sensibility, where self-love and self-respect multiplied within me, and I was empowered, blossoming and blossoming, rising up, ready and willing, to meet all the very best of all sorts of things, holding all kinds of possibilities, all awaiting to serve me, in my forthcoming and hopeful future.

> *"But behaviour in the human being is sometimes a defence,*
> *a way of concealing motives and thought; as language can be*
> *a way of hiding your thoughts and preventing communication."*
> *~ Abraham Maslow*

Part Two

~~~ooOoo~~~

Après Paris

(After Paris)

Chapter 12

Step, Because We Must

"A wise man will make more opportunities than he finds."
~ Francis Bacon, The Essays

Past the boundaries of 'gay Paris' twenty-one regions lay, with a further 5 territories located overseas, all enjoying a healthy tourist industry, but non so much as Paris, where quite astonishingly, in 2010, a staggering 79milion visited that fair city, making it the worlds most favourite place to see. And through history, creative artists have often rested there, writers and sculptors flocked to its café lined streets, as beneath the canopies on the pavement terraces they may have sat, to ponder the world, to gather, or wait upon, inspiration, where to wallow, perhaps without a care, or perhaps with small anxieties, but of it all, to constantly, dispel those naysayers, as they followed their individual dreams, for Paris is magic, it totally seems.

But that place, featured in numerous movies, surrounding romance or intrigue, what a joy it is to view, those magnificent monuments as the camera flashes by, the hoards of crowds, the dirty streets, those oppressive vehicle fumes, the odour-filled *Métro*, of it all, time rolls on, as alas, the last song was sung and the last curtain was to fall, and I was to leave, for my time in Paris was done, and my life's pit-stop along my journey's spent there, was drawing to a close, and it was time to bid a fond farewell to that great city, but "Oh, how I was to miss it so" and the friends I'd made there, yet worry I was not to do, for Paris had captivated my soul, and I knew I would return, and until I did, I was to carry my sweet memories, all wrapped up in my heart, for security.

Yet my question to ponder, "What was next for me to do?" So I examined my talents and my skills, what I enjoyed, and what enthralled and gave me thrills, what came easily when to others perhaps not, and importantly, what encapsulated my character and personality, as with eager interest I did recall, those free weekend seminars in Melbourne I did attend, and "Oh how that information resinated as it hit a cord," and so I began to search for more, books and journals of the same, weekly newsletters to sign-up for, to immerse and educate myself, and as I comprehended all, I came to a conclusion and devised a perfect plan. For my interests, they certainly include travelling, and I so enjoy meeting other traveller and hearing of their tales of triumph and even woe, are educational, to learn of cultures, the good and the bad, the highs and pitfalls. And that race of life, well I prefer more of a stroll, and that being my aim, to have a boss again, who may be potentially to bully me, certainly not my goal.

As my passion remained, a preference for renovating properties, to *trouvère*, search the thrift stores to find bargains galore, as a skill I have to create something out of nothing, to buy an item and magically reuse it for a purpose other than its design, to make a feature where so little, appears to be so much, and what wonderful side benefits, as one for my health practically, to nurture my soul emotionally and to admirably increase my funds financially. Now that is a wonderful side-benefit and well worth the searching and seeing of all that lies inside of us, for us to learn and grasp, and simply, all we need to do such, is be willing.

Remembering 'Perfect preparation prevents poor performance,' and to such an end, back in the UK, with copious books and journals read and perused, to grasp my preferred concept, with my own scrap books being made of the same, as weekends were spent, of sourcing, of renovating, of trudging the mill shops to purchase that perfect piece to finish the ensemble of room design, and a niggling notion remaining, having missed such episodes of property-related fulfilment, I was keen to recommence, as I made a decision, to purchase and renovate an old property in *Provence* in the south of France, to establish, a *Chambre d'Hote*, a Bed & Breakfast, so set in my sights, was that brand new plan, but of it all, "Was success guaranteed?" or "Was I to miss my target, or dodge a bullet?"

For sure in England I was a success, as my toils of hours renovating, my hobby and my pleasure, as up until 2 in the morning wallpapering I would be, then to sleep before the alarm awoke me at 6 a.m. and there, as bright as a button, off to work you see, to earn my money to plough back into my passion, and so the cycle went around, and the beneficiary, well, that was me.

"It is not easy to find happiness in ourselves, and it is not possible to find it elsewhere."
~ Agnes Repplier

"Oh my" was I to wriggle with regret at what I left behind in good-old-Blighty, or more, not to seize the opportunity to grab a business card from that American Frenchman on New Years Eve, who with his team, renovated properties in *Toulouse*, especially when that place came up again, as a woman at the bar, who lived in that district, filled me in with the good and bad of the regions around France, of which were expensive and which were not, which held good prospects and those that did not, and as she sang the praises of that place she herself had moved to, offering caution of care, explaining how some villages accept not strangers into their midst, unless, they were actually born there, having no idea retrospectively, inadvertently, that I was to end up in one.

"Oh my" I did consider, but may not have considered well enough, as I was grateful to accept her name and number, as she offered to be, my help in all systems of Real Estate when in Toulouse I arrived, but more importantly, had I missed the point of all she said, as basically she took on the disguise as a naysayer, telling me, absent of any firm criteria, that I could not afford to conduct my plan in that place, where so often of those glossy photos I perused in that *petite ville* in Melbourne, of cottages painted pink with pale blue shutters aside each tiny window, with roofs of red tiles and side by side nestled within those rolling hills of lavender, in that southerly region, of *Provence*.

"Oh why?" Was I dissuaded by her, and why did I take notice of a person, who epitomized a persona of a half empty glass, when her spirit inside of her, she permitted not to rise, so why did I ignore mine which was soaring high with the desires of my heart, wanting desperately for it to touch the sky, for just maybe, she dissuaded me, for she believed not in the supernatural, but I do, for I believe, when we hold our personal dream, for each of us, our skills, our talents our resourcefulness, can cause magic to happen, using our strength and commitment from within, to pursue our goal, as mountains can be caused to move mysteriously, when our commitment to it we determine to amass.

"Good night, good night! Parting is such sweet sorrow...."
~ William Shakespeare, Romeo and Juliet

Her name of formality "Vodka," but more fondly known as "Princess" a valued feline pet of my dear Parisian friends, who opened their home to me to in a manner so *gentile*, gentle, so kind, in a way, never in all my years, extended to me, certainly not from my mother. Encapsulated by comfort and security, such a pleasure to receive, peace and no pressure, what a precious gift they gave me, for my joy was wrapped up in a freedom of emotion to be just me, for they judged me not, and complained not at all, they were simply unpretentious, what happiness as never before such contentment had I experienced in a home so relaxed, as I felt so at ease, so comforted, all wrapped-up in soothing joy, from their ease of sublime, emotional giving.

The present, and a gift, as I seated in their elegant apartment in the 9eme *arr* through those days organizing, prior to my Parisian departure, where I pondered the relevance of those lyrics from John Denver's 1966 hit song, "I'm leaving on a jet plane, don't know when I'll be back again," as I contemplated, unable with my luggage weight to catch a plain, and "When I'd be back again?" "I only wish I knew." But what I came to realise, my previous thought, of piling all I had into a campervan and touring around France, turned out not to be such a good idea, for my anxieties of such added up to more than a few, missing my routes, getting lost, how to find my way back, understanding the 'Highway Code,' all a little problematic, when, even if the French, could, "Would they understand what I asked?" and "Would I be able to comprehend the answer they'd reply to me?" and so sadly, as the answer I was pretty convinced was "No," I kicked that idea to the curb, and through necessity, reviewed all my transportation options, and my new strategy, for "Where to from here?" Was to be the *gare*, railway station, to take the *TGV*, *Train à Grande Vitesse*, train of high-speed, away from 'gay Paris.'

For sure, a plan of some sort I needed to make, or by withholding such an action or refusing to undertake that necessary process, by default "Did that mean, that by my non-action, that I was planning to fail, and in, unfortunately would likely succeed?" And so it was, I was to pass by all other options to peruse, at least in a portion of my dream, as I packed clothes for all seasons, my French teaching CD's, and as I spoke my last farewells and gave my last Parisian hugs, to those who 'I hung out with' at the end of the bar, as they partook of Champagne with canapés, while I partook of chocolate finger biscuits, always a wonderful accompaniment to fine glass of red wine, and my delightful *colocataire*, flatmate, and the hotel manager, such a pleasant and polite young man, and if I may be so bold, my favourite of all, Flavien, whom when I remembered, with joy, I gave way to a soft and tender smile.

I was to miss Paris and those amazingly lovely people I met, those sensational friends I made, to leave them, I held sadness in my heart, yet, for of the future I held hope, for that was a new emotion I'd come to know, and how lovely to pack it in my heart, as I set course to drag that larger than life suitcase, without ease, across the cobbled streets to the *gare*, train station, missing the copious amounts of doggy-doo on route, which I was not to miss, and pass those *Haussmann bâtiments*, buildings as that winter sun, on them barely shone, of my future endeavours of that journey I was commencing on, I really held no clear concept of what was to come.

Yet on reflection I may say, toward my next adventure 590 miles away, I sped through the French countryside, and my heart it did sing a little as I was to see fields of green, with cows and horses roaming everywhere, and how I reminisced for a decade or three since I'd seen them in their natural habitat, and a nostalgic trip down memory lane with fond thoughts of my grandma, taking me walking as a child and picking blueberries through nearby country fields.

And at 500km per hour, the train tore across the tacks, rushing by dilapidated farmhouses and crumbling ruins, and petite stone cottages with windows placed not on the side where the wind hailed from, as cradled behind conifer ferns planted in a row, forming a wall of hedges tall, to prevent the power of the prevailing winds ripping across the wide open fields so into their homes it could not blow, as I pondered the unsavoury aspect for me to live in such a place, while I wasn't necessarily that 'city girl' my mother professed me to be, but surely I was to find somewhere in the middle, to suit my desires, my needs and aspirations as to the *côte de azure*, Mediterranean coast, via *Montpellier* I travelled to see, down in the southwest corner of France, and still I did not know, I was on the wrong track, heading the wrong way, as Nice, my unfortunate destination.

But really "Why did I end up there?" For a bargain you see, for it was only 10E extra to travel so very much further from *Montpellier*, and score a first class *'luxe,'* luxury seat, of fine leather and most comfortable, for the cost of a second, so perhaps only astutely sensible it was, but as my card so consistently would not work, as I tried to pay for it, should I have not taken that as a sign that simply I was not to go, and shifted my thoughts to something better and given that one, the 'old heave-ho?'

Most assuredly, "Yes" should have been the answer, for as soon as I hit the send button and the job was successfully done, the money by the railway company received, I instantly got a niggle of a notion, that the wrong thing I had done, and sure enough, in my book of life, I was joining an unnecessary dot, and forming the tapestry of the same, only a pungent-color stitch to be added, serving no real purpose or advantage, always un-pleasurable, serving only as a *faux pas*, mistake in this case of inconvenience.

For really, only a little time was needed, should I have given myself the gift of a little time to rationally think it through, rather than respond to emotions of confused anxiety, as it was neither following my dream, nor included anywhere in what I had amerced myself in, of all things Provence. And the diamond interviewee, his locations he recommended to me, a list I had of them, the quaint villages and those with infrastructure, and the right type, and he of his attitude and well balanced notions, "Why did I not act on his recommendations and calculations, for were his not higher than the naysayer?" But ultimately, I was swayed by the negative one, and ended up, with not such a good job to be done.

> *"To hell with circumstances; I create opportunities."*
> ~ *Bruce Lee*

Arriving in the dark, it was late, I was tied and cold, wanting pretty much only my bed, but without a mobile phone, directions on it I could not get, so asking the railway workers of the hotel I was to say at, and only 5 minutes from the station the advertisement said, but still no on knew where it was, and of what sprang to mind, as over I was told, *"Je ne comprends pas,"* "I don't understand," Mark Twain's words rang in my head, paraphrasing, how "Those French have an remarkable inability not to understand their own language when it is spoken to them."

Patience, tact and smiles, achieved the right outcome, yet before arriving at my destination, I was to calculate the time to walk from the station was a 75% underestimation, yet safely there, and paying the fees I was to find my room, located on the 4th floor, but an elevator there was not, so trammelling slowly up the spiral staircase I trod, on the read carpet wearing thin, as I dragged behind mustering my strength, the 23kg or more, in a suitcase the size of a battleship, and there I was, the door before me, with the same number as on my key, "Arrh, relief" but it was not to be, for further problem arose, as the lock turned out to be rather tricky, with 5 frustrating minutes more, before access was granted, and, orange I was to see, the walls, the bedspread, but the line crisp white, and the wood of the furniture a warm colour of honey, and all neatly laid out, and at last "I was so glad." For there was a bed in my sight, waiting for me.

And so I proceeded with my little way, my habitual routine when entering a hotel room, the shower, clean, tick; the bed clean, comfy, tick; but the pillows, bad, so bad for my neck, too hard and too high. OK, you can tell it wasn't a 5 star establishment I was staying in, as I started searching the room with resourcefulness, taking a towel from the shower, and the bath mat too, I placed them within a pillowcase, ready to lay my head upon, enabling me to get some sleep, and with a fitting job done, my tiredness dissipated, I jumped into the shower, with a quick change of clothes before I popped right on out.

For really, suddenly I had a thought, "Was I not at the French Riviera?" "Well yes indeedy I was!" "So did that not follow that of my 3 night stay there, I should make the very best of it all?" And it was an American who I met in a local cafe in San Francisco, with his career in psychology, who explained to me, that the workings of our brain, enable us to adapt and protect ourselves readily, so in new environments and places, it becomes extremely vigilant, of sights, sounds, people and everything else all around, for you mind so alert, will absorb astutely, to ensure, to us, no harm or suffering ensues. And when of that information he told me, how I ruffled and flicked my feathers, quite pleased as that was my usual format, "Oh my, how clever was I?" For while I lived for a decade passing those years living in the southern hemisphere, when on a 36 hour journey to the Caribbean I travelled, with a 3-day layover which I always opted for, forming a snapshot, taking in all the sights I could muster, and what a wonderful surprise to learn, that quite naturally I had been fulfilling that process, doing the best thing in such a compact timeframe, to maximize and capture all I was able from each visit; how awesome; 'Go figure!' & 'Clever me!'

So there it was, utilizing what I could, a question posed, "Are any venues around here playing jazz tonight?" or "Perhaps a piano bar?" As for sure, certainly my tastes had changed since my hip-hop days, and with the affirmation "Yes" there was, I was on my toes down the *rue*, and "Oh my" the lined pedestrian-ways with large bland colored flagstones everywhere, and café's and restaurants, lining each side, posed such a startle change from Melbourne, for it pretty much looked the same, but the atmosphere, definitely not so, as in that *ville*, the vibe most threatening, heavy, tense, and feeling safe? Most definitely not, as my eyes alert everywhere, examining who was walking toward me, and who was coming down the street, who was walking to my side, as my handbag, tightly under my shoulder, close to my body, I tucked it tight. But "Oh my" what an amazingly stark and huge contrast to where I was just 5 hours earlier in the middle of 'gay Paris,' where not once had I felt the need, to protect me or my possessions so, and of Nice "Was keen to hang around?" Definitely "Not!"

But then I had lived in Manchester, so with all senses engaged and astutely aware, in the absence of finding a jazz bar, I chose one with a large flat-screened TV, which normally I'd avoid such, but with the nostalgic tunes of the 1980's videos, with the chart tunes playing as if back in the days on "British Radio 1" playlist, possibly usual but not my preferences as I always preferred the beats and particular melodies, of Stevie Wonder, Luther Vandross, George Benson, Lionel Richie, with old-school, Whitney, Nat King Cole, Gladys Knight & The Pips, The Temptations, Four Tops and so much more music of Town of Motown. And nostalgia hit me with another blast, as I thought of my finely decorated living room in northern England, and my preference, my precious peace and security I revelled in, "When was I, to ever going to enjoy that again?"

Pleasingly I watched the screen, as a nostalgic trip I took down memory lane, as I observed those unsymmetrical hairstyles, with gel galore, stuck up high, with makeup bright, of deep pinks, light blue or green of deep emeralds, all shimmering without the trick of light, and clothes for the ladies and the men, adorned with shoulder pads quite intense, so brash and bold and all masculine, yet not so the astonishingly high patent stiletto heals that of your toes, did pinch in tight. "Oh my" what a trip down memory lane, and oh what a shame, as I contemplated for more than a moment, that which I could not quite build a bridge and get over, as that precious pristine collection of all those clothes and accessories I was viewing on the screen, I was so glad to have and so missgivingly gave away, but surely one day, I had to remove that foot that was stuck in the past, and continue with relief along my way.

The restaurant I chose, most deliberately for it was quite, and comfortably filled mainly by tourists, and I felt safer there than anywhere else, so ordered a fine red wine on which to sip, with canapés given on which to nibble on, and I was left to rest and wonder, why had I paid in advance for all my travel plans, for that afforded me zero flexibility, unless further costs were to be endured, and really, I wanted not to loose money, so temporarily I had to stay in that local, yet utilizing a trend I learnt down-under, already I was counting the days down, for absolutely, I wanted to be out of that place in the soonest jiffy.

"We often miss opportunity because it's dressed in overalls and looks like work"
~ Thomas A Edison

Wearily, as I sat, taking care of me, I was to notice a man standing at the bar, who kept looking over at me, his stature short his brown hair the same, and not too noticeable in his unremarkable brushed cotton, dark coloured corduroy pants with a turn-up at the bottom and an almost invisible line where the crease used to be, his jumper unworthy not of note while hidden under his brown leather blouson jacket with elasticised cuffs, and all it may be said, reminiscent of that decade upon screen, and as he talked with another, in Italian and not in French, it was me that he did keep glancing over at, as he leant on the bar, adjacent to where I sat, and as he came to speak with me, it was the language of Italian and not French of which he spoke, yet when speaking with me, it was English he spoke, quite impressively with perfectly formed grammar and well constructed sentences, and of a strong, accent of any kind, noted was its absence and as our conversation continued, after politely introducing himself, he enquired, should he be able to join me, as he offered a glass of red, and true, of his interaction with others which I had observed, I saw no reason to say no, so gladly I accepted.

An interesting man he proved to be, as his story unfolded, born in Canada 4 decades earlier to Italian parentage, and he taking a 12-month sabbatical from his quite stressful job, to immerse himself for of that culture of his heritage, yet "Why Nice?" For it may be on the Italian boarder, but indeed remains in France. More we explored, his rational for all, and his job quite fascinating, and I became quite enticed as one I had not heard explained before. But then making his apologies for he had to leave, "Well it was nice to meet you" I said, but quickly he insisted he was soon able to return, for our conversation to continue, also he was pleased, and with having nothing more pressing to do, I easily agreed.

Our *rdv* schedule for 30 minutes later but he was quickly returned in half of that, where upon, a tiny walk we went around the *ville*, and he was to show me, a shop that dealt in rental properties, for I was still considering, how wide sped was their data, and if there was a place somewhere that was to be suitable for me to idle awhile and do some writing, that I could book on ahead, and to that some goal I was to visit the *bureau de tourism*, Tourist Office the next day.

So engrossed I had been with my companion for that night, surveying his rationales, concepts and motivations for his midlife decisions, taking him from A to B, and contemplating, 'see, its not just me, who seeks for something different, something more.' So with telephone numbers exchanged, I bid a *'bonsoir,'* good evening, and I was to leave and be on my way as I was to walk briskly back the fresh night air, most congenial for that early part of the year, but relaxed I was not, for the atmosphere, notably not the same, for it heavy and bad, appealingly dangerously raw, and my instinct had kicked-in, for which I was most glad, as I felt my safety unassured, as I raced back to my hotel room quite fast, for behind me I was keen to lock the door, with a good nights sleep my goal to keep.

So keen to gain valuable rest, to get a good nights sleep, but not quite it was to be, as the pillow I thought I had mastered quite well, proved to be far too hard you see, and at the early hour when the clock was only striking two, it was the neighbours above who were to disturb me, as through the ceiling the noise came bounding though and again at a quarter to three, and then should they have been sleeping fast, but not I, as it was at 6.10 in the morning from those below whose noise, through the floor came their hollering chatter, rising me from my slumber, so all in all, recovery from the previous long-day, unable was I to regain.

A sundrenched day, but no, the atmosphere unimproved, I could not say the same, and as I walked around the *ville*, I was to notice, that all the streets had been cordoned off, and so an enquiry as to why, "Oh my" it was a festival that was to pass along the promenade, the *Fête de Fleurs*, Flower Parade, an annual event where trucks designed and assembled extravagantly with flowers, and driven at a slow to stop pace, where 'flower girls' perched high on top, dismantling each display one by one as they went along, and all those flowers they threw into the crowd, until all were gone.

The price, only10E, and as we say in the UK, "You pays your money you take your choice," yet how much wiser I would have been, should I have considered more, why one cue was so much longer than the other, but I did not, as with reduced patience into the empty line I shot but all was to become crystal clear, as all through the parade, at that time of day, to view all, it was a little uncomfortably difficult, as our eyes directly facing towards the beaming sun.

Those costumes of the flower girls fantastic in representing centuries far past, and appreciating their efforts I totally did, but over it all, much of a muchness, as most un-captivated by the carnival certainly I was, but 'only boring,' that was going to be to prove not the worst but the best of it, for worse was to come, as a couple of middle-aged Italian ladies started physically pushing hard into me, but why, there seemed such little point, for only a few inches more of vision it could have given them, but rather than walk away and give up my spot, I continued to hold strong, and so strong I had to be, to induce my muscles to hold straight, and not weaken to fall into those people in front of me, and push them into the metal barrier gate. But no more could I take it, with my back aching, hurting and quite sore, with the strain I placed on it, so eventually, I turned and asked them to 'please stop,' in the best French accent I was able to adorn.

But surprise surprise, for realising perhaps their mistake, they did not, or be apologetic, how pathetic to realise, that was never to be something they were to do, for aggressively angry they instantly became, turning to the crowd all around, shouting in an attempt to align the crowds with them, but the onlookers only did just that, and of all other, appeared not to care. Yet the deal was not complete, for those 'two old ducks' to coin a northern English phrase, were to send their husbands across, who of greater height, were to push into me from the side, nudging me so purposefully and even stand on my feet, and for what? I do not know, but they also, in Italian, as their expressions were to testify to, shouted obscenities at me.

But "Were they kidding?" Perhaps, any moment, there was a hidden camera somewhere, where a TV host was to jump and shout, "Got ya!" Well, that was to be "No." As more credibility, as all 4 of those adults in unison, chose to stand formidably against a wall, perhaps 5 metres away, and continue to shout, moan and complain, but "Why? What were they possibly accomplishing?" and "Why did they act so *gamin*, childlike or juvenile in their performance, as their behaviour unfolded to hold far greater suitability to a school playground, than that venue they attended, as I do believe, for all to see, they made a sceptical of themselves, not me, as I remained quietly refined, saying little to nothing, then a memory sprung to my mind, of the opinions held by Jamaicans or Parisians of that nationality, which previously, I thought a little harsh, though now, post Nice, with so much more information onboard, with them I felt no-longer inclined to disagree.

The carnival continued into the evening, with another precession delivered to those first who wanted to pay another 10E, as behind the barrier a seat could be sought, but for me, desiring hugely not for an encore of that afternoon, and believing at the late hour past 8 o'clock it was already drawing to a close, so I decided not, so my option chosen by default, to walk along the bustling public streets between throngs of people pushing everywhere, all rushing to squeeze between the smallest gaps, around sharp corners and through the dense populous of the colossal crowds. The vibe, most unpleasant, certainly never experienced anywhere before, threatening, harsh and hostile, deteriorating to a level far below my comfort range, not at the annual Christmas Parade in Melbourne, or anywhere in New York city, nor at the copious Reggae parties in Negril, on the west coast of Jamaica where I have been to, but only, in that southern French seaside town, *ville*.

Trestle tables lined the streets, permitting for only the narrowest of walkways, where *vendre's*, sellers sold cans of 'silly-string,' a favoured purchase, with bags of metallic paper confetti, angle in shape and bright in colour, equally popular the same, and as tried to make a route through, I pondered, that which seemed such a distant memory, those quiet unassuming countryside fields, and how incredibly, it was not yet two days earlier, but my spirit, so heavy, it seemed so much longer, and eager to escape, how soon before I could find my way out, as those of the baby boomer age, sprayed 'silly-string,' into my eye, to which I received with a smile and a *"Désolé,"* "Sorry." And as I continued on, I stumbled upon those canisters and caps as they rolled underfoot across the floor, and more, as I was unable to get out of her way quick enough, for coming my way I had seen her intent, and "No" but yes she did, with a hand full of sharp tiny metal pieces, throw them directly into my eyes.

My reflex action was good, and of the second event I was to close my eyes, but the first not so, and as it congealed to the corner of my eye and on my lashes, knowing I only had two eyes, and unlike a false leg which you can walk with, or a false arm which you can grip with, still with false eyes it is impossible to see, and so, of all the eye baths I had given in the medical field, to employees injured by not wearing safety glasses, as I tentatively, gently pulled it out, I held more than a little concern.

And "Where was my way out?" For one I could not find, yet I was well used to rushing through tourists on busy streets as being brought up outside a seaside town located along the Irish sea, its colour grey and not aquamarine, the sand, beneath the feet rather too chilly, but, the sensibility of visitors that night in Nice, appearing so different, more than a tad horrible in my opinion, severely unsettling, even mildly frightening, feeling trapped, holding a healthy caution for my safety, I tried to rekindle my technique from my youth, to quickly as I could sidestep all, and get myself out of there as fast as I possibility could.

Had those people not been told not to play with sticks as a child, of the damage they can cause of the susceptibility of eyes, for the truth is, it is possible to walk with a false leg, grip with a false arm but you cannot see with a false eye. For sure to quote another English phrase, I was "Well not happy" and just wanted to go home, but at that time, where was that? For I had one not, so for that time, all I could supply for myself was to return to the hotel I was soon to be free to leave and just hope that of a good nights sleep I would achieve.

And at last, I was securing that job, and en-route I discovered a petit and quiet position by the railings, where stopping briefly I was to take a rest-bite, and to my side a young French gent and to the other a young French lady, and they, maybe only in there mid-twenties, but still a gentle smile of acknowledgement each of them gave, and as we stood in unison to watch the "Oh so slow" parade go by, all was easy, for there was no pushing, shoving or complaining, as we were simply resting, and at that late hour, enjoying, all we had ventured to see.

"Triumph can't be had without struggle."
~ Wilma Rudolph

A good night sleep was on its way, right? Nope, my neck hurting and my hotel neighbours noisy, a recipe for peace, certainly not, but the days were passing, "Hurrah" I shouted and to celebrate, throwing caution to the wind, I chose to spend 1E, and "On what?" A bus ticket, to take me all the way to Monte Carlo, Monaco, situated on the *Côte d'Azur*. A jolly good deal, and a day trip I planed, for really, "Who would say no to that?" But missing the bus stop even closer to the Italian boarder I was o travel, to a French town, *Menton* where, with another fête that day, I was to idle a while, but then with boredom being a burden, well at least to me, I had been there less than an hour, but any longer, chose not to stay, so checking the bus timetable, one was leaving I just five minutes, so down the road I raced, to make sure from that place, I was surely to get away.

But was it through fate or folly that I arrived in that tiny town sporting, at what I would describe as a skinny pebbled beach, at the Mediterranean Sea, officially, the French Riviera, yet how disappointing it appeared to be, reminiscent of New Caledonia, a French territory in the Pacific Ocean I previously visited, and to say I saw I was enthralled by what I saw would have been a lie, as even the local building, prime for renovation projects, failed unusually so, to inspire my spirit to raise itself, but then, I noticed a garden close by, hosting their annual event, the *Lemon Festival*.

And in my hand for the magical price of 10E, I was to gain access into that mini park, rectangular in shape and all fenced in by high hedges of green foliage, and there behind, lay scenes replicated of wild dragons, French *Château's*, ancient Egypt, and much more, and all binary in colour and design, dependant on the other fruit, oranges where used, and skill required to meticulously achieve such I was not quite convinced, as perhaps predictably placed one of two fruits all in a row, could much go wrong with that, or perhaps my imagination just simply didn't hold the concept for meticulous appreciation.

The best part of all as I traversed a bridge, its structure plain and industrial in design, joining those two areas together, affording me a better view of the surrounding buildings and architecture, and right there, that was where my interest nestled for some moments, and when I had finished seeing all on offer, which took surprisingly little time, I found a shelter beneath the spreading branches of trees next to large and flowering bushes, with leaves of texture and colours quite different, growing effortlessly in harmony, and there taking a break from the strength of the midday sun, such a treat to share in the coolness of the shade they did provide, as there to enjoy for just 5euro, something I'd not been able to find in Paris, perhaps a 'special' of the region or perhaps for the festival, but either way I thoroughly enjoyed my crêpe topped with liquor.

And that *Fête* quite extraordinary it may be said, a precession of floats it also had, were a further 10E would get you into see them, and as they also were made of the same, and English couple who I bumped into on the street, were to share a piece of our Englishman's humour, as we contemplated, should they do the same as at the *Fête de fleurs*, and throw the produce off the floats and into the crowds, there may well be, more than one or two head injuries.

Keen to get out of there, I checked the time, quick, if I could run, I could make the next bus, or for another hour and a half I would be stranded there, so I picked up my pace to a mini-jog, and "Phew," I made it, with such a sigh of relief, I jumped on the bus and took my seat, and as I caught my breath I was to contemplate, "What was next?" And throwing caution and abandonment to the wind, a full further 1E I was to add to my trip, I decided to ride only as far as Monaco, my original destination, to take a tour around, to see perhaps what all the fuss was about, that regency and elegancy, of all that money could buy, but a mild *faux pas*, as I arrived on a Sunday, and like *Menton*, all was closed, with the exception of what was going on at the coastal edge along the seawall, where at restaurants most fine, sat their clientele most refined, and "Oh my" the vibe, it was serene, though somehow electric, with hotels of opulence, and certainly, on that big silver screen, those tales depicting Monte Carlo as most paleaceous and grandiose, certainly had got it right.

Then seated at the promenade, I requested the *carte des vin rouge*, the red wine list, but the waiter, an Italian man, 'assured me,' such a thing they did not have as only one red wine they sold, and I composed a thought of how extremely odd, and of truth, how highly unlikely, yet a question I continued to pose, "By chance, a *Boudreaux?*" but of cause, "No" it was not to be, and you may have guessed it, the wine was also from Italy. Yet I could not complain, as an extra large basket of crisps were placed on my table, and with the absence of another food store available, grateful, I gladly tucked right on in, and the wine, actually wasn't half bad, quite a good tipple, and a generous portion too, so all to enjoy, as with quiet captivation, I revelled as I gazed wistfully upon all those seated below, their clothes so casually worn, yet easy for the eye to see, exuding well-crafted quality, exquisite in detail, of their tailored clothes made of fabrics of finery, in designs most chic, with jumpers thrown nonchalantly over their shoulders, and handbags placed neatly aside the feet, drawing the eye to their shoe ensemble, with their 'crowning glory,' their hair each one appearing as they had just left the hair salon, with sunglasses princely worn on top, and soft scarves of pastel colours blowing beautifully in the wind, and their jewellery, from afar easy to see, and for men and women alike, 'subtle,' it tended not to be.

But the sea breeze, turned out to be more of a blustery and blistering wind that won the better of me, so requesting the *l'addition,* from that quite congenial waiter, I promptly paid, preparing to engage in one of my favourite pastimes, setting off to wander along the waters edge, the seawall of the Mediterranean, gazing harmoniously into its clarity, crystal clear, as the winter sun, gently warm, cast its rays of soft shimmering diamonds through the water as I scanned its graceful depths below, appreciating all of its magnificence and glow, the rocks, how beautiful their vision, something so natural yet I imagined placed there by man, as nature so easily coincided with our demands, and how amazingly similar, and so reminiscent of that coast left so long ago, the 'Land of the Long White Cloud,' that of New Zealand, and so appreciative I was for those welcomed warm memories.

Walking away from the waters edge, with a lighter heart of some reminiscing of my time spent living on the north shore of Auckland, I commenced to return back up that winding and very steep hill, where visions women in convertible cars wore silk scarves wrapped effortlessly around their heads, and as a strong breeze blew in from the sea, perhaps not just a pristine ensemble of style but most purposefully functional, a feature of so many movies, which on my way down, had afforded me such gifts of bright encapsulating euphoric visions, and it was not through lack of good health, but a willing capacity to pause, and before I was to meander around the petite city, the Principality, to wait, exactly as long as I needed for the next bus, I permitted my soul to rest, recover and soak-up all the expansive and glorious vistas, that I enjoying seeing twice, and the rest-bit that gave me to me, I was grateful, for if you forgive the pun, it was far greater than a little nice.

Yet awaiting the bus there was no luxury, for it was to return me to that place, I wanted so not to be, Nice, where, strange and bizarre in my concept, and racially prejudice I considered inhabitants to be, and 'if only,' I had not been seduced by a 10E bonus package, for really was it benefit, or blunder? For me, in the right place, I felt it not to be so, as unravelling that concept of killing-time which had taken on a life all of its own, if you forgive another pun, as counting down those last 36 hours, before most happily, I could leave as off to the train station I was to race.

> *"Set your light by the stars and not by the passing ship."*
> *~ Gen Omar Bradley*

Arriving safely back to the main pedestrian street, but almost by definition, that concept, an oxymoron in that *ville,* but leaving my differences behind, I was to splash out on something I rarely permitted myself to eat, but then, that evening, I deserved a jolly good treat, and so choosing the restaurant most carefully, I chose to forgo, that what I came quickly to accept as most palatable, my favourite a crêpe, filled with rocket and Brie, and over it, a delicate dressing dripped, with a fine wine as an accompaniment, with a delightful plum bouquet, where I had given up my request, to "Please hold the Mozzarella cheese" which agrees with me not, as the French, as many times as I re-jigged my sentence and verbs, even *"Ne Pas"* = "No" satisfied them not as they appeared adamant that they didn't understand my prolonged explained request, incorporating hand signals to match, and even though the same I requested in English, a language they clearly understood, and perhaps awkwardly, "Were they deliberately toying with me?"

And there, me, being watched by a gentleman whose attention I was not happy to receive, from his position beneath the heater in the *alfresco*, area, he commenced a trick to walk pat my table multiple times, before unwittingly by mistake, I looked up at the wrong time and his eyes met mine. "Oh a *petit faux pas"* for that was what I was trying to avoid, and there it was, he saw his way in, as he stood to my side as he leant on the bar, and a one sided conversation did begin. Of what he spoke he enchanted me not, and without appearing to be rude, I did not know how I could get rid of him, for I had not a book with me, which ironically, serves as a lead to commence, and a format to end, an unwanted conversation, but then, it was he who was rude, as suddenly, without an invitation or a request for the same, he suddenly plonked himself down, at my extremely petite round table situated along bar wall, and he, inconvenient, unpleasant, though not threatening in his persona, and ask him to leave, for some reason, I was unwilling or unable.

His topic, I had no idea why he chose it, as his perspective he unfolded, or his historical rational for the same, I held not a clue, but insisted, "Its this way, a manual-worker must marry a person of higher intellectual-capacity, must always be done, because that is the only way they have something interesting and stimulating to talk about," and continuing, "When 2 people be equal in capacity marry, the relationship won't work, because they will both be board and have nothing to say to each other." Out of the blue, why was he to think to share that with me, a little bizarre, but then as he continued on his rollercoaster ride, it became unnervingly clear, I add without conceit, for some unfound reason, it appeared he had in mind, 'he and me.'

"Oh my" how odd, how unwelcoming thought, as "Was I interested?" Most definitely not, for in his notions had he created a hypothesis, had he placed the cart before the horse in some mysterious way, and not to be cruel but realistic, he had to chances of such, and they were both 'no chance' but "Why did he pinpoint me for such an odd game to play?" And of no concern, for then, instead of ignoring him, I spoke freely of my opinion, expressing clearly, that I held no-stock in what he thought, and that it is love, patience, values and virtue which lies within the heart, as one for another freely gives and receives, and should his cap have been set at me, so quickly that notion, I was to dispel, making it abundantly clear, that at that time, I had no interest or care, to enter into a relationship with any man of intellectual status or not, for I had work to do, and of it, nothing or no one was to interrupt, and possibly, something in my forthright-fullness appealed to him, as he left my table, and gladly alone I was in peace again, but I was to be quiet and wait a while before I was to leave for my hotel as up a very quiet street, and while on my way, I cared not to bump into he, as so I considered that prospective and action quite cautionary-worthy.

> *"Never interrupt your enemy when he is making a mistake."*
> ~ Napoleon Bonaparte

"Hip hip hurrah!" It was, "L Day," 'Leaving day,' and although I had yet another poor nights sleep, I mind I did not, for I knew, in just a few short restless hours, I was to be out of there and to a better place I was on my way, and with a spring in my step, it was my last breakfast as a thousand, "Yeah's!" I could have yelled, to that only mini sanctuary I had found along the paved walkway. But no, as around the corner turned, it was him from the previous night's venue who I was to see, quickly with thoughts of how to avoid him sprang up, as I searched for doorways and alleyways to hide, but non in the vicinity, and in that early morning, the workers already arrived at their jobs and tourists not yet mulling around, and there it was, a collision course to say hello, and so I did, *"Bonjour"* quickly socially identifying the difference of, not friendly but formal status quite deliberately, but what of he, ignoring such French and my personal protocol responded with *"Salut,"* "Hi," but either way, I carried on with my step, but he postponed my continuation, as I kept my distance, but he stood in my way and in my personal space, as his words to me, as he looked me up and down, his eyes gleaming, a smile across his face as he spilled out his words, "Wow you look sexy!" "What?"

"No, that was wrong!" For I knew him not, he had no right to speak to me so in such a familiar manner, for of the French etiquette, "Did he not know it?" Really, I am not a stick-in –the-mud, but shallow and disrespectful, I considered him to be, and I refused to be an object for his amusement or imagination, for his intentions abundantly clear, likely of the same, for a gentle-man, certainly, I considered him not, for I know I am so much more than something simply to be pleasing to a man's eye, or to sooth his libido as he walks by. And "Prudish?" "Certainly not, as graciously I receive compliments," but that was not his intent, in his mind, for his accompanying actions delivered his message, so stemming from a place of love and not fear, I engaged my *inner powerful prowess,* as quickly I reflected on a line delivered, by Renee Zellweger, in the 1996 movie, Jerry Maguire, true, I twisted and turned it a little, but I knew, "He lost me, at 'sexy,'" and with that, grateful I need not see him again, I bid him a *"Bonne journée,"* "Good day," as I turned on my heels and walked away.

For women have tied themselves to railings for me, put up with cultural hostility, beaten and locked in prison in that land of England, and they were only the lucky ones, who were not locked in the attic centuries earlier, while their husbands took a mistress and spent all her money, and more the woman, to be owned like a dog hence in the marriage ceremony as it used to be, 'Man and wife,' and not husband and wife; or beaten like a horse, as in the Victorian era, where in court they passed a law, decreeing, "Yes" the husband was permitted to beat his wife, with an occurrence regime that suited him with anything he liked, a riding crop, a poker from the fire, anything of his choosing, all was lawful, with the only proviso, he was prohibited from using anything 'wider than his thumb.' "Yep!" under that law, created by men, with anything else, those men, sanctified, were good to go.

And don't even get me started on the 'scold's bridle' from back in the Medieval days, where "Yes," evil. As iron corsets with jagged tongue depressors were placed on the wife's head, as she, for the duration in days or weeks or more determined only by her husband, as she of the horrendous weight of it, unable to eat, was only 'put her on display' to be paraded 'in shame' on the length of a chain, through the towns streets. At the whims of men, how homogonously wrong, how dreadfully sad, that those women from our history, went through all that, and of their prolonged suffering and courageous sacrifices to try to change it. Their strength, their stamina, against all the odds, they pushed on through, and even disparaged by other women, who believed as society decreed, that their worth, was only ever to be, as much or as little as men, dictated it should be.

All still relevant to this day, and for all my sisters who went before me, who fought so very amazingly hard for my freedom, for that I will always remember, and hold gratitude, so of a man in the street who calls me 'sexy,' as he decreed that was my worth to be, as so equally, he could have easily decreed, I worthless. Of his deliberation, was I to change my considered "Worth of *ME?*" "Absolutely Not!" For the sum of my self-worth is far greater and higher, than his multiplications, of his summarizations. So *I REFUSE* to jump to *their* tune, or permit them any longer, to determine 'who I am,' as I 'know' of that, I am, *TRULY WORTHY OF SO MUCH MORE!*

"Only the shallow know themselves."
~ Oscar Wilde

That *ville* that in my heart I perceived as horrible, was to deliver the icing on the cake, pertaining to my visit, as the previous night I decided to offer myself an emotional pick-me-up, though by comparison ended up, with a knock-me-down, as a petite coffee house up a side street, where I was to linger for a while and rest before heading back to my hotel room. So it was a larger than life slab of cake that I was actually going to partake, though normally never would I permit myself such a thing, for the calories to be worn, or the money from my purse to be torn, neither fitted my preferences, but that was a desperate evening and caused for drastic measures, so I was to throw the proverbial caution to the wind, but was the result, not realizing, they were gale force and heading straight for me.

So I commenced tiptoeing, not through the tulips but the doggy-doo that was so incredibly sited centre stage not 12 inches from the café door entrance, yet no one had thought it necessary to pick it up, but that also it appeared, of faeces on the street, quaint essentially French. So ignoring such, I opted to walk to the rear of the store, so the confectionary and gateau's I could feast my eyes upon, deliberating which I was to choose. Then with my mind made-up I sat back on a long bench with a high back, and there to see, two ladies of maturing years, feeding their dogs, one a piece with nibbles from dishes placed in the centre of tables, as into their dogs mouths they placed their fingers, and the dogs would lick them as they came out, and then the same would do to themselves, and hygienic I thought not, but of my business neither, so I sat and relaxed waiting for the waiter.

My order placed, waiting patiently, I decided to take the edge off my nail, as chipped it was catching on my stockings, so innocent I thought it to be, as the dust fell over my knee, but no, as before the file had barely touched the nail, I heard, so harshly and abruptly shouted, "Madam, NO!" Surprised, quickly I looked around, remaining forever in my OH&S nurse's role at heart, where I worked for so long, and of that job description, I still preferred it the best and miss it, as I, responsible for all accidents, injuries and emergencies onsite, I still have a tendency, to alertly stop whatever I am doing and prepare to fly into action, to act responsibly to prevent injury and promote recovery, should there be a necessity, yet, that occasion was somewhat different, as the warning was not pertaining to another, as that warning was directed at me. But "For what? What had I done?"

That lady, with a superior attitude of conceit, with a pre-formulated bad attitude, speaking in English, shaking her head and waving her finger closely at me, domineeringly commanding, "No. No, you can not do that madam!" *"Pourquoi?"* I asked, in return receiving another stern command of, "No. Put it away." But I was intrigued, interested in the stark contrast of reality, their fingers in dogs mouths, the dogs-bottoms depositing its bacteria, on seats where children sit to eat, where little baby, toddler maybe, sweeps their contaminated hands across their face on the way as they slip them across their lips, or the child, whose little hands brush across the surface where the dogs bottom was, before placing their tiny fingers in their mouths.

"Mmmm! Oh contraire." The nail file already gone away, my cake still being waited upon, but they were not settling, as it was a waiter next one of that duo called over, who incidentally was Italian, coaxing him, though not unwillingly, into their apparent battle, and "Why?" Perhaps, simply because they could! So in my very best French, which was tested well, I explained that the *chien sur la chaise*, dog on the seat, in its faeces, held harmful *les bactéries*, bacteria. True, by the Environmental Protection Agency (EPA) in 1991 categorized 'dog waste' equally as: herbicides, insecticides; toxic chemicals; and acid drainage from abandoned mines. With the eggs of Toxocaro Canis, of 15,000 eggs able to-be-passed, in just one gram of dog's feces; rendering it significantly, highly potent.

So, as an OH&S Nurse who assesses risks and hazards, formulating potential outcomes, calculating a ratio of 'likelihood verses consequence,' so I was then to wonder, from the bottom of a dog sat upon the seat where small children play, of for adults, with a transfer of doggy-doo bacteria, their symptoms from such potentially severe, especially in the case of a child or adult, perhaps a fail person having a weakened immune system. So with the consequence of such verses the edge of my nail filed over my lap above my own skirt, really, I thought with age as a barrier to so little, that those 2 elderly ladies behaved, well, quite bizarrely.

A little perplexed as certainly there appeared to be more than a tad of indiscrepancy, for could a nailfile offend so, when it was nowhere in their vicinity, or held the possibility to a child, potentially susceptible of illness to cause harm, what was their reason for complaining. My query I believed valid and worthy of an answer, for certainly I was keen to understand, was it the French way, was it the Italian way, or perhaps another way, for someone who was not happy with 'their lot in life' to intimidate someone who was peacefully alone, perhaps it was because I was a tourist, or a young woman, and with their life receding in years, they had nothing left to gain so began to inflict misery on others. But of cause I surmise as to their rational I was not privy, but more I wondered of that most unusual occurrence, in their eyes was my worth no more than what they thrust on me, and "Why, were they continuing *their* fight?"

Of my question of the seemingly non-comparable, harm verses consequences, of nailfile verses doggy-doo, perhaps unsurprisingly they wanted non-of-it, and more, surely my curiosity should have ceased, and the price for it not, was their rapid escalation of their tempers soared in unison quite severely so, then talking amongst themselves, the old ladies increased in agitation, as misunderstanding some English words I spoke, irate, protesting to the waiter, who most rapidly pulled out the tiny square table placed in front of me, repeatedly demanding, *"Vous partez maintenant,"* "You leave now!" *"Immédiatement,"* "Immediately." No need for me to query their rational anymore, as I was board and over it, though humorously but not outside the realms of possibility, with what and how it had unfolded, when I get to the door, would there be a TV filming crew and a man with microphone in hand, running up to me, excitedly pronouncing, "Got ya!" But back to that moment, without a grumble, though with decorum, I rose from my seat as gracefully as I was able, and with the best French pronunciation I could muster, I spoke, *"I'l me fait plaisir,"* "It is my pleasure."

Then the correlation struck me, of how that situation was a little reminiscent and a little too close for comfort, of that unfortunate customer on New Years Eve, in that bar on the corner in Paris, and how he had suffered as all the staff all turned on him. Wistfully I joked with myself, "Oh how lucky" that the *Bastille* was no longer in use, and true when it stampeded in 1789, there were less than 10 prisoners within it, and "How lucky am I" that the guillotine they no-longer use it, or by that team of 3, I'm pretty sure I would have been escorted there, as so gladly they may have been to have seen my head roll. But also, of that experience and the peculiar set of circumstances in their behaviours that unfolded, and indeed the whole event took only a few minutes, I remembered while in Florida, a lady who hailed from an adjoining European country, was to tell to me one day, and in those moments they rang rife in my ears with clarity, that really, "You cannot argue with stupid."

And as I exited that establishment, sidestepping back over the doggy-doo as I had when I walked in, of that experience of conundrum and my assessment of that nasty place, and "Oh" how exceedingly eager I was to escape it and so grateful that I was able, yet a greater heaviness fell on y heart, with a heavy contemplation in my soul, "Why was I receiving so much hostility and rejection?" and "Why were my mistakes perpetuating me along a road I cared not to venture down?" And then, like metal filings to a magnet, one negative thought attracted another, and before I knew it, I was freefalling into a great big hollow hole.

Disheartened, feeling heavy and sorrowful, as that "Oh so" pointless question that serves us only badly, "What if?" suddenly popped up to capturing my soul, like on a merry-go-round my thoughts rolled on and relentlessly kept coming of; "What if I hadn't gone to Nice? What if I hadn't been so easily persuaded by a friend to retry to book that ticket?" Then adding in ferocity of turbulence increased their flow and significance, "Why does this keep happening to me? When will I become better at making decisions?" and really, "When was I going to be a wiser woman, with better and improved decisions freely flowing?"

For multiple and costly failures bombarded my mind, impossible for me to escape free from them, as I was trapped within their lair, for really "Had my 'money grabbing' for 10E, placed me in such a predicament?" and "Had my high Australian disposable income, with the exception of only a few great vacations, certainly with no great or small 'events,' that I spent my money on, got wasted?" As "Oh so sad" the absence of any investments, as easily I disposed of my salary, on only of depreciating items, of non-assets, all posing as a waste of money, as when I needed to sell those items, I was unsuccessful, as in just about every thing, not withstanding my emotional attachment and financial commitment, was mostly all given away. True, all were beautiful, all were bargains, all were of exceedingly good quality, but "Were they any use to me?" "No!" And there lay the crux of the problems, as financially and emotionally I was suffering a double bombardment, regurgitating my miss-haps, mistakes and blunders, all rearing their ugly heads up in mine, as in quick succession, nay, simultaneously, I was caught up in a whirlwind, trying to escape the havoc, they were creating, within me.

My emotions so strong, almost a grieving process I was going through, of all those mistakes I made while living in Australian and more as I was leaving, I had made such errors of judgment that I had sought refuge in the wrong places, spending money and buying clothes and accessories, that I didn't wear, them failed to ease, but only added to a growing emotional handicap, which I was having bear. For really, my behaviour equated to, pound-astute or penny-poor, pound-rich or penny-somehow-let-me- find my way out of this deep ditch. "Had I permitted money to simply drip through my fingers into and endless unrewarding never-ending pit?" and "When was 'enough was enough,' ever gong to come?" Sure, my vintage collection and all the clothes I piled up as high as I could 'squash them in my draws' and squeeze the handbags together ever more tightly on the shelves, so they were still always neat and in their place, but never were they used or see the light of day, so the fact, that they were beautiful, "Did that really even matter?" "Yes" I treasured them all, but "Yes" like an addiction, never was I satisfied and like an ill-serving, self-perpetuating system, always, I went searching for more.

I remember my health was bad, and to make a decision to go out, it was likely that I was unable to keep the date, and exercise along I did sometimes and along the waterfront or around the roads filled with all strikingly wonderful houses was equally as enjoyable, but of inclination to keep up with either, I did not really hold it, so it was I guess, with not friends or interests, a default mechanism that also kept me going back for more, and perhaps I should not ignore, messages of 'lack' that propelled me on to hunting and gathering, to make my store cupboard be full. But there I believe lay part of my problem, for when the issue arises in our inner-self, because of words of criticisms that were spoken over us when we were young, or possibly a 'lack' of control we feel in our lives, until we work on our internal rationales, our external behaviours of ill-serving habits may not be rectified.

The angst I lived with in France, my worries the result of those chain reactions resulting from poor decisions, For really, why did I choose to take clothes to France, to learn French instead of a purposeful book found in an Oz thrift store, but from an American school, "What if I would have packed it first?" Now that would have been most wise, as how it would have enhanced my possibility of easy and enjoyable learning, with those direct comparisons of words and pictures with translations for all. "What if I had not volunteered at the thrift shop and met Bertram and chosen to utilize his blueprint to move to France but chosen another more suitable, pertaining to me and not him?"

In a place filled worries because of decisions I made back in Australian, and indeed, before I left New Zealand, and even further back they went, as the chain reactions and consequences resulting from each one, unfolded and so much effort needed to eradicate each one. As the mental calculations commenced, and like a proverbial rolling stone gathering moss it gathered momentum. "What if I had not undertaken nurse training at North Manchester? What if I would have trained in the quaint and peaceful town of Ormskirk? What if I had not gone on that fateful date of horror? What if I would not have bumped into the rapist friend who told me he was searching for me?" from where decades of insomnia ensued. "What if I had not worked on that 'fateful day' I suffered my lower back injury, or lift that patient or worked with that nurse? What if I had taken the opportunity and married for money, to a man who I liked him a lot, who I respected and was proud to be with? What if I had-not have married for love? What if I hadn't been persuaded to sell my 'castle,' aka, my house, to give-up my financial security and my independent attributes existing in my life, therefore, so wrongly, transferring them all to him? What if, I had not chosen that man, that one who was so nearly, to kill me?"

"What if I would have bought the first and perfect house I found in NZ, and not swayed, by a person, a Realtor, a friend, whose opinion I trusted, who let me down so badly?" As I knew not then, that he had a rotten and inner, self-serving agenda, which was to cost me, hundreds of thousands of dollars, causing crumbling ground where to place my foot on the property ladder. "What if I would have bought the apartment next at the beach in Melbourne?" and primarily, "Why was I in rented accommodation and not owning a home, to positively plough my money into, instead of squandering it on clothes, non of which were worn, for which I have nothing to show, rather than paying a perfectly suitable, and to profitable mortgage? What if, wisely, I had not bought, that sports car, yet another in my list of depreciating assets? What if I would have been born to parents who were to love me, or even care for me?" "Hey," actually, them simply not harming me I would have gladly settled for. "What if I'd just had, *just* one person, to mentor me? What if, just possibly I could cease burdening myself so indiscriminately, with those choices I'd previously made?" So wrong, they may have been, but they were done, with resulting negative chain reactions, yet I became resolute, to stop resenting them, and of my life, leaning from the past, I was to meander-on, nay, forge-onward!

"What if I had not spent so much time and energy blaming others for my behaviours, emotional predicaments, my low self-esteem, and my self-hatred? What if I would have recognised my problem and sought a better way sooner? What if I'd searched for my path of exploration and self-discovery, which I deserve to be on, sooner? Would I be further along and healthier down my path of healing I travelled?" and really, "What if I dared to take responsibility and accept all that I'd done, decisions, choices, costly mistakes or not, and just then perhaps, with resolution in my mind?" I may be able to let-go and blame no other, and resolutely with my own life, eagerly seize, and move on.

"What if I hadn't come from an abusive family or suffered the pain and disruption to the brain I endured because of it, with the legacy of emotional harm potentially propelling on into more of the same?" "Arrhah" a good question for sure, but what I have come to realise, not only was there nothing I could do about, that which I was born into, should I not have experienced so much, never would I be able to feel, the exhilaration, of overcoming so much adversity, nor would I have the privilege of this message to share, with those who are not yet out of the other side, but they too, are able to, experience substantial 'Victory.'

In France, I was absolutely overwhelmed and exhausted from considering uncontrollably to consider, so many negative, "If's." The burden was so heavy to bear, pushing me down. With a multitude of regrets and remorse I was going under; panic was setting in, I realised my fate, quickly I needed to compartmentalize those debilitating issues in my mind. I needed, to take a deep and saving breath, to prevent myself plummeting further, I needed, to push myself up from the depths of where I'd sunk. A metaphor for sure, but I was to choose life. I wanted life and chose to leave the dangerous, destructive and hurtling waves of anxiety, panic and regret all behind me. I had become a rescuer of me, for I, having survived so much through the decades of my life, and I deserved to recover, and to thrive, so I chose, not to loose sight of my goal.

For I considered how it should be, that our worth, our right, is to replace regret with reward, after we have navigated through the harsh painful regrets of "What If" from the past, as this is the present is called a gift, for we init, are all wrapped up, in beautiful paper and delicate bows, and able, with just a little encouragement from ourselves, to seize those lessons learnt, from the trails we went through, so relinquishing any need, to travel though it again. And surely that must be right, as the hard-yards, I had already completed them through the trials and tribulations that presented themselves, so surely through passing those tests, it is our privilege and right, to reap all, our deserving rewards.

I considered how, '*if*' looks-back while '*reflection*,' looks-forward, of great and immense value, and a truly marvellous great for progression, from were, positive attributes and logic can be incorporated, while never to overestimated, as when mastered can aid toward healing, growth and wisdom. And important to remember, it is so different forever glaring-intensely in the rear view mirror of life, lingering on the bad, festering with anxiety and debilitating regrets, for that is what regrets does, hold us back, stuck in the past, destroying our prospective, robbing us of our optimism for the future. Yet with pleasure, the opposite I point out, the same mirror, how glancing-briefly in it, to see where you've been, only to remember the good, and happy circumstances, which fed your heart and soul well, dependably, to see those open and wide perspectives, wholesome opportunities, and be refreshed by the new, for having passed along that road before, for the future, you will hold a much wiser clue, to embrace it, and adore.

I had commenced the journey not knowing my worth, but I grew to knew I deserved better, I was no longer fighting for survival, I was fighting for a healed and better me, ultimately I had me in my sights, I was to save me. For I had developed within a strong and unstoppable driving force, I had it and I owned it, it was valuable and it was mine, and once and for all, I had grown to know that I definitely, undoubtedly and categorically deserved it.

As previously my intuition I had ignored and choices I had made, through misery endured, eventually, my lessons were learnt as I made a plan to exit from those experiences of inconvenience, for certainly, that was way overdue, as I was not shaken, not stirred but empowered, as a greater understanding I held of limiting-believes and when planted to cause damage in the mind, it can all be done to those as young as only 3 years old, they will form their own neuro-channels, acting not as a catalyst, but a template for choices we are yet to make.

"A problem?" Certainly, it may present itself as so, but those bygone days are only history, and need not form our legacy, as forewarned is forearmed, and empowered with such valuable information, I knew no longer did I need to blame myself, I needed through education, to break through that haze, and a new path before me to pave, and gold it was not to be, it was to be freedom which I was to walk upon and in, for it was to be mine to hold, for misery was gone and clarity, within me, unshackled breaking free, as through my growth, I was able to recognise, a brighter future awaiting for me, and for a better life to pursue, as persistently I travelled onward toward that place, continuing-on, relentlessly, carrying my own canoe!

"What progress, you ask, have I made? I have begun to be a friend to myself."
~ Hecato

Chapter 13

One More Step

"The most beautiful things in life cannot be seen, not touched but are felt in the heart."
~ Helen Keller

Up the hill I was to drag that suitcase, and so happy was I to do so, though admittedly not a normally a favoured thing to do, but then, I was to reap my reward, to get out of that seemingly oppressive *ville*, and for sure, a good idea to continue, for wasn't that how, I was to reach my goal and succeed in my dream, not surreal, but real? And so it was with relief I boarded the train, for so I wanted to get the heck out of there, and the next *ville* that I was to travel to, I wondered "What was in store for me there?"

So off I did trot and find my pre-booked allocated seat, not first class as on my outward journey from Paris, yet greater amounts of luxury I was determined were to eventually through ceasing many an opportunity to gain, became my aim, and so I sat back, and for 4 and a half hours, as I watched the countryside flash by and wondered, what next was to present itself, or what was I to seek, and more to find, or what else, in what order, what part of my plan next, was I to attempt to try. And there it was, the *gare* at *Montpellier*, another town sited alongside the Med, and true to form, it was a 3 night stay I had booked ahead, but what I was to learn eventually, that in the realms of accommodation, you cannot always believe what you read on the internet, but more "Was it to transpire to be, just the right *ville* for me?"

And there I was at half past three, a little weary after an early start, and as I held my room key in hand, oh how I looked forward to a rest, but was that to be, for when I had opened that door, a pungent smell was to greet me, an odour reminiscent of the days of old when I worked on the hospital wards, of infection or was that the carpet, that my feet stuck to as I walked, and I hated to even think, on that what had been spilt, and left uncleaned, sinking in and festering. "Oh my" not good enough was my cry, nowhere near satisfactory, "Not to be tolerated" was my inner roar.

Superfluous, intolerable, but still I gave it the once-over, that renowned room check, the pillows nasty and repugnant odour, you don't even want to know how I learnt that, a 1960's royal blue nylon bedspread, slightly quilted with a hanging fringe, dare I say, matching perfectly with the curtains, as they also looked and felt to the touch as they not been laundered since the date of their manufacture, and all made my stomach quite turn.

The blankets on the bed, "Oh my" as I touched them so quickly I walked to the bathroom to give my hands a jolly good scrub, but it wasn't there, for in its place quite large space, by name, a wet room so commonly found on many a ward, and there to 3 sides, disabled rails imposing in size, and a toilet so high, never do I recall seeing one the same, and without the polite pan lid, and where the bath or shower should have been, there was just a funnel in its place for the water to spill out, but not to worry if I got into difficulty, I could have always pulled the emergency cord.

A little confused for I knew I had booked a hotel room, but that was not what surrounded me, it was more, the stagnant smell of death lingering in the air, so rapidly down to reception I was deemed to go, to obviously have that room changed, but the 2 young French ladies at the desk, were it appeared mindfully, reluctantly prepared to do the same. But how could that be, I didn't even consider the thought of "Why?" and not until I began to drag my suitcase out toward the street, confirming I was to complain to a higher authority, did they agree as they called me, back, to provide me with a different room, but just how much better was it to be, I was just having to wait and see.

"Oh my" so dark and dingy the room, the air so heavy and stale, almost stagnant to breath, a pleasure, most certainly not, but with the check completed, at least the sheets were clean, and the pillows the same, so there on the 5th floor, the top, OK, it wasn't the penthouse suite, it wasn't even close, but wasn't that something I was to consider, that one day, perhaps I'd have, for surely, I had to have something to imagine to benefit me, to permit my mind to escape, as simultaneously I was to derive and execute a perfectly good plan.

Yet "Bad?" Yes it remained so with a minor interruption of a reality check, but I was not to be deterred, for that was only my geography and a steppingstone of how I was to move, from 'where I was, to here I desired to be,' so I permitted it not to interfere, with my contemplations of 'where I desired to be' as I remained committed to my task, to find a more sturdy and better functional steppingstone along my way, and where I was to stay, that was what I guess I should have expected with bargain basement shopping, and from it was I ever to learn? Well eventually, but not until, a significant amount of repeat episodes had passed, and with information of recognition as one incident added to the next, and eventually, the penny dropped, as memories of consequences, gave way that were fortunately, eventually to significantly last.

Yet undeterred, a notion to cling, only 3 nights and counting, until I was to get the heck out of there, and in the meantime, it was a shower I was so longing to have, so peeling my clothes off, too heavy for the warmth of that day, a treat I planned as under the shower I was to linger, but "What?" "No!" The water pressure so low, only drips fell effortlessly out of the faucet, and I to coin a northern English phase, under the stream, I was running around simply to try and get wet, but worse was to come, the water, only temperate in temperature, and "Oh such a mild travesty," as all too common in reputation, as I say with satire, sadly, that 'shower' after only 4 minutes of time passing, was over and done, as the H2-O reverted to cold, once again.

But not to worry, as Quick smart I got dressed in something cooler and made a hasty walk to the canal, where then, relaxing meandering, as I so adore being close to the water, it was off to *Place de l'Europe,* I was first to go, to find a place to find something to eat, and there it was, a restaurant called 'Ayres Rock,' and so quaint I thought that to be, as the real deal, of coral red sandstone, and to the indigenous population of that land, the Aboriginals, formally known as, *Uluru,* a sacred and ancient monument, in Australia's northern Territory, yet there was I, *aborder,* alongside the Mediterranean Sea, it seemed almost surreal, that I had left that land so recently ago, lived in a city, that in my dreams I had never presumed to do so, and there on my quest, investigating 'what was to come next,' where I was to aim, for sure I had a clue, but whatever I was to do, I knew, certainly, admirably, I was to give to me the gift, of giving it, my very best shot.

Familiarity gained, for don't we all strive for that, my a favourite, spaghetti bolognaise, a fine wine, and retired to bed, to be bright for the morning, when I started my new invigorated surge ahead, and to my aim, a visit to the *l'office de tourisme,* the tourist board lay ahead, as I walked arriving *en centre-ville,* downtown, to discover for the rest of my stay, where better I was to place myself, to continue to write, to get to know the *ville* better, to execute my plan, that had to come sooner or later. But sincerely, was that to be as still, to slow, striving to hard to relax, to wait and see, as I failed to question, really was that to be, for still I had not travelled to that place of my dreams, of my immersion, to that place of *Aix-en-Provence.*

But to care of immediate points of business, and so lucky to find a lady to help, who spoke English really well, and of that attribute in France I was not expecting but grateful for sure, when it was possible, for when not, it only gave credence to my lack of sensibility, and on each occasion I would wiggle and squirm at the choices I made, not of my regrets of selling or giving all such precious things away of the financial, practical or emotional kind, but the kinds of emotions which slowly yet permanently infested me, as my parents convinced me, that accepting violence was not bad, but completely normal, and so upon *their* say-so, I meaninglessly gave up my liberty, needlessly without a fight, to surrender over and over, to those who were to harm me, because of a concept, I held no other sight.

But "Why did those thought intermittently keep regurgitating inside of me?" Yet to push it aside, I was to do, as so much more immediate issues I needed to achieve, and with telephone calls made, at the tourism office, I was to speak with a Frenchman who tried to pull a fast one on me, for so discreditable, as he explained, as a favour he was extending, "I will give you the studio apartment close to *centre ville,* for just 590E per week, if you take 2." "Mmmm" but "No you wont!" I concluded, for that was in greater price than advertised on the Internet, so I discern-fully decided, as he trying to pull the wool over my eyes, of my business he was to receive non, and so the search, it carried on.

Next to be examined, the Bed & Breakfast options, and with various viewed the one I chose, was a sight, that my soul careered to, with such lush setting and bedrooms most fitting, for someone like me, and really, wasn't it time I deserved a little luxury. But a spanner was to come in the works, as the 95E per night after 2 was to shoot up to 115E, and those were the prices, off season, plus 35% exchange rate, plus 2.5% for c/card surcharge, and why, for the cheaper room was taken, but wait a minute, possibly in reality, was that *propriétaire* 'pulling a fast one' for never throughout my stay, did I see or speak to anyone from that room, and only once did I see anyone at all, and more, after I'd dragged my suitcase around the *ville* the *propriétaire* did tell, "I have no credit card machine, cash only I will take"

"Wow" how reminiscent of Paris, which slipped my mind momentarily, and should I have got online and booked the rest of my stay, "Would I have discovered that cheaper room available?" And I hasten to say, "Perhaps I may." As to stay there, I really quite enjoyed, though $2,000 for 2 weeks, retrospectively not the best idea, as after all I was on a budget, and could not magic money out of thin air, or pick it off a tree, as surely, there were fixed necessary expenditures, and perhaps my grandad's words were ringing true, "Everything in moderation" a thought that should have posed as a bigger picture, depicting additional caution, as really, I found myself in a situation, where I was 'Robbing from Peter to pay Paul,' and what transpired, was only grief for my frivolity, of previously, unnecessarily spending money, and as I arrived at the next *ville*, for my choices, I was to pay heavily.

And as I misguided myself, and failed to calculate quite well, seduced by the luxury, I had made my choice, and with suitcase, as I was shown to my room, certainly, the price was not too outrageous to charge, but perhaps just too outrageous for my budget, for the room large and quite exquisite, with ceilings lofty, and light flooding in through the quaint essential French doors, and when opened there I stood at the Juliette balcony, surrounded by light iridescent translucent curtains in charcoal grey, with shimmering sliver threaded through, and hanging from an ornate iron rod to be held in place by ornate *fleur de lys* royal flower, at ether end, and high above, the light fitment custom made, a cylinder effectively, perhaps a metre in diameter and 2 feet deep, yet, refusing to dominate the room, appearing perfectly portioned, and harsh in black, but not so somehow, even though the walls were pained in stark white, the behead grand in size, quite regal too, but not in royal blue, bold and black, padded and quilted with silver bulbuls to secured them in place.

The bedding, beautiful, crisp and perfect perhaps a 450 thread count, quite luxurious, with the pillows packed with feather down, with my head surrounded by softness as I placed my head upon it, the mattress, such good quality I could feel that, but softly sprung so my back it did not support, so many a pillow I placed to the front and to the back while I tried to fight the ache and insomnia, and to do so, I pulled the eiderdown in burgundy, and curled it all around, and there, all cosy, I may put the TV on, and watch a program or two, to try and tune my ears into, but nothing else in that room was to make a sound, with only the birds outside to keep me company, and wake me each morning.

Then down to breakfast, to the dining room, even more tastefully done, and in it at that time of the year, through the long French windows to the end of the 6 seater table, the sun came shining through, and how it glistened on the polished cutlery, a sign of good taste, one that I preferred to continue and enjoy, and the crockery, white and all so dashing, in that formal setting, with petite croissant, filled with fruit fresh or preserved, and then to come, an egg, just as I please, and a piece of fresh ham, and all to relax as I soaked up the ambiance, and even enjoyed the filtered coffee out of the machine, and sat upon quite modern round-backed padded chairs where the lustre of the fabric in contrast to the harsh white of the wood, blended somehow beautifully with the wall of that paper that was so detested a couple of decades ago, of flock, in black, in the style of Damask and to the dark grey background, ideas of sophistication and chic, as I contemplated "Easily I can achieve this too," as my hopes and aspirations, gently, mesmerizingly in my mind, spun around.

Yet my stay I enjoyed, but the level of my emotions, sensible, balanced, or fulfilled, were not a luxury that often visited me, unfortunately not quite so, but I did my best not to dwell, as I scurried around, in an attempt to achieve my dream, but really, how could I when I remained searching in the wrong place. But still that realization had not fallen upon me, as I went blissfully by, yet not exactly wasting time, for as luck would have it, the place where I stayed, of my dream, they had the same, to buy a grand, yet rundown property, tastefully and purposefully, to fix it up as their home and serving as a business equally, and for them quite easy to do, for the husband by profession an architect, and she, a PA, so highly efficient in administration, and using all the tricks, to maximize space and incorporate design, they, I have to say, achieved a most fine job.

And how magnificent, to know there was a blueprint out there for exactly what I was trying to achieve, but hold on one minute, I was to ponder, steady on now, for using another's blueprint, "Was it not that, which got me into trouble not so long ago?" So caution I was to apply, but then not too much, for really, as I learnt more about taxes and working with French *artisans*, craftsmen, but that plan from old, was already in my imagination, and so for a *Chambre d'Hote*, Bed & Breakfast accommodation, as I held firmly to the vision, somehow, somewhere, I was to find the provision.

> *"Believing in yourself is an endless destination.*
> *Believing you have failed is the end of your journey."*
> *~ Sarah Meredit*

The cooler winter days dispersing, giving way to the warmer temperate days of spring, *dans le sud de la France*, in southern France, where the leaves just bursting through, in that hamlet of *Montpellier, en général,* in general, somehow, remained me of my favourite in Melbourne, as in common, so many little things they had, like a few shops to look around, cafes where to idle a while, a fair bit of sunshine, and the architecture my favourite, which as may times as I observed it, in different light, as the seasons passed by and the hours of the day the same, always, something new, something interesting, would come to light.

Endlessly I strolled the streets along the dark and narrow lanes, searching for the perfect gift, for those perfect friends I left behind in Paris, and the architecture I left behind too, the *Haussmann* architecture, not to be reciprocated there, but what they had were many a nook and cranny worthy of investigation, all designed and perfectly planned, for those who needed, as throughout history, purposefully built housing, and more, the buildings perfectly designed, tall with extremely narrow streets, and at lower levels, windows small, most functional, to expel the prevailing winds and the battering rain, and the walls of stone so wide, likely quarried quite locally, and extremely serviceable, for the heat to be retained in the winter, and the cool to regained in the summer, and true to form, through the thickness of the walls, a good and effective insulator is born.

The architecture, likely specific to that tiny town, and for sure, not what I encountered in those countries down-under, for they far too young for that, and perhaps in parts of the USA, the same may be said, so I was to seize the opportunity and revel in what I saw, with my imagination of film set, depicting intrigue or romance, illicit affairs or hard lives lived, and then as I turned the corner, something else caught my eye, or was that someone, as down the lane, a little like the movie with Fagan, and that character who had that dog, OK, a little sketchy I realise, but as a game, try and guess which one, and there he was, whistling as he hurried by, unbothered by the heavy rain, his hood over his head as he walked at the pace of a swagger, in the ever popular camel coloured and dare I say, French duffle coat, knee length of heavy wool, with brown leather toggles, which he left unfastened, as in the wind, behind him flowed wearing jeans and most sensible sturdy laced up shoes, in mat tan, from where the torrential rain, simply rolled right off.

And as his whistle turned into words, what a surprise, as it was English not French the language he sang, and with a smile on my face, and quite mesmerised, a smile was to beam across my face, for there at his side, quite a small dog, shaggy in appearance, spritely in nature and so fitting for many a Hollywood script, with a spiky beige and white short fur coat, with short legs the same, he tottered quickly by at the pace of his master, with his tail wagging wonderfully from side to side, missing not a beat, and I'm sure upon his face, a grin I could see, as beside his master he walked, ignoring the drops of cold rain, as they dripped from his coat onto the floor, and so disappointed was I, as they turned up a *rue*, out of my view, but was I to follow them too, for so intrigued was I, of a man who lived in the South of France, who sang English, with *sans*, no, accent.

So thinking quite quickly, for sure still in pursuit, of that illusive present to send north to Paris, and who was to know, perhaps I would find a shop to sell me such, right up that street, and so I turned, but he had come to a stop searching for his keys, outside a building quite architecturally common in France and deigned many centuries ago called *Appartment Particuliers*, quite my favourite, tall, with a central spiral staircase spinning around, and off it, at unequal levels, one room for each it usually appeared, and so within the workers for the area would live, family by family, but now, unified, one big beautiful house they may make, or alternatively and quite commonly, a *Chambre d'Hote or Gite*, holiday apartment, and most attractive they can be, and for an idea for me, well, it quite filled me with gentle glee.

Then as I walked by, he continued with his dulcet tones, and it, highly intriguing, and me, needing that satisfying, turned around to enquire after first justifying my question, with "I heard you sing, you do that very well, and without a French accent, I'm wondering, if you don't mind telling, what is your nationality?" So pleased was I, that he was happy to tell, for I was so enthralled to learn a quick summery of his experiences and travels, and he happy to tell me more, and so a *rendezvous* was arranged for the next day, at his favourite café down the street, around the corner from where we spoke, and 'hurrah' I did think, how truly magnificent, before quickly considering, "Where the heck am I, and how will I find my way here again?" For those streets contrived weaving in and out like a rabbit warren, with a landmark difficult to find, so taking no chances, as I sometimes did, it was a pen and paper I was to right down the name of the street, the café, and the roads leading back to the main avenue, so like Hansel and Gretel, I could find my way back again.

And so it was the very next day, successfully I found my way back, and foe me, no mean feat, so hurrah again, and "Oh my" fascinating, the venue so tiny, the tables old red Formica from 5 decades ago, and the chairs from the decade to match, and as if in perfect design, the square tablecloths in gingham print, swiped across the table at an angle swiped, with the salt and pepper pots of the same era, along with the cakes display cabinet, wear the cakes, still placed on paper doilies of old, but it was the proportions of the room which was most mesmerizing, for surely not a man of 6 foot could have comfortably stood up in there, especially with the beams poking through, and the tables numbering only 4, with just 3 more alfresco outside the door, and of the width of the street, so absolutely amazingly narrow, of those tables of tiny dimensions and length, yet still managed to portion the street into 2, increasing the café's occupancy by 40%.

And as he the duffle coat man, my first companion in *Montpellier*, unfolded his most interesting story of life, for his journey had been colourful, and he a musician, busking in many a country as a young man, and making lots of money and ceasing every opportunity that presented itself along the way, enjoying the good-life as he travelled widely and played much in great cities around the world, from Scandinavia to England to the USA, and great success was his acclaim, as he teaming with others, playing proper gigs, producing bigger rewards, and at the top, rolling high and enjoying the lot, thought it would not stop, and more the money he made, all tax-free.

And there he was that man sat before me, tall with dark wavy hair, well, it was France, as his tone changed a little and his expression the same, with nicotine stained fingers he reached for another cigarette, as his story rolled on, as perhaps unwise he and been for he splurged and fluttered all his spoils away, not saving even a farthing, a dime, a centime, for a rainy day, and he then, a little despondent, a little withdrawn, as he realised the effects of those frivolous actions way back then, so much achieved and so much discarded, for then, he was living without options for those he could not afford to pay, as no investments and no security, he admitted to me, should he have a choice, resolute, at the age of 50 or more, and to do the same, he would not take that action, all over again.

> *"Even if you are on the right track you will get run over if you just sit there."*
> *~ Will Rogers*

A case certainly worthy of consideration, for on the list of things not to do, I remained determined to learn by other people's mistakes whenever possible, therefore, avoiding my own. And true, it was not enlightenment I received inadvertently from him, but confirmation for me, "Where to from here?" I needed deliberation, to be wise and get it right, for is it true, there are only so many chances in this world, and when they run out, that is us done, or is it m ore a case, of exploration of bigger and greater, or milder and softer, depending on what we learn, and more what we learn of ourselves of our preferences likes, and dislikes, that help us out, and refine, remodel, or fix us up, as we travel along our way.

My companion then extended what I consider the normal hand of French hospitality, inviting me to his home to share a meal, and although this is not my culture, or an attribute I have to entertain those who I know not well at my home, to the added irritation to a Frenchman that I knew in Melbourne, but more, at the back of my mind, perhaps I worried of his true intention, but "Did I need to do the same again?" So quickly, a Risk Assessment, which had become an excellent trick for me to do, after all my life experiences, utilizing the World Health Organization motto, 'Prevention is better than cure,' so that system I grew and lived by, for in the realms of men, evidence had proved, that to throw caution to the wind, was not a wise way to go.

Arriving punctually, knocking of the oak door of centuries old, but painted in an underwhelming dirty green, safety should have shouted as my first priority, as a man, rather worse for wear, unkept and unclean, with lack of hygiene, opened the door, and beckoned me in, but instantly the vibe wasn't right, and right then, before behind the door I stood, same on the street, I should have acted on he gut instinct and instantly, taken flight…and "Why?" So foolishly "For I didn't want to hurt his feelings or appear impolite?" "Oh my!" Really! "Had I heard myself?" and "Leant so little?"

My mind unsettled but still I did not make my excuses, and get the hell out of there, as slowly I wound myself up the spiralling staircase to the 3rd floor, and I placed my hand still in my black leather gloves, but still, the chill of the pervasive damp permeating through that wall of stone, and without a handrail, quite treacherous the ascent, as the steps so narrow, so precarious underfoot, impossible to sidestep and avoid the trench worn away by those who quite ordinarily, for 3 or 400 years, had passed that way before.

And reaching our destination, an outstretched hand directed me in, the door, it appeared to bang shut behind me, but what of may safety, for suddenly I became so pleased of my precautionary measures, how I had told my *propriétaire*, where I was going at 4 o'clock and who I was meeting there and indeed why, so a safety net to some degree I believed I had provided for myself, but it appeared that was the only one I had, and as I looked around, in that amazingly square room, of 4 metres wide, long, and even tall, another exit there was not, so precautionary, I checked out the distance from the window down to the cobbled ground, and decided as an action plan, it was not at all, and then so missgivingly, I rationalized all the unfolding events, but hugely, importantly, as an American Court Judge, through experience, completely convicted in his opinion, "When your instinct kicks-in, *never* second guess it, simply, just get the heck out of there!"

Was it too late to implement a portion of caution, I considered not, but a good thing to do, and as I sat on the chair, with he eating food sat on one separating me from the exit door, and did he lock it when I walked in, I didn't notice, as I contemplated, was I trapped and when would I be safely at the other side of it again, but in the interim, for I cold not make an excuse, for he knew I knew no one in that *ville* and had noting else to do, for I had failed to leave myself open a get-out clause, so I was to implement my Mental Health nurse training, and keep calm, talk of subjects that were to cause zero emotions or stress, and a good job I believe I was doing, and then, a telephone call he received, and he became instantly extremely emotive as his temper soared, as so angrily with force, he threw his pen across the room and why because his mother had called.

A flash back I was to have of my ex-fiancé, how his levels of violence so gradually escalated, and true that was over months, adding up to years, but first it began with him throwing a china mug against he wall, and then a hairspray canister at my head, I watched him lie so effortlessly to people and with such skill, even I who was supposed to know him best, even believed what he said, and that all before, his threats to me commenced, then increased, then one night angry, his temper flying, I tried to run away from him, but he caught me by my ankles as up the stairs I tried to escape, and ignoring my pleas and shouts for him to let go, with force he tugged on them hard, causing me to fall flat on my face.

Then relenting not at what he'd done, he began to drag me backwards down the stairs, and as my nightgown rose up, and form the carpet I suffered mild irritating burns, and that night I slept in our store room, as I cleared boxes and made a place on the floor, and you may have guessed it, they next day, he came crawling all over me, with kisses and hugs and smiles, and what did I do, you may have guessed that too, consumed by low self-esteem, which he willingly enforced, with lack of worth, compounded by his heavy influence, and at my deepest core, seeking not rejection, but love and acceptance, desperately, so hard I am trying not to scream, as not reading those tell-tale obvious signs, quite 'pathetically,' the start of too many, as 'I gave right in.' So I urge you ladies, to take note, and never ever, underestimate those smallest things you see or notice.

"Oh my" it turned out that niggling gut-thing was right, and I quick-smart had to get out of there, but what to do, thinking fast on my feet, about 45 mins had passed, and I thought that was good enough, not to vex him to much, so with my gentle reasoning's growing, and my conversation in self-preservation flow, I was to say goodbye to those cool blank walls, and that rather too hot to touch character, and see myself, "Wahoo" with relief safely speeding as fast as I could down those slightly slippy stairs, and safely out on the street, where the air, never, had it felt so fresh.

"Phew," my strategy complete, I was out on the street, safe from harm. I wondered the warrens of the tiny rue's, wondering again, how I managed to manifested that scenario in my life. "How could I have got it so wrong? Had I made a big mistake? Should I have shown greater caution?" But I thought I need not, not in daylight, not in a downtown apartment, but then, still alone, isolated and so with someone I did not know, potentially in a threatening environment. But "Was I wrong to trust that man, or foolish for considering to do so?" I had so many questions, but no immediate answers. For I was doing the best I could, or "Was I?" "Was I growing, or just standing still? Was I learning to trust others when in fact, I should have been learning to trust in myself, to make increasingly wise decisions, using not incremental portions, but doubling on, great big dollops of discernment?" For perhaps that experience was less attached to my instinct than it was to a simple choice, but "What of common sense? On that day did I let mine slip away?" and you know what they say, "If common sense is so common, *why*, do so few people have it?"

For sure, it was not low self-esteem that trapped me on that day, or low self-worth, it was more simply I do perceive, that really, my common sense took a day off and refused to come out to play, yet should I have refused to permit it to do so, simply I may have been saved from another mistake and lesson requiring to be learnt, for actually I do believe it was unnecessary and along my way, completely avoidable.

And only when safely walking back along the street, toward the light, my imagination in full flight, "Oh my" how I would so adore to own such a building as that, or just a portion, or anywhere maybe of those proportions of size, where how marvellously a trendy and purposeful mezzanine level could be put right up in the eaves, yet still permitting for such grandeur of space underneath, and its construction of industrial steel or equally appealing, that of thick and hefty blocks of wood, all held such appeal.

But so sad, for there seemed little to cheer up the duffle coat man, for his imagination, may have been trapped from flying, as his reality a dark blank, rejected space, most notably, his mattress placed in the far corner on the cold stone flags, his sheets all tattered and torn, with a small chest of draws at an angle across the corner, where placed and old, small TV, disappearing into nothingness in that cavernous space, and his shower old and dirty and visible to see, as only privacy was afforded by a piece of shoddy fabric swung over a tied up piece of string, and the kitchen hustling to be noticed, trapped in such a petite space, beneath the curve of the spiralling staircase above, with a cooker ring of only one, and the sink, not close by, but positioned to the side, in front of the old fireplace and piled high, with multiple pots and pans, from an era of my grandma's, and the fridge, infection may have resided there and all the heaps of rubbish that were close to his square table and 2 chairs, may have been piled up as rubbish previously, yet for purpose, fitted perfectly.

"Oh my" I was to wonder, of the conversation we had the previous day, and all what we talked about, really, what would he have chosen to do differently, to rollout a different scenario, created by a different chain reaction, from his choices in-between, for that money he so gladly earned, wisely, it was not just to spend it randomly, for it was a tool of prosperity, it was give him choices, to buy him options, to form his on flowing wealth, of fulfil his heart's desires.

> *"Know thy self, know thy enemy. A thousand battles a thousand victories."*
> *~ Sun Tzu*

The days of torrential downpours gone and the pale blue sky, clear with not a cloud in sight, seemed to cheer everyone's sooth peoples mood in that lovely *ville*, quite remarkably so, and more smiles could be seen as I passed by the café's and bars, dotted around the centre square and the rue's, and filled with those sipping on a short black, or a tipple of wine, but me, I only ever partook after lunch, and an afternoon habit I created, was not the traditional English tea and scones, but a glass of the wonderful *Bordeaux*. But where to rest and idle a while, I was unsure, for I had not discovered a preferred venue, but as one I walked by, street appeal it seemed to have, and on an angle from a bend in the road, sheltered from that brisk-full breeze, and beneath the heater I sat to eat a baguette, I was to take a weight off my feet.

And there, although I was not looking at him, through my peripheral vision, I could see he was looking at me, His stature about 5foot eight, his hair slightly greying, but loose and flowing and so I observed him as he passed on by, but wait a minute that was him again, and he looking more intently at me, and as I turned to look his way, his smile, larger than life as they say, and his gleaming eyes to match, he paused in front of my table, and in French spoke to me, "Arrhar" that language I did not quite understand, so in my best accent I could muster, I gave it a shot and relied apologetically, *"Je suis désolé, je ne comprends pas,"* "I'm sorry, I don't understand." "Oh my" then how thrilled I was when he in response was to pass me a compliment, announcing, "Because of your style, I thought you were French."

"Arrhar," he understood every word, and I quickly contemplated, 'if only' my well rehearsed phrase of *"Un verre de vin rouge et une tasse d'eau chaude s'il vous plait,"* "A glass of red wine and a cup of hot water please," was so easily understood, yet so unfortunately, recurrently with frustration, that forever surpassed my pronunciation skills, and never before had I not been required to repeat it, several times, so to coin northern English vernacular, " I was well pleased." But in the interim, I wondered, "If it's true that the best way to a man's heart is through his stomach, "What was the best way to mine?" To complement me on my style contrived as a French chic, certainly it proved as no guarantee, but still, it was a very good start, and one I have to say, quite unusually so, I did enjoy.

Gracefully I accepted, but cautiously I suspected why he spoke it, as a 'Casanova,' he might have been, but there again perhaps not, for it was not the first comment on my style I received, as on a most chilly and highly humid typically damp Parisian day while I, searching for an Internet café, as no access which I was told by that landlord there would be, that was until he received his princely monthly sum, and then miraculously, it appeared not to be. So up and down the extensive boulevards I travelled, as I was assured, "Up there you will find one," yet no, for it remained illusive.

But then not to worry too much, for I, most sensible, rugged up warm, dressed in my pink thick cable-knit wool dress, to the knee in length and of contrast, I sported a fine woollen rib black pantyhose, with black patent leather boots, just finishing short of my knee, with of cause matching handbag of patent leather with faux fur grey trim, and suede leather gloves of the same in colour, and hat with fur trim that cradled my head, and you guessed it, in black. The ensemble completed and classically untinted, by a vintage fur coat, 1940's in design, the colour a deep warm burgundy in length rested neatly 6 inches above my knee. And to top it off, in a way of contrast, a scarf in cream, tucked beneath, only just enough, so with a peak, it could be seen.

And me, minding my own business as I went on my way, that was until I was passing a restaurant, where the warmth of the inviting air inside could be felt as the couple close by, a gentleman and his lady companion me were to leave, and as I approached, it was she who approached me, and although I knew not of what she said, with communication being 93% non verbal, and only 7% accounting for the words we speak, I need not to be a rocket scientist to understand her intimation, as she passed her camera into my hand, so happily I obliged, but I was no David Bailey but hoped he would have been proud of my efforts, or perhaps he would not, so to edge their-bets for a good photo to be assured, I took a couple of shots.

It was impossible to miss the style of the gentleman, his of utter sophistication, a man of a 'certain age,' and dare I say, a 'certain class.' A traditional or Renaissance man I dared to presume, somehow the manners of the former, but the attitude of the latter, but either unnecessary to presume, as the words he spoke, less clear than his big smile which he delivered with his eyes, and his French accent wooing me, although I understood not what he uttered, and so implementing my over used phrase as expressing, sorry, I understand not what you say, with a tilt of his head, with a unmistakable nod of appreciation, his eyes telling the take, as smiling gently and admiringly, in an accent of the most exquisite French, a phrase that induced my mind to wallow his words, *"Votre style c'est très chic et sophistiqué,"* "Your style is very chic and sophisticated." "Oh my" my smile must have travelled from ear to ear, not because of the complement, but of who gave it, for he, of so much style and sophistication to think that I had my own, now that was a complement, I was so graciously and happily to receive.

And in Paris, of that *Renaissance* man's companion, I noted her style, most of modern, and she taller than he, in her black leather high healed boots reaching to her knee, with her denim jeans tucked in them, with her modern white and fawn, blouson jacket, not in *faux* but real fur, not vintage but brand new, and no hat was she waring, as her long straight blonde hair blew briskly in the breeze, then missing her gloves on that bitterly cold day, her manicure of distinction, was easily seen, then her bag, clearly expensive, she swung nonchalantly across her shoulder, as not even a *foulard*, flimsily scarf, did she ware to keep her warm.

But then again, she, quite young, perhaps keeping warm wasn't her goal, and after casting a sigh, she stepped towards me, as I contemplated, such a delicate balance, she so pretty with makeup so refined, yet her face, depicted an expression dejection and deflation, as her companion even momentarily, placed his attentions elsewhere, other than on her, and a surpassing thought sprung to my mind, in the concept of love-verses-money, or peace-verses-security, or maybe, she was just having fun, for as they turned, she linked his arm, and down the boulevard, merrily, they seemed to stroll.

I must say, so thrilled am I when people mention my style, for unlike looks, they are not inherited, they are something that I have personally cultivated, and "Oh how I enjoy" putting together an ensemble that is chic, classy and a little funky simultaneously, for inject a petite piece of *je ne sais pas*, I don't know what, but really I do, for its just a little added piece of my inner spirit, making something out of noting, in the realms of making the ordinary appear extraordinary, like luxury.

And true, when I was in Melbourne, so thrilled was I to be asked while gazing upon those coloured photos of France, of Parisian lofts and Provence farmhouses and copious copies of those depicting castles and more, when a customer who I noticed casting an eye at me, was to eventually to speak, and her far younger in years than I and looking rather quite fine she asked, "Are you a designer?" Flattered, surprised and perhaps recognizable in my voice as "No" I replied. Continuing, "Oh I thought you were because of the way you are dressed, your design, you've put together." Certainly I was grateful for her comments, and I accepted it as a huge and inspiring complement, for when one women compliments another, it means so much more than when a man does the same, for unlike him, its pretty much certain she is genuine and has nothing to gain. And so I ruffled my feathers, for she looked pretty stylish herself.

"We cannot teach people anything; we can only help them discover it within themselves."
~ Galileo Galilei

James with his appealing smile and his outstretched arm, pointing to the petite circular table beside me, should he be able to sit there, well, sure, it was empty, and to passing time with him, certainly I held no aversion. And then a lovely conversation did ensue, the topics I remember not, but I remember how I felt in his presence, relaxed, welcomed and feely able to be myself, and more, he permitted me to speak in French, which so often others did not permit me to do, at least no without minor or extreme criticism on each attempt, of how badly I was doing, stabbing with scorns of the same, and after so many months I was unable to bypass, "Don't speak my language you make it sound so bad," or "French, you think you speak it, when really you don't speak it at all!"

Really, "Was I ever going to surpass that level?" but I shouldn't complain, when the French said to me, "It is not to speak French, why I am speaking to you, it is only so I can, practice and improve my English." But really, did I have cause to be disgruntled at them, for as time went on, and my proficiency failed to improve, even with the most mundane and practiced phrases, my pronunciation the same, and so often did I return to communicate in that language from my birth I knew so well, and sincerely hoped, nay desired that they knew it as well.

And a double edged sword it was to be, as my *propriétaire* told me, that when the French are outside Paris, little opportunity is presented to practice their skills, so maybe that was why, so many at stores or cafes, comprehended so little in that *ville*, of what I did say, but hey, a tact I was to learn, from girls so much younger than me, who were staying in France only to practice the language in their gap year informed me, "When we are with French people that is the only language we speak, and they just have to be patient and help" but "What if they don't?" I enquired, reflecting on my experiences, "Well that's all right" I was told, "If they ignore our request to do just that, its easy, we simply move on and speak with someone who will."

"Wow!" So young so bold at only 20 years or so, and how sensible, and my heart panged slowly, as I did contemplate, "If only" I could have been as wise as that, as confident, or hold such self-esteem." And clearly they did, as they told me, they were from Sydney in Australia, and when I commented, "But I don't note an accent" it was pointed out to me, that in that country, "Our accent is more noted by our class and the money we have rather than the state or area we come from." And 'if only' where we come from, of our experiences there, were one way or another, only to benignly affect our ascents, "Wow!" How much better off, many of us, like me would be.

But not so for the anxiety she did provoke, as on the 2 close friends continued and explained, of where they lived, and the allowance they received, of what they were to go back to, friends, family relations unbound, and like the Swedish girls at *la Sorbonne* revealed, their own precious things collected over the years kept safely within their own private rooms, and hobbies that they were to resume too, all that had been paid for by their loving parents, and "Oh" what a cavernous gap that did open, but in honesty, it needed little encouragement, for in existence, it already was, and their security, their homes of love and acceptance of support, financially and otherwise, that through their tender years, all had cradled and weaved together a picture most pleasant, that was easily clear to see and of it, too easy to covert.

For they with no responsibilities of bills to pay, no insurance to consider, a network support system and safety nets they had in place, all importantly providing comfort too with no worries, of how long was my money to last for, and was I to be destitute, or run out, before I had even a chance to conduct my plan or follow my dream, and never as they hated themselves for the choices they made, to choose so badly, that the man whose engagement ring they were to wear, as to almost murder them, and the other of cause, seemed so silly in comparison to consider, how he took my castle and my livelihood of independent security, and "Yes" that was right, I hated myself for I chose him too. So as they spoke of their good fortune, and how fortunate and pleasant their lives were and had been, though they recognised it not as such, but merely as simply normal, and to them, sure enough, it was, but for me to claim the same, "Could I really dare, on a permanent basis to harness to hold, such hope?"

And "Why were my emotions not ceasing to cripple me?" For as they talked of the abundance, I could only concentrate on my lack, of a lifetime of regrets, wheeling up pain, panging and devastation of such misery at the deepest depth or my core, where the flame of turmoil still flicked in my heart, refusing to go out, as those emotional continued to create physical responses that I still felt, those spreading throughout my body and causing involuntary adrenaline surges, and as much as fought it, as I tried so much to embrace hope, moving from that darkened place toward the light. Yet periodically, I'd loose the fight, and sometimes the repercussions of enduring horrendous pain, through those decades, dragged me back again, refusing to permit my escape forwards, to a place, healthy, nourished, loved, where the light truly does shine, where I, like those young girls, and the girls at university, will hold something so valuable, to be, grounded, balanced with well-seated emotions, and to dwell in me have hope and peace in abundance, and I, able to proclaim their permanence.

As their security, only served to highlight my lack of it, but really "Was it reasonable to consider, that those rollercoaster emotions served as a part of my healing?" or "Was I simply wandering again down the wrong track again?" for "Was it reasonable to believe, that following decades of abuse and its unfolding blueprint, almost predestining me to receive more of the same, and indeed of such a history, so long in the making, how was it to be eradicated overnight?" or perhaps "With myself should I have been more gentle and realistic, not in a notion to abdicate responsibility for helping myself, but in the realms of time, to allow myself to heal to cease being harsh toward myself, but to be kind and tenderness, of these attributes to manufacture and allocate?" as "Where to from here?" was knocking at my door, and for sure, it needed an answer, so I needed to push on through, for nothing else there was for me to do, and all the regrets of a life, spent less well than I ought, and my parents spell, I was to practice everyday to kick it to the curb, and the shame and guilt they disposed upon me, well I made a choice, I was to do all I could, to make completely sure, from my body and my mind, I was to let go of their crippling blueprint and all their screamed disparaging cures of ridicule and mockery, once and for all, that I had ever heard.

"The greatest accomplishment is not in never falling, but in rising again after you fall."
~ Vince Lombardi Jr

Toulouse, was to be where my next *billet*, ticket was to take me to, for it had come highly recommended for astute property investment options, and I needed to leave, for the 10 days I'd past in *Montpellier* proved to be nothing more than a little break, and really I didn't need on of those, I needed more, "Where to from here?" so off to the *office de tourisme*, I did go, and walking across the square I was in fine-fettle, and good sprits as always had I received such good assistance form them, and never did it occur to me that there, I would receive anything else.

And while I waited in line, I noticed the two lovely people who helped me before were nowhere to be seen, so I was happy to speak to a lady who wore a Union Jack badge, the flag of Britten, for that served to all the tourists who needed assistance that English she could converse, so I believed I was good to go. But first, it was my very best French I tried to speak, but her facial expression indicated that of assistance she cared not to give me, as it was that, my father used to get so angry at me for, one of dumb-insolence, but "Why? Wasn't I just a customer, trying hard and being polite?"

I needed to know, "Do you have a map of Toulouse?" Perhaps not a stretch too great, for they all were tourist offices of one Government body, and the town was only a swift 3 hours away by train, but that was not to be, not to worry, but onto my next and more important question, "Does the *office de tourisme*, in Toulouse, provide the same service as you do, "To telephone *propriétaire* on my behalf, to assist in gaining suitable hotel accommodation?" but "Why was that so difficult for her to answer?" and "Why was she telling me, 'No office may do that for you'" when clearly she was so wrong, as at the office she was sitting in, twice, already for me, that service had been provided.

But accidently or deliberately, that young girl was a little awkward and obstinate, but the main problem she was not helping me at all, but worse, causing frustration, with her inclination to tell me I was wrong, when I knew myself to be right, and then, hope, I thought was at hand, as a man, a few years older than her, but younger than me, who had heard the extent of the conversation, and once he interjected, but I have to say not helpfully so, and then as he put the phone down, he in an instant stood up, with a most harsh interjection, as he waved his arms around declaring, "At this office they have never telephoned hotels or any other accommodation to help the client." "What? Hadn't he been listening to the conversation for 10 minutes, and didn't he know my testimony to be to the contrary, and didn't he recognize how unhelpful, nay, obstinate that girl had been, failing to adequately assist a tourist like me?"

His instruction, delivered by his tone and pitch of voice with indignation, with a look of intolerance upon his face, his body language, tense and fraught, as angrily he said to me, "You will have to go away and telephone them yourself." Then, quite ashamed, as for after 3 months at university and further in immersion, I considered my skills would be far in ahead than where they were, but amidst my regrets of misfortune, and little to no advancement, I served myself, more than a generous portion of reignited, self-belittling self-flagellating, negative emotions of insecurities, all hindering, lurking and taking up residence in the crevices of my mind. But "Did I tell him all that?" "No" I kept it hidden, simply admitting, that 2 nights earlier I had already tried to do as he suggested, 3 times I called, but on each occasion the French person, on the other end of the line, unable to decipher my words, my struggling phrase, simply, hung up.

And true, I had not focused on it, but tried to give it little thought as possible, preferring to concentrate on keeping that episode like so many others, compartmented in a neat little box, and never letting them mix, for should they compound and multiply, or should I examine it all too closely, that remorse, those regrets, created by unlevel emotionally-charged choices, which only I was responsible for, where forgiveness, not for others of what they did to me, but of what I have continued to do toward myself, with my self-esteem so low, my self-worth the same, trying so hard but apparently too frequently failing miserably to rectify the past, and produce a more pleasant future, as I tried so drastically hard to prevent history repeating itself, and me tumbling to the bottom, of really how knew where, or how deep or how long I would be there, and the answer knew not, should I within, hold sufficient willpower to ensure a resolution, for those compounding catastrophic emotions to disperse, repair or fix.

But then, as that Frenchman standing tall and for all around in that busy tourism office declared, sarcastically with spiteful ridicule, with the toss of his head, laughing, "You have been to school and had a professor at *la Sorbonne* and still, you cannot speak French!" "Really? Had I lost my way and ended up in a children's playground?" For it appeared so from his intimations and hand gestures of his actions, of *his* dogmatic opinion and offensive persona, perhaps designed to enhance his superiority or demoralize me, yet either way, in front of all those non discarnate onlookers, his perceived goal achieved, as I felt so terribly embarrassed and so ashamed, he put on quite a show for staff and tourists alike, for which they needed not to buy a ticket, but I was to pay the price. But "Who was I to passively accept his disparagement and prejudice he passed to me?" As I had done no-wrong thing to him, I had only and simply, sought help, the kind in his workplace he was supposed to provide?"

Winds of tornado proportions swept through my mind of inferiority, as his stinging sarcasm overwhelming, his arrogance undisguised, his professionalism nowhere to be found, and yet, too upset to fight back, softly, timidly, but definitely I was to speak, as explain I did in my defence, "I did try." But then I did not argue, I had nothing more to say, I turned to leave, my spirit broken yet my head held high, or sadly, "Was it?" As I walked past all those who stared, who had enjoyed his wonderful show, as I refused to justify myself to him, but like the escalating lava of a volcano, a crescendo of emotions were about to erupt and I was going to have to justify it to myself. For he, with his unnecessary superficial insults, that he randomly tossed away were to cut me deep, for recognition flooded to my mind, of my inability to learn, not created by stupidity as my father spouted at me, but by an injury from a man I chose to love, as a direct consequence of the abuse I suffered at the hands of my father, for 19 years, resulting in that reduced cognition, so learning physically a problem, and more thoughts of negativity attached in an instant to those, where I thought, "My castle my castle, my love for my castle."

And that too gone, as a consequence of parental harm, where me, not understanding love, not even in the slightest way, had mistaken what I presumed to be the love for a lover for that of a brother, and friends there were non, to steer me to the right path, and when I realised something was wrong and tried to call it off, true to parental training I did what I was taught to do, put myself second, in any and every circumstance, and as I had desperately dragged my way through, to just survive, for my own life to benefit and enhance, for that curse of old trapped in my brain, harming my progression, full of self-loathing, and self-condemnation, resilient, resisting my attempts to break free, refusing to let go of me, trying, succeeding in pulling me back again, as all consuming, the pain of the past in that moment, tangible, twisting at my digestion and tugging at my nerves, as so many moments I was fighting each moment not to hate myself with even greater fortitude.

But "Was I to mention a snippet of a word of my private world to him?" "Absolutely not!" For he deserved not to know those circumstances that got me to where I was, to that destination, so ready for rejuvenation, escaping that cesspit of a dark dungeon, where life had tightly bound and gagged me, in chians, oppressed, depressed, but it was time to repel that faulty programming, to break free, and walk most definitely in my, majesty.

And that a notion I clung to as I walked across the square *en centre ville,* unable to hold back the tears, as sorrow filled, spilled, overflowing out of my heart, and as I placed one foot in front of the other, the flow of tears began to tumble like a cascading waterfall from my eyes, as my heart overfilled with sorrow. As the warmth of the tears chilled in the air, uncomfortable upon my skin, uncomfortable were his taunted words, apparent of malice and vengeance, void of comprehension or dignity. But for "Why, why had he harmed me so?" and through the enormity of those gut emotions, I contemplated, "Who was he to judge me?"

Yet something else was to rise up on the inside of me, a new, and worthy strength, overcoming those of debilitation, and I was to declare, "No!" "No, you cannot judge me so!" Fighting back those uncontrollable tears, opening up those festering wounds, I, gaining composure, returning to that tourism office with dignity and decorum, and walking up to the counter, my request simple, "I'd like to speak to the manager please." I was told, she was at lunch and in 90 minutes would need to return, and "OK" I was not swayed, my concerns were to be heard; and so it was, I set my clock and I was prompt. Greeted, before I was escorted to an upstairs office, where my complaint was listened to, and so pleased was I, that the young man who had initially helped me, who had offered and did make those telephone calls to the owners of the *Chambre d'Hotes,* and *Gites,* accompanied us to assist in that investigation, for I considered with him I had already proven my credibility of politeness and a grateful attitude, therefore contradicting anything to the contrary that the assistant to whom I held the complaint could say, and so believing, I, at last, deserved to stand up for my rights, I commenced to unfold the tale of my distress, not only to help me, but hold he, accountable, so he, would not again make an other suffer as he did me.

Perhaps, they were bemused, uncomprehending "Why?" I was so effected by that man's behaviour toward me, and so I desired to explain that I was not simply, an 'emotionally frail lady,' or in truth, really, how quite resilient I could be, as it was not for them to know, neither for me to explain the reasons I could not learn French easily, of my cognition effected by fighting for my life, as all of it, by that government employee, who criticized and scorned me so didn't need to know.

So I kept it hidden, my neck injury and the reason for that neck injury, the assault of grievous and actual bodily harm, my life threatened and my fight to survive, my physical and emotional abuse that I marinaded in by my parents, and seasoned by my brother, then my taste for abusive men was sealed, and baked to a crisp by my husband then almost dissected by my ex-fiancé, and all those mistakes rolled on, for a recipe I was given as a toddler, that was poured over me as a child and teenager, so as I entered into womanhood, that recipe, the only one I had in my book, was to prepare a banquette of disaster.

Inwardly, perhaps I should have justified my emotions by declaring, I would rather move houses, move countries and continents and live in a country where I was unable to speak the language, than remain where I was and possibly end up dead. But of cause, they remained hidden too, and true, those floods of sobs I'd been unable to hold back, had released 'something' and I was feeling better, stronger, more determined and confident, with greater insightfulness of my own worth and capabilities, that truly recovery was possible, for it was not the past I wanted to live in, for I was pushing for the bliss, I aimed to gain in my future.

But of it all, not an ounce did I share with them, for really, my only concern and point of reference for that meeting, "Who was he to criticize, demoralize or throw accusations on me?" and for us all, "Who are we to presume to do that to each other?" For what I have learnt through walking so many miles in my own shoes, over the rough, treacherous and damn right dangerous terrain I have travelled along my journey, judge not another, for in their shoes, we know not, what they have walked upon, nor what, they have suffered or overcome.

As when we look at others, our first perceptions of our observations, often their clothes, but "Oh my" how they can form a disguise or identify who, on the inside they really are, perhaps deliberately or by default, as you see, only what they want you to. Their actions, equally their non-actions or reactions can be derived from a history, that really, they choose not to tell, and we, have no idea of the footsteps they have trodden, willingly or cruelly, maliciously forced by other to take them toward a certain destination, where really, certainly they preferred not to be, and from it, they may have tried to escape, 'if only' they knew they could, or they should, or there really was, another place for them to be.

For their journey, pleasant or horrendous, we know not, what that is, and of themselves, sadly how badly, as their normal, oblivious, they may not recognize it either, as their smile, can conceal a world of pain too heavy to bear that hides behind, but they eyes, they may reveal the anxiety of the harm and hurt they live in everyday, 'if only,' they stay still long enough so in them we can see right, and is this true for everyone, or "Am I, just talking about me?"

Then that manager when my concerns were aired, asked me, 'what I thought she should do.' And perhaps because of my OH&S safety training or perhaps because in my life I was beginning to come up with my own recipe filled cookbook, I focused not on the negativity of his misconduct, but of actions to move positively forward from that spot. Training, education, of personal and development courses, concerned with identifying 'inter-personal skills,' respect and 'team building exercises,' sprang to my mind, for surely to goodness, it appeared that man was in need of some, and who knew at the beginning and the end of the day, what the reason was, that he behaved toward me in such a way, I knew not, but possibly was it because, of some terrain quite terrible, that he himself, had been forced to walk upon.

And what I knew for myself, I had walked away from that tourist office, believing I had stood-up for me, and given someone else grace, I had taught myself to do what I was worthy of and what right for me, and my emotions were as different as night is to day, from when I walked in that place to when I walked away, for my actions were not derived from a place fear, but out of self-worth, self-respect and my forever growing, self-love, and there from within, empowered and encouraged, I knew that so much more, I was able to overcome.

"The only journey is the journey within."
~ Rainer Maria Rilke

It was damp and drizzly as for the last time I walked across the main square, and although quite pleasant, certainly, I was not to miss that quite small and tasteful *ville*, but of those people I met who were kind, of the lady at the *Chamber d'Hote*, and the lovely couple who having met them in the movie theatre, where I watched an English film, generously invited me to their home. And such a pleasure that was for our discussions surrounded my two favourite topics, first we discussed the wine, the vine the soil the region, as it was poured into large bolus glasses, and then what a treat as infolded, then story of their renovation proposals, of their new home, a property centuries old, of a dream she held tight for several years, what seemed impossible, magically came her way, as strive she did through her inner-personal commitment, she swayed not, perhaps a little bit scary, though resolving to seize her opportunities, come-what-may.

As I wondered what was left for me to do, except just pass time away, as in the chilly air, all rugged up well, in wool and silk, as I simply had to sit alfresco, for I so detest sitting in, and there, suddenly from around the corner, my French friend came, wearing one of his big brimming smiles sufficient to brighten even the gloomiest days, and so pleased as he passed by to say hello, and his apparel like his smile most appealing, in his rustic jeans, that somehow look kind of extra cool, a double breasted wool jacket, with bold, but not garish gold buttons, exposing an emblem, of who knew what, but they too looked kind of hot, his grey and blue check scarf nonchalantly strewn around his neck, that really, no Frenchman would be without, and his well stylish black leather lace up shoes, highly polished, for isn't that the way to permit the rain to roll off and right away, and his matching gloves, somehow extra masculine, and "Oh my" of an ensemble how absolutely fine and in taste, *tres*, very chic.

And I permitted my eyes to meander wistfully over him, as they paused on his grey hair of loose curls, unusual for a man of his years, who may have been 10 years younger than me, but mature, and dare I say sexy that his eyes could testify to, for they I could quite swim in, and his smile, well that could melt me everyday. But swooning, not a good luck, so I chose to maintain my composure as he seated himself opposite me, as he partook of a 'short black' coffee, an association I find, just so French. For sure, I was pleased to see him, and as we talked, me composing my very best French and he responding in his best English, and in fairness, he held greater in competency than me. True I liked him, but I knew my stay there held an expiry date, so Caution was the name of my game, and I think, in reality, Player, was the name of his game, and either way I was scheduled to leave in less than 24 hours.

Interrupting what we spoke, a telephone call he was to take, followed by a hasty departure, but not until he had invited me for a *rendezvous*, and "What's that about?" I wondered, and there it was, an invitation that evening to his home, but quickly I was to recall, what my *propriétaire* had said, that when a Frenchman invites you to his home, it is on his mind, and in his intention, to take you to bed. "Really, was I to be desert?" and more, "What of the logistics?" For I knew not where his home was, and although he said, "Don't worry, you just get on the tram, I'll tell you where to get off." "Really! Chivalry?" But so easily on the way there I could get lost, and on the way back, a 25 minute ride, in the dark, late at night, extra cold, followed by a 10 minute walk when I get off at the station, down narrow roads, and of safety I could not vouch, or the time the trams stop running, so then I'd need to get a taxi. "Mmmm," my mind was a wiz with complications of inconvenience that faced me, but what of he, 'all wrapped up and cosy.'

Somehow that didn't seem chivalrous at all, so I suggested meeting in the Square, for I knew how to get there, and no logistical or safety nightmares, "So what do you think?" And then a petite barrage of determined excuses, and to change his offer, possibly aka agenda, there was to be non of that, no discussion, no compromise. "OK then" I said, improvising with my own *Gallic* shrug, and serene shaking of my head, vowing that his desert was not to be me, then sidestepping his cloak of gallantry, that slipping, as if by design, onto the ground, as gently, though quite confidently and comfortably, I declined his unscrupulous offer, speaking softly *"Je suis désolé, il n'est pas possible,"* I'm sorry it's not possible.

But James, undeterred, by my decline, missed not a beat, as he rose from his chair, his eyes, gazing fixed on mine, as slowly and purposefully, dare I say seductively, he, took one step toward me, before slowly learning forward, and in one smooth motion, placed his lips, soft and sumptuous, gently onto mine, lingering, he paused, applying the smallest amount of pressure, so sweet, so sensual. "Oh my" it was almost enough to make me change my mind.

And I, leaving that *ville* on the Med the next day, and the lessons I had learnt there, all wrapped up for my safety, as I keeping the knowledge and taking it with me, of overcoming the of the bad and achieving the good, and with progress made I was happy to see what my tomorrow was to bring, and my future the same, to live perhaps with not just marvellous days, but the memories of those precious moments tucked within them, for those are the things which we truly remember, which create our wonderful lasting memories, and for me, in *Montpellier*, there would always be that kiss, and, "Oh, what a kiss!"

"Belief fuels passion, passion rarely fails."
~ M. Anderson

Chapter 14

Step, Remarkably Onward

"Nothing happens, but first a dream."
~ Carl Sandburg

"Oh my" "Where to next?" Was my increasing conundrum, with so much to choose from with a blank board in front of me, I was a little like, pinning the tail on the donkey, that decision should have been easy, though with so any avenues open to me, surely, but not quite so, for it was difficult to know where to go, or which direction to take, as I was seduced by the possibility of ease of how far my money would stretch, so possibly, a wise and good option to adhere to. Yet without sufficient due diligence of even minimally surfing the internet, I was to visit that city that I was told was such a great investment opportunity, by a French lady, while resting at *Café Laurent,* near *Métro Odeon*, the prospect of buying a run-down castle which to renovate, nestled in the country for so much less seduced me, but really, of that 'naysayer' who told me, that my dream, as I dared to dream bigger, could not come true for me in that wonderful place I'd meditated on, of *Aix-en-Provence,* was to mislead me greatly, yet too late was I, to reconsider her doubts of what she spoken, which she willingly infected me, and how slow was I, before I travelled there, to have realized, of what she spoke was not true, but blowing in the wind, just hot air, for which, I never did quite fine the antidote.

Yet true, Toulouse as a *bon affaire,* good business prospect, held value, as infrastructure served it well, and tourist attractions it had plenty, with the *TGV,* regular passing through, with only a 2.5 hour journey to reach Paris, and castles and museums, with weekly markets and other attractions, were there to please the locals and tourist, serviced by several major roads and an airport too, so really, for inclusion into my decision process, it was not a mistake, for really I needed it begin, to wed out and investigate, those obvious options first, but then in fullness I did not consider, as so many options presented themselves, that in reality, to look not at the blank canvas in front of you, but for the hidden gems, not obvious at all, for they are the ones, that may posses the greater gift of a ripe opportunity, yet I didn't look there, for I was simply in circles contorting and appearing to get nowhere, as in a conundrum, I remained in mild despair.

And no surprise, the train I travelled upon, a delay in departure, but I'd come to view that as normal and the timetable not as an accurate document but more as a casual guide, and so it was, before they closed, I reached the *Accueil,* Information kiosk, to take the *Métro* to another station, and how super marvellous when I arrived on the platform, to hear a gentle rendition of "Waltz in Matilda," now that certainly gave me a smile, to last the was, as I was to hunt for the *Office de Tourism*, as my muscles grew larger, my triceps and biceps, as with no elevator available, like Little Bo Peep, who was becoming me, as forever, I was dragging my suitcase behind me.

And how bizarre it turned out to be, for that journey took over 45 mins to get from point A to point B, and the very next day, I was to realize, I could have walked all the was in just 10 minutes, but not to worry, for to great me there was a young man who was married to an Australian lady, and he, speaking very good English and he, understanding my predicament of rapidly needing a place to stay as the night was drawing in, was happy to help and explore through his lists and website, different options with me, such a different scenario to that unpleasant situation in *Montpellier*, and so all seemed good, that was until, I was to agree, to spend 100E to stay in a chicken hutch.

"Oh my" how terribly bad, and how bizarre, for it wasn't clear "Why I would I do such thing?" but perhaps with having so many decisions to make, and my mind, was not filled with clarity, but confusion, for it didn't occur to me, perhaps you guessed it, until the next day, that I could have stayed in the city, at a fine hotel for 35% less, and then, there would have been no requirement to drag that suitcase another few times, not up hill and down dale, but along a few more roads, and down stairs, along platforms and up again, before I was to arrive, at a place that even in nightmares, I would never have been.

On the outside, it was grubby and noisy, and the street, not one you would want to be in after dark, yet I, dehydrated, by this time, just wanted to get shown to my room and change out of my leather and wool travelling clothes, and put the kettle on for a good full mug of hot water to drink, but the *propriétaire* of that establishment had other ideas, as she sat me down, and began to ask me questions of 'this and that,' intrusively, with which I felt most uncomfortable, and sidestepped the answers, but that was, pre-positive healing, as what I have become since that 'job in progress' that I was, has been further overcome, as to anyone who tried to do that to me now, would have a polite though most certainly a refusal to do such a thing, as I would insist on being shown to my room, but then, to jump back even further, it would not have been a 'rat-a-tat-tat' on the door I made, but, in-spite of the declining light, a trip back to the *Métro* and a swift jaunt to the city, to find me something so very much better.

Her attitude domineering, and somehow offensive, her tone and facial expressions abrasive, as she was determined to manipulate my time, and perhaps I was to decide, that perhaps it was all apart of her cunning plan, as she insisted on the map to show me places of interest, even though I insisted I didn't need her to do so, but that was it, how she could prevent me seeing too early, the disaster of accommodation that awaited me, so I would not have accessibility of time, to turn around and quickly, 'tail it out of there.'

"If we all did the things we are capable of, we would astound ourselves."
~ Thomas Edison

And so, 100E only secured me a spot at the end of the garden, and only 6 feet way from the chicken pen, also with a cockerel residing there, and indeed the box that I was shown to, although much higher, looked also, that it certainly could have been back in the days, a hen house too, before the plumbing was instilled. "I jest?" "I only wish!" As in that dark and gloomy box, the stifling dense extremely heavy air, made it difficult to breath, and it appeared as though the odour from those chickens had been absorbed into every molecule of those wooden walls, and without a window, the only solution, through the night while I tried sleep, to leave the sliding door ajar, allowing light and that much needed air to come in, to cool and freshen and give me something pleasing to breath.

But that situation, only added to my problem, for the fear and anxiety for my safety became my instant priority, and of no surprise, I was unable to sleep, as too worried was I that a person would break through the barricade I'd made, by dragging from a make-shift desk the only furniture in that room, a huge and ugly iron chair, and placing it with precision by the range-slider door, with my heavy suitcase wedged behind it, disguised by the curtain, before ugly metal ornaments I placed on top, serving in my mind a notion, that should an intruder, chance their luck, and try to get in, they would disturb my little trap, the noise would alert me and scare them, then desperately rapidly, the police I would call.

The daylight, afforded me a clear view of what I had, well, had not, slept in, as the décor with the morning sun became clear, what was all around in that box they called a *chamber* was eclectic, I presume they would have like to call it, but more so, a miss-mash of what on the street they reclaimed from the skip, forming an apparent, improvised collaboration, appearing of 'particular' taste, quite rare quite horrible I suggest, where, a desert harem, brothel, country farmhouse, French colonial, amalgamated most poorly, with nylon fabrics hung from here to there, and brass bells swinging from the ends of gold tassels strewn from her to there, and just about everywhere, ornaments of chickens, in iron, ceramic steel and wood, with pictures of moving parts adding to their number, cluttering up everyplace, but how bizarre, for really, if you were so interested in chickens, you only had to look out of the door and there they were, as certainly at 6 in the morning there was no doubt, for that was the time they started their, cock-a-doodle-doo-ing.

"Oh my" I new I needed 'fresh' air, did I need some good food too, as after a poor sleep, I hadn't eaten since the night before when I had returned to the Toulouse centre to treat myself to a steak, 300g that basically equated to all fat, I was famished, and recalling those breakfasts so peaceful and serene in *Montpellier*, I was so much looking forward to more of the same, and just getting over such an unpleasant night, I was so very eager to start a brighter and better day. But at least initially, that was not to be, as lady who owned the *Chamber d'Hote*, whose vibe somewhat troubled me, was in my space, speaking interrupting, annoying, my much search for and required peace. As I did my best to ignore her incessant, unpleasant, unnecessary ramblings, a stark absence of fine cutlery, or pleasant crockery to eat from, as what lay before me on the table, again, looked more like it had been pulled out of a skip, and the boxes of cereals so unceremoniously planted with torn packages on the plastic gaudy coloured tablecloth, with a not so clean glass to the side, and so much better than all that before me, gladly I would have given away, and she that women, who I so whished would disappear, painstakingly pointed out piece by piece, which jam was in which jar, and if I wanted warm milk "There's a microwave over there" and stale croissants, most unappetizing, though she described it all, so misguidedly I thought, as though she was a serving up a Waldorf Salad.

Sure, no contemplation necessary to know I needed to withdraw my pre-surmised 2-night further to stay there, so back to the drawing board it was to be, to find a place to stay, not too expensive but pleasing to me, as I had miss-joined the dot to dot in my picture, nay, growing diagram of life, it took the mastering of another hurdle or 2, just to get-back to point 1, as I strived to make it better, and fill in colours, not misty or dark but clear and bright, and so it was to be, I continued along my way, bumping into yet another learning curve I was to ascend, as I stumbled inadvertently, where disruptions and disillusionment were to accompany me, yet fervently vowing, not to give up, so "Why should I worry?" for was it not all, to take me to, "Where I desired and chose to be?"

"Oh" how, words and reckonings were to resound in my head, as with one *Chanbre d'Hote* or *Gite*, I stayed, the lyrics of Paul Young 1980's song sprang, too frequently to mind, of the words I used to sing along to, and I wondered, had they rendered a prophecy to form within me, "Wherever I lay my hat that's my home." "Was that to be so?" and "How quickly could I undo those words I'd so often sewn, and to get myself to a place, rested, settled, where my hat, was always able to reside in my closet?" and "Just how soon, was it to be, before, I could blissfully, achieve that again for me?"

"Once you learn to quit, it becomes a habit."
~ Vince Lombardi Jr

So rather than the internet, it was another French government store, aka the tourist board, I was to visit, who helped tourists find accommodation, which periodically referred my thoughts back to my experience in *Montpellier*, for I was still a little bruised of that episode, not of he, but of what his actions enflamed my emotions in me. Pushing open the heavy glass and steel door I entered into what appeared to be an office space, and there in Toulouse thankfully, I was to meet an assistant who spoke quite good English, a relief for sure, at least relieving some of my stress, tough really, I had quite wrongly almost I do believe, fallen into a bad position, of looking not what was ahead of me of the destination I was heading toward, but what was directly in front of me, therefore missing the biggest part of my overall designed picture, as it was lanes and cul-de-sacs I was venturing down, as I fell into a trap of micro and not maxi-managing my situations.

Reactive and not proactive, now that certainly wasn't inline with my job I loved so much or a way of life I had carved out for myself, and exactly "When, was I to stop fighting the emotions of what I had left behind, and start looking forward for all my desires to come to fruition?" Though I was too stressed to think so rationally, as when was I to be able to relieve myself of that disabling weight of regret, and allow my sensibly of productivity to flow, and all my plans so positive in nature, to grow, really, at that time, confused, filled with uncertainty, muddling through, of a clear answer, I didn't know.

And with the season warming up, accommodation options were becoming less, and with only 2 choices available to me, the decision should have been easy, as I had grown to know, greater choice, does not equate to greater ease, and available immediately, a studio apartment downtown at 250E per week (pw) or alternatively, 2 days later, 1 in the countryside at 350E pw, but I was to discover as I chose the latter, to advertise something as the countryside, does not make it so, as I was sincerely mislead me, as after careful considerations of which will provide the best means of 'moving forward' with the writing of my book, I reminisced, how beautiful it would be after partaking of morning coffee, to meander along country lanes with the freshness of the spring air, while smelling the freshness of the flowers as I passed them by while listening to the tweeting lullabies. "Oh how idyllic?" Yet "No. All just a dream." As what was to wake me at 6 in the morning, as through a flimsy ply board wall, all I heard, was a baby, and 3 children under the age of 8, and all their, shouting and screaming.

Then worse, the accommodation I did not choose, only a 5 minute walk away from a delicious latter, yet the other not so, as a train ride was required, before a 2 hour wait for the first bus and a 1 hour wait for the next, and on my arrival date, that most uncommon sunshine for that time of the year, turned out not to be my friend, as I was wearing my heaviest travelling clothes, avoiding the need to drag them around, yet I was getting more than a little hot and uncomfortable, and my unpleasantness was not done, in fact it had only just begun, as a half a mile I climbed dragging that suitcase behind, a hill of sufficiently steep gradient, to find that house, not to be in the countryside but suburbia, where many brightly coloured toys and cycles by the pool and in the front yard greeted me, and at all that I looked, dashed were my plans, my dreams of pleasant mornings, of peace and quiet and working hard writing my book, as the only sounds to come my way were children playing and crying.

I dared to have hope, that one morning something would be different, but evidentially my optimism had proved futile, and then it wanned so miserably, as what a cold dark apartment it was, with the kitchen being made not from a room, but a closed-in veranda, with a sink, a cooker and a cupboard put in there, but the coldness of that space, seeped in everywhere, and ill-stocked, with not even a tin-opener working, how horrible it was, clogged up with who knew what, everything about it, as the vibes jumping out of every corner, screaming at the renter, "You're unwelcome, we don't want you here, we just want your money!" And how mean and dangerous it was, as it was a normal drinking water bottle, resting in the cupboard, and "Oh my" perhaps I could have drunk out of it, for sure, "Why not?" As in the accommodation in *Montpellier*, the guests were provided with bottles of water. But how extremely serious it would have been, for me to take a sip from that, as it turned out to be nothing other, than bleach disinfectant, that 'dangerously unmarked, just waiting for an accident to happen,' bottle.

And the disasters not over yet, for the bedding after I arrived I was informed, for that, I had to pay an extra 20E, and not even towels were provided in with that price, and how bizarre or "Was that just me?" And keeping warm was not easy, as there was only small eclectic fan hearer that required to be moved from room to room, and should I use over a certain wattage of electricity, they were to charge me additionally, and "What could I do?" Only have a shower in attempts to keep warm, but you may have guessed it, not easy to do, as the bathroom, dark and dingy with a tiny cracked and immensely dirty window and only lit by a 25watt bulb, and no light outside either, in that thin as a pencil strip of space they called a hallway, and the only mirror in that apartment was also situated in there, "Oh my" the whole affair, it 'hummed danger' and 'whispered mean-mindedness,' possibly its origin, the *propriétaire*.

> "If a man does his best, what else is there?"
> ~ George S. Patton

The bath, most hazardous, as I stepped in the bath, that appeared to be recycled from a demolished hospital, perhaps one built circa 1900's but not of a beautiful or historic antique, but an instrument primed to cause danger, less than 3 foot in length and really quite high, the trick was getting inside, for underfoot was quite difficult to gain stability or balance, as moulded in that white enamel where featured its base were 2 raised rectangles of 4 or more inches high, where from the middle each sloping backwards and slanting towards the edge, and a groove separated them in the middle, which would fit easily the male genital parts, and bearing mind how much of design used to be gender specific, perhaps that is not outside the realms of possibility, and to the opposite side was a tiny flat part, which "Yeah" it was hoped it be able to stand upon, but so unfortunately not, as the big old and yes grungy taps that were sited there, and maybe even came out of a different part of the hospital, and where I draw my knowledge from, that is an old Victorian Workhouse in north Manchester, that became a hospital where I did my nurse training, and those taps protruding into and over that space, so feet may enter, but the legs unable to follow.

Treacherous is was getting in and out and even standing there, as the shower curtain, compiled of 2 different mismatched ends, unevenly and jaggedly cut from others, and their placement proved quite hazardous, as they hung so low crumpled and tucked up at the bottom of that space, and my attempts to fold it over the lip of the rim failed as the ridged harsh plastic was not subtle enough to do that. Slips, trips and slides, how I tried so hard to avoid them all, but one night I that precarious balance that I afforded myself was to wane and a tumble I took. How fortunate I was, that toilet of pale blue, situated perhaps only one inch from the side of the bath, and the sink in aqua green, perhaps 4 inches form the end, and the windowsill with sharp edges jutting out in between, with rusty pointy little metal iron railings, covering the broken pane of glass, and what a mini-miracle occurred, as in that second as I stumbled and fell while desperately trying to save myself, of all those hazards, ready and waiting for me, poised to cause me specific harm, 'somehow,' I wonderfully missed them all.

"Oh my" washing my long hair, wavy but straggly, after the basting in the Australian sun, you guessed, it not easy, for on top of all that, the shower, was actually no shower at all, as with a plastic hose it had been attached to the tap, and too short to hold above my head, even if I had 1 hand to do so while I was trying to soap my golden locks, then rinse it out while I held the attachment, probably dating back with its garish yellow and diminished water flow, to the 1960's and "Oh my" I was so, so wanting to be out of there. But paying in advance and having no way to get my money back, I was stuck, doing the best I could, with only the 350E fee, to provide to me that lesson, though true, a portion of regret, as ironically, the reason I didn't choose that other available apartment, was because I thought the potential noise because of its location would be disruptive, and I preferred the prospect of seeing roaming cattle and get back to nature, now certainly, that seems to pose as compelling absurdity.

A little trick I'd picked up in the southern hemisphere, I counted down the sleeps until I was able to leave, and the only silver lining in that grey cloud, how ironically, I had paid to settle over me, was a rest-bite I found, well at least until 3 o'clock in the afternoon, where to visit a restaurant, run by a lovely family of Italians, and how pleasant were they to me, as I sipped on one coffee before the next, and treated myself to their daily special, which I have to say, was very well priced and tasted so very good, as there I camped-out, from about 8.30a.m until they closed each day. Their mother who spoke no English or French, yet her and I on more than one occasion enjoyed a 'jolly good chat,' for so true as they say, communication, is less than 9% of words, and her and I, both seemed to part, content, with a smile that filled our face, and "Oh my" I would have been lost without that place, though I have to say, being stuck in suburbia, did nothing to help me, to reach my dream, of finding a property to purchase and renovate, so aimed in part to meet lots of other travellers similar and different to me, through my Bed & Breakfast business, that I so desired to create.

> *"The two most patient warriors are patience and time."*
> *~ Leo Tolstoy*

Yet true, something good did happen in that unpleasant suburbia place, thought I doubt the local played any sort of part in the unfolding step forward toward my healing and recovery I made, for likely it would have been an accumulation of previous events of my learning curves of recovery and perhaps, something, of what, I am not sure, as I communicated with the caring family, as they showed that curiously to me, that quite unbelievably one morning, as I prepared my boiled egg, croissant and piece of ham, I found myself, quite miraculously sat at the table. A milestone lay right there! "What?" you may be saying, "What's so special about that?" Well let me tell you, over 4 decades I had lived on this earth, and to do such a thing wasn't in my psyche, for the only association my brain had of sitting at a table in the place I lived, should a piece of potato fall off my fork or my father perceive it did, instantly, with force I would be hit, or if he accused me of slouching, for sitting up-straight was what I must do, or heaven forbid, he should hear a noise from my knife or fork clinking on the plate, another 'hit' from him would come from just 10 inches short away, was always guaranteed, as the flying hand of his violence, as a 'backhander' would visit my head or face, he would quickly race, and the pain, not minimum but severe, as usually it was accompanied by a red and smarting handprint, of my father's palm and 5 fingers, where an outline could easily be traced; but still, until I'd finished my food, he forced me to remain there and keep eating through his ongoing threats, "Be quick! If you don't eat that up *now*; *you* just wait to see what comes next." And make good on them, certainly, scared, for of cause, I knew he could, and if *he* chose, would.

Eventually, dismissed from the table, though he could have me waiting there for quite a while, I continued to show no weakness, for he would pounce on that, and forever not permitted to cry, though really, to let me see me cry, never, I refused to ever give him that satisfaction, for surely, as this survivor knew her aggressor, he would have most definitely wallowed in the superiority of his accomplishment, so I made it my goal to deign him that. One so young, "Oh so sad." Walking to the bathroom, I'd go and examine my face, to see the damage he did on that day, the palm print fading and the stinging the same, externally the physical signs of what he had done, were disappearing, no one would know they were there, but it was what was going on internally that was not disappearing as easily, indoctrinated to expect fear and fright, festering, mutating, depositing its damage and toxicity within that young girls body, turning in on itself, causing bitter hate, that were to effect her relationships with, food, people in authority, men {always,} but worst of all, herself! ... & she, who is me.

And don't misunderstand, that he may have thought he made a mistake, for evidentially, that was not the case, for never did he show remorse, for any occurrence, and never, how bizarre to consider, that he would apologize, for the only company those treats and violence kept, were more of the same, delivered by him in a package to his choosing, when ever his mood took him. Part of the fear was, you didn't know when and you didn't know where, so you were on-guard, all the time, and so it was, that relentless flow of adrenaline surging, raging torrents 24/7 around my mind and body, in and out of all my bodies organs, my digestive system, my nervous system, yet I still too young I knew not of the hazards, unaware I dared not to think of the damage that was done, as a far greater, and a much closer danger, I was only ever left in fear, wondering, "Just how soon before, he was to do it all again?"

My milestone so gratefully valued and appreciated, it stimulated a thought, as that inner-progress came quite naturally and was not forced, I began to review, of my actions taken, or thought processes changed, what had been the catalyst for that fortuitous and quite profound change. Perhaps it had been my time in Montpellier while staying at that *Chambre d'Hote*, most expensive but luxurious, where I had passed such amenable times, sitting, and relaxing with ease at the breakfast table where the *propriétaire*, we enjoyed each others company, talking normally, no loud voices, no complaints, only discussions of topics that were relevant or pleasing to us, no discord, no testiness, only pleasure, even humour, and how enormously comfortable it was, from that point to start each day, relying safe in the knowledge it would remain the same on the next.

Of course there were the family in the restaurant were I visited daily at least for a week, but their kindness they gave me, reached to a far greater depth than that petite timeframe, would normally suggest, and when I reflect on it, the environment where our conversations took place was in an environment connected to food, with its vision, its smell, everywhere and even the aprons they wore, and there also, I sat at a table comfortably so, relaxing, not the norm as I used to do, as usually I would always anticipate and pre-disposed to someone coming to me complaining, angry, ready to punish me in some way or other. How amazingly wonderful, that as a barrier to simple comfort in my life, that barrier, which indeed I hadn't recognized as such, has been so positively eradicated and overcome.

Perhaps it was there when a mini revolution began, as somewhere deep inside my brain, leant by example, how it was safe for me to sit at the table, and as I forever push forward, and do kinder, nicer and more pleasant things for me, I hope that my brain will keep up, as it is able to release from its physiology, the destructive programming of the past, so gladly enabling it to heal, "Oh my" horses for courses as my grandad used to say, and how valuable it must have been to spend that money and visit those places, and of the mild adversity, through the money spent on luxury or the dis-concord endured in the suburb, and although on neither occasion did I have an idea way back then, it appeared, my experiences were preparing and benefitting my future.

What a fortunate and worthwhile observation of my progress, and worthy to take more than a minute to congratulate myself, on a 'job well learnt' and 'a job well done,' and from that point on, my tool of preference I placed in my self-help box, that of *Reflection*. As with reflection it is not a case of looking in the rear view mirror to look and stare at a past at all that which was grossly bad, but, an from as casual looks to enable you to see how far you've come, and an opportunity to showcase yourself, what you've learnt,, what you've moved on from, and how now you know, what we need to avoid running into again, as we choose the best we can, to leave the pain behind, and let it fade from view, as to the front we cast our sight, looking with anticipation, straight ahead, realizing, that the pain can act as a springboard we can jump upwards from, recognizing that those stumbling blocks have transposed into steppingstone, and this a free process, we can do to help ourselves.

So fear not, be bold and take courage and seek out that road before you, to a healthier future, as in our minds and in our soul we are able to determine what we 'grew up in' was not normal; and "Yes," to move away from it, is our right, and discernment becomes our friend, so as improved decisions becomes a way of our life, with fewer miss-haps or mistakes, more marvellous situations can unfold, and as 'like attracts like' for each positive thought we have, another 7, equally so, will be attracted to it and so the process goes on, as with self-worth and inner-strength accompanying our days, and of progress through this process, as we learn to be patient and kind our ourselves, always be assured, that come-what-may, on the-inside of us, we can always start this, afresh and anew, every single day!

"Time flys, its up to you to be the navigator."
~ Robert Orben

So I carried on as "I picked up my troubles in my old tin hat and smiled smiled smiled," in the words of what maybe considered a war-song from so many years ago, and perhaps how poignant, yet on a much milder note, that was exactly what I was to do, as when the Saturday swung around again, and I was to be out of that dreadful apartment, as it was back to the town centre I was so gladly to go, to resume normality, at whatever the cost maybe, I was to pay it, as I was learning quite quickly, perhaps I should re-think my career path and become a travel writer, specializing in hotel accommodation, though I thought it with satire, though later, it became a notion with perhaps less humour attached, though not to digress, a prospect, I opted not investigate or pursue any further.

And so it began, my quest to find somewhere else, to stay, as the season was coming on and prices were rising, but first the logistics, of the trip on the public transport, didn't sway me from being "Oh so pleased" when my bags were safely lodged at a hotel at least for the night, a week I considered spending at another place I went to view, but the couple who ran it, I'm not sure I trusted their vibe, the toilet, not separate but inside the bathroom was to be shared by all, and the only other, wedged in-between the living room and the kitchen, so extremely tiny perhaps a pantry it may have been, and just beside it, the dining table where they showed me they sat to eat breakfast and every meal. The smoke it was dreadful, lingering in the air everywhere, and I could only think, how horrible that would be, to inhale that smell at the beginning of each day, and how really, it goes not with my philosophy of staying healthy, so all in all I decided to say "No" and on that choice for consideration, firmly close the door.

Yet seriously, how could I possibly do my 'ablutions' when they would know what I was doing, they would know how long I'd been in that smallest room tucked in the house, and true until recently, I had severe and unresolved 'toilet issues' from when I was a child, as I was unable to use public conveniences, for anything other than a number 1, even in the case of emergencies, for in the household I grew up, as fists were banged upon on the door as shouts and taunts were travelled through the it, of "What's up with you?" "Haven't you finished yet?" "You've been in there too long, now, get out!" and really 'if only' I could have got what I wanted, out of me, but that "Bloody awful smell," they accused me of making, was not me, for constipation plagued me, with relentless stomach cramps, randomly, frequently troubling me, the doctors verdict always the same, he couldn't find anything wrong, so for years, that dance with the doctor of my toilet syndrome went on, but nothing positive was ever done.

> *"There are two ways of exerting ones strength;
> one is pushing down, the other pulling up."*
> ~ Booker T. Washington

Then always what my mother had taught me, never to do a number 2, ever, while I was out anywhere, or ever sit on a public loo, not even the one at my grandparents I was permitted to do, for germs linger unseen everywhere, and with my digestion tricky at best, and I guess because of at least their complaints and restrictions a further problem was to accompany me, as fear set in that everyone was listening and checking their watches when I went out of the room and until I returned waiting with ridicule and complaints, so it was an extra dysfunction was added to an already dysfunctional system, and when travelling with friends in New Zealand, for those weekends of 4 days, to the bathroom for a number two, not even once, I was unable to go. And it transpired with boyfriends, in those bad old days when anything went, I was unable to use the toilet when we went travelling, or even use my own, when they were staying at my house.

Not so funny really, s when I was staying at a friends house when I was between accommodation, a room upstairs with private bathroom was for my convenience and with him downstairs on the lower level watching TV, still so ingrained were my limiting beliefs of what I had been scorned and indoctrinated with, surrounding toilet issues, even late into the evening, I would get in my car, and travel 5 miles to the closest public bathrooms at the beach, and only there, with no one around, and no one to hear me or time me, observe me going in or shout at me coming out, I would place toilet paper all over the seat, before I sitting down, and as I tried so hard to do that necessary thing, but believe it or not, as the dark settled in, with thoughts of my friend back at his house timing me for when I was retuning, wondering where I'd gone or waiting to question me accusatorially so when I got back, so many worries, concerns of my mothers, brothers and fathers words and their intimidating accusations rambling around, all those and all those decades later, and so amazingly, sometimes I found it still impossible to do, that very thing that I'd especially, specifically gone there for.

But there is good news was to come, "Harrah, Hooray" for I worked hard on this matter and rationalized all, and then as time passed, I told friends of my predicament, and together "Oh how we would laugh," and make a joke of it all, and that was quite successful as a strategy, as through the humour, what they were doing was not, criticizing, but rather, wilfully, supporting me, and what a difference good friends can make, for sure, of an easier life, they positively helped mould mine. True, it didn't happen overnight, but patience is a virtue, and they and me, simply, kindly and gently persisted, by any other name, supportive, and "Why?" "Just for me!" "Can you believe that?" They did it, just for my, own sake.

"At every single moment of one's life, one is going to be no less than what one has been."
~ Oscar Wilde

Another week, another new apartment, and like the proverbial driftwood, aimlessly going nowhere, with another week living out of my suitcase, and how uncomfortable and tedious that was swiftly becoming, with, wherever I was to lay my hat was home, a weary and tiresome concept, old, outdated, uncomfortable and most unwelcomed. And long since had I attempted to empty my suitcase, to neatly place my clothes on hanger or shelves, for in propriety of ease, I left them carefully folded, in plastic backs sealed with bows. And a spanner in the works was apparent immediately, for the lift, that was specific to the requirement of getting my battleship sized case up to the 5th floor was broken, and me, with that tricky back, still in pursuit of causing me potential suffering from that industrial injury suffered and a newly qualified nurse, I was unable to do it myself, and what a relief, that the lady who was to hand me the keys, was to do that job for me, and not to worry, for when I was to leave, should the lift not be fixed, I was to let gravity, sort out, taking it back down again.

So there I was to rest, in that apartment where the bedding, I needed not to pay extra for, or the electric the same, and there was internet access for telephone calls, a bonus, not that I contacted anyone, and the gadgets in the kitchen of only 4feet long 2 foot wide, and no work service left to prepare anything, but not to worry, for the absence of a car, made it impossible with ease to travel to a supermarket, as the residence, that "Yeah" had sheets and pillows that did not look and feel as though they'd been pulled out of a skip like the one before, located on the outskirts of the city, it was further afield to access what I needed, so I decided not to take my stab at preparing the cuisine, but no problem there, as I chose to eat out, rather than try to turn my hand to something that I knew from recent experience, was not my supreme forte, so I chose to relax, as I opened the Juliet doors and step out onto the veranda, thinking how wonderful it was, that the neighbours from the industrial building facing, were not to cause a ruckus that night.

And how wonderful, there was no noise from the neighbours aka, owners, children, jettisoning through the walls, early in the morning, for the industrial property at the end of the street, it was the hugely large trucks, which were to pose as a mini-problem, to exceedingly good REM sleep, though in fairness, the luxury of the mattress and the softness of the feather pillows, did do there best to accommodate that, but perhaps I would have swapped it all, for that which I had not yet discovered, *une douche*, a shower, refreshing and hot, impossible to have, as it appears to be the French way, absent was the hook to hold up the showerhead, and so, it was a piece of twine I was to find, to masterfully improvise, as I made do and mended, yet worse, the *bouloir*, bath, it was blocked, and the water took over 10 minutes to get hot, so it was to fill the bath and mix with the regurgitated pipe water, not yet completely run away, and how horrible to think of that water refluxing, germs lingered there, and how so quickly it filled the bath and gathered around my feet, the temperature transferring to instantly cold, and "Oh my" how I was to reflect, how while watching an American TV show, firstly, customers seek comfort and convenience, and how sad I thought, that on my budget, it wasn't even able, to afford too much of that.

But, really should I complain, as I was to find no towels and so improvise to use, felt pillowcase protectors, found in the cupboard to substitute for the same, as I examined the silver lining amidst those gloomy clouds, as a perfect opportunity in disguise, to establish the good, the bad and the ugly, of what is to be served up, to well intentioned tourists spending their hard earned money, with that magic number appearing to be 350euro pw, so "Should I be glad?" That those recurrent, unfortunate situations I was encountering, could serve me well and form an excellent opportunity for my own piece of market research, for when I established my Bed & Breakfast, with environment, tranquillity and rest all important, with value for money forming a main portion of my business ethos.

So it was, I was to create a mini check-off list for my accommodation requirements: First, a joint tie for budget and location as within my price range they are extremely intertwined: A swift second, a shower to refresh me in the morning and welcome me into the day, and in the evening, to slumber me back in the reverse way: So close is third, really it needs to be joint second place, as a comfy mattress, fresh pillows and bedding the best to sleep in, but so surprising how often in France I haven't received them: Cleanliness, well I don't think that should be given a number as perhaps it should be a given, but then again, I have stayed in hotel rooms where that 'given,' wasn't at all so forth coming: Safety, surely that should be a priority and guaranteed and supersede any number: With transport certainly necessary for convenience, unless all you need is close to hand, as by foot you can find that important café for partaking a fresh latté. Now surely, that needs to e a priority: OK; so all seems so obviously and simply easy, so no longer should it take so much of my time to jingle jangle options of accommodation, as I try with all my might, to next time, get it perfectly right!

"To most of us the real life is the life we do not lead."
~ Oscar Wilde

Searching for the next café, *pâtisserie*, cake shop or a *boulangerie*, bakery, to suit my preferred ambiance was definitely next on my agenda, where to *boire une café*, drink a coffee, yet unlike Australia, Toulouse was more like England, where at lunch time, a table would not be given, to a person who only wanted to drink, requiring in order to sit, a higher bill needed to be paid, to include food as well, so that was out for me, so wander around I did, until that magical 2 hours had passed then once again, I would be semi-welcomed into a coffee house, perhaps to read a book and linger a while, though never for such a thing in the *ville,* town centre, did I feel welcomed to do such a thing, yet in different countries in the other hemisphere, such an act, is generally a cultural habit.

And while time passed, I made myself be patient and accommodating to that fact, for sure, it was out of my control and nothing about it I could do, so my new strategy, to rearrange my day around that event, so, I was not caught out again. But "Oh" how that time to wander made me contemplate and think, of what life had made me, where I first began, my parents, and where under my own commitment to myself, how I had achieved so far away a place to stay, to live life, and gain my dream, or was it to be only something different, and was I ultimately to attain something better or less than what I had before, or perhaps marvellously, it was the desire of my heart which was ultimately to be mine. Yet what a cry of sorrow was to escape me one day as I recognized, what I had let slip away, as through all my extensive travels while moving from point A to B to C to; well, you get the picture, a casualty, my list of friends, which true, was never very long, but so much shorter it got, as I failed to put in the necessary time and trouble to keep in touch with them, and how sad, that I had previously been too occupied with 'this and that,' to prevent them from slipping right out of my life, and then I made a decision to take action, to rectify my mistake.

And so it was, a new friend I thought I made, Claudia, who I met at *Café Laurent* in Paris, near *Métro Odeon,* who volunteered and offered to help me, choose a house in France, and with French real estate agents act as an intermediary, but alas, as many times as I texted or telephoned her, other than the once, when I was in transit, not a word from her was ever to be returned, but how bizarre, a concept I posed to myself, for why would she take it on her self, to offer so much and be so willing, only in that allotted time to come around, she was to disappear, and not give a care, to the difficulties she may leave someone in. But was I surprised? Not really, as I reflected on what a man, a Sydney-sider once told me, "Fiends are like parachutes, the first time they let you down, they are not good for you ever again." Now I had to see, a certain irony in that, in fact, I was becoming to see quite a lot of that in my life, as I let go of the past, and headed toward my future, with an opening mind and a lighter heart, and how absolutely wonderful, for though that process, I could see, so much more clearly.

> *"Only the shallow know themselves"*
> *~ Oscar Wilde*

Yet how bizarre, as my perception of her was, she was genuine, but that was not to be, as she eventuated to have more in common with my mother than me, as my mother, the master at falsehood, rarely meaning what she said, unless it was nasty or mean, for then when talking about me, I knew although it may be a lie, in her eyes she meant her curses of accusation, which she, so passive-aggressively spoke, yet I, was not the only one who she cast her curses upon, for someone in the family was often in her verbal range of toxic fire, usually her sister, certainly my father's mother, and me; "Oh that was constantly," but my brother, "Oh no, that situation was never to be," as she so cosseted he, and thinking about, he also had blue eyes and blonde hair, so why such a difference that she loved him so, while so intently and obviously, while she, that appearing only an empty vessel only filled with spite, so disparaging held such vengeful distain and resentment, against me, denoted clearly, by her rants and wailings of morbid negativity, with behaviour of hostility appearing fresh everyday, though hope, I should have held, for eventually, I was to succeed in placing her unbridled declarations, positively behind me.

True, no offer of help offer did come from her, only her intent, appearing to place another obstacle in my way, and "Why?" Well that was never clear, I just simply learnt to live with it growing up, and accepted that one of my most difficult jobs of the year was to find a Mothers Day card, that didn't mention, love, support, sacrifice, or thanks for it all, for history had taught me, those attributes of family life or a mothers love were not mine to enjoy, as even cleaning my school uniform each weekend was a list of great length commencing each Friday night, until I was about to walk out of the door Monday morning I was forced to endure, and cleaning the bedding once a fortnight, don't even get me started there, and now I wonder, to my brother, "Did she do the same and always complain?" Though I think it unlikely, as I saw not evidence of it, as to him, she gave everything, and to me she gave nothing, and yet strangely it was I, who tried so hard to help her and please, her, until one day, she decided she'd had enough of me, as she chose to dis-own me, and out of my life, walk away.

So just possibly, it is a poor prospective I had on relationships, for those with family were confusing, dysfunctional and disastrous too, so why would I even think to put time or effort into friendships, for didn't they have an expiry date on the, just like my mother and father had shown toward me, and with still, no other benchmark to work from, I was only going with the information available t me on the template I'd been shown, and how terribly sad, I now reflect, that I missed so amazingly much through my life, simply because I knew no-better, or knew that another I should be searching for, but of a concept of life, that it could possible reap different fruit to the ones that I and harvested from the seeds planted earlier, in my youth, and even in the cradle, I was ignorant and held not a clue, that 'things' anything in life could be different from my experiences, so why would I put up a fight, or seek the light, when I'd always lived in the dark, and knew no more than that, and, should such a notion have entered my imagination, "Would I not have simply dismissed it, believing only, it was a benefit which others, were to hold and enjoy, as I, in my concept, of such, wasn't possibly worthy?"

But a new time was coming where realization of my worth was to envelope me, and I was to discover, through my journey of exploration and self-education, with the library and second-hand bookstores being amongst my best friends, as my poor perspective, on what true socialization was, and basically, how other people were not out to destroy me, as their first intention, and I, was to amazingly receive emotional warmth though the process, of permitting me to be apart of another, not in a continual expectancy of battle, or one, determined to master the other, with cart-blanche to let cruelty slip-in, but a notion, that they liked me, and meant me no harm, and "Oh my" from whence my journey of self-discovery and self-recovery began, I was clocking up a decade and beyond, before the nugget of treasure came as a wonderful realization of faith to me, and leading from it, truly marvellously, as I vowed to try and do better each time, I was to live and learn even more about healthy relationships, and my reward for such, was to be huge in return.

> *"Seek freedom and become captive of your desires.*
> *Seek discipline and find your liberty."*
> *~ Frank Herbert*

How wonderfully I began to observe my own behavior first, and so gratefully, through that emotional recovery, I have learnt what my friends meant, when insistently they would say to me through times of trouble and strife, "You deserve better," for previously I held no clue as to what they were talking about, and when I dared to ask, "What do you mean?" As their answer never made sense, for I simply, didn't believe what they said, and with desperation inside, I thought sincerely, as my stomach got contorted in knots, that even though they were sat beside me, they were getting me mixed up with someone else.

So the tide of change did come, slowly, yes, but surely, as I was to transpose into a whole new me, as I continued my commitment to positive change, and less intent I became with climbing the career ladder, or buying bigger and better houses, filling them with beautiful things, as no longer did they fulfil me or give me what I needed for the tide of change had arrived and I was to do for me, what was healthy inside, as I began to loosen and throw away that mask I'd relied upon, forming my disguise, to conceal my true identity, and a smile and perfect makeup I used as my body armour, preventing anyone for seeing the crumbling and real me, as I drastically tried to get through each day, just hoping that no one else would be added to the list of, those who hated me, as deep within, in that darkened broken place, all tattered and torn, where helpless, there was no easy access, to mend those generational curses, which must be borne.

"Oh my" a revelation came to pass, at the transgressions I had committed against others, and true, they were only done, as a mode of self-protection, or ignorance, for I knew of no other way, but that was not excuse, once I knew better, to perpetuate more of the same, so a new road I began to trample upon, to mend my wrongs, as I vowed to do better for my future, and as many opportunities came my way, I was to say sincerely, "I'm so sorry" to those who emotionally I offended, for really, shouldn't I have known better, for to be treated badly, I knew first hand the emotional pain, and for sure, it is not to be taken lightly, but there lies the mystery, for so surprisingly I found myself to be in the midst of domestic violence, and "How crazy was that?"

For I had fooled myself into believing, that should *anyone* was to see the onset of violent behaviour, it was me, but "No" I saw it not, and as episodes of severity escalated, still I recognized not, that certain disaster was coming my way, and "Why?" Because accepting raised levels of violence through the example of my father, had been delivered and accepted as normal, and when I escaped him, my mind, failed to get-better or reset itself, for truly, I absolutely knew of no other way, and how catastrophically sad, that we who have suffered once, unless we enlighten ourselves to the tell-tale signs and recognize, that through our anatomy of the brain, we are so susceptible to continue in those relationships that will replicate the same, as 'depilating disaster,' too frequently, will call our name.

My father, the way he treated me, he had a choice, and he chose not to do anything different for me, than what possibly was done to he, and so many excuses I stared to make, believing it wasn't his fault, for he too, may well have been damaged emotionally by the age of 3, and there the neurology set, lives a disaster to be waiting, how sad it was, that he illegitimate in the 1930's to an Irish Catholic mother, who was ostracized and sent away to England, ending up in Manchester, and how hard it must have been for him, as I counted the ways.

But then a revelation was to come my way one day, as speaking with the late, gentle and compassionate, Reverend Turnball, from St Pauls Cathedral, Healing Ministry in Melbourne, who was to tell me, there was "No justification for what my father had done." And more, a Salsa dancing friend in NZ, told me more of the same, as he also back in that era was also illegitimate, and no excuse did he ever find to be cruel or his children, and quite shocking to tell the truth, for was that a false safety-net I made for myself, to find a reason why my father did what he did to me, for otherwise, "Why would he, everyday, wilfully cause so much hurt and pain, to descend on me?"

"Hot heads and cold hearts, never solved anything."
~ Billy Graham

From way back when, I have no idea where my determination to get through each day for survival came from, and true, there was a stumble in the middle, that nearly made it possible, and so, to reach this point maybe I wouldn't have, but I chose not to be a victim or live in that mentality of that, as I forever pushed through, refusing to be the sacrifice that my parents made me, no matter how scared it made me or lacking confidence, I prohibited it from forming a barrier to what I needed to achieve, for I knew, I was to move from point A to point B, and that was never up for misunderstanding or interpretation, as resoundedly I gave full commitment to proving what my father said was wrong, for although I believed his words, something magical happen inside, where I was always, forever determined, to prove him so utterly wrong.

So young was I, I still played with my teddies and dolls, and me so innocent, as her plan 'of maturity' or was that of humiliation, to make me stay, was not to tell me how much she loved me, certainly not, for sure that was not ever her MO, as so much more, suitably demoralizing she found it to be, to dictate her instructions of what she was to let me pack in my suitcase, was no-thing that she or my grandma, her mother, had bought or made me, disparagingly snarling, "I'm *only* allowing *you*, to take with *you*, what *your* father gave *you*!"

True, I looked around my bedroom, through my wardrobe and in my chest of draws, even behind the cupboard and under the bed, I searched quite frantically, for just something to take, yet, what my father bought for me, I found nothing, but of cause that was her intention. But then again, wasn't she, that mother of torments, being wilfully and deceitfully misleading, for sure, anything that came through her, came from him first, for he, in the household, was the only breadwinner. But she made her point, quite deliberately, intentionally, as was possibly her desired side-effect, or maybe the principal point for her exploit, was that my father truly didn't care for me, that he loved me not, and his dislike of me was quite great, and they were the reasons, why all I had, though it was only little, had come from what *she* had given me.

Yet really, a notion that did not occur to me, as one so innocent of such few years, I was still played dressing-up my toys, and how misguiding she was, as she cast aspirations on him, her mission, deliberately by purpose to prevent the possibility that I may realize what the emotional destruction to me, *she* was causing, and so much satisfaction I surmise that must have given her, to add such corrosive destruction as she tore even wider open, those crippling emotional wounds I bore, and her bitter intent, leaving me in no doubt, that I was unloved by him, my brutal father, whose blood she forever reminisced, ran in my veins, as she dismissed him, as worth less than nothing, for not even 'smalls' had he bought me, and for all, she led me to believe, it was because, he didn't, he never had, nor ever would, care for or love me! And with her accusation common, "You're just like your father" who by her words and opinions hated so very much, leaving me in no doubt, to her venom she passed onto me, it took little figuring out, for me to believe and internalize, that of my value, according to him and according to her, was decided to be, less than, none.

"Oh my" "Way to go mom!" So lonely I felt before I tried to run away, but after she was done that day, after my attempt to leave that horrendous house had been fraught, even greater my sorrow and less love than ever, if any, was I able to hold inside, as the cavern of nothingness was becoming larger, and my self-worth meaningless, as it rapidly began to fragment and fail to be of anything of value to help me, and my soul, was casting adrift, as through the progression of hopeless, from deterioration to disintegration, where only wrath and fear, lived in me, and shame and guilt, I guess made their job complete, as I, no longer a little girl desiring, or dare I say, deserving of love, comfort or support, as I 'metamorphosed' into a being, distraught, with my demise certain as their task was to be completed. So terribly young yet held only, an emptiness, that lingered in my heart, as nothing healthy lived within, as so falsely I accepted, their wrong as my right, and how debilitating so, as even when I was geographically moved far beyond the reach of their grasp, though what lay inside me, held no capacity to move clearly away from their reach, as I remained flawed for such a long time, but, that was all going to change eventually, as wilfully, at last awakening from those nightmares of their false facts of 'untruths,' as seeds of 'true beliefs' about me I was able to plant, and my fruitful harvest was to come, as I nurtured what I need, as slowly I nurtured those seeds and through that patience and kindness to myself that was growing, increasingly, and with my heart healing and my soul returning, I got to know the real me, as I became the person who quite rightly, I deserved to be.

"A good head and a good heart are always formidable companions."
~ Nelson Mandela

For how wonderfully I grew, as I began to thrive, breaking free of their cycle of the residual effects of childhood abuse, and not by mistake, but deliberately transferring me, from a life, overflowing with hostility, seeping into every cell in my body, to a healthier life, where I, no longer within those tattered emotions, was I trapped or held hostage, for I did not give in, but give up the dishonourable reign of dominion, as chose to separate myself from it, for I was deservingly worthy, to break away from their authority, and so spectacular was my reward for all my effort, as I surpassed their unbearable captivity, to live free, and become, a better me.

Yet how ironic, or sadly, it all turned out to be, for as I got older, she tried to through me out of the house, screaming, "You leave here now!" But I a little smart at that age of 17, older and wiser, and standing on her words she'd so often barked at me, pertaining to that house where we lived, "This house is half mine!" OK! So being a bit of a smarty-pants and choosing to use her own words right back at her in my defence, "Don't worry; I'll only live in the half that doesn't belong to you" "Oh my" at that she was even more angry, "No you wont!" was her harsh reply rapidly flying back, but for the first time ever, her words, her intimations against me held no power, for then I played the trump card, "We'll see, I'll discuss it with my father when he returns after work" "Olalla!" Rapidly she spouted, with the force of a damn breaking, "Oh no *you* wont!" Relaying her mantra, "Remember! What goes on between the 3 of us, {her, my brother and I} stays between us, with *nothing* to do with him, at all!"

"Phew," and so it was, a little more time I was granted to stay in that house, that was not a home, and not safe either, but I was only 17 and believed I needed to stay, for I knew of nowhere else to go. Yet how ironic that golden boy, her first born, 15 months older than me, "Who could do no wrong, while I could do no right," who at 19 years, had somehow upset my father in the extreme, and father from under his roof, was throwing him out, but my mother she wasn't having any of that, and after all I'd suffered, when to protect me, she had done nothing, and even though I took those little blue pills, yet suddenly as a threat was posed against her 'precious one' her son, it was off to the Lawyers she ran, shouting 'divorce,' so the money she'd have, to provide a roof, to cover my brother's head.

"Oh happy days" yes, that is sarcasm; but post-living with my mother, I learnt to reflect on a newly created philosophy, as an antidote to her gross negativity, "Don't tell me what you can't do, tell me what you can," and then, of any disproportionate offence, we may muster our forgiveness, through emotional strength, and take a leap over that of-fence, leaving the past behind, as we head off, into our future to a far better and happier place, which has our name etched upon it, where we with greater peace deserve to be.

Yet how unfortunate, my mother could get over nothing, she couldn't even get over herself, though possibly, as forever she relived those torments of when she was a child, how the teacher used to rack her knuckles with a ruler, but really she never should have done, as she couldn't read the blackboard because she needed spectacles. "But that was over 40 years ago!" It never crossed my mind to reply, but really, while she never took her eyes away from the rear view mirror, which she polished and magnified everyday, how did she ever expect to leave the past behind? Though maybe, sincerely, she really never tried, for her aim not to move wonderfully from A to B, though with the absence of friends for good advice or counsel, or that inner-strength, that gut-barometer, or internal GPS in preference to a map to guide her, and with only her own complaining voice for companionship, so unfortunately she never ventured far away, from where he experiences of her youth had placed her.

And it was scorn, not admiration that forever accompanied her attitude toward me each day, and too oblivious was I, perhaps thankfully, to recognize what she did, though hissing words, "You're just like him" cut me like a knife, with more in the same genre, she forever outpoured, as story by story, daily, that heart of mine was broken a little more every time, and with no way to mend as it only compounded that damaged which was cast into my soul, until unable to survive any longer, dead, it left that place from inside me where it used to call home, and I was left emotionally lifeless in any realms of positiveness, struggling, as she alone, well along with my father, brother and all those to come who chose to cause me misery, under her power, was able to freely to mould me, and without defence to filter and sweep clear away the infectious debris she wove into me, by my misfortune and default, I became the woman that her influence made me.

But really, "Could I, with her as a role model, love anyone, anything better than her?" Well that, I was to give it a blooming good try. After contemplation and looking around my house and realizing, other than me there wasn't another living thing in it, as not even a plant did I have, so a thought became a decision and I was to give a home to someone like me, who was abandoned, possibly rejected and may have suffered, for they needed love, and in my heart, I considered, "Yes" of giving and sharing love, of being kind, loving and patient to another that needed the same, so gentle steps, I was to get myself, a rescue cat.

So in the Yellow Pages I looked, for that was in the days before the Internet was commonly used, and there I found a lady, self-funding, a one man band, who rescued cats, who *saved* those who were in danger, rejected or unwanted, just like I was really, then after making them healthy, found them a *good home*. And "Oh my" I dared to believe that I could provide one of those for a four legged friend, so, I placed my order, for a cat, all white and fluffy, and when one arrived, how ever long that was to take, I was to totter down in my little car to see her and greet her and bring her back with me to, my, loving home.

So arriving at the Cattery, I was led through the house and down the garden, and there in front of me, a rather grand wooden shed, bright and breezy with many a window, and as the door was opened, right before me, sat proudly was the most beautiful cat I think I had ever seen, and as the proprietor gave me the gab on the merits of the cat I'd asked for, and as I looked interestingly at her, it was in my periphery to the corner that I was drawn to, as I was unable to tear my eyes away from another cat, petite, short-haired, ginger and white, and not at all what I'd been looking for, but, there was something so marvellously interesting about her, and it was confusion I caused the lady, as I asked not to hold the fluffy one I had patiently waited for, but the one, that previously I would have, in logic terms refused to consider. Yet there was something intriguingly wonderful about that feline, her personality captured me, as I was innately drawn to her, and there, as she was placed in my arms, and tenderly I stroked her, the sound of gentle purrs, I heard with my ears but felt in my heart, as instantly I announced, with an inner joy I'd really not felt before "I'll take this one." And a little confusion I caused, as the rescue lady asked, "Are you sure, for that's not the one you came for?"

"Love is the only force turning an enemy into a friend."
~ Martin Luther King Jr

But my mind was made up, so paperwork completed, to purchase my new feline friend with the magnetic personality, as I went off to the pet shop to prepare for her homecoming, and what a pleasure it proved to be, to be blessed to care for something else that was living, and place their needs above my own, and "Oh my" the rewards that I inadvertently received from that were huge, and every night when I got home, there on the doorstep, she'd be waiting for me, exactly like she was, when I saw her in the cattery for the very first time, and as soon as my car engine turned off, the commencement of her gallant work, nay her swagger, as she walked over to me, and as my feet went on the floor, she was there to greet me as wrap herself around them was her welcome home to me, and "Oh my" those memories, I will treasure, for all eternity.

One such night, I was getting out of the car, while an Alsatian dog, off its leash dog walking down the street, and suddenly its eyes set on my best, ginger and white friend, as its body posture altered and it started moving quickly, coming toward her, so instinctively, stooping down to pick her up, to protect her, to save her, to place me between her and harms way, even tough, as a child at only 7 years of age, one such bread bit me on the face and shuck my head about, and since then that is the dog I am most uncomfortable and wary of. Yet, I hesitated not, to bend down to pick up, that little precious being that meant so much to me and was worthy of saving, and so frightened was she as I cradled her in my arms, she startled, as her eyes and ears on full alert, as she knew the treat was real and she needed to get away from there.

Emma, in my arms, still, not moving, almost frozen until the owner called off his Alsatian dog, and I, for my cat's sake, began to relax, and that, to protect what I loved, which proved as an automatic and intrinsic reaction for me, caused me to ponder over a decade later as I began to realise, what I did, was to make a choice, a choice to put myself in harms way, up against the breed of dog that really, since one bit me on the face, barely missing my eye when I was only a child, I cross over the road to avoid them. I loved Emma so unconditionally, and it occurred to me, how I was willing to put myself in a degree of danger, facing something that in essence created fear in me, to protect something I loved. Then suddenly it hit me, my mother, she would not even walk to the gate and the end of the garden to protect me, not once, not ever. And so immensely prominent and illuminated, became her treatment of me, her apparent neglect that seemed so sadly and destructively worse, for I knew then in that moment, of another way there truly was, intuitively so, and as I reflected more greatly of my mothers actions to re-access and understand, her concepts, her behaviours toward me, I considered surely of what she gave me, "Truly I was worth more!"

Poor Emma, my dearest cat, but of all that, a silver lining to that cloud quickly began revealing itself, and there at the age of 30-something years, revelation was to pose as a dear friend, for light had started to shine bright, and remarkably quickly shedding insight to my plights the I unnecessarily suffered through childhood and in adolescence, which effected my habits, relationships and indeed how I lived every facet of my life, in part by she who always denied any responsibility of ill-doing toward me, my mother, and her choices, to abstain and abandon, removing herself from the responsibility of my protection and safety. But suddenly: all my previous notions and concerns had all transferred, out of the realms of my imagination or explanation of embellishment, into something fundamentally real, for evidentially it was so, and through that scenario, involving my adorable cat I was able to receive, such *treasured* and *meaningful validation*. Then the rays of hope, they beautifully shone so very brightly and awakening me in that moment, that what I had endured I knew for the first time in my inner and rising spirit with the very essence of my being, as every cell and tissue was in unison agreeing, that what I been forced to live in as one so young, *was totally wrong!*

And so it was, a wonderful revelation, that set me free, for I absolutely refused, to tie myself to that pain of the past any longer, or permit it to radiate through me, as born and ignited that snippet of a notion, that I was more worthy than what my parents had shown me, so casting their assumptions, of that 'blame train,' so many moons ago I jumped onboard, I was to relinquish my first class ticket, and of those endless circles, never permitting me to de-board, adamantly I was to pull the emergency cord, and pull it hard, and there, at the station where the train came to a stop, where at last, I was able, willing and pleased to get off, as I arrived at a town where I was so glad to be, named, "Opportunity!" Where I was to do all I possibly could do, to explore and enjoy, getting to like and know, 'the real me.'

> *"Forgive your enemies, but never forget their names."*
> *~ John F Kennedy*

My mother's benchmarks set so low, but me, once enlightened, I was to set mine most high, for I was worthy of so much more, and quite magically a chain reaction ensued, as I grew to understand, others were worthy of so much more, from me also, so I was to break her bad habits planted in me, and replace them with a life, whole and healthy, that was awaiting me, as I learnt through those learning curves that taught me, not only a better way to be, but also, right from wrong. So then, learning to know better, leaving behind, my 'previous' life where the love that she and he, my parents withheld of love support and all those other beautiful childhood requirements, I was to be the best person to me I could be, making no excuses for myself, nor accepting any for I was to push on to a life restored, and the life, rich in love, peace comfort an pleasantries, all I deserved, and all revered.

A magical emotion, refuting and removing their power, and replacing it exactly where it should have always been, with me, as I simultaneously dismissed their actions while accepting and taking responsibility for my own and adding on my welcomed personal growth. For it became far less important, to consider the 'whys and maybe's' of what they did to me, perhaps deceitfully, wilfully or unwittingly, but true, that had gone as I was then outside their geographical location of reach, so then I needed to get them out of my head, thoughts and behaviours, for there also, laid a further chain reaction. So acceptance was the route that insight had eventually enabled me to take, as increasingly I began to realize that horrendous and cruel place with malice permeating freely through it, of shouts and commands filling the air which I breathed, everywhere, bitterness and hate woven in the fabrics of that house, so much, I remembered I felt, but, I was moving toward my future then, where in-spite of those previous circumstances, I was to search for and discover, a better me, to be.

My father relentless, written all over his face, such apparent satisfaction, the torment he created gave him, to deliver his info by poisoned arrows, "You think you hate me! Well you don't, for there is only a fine line between love and hate, and more they are on the opposite side of the same coins!" His deliberate intent to steel away every glimmer of hope for an independent spirit I may have held, to rise or float, as he crushed it and broke me, pronouncing his crippling control, over my thoughts, feelings and emotions. I was battered and knocked about, but no longer lost, as inquisitive I became and began to accelerate that knowledge of self-acceptance, where love was eventually to bloom and blossom in its attributes. True in my history for so utterly long, I had been put down and left in dark and dingy place, with nothing to positively feed me knew of no other way, but "My oh my!" I saw the light and spelt the roses, and so from my past I sped away from it determined to recover, as time had proved to be a friend to me, as clearly it revealed that they lacked credibility in all they said and did, and of my nature in the absence of positive evidence, I will examine more closely and choose a different way, so their words lost their power, as I refuted past horrible history, while waving in the tide of change, onto a legacy, wholesome and healing me, as so much more able was I, without their lies to hear, my own words I head, speaking of *knowledge* and *congratulating* me, on my new *self-worth* and so much more, for they may have won the battles in yesteryear when I was weaker and impressionable, but I, was to win the war!

> *"Faith is putting something to the test.*
> *It is better to try to do something and fail, than try to do nothing and succeed."*
> *~ Dr Robert H Schuller*

"Oh my" I was to be on the move once again, leaving Toulouse where possibly I had stayed longer than necessary, as in my mind, it had little to recommend it, and I didn't really feel too comfortable there, and the residents, well they were OK, and the architecture fine and pleasing on the eye, but what I really couldn't live in a place with stale air and in-spite of Toulouse, having the river Garonne, named after the region Haute-Garonne which it is the capital of, running through middle of it, curiously oddly, there seemed an insufficient abundance of fresh air.

And in-spite of my endeavours, those doors that I was looking for were simply not there to open, and my due diligence visiting the real estate agents, revealed noting positive as not a one to provide me any information, certainly not a helping hand, so really, all in all, I thought I had given it a good shot, but opted to return to the drawing board, contemplating with greater determination, as I continued to choose, what I wanted to do with my life, to follow a dream, to renovate a property in the town or countryside, where best should I go next to achieve my goal. But "Oh my, had I lost my way? Why was I heading next heading toward *Albi*, and not toward *Aix-en-Provence?*" That place, I had meditated upon, so deep-fully and wilfully, so positively in-awe, for so long, before I left Melbourne.

"My oh my!" Really; "Had I made any headway at all?" Was an included in my perplexing thoughts, as I dragged my bigger than a battleship suitcase, back to the *gare,* train station, heading north, in the wrong direction, for where I should I not have been going toward the south, where to meet those fragrance hills of lavender, which the mere thought warmed my senses, so why had I so easily, as if the waving of a wand forgotten it, as those naysayers in Paris, had almost put a spell, nay, a curse on it, or why else I now contemplate, did the notion slip from my mind, believing their negativity, of "Oh its very expensive, you wont be able to afford that." But "How would they know what I could afford and more, who ere they to surmise?" For seriously I do believe, when we are in following our deepest desires, in pursuit of our dreams, in the right place, doing the right things and taking the right steps, as we take-action while remaining patient, as time goes by, wonderful situations may quite supernaturally occur and unfold to spur us on to achieve its accomplishment as it comes to fruition; and right there for me lays, a most retrospective lesson.

"Exert your talents, and distinguish yourself,
and don't think of retiring from the world, until the world will be sorry that you retire."
~ Samuel Johnson

Chapter 15

Step, Encore

"Love doesn't make the world go around, Love is what makes the ride worthwhile."
~ *Franklin P Jones*

I wanted, I desired, I dreamed, I believed, as I believed it is possible to meet our dreams, to flourish, to thrive, to be alive in the midst of all our positive affirmations afford ourselves, in my mind more perfect than a masterpiece, to be painted upon a clear canvas with brushstrokes of glee, of lavender, upon lush rolling hills, where the landscape only interrupted by petite cottages of pastel pink topped by roof tiles in rouge, window shutters of blue, shimmering beneath the sunrays peaking uninterrupted through the Provincial clear sky, as all the dots are joined in proper sequence, to form my preferred picture of life. But really, *un problem,* a problem, as too late I was to wonder, as the train was whisking me away in the opposite, the wrong direction, "Was I being astute to investigate elsewhere, or going against the desires of my heart, committing a huge great big blunder?"

As "Oh contraire," *"Un petit problem,"* as sensible it was not, as I was not heading toward the direction of my so falsely held dream, manufactured so long ago in my heart, so "Why, then from it was I permitting it to depart and allowing that train to whisk me up north in France?" Perhaps, in-fact only because, of those naysayers I had fallen victim to, which I had permitted to falsely get inside my head, but why was I so easily influenced, and why was I allowing them to take my dream away from me, with words and phrases amounting to, "No, not possible, to expensive for you to do," and so negatively, those how held not the power or authority to say "Yes" to me, "Oh why oh why," did it take-onboard and their "No." absorb?"

"My dream?" My dream, my kingdom for my dream! "So was I misguided, for how could it flourish, and why was I entertaining such defeatist aspects of those?" but really, "Was I acting foolhardy at best, and at worst, well worse, or was I on the right path, conducting valuable market research, exploring the good the bad and the ugly of Bed & Breakfast accommodation, of what attributes would encourage me to stay and those that would propel me to leave?" And what of my ability to speak French, or not as the case may be, will I had already devised a plan to design that problem out, as it was not the French but foreigners you see, who I was to market as potential clients, from English speaking Europeans and Scandinavian countries, who spoke English so well.

"Was I learning a lot?" or simply through those exploits, "Was I only, as if in revolving doors, spinning around and around in ever-decreasing circles, and only, becoming dizzy?" But that which was really expensive and that which was really bad, what I concluded most of all, and from deriving what I read, the venue, the *ville*, it had to suit my needs, to suit my hobbies, of walking and cycling, the water, that must play a great part, so all of my hobbies I was able to do, a cinema was important, and the 'arts' that would be truly magnificent, but more simply the air I breathed, all those ideas to encapsulate, to a lesser or greater degree, to sooth my soul, definitely, I was in need.

So "Where to next?" I was to reflect on the to set aside the idea of pinning the proverbial tail on the donkey, such a well played children's party game from the 1960's significant, as blindfolded, led to the board, it was a guess, and the closest to it won, but I considered, perhaps a little more methodical or scientific I needed to be, perhaps, as it was turning out, that may have formed a re-jump of an old strategy, and so it was, refreshing my mind of the diamond interviewee, of the infrastructure he informed me may play an important key, for the destination I chose, as "Would it please me, would it encourage easily through ease of accessibility to encourage tourists to come and stay?"

So getting wiser at last, a map I began to scan, to pinpoint airports, of international or those that flew to just the UK, major road links, major and minor, or hubs where several converged, places of interest, perhaps historic in nature, those that had beaches or canals, or mountain ranges for skiing or more, I explored so many, but still likely, too few, and all possibly a little bit too late, for note I did, that really all what I was doing, I was grossly under prepared for, and far greater due diligence I really should have done, before my quest I set out upon.

For I thought to some degree I could 'wing it' and see how I went, and that all would turn out right in the end, and the solution to that matter is really quite clear, that if I had followed my dream it likely quite would have, but I was off its beaten track, following the wrong path, joining all the wrong dots, and the only person I had to blame was me, for so often I was pleased to tell those who asked of my plan of my dream, and too intent was I in listening to their advice, thinking they knew better, what was best for me, when really, clearly, of that notion I should have thought more than once or twice, and clearly ignored, for it was my dream, and so, should I have stuck to it, and deviated not in an instance, I am quite convinced that everything would have, in the smoothest of way, magically taken place.

But that was not to be, and as it turned out, lost, on a road I should never have been, I began to contemplated less of my dream but "Was I foolhardy and had I lost my marbles?" And still my misery unfolded, as go back to the beginning and start again I did not, I gave myself not to opportunity to realign myself with it, for I was running around it appeared in decreasing circles, and for sure, forever in the wrong place at the wrong time, me they did not at-all-well serve, as like Little Bow Peep, it was not sheep but that larger than life *valise*, suitcase, I trailed cumbersomely behind me.

Designing a perfect future but was I failing, for that plan of validity had escaped me, and like a string of a jumper falling apart just slightly, the whole, serving as something, was to disintegrated to form absolutely nothing, as emotions unravelled the same, as I was becoming so unsure of so much, as I found myself encompassing, or was that becoming injuring, another leg of my journey, where ever-increasing episodes of loneliness were circling me, where I, devastated and distraught, embodied exactly the scenario, depicted by Tom Hanks in the movie Cast Away, when lost, isolated on a desert island, no companions, no comfort, alone in the world, and finding a ball, he pained a face on it, and his attachment to that became huge, as it was his only connection to his other world, and the emotions he portrayed, of emotional deprivation and more, so very well, were reminiscent, in their exact content of those I faced, increasingly so everyday.

For really, now I could commence adding up all the errors I made, and just another to add to the list, was to follow a concept I once read, "That when to a place you really don't wish to go back, burn your bridges and it will be impossible to do." Is that what I had done with Australia, and my regrets were they adding up, perhaps that was why I could not eradicate them, for as one tried to go, so quickly it was replaced and multiplied where in despair in the pit of my stomach, they set up home and wailed and hollered.

"Good judgment comes from experience, and experience comes from bad judgment."
~ Rita Mae Brown

Yet I remained committed to joining the dots of my picture, and "Why?" For quite amazingly, I remained oblivious and had not woken up, when really to myself I should have been shouting in the loudest voice, "Hello!" And so, as I had not learnt to 'Stop!' and cease going on, for really my emotions in so much turmoil should have really provided me with a clue, the picture I formulated and the tapestry I created, not exactly a Monet, as rolling around the southern French countryside, a case of *déjà vu*, already seen, on a carriage comfort not of luxury, but of bargain basement, with only the tune from the 1960s children's show Jessie James, of what next, I was to go, "A steamin and a rollin," unceremoniously, all the way, to my next destination, the historic town of *Albi*.

Another day another *gare*, another French railway timetable, served only as a loose guideline and not as a guarantee, where escalators, to aid my transportation of my luggage, rarely seen, as I dragged around clothes for spring, summer and fall, and more, books to help with my writing, so light it was not to be, but I must say, so many gentlemen did offer to help me, and indeed even women, as they saw me struggling, and offered their assistance when men had not, yet getting it off was so much easier than putting it on, as it was Mr Einstein and his theory proved a good friend to me, as so often, it as gravity which was to serve equally to all.

"Whoops!" "What to do?" As my Russian *colocataire*, would have asked in Paris, as I, about to disembark, realised far too late that in fact, not one but two railway stations in that petite *ville*, but how could that be, the place was so tiny, but too late to panic I had to estimate what to do, but as I pursued my printed map, it gave me not a clue, so logic I embraced staying calm, and there wonderfully I made the right choice, well, I guess I had a 50/50 chance of getting it right, and as I departed the steps of the station, no need to ask where it was, for so pleasingly, it was clearly visible facing the exit of the railway station.

What a prime location I scored as I booked my accommodation online, but as with so many things, words can be cheap and pictures deceptive, and so it was to be, as I big-upped myself too early thinking 'the girl did good!' as there Little Bow Peep, again, pulled her temporary home on wheels, "Oops, sorry she was me," only a few hundred yards until I arrived at the door, but was it to be, cheap-and-cheerful or cheap-and-nasty, and I wondered was I, with the weeks accruing since a good nights sleep I'd enjoyed, and so much really did I need one, there, was I to receive it?

Approaching the hotel front door, looking up I noticed above, painted 2 stars, identifying the calibre of that establishment, but was it worthy of the non-princely sum of 35E per night, or had the *artisan*, tradesman had a sniffle or a cough, perhaps sneezed and placed an additional one there in error? As force I had to muster to push open that badly hung door, which swung not easily, and likely held together by the layers of paint, chipped, the green seen beneath the blue, the brown beneath the blue, and so onto orange and yellow, all showing through, depicting décor fashion choices along the way, and all the brass ornaments, and there were many yet not polished in more than a decade or two, and how I considered, the age of that building and its proximity to the station and *ville*, and how it must have been so absolutely bustling in the times that possibly history now can only testify to, of horses and arts, and all people of industry and agriculture that made their living, from the canal that of that petite *ville*, passed on through.

Such a small place before me lay, but it was not the sight that grabbed me first but the odour, but too, late to turn away, for I'd already paid in advance, and as I closed the door behind me, up to the ceiling I glanced and noted its extraordinary and lofty heights, where the globed light fitting was lost, and disguised under years of dust. The narrow hallway, its décor dark and gloomy, the light sucked from it, with burnt orange painted over embossed wallpaper and in abundance, above the higher the height than usual door, with a dusky brown beneath, and separating the two, that freeze of the colour of almost red, and not at all pleasing on the eye.

As I ventured I further, the Linoleum all tattered and torn, of jester squares of black and cream with a gold fleck in between, but cracking underfoot, revealing, other designs chosen in decades gone-by, and to my left, such a narrow and underwhelming staircase for the size of that building, but quaint and original and easily conceivable it was in my mind, of all those in the tails of their crinoline dresses dragging behind or their husbands perhaps, winding their way up, smoking maybe a cigar or a pipe, as they held on tight after a night in the adjoining bar to that rich mahogany handrail, as not to fall, as they curved their way up and around to the second or third floor.

And there squeezed in at the bottom of the stairs, where really there was insufficient space to do so, a tiny quarter moon lounge bar, the design and purpose straight for the 1960's where embossed on the front, gold tiles, of squares of geometric patterns, with a curved Formica top of glossy imitation wood, and edged with a strip of black plastic which with yellowing glue visible was falling off, such a sorry state, really it was to see, and normally, in such a place, my mind would buzz an embrace all possibilities of how I would renovate it, and the fun I would have exploring all possibilities, but astonishingly, in stark absence in that place there were non.

A delectable vision to be seen in Home and Gardens, I think not, and almost an irony, as sited on top was a traditional porters bell, depicting maybe, notoriety or class, but neither I was to find were to amass, but when I rung, a sketch from Faulty Towers almost unfolded, as a lady approached, certainly much younger than the shabby décor came to assist, whose apparel was ordinary, but her hair colour exceedingly bright, but no more so than her welcoming personality. The formalities taken care of, I was given a key, quite extraordinary in size, weight and design, and as I wondered, who before me had used that, and would they through their day used a horse and trap?

With our best communication taking place, her best English meeting my best French, quickly it was established, that no elevator was there in that hotel, but she had a solution, she was to ask someone in the bar, and 'hey-presto' a gentleman offered to carry it up, but caution I did give him, not just because of its weight, but because, the stairs, like everything else in that quite bizarre hallway, had layers of lino all cracking up under foot, a bit of a trip hazard really, and I was concerned for his safety, but of no concern to him, and there it was like so many others before he dragged, pushed and lifted the case, colliding with the Formica in mottled yellow that had been glued to the wall and nailed over the spindles, and you guessed it though quite remarkably, for really it is most hardy and study, it also was wearing away.

Wow, safe and sound or was I, as I unlocked the *chambre* door, though really, the lock, the latch, all fitted so precariously badly, it hardly fitted even at all, with half an inch of light beaming through between the door and its frame shining through, and an association I instantly made, of many a great movie script, as I could have pushed my shoulder hard against that door, and instantly have fallen in. For sure of security I considered it provided little to none. But sill, thanking the man, I waited in hope thinking that all could not be as bad as it appeared, but with nothing to feast for the eyes, but for the imagination, bland misery, it appeared, I was to be wrong. Yet simply, was that my price to pay, for that frivolous exuberance of expenditure for the previous 14 days? Where with an unbalanced extravagance, taking more than a partial pittance, it was not a proposal of, 'Everything in moderation' or alternatively 'Save something for a rainy day, but an unnecessary and misguided hiccup, of financial outlay along my journey's way.

That building, built in a different century, yet unconceivably had all its historical details stripped away, with all fixtures and fittings looking as if they'd been dragged out of a skip, the furniture, mainly Formica or ply-board, crumbling away at the edges, likely unfit, for a roadside collection, and nothing looking grand against blank walls that once, likely magnolia without a picture or an ornament insight. "Oh my!" "Was there anything that could curve the disappointment or ignite my imagination?" There with the exception of the black marble with speckled white fleck, but in a design, so terribly basic, not appearing in form to fit the building at all, and so awkwardly it was set, as the space to its left, had been taken to utilized for a shower, and I was to walk over to commence my routine room check.

And there I realised as the floor beneath me, which the deep green lino, the preferred covering of choice in that establishment, cracked and peeling upon that wood floor, rippled and rotten, toward the window, far beneath the level of the skirting board, completely rolling away, and so instantly it took my back to when I was a child, and to my fathers mothers house in Manchester we were taken, and the floor, represented by the same, but her home, a two-up two-down terraced houses had been condemned, considered slums, as streets after streets, knocked down, and whole communities, displaced, as high rise blocks of flats were to take their place, yet by a twist of fate, 4 decades later I was to pay money to stay in the same.

The room, really was there any point checking it for it appeared everything glaringly obvious, that I had slipped to an all time low, as penny-pinching had become a format of choice in order to preserve all those funds I possibly could, to invest in order to become, pound-rich, which perhaps I was making into a practiced fine art, or perhaps I should have formulated it into more of a science, particularly on that occasion, as on balance I considered, "I was to get what I paid for?" As sorrowfully, worriedly I pondered, how far down was there left and, exactly, "How low could I go?"

Nestled within the corner, and quite ingeniously I must say, at an angle across it to afford for a window too, cautiously I looked with a little trepidation of what I was to find, and the shower cubicle, clean and white in presentation, but chipped, cracked with seals of mould, and rough as the hand was laced upon it, bacteria sprung to mind, and so pleased as I often am, that to work in NZ, I was required to have a Hepatitis B vaccination. The colour palette, from festering green to charcoal black, something you might find in a sputum pot, but hey, as long as the water from the drain wasn't to feed it way back up, and then as I turned a tad of excitement I gleamed as I spied the towels, white and clean, just for me, so no need to dry myself with the pillow protectors as also in Toulouse. "Oh my" "Was I to be, ahead of the game, and quids-in, or was an opposite scenario out to win?" Well, I was just going have to wait and see.

The mattress, really I shouldn't have bothered, but it seems we have our own little habits and idiosyncrasy, I was to check it, I was to consider, a great big bear ate the porridge and slept in the bed, for an excessive amount of time, as the bear's weight, had left an indentation that could have been used to berth a proverbial battle ship, but shipshape, it most certainly was not. And the pillows how I laugh, for not pillows at all, as cotton bags filled with pieces of foam, jaggedly cut, sharp and catching on the face, that was until they separated apart. "Oh my!" Comfort becoming illusive, my home, my belongs, my choice, my preference, my freedom, was I ever experience creature or home comforts again? As with sincerity, I dearly desired to.

Yet melancholy slipped away, as I had not time to contemplate "How sad" as momentarily I surveyed the room, thinking of that once, quite well-to-do establishment, how disappointingly shabby it had become, and, 'oh how the great fall.' For I had better things to do and places to go so on that extremely hot day for that time of year, first off I took my boots, before I began to disrobe my self from those leather travelling pants and peel of the thick wool tights that were hidden below, for it was a quick shower, to freshen up, to wash underarms, which proved a bit of a nuisance sine I had ceased wearing deodorant as I was found to have a raised aluminium levels, and natural alternatives, at that time, I had not found, so a spruce-up it was to be, as was regularly necessary. And to follow, a quick 'pee,' "Yippee" a toilet roll dispenser sited on the wall, OK, there were screwed in with industrial sized bolts, but "Hello," I had far since become less fussy, and after all, it was on the wall and not on the floor. But hang-on one minute, "What was that?" It was the toilet, it was clean, it was fresh, but it was not, functional. "Flushing?" "Nope, no-way!"

> *"The man on top of the mountain didn't fall there."*
> ~ Vince Lombardi Jr

Really, it was not the Ritz, "If only!" "If only, 'money grew on trees' rapidly, I would have reached for the fertilizer and ploughed it in ever so quickly," but no, from tender years I knew that was the case, as my father forever screamed, "I'm not Rockefeller" followed by "I'm not made of money!" concluding, "Don't dare ask for anything else, now shut up and get out of here." And my mother, not far from the same, as he forever response to "I want" was "I want never gets," and true, she wasn't right about much, but it turned out she was right about that, for never did I get what I wanted, but more unfortunately, her scorns of the same, imbed her condemnation in my brain, and before I knew it, I an adult, with fixed and limiting beliefs, that 'what I want I can't have,' and worse, 'what I want I don't deserve,' for after all, money doesn't grow on trees.

And so my mother continued, "Money burns a whole in your pocket, you'll never be able to save," scorned so disparagingly, with no hope of reprieve, and he, "You have to learn to lower your sights because your tastes are too expensive," and for sure, topped off with, "Beggars can't be choosers, so you better get used to it now." but goodness gracious me, "Who was she to condemn me as a beggar?" When I, so young, had my whole life stretched our before me. Just maybe that was her concept of what she had, maybe she even believed what she had she deserved, but I deserved not her downward spiralling condemnation, "You'll never have or amount to anything, because you're useless and stupid!" And so variants of the same theme, day by day went on, until their evil curse was spun, and their seeds of a bad and damaging job won, but really, "Was that going to be forever," or "When were those curses to die, and what could I do, to make that happen?" For really quickly please, for life was passing me by, and really, I knew they were wrong and I needed to prove it to myself, before anymore of life, passed me by.

Dispelling their myths of how I arrived at that point, was of far less concern than the 'what and how' of preserving and multiplying my funds, before as an investment, they disappeared, for spending it on only what I needed, food and shelter, predominately, and a coffee at a café, so I could rest, write, and always, 'get myself together.' Trapped in a cycle, I could see no way out, except, to give up and go back, returning to that hamster-wheel which I had relinquished several months ago.

But, "Was I actually going to permit those thoughts and fears to delay me, to disturb my progress, for doesn't hard become before easy?" Reflecting further, "Did I deserve more? Did I deserve better? Did I not deserve to persist, to resist, giving into those voices of that pre-programming by my parent's, values concerning money?" or actually, "Were those condemnations not money matters related, but more specifically orientated toward me?" and really, "Their money-values toward me, should I succumb and inadvertently agree?" Well actually, "No" as to do so, there was no good reason at all, and so I chose to push on, and cast out *their* limiting beliefs, for one last thing I was sure, in-spite of my anxieties, my fretting, rolling around my head, their vibrations of collisions echoing downwardly into my heart, yet away from that uncomfortable emotional nature of my search, but ultimately from my dream, I was not to depart.

> *"Change your thoughts and change your world."*
> *~ Norman Vincent Peale*

Staying cool was what I must do, to eliminate the onset of one of 'those' Melbourne headaches, so grabbing something from my mobile wardrobe, my suitcase, my short denim skirt, but not too short, teamed with a little white T-shirt, excellent for the beach or a cosmopolitan city, always so easy to wear, and though my tan needed topping up, not the first on my list, as that was *epilation*, waxing needed to be done. And my only footwear available other than flip-flops were my ¾ length black boots with a small heal, bought in Montpellier, and most importantly a colour and design to match my handbag, so there it was, in a jiffy, with a good job done, I was on my way.

And so, needing directions to *centre ville*, I walked into the adjoining bar, with the larger than life TV, which it turned out, each morning at 6a.m. was going to wake me, and greeting by the lovely receptionist once again, and smiling I spoke my best French, receiving a warm welcome from her, but of the man who had been kind in carrying my suitcase to the upper level, his persona, significantly changed, and suddenly I had the vibe, that I became the 'elephant in the room' that Annie in Paris had told me about, for it appeared it was not my apparel was not the only thing to have changed. Surprised, for such a stark contrast, from the kind man who was so welcoming before, but really, it was only my clothes that had changed and not my personality.

True those clothes chosen, not shabby or expensive, but for financial feasibility and functionality, and altered not my ethics, values or morals, but somehow it appeared I was being judged by so, and was I being judged too quickly, unreasonably, undeservedly or unfairly, perhaps, instantly, partially or completely? And I pondered as I walked with directions in my hand, was I also a culprit of doing that to others? As I contemplated, was it not Oscar Wild who wrote, "Manners that maketh the man." Perhaps women too, but defiantly not, clothes or shoes.

Amazingly interestingly, for I found it to be true, as soon as I swept away their stares, and guarded myself from their glares, and threw their judgements aside, reviewing what I had been told, so many moons ago, 'that no one can make you feel bad without your consent,' so my, attitude I did change rebuking their notions of unimportant opinion, and astonishingly, significantly and instantly I have to say, something else profoundly became obviously true, as I began to think better of me, they did so too.

With directions in hand, I headed toward *centre ville* on a quest, armed with a list of things to do, and with my first port of call, an appointment for waxing secured, I was off to find that apparently illusive present as a "Thank you" gift for my Parisian friends, for their kindness, never before had I received, and seek and ye shall find, and so I did, as what suited so perfectly in a *magasin*, shop window staring back at me, and so with gift in hand, it was of to the post office I swiftly went, to send it to them, void of any further delay.

And so onto the purpose of my business, to discover the Real Estate agents for the acquisition and restoration of a property, and so to explore the *ville* for viability of the same, I wandered the alleyways and byways, and happy to see the testimony of time, where trough the years renovations so clear, where a wide open space that once the horse drawn carts would have entered, and offloaded their produce and wares, long since redundant, blocked up with rows of bricks, only permitting for a small door, or as so often seen, a feature made of such a loft space, with huge pains of glass, reaching from ceiling to floor, and doors became windows, and those long and narrow may be adorned with a Juliet balcony, and the pullies above stripped of their ropes so long ago, ignored and disappeared into the wall, or painted as a feature, in colours most bright, and all to be gleamed, as those decades did come and go, and changing the purpose for a brand new business, through the progression of all, it enthralled and amused me so.

Time to take a break, for hunger was knocking on my door, and to save a buck or two, I wandered to a *pâtisserie,* cake shop, and cheaper than sitting-in, through the hole in the wall I gave my order, and received quick-smart a French roll, full of chicken, though *sans* no, avocado, often a duo seldom apart from my experience in Melbourne, and as I wandered around the blank square in search of a place to sit under the gentle sun, so upon my tan to work, a double job could be done.

And as I sat there, perhaps not most comfortably, I was to reflect nicely on the words I had listened to on a TD Jakes audio CD, 'Repositioning Yourself,' as that dollar to two I saved and put in my pocket and saved for another day, and my grandad I thought would also be proud of me, for his caption of note, as thrift he was, where 'make do and mend' was his policy, and so often I heard "Look after the pennies, and the pounds will look after themselves," and so I did, for intuitively I knew, that was not critical yet good advice, so happily I did, so consecutively along life's way.

Then after my rest, further explorations were mine to achieve, and walking around I found myself, a little underground, but not to worry, soon I was out of the tunnel and facing the light, and there before me, as the opposite side to the underpass, a gentleman from a wedding party, tall, slim and fair, dressed in a formal suit of black, white shirt and dickie-bow tie, and he waving his arm pointing at me, but I a little bemused, turned to look around, but no, no one behind, but I quite mesmerized for what was on his mind, as he ran back to the Cathedral steps, where the couple were to receive their marital Blessing after the French legal obligation, the service held at the *mairie,* Town Hall, of that oppressive, domineering and imposing building, but nothing admirable or appealing, and as he called to is friends, causing a 'hullabaloo.'

Receiving no response from his friends, with his tuxedo tails flowing behind him, up the Cathedral steps he sped, shouting still, but "Why?" I bemused, for I only wore an 8E skirt and a 2E top, but was it something about my silhouette in that darkened underpass that effected him so, as I considered curiously, "What was his problem or what was it about me, that effected him so?"

Then around the corner the bride did come, and her ensemble, what a beautiful vision, gentle and elegant, her dress, flowing in soft chiffon, in colour warm cream, in tulip design cradling neatly around her knee, with her hair of lush dark curls pinned up, and nestled between each, pretty flowers of rose petals, and echoed in her bouquet of delightful sophistication, held in her gloved hands an adornment by beautiful blossoms, soft and cream of monotones, with foliage sweeping down to the floor and trailing behind her as if a bridal train, and with each dainty step she took, in her shoes of silk or leather with heels so amazingly high, yet she still maintained her poise, perceiving that it was her natural grace.

"Oh those shoes!" How I missed my high heels, not able to be worn since my industrial back injury suffered after newly-qualifying as a nurse, and how I used to love wearing them, for to the supermarket in them I would also go, but perhaps not unusual, for my grandmother who died at 82, was wearing them just the day before she died, and my mother, never did I see her wear anything else, so and natural as taking a breath it was to me, but of cause, that did not make it right. Yet with sadness that I bid a sad a fond, *au revoir*, bye bye, to those that later only served to cause me pain, and so how lucky I thought it to be, when in a Community Health Nurse job, I was to work with Podiatrist, and from them I was to learn, the significance of shoes bending in perfect place where the ball joint does on our foot, for this will make them so much healthier to wear you see.

The heals of a shoe hold great significant, for their different shapes effect our posture so tremendously, and the best shape I was to read about, those of the 'kitten' or 'Louis' in design, are the best for they place the least problem to the pelvis or the back, so now my format, to check the colour and design, and once that appeals, I shall pick them up to check the heals, then all so far so good, I give them a jolly good bend, but should they fail to pass that bend test, no matter the appeal or bargain they may be, back onto the shelf I let them rest, and keep on searching, for with shopping for me, that is what provides most of the fun. And one last thing, it was not a medical person but an entrepreneur who said to me, some years previously, "The 2 things you should spend the most on in life, are your shoes and your bed, for you will always be in one or the other of them." Now that, a piece of valuable advice I always adhere to.

And I contemplated the months of preparation, preparing the bride for her pristine appearance, and a little surprised that my outfit so cheap would attract so attention. But was it Coco Chanel who said, "You can't buy style." For you either have-it or you don't, or was I simply barking up the wrong tree?" And for sure, just an adornment of one, of my many beautiful, bargain silk scarves, would have added a certain flair and sophistication, and such a cost-effective strategy to add a certain panache, and so a different look so easily achieved and not another person would have, that he so curiously stared so.

"I never think of myself as an icon.
What is in other people's minds is not in my mind. I just do my thing."
~ Audrey Hepburn

Alfresco, I was to enjoy beneath the sunrays, at a restaurant in a building centuries old, for the second part of my extremely late, *déjeuner,* lunch, and was it to be a *une bouteille de bière ou un verre de vin rouge* a bottle of cold beer or a glass of red wine, always fine, for the latter certainly cheaper than a recurrently, not so fine coffee. And the ambient temperature sped my mind to the Red Stripe beer I had enjoyed sat at a bar at the beach, staring out across the glistening Caribbean Sea, with sunset my preferred time for such, so mesmerised by that changing shades of colour, pink to orange to yellow and red, as sailboats casting silhouettes before the setting sun, and a fine photo was taken of more than one or two, one of which in an exquisite frame, sat placed upon my bathroom sink in New Zealand, with Maslow's euphoric experiences realised, which I gazed upon last thing at night and first each morning, setting my thoughts and emotions everyday along my journeys way.

As I sat sipping I stared noticing the tourists, so early yet they appearing all spruced up returning to centre square in their eveningwear, it occurred to me, "Why so soon?" Then quickly my answer became apparent, there appeared little else to do. But it was the locals who caught my eye, as a smile to my face they brought as whizzing past my eyes, a scooter, a favoured mode of transport in so many French towns, and sat upon it, *jeune,* young ladies x2 riders, in bright pink with their helmets to match and never to miss, but not the most noticeable of what they wore, it was not the pastel coloured ribbons tied around their lashings of thick and strong curls, flowing behind them in the wind, nor their choice of classic fashion, or their footwear of the same, not even their stylish bags which were strewn across their bodies, no, not at all, for it was their large smiles they wore, lit-up by their eyes, and the transparency of *la joie de vie,* the joy of life, that which they appeared in abundance to reveal and a thought, of their expectations of life, of their future, "Was that also to be tickled pink?"

As quickly as they passed by, another treat was to fall upon me, as 2 ladies from a bygone era were to strike a pose in my minds eye as they sauntered on by, their transport not motorised but driven by peddle-power, and elegant in appearance and perfect in poise as along the roadside the duo strolled, with their style-of-dress quite reminiscent likely of the date of the manufacture of that bicycle being pushed, up a small gradient hill. Her cycle of dark green paint, with polished chrome, it was a wicker basket centre stage, hanging from the handle bars, and from it standing proud, her big leather bag, appearing well used though well taken care of, its colour deep brown, and perfectly matched her lace-up Cuban healed shoes.

The rest of her ensemble, of simplicity and elegance, so neat and most tidy, as a fine figure she cut, revealed by her tailored jacket nipped in at the waist in cream woven wool in cream, with her ankles and calves, slim and shapely, defined by exercise of regularity, but barely visible beneath the mid-calf length tweed-plaid pleated skirt of her blue and green, neatly laundered and breaking with each soft but purposeful step she took. Her 'crowning glory,' silver in colour and most sleek, placed pristinely up, tidily in a French style bun, but perhaps untraditionally, a hat she did not wear, yet what most profoundly obvious of what she did wear, was her youthful spirit, alive and free, exuded effortlessly from her, visible for those who chose to spare a morsel of time, just to see.

I feasted my eyes with appreciation as I contemplated, her unmistakable charisma and timeless grace, and her friend beside her, as they chatted genially, I wondered, as the years had passed effortlessly away, how maybe their friendship had spanned for over half a century. And "Had they sought and they had found? Had they knocked and found the door to be opened?" So long ago, "Had they suffered unrequited love, or seized all their opportunities and experienced love, the love that lasts a lifetime?" Their regrets and successes, of "What they did and equally importantly, what they did not do, but rather wished they had, and of what of their secrets, were they always remain so, until one day, when their last breath is taken away?" Really, "What of their past, a hidden history, a conundrum or a mystery, or was it, a past happily revealed, happily relived from those situations that formed and molded them into what and who they did become, and I wondered, of their twilight years, were there many, or any tears?"

> *"I never stop to plan. I take things step by step."*
> *~ Mary McLeod Bethune*

Time to move, but not too far, just as far as that hotel, where to return to, really, I did not want to go. For really, I posed in my mind the possibility of feasibility, of the toilet being fixed and flushing, "Was it likely?" And the answer to both was, "Not so," as my slow meander began, but to utilize the time well, as I was to explore, missing not an opportunity to investigate all those nooks and crannies, and on route I contemplated, what exactly defines a 'street'? As those, so short, so narrow in width, I pondered to define them as such, may be quite a folly, yet I stood, marvelling, observing, the architecture of multiple centuries gone by and even those, defying gravity. As a quaint characteristic so blatant to see, the angle which the top floor of those Tudor dwellings, and so incredible they were still standing as great was the lean toward each other, that just a few degrees more, and I'd think they'd topple in and end up crumbled on the floor.

Of fine engineering in their assembly I considered them to be, and the place tiny but eerie and dark, the space lingering in the air, bearing a heavy pungent, repugnant odour, which made me ready to escape. And what a purpose the acute olfactory nerve serves, that of smell, so it can warn us of danger, and as if a cruel trick, in a moments instant, I was sped back 4 decades to that time in my childhood, to that place we hardly went, but obviously, though I had not realised it, I was returned to the 'slums of Manchester,' a term of commonality, or so I believed, predicting not only habitation but the culture and class system so staunchly lived under, of English traditions and expectations, where the class you were born into, you were expected forever to stay.

As 'to better yourself,' was not easily accepted, not even 'by your own kind' were accepted, as you were expected, to "know your place and stay in it," and 'think no better of yourself than what you are.' As class-orientation constrictive, and participation not optional but unavoidable, yet my father, tenacious, determined, stubborn maybe, unable to be told anything, certainly not what he could not do, as he chose and made a decision to break away from his 'lot in life,' to escape those captive restraints, of social standing and class, daring to do, to achieve, exactly what he wanted to. As he, his personal driving force, propelled him forward and out from those slums, out from where he began, for he knew that was only a place geography, for he knew he was not to finish there, for also he knew he was to permit no one to say "No" to him who had not the right to say "Yes."

He chose not necessarily an easy road, he chose a road less travelled, he chose to battle up stream and face the naysayers, and true, intelligent, as he passed his 11-Plus school examination, breaking his first of many unexpected predetermined social moulds, as off to Grammar school he went, but of acceptance there, I dare declare there was little to non, and when he got home to his neighbourhood the same was likely, for the 'class' that he stemmed from may have perceived him, as believing he, was too good for them, then like a two edged sword, both sides of the equation, held to his success, the potential to cause emotional or debilitating harm.

But my father, fought on through, his strength, his determination, his belief in himself, to have, to hold, against the odds, moulding and creating his accomplishments, significant in theory and in practice, but really, was he simply masking his personal pain, and was he on a road to self-destruction, while he tried to escape the confines of where others had put him, as he strived so hard, to do, and be better, than he was ever, told he was. Yet I wonder, could he ever possibly really have succeeded in multiple avenues other than work and career, when possibly, peace or pleasure were never his to call his own, when forever he was standing in a place, where fear of moving forward may have acted as his compass, as he misguidedly embraced as his driving force, delivering him into his life's spiral, where not-enough or maybe not good-enough, became mantras with to rule over him, as self-love or self-worth were superfluous to his self-focused requirements, as perhaps sadly, it was more debilitating bitterness with an inability to overcome his past, that drove him on with ingrained hostility.

True, what you don't have, you cannot give away, and so his family was to suffer, as the negative, destructive cycles he did not break, or do I entirely presume and speculate over what created his thoughts and actions and moulded his expectations and aspirations. And of it, through of all the abuse I suffered at his hand, I so would like to comprehend, the anguish or trauma that perhaps he felt, that he carried on his back, a heavy sack from his childhood, but yet never did he share or discus an ounce of himself, or let me into the crevices of his inner-psyche, but never, yet may be it may have helped him, dispel those curses that as a little boy may have been set against him, and possibly, of his actions towards his children, his wife, his family, he may have shone a gentle light, of hope, of realization, then maybe, happily he could have eradicated and destroyed them.

But no, that was not so, and of his dreams I knew not, of his efforts, of the dots he joined, the sacrifices he made, the troffs of his disappointments, and accomplishments at his mountain tops, I knew not; yet, I wondered, "Was there someone he confided in, a friend possibly, but never did I see any, and phone calls, he never made, and what of his mother?" I think not, for indifference and distance seemed to sum up their relationship, but maybe his Aunt Mary, his mother's sister, but then she lived in Ireland, only ever visiting us, just the once.

His mother, the most I knew about her, whilst making bombs working in a munitions factory during the second world war, she lost her little finger, as it was trapped in a machine, and no more was I told, or invited to ask, and rarely we saw her, except as if ceremoniously she would be rolled out each Christmas for a visit of several days, a visit my mother would complain of in advance for several weeks, and somehow, mysteriously, continue to complain after she had left, and why she quite hated her so, I never did find out, but I wonder, what exactly had gone on, when just after my parents married on the coast, that sometime after that, they went to stay in Manchester, but I have no idea how long for. But her complaints seemed to include nothing more, though incredibly 30 years post event to her, the inconvenience remained raw, "I would peg the washing out on the washing-line, and when it came in, it was dirtier than when it went out," and "Your father's mother boils a cabbage whole in one pan." And never did I enquire, but then as a young child "Why would I" that of all she spoke, with such intense hatred of it all, but as an adult, I wonder of her significance "Was that all a rouse, to redirect it and pass her hatred toward me?"

But alternatively, my great Aunt Mary was never really mentioned at all, and if a blood relative, I don't even know, and nothing more I know of her, but how extraordinarily delightful she was and what a wonderful old lady, and how incredibly, she touched something so gentle and protected within me, as short in stature, with a dress code of a certain panache, of the design dated, reminiscent of the 1940s, and wonderfully I encountered her at such a young age, as it gave rise to a changed perspective, for my father never mentioned his family not ever, not even the history of his mother, not once ever did he mention his childhood either, but "Was I to be challenged in my belief?" as I liked Auntie Mary straight away, though I knew it not by name, her spirit, appeared light-hearted, she happy and contented, "So was there some kindness surrounding him, and could that be transferred to me?"

But alas, of cause, in my desperate and naïve days, it was never to be, as he fleeting tenderness, from that day, when she gave me a magnificent dress, from Marks and Sparks in blue metallic, that fit me so beautifully, and a little card she gave to me, such was her impact on that tiny child, me, that as many times as I have moved location, of house, continent, hemisphere or over the dateline, I have always held tight to the tiny gift card she gave me, as each time her I read her inscription, I was transported back, to that magical moment, when I felt special, I felt loved, I felt liked, and I felt accepted as never before, and so significantly, nearly 50 years on, I still hold that little card dear, as it reminds me of her genteelness she showed to me, and that single moment, captured in time.

The positive emotions associated with such warm-heartedness, striking but so in misery was I, remaining so sadly insufficient to weave its way into my psyche, so unable was it to survive, perhaps subconsciously I felt unworthy, or perhaps I had already at that tender age, learnt to condemned myself, as already found guilty as charged by the judge and jury of my mother and father. And in the house, 'his house' as we were always told, inline with his Victorian values, of 'children should be seen and not heard,' where never a civil word was heard, no love was held, no laughter to cradle, only silence of the deafening kind, with the only exception, of colossal and virulent shouting.

How terribly sad, that outwardly my father loved only money and what it could buy him, as his family and she who he married and the children he bore, his emotions of such, unworthy, nay inconvenient to his concerns, as we were only casualties of his inner-war he fought, likely daily, but of it, "Was he winning or loosing?" Yet I contemplate, trapped within him, was there the remanets of an emotionally injured child trapped inside, and unable possibly to deal with his injuries, and not recognizing how to recover, or simply not trying to hard enough, or using the wrong strategy, to break his chains and curses from so many moons ago, but his format seemed incorrect, as mindlessly and needlessly, he seemed minimally by default, maximally by trying no better, but either way, his rational unknown, my requirements superfluous, his love illusive, my existence sorrowful, and all of the above, he passed them all on to me.

So the years rolled on, and of my father's catalyst for change, for his choices of cruelty surpassing those of love, I never did discover, maybe a primal instinct to protect himself, or perhaps ignorance or simple indulgence or selfishness, but of all his striving, inwardly partitioning himself to achieve all that which they naysayers told him he could not, but until he chose to stop his battle, and chose to start to heal, for himself, "Would he ever find personal-growth or freedom or peace?" Perhaps unlikely, for under those circumstances of perpetuating the same hostility that was done to you onto others, as all around you remained the same, so a better way of life, he would never, be able to call its name.

"Too often we underestimate the power of touch, a smile, a kind word, a listening ear, an honest complaint, all of which have potential to turn a life around."
~ Leo Buscaglia

But all too innocent or was that naïve, for during those years, I held not a clue, of what I was being 'put through,' but the revelation was to reveal itself one day, when a bullseye was to come along my way, in the form of a medical report, from a doctor concerned with the mind, the psychiatrist kind, who I was commanded to see, as part of the process of the legal action I had taken against my employer the local Health Authority, for my lower back injury which I had sustained, but from it, not recovered.

Yet through all, I had managed to save my house, but eat, well pretty much I had to give that luxury away, for I had not the money or the ability to walk the short distance to the shops, and to stand and prepare the food, well increased pain would kick in, as for not even a few minutes I could stand in one place, so it was jam sandwiches that transferred to my stable diet, but I did not complain, for I was safe from the beatings of men, and the 'roof over my head,' I did sustain.

Then one fine day, a revelation, as a physiatrist report popped through the door, from that doctor, which I expected not to see, but there it was in front of me, so a seat I took upon the staircase, my favourite place to sit, a hidden, quite spot in my terraced-house, and as I opened the letter and commenced to read, with medical jargon, and all seemingly normal and easily understood, until my eyes gazed fixed, staring, unbelieving at the incomprehensible sentence, where a new realm having opened up as if in fairyland, where nothing was any longer as it seemed, as there in front of me in that legal document, it was stated, that I, *me*, as a child, I was abused. "WHAT! WHAT! WHAT!"

"WHAT?" Was that Psyche doctor confused and thinking, quite obviously he'd made a mistake as on that 3rd step up my preferred, over and over I reread those words, "This young lady was severely abused as a child," uncomfortably stirring, twitching and wiggling, trying so hard to make sense of that succinct sentence, believing, "No!" Absolutely that can't be right! He must be wrong! Surely I knew, I had never been told I was beautiful, pretty or cute, never had anyone utter the words, "I'm proud of you," and be called a Princess, certainly not, but as an effective prescription relevant to my life, that I, me, was abused. Absolutely absurd! Impossible to comprehend, I was an adult, I was a Registered Nurse, so surly, 'if' I would have suffered such, "Wouldn't I have been aware of it? Have recognized it? Wouldn't I have known it? Wouldn't I have been aware of it?" But, that was to be an absolutely resounding, "No!"

Squirmed and unsettled, standing up, walking around, sitting down, not quite knowing what to do or what to do, considering, 'surely that doctor had misunderstood me,' as 'he jumped to conclusions,' and as I continued to think how "He must be wrong." as paced about my little house, for all those horrendous things that happened to me, that were done against me, and forced on me without my consent, incredibly, at last, my suffering and pain was given a name, a title, a diagnosis, "Oh my!" "Was I to be reborn afresh and free?" or "Was that hate, harbouring inside of me, so deeply entrenched, nay intrinsic, was it to continue to be part of me?" or "In a most bizarre way, should I now celebrate, as for the first time in my life, how astoundingly grateful I was, for I had received validation, for all that in my life, I had gone through?"

But then perhaps, should I have known of this deception, or was I at last receiving a well over due explanation, for my parents or myself, perhaps I would not have purchased my first class ticket on the 'blame train' and settled myself in so nicely, tucking up my feet, which never could I do at home, and that word I use most loosely. And, included in the price I paid a buffet, 'as much as you can eat' free for consumption, to feast on a diet of resentment and bitterness, lack of respect for self and others, with aspects harm to be readily dispatched, and delivered to each, on platters with unhealthy portions of denial, fuelling a fire, of shame and guilt, yet worst of all, in their most formidable capacity not to dwindle sufficiently, "Did they not pose as most oppressive companions to peace and forgiveness?"

> *"Ordinary riches can be stolen, real riches cannot. In your soul are infinitely precious things that cannot be taken from you."*
> ~ Oscar Wilde

The swinging sixties the decade I was born, and living in that three bedroom dethatched house, when I was only young, and my father wore tailored suits and brought a brand new car every year, and before the days of credit cards, so perhaps not a person would have presumed my instructions each morning, "Go to the cupboard and get one of those little blue pills." But those, so tiny and round, I had to pinch them tight between my fingers so they did not fall out, but left to take them on my own, I would suck of the powder-blue enteric coating, that which protects them to be digested later on in the digestive tract, and when I did so, like sweets they were, and what a treat, for we were never given those, but then, a bitter taste would enter my mouth, so out I would spit it, and the reason I was given it, as my mother so often complained resiting *her* inconvenience, "At the age of 7, you were the most mentally disturbed child the doctor had ever seen!"

But an interesting part of that all, those pills were only for me, as my brother didn't take them, and never before had I experienced something, 'just for me,' and somehow, it felt kind of special, kind of nice, as never had I received personal attention from my mother before, and of it, I liked it. But for her, apparently it was not reciprocated, for knowing the truth, still, nothing did she do to change or improve my circumstances. Yet so young, I held no significance to the fact that my auntie, my mothers sister, 6 years younger, had divorced her husband just because he was boring, but my mother, to protect me or save me from harm, would not even walk the distance between the front door and the street, and I, always knew somehow, that I was an inconvenience to her, and of that true extent I was to see, when 3 decades later, she was to come to my doorstep, and ceremoniously disown me.

So innocent, so young, so helpless, so hopeless, really, was no one to help me, not at Church not at school, was I ever to be like driftwood, passing from one raging current to the next, battered from bank to the other, spliced, colliding with rocks of jagged edges on route, tossed, tattered and torn, no harbour, not even a sheltered crevice for comfort, no life raft to call my own, no net to call safe, to be rescued I was not, a resource to help myself I was unable to find, and not even a mother, for she was part of the problem, never to love or protect me.

And "When was that day to be, when I was to come home and find her, with her head in the oven?" and "Believe she would do it?" Absolutely so! For she repeatedly told me so, and according to her it was to be all be my fault, my penance, as she'd continue, her spiteful tale of mockery and sneering adding pain to my deep wound within, where incredibly, more could be added and remain, as so often was her critical acclaim, "Yes, then you'll be sorry, and your brother will come off worse, because he always does, and it will be all *your fault*, and you're father, well, he'll take you to live with his mother in that dirty and horrible grimy place, Manchester, and you won't like that, then what will you do, you'll be all alone, and don't think for one minute he'll let you see your grandma, because he won't, and you'll be worse without me there to protect you!" "Was she kidding?" That was "No!" But then I was too young to speak or consider such a notion to the contrary, and with no information to rebuttal it, her seeds sewn, I simply believed every word she said.

Then pausing, only momentarily, before continuing along with her regular raging rant, "It's your fault that I had to give up Night Scholl! Because you were too frightened to be left alone with your father! So I had to stay home to be with you." And that was true, and that was my fault too, as was apparently everything bad or inconvenient that happened was, and those bad things yet to come the same, were also to be, as she clearly pointed out, somehow, all-my fault. But "Oh my" "How could someone so young cause so much harm and how?" I never did work it out. And I like an empty vessel, just accepted those seeds that were planted in me, and with daily affirmations of the same, they grew, for whatever it is, good or bad, gentle or evil, those seeds will multiply and grow, and of all her stories told, they were done so with such seeds of venom, delivered without a smile, and so sadly, not a one ended with, "And they all lived happily ever after."

"Follow your honest convictions and stay strong."
~ William Thackeray

Documented, in black and white, my hands almost trembling, my insides unreservedly doing so, as I tried to contrive, a format for which compartment in my brain I was to place that portion of knowledge in, for it was fresh and new, I had no previous experience or evidence for where it should go. "With it, what I should do?" As I dissected and digested those episodes of childhood devastation, "Was I even worthy of a title or a diagnosis?" or more, really, "Had that doctor, simply got it wrong?" Yet in *TRUTH* he'd shone a light in a darkened place, one I knew not of its existence, of the harm done to me, that of each stroke of the hand, or the fist, each word spoken, delivered with such immense toxic and corrosive scorn, so acutely influential through those tentative years, in their fullness, erupting hopelessness, helplessness, anguish, self-loathing, self-hatred and tears, sufficient to have 'cried me a river,' perhaps an ocean, where only emotional pain reigned, and "Oh my" the sweetness of humble validation, but "Oh, what bitterness!"

Release! As I began to digest what I'd read, distress rose up from the deepest of my inner-core, and flowed effortlessly out, as after several minutes passing, I began to cry hollering, desperate for help, as those hindering, binding and crippling emotions that were so securely entrenched within, those that I was so familiar with tried so desperately to escape their confines, as that tender little girl, trapped inside that damaged adult, relief was to come, as life a bolt of power, a sudden realisation, with force, hurtled and whirled upwards, expanding and spiralling out, that 'she' and 'he' who had done 'that to me' were both absolutely and utterly wrong, as wrong as could be, as *"It was not all my fault what happened to me, I was innocent, guilty of no sin."* Yet "Relief? Did it bring me any?" So devastatingly sadly, there was none.

Spanning almost 3 decades, I was found guilt, but of what, being born, and agony and torment just 2 suppressed companion, where I understood so little of so much, of life, relationships, but predominantly love. "Could I heal? Could I ever be free?" or "Were such questions premature? Was I ever to stop so timidly trembling, when a piece of food fell off my fork onto my plate?" or "I spilt water on the kitchen bench, as expecting, waiting for that hit with force from his hand to land upon me?" or "Was I ever to be able to relax in my own house, put my feet up or grab a duvet, and slumber, to slouch in a chair, sometime before I arrived in my 30's?" "Oh my" how astoundingly marvellous that would have been, to even dare to do it, or without fear of being hit, or accused of slovenly behaviour, the latter just about a 'hit-able offence,' and to lean with my chin resting on my hand most definitely was, for then, "Stop biting your fingernails" was shrieked as an accompaniment, my father knocked my arm violently out from beneath me.

As to turn a light switch off, "Be careful!" For it was almost impossible, to do without fear, wondering from which corner 'he' was to come, to hit me once more, accusing me of not taking care, and dirtying the paintwork around the door, and a door would I ever be able to open one, without fearing that his hand was to come and swipe at me, from really anywhere, for really everywhere was his hiding place, as he crept around, and never did I know, at any given moment, of 'his' choosing, I was to be accused of 'dumb insolence' and at a glance, a swing with an instantaneous sting as his hand swiped across my face. "Oh my" what a web he weaved of violent authority, for me to be scared of him, and so I was, and that 'flight or fight' mechanism to protect me, with such total immersion in gross emotions encapsulated by anxieties and fear, trapped in my mind, and fed since the age of 3. Damage so severely done, my recovery, I determined that was due, in process, it was not magical, but it was, achievable.

"Don't spend time beating on a wall, hoping to transform it into a door."
~ Coco Chanel

Desperate, I reached out for help, there was only onetime, and once was enough to teach me, what a futile exercise it was to be, as it was not understanding I received from that popular girl, blonde and petite in structure who sat always on the back row in class, and why I told her, I really don't know, but there I was at 13 years, the first time I had ever mentioned anything to anyone other than my mother, who of cause already knew, and as I told that girl what my life was like and what my father was doing, quite quickly she became so hostile, and although we never talked, even though we were in the same class, for some reason I was to confide in her, and somehow, it was another punishment I was to receive, as in the playground with everyone around, her words of condemnation left her mouth, fuelled with anger as she shouted, "Liar, liar, shut up you're a liar, no one does that!" But "What!" How could that be, that wasn't right, for she was from the 'other side of the tracks' as my mother always said, and such people were 'this and that' so I felt sure she'd understand, but "No, alone, how could I get it so wrong?"

I had mustered the courage to speak, I had found it from deep within, but she angry with me, pinned me against the cold brick wall of the quad and forcing my torso, bending it forward, immobilising it, within her bent body over it, and then up and down she threw her punches, as my arm I tried to use for protection. But it was not physical pain that was to serve me so ill, it was emotional, for only that once, ever, did I try to come out of my shell, and speak about the unspeakable, trapped so deep inside, yet then, was I really to consider that my father was right, that no one will believe me if I speak, and so incredibly unfortunately, her actions, certainly sanctified his, and I remained accused, and found guilty again, when I was lost and so helpless, but between them they did a good job, a final job, for I shut right up, or was that right down, drowning, plummeting like a piece of dead and cold iron to the pit in the ground, void of feelings or possibilities, nowhere ever to turn again, no one to listen, no one to explain anything to, yet I knew not, that I was, "Dead girl walking."

Time was to pass, that great healer and revealer of us much, before the contents of that letter marinated on the inside of me, and I'm guessing with some realisation of 'what was what,' I began to open up, to tell a friend who I'd met several years earlier while nursing during my 'paediatric placement' on the Burns Unit, who came to visit my tiny terraced house, void of damp, as in the little living room we sat, on my £35 lounge set, a 2 seater with 2 matching chairs, solid square in shape with low backs and quite tough brown hessian fabric with a narrow cream horizontal and vertical lines going through it, I bought from a flee market, how well it fit that space and how terribly proud I was to have it.

Then sitting as comfortably as we were able, sharing a glass of mellow, quite weak wine really, as I would tell her tales of woe from so long ago, and as she listened, shocked, often would she become, for never in all her history or experience had she met another, who had been through the experiences I had, and quite astounded and with intent to support her words of affirmation, "It's amazing that you've turned out as normal as you have." "What a relief!" For her to think that of me, for I so highly respected her, and a happy family she came from, and many friends she had, good at her career, so well balanced was she, criticizing no one, not even when quite possibly, it would not have been unreasonable to do, and so grateful is my memory of her, as over and over she was there to support me emotionally, as my traumas, that unfolded in my life, I was unable to get around, for I held no emotional or stable base to return to.

"Oh why?" I mused, when there are so many variations on the best teaching methods, "Oh why could I not be a dolphin?" OK, I say in jest, though really their type of training, 'Operant Conditioning,' developed by BF Skinner, which basically means, 'positive reinforcement' is used, as punishment is never given for getting anything wrong, and praise, treats and affirmations are given when something is gotten right, and with whimsical imaginings of a childhood completely different, "Oh!" how I sighed; and musing more, composing notions in my mind, as it is good enough for dolphins why was it not good enough for me and why did my father not think, that I was worthy of that also, instead of inducting me into a school, not of praise but punishment, not positive but destructive, where I was confined to that status of stupid, worthless, and each and everyday, worth-less!

Living beneath a doctrine of fear, not easy, delivered by he, my father who was supposed to protect me, and so pervasive were his negative attributes, that it was not only he, but all men I learnt to instinctively, intuitively distrustful, for all I perceived to harm me, and "Why not?" As my brother had his own little ways of nasty behaviours to affect me, deliberately, inadvertently, but for sure dishonestly, my grandad, he too processed ways that were less than admirable in the way he treated my grandma, and men in general, all twisted and torn within myself, I tared them all with the same brush, harbouring festering and utter distain of contempt fort them, while resolute, respectful of none though fearful, of them all.

So 'many a man' was to pay the price for what my father had done, but I was the one who paid the most ultimate price, as should a 'nice, respectful, caring or honourable man' trouble himself to pursue me or idle a while in my vicinity, I was sure to send him away quite unpleasantly, recognising not his strength of character, but purely misguided, misjudging unknowingly considering his persona as deficient and weak, and how terribly terribly sad that false belief served me, prohibiting my recovery and sending me far down the wrong track. Mostly it was 3 decades that were to pass, before I saw the error of my ways, and then it was regret that set in, for the terribly terribly significant *faux par's* that I had participated in. So non-progressive and non-productive inhibiting my hope for future, as geographically I'd moved away, but my GPS signal was still tuned into all my parents used to do and say, holding me back, lost, trapped, unable to find my way out to find my route, to take me far away, to a place safer and brighter, where a good man, I could value.

Yet emotionally and physically within relationships with men, I had good cause to pause and mistrust them, so desired none, for my father with me a relationship with me, he wanted not, and to what extent a surprise was to come to make that notion astoundingly relevant, as on one Saturday when my brothers 18th birthday was approaching, a big deal back in the day, and my father's enquiry to him, "When do you want your 'coming of age,' now, or when your 21?" Well of cause my brother chose the former, as was the developing tradition for his celebration, and my father, having decided what he was to buy him, was to take my brother to the shop that morning to choose one, and shortly before he walked out of the door, an instruction he gave for me to accompany them, surprised, but quickly abiding, I grabbed my coat and swiftly put it on.

Poulton-Le-Fylde, a small but growing village, of ancient, and some petite buildings dating back a couple of centuries or more, with a magnificent church at the centre of everything, and there we stood, on that narrow footpath, where passers-by and their dogs brushed against me, and the three of us, spanning the full window width of that quaint shop, as we peered viewing the polished antique jewellery it sold, and there before us an array of a 'gold sovereigns,' an investment they were perceived to be and from a bygone era, a value of English currency. Some sold separately and displayed on top of little velvet pockets, in rich reds, blues or greens, all associated with monarchies, while many were mounted in rings or hanging on pendant chains, all in an array of various settings, while some had been made into earrings, but that was not my brothers thing, and it must be said, all quite trendy back in the day, and in price amounting to quite a 'pretty penny.'

The window so small, the three of us covered its breadth, filled with such beautiful things visible in my sight, admiring miniatures of watercolours and silhouettes all displayed in the finest frames with glass and crockery of pretty followers and delicate designs or resting on antique crocheted doilies formatted as if in a strikingly plush Victorian dining room. Yet sill, it seemed so mighty peculiar, really "Why?" I was included in that little event too, as I was not to reach that age for another year and a half, that was until, those words suddenly, passed my fathers lips, not spoken softly or with remorse, not with a tinge of regret nor even a tad of anger, nothing; "No" his words, void of any emotion, only the facts were given, and not even saying my name, because he never addressed me by that, but believe me, by his voice, his tone, his pitch, his projection, I always knew when he was speaking to me, for it was significantly most prudent to do so, for making such a folly to miss it, could likely result a in a punishment, and there in that busy street, mulling with weekend shoppers, nonchalantly his phrase delivered, "You better choose one too, because *I won't know you,* you won't be in *my life,* when *you* turn 21!" "Was he kidding?" "Oh my!" "No!"

"Surreal?" "Not really." "Did I believe him?" "Oh absolutely!" "Was there torment or anguish?" "You may think, but NO!" Should I have screamed, "WHAT?" and "Was I not to wonder, because of what he said, should I not have crumbled in the street or cried uncontrollably or minimally been mesmerised? Why did he choose that moment in that location, did he mean to surprise, shock, injure, the most or maybe the least?" But "No," unperturbed, it was life as usual in the reams of living in 'my life.' It was simply more of the same just wrapped up in a different way, as the same as his smacks and his thumps, his pushing and pulling, his knocking me here and there, his threats of fists, that I knew he was good for, landing on my face, it was 'just another' splotch in my life, likely designed by him, my father, who my mother refused to let me forget, that his blood ran in my veins, aka, I was just a chip off the old block, to cause me maximum havoc, that's of cause, assuming that he troubled himself to place that much thought into it. Like a whirlwind causing emotional distress, I was used to it, and perhaps quite immuned to it, but then rationally, as such injuries, hurting on the inside where the wounds are not visible on the outside, so much harm had been done and so many layers of smarting, stinging, distraught distress piled on, and with such velocity, it was difficult to feel the weight of an extra one.

My 'lot in life,' "Was that to be prophecy to come true, that such neglect of any emotional wellbeing was to be cast against me, as that was to be the only sum of my worth?" How terribly sad, that in my world such apparent abnormalities portrayed as normal, carried on unchallenged, perhaps its no wonder why my communication skills were zero, and my trust of people sunk to a value even less than that, but maybe the saddest part of all, that the information my farther gave me, on that day, in the middle of that village, my life as I knew it, uninterrupted, unperturbed, not missing a beat, as the severity of it all, simply slipped right off, like the water off a ducks back.

> *"My life didn't please me, so I created my life."*
> ~ Coco Chanel

Weeks turned into months, and months into years as I progressed through adolescence into young adulthood, when 'he' true to his word disappeared from my life before I'd reached the age of 19 years. "Good?" Surely it must have been, for wasn't that what I always wanted, or was it that I simply wanted the pain to go away? But he was my father and so him, I desired to know, so a letter I wrote, and a reply came back stating a time and place, to him, and I agreed. It was a pub, where he told me to go, on a busy Friday night, so I enquired "Where's your favourite spot and where shall I find you?" To be told sharply, "I don't have one, I'll be anywhere I choose be and you'll just have to keep looking until you find me!" And so I did, though back in the days, it wasn't the 'done thing' for a lady to walk in a pub unaccompanied, that pub was packed, filled to the rafters with people enjoying frivolity, as I weaved my way through the people with "Excuse me" being muttered loudly more than once, and spying my father stood leaning on the bar, I pushed through the crowd to meet him, yet not a muscle did he move to accommodate me to squeeze in a little into a space, nor exhibited on his face, a trace of acknowledgement of my arrival with 6 months passing since we last saw each other, time it appeared had not pertained to mellow his staunch attitude, or adorn a higher regard toward his daughter.

Mild hostility he portrayed, with certainly a high degree of superiority in displayed with a tad of condemnation thrown in, but for him, non struck me as unusual, his silence, one hand resting on his drink, he just stared at me waiting for me to begin, making it abundantly clear, that of niceties of small-talk or catching-up, he certainly was not to adhere, so as everyone was around me, happy, pushing and jolting me, trying to get served, stomach churning, bypassing the vibe to me my father was giving, I delivered my question, unrehearsed, "You're my father, *please* will you have a relationship with me, can we see each other sometime?" My stomach retching, it could of done as I waited upon his response, as a pregnant pause ensued, perhaps for effect, though likely deliberately, for that way he held the control, then, not nonchalantly, but precisely, decisively, with his eyes staring coldly into mine and the corners of his mouth, contort and turning down, with precision, succinctly, his reply he delivered, "No!" Him pausing, perhaps to gloat, or awaiting my emotion or petition for him to reconsider, but I knew him from old, and his parting line, dismissing me in disgrace, "You had your chance and you blew it, I don't and wont have a relationship with you at all, your dead to me!"

My stomach, it had been jumping into my throat, but then, with a thud, it fell to the floor, and the 'going-rate' for him to annihilate his daughter, less than 5 short minutes, but true, not a record for him, he must have been slipping. "Was I shocked?" Certainly not! "Surprised?" Not that either. But I was to wonder, for annihilating his daughter in less than 5 very short minutes, of himself, "Was he proud?" Despise and disgust and an inflated personal reverence, those emotions displayed on his face, his preferred intention, that I clearly read them, yet then in an instant, everything became so transparent, as realization stuck me, with his perversion of character, his purpose for agreeing to that meeting, was not for a reconciliation, as never could he bear to have me around, to see my face or hear my voice, "Why he hated me so?" I never did learn, but I was pretty sure that evening he'd achieved his goal, to watch me squirm, and as I left that place his displayed expression slightly altering to an unpleasant concoction of indifference with contempt and condescension, and that man, whose blood runs in my veins, he, my father, I was never, to see again.

Holding back the tears with all my might, I was to fight my way out of that bustling pub and into the coldness of the night air, but really was I ever to successfully fight my way out of all the pain and debauchery that he had caused me through the years, and true, it was a facet of my life that as yet had not dawned on me, so at that point, I had never posed the question or summarised the answer, of when or how could I ever accept what he had done to me and from it all, when to be free from it all, finally, was I to be? But could I? For his DNA was in me, he was apart of me, that very thought produced tangible pain, his callus of malice, his apparently of hate of me, spinning around me so greatly, it could have made me dizzy.

But "*If* I was to hate him, with so much of him inside me, did that really mean I was hating me?" So many moons were to pass, 3 decades actually, before I was to see a wonderful dramatization of a novel entitled "He Knew He Was Right." In it, the husband, the father, commenced doing some mean and rotten things, and his son, only a little boy, already worried that he would do the same horrible things as his father, but how caring his mother, as she crouched down before him, and holding his arms gently reassuring him, with love she looked in his eyes and not quite word exact, "You are the very best of parts of your father." "Wow! What a wonderful revelation, not guilty by blood, as my mother always told me I was, as truly I could be, the very best parts of *him*, and from thereon in, that's who I, was always going to be.

I had miss-judged that public transport timetable, or rather, I had miss-judged the time I was to spend with my father, as 90 minutes was to be my wait upon the bus, but really, I so wish I'd done a far better job at judging my father, as true his actions didn't surprise me, yet still, most unlike me, I didn't see them coming, I thought he was genuinely pleased to be meeting with me and I didn't realize he had a hidden agenda. That emotional physical pain, real, was what I was bearing, it hurt, and was not subsiding, and unable I seemed, in those following minutes to drastically 'pull myself together,' for there lay another problem, as I was on my way returning to the house where I lived, my mothers, and she so fervently *warned* me, "If *you ever dare*, to see your father, I will throw you out of here, so fast, that you're feet wont touch the ground!" Believe her? Absolutely!

The companion for her preferred regularly resited duo, as though really, I could ever forget, "*You* live 'under *my* roof' as a privilege, not a right, and you *obey my* rules, and remember, I can revoke that privilege any time I choose!" "Believe her?" Well of cause! For already before she left my father's house she had tried to throw me out twice. In fact, one day she did just that, telling me on morning "Be out by the evening and take all your 'things' with you, or they will be in the dustbin." "Believe her?" Certainly! But not that night, as my horrendous secret from her I concealed, and took all the time I needed as I strolled, as so desperately I just kept on going, trying so hard to walk off that pain, and as the headlights from oncoming vehicles shone brightly in tear stained face, as if they all knew the truth, I'd hang my head in shame, as tears tumbled down.

How careful I had to be when I walked through her door, really hoping that as I spoke after all that crying, a crackly voice wouldn't give me away, and as I entered the hallway, avoiding going into the lounge and commencing to climb up the stairs, a shout came from her, "Why are you not coming in to see me?" Something I said appeased her, and I was able to go straight to my bed, and "Oh how I needed it?" I was exhausted, it took me 2 hours to walk all the way back, hiding in doorways or bushes, so dog walkers and others weren't able to see the sobs, of those tremendous torrents of tears, erupting from my heart, breaking.

So quietly I cried, I daren't let my mother hear, but "Why wasn't I allowed to see my father and still have a place to stay under her roof?" and "Why would she throw me out because of it?" Yet 'oh how very contraire' of a seemingly double standard going on, as reverse was the case a couple of years earlier, when my father was to throw my brother at the age of 20, out of the marital home, onto the street, and to protect my brother from that, she took the huge action to see the Solicitors to start divorce proceedings. More sobs as I laid in bed and images of memories flooded my head, for why would she do that for my brother, when he had an enormous amount of friends to lean on, and my grandparents the same and she did that for security and safety for him, but so unequally, ignoring the plight of my life, where only suffering, hurt and fear were rife, when at 7 years take those little blue pills I was by the doctor told to take, but to protect me, she did nothing, not even trouble herself to walk, as far as the garden gate.

But "Was I to give up?" Absolutely not! For a story I was to call to mind, of a donkey unwanted, considered useless and superfluous to requirements, and when he fell in a pit, those who were supposed to take care of him, chose to not to, as the donkey was left there to die, and worse, to get rid of it faster, the one who should have been first inline to do such a thing in fact to do the opposite, as a he shovel he took up and began throwing dirt on top of the poor donkey, to cover it and make the problem go away. But the donkey, believing in himself and smarter than the owner, hatched a strategic plan to help himself and turn that adversity around, so when each amount of dirt was shovelled upon him, quickly he trampled it down beneath his feet, and as he carried on, doing the same with everyone, maybe tired but still, refusing to give up, to everyone's amazement, that depth of the pit he was in became shallower and shallower, as the donkey was rising up higher and higher, and all the way up out of that ditch, he managed to get himself, and then, just a couple of extra steps, and with them, there he was on solid ground, and he was able to walk, safe and clean away; and of all those onlookers who'd stood-by and watched his suffering and adversity, so surprised were they, at that wonderful accomplishment and a good job well done, as that captive was set free.

So I, I made a choice, with increasing empowerment, that belief in myself that somehow shone through, I was to rise, up high, as I was to learn to leave all the blame, all the shame, all their rejections, their hurts, neglect and abandonment of behind me, refusing to continue to walk in their world, for I was determined to walk in my own, increasingly so was to manufacture, to make a brand new life just for me. And "Why?" For like the donkey, I jolly well deserved; to survive, then, thrive!

> *"If you were born without wings, do nothing to prevent them from growing."*
> ~ *Coco Chanel*

Then as I walked on by, I was quietly mesmerized by all those buildings with boarded up windows, in streets of only 3 houses long, would make for such a good business for me, but then again I though I unable to survive in that, well at least in my mind, quiet unremarkable *ville*. But I was not to give up straight away, still eager for what it had left to reveal, and as I wheedled my way back to the hotel, a different route I took and with the sunrays giving way to dusk, it was an amazing architectural treat, a feat of industrial engineering I happened upon, the spectacular splendour of a design fit for purpose, a Viaduct, tall and imposing, slashing through the vista of the landscape, functional in its requirements to transport goods and men around the countryside, it appeared first as a canal, but then possible transferred to accommodate trains, all with greater speed and ease, and like the rest of the mini-town, as history and change did overspill, and in our lives, we need to take care, for never, does time stand still.

Its vision pure *magnifique,* magnificent as the night light was drawing in, so I paused to marvel and admire its large sweeping structure as it curved across the landscape, bold while mildly domineering, yet softened in its presentation, as generous beams of light, cast high and bright creating dazzling shadows against its ancient stone, in shades of gleaming yellow through to deep terracotta, which that marvel of engineering from back in the day, was absolutely so rightly it dissevering, to display the simplicity of excellence of its natural beauty.

How poetic it all seemed, and as I commenced to leave the vision of the Viaduct, crossing over the small bridge on which I stood, the Church bells that began to chime such a sweet melody, and as I continued to stroll with a spring in my step and a lightened heart as my companions, a smile suck up and embellished my face, as it occurred to me, how absolutely marvellously, my health had surpassed all my expectations on that day, with ill health avoided and not a small feat I must say, because as the sunbeams slipped away, and the stars came out to play I was so pleased that my energy remained so high; but another note that quickly became obvious, my outfit, with the casting of shadows in that small *ville* it quite apparently appeared a little risqué, and certainly no-longer fit-for-purpose as it had been some hours earlier, so making a wise choice, I was to deliberate less on those favourite topics of mine, the ebbs and flows of industrial, medical and social histories, as I hasten my return to that, only-just purposeful hotel, where I was to be safe and a change of clothes was on the menu.

Yet the night, it seemed somehow still young, at 7pm so with a quick change of apparel, well just the denim, from skirt to jeans, I was to grab my *ordinateur,* computer, and there, ready to explore a little more, I was armed, just in case I found a place I could get some work done. And so in the opposite direction I walked, and passed the first bar on the corner, which appeared full of young people, having a really good time, and the atmosphere, felt really safe and congenial, but never would I get some work done, so up the road I carried on, then, there in front of me, that hotel, that on the net I so wanted to stay bout of its location and proximity to the station, I could not work out, and more, the price, 60E a night, and that for 3, plus tax 100E, add tax, add 35% exchange, and even more, plus premium for credit card use, and there, a decision not to stay where I really desired to. But really, was I positively being a spendthrift and watching my pennies-make-pounds as my granddad would say, or was I just unnecessarily, being mean to me along my way.

"Oh what a beautiful place" it was one of those, as soon as you walk in you feel right at home, and "Oh my" how I could have done with some of that, and as a most pleasant a *Maître d'Hôtel*, head waiter, was to seat me, as I requested the usual, the red wine menu, it was to eventuate that I was to receive service quite exceptional, for seeing my computer, he asked in such proficient English, "Would you like to use the Conference room?" Well, *"Merci beaucoup*, that will be extremely nice." And so I accepted, and his kindness continued, as I began to enquire of the wines on the list, for some I had not come across before, then he enquiring of my wine preferences, and I quite surprised myself at how much I had learnt, not only the product knowledge but also my preferences I acquired along the way, for I had no idea I had become such a connoisseur, and such a pleasure I was to receive as he graciously offered to let me sample a few.

"Oh my" never had I been treated so well, as upon the conference table, lined up stylish crisp sparkling glasses and the fresh uncorked bottles behind, and with his white crisply starched napkin draped over his arm, and another wrapped around the neck of the bottle, in turn, each he picked up, and poured professionally into a glass of distinction, and with each he poured, rolling the wine around the glass, admiring its bouquet before sipping and tantalizing my palate, and so generous he was with his information of the region, the grape, even the soil and the particulars of the harvest, and how all in turn effected the flavour and maturity of all, I was to try. For his kindness I knew not, or why I was given the very best treatment, and gratefully I received the best of service. I was a novice, but I felt special, I felt validated and appreciated, I had never experienced such before, but what I already knew of it, I liked it and I wanted more.

For sure, I have no idea of his rational, I just knew that I liked it a lot, and in future that is the kind of service I chose to aspire to and accept, and one more thing, I wonder, as I was high on life that evening, for sure, I had achieved a 100% of my to-do list, I remained healthy and with energy, I discovered a place I wanted to be and felt good being there, evidentially, proving that some system inside of me, is worthy, right and correct, and that so much aided my confidence, and I focused on that, and not everything that had turned out to be a little less than perfect and maybe a little wrong, so just maybe, it was a resort to the new, I had learnt earlier that day, "That what you think of yourself, others will too, and they will like a mirror image, treat you that same way."

So I began to reassess of my nature, how it does appear sometimes that people mistake my meekness for weakness, of how people will treat me not well, but "Is that only for I permit then to do so?" I reflected on my hotel room in Toulouse, where for my 3 night stay where the electric blind was stuck, broken, insufficient to let in the natural light for the day, necessary for my writing, for I loath artificial light, or sufficient to block out the exterior lights of the night, and how, my friend in Paris who works at a rather fancy hotel, in proximity to the *Champs Elysées*, told me, when things are not as they should be, that customers, to gain compensation, regularly complain, and surely in stores that's what we do. So surely, at my hotel, "With confidence, I should have requested with a generous helping of self-worth, at least a complementary continental breakfast, or a Spa treatment perhaps, and not been put-off by the unhelpful and rude, dismissive staff, to ensure I received in equal value, that which I had paid for?" So gladly, I concluded, perhaps that wonderful encounter of happenstance was there to teach me a lesson, to learn to shift my mind-pattern, to make it new, for is it true, "Before *anything* can change, *first,* we have to change our own minds?"

Of that beautiful hotel where I was treated so well, I so wanted more, but for me, it was off down the road 500 yards away, I was to go, while pondering the conundrums: A) Had the toilet been fixed? B) Could I have a shower that would last for longer than four minutes? 3) Was I to be woken at six o'clock the next morning by annoying and unnecessarily loud television? Well, that was unnecessary to me! Only time was to reveal, and soon, unfortunately I discovered the answers to be: No! No! Yes!

"Oh my" my tolerance for accepting situations that were not good, in fact those appearing on an unbalanced scale, sliding forever downwards, quite miserably so, and with it slid my comfort, and I, with each new lower levels I had sunk, which previously I thought impossible, but grew to accept as my new normal, where bargain basement wasn't something to relish, for a dollar saved here and there, but an uncomfortable necessity of life, and I wondered, how much more could I take, financially, emotionally, before a more determined choice I was to make, "Of what to do?" And for the second time that day, I contemplated "Do I give up or give in or turn back to return to where my journey began?" or "Do I continue on my way, facing adversity where necessary, of valleys low and mountains high and everything in-between?" and "Why not?"

As from its peak I would enjoy a view of crystal clarity, of those paths I had trodden, where my footprints of accomplishment were clearly etched within them, and through that process of my progression, resilience and persistence stood as sturdy companions by my side, as I became adapt, at mastering those unravelling circumstances, while that uncertain terrain and those pitfalls I was unaware of their location, but that held not a barrier to me, for still without a firm plan, yet indeed one for investigation, as I moved further away 'from where I was' and 'closer to where I chose to be,' I knew with an inner-determination of utter strength, somehow, until I succeeded in all my endeavours, I was to continue-on, to carry my own canoe.

Reflecting on 'observing thyn own behaviour first,' I was to wonder, were my criticisms of me, by me realistic or was I being too hard on me, unduly criticizing myself, as in the realms of finance and investment opportunities that lay ahead, simply, "Was I sensibly, doing what I needed to do, to preserve what I had, to make my business plan affordable, achievable and available to me. For that's only astute, right?" For surely the best reason, for my future, my dream, my endeavours, that must surely pose as a normal part of that process bearing fruit and coming to fruition. Surely, I was being wise, and 'cutting my pattern according to my cloth.'

A notion that is in stark contrast to scrimping in the wrong places and resulting in being penny-rich pound poor. For such a *faux pas*, and such a false economy, when travelling to Hawaii I saw the perfect purse for me, "Oh my" pink and metallic inside and out it was perfect for me, the right size and the right number of 'this and that' compartment for all I wanted to put in, "So why did I not buy it?" Because it was $10 more than I wanted to spend, adding up to 10% only. So that perfect item for me, I left the island without buying, and although I searched, it was to be 3 years more, before I was to find a purse that I liked, only half as much. Extravagance, false economy and value for money, so much more careful now working within my budget, as that was the very last time, I was to get those 3, mixed up.

Perhaps in my perceptions I needed to be more reasonable, level-headed or balanced, after all, "Was I developing a fear based mentality in regards to money, was my spending, predominately, all the wrong places, only adding to my fear of lack, giving birth to the notion of scarcity with my deepening concern for my future, of what was evolving, what was unravelling, what was taking so long, and when was I to find, 'the place' for my business, and what funds for the project, were still to be available?"

Yet, true, perhaps my worries were exacerbated, as all the travelling I was doing, of going here and there, of resting in sub-standard accommodation while I did so, perhaps part of the unease, my unrest was that I was searching all in the wrong directions, for really, "How did I allow myself to listen to such bad advice in Paris to be so easily swayed by those naysayers?" just "How could I have been so enormously off target?" and "Was the real reason for my unrest, my unease, a result, that I was too busy, frantically running around, all wrapped up in the nuances, of those situations, so failed to stand back and take a look, to surmise the *faux pas* afoot, as surely if I had, I would have recognized my physical bodily symptoms, and understood what they were telling me, "Hold up!" You're joining the wrong dots. You're drawing the wrong picture, as the picture you're manufacturing, doesn't look anything like the picture from your dreams. "Remember?" Those rolling hills of lilacs, in that land known as *Aix en Provence*, in southern France, where you're should be heading.

How misguided I must have been, so far off the mark, of my destination, the one that was in my sight, the one that set in my heart alight, so odd so strange so bizarre, so far off my beaten track, how could I ever hope to hit a bullseye with my target when not even in the vicinity of where I wanted to be had I then, not even ventured close to, to nestling down in that idyllic town, as unrequited was a melodic tune that was to play on the inside of me, as absent of pain or pleasure in my life, nothing to stimulate me into action, weary of my goal chasing, and after expending too much energy, for too long, searching in the all the *wrong places*, passively, it was mediocrity that turned out to be the jailer of me.

Preparing to leave *Albi*, where my research had revealed, that 'there wasn't the place for me to be,' and the possibly overrated 2 star property how I enjoyed my experience at the hotel, the nice one down the street that is, with the waiter the same, and the comfortable emotions and sense of calm and worth, I felt there, for sure, it taught me a little more about myself, how I could 'accept' when people are kind, accommodating or other such pleasant ways they extend to me, and not 'wonder' with worry, of that new experience, "What is it I'm supposed to do' and 'how much will they hate me if I get it wrong?" But so pleased I am to say, that those questions that created devastated emotions, as relax in situations I could not, as adrenaline was always battering my organs and my mind, as I struggled drastically to work out what in each instant I needed to. Yet no longer, for through my inner-growth, my self-worth has grown, and peace has become a companion of mine and freedom in such situations has been mine to gain.

"Oh my" how absolutely wonderful, I was already so much further along my journey than I ever anticipated or thought was possible, as from those British isles 12 years earlier I was to part, tough I held not an inkling back then, that my journey of adventures, to achieve inner-progress was just about to begin, and from there, the world that I lived in was wonderfully irrevocably to change, yet my journey of such great magnitude, held nothing to do with those 11,272 miles I was to travel by plane to New Zealand, for the journey I talk of, its length miniscule by comparison, though its significance, held such great magnitude as upon that journey I was to discover, that the bigger and better houses were I bought were incapable of filling my inner-void; and those clothes in my closet, posing only as ornaments, as I didn't wear them; nor that next new rung on my career ladder that had my name etched on it, insufficient to bring me happiness; and those primaries that used to be in my life, all faded in comparison, as that most important journey of all I was to make, and only a short 18 inches in length, was to reunite my head and my heart, and from there on in, to stray from such a notion or accomplishment, never, was I to depart.

Transformation, on the inside had begun, and what was dead, magnificently was being brought back to life, as from my past, I was to dissect the 'bad' and reconstruct it as 'good' and as that path I travelled upon, the more steps I took, that lingering emptiness and helplessness, that from *their* curses of spoken words, which I had accepted as limiting beliefs, as each one, set within me like stone, but then, as I traversed those 18 inches, and became far more enlightened, as I knew at last, for all those years, what they did was wrong, so of their concepts I was to start chipping away at them, and woe is me transposed to woe is them, for truly, I had discovered, that the acquisition of a whole array of items, was not to fill the void, or held the capacity to heal me on the inside, for effectually, those items only serve as a bandaid.

Interesting too, that those revelations did not come in a flurry, but slowly, and the make-up I dare not leave the house without, for truly it formed apart of my armour to hide behind, a mask to wear, so onlookers into my soul were unable to stare, and my ensemble of outfits, so pristinely put together, just in a hope, that somewhere by someone on that day, I may just be good enough for them to like me, nay, accept me would so, yet little by little, that fear and worry was to slip away, as the most magical thing of all, I began to like *me* and accept myself; and through those baby steps I was taking, I became strong, nurturing myself, as after all, that journey had taught me of it, I was, truly worthy.

True, I had a choice, I could choose to stay the same or I could choose to change, to change my thoughts, consequently changing my behaviours. Oh how I thrived. "Was it simple?" "Heck no!" "Yet was it worth it?" "Yes! Astoundingly wonderfully so." And as I grew to do, what served *me* the best, to do what improved *me* the most, to manoeuvre and make *my* efforts to count and amount to something, everything in effect, for my health, my future, my fortune and importantly, to help others, for they like me, deserved the very best of what I could possibly be, and with genetic and generational curses severed and destroyed, I was ultimately free, for I had discovered, and found, *me*!

> *"For beautiful eyes, look for the good in others; for beautiful lips, speak only words of kindness; and for poise, walk with the knowledge that you are never alone."*
> *~ Audrey Hepburn*

Chapter 16

Step Unconditionally

> "Change and growth take place when a person has risked himself and dares to become involved with experimenting with his own life."
> ~ Herbert Otto

Lost! Whirling within my own world, I became, swirling in ever-decreasing circles, consistently considering really, "Where to next?" and striving for a sensible answer, as my journey almost spontaneously transformed, but into "What?" no longer was I totally sure, and I was to more than casually ponder, of that notion given to me, written on my leaving card, as I left Blighty and the town of Bolton, given by Tony and Betty, where on it they wrote, "May all your stumbling blocks turn into steppingstones," and of that concept, I had freely, gladly and gratefully grasped, but "Onto me, when was it, going to latch?"

As I investigated more, and trials and tribulations became mine to unhappily explore, was I becoming stronger and wiser, or simply loosing the plot? For still I had not stopped, in silence, I had not even paused, to let the fact permeate my mind, that "Hello!" In reality, it was not Provence, my dream I was on my way to, but another *petite ville* only 56 miles from the Med, close to the *Côte d'Azur*, where I was heading toward, but "Why was I so wrong, so misguided and what was getting in my way?" "Oh" I think that was me!" For I had been too easily detracted by what the naysayers did spout, as wrongly, their negativity, dodged under my awareness barrier, as I had not risen above it, and worse, unwittingly remaining unaware to the contrary, I had accepted and believed, what they said of me was true, that I was incapable of achieving my dream, but "Why was I so blooming slow?" To reject the flawed and false judgment, of their, perceptions of limitations, and declare, through my personal review, those as unnecessary and redundant.

And so it was, still no heading toward that destination of my dream, I was heading toward a town, previously sited on the French and Spanish boarder, but then reached after just 2.5 hours drive, and in an exceptional little province, over that boarder, tax-free shopping was available there, and more, on paper, all the boxes were ticked, for it had a canal, a river, a medieval castle, of importance, an airport serving at least the UK, and Paris, well wonderfully by *TGV*, that was only a few hours away.

But the importance of the people, I had not thought to include them on my list, and quite amazing that my brain was to take onboard the negatives of the naysayers, but she from Toulouse, who offered her telephone number and to help me when I arrived, but effectively, refused in the end, as phone calls not returned, "Why did I not reflect so much hugely greatly, on what she was to say?" "Be careful where you choose to go, for some towns in France, the people there don't even accept other French unless you were born there, and a foreigner, they'll be quite hostile and never accept you living there!" "Oh my!" "Why oh why, did I not pay more head to that?" For time was to be the great revealer of all, as I, had failed to contemplate, was I heading toward an avenue of possibility or a dead-end street, and France, in that relatively small *ville*, "Was it to transpire to be, good, or miss-fortune?"

> *"If we're growing, we're always going to be out of our comfort zone."*
> ~ John Maxwell

Arriving at night, leaving the *gare*, I liked what I saw, as I cast my eyes across the canal, to the Village Square, rectangular in shape an enclosed by tall old trees, lush in leaves, with fountains numbering 2, each with three tiers, and bowls from where the water cascaded, large and ornate, yet refusing to dominate, and the water it glistened, but lit not by moonlight, but the lanterns, modern and tall of black pained iron, casting a shimmer as the water from one tier to the next did fall, and the sound, how magical, for at that late hour of the night, with no one around, the gentle flow and patter whispered in my ear, and after that long confined train ride, what a pleasure.

Finding my hotel, not a problem as my skills were increasing, of course, close to the *gare* I was quickly to rest, restored by sleep and in the morning start afresh, but too tired to do my usual room check for I so longed to rest, so after a shower slipped quickly between the sheets, but in the morning, I was not so sure that was a good thing to do, for "Oh my" the check revealed, for a good nights sleep I did not have, as the mattress so many decades old I dare to say, and the crevice in the middle, could have in another world be used to birth ships, and the pillows, don't get me started on them, so dirty, even repulsive, I was to sleep with a folded towel over them, the sheets, they were crisp and clean, but the blanket that lay on top, of a polyester type fabric that may have shrunk, when it was last washed maybe 20 years ago were so terribly grubby, and look like they'd been taken from a dogs bed, and more, as I tried to tuck my sheets in, it was other peoples hair that I was found to be lying there, "Oh my goodness" all rendered the tape holding together the toilet door handle by comparison look so amazingly, not bad.

The curtains in a nasty fabric, probably popular in the 60's judging by the pattern, and the nicotine walls, yellow, nay almost brown of years that it had seeped into the paper, but of dangerous that was not, but the leaking of the shower, I could not say the same, as two large bath towels I was to use to stop the flow of the water on the floor, but somehow, I could not seal the leak and stop the flow, but as treacherously it sped across the bathroom floor, that in two weeks I ended up being there, not once did it or the maid ever reach the large obnoxious pile of dust and more that lay, near the radiator unconcealed on the floor. And I, I think I was loosing the plot, for I had settled at a point where somehow, I was putting up with more and more, of all that was bad and substandard, as I placed so much effort, trying to search out all that was good, but of 'seek and ye shall find, and knock and the door shall be opened was I simply doing it in the wrong place at the wrong time?

So quickly I got out of there the next day, to find a place to relax, to get a map from the tourist board, but part-time hours, it was not to be, so it was off for a croissant and a café latté, and there almost immediately I began to notice of the locals, a little unordinary, and on the narrow roads, cars would simply stop, to share a yarn with someone, not so much a chat as a full conversation, as in the car their head would pop, and a kiss to the side of each cheek, while all the vehicles would wait behind, and toot their, horns? Amazingly no, as no one made a peep, but eventually the reason became clear, for the next time, it may be them, holding the folks up to the rear.

That French kissing thing became a bit of a minefield, for in Paris it was so easy, a kiss to the right and then the left, but in that small *ville* in the south of France it was the opposite way around, but an added complication was hit upon, as when I was introduced to a friends friend who effectively I didn't know they would also want to kiss me too, but then there husband or wife would not, but was that gender specific, or more to do with the proximity of the relationship, I never really did attain the reasoning, and an observation I did make, watching intently of introductions of other people in the square, never did clarity strike, so a tactic I began to use, simply hold back and be passive, but somehow with lingering intent, to jump in and respond quickly to the action that they in front of you did take.

Of interesting note, it was not the 'elephant in the room' that I was to be in that small *ville*, but of obvious note, when I wore my short skirt and walked around the town, as the sun shone down, less attention did I receive, than on those winter days, when I rugged up in my hat and my scarf, a long coat and jeans, and my figure disguised, so of the message I calculated from that, is that my figure, was not 'all-that' or it really is true what they say, that men, like something left to the imagination. But something most bizarre was to happen to me down there near the Med Sea, for though it initially appeared, that *ville tranquillé et calme*, peace and quiet, though it transpired to me to be only superficially, as my perspective was to reveal, that place had greater in common with the movie, 'The Stepford Wives,' than anything else I had ever known.

But then at the beginning of my stay, as I wandered and meandered, not trying so hard for 'what to do,' for I thought somehow for some reason, there I was possibly able to make a 'place for myself' and investigate all options, sitting and resting, a man I noticed commenced from a table across the way, to take a particular interest in me, and as my napkin from my knee blew away, he forty something, in beige canvas slacks and a well pressed tailored striped pale blue and white shirt, sitting beneath his well-worn, blouson jacket, larger than suited him in leather, heavy and thick, in the colour of tan. His face ruggedly handsome, though his skin had not stood well to the test of time, with fine fair hair swept back and his eyes of blue, introducing himself as Pierre, took that opportunity to walk several feet and pick it up, then hey-presto, a conversation he struck, a gentle kind of man, at first-appearance he appeared to be, but really, as time passes by, I wonder more, of such a concept, "How much trust should we put in store?"

And so often, *en centre ville* village square, commonly we would bump into each other and he, generously would offer me, *un verre de vin rouge*, a glass of red, "Well, thank you very much don't mind if I do," as gladly I would agree, and there we'd sit, he spoke, *la langue anglaise*, the English language, and I replied in *la langue francaise*, and happily we would pass the day. So a friendship we began, but to me, though I spoke not the words, for I knew not that I needed to, but no more than that, never would it ever be.

A confident man, he was not, more a little desperate and slightly sad, and forever lived in the past, as each *rencontrer à nouveau*, another meeting, he was to reveal, his deep-seated concerns, his wishes and his aspirations, as his character came glistening through, that by design, he desired a woman to take care of him, financially and actually in all-ways, as he deemed her to be most active taking all the action, where it appeared from what he divulged, he intended to take non. And he spilled the attributes of the well-rehearsed woman he sought, of what the lady, should have and be, but hold up one minute; "Was he talking about me?"

So it was, he continued releasing his needs and wants, "The right woman, she will help me give up smoking," but my abundant thought, "I'm not so sure she will," for that wonderful and patient woman who was 'alive and well' in Pierre's imagination, as a non-smoker, may just be looking for another, and more, in a relationship and the roll he wants her to play in his life, unsure, "Was he seeking a guardian, provider, lover or mother?"

True, he and I held on life a completely different view, for sure, a smoker in an instant, holds different values to me, in the realms of health an money, to name but 2, with time not spent on fitness or investing wisely, or at least trying, rather than using it not wisely but effectively, at least eventually, causing problems and throwing money down the pan. And as for any addictions that may hold me tight for a while, that serve me ill, I'll find a strategy and put it in place, to overcome that which I really desire to, and until I succeed, over and over I'll try again, until I've achieved something increasingly better, something more helpful, something wiser or brighter, and until I get to my goal, nothing will enable to give my power away, for I have done that once or twice before, but no more, for now empowered, my life, is may game to play.

But Pierre, he appeared to have given all his power away, seeing not a reason in the world to regain it, claw it back, of do anything positive by taking any portion of action to help him to hold along life's journey, but "Why?" For just a little empowerment he would have benefitted from, and support, well, he seemed to have oodles of that, for he had 2 daughters, one who he spoke to everyday, and spent lunch with each week, at the very least, he held a government job, with plenty of security, they type the French prefer apparently, "So why was he living in a state of misery?" As really, effectively he was doing nothing to help himself, and although we had not really passed from more than casual friends, really, more like acquaintances, support by means of a listening ear, and words of encouragement I freely gave to assist him through his days, but cautiously observing I gained an insightful glimpse, of the road ahead so subtlety he was trying to have me travel upon, but I refused to be, a crutch for him to lean on.

Really, should I have tired a little experiment, and asked him, "What are 3 words you'd use to describe yourself?" I wonder, how negative, and spiritless they would have been, and a good tool perhaps this is to do, to simply and succinctly gain insight to what goes on in the perceptions of another's mind, for it is not trickery, but simply easy, to reveal a potential minefield that may linger below the surface, or perhaps the gentle flow of a babbling brook, for subtleties of how they perceive themselves, may release good and valuable clues, for the road ahead, on it do you choose to travel or from varying aspirations, quick-smart to slowly-does-it, we choose to release it.

"Don't spend time beating on a wall, hoping to transform it into a door."
~ Coco Chanel

At first, quite gallant, I thought that Frenchman to be, as he walking me back to my hotel, when late at night, and appearing concerned for my safely, but beneath his flimsy exterior potential trouble loomed, and surprisingly his veil fell suddenly, collapsing with a thud to the ground, as he ignored my repeated requirement, "I must go right now, my head is hurting and I feel unwell" while those Melbourne Maladies I was recovering from, I had experienced a small relapse, and ignoring my needs and manipulating the conversation for continuity, but eventually, I had to insist, and as I turned to walk away, he grabbed hold of my arm in a hostile way, pulling me back, harshly and firmly. "Oh how in an instant," how memories came flooding back from my childhood, for always I was being pushed or pulled or tugged, in this direction or that, with jarring my body, as my little head from side to side and up and down, floundered around.

As Pierre with his fury increasing, and preventing me escaping, increased his efforts, placing his other hand with force on my opposite shoulder, his method to prevent me from breaking free, and in that moment, I had, had enough and was free from fear, and with confidence spoke, in a tone that was definite and concise, "Let me go now!" with my facial expression clearly indicating I meant what I said, and trouble, I was going to have non, and suddenly, he changed his response and released my arm from his upward pulling grip, but for him it was too late, for the harm had been done, as his true colours abundantly shone, for that was on the open street "So what would his intent be, behind closed doors?"

My tolerance levels to violence reassessed and tuned in, to what first they should have been before, so badly programmed by my parents was I, and from there on in, knowledge and reflection became close compatriots of mine, as my choice, as often as I saw him around that unamusing *ville*, not to spend time with him, until one day, close by he did come, and with his friend, invited me to *manger*, eat a croissant and partake of a coffee, wrapped in a proposal to fatten me up. But "What-to-do? For had enough water passed under the bridge, but remembering it had, passed through, but a coffee, what harm could that do?"

But "Was reflection my instigator and knowledge my protector, for something safer, something better, and if so, what was I doing sitting down?" For sure, there was no such thing to kiss and make up, but really, was I giving in unwisely, and was one thing to led to another, and what message was I even giving to sit right there, and really, should I have been making good my escape. For it was not rocket science, the theory had jumped into particle and the evidence was clear, I knew, to keep my distance from him, but rightly or wrongly, on that square on that cooler afternoon, I was to sit to idle a while.

"Know thyself means this, that you get acquainted with what you know,
and what you can do."
~ Menander

He introduced me to his friend, much older in years, whose English was a little better than Pierre's, but as a second language, both proved in advance of mine, and he, a hobby a business, buying properties, and he a landlord, and Pierre thought a few tips that man may have for me, and gladly as a notion I was pleased to explore, for perhaps some information I maybe able to accumulate, but to slow was I to consider, the notion of 'birds of a feather flock together' and 'lye with dogs and you'll catch fleas.' And more caution I should have shown along the way, and paused for greater consideration and consequences, before I agreed to accompany him, while he showed me his house perched the hill overlooking the *ville*, but he said it wasn't too far, and I concluded it was day so no harm would come my way, and he was a little infirm, and quickly I could escape that vehicle, but a question to ponder, when I was so highly concerned, "Why did I even think, about getting in his car?"

Then he, true to his word, in 10 minutes, dropping me off in the reported time slot, in the reported place, that man, building-up credibility, so when an invitation was presented, to accompany him to his village fête in his street, after balanced consideration, I saw no reason to reject it, for he had shown me his house, and of its location, I knew I could independently walk there and leave the same, so I accepted with little hesitation. But really, isn't that what bad people do, when they are deliberately trying to suck you in, they make sure at first, they do something right, so when they do something wrong, they forever are able to revert back to, well remember when I did this for you, as they twist and turn the truth, forever referring us right back to it, as though, that was all they ever needed to do. And more, with precision-persuasion and the power of word suggestion, and phrases the same, they, not weak in achieving their aim, their goal, to place us like a puppet on a string, right back, under their lethal and oppressive spell.

But there it was, I did have some, and I ignored that little niggle, discarding it as me imagining it, but "No, of cause I wasn't" as things started to turn a little awry, as soon as we met for our rendezvous, for his car, he turned it not to drive up the hill, but quickly drove straight on, away from the *ville*. "Where are you going?" I quickly asked, "To my house" he snapped right back, his attitude, *tres mauvais*, very bad, but to blandly for my own good ignoring it, observing, but "Your house is in the opposite direction" "Oh no" he said, "I'm taking you to my other place." "And that would be where?" he carried on, "Oh just a few kilometres away." So there it was, as we passed the rolling fields of farmer's crops, I found myself in a French village that I held no joy, and I was thinking more badly of me, and really, more often "Was I to transpose to something else?"

In his other house, at the top of a hill, so proudly he showed me around, but his heart was sagging as his ego bragging, and as he showed me the roof from the rooftop, he began to boast, how he and his friends, one he overly repeated was a doctor, and perhaps then I should have spoken, "Sorry that doesn't impress" and it did not appear bravado, but sadly appearing real, like a teenage boy gesturing with his hands, that the group of them hid quietly, to ogle at the lady next door, sunbathing in her bikini.

To the kitchen he then took me, to sit and wait for the time the festival began, and I, far from happy, for I considered, he had wilfully, deliberately manipulated my time and my attendance, and as I sat opposite him, my thoughts were going back tying to formulate a plan of escape out of that rabbit warren of renovations, calculating all the exits, and strategizing a plan, for how fast I could get out of there. And then, it was his wedding photos he took off the walls and the photo album he collected from the draws, and painfully describing each one, of pictures I cared to see, and declared as he pointed at his pretty wife, defiled with venom, flying from his mouth, emotion so raw, it could have happened yesterday not 40 years ago, "She was such a disappointment to me! And look at her, she's ugly!" "I really stooped when I took her. Because look, I am so handsome and great!" "Mmmm," it appeared abundantly so, that he held an extremely grandiose and distorted opinion of his self-virility. True, it is said that beauty is in the eye of the beholder, but really, of his self-perceptive vision, he likely needed, a new lens prescription.

His insults on that day not just reserved for long-gone wife, for a few he threw at me, for as I tried to speak in French to him, "Don't do that!" sharply left his mouth, and as I explained, "I don't understand" with a prickling intolerance,

"You speak my language so badly, it offends me!" "Well don't be shy, just say what you mean," I could have joked and laughed, but I recognized easily humour wasn't his best forte, as I realised simply, with malicious spite, he, was just mean.

A bitter man, and one I longed not to be around, as I hasting-on our timing to go the fête, suggesting, "It might be nice to get there early, and to set it up, lend a hand." And eventually I persuaded him so, and such a relief as we arrived at that fête as I considered, 'safety first' and how when we 'listen to what people say' and they will easily and inadvertently, weather they mean to or not, tell us, who inside they are, but most importantly, the key to this tactic working, is that we do not tell them we're looking or listening closely at all, and him, I listened and I knew his measure, and it was one, I chose not to close to, not even with a bargepole. And better late than never, as a master at this previously I was not, but after practice and precision, as I can practice with people anywhere, on the bus, at work or in the supermarket, I have perfected the art, and now, it is not after a relationship has begun that I activate this process, but wilfully, wisely, before they begin.

> *"What progress, you ask, have I made? I have begun to be a friend to myself."*
> *~ Hecato*

Could that man really have been so misguided in his concepts, with his personality of superiority, how much authority did he missgivingly wheeled, and I wonder, was it before or after the marriage, he revealed unsuspectingly to his wife, "Before her spirit he did destroy?" For is that often a format of men, and was that true, or even partially the case of my father, for did he do the same, and did my mother not recognise his disguise, that really he 'wasn't nice,' and really she should think twice, before walking off down the aisle.

For once, she had sent him a "Dear John letter" calling the whole thing off, but what was her reason for getting back with him, and really, "Was it worth one considering?" Perhaps it was simply loneliness, perhaps her thought, through low self-esteem or low self-worth, other than that relationship, nothing better was to come to pass. So was it by flawed decision making or by default, simply desperation, or perhaps a curse she passed on to me, that ultimately, rather than call the whole thing off, she gave-into his persuasion.

For my father's cloak, so soon it must have dropped, for my brother had suffered bruises, while he was still in his cot, but "Why did my father hate his own children so?" And what a shock of desperation was to fall on me one day, as most unusually and only on one occasion we visited a work colleague of his, and that man's children, he so happily smiling and playing while still ignoring me, as I stood close by at the side of the lawn, bewildered, my heart torn to pieces with a strange crippling feeling in my brain, as at the age of maybe only 10, never had I ever seen him do such a thing before, and could not comprehend what I saw, as stifling anguish of pain feeling real I was to absorb, as tears welled up stinging my eyes, as uninvited and knowing better to invite myself, my inside *cried*, "Why! WHY? Had he never once, ever done that with me?"

For until that day, I had no comparison of only angry words he spoke being thrown my way, and to his character I knew not that there was an alternative, so by default, I had accepted it as so, for sure, not a pleasant or kind word ever passed his lips, or a quiet word spoken, only aggressive shouting, but really, "What made those other children better than me?" "Why were they more special than I, and why did he prefer them, and what in all the world do, could I possibly do, so my father, may just play with me, and like me too?"

And from there on in, there was never to be any peace only, comparison, stemming from his action, and then I tried so hard to be something else, to turn myself into someone he wanted me to be, and then just perhaps, he might smile and be happy with me too, but then again, I knew what he liked best of me, nay expected, as his words forever yelled, to "Shut up!" and simply, "Be quiet!" and "Don't trouble me!" and never delivered with a smile. With "Don't talk such nonsense!" being hurled in my direction, and should I have ever surpassed his first level of defence, of cause, his last line of resistance, if I was ever to forget myself and mistakenly ask "Why?" his forever retort, "Don't ask me your stupid questions, ask your teachers," continuing "That's what I pay my tax's for!"

"Oh happy days" I say with more than a note of sarcasm, as "Yes" I clearly understood all that, for never was I permitted to forget, and "Yes," I had accepted it as normal, until that day, when I saw with my own eyes, that he had another way of being, and with sadness in my heart, I began to wonder, "He is my father not theirs, so why is he not that way with me?" and "Why was it one rule for me, and another for those children he didn't even know?" and "What made them so good, so special, and made me so terribly bad?" and "Why was it I felt his heavy weight of bitter scorn, he dumped on me everyday, as I searched so hard to try and think, "What could I do, to make him stop him hating me, and make all things better?"

Then my ex-for-a-reason, his cloak concealing his true intent really well, as our first date, how magnificent, as a country pub he took me to, and how we enjoyed ourselves as my spirit came out to play, and never would I have ever guessed, that one day he would be suffocating me on my bed. For he had wheeled me in through his persuasive charm, and coercively, breaking down and pushing though all my boundaries, with perhaps his deliberate intent and disguised MO, to achieve his deception, "Gently as I go."

For through his dominance in the relationship, he had secured so long ago, I transpired to be, an unwitting participant in his master plan, to do as he pleased, and whatever he liked, and like a horse in days of old, he had harnessed me, and put blinkers on, so to the left or fright I could not see, so forward along my path, only what was to be in my vision, to the exclusion of all else, was only to be he.

Then worse, retrospectively, how foolish was I, for no matter what harm he'd done, while calling me his pet name and wrapping his arms around me again and again, until he had achieved his forever goal, as another false apology and lie he spun, and as I gave in, my actions only served, once again to give him cart-blanch, to deliver to me, in any way he chose, whatever he wanted, and however he wanted to deliver it, so to his tune and his dance, I remained somehow grateful he was mine, as I lived in a bewildering trance.

For he knew I loved him so, so when his critical names began, as along the canal side in Cornwall, we saw a Moorhen, and he calling it me, as a joke, yet in inclination and intonation, equalling a Moron, so perhaps not so funny, as timidly, I begged him to stop, because so disparagingly that was a word my father called me, and so with emotions afresh, it made my spirit tumble, but he ignored my request of "Please, please don't say that." Yet because it was what I wanted and not he, skittishly he continued, and "Why was I so blind I could not see?" For that was at the beginning of the relationship, and still not so much time I had invested, so surely I should have 'quick-smart' made my escape. But the unfortunate hazard there, was that 'to be made to feel so bad, was in my training from my mum and dad,' normal and acceptable, for hadn't they taught me, 'that was what love is,' so "Why would I have expected anything different or better?"

And true to form, with the passing of years the hugs and kisses stopped after he had done something quite bad, as they then transferred from the exception to the usual, as like my father, he began to control me with an iron fist, as without question, I learnt to do what he said, nay, anticipate his needs, to prevent his mood from rising and his temper increasing, and to try to reduce his wrath, just so I may simply have, a less stressful, less risk-full and easier day.

Appeasing him surpassed, proactive and preventing-harm, became the master of each of my days, of carefully speaking my words to conjure up no ill, as each day on my path, on those eggshells I walked upon, as I tried so hard not to crush any more, but "Why I had not done my math and calculated?" That his, anger and hostility, caused my ever increasing restrictions through his delivered unconcealed manipulations, while I did everything I could not to step out of line as I did his bidding, and although I knew I was unhappy, still really, I did not know totally that all was wrong, and that there was, a better, kinder, more deserving way of living.

As too late was I to question, "Why I had not read the writing on the wall?" As I got to the end of the game, as I bought my house in secret my new castle, as each morning before I had started my 35 minute journey to that responsible job, where for peoples health in the realms of accidents and emergencies I was accountable, and for my employer the same, to ensure all legal requirements were covered and adhered, and as I rocked up each day, not a one had even the slightest clue, that I void of feelings, dead of emotions, for those I cold no longer afford or spare, as like a robot, in the shower I would get, with that man who I detested, yet please him as I relieved him sexually, and give me the very best chance for me to enhance, in just the hope, that it would calm him sufficiently, to benefit me.

And with my job of the day complete, as I went about my business, I was to keep it a secret, for no one was to know the turmoil or trappings of each day I faced, or how my adrenaline daily raced, and how I longed to get out of that place, to be secure, and perhaps who knew, one day, be emotionally healed from all the trauma of my past as around my falsely wired neurons it reeled, for realistically, still at the age of 30-something, I knew not, that I needed to survive the pain and prejudice of my past, and start living a different, a greater evolved life at last. But of the consequences, memories and trauma, trapped in my mind, free loading and hitching a ride, really "Was I ever to fully become aware, and when was that ever to be?" For from the devastation and strangulation o f how it affected my life, of lack of connectedness to others, for my heart to be healthy, for hope of any compatibility to join the human race, *all* of what passed previously, I *needed*, desperately, to surpass.

For it appears the story of the Frog, I'll call her Freda, and I have much in common, as she, who was placed in a pan of tepid water, quite comfortable, not astonished or alarmed, she rested, perceiving it not a place of danger, and then when the pan, was placed over the heat, obliviously she continued not noticing, taking no action for protection, and as she noticed the water getting hotter, she decided to put up with it, possibly thinking, "Well, I've been here this long, and really, nothing too bad has happened so far so why would it now?" So aware, unalarmed, passively she lingered, until, suddenly it was too late, for the water surrounding her had become treacherous in temperature, draining her of energy and her capacity to escape, for she had ignored the clues along the way, and the warning signs, and all contributed to her demise.

But a different scenario, as time passed, she recognized things were not so good, in fact quite bad but didn't feel she could complain, possibly believing "Well it's OK, I don't like to make a fuss or complain, and really, is this not acceptable?" For she would have recognized the danger she was in, through the subtle signs of the pot being moved, or the changing heat, or the increase of its intensity, and at the very first inkling that "Something is not quite right here, I'm going to jump out while the goings good" and the story, then it would have a different and happy ending.

As danger, it does not wave a flag and announce "Here I am" and those who are to cause it, will conceal it and tell you the opposite, so to stay astute, may serve as one of our best friends and attribute and, so along our way, of miss-happenings and miss-takes, that unfortunately come out to play, a larger price than we need, never, do we pay. For progress I became determined to make, as a young women in her 20's was to tell me "No man has ever hit me, not my father, brother, lover, or stranger." "Yeah. Right!" Was my instant reaction, believing, she was lying, but then I knew her and had no reason to disbelieve her word, though still, at the age of 40something, as so sadly from my past of those who wove a web and trapped me within it, it all seemed quite inconceivable to me, yet, unravelling my future, "Could I possibly have a happy ending, pending?"

> *"How many cares one loses when one decides not to be something but to be someone."*
> ~ Coco Chanel

True, I had not escaped unscathed from my poor choice of men, for it was a Consultant who diagnosed a slipped disc in my neck, causing debilitating headaches, requiring 4 sick days in bed, where I, unable to even tolerate sips of water, his diagnosis, from mechanism of injury, likely as a result, as I fought for my life, during that assault of suffocation, and "Oh my" as he benignly passed his judgement, how a flood of emotions rose to consume me, as I reminisced so un-intentionally, the condemnation from colleagues, the debilitating pain, a social life forgone, disturbed cognition, and huge volumes of financial expenditure on doctors, practitioners, therapists, pharmaceuticals, and non-pharmaceutical medications, and so the extensive list could go on, and in the pit of my stomach, tumbling, as I could only hold more umbrage against myself, than anyone else, for all those terrible decisions gone by, but completely missing the point, that the real wrong was done, by *they* who had caused that harm and injury, toward me.

With self-criticism and self-contempt rampant, I captured and calculated all of those ill-informed, past choices, as I failed to recognize the significance of them in my life, at they, all in advance of my inner-revelation being, when the light in my mind eventually shone, preventing my inner-suffering or disparagement to be prolonged, as at last, to it all I was to decree, *"NO!"* "As for me, I make a choice, permitting that badness, to go on, no-longer!"

It appeared that to trust my own judgement of men I could not, of their all-important values and morals, their deceits and undercurrents, I appeared weak from battling a lifetime of all things men. I was to reflect how relationships were not for me, and of a strategy to keep me safe from harm, was simply and effectively to avoid them. And true, an aspect of thought, avoiding something, is not the same thing as dealing, resolving or healing from it, but at that time, it was the best strategy I could have, and actually, it worked perfectly well, for space, it gave me to breath, to reassess, and regroup me, myself and I, and one I considered I had no option to, for really, until I could trust myself, to choose a better calibre of man, I resolved to choose non at all.

So, the drawbridge came up, for nothing was I to risk to penetrate, that which I had fought so hard for, effectively my life, and so, resolute, I was to permit nothing and no one to penetrate those dense wall of stone, and the moat, too treacherous to row, and alone I stood, but safe, as I struggled with my emotional impairments, delivered by my farther and seconded by, well really, many another, before the motion was carried, but I, was not to be knocked down or imprisoned by others anymore, as in my kingdom, *Carole-dom*, protected, I was to commence upon a quest, to commence the process of dealing with my healing, where knowledge was to serve as my key, to a live, better spent, with love, peace and free, living in harmony, coming, perhaps slower than some but quicker than others, for this journey we are on, it is run, or walked at our own pace, and through all those books read, and there were many, they so fortunately enabled me to gather and encompass that which can live within, *empowerment*, and armed and fortified, I carried right on to gain a portion of wisdom, before learning, that I in fact was already strong, for I had survived so far, and I, was capable to recover some more, and eventually, through my *commitment* to me, certainly for I deserved it so, I was to *thrive*, absolutely.

And so it came to pass, as I was kind to myself, through that process as my decisions improved, and I was to let go of that self-imposed prison I had created to live in, as I chose to be an island no-more and lowered my drawbridge and emptied my moat, for my confidence levels in making discussions had risen, through inner-strength and inner-healing, and so happy I was to become, as that freedom from within was won, for self-esteem and "Yes" self-love, knew how to call my name, and I holding newfound confidence and self-assuredly, I was rising in my ability, to banish the pain of the past, and that anguish assigned from everywhere, as consistently, positively as I moved forever in my new purposeful direction, for emotional recovery, where I relinquished the need to make excuses or assign blame, and along my way, most importantly, I remembered to be, patient and gentle with myself, along my journey until I rested at my new destination.

My quest complete that I enrolled myself on, and then a strategy to move forward was to really 'listening to what men say,' and most importantly observe what they do, and ask more questions than you answer, and commencing this format, and through a trial and error process I eventually learnt to excel, in using my one mouth to speak less, and my two ears to hear twice as much, so simple, and true, so soon, it became abundantly clear and quite amazing, how they may 'run their mouths' when they don't realise that you are truly listening.

And so well it this tactic serves to reveal their likelihood of compatibility, and you guessed it, quite quickly establishing, their values, morals and ethics, not only by what they say, but their tone and gestures as they do just so, as so unwittingly, they may serve as their own worst enemy, as they let slip, their cloak of disguise, which they may be trying to conceal from you. And true, a foolproof scientific system this may not be, perhaps more of an art-form, but non the less I suggest, being purposeful in providing an advantage, in assessing their character, so next time, when in a safe place a man strikes up a conversation and you feel like participating, "Why not try it, and give this idea a go?"

> *"The most difficult thing in life is to know yourself."*
> *~ Thales*

Ok, that marvellous tool of reflexion, was certainly to be implemented to serve me most well post that rendezvous, for sometimes, true, we slip a little backwards, but eventually, through our determination, we successfully end up at the top of the hill, and my experiences on that day were to be no exception, as I knew to pay added attention along my way, and not disappointed in me, as previously with a folly I may have been, but resound, that there, new knowledge of signals to take notice off, new instructions for myself, to say, "No, you're not doing that which we agreed, and now, of the car, I choose to get out." and "Why not?" For this is 'my life,' I need to be empowered and strong, so to benefit me, so I may journey more easily along.

But the day was not over, and there was a Fête to enjoy, and so I set about that as my next task, as there in the middle of the French countryside, a village surrounding all sides of a hill, was to be my entertainer for the day, and how wonderful, that to share in humour quite rare, an English family I met along the way. And entering a very large barn, owned by the village and not privately I thought, so lofty in height, never before has such come before my sight, the door so tall and the rafters so far away, the dimensions gave thought to an amazing renovation, to make such a beautiful home, should someone wish to take that task on, but for me, that location, worked least well of all. So in that huge and hollow barn, my unwelcomed companion for the day, began introducing me to his village neighbours, but not by my name, but as his English professor, and then inadvertently I do believe, that was his inner intent for precisely that, and I must say, normally I would not be vexed, but he with his attitude in his *maison*, home had done, insulting me so, of his notion, I felt, most unagreeable.

And so to sit, anywhere was on offer along the either of the 2 trestle tables, stretching 20 meters or more, where fortunately I was to sit with a family for up north, but hailing from closer to the Scottish boarder than I, and they like me were un-enamoured, with he who sat I sat beside, particularly to his nasty comment that "English women cannot cook and they cannot…" Well, I'll leave that word to your imagination, but it rhymes with duck. A "Gentle-man?" "No!" Certainly, he was not. But "Crass?" I surmise, absolutely yes.

First to be served on those paper plates, resting on red and white gingham print plastic tablecloths, big boiled brown sausages, served with, well something else that neither could I eat, and of the cheeses placed before me, just the smell was enough to put me off, so strong and unpleasant, their pungent aroma, at least to me, rancid, and of those copious cheeses available in France, on that day I, with hunger, was so wishing they'd chosen others, as for sure, I was unable to partake of them. And with satire, in that moment, of English Cheddar, not necessarily so remarkable, but I would have given quite a lot right then to eat more than a morsel of it. Then thinking "Oh my" I can fill up on that gateau I bought, at the price of 18E that he, that nasty companion that day, leaving it in his refrigerator, refusing to being it along, with his words of indignation upon my request for him to do the same, "It is unnecessary, there will be plenty to eat there." "Really!" For while others all around me were tucking-in and enjoying a great feast, I remained famishing.

With the food, done it was time for the afternoon festivities to begin, and so requests were made for people to play *Boules*, and that quite a tradition and a most popular game, played by teams of men, for sure, never had I ever seen a French women included in any teams I'd observed, playing in Paris, or in the south of France, by the river or near the market place beneath the trees sheltering wisely from the midday sun, and true, not even when I visited New Caledonia, a French territory, and being played *à côté de*, beside the Pacific Ocean, never did I see a woman included.

The rules, teams generally of 2 to 4 or so in number, first, a small ball called the *cloche* is thrown, before larger heavy and silver balls are thrown toward it, the closer your ball the more points you accrue, but watch out, for your opponent then throws their balls and can knock yours out of the way, that that whole point of the game, and so your points become theirs. And distinctly true, ball games have never been my forte, and always getting picked last at school for anyone of them really didn't do anything to enhance my enjoyment of them, and just for fun, I decided "Why not?" But that was after a little persuasion, as I walked up the road behind the Frenchmen, though by him, pretty much being ignored, but I paid no heed, as I was basking and enjoying the unusual nature of that petite village, of its winding lanes and buildings most old while inhaling that excessively refreshing air, and admiring the plants and trees most everywhere.

"Oh my" on that bright and sunny day, what a wonderful surprise awaited me, as I was to discover that game, aka, *Platongue*, as it turned out, I was a 'dab hand' at, 'go figure!' "Who would have guessed it?" Not I. Of cause back then, I didn't know what I was doing, I was just told to hit that little ball with the big one and simply, I did! And true, I was amazingly good. Though of the lead Frenchman on the opposing team, of his apparent discord to me being placed there at all, it appeased him not, for so testily and complaining was his retort, first demanding "You're lying, admit it, you have played this game before." And to my denials, he became quite bizarrely even more vexed declaring, "You have no right to be able to play like that, when..." pointing to his medal-winning friend of 20-30something years... "He has been practicing since the age of 4." Well, perplexed somewhat by his hostility, I added, "Hey it's only a game," which angered him substantially, swiftly resorting "Yes, well, its only beginners luck!" But "Oh contraire;" for I had to disagree, stating quite boldly, "No! I think I really have, a new-found skill."

The progression of that afternoon and my skill really was to deliver a prize, for there, with all the teams dwindling, and I ended up competing in the semi-finals. "Yippee, hip-hip-hooray!" For seriously, in those decades preceding me, the only competition I'd ever won before, except only once when I was maybe 7, and I was invited to a school friend's birthday part, held in her in her living room, and as the music was turned on, and we all did our best, and adjudicated by her older sister and cousin, it was me, who they were to announced as the winner for that dancing competition, and my prize, a whole shiny silver 6d, 6pennies. Yet how terribly sad, for decades were to pass, and on my recall of that day, on the inside it only made me feel sick, for I worried so immensely that they had given it me, not because I was worthy, but because they felt sorry for me, as non of the games I'd been able to win. Then I grew to contemplate, was that apart of my legacy from my father, that I was as he said I was, "Good for no-thing!" And has his lies settled as my truths, had I took onboard that job of his, as always belittling myself, and only vexed at myself for I was "Too stupid" to win anything, and embarrassed that those girls had done that, because they must have been so bad, that they thought they better make-up something or she'll leave with nothing. Feeling inferior, certainly, and really, "Was that view of my self-esteem so low as the result of what my father had done, and more, could I never give myself a break, not through all those years, where I was still hoping, somehow that my father may stop being cruel, and dare I ever dream or aspire to him accepting of me, and cease resenting that I'd ever been born?"

But 'not to worry,' for there in that France village, as the day drew toward 9 o'clock, it was decided the final was not to be played, so there I was, standing so proud of myself, at the top of the humongously large, tall and wide, village barn, on stage, with my team mate, quite ironically, at that late stage in the game turned out to be, that man who was previously so vexed with me, and *I* was *awarded*, for the first time ever, a great big cup, and how ecstatically and immensely thrilled I was!"

"Oh my" I could feel every cell throughout my body jumping for joy, and my heart revelling in rapture, and my mind, as if alive somehow for the very first time, for I had done something good, I had been justified and my worth had been recognised, I was no longer a failure, I had excelled in something, 'if only' I could have taken a deep breath, but I did not, for my excitement self-propelled, as if as a student who had excelled, I was at the front of the class, everyone before me was clapping and cheering and for the first time ever in my life, I thought for my efforts and accomplishments I was being appreciated.

So as the day drew to a conclusion, a mini-prize, my chocolate Matchmakers that I'd shared and handed around, and with my silver 12 inch plus trophy in hand, with which I, was to clean then literally, with a big, nay huge smiling beam, drink red wine out of that very cup, that very night, for *the celebration of my life*, for really, in it, could I have more good luck? Then by comparison, the contemplation dominating my thoughts, as that horrible companion, so rude, so arrogant, 20 plus years my senior, who actually was the person who persuaded e to enter the competition, so really, I should have thanked him; was to drive me back the 7 miles to *centre ville*, who when we arrived tried to kiss me, "What?" "No!" "Oh my goodness." He must have been having a joke, only he wasn't funny, yet safely back, with so may new lesson's of life, all tucked up securely, for me to nurture and take care of, to ensure fewer and fewer sub-standard, unsatisfactory or inferior situations were to come my way. And resoundingly, on balance, I was to conclude, that *dans la sud de la France,* it was not a bad day!

> *"The funny thing about life;*
> *if you refuse to accept anything but the best, you very often get it."*
> *~ W. Somerset Maugham*

It was a beautiful spring day as I walked by the river, the temperature perfect, and all to enjoy, as beneath the basking sun I paused to look over the bridge, and there an otter who was just going about its normal business and being, he, was delighting me, and the trees with their heavy set leaves swayed gently in the breeze, and the ducks close by were easily heard, and all, such tranquillity to admire, and even more, in life, on that summer afternoon, to enjoy all for free.

And there, between the mild multitudes of tourists, there he was, again, walking toward me, sometimes it seamed that there was no escaping him, the Frenchman, who I perceived had so much and he perceived had so little, for I was viewing the aspect of having many loving family members, while he viewing it, well, with his apparent grumbling hefty in weight, anything negative really, and I had remembered the issue outside my hotel of his episode of aggression, and his friend who he introduced me to, who also was not to be trusted, so with all balance, I was to turn and run, but with nowhere it hide, it looked with him along that footpath I was to collide.

So I, commenced with a formal *Bonjour* yet he responded with an informal and familiar, *"Salut."* Then commenced the language dance, he speaking *Anglais*, and me French, as termed in up northern England, *"Ca va?"* = "All right?" With *"Oui,"* "Yes." In response, and the formalities of a reencounter over and done, I could not escape his gloomy persona and a most depressed facial expression with even weak shoulder shrugging, completed his ensemble, then a job of listening patiently, as my ears tuned in hard to understand his unfolding broken-English, telling of how bad things were for him and how very depressed he felt; but just hold on one minute, he had family, he had just finished lunch with his son, and a daughter who visited weekly who telephoned more often, who he doted on so really, "How lonely could he be?" Or possibly in my concept of having, well, 'now one,' while not meaning to, was I a little self-righteous, peering through distorted and fragmented lenses, with sorrowful resentment, perhaps pondering for valid consideration, really, "Did he have the right to be?"

For true, I was happier than he, and my father, abandoned me 3 decades earlier, and my mother almost 2, and a brother who also chose not to know me, so "Why was he so miserable, for it was not him suffering maternal deprivation, or isolation or lack or connectedness, or kisses of affection, or hugs?" And should research be believed, we need all those to thrive, so really, me, a little incey-wincey bitterly I thought, of his self-indulgence, "What gives him such a reason?" For so easily I could have said, "You think your life's so bad, try having mine!" But of course I didn't, for that would have not helped him, and of my emotions I cared not to share and kept private, as I reflected with patience, as each of us, hold varying capacities of what our minds may perceive within our emotions fields as good or poor, and more, our toleration for such, is not only dependant on our history, our character, but also physiology, our resolve and determination. True non of us are perfect, so one may succeed in one area where another may fail miserably, but within humility I make haste to remember, best not to, judge our weaknesses to another's strengths, for under different circumstances, in different chapter or another scenario of our life's, situations maybe turned upside down or inside out, so really, "Who are we to say or judge what is bad or best?"

Pierre, complaining how "I don't want to go back to my empty apartment," before inviting me up to the *castle medieval* for a 'glass of red,' and with reservations, still, I reluctantly agreed to his proposal, but really, after his previous behaviour toward me, I believed he deserved it not, so maybe, it was mercy I showed and not good judgment I exhibited, as I commenced the walk up the hill with him. But then again, "Had I not learnt my lesson on that subject already, and why was I giving him the benefit of the doubt, and by my actions, setting aside what in his character he had exposed, was I sanctioning his behaviour, or worse, inviting more of it?" As my ex-for-a-reason, who cried like a baby when I told him I was leaving him, until I wrongly gave-in and he came with me, and clearly with magnified sight, my testimony of that episode is that truly 'a leopard doesn't change its spots,' so "Why, was I giving-in and doing for another, really something in my heart and mind was against all sensibility and, truly I didn't want to? For really, surely, history dictated that I had already learnt that lesson regarding my ex-for-a-reason…Right?" So "What was wrong with me? Why was I making the same mistake twice?"

But then not troubling myself too much about it, as a most significant aspect, was that I recognized my actions, so was stronger and wiser and could choose more carefully next time, plus I had my own transport, my own feet, and they could easily carry me back to the little place 20 minutes away I stayed, so my Risk Assessment completed, I considered there was no significant threat, with so many others around, but that concept was soon certainly to be proved a great error of judgment, yet most importantly in my contemplations of all as I made that decision, at the beginning and the end, my actions were sanctifying his behaviours, telling him, "Oh that's all right." When, "No! Actually they were wrong!" And accordingly, therefore I should not have been swayed from good judgment, and 'stood my ground,' throwing away that designation of 'people pleaser,' been unable to be coaxed into submitting to his wants over and above my own. Another lesson learnt, and I vowed to do better, in advance, on any consecutive time, with anyone.

And on that day, I was to be shown a new way to ascend that hill, as we turned to *traverse*, crossover a low-stone bridge, hovering only some 24 inches above the swell of the river, and without hand rails, it was a little weird for when I admired the water too much, it made me almost fall back as though I was to ramble along with it, yet safely at the other side, through a park laden with trees, and over the bustling water of the weir, until coming to, an ancient, narrow and winding staircase we were to arrive, seemingly hidden and merging with the castle's lowest wall, its first line of defence, made of stone, encased by stone, which had not seen a repair more many a year, all uneven, cracked and slippery, where careful footing was extremely necessary as the way to go, and what a wonderful discovery, and to walk that way again, surely I was to enjoy the pleasure to do so.

Really what a bonus that turned out to be, for that got me wondering, just how many alternatives are there to reach the top, and a concept born, as I so commenced, my *comme d'habitude*, usual habit, of quite tantalizing exploration, as each day I was to discover another new way, and then with them I began to play, mixing them up, and even more, I became quite skilled, for depending on the weather, be it sunny or windy, or damp or other, my route I could change effectively so those elements to reduce the risk to me, and oh so invigorating, for it was not just my physique that was benefiting, but my mind too, and to enjoy nature, the sight the sounds, improve my stamina, and of those simple, succinct measures, I was to consider, "Why with the rest of my life, do I not transfer, the principles learnt there?"

How absolutely marvellous, I was reinventing myself, I was changing from a 'fine weather girl' as I would have termed myself in Melbourne, only walking when my mood was 'just so' and the sun the breeze was just right, to an 'anytime weather girl' that I was to exercise with all my might, as I grew to know myself as so. And "How good did that feel?" "Oh my" outstandingly so, for what I gained was freedom and options, from within and not restrictions or dictations which lay outside all around, and so I embraced, the snow, the sleet, the hail, rain, winds and blustery gales, for they all had something to hold, and as I trudged up one side and down the other, being very careful underfoot, I felt revived, and through all my health issues, glad I survived, and how grateful I became that my life was not slain, for I was able to live, to walk, and even reverse my osteoporosis diagnosis.

> *"Keep your face to the sunshine and you will not see the shadows."*
> *~ Helen Keller*

Finding a café, an ice-cream parlour or a high-end hotel, not difficult for they lay all around those cobbled streets and old courtyards, which back in the days used to be, villagers homes, and so many, to choose from, simply we just take our choice, and surrounded amongst thongs of tourists busily eating their lunch, usual for he and me, a good glass of *Bordeaux,* I was t have, for really I had never tasted one that was bad, and he his small black coffee. And then as I was tried not to get caught up in his rapture of negativity, his pendulum swung, then suddenly, tough not really surprisingly of his self-indulgence, out of the blue said to me, as his held and wafted his cigarette around in his hand, with a seemingly cocky attitude, "You are beautiful, I want to have sex with you. When can I?" Really! "Was he kidding?" that was to be "No." But really, "Hello!" For he had trampled down that road before, and the answer hadn't changed a jot. My face clearly displaying my thoughts, at my intolerance of his blatant request or innuendoes of the same, as nowhere in his and mine association has such a situation ever been suggested or even hinted at, in fact the intimations was always that, never, was it to be a scenario he was to encounter with me pass, his exclamation, rude and tiresome, and his retort when I enquired, why he persist to go on, his response "Oh I like you!" That was it.

Continuing, he told me, "You are like a mannequin. Your style is exquisite, your hair and your apparel" as he not realizing, that all of my purchases originated at thrift stores. And he, not for being quiet, or quitting while ahead, "I thought 'why not,' I will give it a try, as I want to take you to bed." "Oh my" enough already, I was instantly board, and of insulted a little for sure, he knew me not, and had no-call to be so familiar, and what of that 'formal' French etiquette they talked so much of, does that suddenly fly out of the window, when greedily they try to seize anything that takes their fancy? But whatever the answer maybe, he had gone way off ballpark, chances, he had 2, sensibly I refused to give him three, for his character, on so many levels had failed at every test, and then for me, I was to serve my needs best, and from him, stay clear-away.

Though true, I had not always been so discerning with the men I slept with, for back in the days, when I held less respect for myself, it was not 1, but 2 male friends in NZ, who were to tell me of the '6-date rule,' and how, I should not consider sleeping with a man, at least until that milestone had been surpassed, and my reply to that concept, "Arrhah, I won't be sleeping with anyone the, for rarely so I surpass date 3." Their eyebrows raised in astonishment with my reply, but really, that was all so normal to me and for sure, back in the day, at different behaviours I exhibited, as no longer, nonchalantly, "Shall I sleep with this one?" is a passing concept I throw away, affording far less credence to it than calculation and examination, I imparted before choosing which new jumper to purchase, and thank goodness, those outdated ways are behind me.

Even my friends I hadn't really told of my history, so they had no idea that I fervently ran away from relationships, and true, should I ever have reached 6 dates, I would have contemplated that I was in one, and far to close for comfort, still scared, still injured, only a decade ago, that was something, I could never possibly do, true, my prescription for protection wasn't perfect, in fact it had many flaws init, but at that time, it served me perfectly well, one strategy I had, was to find fault with them before they could find fault with me, and hey-presto, simultaneously, a relationship averted, and the risk of assured abandonment or further rejection from me diverted, as I, so healthy and safe, was to carry-on along my way, all alone.

Though interestingly, most of my friends, able to hold relationships of the steady and dependable kind, they, not scared, not frightened to get emotionally close or even emotionally attached to some other person, amazing to me, that they held not an inkling of a belief, that the man would hurt them, as quite different my staunchly held and debilitating belief as I seriously could not, and indeed I think

I gave the notion a try once, but "No," I could not conceive the notion, that I would be in a relationship with a man, and not get beaten or harmed in some way. And although they could not conceive my point of view, if forever I dared share it, I could not conceive that there was another alternative, "Oh my" how terribly sad it had been, at the hands of so many men, mine had been a lifetime of ongoing abuse, and evidentially so had drawn me to the conclusion, that it was to be most likely forever resoundingly so.

So simply, unfortunately I had at that time, I has such a long way to travel, to rise up to a valuable stage of welcomed recovery, for limiting beliefs were so entrenched and trapped in my mind, subconsciously they self-perpetuating fear, so by definition, as that was my belief that governed me, I was unable to grasp the concept, that in a relationship with a man, of the emotional and physical kinds, I would never be free from pain, suffering, or violence, or free from financial deprivation, as so 'Slowly does it' became my goal, as they were to take what I had and make it theirs, to steel and deplete my independence, while enhancing theirs, so trapping me, into what and who they expected and conceded, I was to be.

Though true, as the years went on and my inner-healing and growth came on, though it came slowly and unannounced, and it was only through the attributes it brought me that I realized, I was indeed recovering, and that great iron drawbridge to my castle that for my protection I had welded shut, well, eventually, I was able to lower it again, and that shark-infested moat, well, those fish I was able to dispense with, but the deep cold water, well that stayed, so as they paddled to where I stood, still wearing my heavy body armour, I was able with caution to observe them as across it they rowed.

Deliberation still remained, though really with my past history I thought it only astute, for to get side-swiped again by another man wearing Little Miss Red Riding Hoods cloak, I refused to be served up ever again as my fate, for wisdom has taught me that a man's personal agenda can be hidden extremely deeply, and we need our 'wits about us,' to ensure, they are unable to trick us, or maybe possibly that was just me.

But of truth, since my childhood, violence against me had risen considerably since my youth, with different men and consecutive relationships, proving that each somehow knew how to, harm me a little more than the previous on. And the pattern, while in it, I had not recognized it, or picked-up on any type of significance to it, but of cause that was until, the one who came so close to steeling my life from me, then began to threaten me more of the same, at last Halleluiah, that was my pivotal and defining point, for my ultimate and set in stone, not to be altered message, addressed to me, "Well! As I cannot choose any better than that I am not to choose at all." And just maybe, positively, perhaps certainly, that decision is what ultimately, saved my life.

Not such a good shot, as those men who I chose, even when they were not hitting, controlling or generally being the master of me, several stole from me, money out of my purse by the £20 at a time, a pretty sum back in the day, and CD's, my favourites too, stolen from my home and in England, when their invention was still quite new, they cost a pretty penny too, then sunglasses that had lovely mirrored lustre sheen, and jewellery, really and even my old 12inches, 45's and LP's nostalgic, Town of Motown and one with the Onedin Line theme music on it, more significant than you can imagine, all from when I was doing my nurse training and first escaping my parents house, they disappeared too, but "Why?" It simply got that I didn't understand, for when telling friends about it, asking, "What men had stolen from them?" No, nothing!

For sure, in the regards to men, Postponing choosing, I decided was uppermost, the best thing that for me I could do, for I was learning, that my worth was equating to far more than they dictated it was and as such, I, no more, was to be pushed down, to that place where they determined I should be, for I had grown, and I knew for me, I was jolly well to pull myself up gain, to a position, I was to maintain, refusing to be waiver from my stance, or be swayed by any of their sweet talk or romance, which may only prove to be a smokescreen of magic, while they may trick you into bed, and while your looking for love, their looking for sex, and the strength of their ultimate goal is not to get you between the sheets, but their feet under your table.

Well I had a yet unspoken message for all those men who were to come, for I knew then, kindness goodness, gentleness and faithfulness were to follow me or the rest of my life, and if they can't supply, "Keep on walking," to them was my cry; and in the lyrics of the Janet Jackson song from back in the day still relevant today, "What have you done for me lately?" True, if any of those men don't believe I deserve any better, "Well, categorically, I don't deserve them at all!"

So it came to pass, those outdated self-defeating attitudes, of such notions no longer were they able to flourish, for I chose to give them all away, and so I did, all the fear, all the shame and guilt, feeling lighter unencumbered I rose to a higher and new level, as those bygone days were to slip away, as slowly but surely, gladly I began to think so much more of me, successfully, recognizing my own and true value, the days got brighter, the roads got wider, the cul-de-sacs dwindled, and avenues gave way, to wide open tree-lined boulevards, my vision stretching far, as into the distance I could see the path beckoning me, for my journey, more peaceful, to continue on.

"In learning to know other things, and other minds, we become more intimately acquainted with ourselves, and are to ourselves better worth knowing."
~ Philip Gilbert Hamilton

Chapter 17

Step In, One's Own Truth!

"I have tried to lift France out of the mud. But she will return to her errors and vomiting, I cannot prevent the French from being French."
~ Charles de Gaulle; French President, in Office 1959 - 1969

Memories of Paris, came flooding back, from not so long ago, and "Oh my" how I missed it so," I wondered, those friends, "What were they up to? Were they happy and healthy?" and "Did they think of me for even a minute or two?" and my old flatmate Anastasia, "How was she faring and did she ever overcome the French bureaucracy?" She at half my age, who helped me with my *travail à la maison*, homework, as I encouraged her and gave her mechanisms and strategies, to overcome her nocturnal ways, and we enjoyed the odd day out, to the movies, or the *pâtisserie*, or walking along the river *Seine*, especially on that day, when the tide was so high, it swelled so much it's banks overflowed, yet we had so much fun jumping here and there, navigating and manoeuvring our way around.

Then reminiscing, over visiting those *grands magasins*, department stores, located in the *IXeme.*' 9eme arr, of *Galeries Lafayette* and *Printemps*, on *Boulevard Haussmann*, while admiring their architecture, as from the ground to the high distance to the domes above, with such bright guilt finishing's and there, as we walked our way to the top, my imagine began wildly running, of those who had trodden those steps before, and the *artisans*, whose skills had made such amazing beauty, "What were their life really like?" Holding onto the banister rail, we trundled our way up, and there at the top, a café, where we were to sit and enjoy a wonderful view, of the close and distant vista, but a reality check as, back at the apartment, while chatting and laughing, as we remembered the fun we had, before our landlord returned and observed our joviality, of our conversation and light hearted spirit, and that displeasing him, so to break us up, he hastened, with interruptions of nonsense.

But never to worry, there was always the oasis of *Café Laurent* where I was able to go, so welcomed on those snow filled winter days, where battling with, trying my best not to be swept off your feet on that slippery ground outside, and there I may order a teapot filled with hot chocolate, so thick and steamy, that I could stand my spoon up init, and so-many new my name and welcomed me as I strutted right in, and "Oh my" how those memories still so fresh, wrapped around me so warm and snugly, but of those to recoup or enhance, nothing was to prove so positive, from my emotions or that time passed, in that small southern *ville, dansl le sud le la France*, down the south of France.

For trials and tribulations were to fall on me quite unexpectedly, in a way, in my wildest dreams, nay nightmares, I could never have comprehended, though it is fare to say, many a crack I had seen begin to show, in that place, where I became to wish, never did I go there, for as I took a walk one sundrenched day, up to the shop that I went, true, the service was bad well at least to me, as there I would wait in the queue patiently, only to reach the front of the line, where rudeness reigned, as the manager, with her long dark hair, turning around, really would do anything, rummaging on the shelf behind, making a telephone call or simply, walk away, while deliberately appearing, to ignore serving me.

And surely, I would never have gone in that store again, but unlike Paris, where there was such a franchised store in each *arrondissement* for the products they sold, but in that *ville*, there was only one, and of another, more than a short car ride away, and needless to say, unachievable on my bicycle, so perhaps foolishly, I continued to frequent the shop, for I liked the products, and I so enjoyed building up my loyalty points, but really, I should have conceived, with greater discernment, as a *client,* customer "What was their loyalty shown to me?"

As on one fateful day, deep ditch and falling sprang to mind, as everything, was about to get a whole lot worse, as a beautician served me as I bought my usual, 3 bottle so body lotion, and in Euros that assistant short changed me, but refused my requests to recalculate and make right her wrong. Her refusals absolute, punctuated by *"Je ne comprende pas,"* "I do not understand," thrown my way with an unhelpful expression of disgust on her face, perhaps her exaggerated tone was to embarrass me in front of the other customer, but sincerely, that, was only to be the start of it.

A receipt I requested next, as it is unlawful in France I found out not to be given one, but that she refused too, her excuse, 'the register' was broken, yet she'd just provided one to the customer in front of me. Knowing I was right, I held my change in my hand tight, until I reached *ma maison,* my house, placing them safely there, before getting my calculator out. True enough I was right so back to the shop I wandered just 15 minutes later, and there as I walked through the door, a long till receipt from that broken till she was providing for a customer. But what of that employees deceit surely so another wouldn't be subject to the same, to inform the manager became my objective. Yet a name badge she did not wear, so I considered, "Arrhah," a photo will solve that issue, so to use my tiny flip phone, 6 year old, Nokia, pink and terribly cute, I was to snap a shot, though normally used only for calls, I knew not, even how to save it, so simply, I flipped it shut and left the store, then walking out onto the paved street, *"Madame, Madame,"* I barely heard called, so had not a clue, it was being addressed to me, then suddenly, I felt my arm in a tight grip, as sharply, I was spun around, as aggressively, that beautician demanded of me, *"Donnez-moi votre telephone maintenant,"* "Give me your telephone now!" "What? No."

"Leaning is not compulsory and neither is survival."
~ *W. Edwards Deming*

Then *their* performance began, "Oh my oh my!" For there were to be 2 of them, as I, an unwilling participant, was that morning, to become the street entertainment, so the juggler, unable to reign over that completion, after a while packed up his skittles and disappeared, as there on the paved pedestrian way, that rather rotund dark-haired girl of 20someting years, dressed in her white trouser tunic trimmed with green, with her strength and certainly her weight, I suggest, in greater excess of double mine, pulling, tugging and dragging me about, from one side to the other, and everywhere in between, grappling with my arm, and drastically trying, to grab my phone from out of my clasped hand, and of the swiftly gathering crowd, not a one, attempted to intervene.

Her colleague quickly joining her, she, blonde and petite but only in stature, as appearing overflowing with viciousness, because I didn't need to understand the language, to know how seriously she threatened me. Then each of them, with their 2 hands, took one of my wrists a piece and grabbing so tightly a-hold of it, it was impossible to escape, they, cajoling, pushing pulling, jarring my body from side to side, while simultaneously trying their best to seize my phone out from my hand. To break free was impossible, though I should have laughed and declared, "OK, where's that man with his film crew, preparing to rush out and shout 'Got Ya!' Will you please tell them to hurry, because this really, isn't funny anymore!" As surely, "They must have been having a laugh, right?" Seriously, sadly, "No!" In broad daylight that occurrence unfolded, then I got to thinking, "What about that man in Paris on New Years Eve? What about Nice" I was left wondering, of such incidences in France, of that type of behavior, were they frequent, are they common?" and "Was that just 'my time,' for it happened to be me?"

Likely 20 minutes and counting, being put on show and assaulted and trapped in the street, and all my escape attempts failed and my only hope for additional evidence, I pleaded to the onlookers, "*Téléphone à la police, s'il vous plaît, prendre des photos,*" "Please telephone the police and take photos" I begged as I, so innocent, and falsely held hostage, suffering with increasing neck and shoulder pain, with that situation of uncomfortable and additional public humiliation, but really, things could have been so much worse as some centuries ago, likely I may have been taken off to the guillotine, so they could see my head role, or as the War History Museum confirmed, should I have been a Jewish, by the pact France made with Germany in WW 1, they could have sent to a concentration camp.

Time more of it was passing, "Why was no one helping me? Why was no one intervening on the wrongdoing and my suffering they were seeing? When was I to be set free? Where were the police?" and "How soon were they to come to save me?" Then suddenly, noticing that one of the girls only held my wrist with only one of her hands, in an instant, my mental health training, burst in my head, that whenever a person grabs you by the wrist, pull your arm, in a downward and outward direction, as that is the weakest part of the grip, where the thumb and index finger meet at the tip, and with pressure applied, it will separate them." "Would it work?" In an instant, magic, one wrist, I broke free.

My instant relieve and celebration, too short lived, as those 2 young women of 20 something, were instantly outraged, I mean, outraged, the penance I paid was for them in unison, with excessive and extreme force, erratically, as several meters they pushed me, where I was stumbling, trying so hard to keep on my feet, while they appeared consumed, by tremendous vengeance, and one had her hand on my head, slammed it side on against a brick wall, continuing applying oppressive force, holding me there as my shoulder collided, as they dragged my body along, and I, suffering scrapes, grazes, and bruises, but still, no help came, no tourists or locals did no-thing at all to help, only passively looked-on, seemingly with no-thing better to do, they just simply stood by and ogled at me.

Yet I contemplated of those 2 females, so young, but appearing absorbed in so much hate and rage, perhaps triggered so intrinsically, as it appeared by their attitudes and actions, that was not the first time they had behaved, 'just so,' for really, "What did they go through, or what did their parents do, possibly, how did they train them, or possibly didn't, as in that case, maybe inside, something so very bad was hiding or lingering, I was left wondering, "How, why, where, could so little, provoke so much?" Perhaps it could have been prejudice, or individual, or appearing from experiences, perhaps, "The French way?"

Stunned, shocked, with my neck and my head suddenly hurting more, as I, was abruptly snapped back around facing them, as they continued to exert their control, and then, such a relief, a 'ray of hope' as the police came into my view, but "Why were they not hurrying, why were they, meandering?" For the place that the onlookers had formed a loose circle around me as the centre show, the police could not have failed to see what was done to me, so I could not understand, for the police in England and NZ had always been so appropriately helpful, but of those French, "Why they were not rushing to protect the victim?"

My relief certainly proved to be premature, as when the young beauticians left, my legs weak, I stumbled more, but first remembering to ask the police before I collapsed to the floor, and as I handed them my mobile phone so they could see, no picture I had on it, they seeming totally disinterested, insisted on seeing my bag instead, "Well of cause," "But wasn't that unusual for it had noting to do with my phone?" So low was I to catch on, as every pocket they examined in detail, but for what I knew not, thinking only that it was the normal procedure in France, but then it became apparent, that those young women from the store, to cover up their own deceptions, using the oldest trick in the book, in an attempt to deflect from them, to another, so maybe they cast wide their aspersions, accusations of lies of steeling, and delivering them to the police.

Deceit and dishonesty spun in their web apparently, and in the absence of that till receipt "How on earth would I ever have been able to prove it?" Such a blessing that I lived so close to that little shop, and rushed home first to place my purchases on the bathroom shelf, or I suggest by now as it was to turn out, I could have been rotting in a French jail, for surely, of those French girls, whose apparently, nasty, evil words set against me, to coin an English expression, 'you've got 2 chances, and there both no-chance.' And the reason for such a conclusion, it was Frenchmen, who pertained to such a fact, as by the river one evening we were playing *Boules*, and their descriptive explanation, they gave me, 1) in France unfortunately, woman still don't have the same standing as men, They continued, apparently, a singe woman falls even lower down the pecking order. 2) I was a foreigner in their country. 3) I didn't speak French yet. Then more they were to reveal; "It is most unusual what happened to you, before this, we have not heard about such a bad thing happening, where the police have done, nothing."

"Oh really!" Then an English lady, who I told what happened to me, gave me some quite amazing accounts of information, explaining she read quite frequently in papers, of how, when one person was causing harm to another, off to the police station he/she would be taken, so me in a quandary, considering, "Why did the same procedure not occur in my circumstance?" "Quite bewildered" and perhaps those, *Boule* playing Frenchman, were right in their calculations, as for they who assaulted me, they were not marched off to anywhere, as on that day, when the rest of the multitudes had disappeared, they awaited close by, while the police officers dispensed their instructions, categorically informing me, 'I must never enter into that store again', and that street 'not to walk on it again until the next day.' And when I requested their name, rank or number, each was met with a refusal, I then requested a case number, for I needed that for when I went to lodge a formal complaint against those assailants, at the police station, to hold them accountable, for what harm they had caused, yet he appearing effortlessly bold and unambiguous in purpose, with his instructions directly delivered, "That is not a good idea. It is your word against theirs. So just leave now. Go away and stay away." "What, were they kidding?" "That was to be, "Not."

Then, "Yeah!" "Phew!" To help me a witness came forward! A young lady of only 20 or so years, appearing kind and caring for my safety, fervently expressing concerns of the travesty she had seen, firstly addressing me, then to the police she turned to, with had gestures, expressing an account of the events that had unfolded and how bad it all was, but "What?" Not even a notebook did the officer take out or record those prized details, of her name etc, and as in my defense she spoke, not even once did he glance in her direction, he appearing somewhat superior, totally ignoring her, until a few words he uttered, dismissing her, to go away. Yet me, picking up on the clues, her body language and facial expressions, she appeared, clearly perturbed and confused, at the officers non-action to listen or engage with her. And before he was to follow his instructions, she passed me a glance of sincere support, of wishing she could do more, I was to watch her and my hope for justice, walk off down the road.

But then, as I bent down to pick up my bag, "What! "What was I seeing?" Those 2 officers who had walked away from me, stood only a few feet away, directly in front, of those 2 young women, those assailants by another name, who had just assaulted me and their interaction, clearly indentifying, comfort of familiarity, sharing laughs and joviality, with those who I was to understand later, from further investigations, by speaking with non French policeman, had in fact committed a criminal offence against me. Really? "Was that it, my lot in life, to always, 'put up and shut up,' and for justice never to be received, forever it to be depleted or deferred, as for me, I was not to have it served?"

Really! For that scenario to continue, I was most unhappy, for I was assaulted and they who caused the harm, "Surely must be held accountable?" Yet in the interim, a more pressing matter, a doctor I needed to find, and at that hour not necessarily easy, so grateful I was, when English acquaintance, who she spoke French quite well, agreed to accompany me, yet soon as it appeared I travelled 50 years backwards to a parallel universe, as the doctor with his height less than mine, though his air of conceit considerably higher, as he minced not his intent or words, dogmatically speaking while pointing to my companion, "She cannot come in." "But stressed, I feel so terribly unwell," I persisted, "She is my support and translator," but his replied was not up for discussion, "She is not welcome, I speak very good English, I will understand all you say, you do not need an interpreter, she must go away." Before, continuing in his unwavering authority, "These are my conditions, you accept them, or you leave!"

Obviously, ambiguity was not one of his failings, as clearly it was his way or the highway. "Wow!" It appeared no 'White Paper' for patient's rights or empowerment in France, and being apart of the medical profession, it seemed more than a tad archaic, of such a staunch manner, "Was it his norm or a little unusual? Was he like that with all patients or perhaps just single women or even just foreign travelers?" or "Prejudice?" that was increasingly relevant, that those *boule*-players spoke of. But then that doctor, did appear to took a good history of events, and almost ironically, considering his unsympathetic, harsh behavior, amongst the already visible, bruising to both wrists, my skin scrapes, torn on my face, back and shoulder, "What I had suffered?" His, *première*, major diagnosis, was that of, *'Psychological Traumatisation,'* 'Psychological Trauma.' {PTSD.}

The trauma transferred, to effect my rest, as sleep-full nights became sleep-less, with bad dreams beginning to wake me up, and hearing noises began to startle me, and prolonged were such, then surprisingly unexpectedly, I would have bouts where I'd fall to my knees and cry grievously, and of an outlet of hope, for the police to do something, to address the situation in an appropriate manner, where I was grossly wronged, it still seemed that nothing was being done, yet upon a friends insisting, regardless of what that policeman said, she insisted I must go to the station to make a report. Then with my statement given, I enquired, "When will the surveillance cameras from the street and store be collected and checked, to prove irrevocably, the truth of my account of events, and the officer, appearing ambiguous at best, and obstructive at worst, refused to give me a conclusive answer.

From pillar to post I was then to be sent, initially, following that officer's instruction to return in a week, only to be told, for a month, he had gone on *des vacances*, holiday˙ so no-more on my case was to be done until his return. Eager for that, my friend and I anticipating good news, ventured again to the station, but "No," as I was informed, he was no longer dealing with my case, and it had been passed onto another officer, who, you may have guessed it, when I asked to speak with him, was told, "You cannot, he had just started his month long *des vacances*." "Well who else will help me, who is to take over while 'he' is away?" "No one." Was to be their dismissive reply, apparently, 'I just had to wait!' Surreal! The situation could have been a sit-com, only really, it wasn't funny.

"Were they joking?" "If only!" Though absolutely not! Time passed by, still, all my pleaded questions remained unanswered, "Have you got the camera footage from the street, is it recorded safely on file? The footage from the shop is that the same? How frequently are those tapes re-used?" Yet the officer's, appearing preoccupied, only replied, "I don't know." Somewhat distressed and wanting to know something, "What is the protocol for obtaining the camera footage? Who does it, that officer or another? Where are they stored? What of documentation, has that been completed? Has someone put hold on them?" Though the result consistently the same, apparent disinterest coming my way, and one time, the trauma of it all got too much, no justice for me and those 2 French girls still out on the street, the sleep problems, the emotions, being pointed out in the streets, as laughing, sneers and jeers were sent my way, by teenagers and their mothers, and worse, was refused to be served at a café I used to regularly frequent, it all got too much, I was overcome, and unable to hold myself up, in the corner of the police station, I crumpled, into a heap on the floor, sobbing uncontrollably, with my biggest question of all, "Why: were they appearing so terribly obstructive and not helping me, *not* at all?"

Months x 2 had passed since that vindictive assault, and I the innocent one, the victim, still I remained, void of the police force rallying to my aid, and above their apparent inertia, "Was that day ever to come?" Then as the sun was shining, to the seaside three of us rode in the car, a friend who on my behalf had been liaising with the police, "Oh yes I spoke with the police this morning" she said "And?" "I got an answer to your question," for a moment, relief, instantly my spirit changed and with an urgency of positive expectation I enquired, "What did they say?" explaining, "It's all bad. None of the camera footage was collected, and after 14 days, it was re-recoded over, so your evidence has gone, and the police on your case, are taking no more action."

Distraught. Worrying about justice, asking, "Why was the footage not tracked and saved?" she continuing, "This is what happened, the police personnel, seeing no value in doing so, chose not to complete the necessary paperwork or pass them along to the appropriate office, for further investigation of your case." "What?" With exacerbation I cried out, "But why ever not?" Seriously, having suffered too much of it in life, I insisted, "Violence is a most serious matter for investigation." Still, her shoulders shrugging, my stomach wrenching, she delivered her final blow, likely of facts, "You may be upset; you may be distressed; you may have reason to be; but you are not French; and in their investigation process, they decided *you* were worthy of justice. That is it, you need to accept it!"

"POW!" Sadness gripped me tightly, "What! Was she kidding me?" So sorrowfully, absolutely not! Tears flooded down my face, her stern expression remained firmly in place, and then from the back of the car, her elder brother who visiting from a neighbouring European country, an outsider, yet after hearing about the unfolded situation, and unemotionally examining only the facts, he delivered his mature and professional opinion, effectively 'his verdict:' "This is what the police have done; simply, they played a waiting game with you, they would have known that the camera footage would automatically be re-recorded over after 14 days, effectively, wiping your evidence clean away and negating your claim." Continuing, "It does seem most odd, that they interrupted their normal reporting processes, but whatever their reasons, for you, justice was not done."

"Wow!" "Was he right? Had they deliberately done that to me?" Certainly his logic, his verdict, was the only one holding substance of clarity, or since that assault, a sound rational, and "Was I to give up without a fight for justice, for was he right, was that all *they*, determined I was worthy of?" as "Oh my" distraught at the revelation the apparent injustice of so much, physically sick I felt, and my gut jumping up into my throat, severely wrenching with anxiety, as suddenly, my instinct, struck a cord with every cell in my body, vibrating, through my heart and to the largest degree, causing such sorrow in my deepest core, for "Why was it, as seemingly always, forever-more, no-one, not anyone at anytime, would ever in word or deed, be on my side, or stick up for me?"

> *"The great thing in the world is not so much where we stand,*
> *as in what direction we are moving."*
> *~ Oliver Wendell Holmes*

For really, "How many decades were to pass, that apparently no one considered *ME*?" or held an inkling of *my self-worth*, as I, was void of value, and seemingly unimportant, unworthy of protection," yet surely, "As I strived for acceptance, by somebody, anybody, had I not demonstrated, at least outwardly, that I thought myself worthy of so much more than I given?" Yet never had I gone to seek justice for those who transgressed against me, and "Was I at last to 'stand up to be counted?" For had I not grown sufficiently, as I travelled along my journeys path, to know that of self-value, as a minimum, I deserved that, *surely*, I deserved better, than I had received in the past, then in a blast, a puzzle formed in my head, where questions I asked; "Was I to be made scapegoat, or 'sent to the lions den?" and "Why were such scenarios in my life not ceasing? Why did people view my needs as expendable and never meet them? Why were all my actions and deeds dismissed or devalued?" and "Why was my safety appearing forever superfluous to other peoples requirements forever an apparent, living sacrifice?"

As a pattern emerged from back in the day, when I at just 17 years, where in a brown little old Triumph, the car that my father bought my mother, and in it, up and down the driveway, I was practicing my foot control, with the test for my provisional licence hovering on the horizon, drive, and for sure, I knew no quite what happened, as the lock of the steering wheel was on the wrong way, and "Too late" was my cry, as, it was all too late, to break or quickly turn the steering wheel, as shattering glass was all I heard. And "Oh my" my adrenaline profoundly pounding around my body, as I quickly started calculating how angry my father was to be, and what punishment he was to deliver to me, for I knew I would be in serious trouble for that huge mistake, so scared was I, as I walked in through the backdoor, to find my brother and mother standing there, their words, not of support or encouragement, but those inducing added distress, with my brother skiting "Huh! You're in for it now! You better get in there and tell him what you've done," as he pointed toward the lounge door.

"No" I hastened, "I'm scared, and besides he's sleeping, if I disturb him he'll be even more angry, so I'll wait until he wakes and tell him then." "No you wont!" my mother said testily, "I don't want this hanging over *my* head; until he decides to wake up, wondering what he's going to do next. So you'll get in there now, and get it over and done with." And so, the two of them stood in unison, fortified in their conviction, that I must go in, so I grabbed a hold of that metal door handle, gently lowering it, my spirit plummeted, as I wondered, "What on earth was he going to do to me this time?" So daintily and tentatively I placed one foot then the other on that dark green shagpile carpet, and then, as I stepped in the room with both feet, as quick as a flash, in an instant, my mother pulled that door boldly shut behind me, making sure, from his wrath, her and my brother were protected, as I, ended up, alone again, thrown to the lions den.

Standing at the foot of where he lay, on the floor with his eyes closed, vulnerable, exposed and susceptible, as I was easily within an arms length, and trembling in my boots, as I gently spoke, but not daring to do so too loud, for surely that would vex him more. But "What was that?" bemused, he wasn't angry, he did not hit me, or call me names, or push or pull me around, not even a threat came away from his lips, and I, quite bemused, yet my guard I did not let down, as he raised himself from the floor, with his instructions, not spoken too nastily, "Show me what you've done." So I walked past that duo of my mother and brother, who were squeezed into the furthest corner of the kitchen, certainly determined, not to get in his way, and as out of the door we walked, I wondered, "Is it now it is coming?" Now he's tricking me into a false sense of security, for his hand is only a couple of feet away, and even if it was further, he was good at racing, to hit me across the face, or somewhere else," so my guard remained up, ready, on alert, at any moment, just to try and protect myself.

My adrenaline pumping so rapidly, so fast that my heart and lungs were almost unable to carry it, as just in preparation, awaiting for that inevitable moment, when he was to strike-out at me and hit, but that action, oddly, bizarrely he did not make or take, and how confused I was, for I knew not what to do, "Was I supposed to stand still and ask for him to punish me, or ask him how long it was to be before he chose to do so, as for sure I was in new territory, and I knew not why I escaped his wrath that day, but I did ponder along the way, with my only conclusion, perhaps his concept; he held greater power and credence, in his world which he ruled over ours with his iron-fist, and to disprove us as wrong, in his own sight, was a victory, his rational, to cause confusion or uncertainty, destabilizing what we thought we knew, assigning himself greater power, to knock us off guard more easily next time, perhaps aiming to make us increasingly weak, or perhaps, just on that occasion, "Why" he was being, kind!

But "Only if" I'd always been so lucky, but for sure that was not the case a year earlier, when then, the 3 of us, mother, brother and I, stood in the kitchen, that room so small, as the burners lit and huddled around it to keep warm, for we had central heating, but were prohibited because of the cost of running it, from using it; but suddenly, the backdoor was flung wide open, so aggressively, that it banged and bounced again off the wall, and I clearly knew, a slam of the door or something else, often preceded him, slamming some punishment directly at me, and then his, my father's instructions, with his raising temper, with his anger rampantly displayed, with his finger fiercely pointed in my face, "*YOU*! Get in that room now!" And of cause, no questions were to be asked, only obedience to the dogma of his instructions, as always, I did exactly as what I was told to do, and as through the door I walked, and as my feet stepped onto that dark green shagpile carpeted room, in an instant, I was almost knocked right off them, as the force of his body weight, he transferred it to me, as he pushing me so hard.

Again and again violently, backwards he pushed me, while my petite frame at only 16, I tried as hard as I might to keep my balanced feet, as he as usual, his face a blazing red, his veins all popping out on his forehead, his gritted teeth, yellow and nasty, as his face only a couple of centimetres from mine with his finger pointing into the side of my cheek, his temper raged out of control, and the clouds in the sky how funny they concealed the sun, as he propelled me further down the length of the long 'L' shaped room, past the G-Plan furniture suit, and into an open space, as his vengeance carried on, and as he had pushed me so far, I struggled not to tumble to the floor, until under his strength, at the far end of the room, my body all twisted and hurting, my neck, at a most awkward angle, as there I laid on my back, pinned down, beneath the weight of his body, as on that family, 3 seater sofa, with his left hand pushing hard into my chest, immobilizing me, as not an inch, I was able to move, or even twist my head out of that contorted position, just in the hope that it would cease the pain, but no, that was not to be, as he, my father, had me totally trapped, as his right hand, clenched in a fist, he held it, hovering above my head, as he was yelling and hurling abuse, but about "What?" honestly I didn't know, for non of it made any sense, and all I could see was his face so angry, and his fist as I wondered, "How soon before it landed on me?" and me so helpless, I was only to worry, "What was he going to do next?" and "How long would it go on for?" and "When, oh when, was he ever going to stop?"

Yet I did not scream, I did not even cry, for in the world I lived, that I was not allowed to do, not even as a child, such behaviour by him was not tolerated, so my default in times of trouble, was to let the adrenaline bubble and internalize all the hardships of the emotion and pain, where it only multiplied and festered, and in my life caused such a strain, for really, I had no idea what was normal or acceptable, for really, "Wasn't that it?" For no one had come to my rescue, no one in the world cared about me, as I was always sacrificed, always dispensable, never held in care or considered worthy of any good, and so demonstrated as my mother and brother, who that day, so swiftly pulled the lounge door, behind me, firmly shut.

Really! "Was I ever, ever in the world, perhaps possibly somewhere by someone, ever thought to be special, or even in the very basic of needs, worthy of protection?" But so young and knowing absolutely no alternative, that was not a conundrum or even a very simple question, for evidence I held absolutely non, no provided data or to support to the contrary, my only living destiny, in that in the world, I was all alone, all lost, that little girl, with nowhere to go, nowhere to escape, no mentor, and no one to help, only suffering so terribly much, but she remained the same, for their was nothing she could do, and so sorrowfully she grew, passing from a child into adulthood, remaining helpless, rejected and desperately unloved.

And so, my father, eventually took his body weight off mine, and there an agreement somewhere in my brain equated to, "That's what love is, and that's what people who love you do," and so tragic was that days work that he did, leaving his little girl, me, with his destruction seeled, and my heart my mind, spirit and emotions, for decades of health or healing, never to see the light of day. But really, "Why had he done such a thing?" And eventually, after he had lowered his fist, and removed his hand from pressing on my chest, his story he was to continue to shout, and as it turned, out, it was a lie, a rouse, he just made the whole thing up, telling a story, as he was on his way back after dropping his car off at the mechanics, "I was stood at the bus stop and I heard 2 boys taking about your bother, and telling each other, that they'd both had sex with his little sister and that you're a slut!" Continuing, pointing his finger harder into my face, "You slut! You bloody slut!" "If only" I would have had more confidence, but I dared not to 'answer him back' for I knew his rules of old, of that, I was most definitely forbidden, but so much I wanted to declare, "But; I'm a virgin!"

How sad, I had to put up with all that, and not even cry out my defence, daring to tell him that he was wrong, but "Simply I 'dare not,' as if my life depended on it, never ever under any circumstance, to contradict him," for that in itself was more-than a hittable offence, so you see my dilemma I was on a bit of a sticky wicket, but I did deny the accusation, fervently so, pleading, begging with him to believe me, that me, his daughter, "I'm not a slut, I'm really not," but he would not, or perhaps just because he simply didn't wan to.

Perhaps, he thought that that in house over time I wasn't being sufficiently submissive, so he upped the anti of his wheedling command, perhaps I failed to guard my face expression on when I had to look at him, or my tone of voice, perhaps I spoke 'goodnight' to him wrongly, for all I knew so very well, I had to 'watch myself' and be most careful, to ensure that I never did divulge or give a clue away by mistake of my true feelings, certainly not one that could be miss-strewed as 'dumb-insolence,' as certainly when accused of that, 'something' was a-coming at me. But maybe I made a mistake, maybe I miss-calculated, maybe he guessed the emotions toward him I was harbouring, my increasing almost-hatred for him, maybe he thought I was 'getting above myself' in some other way, having too much confidence or self-determination to achieve my goal of becoming a nurse, and he was determined to make me 'know my place' and 'not get above myself' and to remember to dance to his tune and not other, with his ultimate aim to 'bring me down a peg or two!' Any of the above conjured up so easily in his mind would suffice, he didn't need a reason, he just needed his intention!

So young, so innocent, tears hiding behind my eyes as agony and living in my heart, with such a burden of pain, so real to bear, through the cruelty suffered at the wilful hands of my father who didn't care, and "Why, did he deliberately choose to do such things to me?" I wondered, "Was it simply because he could, or perhaps he cared not to apply effort into making different or better choices, concerning that attributes of not, harming me, his daughter?" And forever reminding me 'who was in-charge,' for that was always to be him, as he disempowered me by surprise, and the uncertainty, from behind which wall, or around which door where his next strike was to come from, for the forever certainty was, that it was always going to come. The physical bouts of violence only interjected by his daily accusations spouted, "You Dunce! You Moron! You Imbecile!" Banded about like confetti at a wedding. Yet now, as an adult, I reflect on how his attitude and behaviours encroached on the ridiculous, as how counterproductive, he consistently punishing me for not excelling in class, sparing not a thought of how his actions were the reasons, as now, to that research, will attest.

True, of his certain intent, I know not, yet fortunately to some degree, I had learnt what made him tick, for I was not a victim I was a survivor, and that as a mechanism to protect themselves is what we do, so perhaps I became a mini master at that, to serve me the best way I knew how, but on that day, the lie he told the accusation against his me, my brother was to tell me, afterwards of cause, as they, my mother and my brother, 15 months older, like the onlookers in that *ville*, never did they get involved or come to my rescue, afterwards my brothers words, "I know that what 'he' said was anywhere remotely near the truth." My friends never call me by my Christian or surname, only ever my nickname, and with 10 or more of us with cars, never would we leave another stood waiting for a bus, so what 'he' said, no way could it be true. Confirmation that my father had prefabricated a deception of lies, of where he was stood and what he heard after he had dropped his car off at the mechanic that Saturday morning. So I begged my brother, "Oh please go and let him know, that they weren't talking about me." "No way!" was his distancing rapid retort, followed swiftly by, "It's nought to do with me!" "So don't expect me to step in!" "Hey!! Thanks big brother!"

> *"Happiness is not a goal; it is a by-product."*
> *~ Eleanor Roosevelt*

Too slow was I to recognize, that my brother, as he grew into a man, was developing some deep-set traits like his father, but inside I tried to dismiss it as such deep sad sorrow would rise from that horrible notion, so as quickly as it hit the surface I would bury it again, that was until one evening when his ex-girlfriend, a friend of mine for a while, down at the river Wyre, after the pub had closed, we were chatting and laughing, and talking over the night, hiding from those cold and dreary elements, sat in her car, with the windows wound up, but then, she dared to say those words I'd dared not concede, "You know your brother is just like your father!" "No. No." I wanted to declare, to disprove her statement, but that was not to happen, as by her rationalization, no longer was I able to dismiss my own theory, as confirmation of that bad thing she'd given, and my heart fearing, that the unthinkable, was actually true, and with that revelation, as I sat beside her, as deafening sounding echoes, bounced all around, as I, sadly, just started screaming.

Stunned, so full of sorrow, that in my assessment, I had not been wrong, but right, and as I return to my father's house quite late that night, still shocked, revolving my thoughts, "He's was my brother, how could he turn out like him?" And there, perhaps not noticing the bathroom door ajar, though I do recall mildly registering the light was turned on, and with a heavier heart than usual, weary I commenced dragging myself up the stairs, eagerly wanting my bed to rest my heavy mind, but, right there, that was my mistake, as I failed to make a connection, that my father was behind that door, so momentarily made and error, as I, missed, omitted to acknowledge him to say "Goodnight."

For that, was a necessary word for his attention, a requirement, a note for his personal respect, and acknowledgment of his authority, and never, to be missed! My nightgown I had put on, before I heard him shout, and I knew that tone, and in my minds eye could see his gritted teeth with the words of his command, "You! Get down these stairs now!" And he used not my name, for really rarely did he, but his voice, that statement, never undiscerning, for I knew it was meant for me, so wearily, opening my bedroom door, one step tentatively before the other, on each wooden steps, descending half way down that spiral staircase I walked, and to that the black iron handrail, holding tight, wondering that night, "What did he, have in store for me?"

My father, by my presence, certainly not appeased, and with his blood boiling, as his veins were nearly popping out of his head, he stood, in partial dress, staring with daggers as his further command viciously delivered, as he fervently, he pointed to the spot directly at the base of his feet, "You get here *NOW*!" And of cause, I did exactly what I was told, for from old, I had never dared do anything else for I absolutely knew of nothing else to do, and so he continued with his spite, perhaps only to serve to cause me fright, as his vengeance unfolded, spurting out from him like blistering laver, and all pouring over me, demanding, "Who do *you* think you are?" timidly, "I don't understand" I answered, "Do *you* think *you're* better than me?" with his finger pushing closer toward my head, so taking 2 steps backwards, replying, "No! Really, I don't!" But not 'good enough,' as he began to push me backwards, his hissing, spitting, words springing forth, "*You* idiot! *You* tell me, what you did wrong! *NOW!*"

My brain, still not thinking clearly it, as those words I heard, shared, sat in the car, had not cleared from my mind, but how fortunate, I remembered, that never ever was I permitted to say, "I don't know," and caught myself in time as that would hugely, exacerbate his perversity for violence, but "Phew" that error I bypassed, or so I thought, but not so on that night, as it made no difference, as he continued to push me into another wall, as only an inch separated his face from mine, his arrows like flames of poison, heading directly toward me, yelling, "Do *you* remember who I am?" "Do *you?*" assuring him, "Yes, you're my father." Though really, "How could I ever forget it?" But my response, maybe not quick enough, maybe spoken without the 'right degree' of respect, or to his commanded, not sufficiently subservient enough, as with such anger, he carried-on knocking me around the hall, from wall to wall, and funnily, I never even wondered, "Why?" he did it, as it was just more of the same, on a different day!

My mistake, quite simple, wrapped up in my stress, I had made a mistake and forgotten of he to be appeased, not to ask, but simply guess, 'how high must I jump,' in the hope that he would not dump a huge portion of his wrath upon me, but Just his format as always was, as I was subjected to at his whim, by his decree, that night he continued knocking me here and there banging me from one wall to the next, and by quickly shifting it to the side, I only just missed him banging my head hard against the wooden stair tread, as he unweaved his web of vicious verbal assaults, "You're stupid!" "How *dare* you not speak to me!" "I'm your father, *remember* that!" "*You* make sure, if you see that bathroom light on, that *you* think on, and shout 'Goodnight father,' just in-case its me in there, because; *YOU will,* acknowledge *my* presence, for *I will NOT be ignored!*" And so it went on, and on, with his accusations as usual, directed at my intelligence, and "How could I forget that one?" "Wow!" for contemplation, "How absolutely, scarily sad to know, that 'I was apart of him, and he, was apart of me!'"

But I was 18 years old then, I was an adult, or so I had always been told, "So did I have to put up with that any longer?" I thought not, so in my distress, I took courage in my hand, and drew my arm across my body to protect myself, and my knee I drew up the same way, and as his noise continued, I began to make a fuss, just hoping that someone upstairs would hear and come to help. And my mother with her bad back, ventured halfway down the staircase, to assess the commotion, and she asking rather loudly, "What's going on?" But my brother, in the bedroom directly overhead, with his door beside my mothers, he venture no where around, though predictable evidentially so, as he never willing to help his little sister, and true, attempts I made to grab his attention and illicit his help by louder yelps, but my big brother, he didn't even make a murmur. "How long did the violence go on for?" Exactly as long as my father deemed it so, until his mission was completed and his job was done, as he had purposefully removed any ambiguity, who was boss within those 4 walls, that house; then, I was dismissed, and sent off back to bed, where I was to get, a good nights sleep?

But there were not so many more to go, until we were to leave that house, for the divorce was through and the financial settlement complete, and although he was hiding, watching somewhere, and though I lingered, and turned around, paused, as my mother told me to hurry and get in the car, never was there a reconciliation, or last embrace, for never did he show his face, and from there, my father was to disappear from my life without a trace. That was of cause, until I wrote requesting a for a reconciliation, and at that "Oh such brief meeting in the pub" I spoke softly, with hope, only daring to receive a kind word, asking, "When I described in my letter, our relationship being like the turbulent sea, with waves crashing against the Promenade seawall, in stormy weather, did you like it, perhaps think it descriptive or poignant?" Yet rapidly, my dreams dashed, as unambiguously, he left me in no doubt, as the corners of his mouth twisted and contorted, "No!" categorically was his retort, continuing with his skilful report "I thought it was stupid and pointless, but then I expect nothing better form you!" Well! I guess if nothing else, of that man, whose blood runs in my veins, no one, could ever accuse him, of being inconsistent!

"Conformity is the jailer of freedom and the enemy of growth."
~ J F Kennedy

I wonder, after all of that, "Why of why, was I a little piece of me pleased to see him?" at the Illawalla Night Club, my favourite spot, in years gone by, where I, passed many a night through my flourishing and newly independent youth, as it an impressive bungalow of its day, the largest in the land, or at least the land far around, was exquisitely transformed with taste and expertise, to a business of reputation, of an exceptional membership list, or so I liked to think, for I was on it. And so captivating its original features, that had all been saved, maintained and enhanced, throughout the renovation, of changing that 5 bed-roomed home, from the old, to a role brand new, with its floor-plan utilized so well, as around the circumference of that building of grandeur, 5 independently named bars with the décor most delightful and inspirational, matching perfectly in elegance to those bygone days, of pristine and plush upholstery, rich in velvets and tapestry and guilt and fringes everywhere, and so young, but such gratitude and appreciation I held, for the exquisite luxury I observed all around.

With drink in hand, walking from each one would lead to a wide and spacious landing, a walkway of where to gather, or promenade, where choosing either would permit a panoramic view of the dance floor below, that large, inviting open space, at the heart of the club, where so many nights full of people enjoying fun and frivolity, onto it would spill. Oh what a joy, as to reach the polished parquet, of staircases numbering 3, while treading so deliberately, as each step sunk into the plush deep pile of the regal red carpet, and down several steps I deliberately almost strutted, while holding onto the highly polished thick mahogany banister rails, the lustre of polished wood gleaming to a glossy high sheen and warm to the touch. And just that simple act, where I almost strut, on each and every occasion brought me so such pleasure, as my posture I'm sure, momentarily stood a little taller as falling over me, an heir of sophistication, and so absolutely exquisite I always felt within myself, and never through all the years I went there, did that notion of emotion, ever become mundane or even dwindle.

And there of a night, I thought to be like any other, into our favourite bar, Alistair and I walked, he a gentle-man, a man I liked greatly, a man who treated me well, though why, I never did comprehend or indeed appreciate, and 8 years my senior, and respect I held for him, quite extraordinarily so, and the barmaid was to greet us in that dimly lit room, which only held a scattering of guests, for the night was still young, Walking into our favourite bar, where our favourite barmaid served, entering the quite well lit room and filled with only a scattering of guests for the night was still young, past the plush upholstered chairs toward the bar we walked. With greetings shared, and smiles exchanged, while waiting to be served, as I turned around, and the greeting was not to be the same, for it was he, my father who I was to see, and what he was to serve me, was not to be pleasant, but then again, I guess, for him, that was not unusual, as only normal, for his personal, routine.

Initially, I was a little unsure of what to do, as he stood alone in the centre of the room, for it had been several months since he had dismissed me, refusing a relationship, so if I walked over to him, "What was he to do?" Yet he, not smiling, but looking directly at me, doing nothing, moved neither closer or further away, just staring, as the prey, having its victim in sight. Then perhaps it was old-school behaviour that kicked into play, as I remembering my 'duty' and 'respect' toward him, which always must complied, so attempting not to be timid, doing my best to hold my shoulders up high, as one tentative foot in front of the other I placed, tedding on that tapestry carpet, as over to him I walked, trying so hard not to be confident, "Hello, how are you?" But his response swift and sharp, with no interest in my question, as gesturing his head toward the bar, where Alistair stood, snapping sharply, "Who's that?" "That's my boyfriend" I replied, and him being a man not a boy I asked, "What would you like him to call you, Mick or Michael?" For you see, his friends, colleagues were welcome to call him the former, but my mother, out of a 'mark of respect,' was only ever allowed and must, call him by the latter.

So, such a valid and harmless question I considered, but that was not to be my father's opinion, as in a rush of hostility, he, standing rigid, with one hand in his pocket, the other holding firm to his glass of beverage, he, instantly vexed as his venom tipped arrows were launched on me, as in that quiet bar, he tilted his head right back, and propelled it forward, with those red veins in his forehead prominent, his teeth gritted and the corners of his mouth twisted, as out practiced precision, he projected his words, not carelessly but deliberately, his intent most likely to harm sufficiently directly to my very core, for wasn't that where his curses, his wounds delivered, would cause the maximum damage, resolutely designed to destroy, "I'm your father *you stupid bitch*!"

What! I was his daughter! And clearly he thought less of me than he ought-ta! Yet still I did not move, for I waited for 'what he was to do next,' as that is what I'd always been taught to do. And I cared not what the onlookers thought, as my new and overwhelming thoughts stood up to take notice, wanting to be heard, that, "He can't be right!" "Thinking; I've moved to a big city, Manchester, I'm achieving my goal, I'm a trainee nurse, I'm independent, I had already proved that I could succeed when he said I wouldn't." And more, I saved my first months salary and bought a portable TV, and with my second, a music centre, so I was not useless or worthless, as he had decreed me to be, and neither anymore was I helpless. For I had already achieved that which he, my father, forever told me I wouldn't, as I had already 'made something of myself,' which he told me I couldn't ever possible do, and so in reality, by definition, that made *his* opinion and attitudes obsolete, and absolutely, unequivocally, wrong!

"If we all did things we are capable of, we would even astound ourselves."
~ Thomas Edison

So "Why was I so scared?" For I didn't live with him any longer, so surely I didn't need to, nay, shouldn't put up with, that anymore, so I plucked up the courage, yet that stopped me not, quaking in my boots, trembling through to my core, my heart pounding in my chest, my stomach jumping into my throat, with every cell in my body tense, for never before had I been so bold or frivolous with my safety to challenge his authority, and as I stood my ground awaiting his onslaught, wondering "What was he going to do to me next?" I meekly replied, "I'm not, I'm not a stupid bitch."

But *he*, undeterred, *cared not* for my disagreement, as his astonishingly-low concept of me was altered not, as he, gathering impetuous from whatever it was that resided within him, as aching from his deepest core, stood staunch, as on his face, vicious intent he displayed, with his eyes piercing like icy daggers, and not satisfied with his first attempt, he *fortified* his commitment, jolting his head backwards, before more sternly, jerking it forwards, his teeth gritted, not pausing, but with his upmost conviction, of his certainty of authority, his words of condemnation, splicing them effortlessly, through that clear quiet air, resolutely declaring for all to hear, "*YES YOU* are! You're a *stupid bitch!*"

Then, quietly, without a fuss, I turned and walked away, trying to hold my composer, as I cast my eyes around the stylish bar, of polished wood and guilt with imposing chandeliers overhead, and as I held secrets in the crevices of my mind, I knew not, that at the age of 19 years, was the last time I was to see my father, and much later, I was to learn, to be most grateful for that. And as I returned to where my ever so placid boyfriend, he so gentle and respectful by nature was standing, I noticed a change in him, something I'd not seen before, as he leaning forward with his elbows, as his hands stretching his fingers wide then clenching them tight forming a fist, I asked somewhat perplexed, "What are you doing?" Through words of frustration he spoke, "If he wasn't your father, I would have knocked him to the floor."

At last, for the first time in my life, validity wrapped in emotional support for what that man had done to and against me all my life, and now I wonder, why I dismissed Alistair's sentiments, as absolutely so sadly, as I had grown to accept abnormal behaviour as normal, as ordinary, for sure, that's what it was to me, so almost blatantly in response I sighed, "That's ok, that's just the way his is, I'm used to it. I'm just glad I got away without him giving me a great big wallop or at the minimum, a heavy backhander." But really, of that offence, "Why was there no middle ground, where simply, my boyfriend opened his mouth and used words in my defence?" Yet, that was, 'my life as I knew it,' so without even really giving it a second thought, simply, I just picked up my glass, and sipped on my beer.

"Oh my" there was certainly, and no lack of clarity, as ambiguity, never my father's way, and really, there was nothing more to say, yet I had stood up to him for the first time in my life, and for that I was truly grateful, and I'd managed to do it, without receiving punishment. And from that episode with my father was not wasted, for of him I held a truer measure, as finally a realization of all his opinions, of all what he said and did to me, that he was a *fraud and liar!* And in his dishonesty, he had deliberately deceived and tricked me all my life to believing something else, and with firm convictions I walked away with concise and firm notions, that I was so terribly sorry and sad, that he was, my father.

Yet it appeared that forever he had begrudged me, my very life, and of it, at l east my spirit, any emotional security, it appeared to be his mission, to destroy it. But he failed, wonderfully and magnificently so, he failed and I succeeded, for I overcame all he did, and now, my heart afresh, renewed, it lives once again, as I learnt to be patient with myself as I went through the process of leaning live and love healthily, and so, of the battle he raged on me, unequivocally and absolutely, the *Victory, belongs to ME!*

"Every block of stone has a statue inside it and it is the task of the sculptor to discover it"
~ Michelangelo

But it was not just human's, weaker than my father who were subject to his wrath, as so sadly, he was to adopt a dog, Whisky was his name, and frisky by nature, an Alsatian mix, a hardy mongrel of which my granddad forever said, the most loyal and healthy of dogs, especially when often, the price may be free, and where he came from or why, I really don't know, he just turned up one day, yet for that poor dog, unfortunately the price to pay was high, for living the four-walls it found itself, it was not to be a sanctuary, but where sanity was wrongly stolen, for the dog too, they also felt the fuming fury of my father's temper and anger, of his relentless moods and unforgiving in nature.

I was only young, and "Oh I loved my dog," and the dog, may just have loved me, but for either of us, a peaceful ride it was not to be. Whisky so wanted to go-to-play with the dog next door at number 3, not a mongrel but an Alsatian pedigree, but they both looked the same. And in his eagerness over and over hole's he would dig under the fence trying to reach what he sought, but of my father, so amazingly angry, his temper uncontrollable out of control even for he, perhaps a possibility, for he was not used to having his word misunderstood or adhered to, but really, had he ever tried to train Whisky, to teach him right from wrong, or as with his children, through all his cursed criticism, as if by a mysterious magic spell, he still expected us to guess, to simply know, everything.

But Whisky did not understand my father's language, so persisted, but his punishment, was to unfold, and almost violently so. And my father, in his tweed work trousers, tucked in his Wellington boots, and the thick woolly jumper he tucked under his thick brown leather belt, to the dog, my pet, who I loved he started cursing and shouting "I'm getting the spade and I'm going to chop that bloody dogs head off." And "kidding, of his intent, I think not," for then, off to the garden shed he did went, and sure enough in his hand, he returned with a spade, with his face all ablaze, and armed with that tool or was it a weapon, gripping it tightly, as though a gun with a musket on it, he began to chase Whisky around and around the garden, shouting so viciously, "Dog! You've had your last chance! Get over here *now*!"

Yet while all that went on, I was held in the kitchen corner, tightly by my mother, as she prevented me from going outside, with her coldly delivered callus words, "Shut up and be quiet!" And as I screamed with all my might, "Please please don't hurt my Whisky, please, stop, please leave him alone, please!" But all to no-avail, as my words were buried in my sobs, as salty tears ran down my face, stinging my skin, as I, completely ignored, and through the frosted glass of the kitchen door, and peered through the kitchen window, I could see Whisky, his tail tucked tightly between his legs, darting rapidly this way and that, sensibly trying, to make good his escape, then now and again my father caught him up, and with the spade raised above his head, wheedling that dangerous tool, dropping it down as quickly as he could, over my dear Whisky's head.

Another favorite, a violent tactic to my fathers usual format, suddenly dragging the dog around by the scruff of its neck, yet with so much more anger, relentlessly, in sharp jarring movements, trying so hard to hurt my dog, my loving pet, and not giving up, chasing Whisky all around while repeatedly, thrust that weapon down again and I could hear the whimpering and fearful yelps of Whisky. My mother tugging at my arm to make me still, trapping me, and ignoring my unleashed torrent of tears, and my desperate begging, "Please please, let me go out and help him!"

But "NO!" she screeched her answer, as to-and-fro she jolted my tiny body, as evermore tightly she gripped onto me, and as tears of distress stinging may face and falling in floods to the floor, fearlessly away from her in that dark and bleak place I tried to make my escape, but she void of caring and ignoring my pleas, while only complaining callously of the noise I was making, and yelling adamantly her clear and concise instructions; "Now Shut Up! You're testing my patience like you usually do!" "Be Quiet! Be Still! Like I've told you to!…"

…And then frequently as was her usual format, 'cautioning me,' she went on, in her tone to deliver a threat of condemnation, "Because if *your* father hears you, as *you* do; *you'll* make *everything worse,* for *everyone*!"

So familiar, in that room with her I was confined, as the harsh reality of how so absolutely cold and alone in the world I appeared to be, isolated and tormented, as comfort or solace, love or kindness, or even the possibility to be free from emotional or physical pain completely bypassed me, as I had not even begun to know of the existence of such, for really, "What were they?" For at that tender age, a concept of such fancifulness was not a part of my reality and had completely failed to seep into my life, and so unfortunately sadly, it was to be the passing of a far greater number of years before the slightest notion of such, was to permeate my thoughtfulness; as I, was only left chillingly cold, lost and forlorn in the vastness of nothingness, in a place where I did not belong nor any one there wanted me to be, not my mother or my father, and my four-legged friend who was affectionate, Whisky my pet, who I loved and loved me back, that only natural living force of normality around me, I had been helpless to protect him, from the cruelty and hurt from my father, that I too felt everyday in everyway.

"Really?" How slow were my parents to recognize that within our 'family' a pet really wasn't a good-fit, and ruining yet another innocent and helpless dogs life, as they were to bring it into, our malfunctioning, contorted family they were to do it again, and what a folly as within it absolutely there was nothing healthy, certainly not in the realms of security of emotions for they consistently failed to thrive, or even barely survive, so incomprehensively, I wonder "Why did they repeat their mistake?" And what a beautiful dog Whisky was, and when he disappeared one day, I knew not where Whisky had gone, or where the new one came from, I was only immensely sad for him, a most beautiful, black and white Boarder Collie cross, so gentle and playful and Major was to be his name, but distraughtly, somehow I knew that for him as for Whiskey, the prognosis was to be the same.

And a liking he took to chewing slippers and more, but my mother, a housewife, "Why did she not keep them away from him?" So then in the morning he would not have to face punishment for the tearing up he'd done, and more, "Could she not have bought him one of those chewy-things?" And perhaps not rocket science but a concept of easy note, for that the ironing pile she left on the top of the low level fridge, Major through the night, had ripped them to shreds, and included was a beautiful red velvet dress of mine, long sleeves and toughing at the knee, trimmed around the neck with a white fur collar, that my mother had made me, that actually fit me quite beautifully and I wore to Church when I was made to go on Sundays. But "Why did she leave everything in harms way?"

Surprising it was not, nor was the punishment for the dog received, and I felt so guilty, for I felt so upset at loosing that red dress, that my mother refused to try and repair, and those tattered and torn, a collage of silk embroidered patches, all collected by my Grandfather from cigarette packets during the war I was told, quite valuable also of pretty ladies in national costume, ironed onto self-adhesive interfacing fabric, from 26 only half a dozen were to survive the tearing rampage of Major's presumed, puppy and bread boredom.

I had never been told I was a good-girl, not by anyone, but a bad-girl? All too frequently, and I thought I'd done it again, for that dress that I cherished so much, I thought if I had not made such a fuss, and not worried about it being damaged or that I couldn't wear it again, Major might of escaped being punished and that harm which was inflicted on him, and at the age of only 9, I couldn't stop thinking, of sorrow of guilt, yet to another I dared not speak, that "Major's suffering and sadness was all my fault." And there it was, another limiting belief was set, that I, should never complain about anyone at any time, only to take what they were dishing-out, or they'd be punished and helpless to prevent it, and of that harm, it would all be my responsibility.

A serious notion stirred in my mind 4 decades later, really, "Would my mother, have deliberately left my things that I cared for so much, in a place so easily reachable by a pet, that she knew could not resist to tear them up, that dogs emotions and its physical wellbeing, were they expendable to her, because her vengeance and harming me was of far greater importance, than protecting another living thing?" For she clearly knew the consequential actions of punishment that for Major would ensue, of anguish and torment he would be subjected to suffer, so again I wonder, is it beyond the scope of her personality, is this pure fabrication of my mind, a concept, unreasonable foolish, imaginary, or just possibly, perhaps true.

Major fared not-well at our house, and my mother, after walking him would return with increasing tales of how he barked at this man then snapped at the next and was uncontrollable on the leash and for such behavior and disobedience, there was a price to pay, as Major, was to be sent away. But of it, I knew nothing, until one morning as I was just about to leave for Infant school that day, my mother announced, as if talking of cleaning the windows or cleaning out the fire grate, or some other usaual task, "Say goodbye to Major this is last time you'll see him. He won't be hear when you get home later." "What!!!" My mind suddenly flipped, feeling so sick with panic, uncertain, "I don't know what you mean, where is he going to be?" And with impatience in her voice, "He's going away" my mother said "Now put on your shoes; quickly!"

"What!" Confused, that was my pet, my dog, my friend, who I loved, was to disappear, to be no more, and I begged to know, "Where is he going to go?" With irritation written all over her face and detailed abruptly in her voice she told me, "He's gong to a farm, out in the country, where he'll have plenty of fields to run around, and fresh air and sheep to heard, he'll be much better off there." A healthy picture she painted that consoled me slightly, and because I loved him so, I so wanted to believe Major had gone to a far better and happier place, and perhaps somewhere deep inside of me, I wished I wished so hard relentlessly that I too one day, could go to that place, where the sun shone and I to could run away. But still, my fury friend, I was to miss him too much, but suddenly, it occurred to me, "What if she was just lying and had Major put down?" Because that sort of thing, more than once, was mentioned, with angrily recited regular threats by both my parent, not in unison but separately, that's what they'd do to Whisky, and he did disappear. So really, "Was anything or anyone to stop them doing the same thing all over again to Major?"

My emotions storming like a tornado, turbulence swirling in my stomach, shocked, bewildered, slightly destroyed I murmured, "What do you mean?" Testily she replied, "Look, the dog hasn't behaved so now its got to go." "But I want him to stay" I pleaded, "Please don't send him away" but as the thick drops of tears streamed quickly down my tiny face, and I could taste the salt water as they cascaded into my mouth, yet undeterred as her inconvenience clearly to be seen, with her scorching words rolling off her tongue, "Listen! This is your father's fault; he sent the dog mad, so now, he's got to go! So you'll just have to get use to it!" and if *your* not satisfied, complain to your father, if *you* dare!" then pausing, only to take a drag on her cigarette, impatiently screaming, "Now do as you're told!" "Leave!" "Put your coat on!" and "Get out of here!" *"NOW!"*

No more happy times, or warm welcomes, no more cuddles to be had, and of the house I lived in, empty and cold once again, of it all, I thought, "It was my fault, why he was leaving." My heart hurt so much for my friend, for was it my fault they were sending him away, was it all about me complaining about the dress, "What could I do to put it right? What could I do to stop them killing my second four-legged friend?" so more I begged, "Please don't send him away?" But my sobs useless and unheard, of cared for they were not and through the breaths that I struggled to take, my mother, stood beyond, in the farthest corner of the kitchen, her eyes shooting daggers, intolerantly tapping her fingers on the work surface, her agitation, tetchily increasingly, delivering her lines, "Now don't test my patience." "Pull yourself together!" "Or *you'll* be late for school!"

But "How could I?" Begging and refusing, in circles we went around, until at last, a ray of hope, when my mother eventually spoke, "All right! Shut up! I'll send him away another day," impatiently continuing, "So stop your moaning, right now!" then me, confirming, "So Major will be here when you come home tonight?" "Yes! I've told you!" *"NOW GO!"* My tears, at first, did not stop flooding out, though really, "Was not convinced of her testimony?" for she had tricked me before, but, she assured me, she really did, "Didn't she?" and after all, she was my mother, so I could trust her, "Right?"

In my innocence, I believed her, for I, in so few years had not yet established the full 'measure' of her, as I had achieved the answer I longed for, I wrapped my arms around his neck feeling his soft fur, and gave Major big hugs and kisses, as in that moment I was filled with instant relief, and ignoring my eyes all stingy, and my face all sticky and raw from those tumbling salty tears, as all alone, I began my 15 minutes walk to school, but I put a spring in my step, as I was so very pleased and already looking forward to, giving Major more big hugs later.

Then racing home from school, with a rapid pace of anticipation and delight, as a reprieve had been assured, secured, and I was keen to greet my loving pet and calling his name, into the house I dashed, but to greet me, from nowhere did he come, so continuing to investigate, briskly I sprinted into the garden searching from one side to the other around the house, behind the tree, and he wasn't there, and neither was he hiding behind the gate, and I a little confused, as really, "Where was he?" Yet still not even imagining the worst, with no idea of my mother's lies and pending betrayal, as I asked her, "Where's Major?"

Delivering her line void of caring or feeling in her heart, she, "He's not here, he's been sent away!" My gut wrenched, ever so quickly as so badly I began to sob, yet so young and so perplexed I petitioning, "But you told me you wouldn't do that, you told me when I got back from school tonight Major would still be here. You told you weren't going to send him away." My tears not yet tumbling, as me not understanding, "So why isn't he here now? What have you done with him? Where is he?"

Without any compassion or consideration for that little girl's feeling, that little girl, her daughter, me, likely under 10 years, he hardly troubled herself to even turn her head toward me, as at the kitchen sink, she carried on peeling the potatoes, dismissive, void of any concept of concern or emotions I was holding, saying without any apparent care at all, "Yes, well, I only told you that so you'd shut up your whining, get out of the house and go to school!" No tears seemed to come, as I stood in the middle of the kitchen floor, feeling so utterly alone, in a quiet tone asking "So why did you lie to me this morning and tell me Major was going to be here when he wasn't?" Her cutting tone, as sharp as the knife, "Because that was the only way I could get you out of the house!"

My loving pet, the one who was always pleased to see me, the one who never got angry or hurt me, the one whose mood was always the same, the one whose eyes were kind, the one who allowed me to touch him, who never barked aggressively, or with a passive hostility ignored me, the one who never viciously sent me away, and never sent me away, and we, could play, he so beautiful in spirit, loving and friendly, and *he liked me* too, he always *accepted* me, but then, Major was gone!

'Cry me a river,' I could have done, distrust, but there was more, for she, whom

I was supposed be able to rely on, I could do so no-more, so slowly was I to realize, that the burden of betrayal, is heavy and mean, invasive, dysfunctional, undetected, so unmonitored, almost by osmosis, pervasive, it effected just about every type of relationship, as unraveling distrust of everyone rampantly entwining themselves in those deep crevices of my mind and soul, lodging themselves deep within and making themselves a home. Sad, decades were to pass, before at last, almost an epiphany struck me, as I wondered, perhaps unwisely, or perhaps not; for other things my mother did, that only over years came into the light, aspects of her personality and character that unfolds as the reality of who she was, and the realism of what she was capable of, a question I began to beg, "Was poor major, simply a casualty, of my mothers scorn toward me?" True, I'll never know, but what I can hope is that when Major was banished from our house, I think fortunately for him, I so very much dearly hope that it was to the country he was sent, and there he'd run around in wide open and lush fields, and there he found love, and was accepted, by everyone.

"Insist on yourself. Never imitate."
~ Ralph Waldo Emerson

"Oh my" only 20 years old, and firmly on track to achieved my cherished desire, to become a nurse by profession, and how wonderfully exciting, yet so much more, how absolutely relieving, to know my safety plan for protection was coming to fruition, and with that achievement ticked off, it was on to my next job, though with significant importance, that exciting job of being able to choose what was to be my brass buckle, to adorn my uniform belt, and my design choice, well that had to be Victorian, as always my desired preference, so attractively, ornate and delicate. So immensely symbolic, with the pride of accomplishment and a good job well done, and life's obstacles overcome, I was looking forward to rewarding myself with such a delightful trinket, so often, in preparation, I had peered in the jewellers window at them.

Then a big surprise was to greet me, while explaining to my mother, my impending joy offered to buy it for me, and true, her generosity most unusual, not just in the money, but never outside birthdays and Christmas did she give me anything, not even a cake from the bakery, without telling me how grateful I should be and how *much* it cost, while persistently inconsistent in her favours, as my brother, who she gave 3 cars to, while not even a trinket or token did she pass my way, and over the decades I had just come to accept that as normal, so I was quite flabbergasted, not even thinking she meant it, for "Why in her behaviour would she do something so out of character for her and what was her unfamiliar rational?" Good questions indeed, for as I gave her the benefit of the doubt, only emotional misery was to be the result.

Time passed, my exams came and went and I passed them the same, and then it was my graduation, where a certificate and badge I received and along them was granted the permission to wear that fine buckle, in bronze, depicting my qualification level, and as my delightful grandma, my lovely step-dad and my mother came to my ceremony, afterwards we returned to my apartment, where I had prepared some sandwiches and coffee, and as usual, only enjoyed superficial conversation, yet still I got my camera out, so of a memory to make, waiting patiently in hope, that my mother was soon to give me, that which she so importantly promised so many moons ago, to commemorate my landmark, my milestone the greatest achievement in my life. I had achieved thus far, and really, if not the buckle, from her a greeting card would have sufficed, but neither on that day, she passed my way.

Such an uneasy feeling in my stomach I felt as I waved them off before closing the behind them, and as they drove away, I just dared to wondered, "Why had my mother to me, not kept her word?" Yet true, as history was a testimony and the future was to prove same, it was not surprising in any way, but hurtful, amazingly badly so, distressed really, I thought of all the other trainee nurses, and the celebrations that were lasting all day that had been planned lovingly by their families, and my mother gave me, maybe an hour of her time, and really it wasn't about the buckle per se, it was about so much humongously more, and "Why oh why, would she neglect to do what she promised, for she must of known how it would hurt me so?"

As a nurse from such an early age had always been my goal, so consecutively, and so often she recalled how frequently she needed to lower the hem on my little girls nurses uniform as I played plastic stethoscopes, and when I completely grew out of it, I started going to the medicine cabinet, with squares of non-grease proof paper in hand, to place petite portions of Germolene cream and more upon them, then fold them carefully, and along with a bandage of two made of strips of gauze, I made my own little personal, first aid kit, where pretending they were hurt and needed care, I'd wrap my doll's and teddies in them, to make them all better.

My mother void of ever expressing care or concern for me, but surely, she knew the real significance to set myself up in my career, to gain independence, so if a man should ever harm or hit a child of mine, I would have the financial means of an income, to escape and take them with me, to a place of perfect safety, for sure, as she had gone through so much with my father, complaining she had to stay for she had not the means to leave him, as my granddad refused to let her go to night school, yet somehow that blame of him, transferred to me, as the lack of her education, also proved to be my fault, with her forever complaint, so frequently, ever bitterly spoken words, forever reminding me, "You, were *too frightened* to be left alone with your father even once a week, for just 2 hours, so its all *your fault*, that I couldn't get an education, a job, and leave him!" Never did she cease throwing those cutting, cursing allegations that so effortlessly, consistently rolled off her tongue, and starting from so young, her accusations, I absorbed and internalized every one, as not even once, never, ever, did it occur to me, to disagree, or ask, "Really mum, really!" "You think *all* this is my fault?"

Surely, as she had received as much deprivation as she complained, surely even more, she understood how important my qualification was to me, and "Why wouldn't she want to celebrate that with me?" As true, "Wouldn't that enable me, unlike her was to be in a valuable position to protect my children, and of that, shouldn't she be well pleased?" But perhaps I was a little too short-sighted, for I momentarily failed to remember, that although my Auntie, her sister, with 4 children one of who from birth was disabled in mental capacity, divorced her husband because 'he was boring,' yet my mother refused to divorce hers, even when her children, he was beating.

So perhaps I wasn't misguided for comparing such inconstancies of what my mother complained of, but effectively did nothing about, and even back then, not examining my past, but looking toward my future, my sincere desire, for my children to have, so much better, of safety and peace in their lives, than I ever received in mine. How terribly sad, my mother, forever moaning and groaning about the past, and always choosing to reside there in her mind, seemingly not trying or learning, to use that crystal clear of 20/20 vision of hindsight, to prepare or plan a better, a brighter, an improved future, really looking what's before me and not behind me, "Where to from here?"

But those thoughts, at that moment bypassed my mind, as mustering all hope, I was seriously considering, true, although she'd never done it before, just maybe, she wanted to surprise me, and left the buckle in a beautiful little box, with a ribbon and little glistening stares twinkling all around it as a surprise by my bed, so quickly in anticipation, I rushed down the corridor to find it, but no, not there, then I thought, "Arrhah" maybe it's a game, and she wants to jokingly trick me, into thinking that she really didn't get me one when she did, so hid it in somewhere else, in the cupboard I looked, under the sink, even in the serial packets, and of cause in the fridge, what about my handbag, but I knew it was forbidden to go in another's handbag, but just maybe that was part of the game, but again, "No," not a token, not a note to commemorate my lifelong, and saving-me, goal.

Disappointed, hurt, a little devastated really, I wondered why I'd dared to allow myself to believe, just for once, that she, would do something for me, gladly not begrudgingly, but either way evidentially, it was not to be, but then I shouldn't be too disappointed for "Hey, that was only August and my birthday was just around the corner in only 3 months, so perhaps, maybe, she was saving it up, to give to me then," and so with the hope of that anticipation, I calmed myself down and contemplated through delayed gratification, what a thrill it would be to receive that gift. My birthday came and went, but the buckle, well that never did eventuate, that gift of significance did not come. My mother, her present was always the past, and from her uncleansed emotional seeping wounds never did she seem to escape into a brighter future, that for her, was eager and awaiting.

Yet was I being too melodramatic, for I may have been her daughter, and her blood too ran in my veins, but fortunately at my core, I was nothing like her, and true, I daren't ask her about the buckle, for that 'sort of think' was never permitted, for to intrude on her thoughts would be outside the parameters of my authority, subject to her, and knowing my place, as her daughter, and more, that question, in her sight, would have rendered me, greedy, so therefore, obviously it was one that never passed my lips, for I cared not at my maturing age to hear those resounding words, "I want never gets," because really, I was so over hearing that, so I consoled myself with the fact, that Christmas was only a few weeks away, and perhaps she was saving it up to give it to me then, as maybe she was thinking with reverse psychology, "She'll never expect it then, so that is how I will keep control by keeping her guessing, of when I am going to give it to her, and do so when she least's expect it, I'll will give it to her then."

I clung to that notion, just in hope that the almost inevitable wasn't to take place, and that I was, from her, to receive that so desirable bronze ornate buckle, and as I remained forever hopeful that my mothers word would be true, every shift I walked on the ward, as I saw so many others wearing theirs, mine was so obvious by its absence, and such sadness I felt, for the first time my mother offered her hand out, and I so believed it was with value of sentiment, but really, it was hollow and empty with nothing in it. For sure, it wasn't about the money, for so easily at any point during that time I could have chosen and paid for one on my own, it was just that hope against hope, I was believing of my emotions, her love, just for once, especially for me, accepting me freely, toward me, she would allow the two to unite.

"Oh my" I never should have been surprised when Christmas came and went, but no buckle, no love, no support, no acknowledgement of my achievement, never did she give, the bond that was never between us remained, still never nurtured nothing of value ever manifested for the hand that only she ever held out once, evolved to be empty, which perhaps unpoetically symbolic of my mother's heart toward me, void of any acknowledgement that then, I was in a position to be able to provide for my unborn children, and of all her complaints about not being able to leave 'him' my father, I thought for that she'd be at least pleased, but apparently not, for her boundaries barring me to be anything but an inconvenience in her life, were never broken and at any risk of any, quickly she's repair them, and while this was going on, still my brother was given this or that, all along, and my grandfather also, with cars and holidays abroad, given to him; so uneven, unequal, perhaps by mistake or deliberately done, but either way, that was my mother and even though I tried, I was ultimately, unable to help her.

And too late for comfort I recognised, through outstretched traitorous and treacherous decades, before finally I saw life through my mother's eyes, and in her world, "My brother could do no wrong, and I could do no right." His wishes always granted, mine only trampled upon before denied, for nothing I could do to please her, and not one thing that my brother could do could upset her, begrudging me everything and begrudging him nothing, not even after her proclaimed humiliation, how he informed to a pub full of people he was getting married, but still, failed to mention it to her, what a surprise as she was stood at the bar, and someone asked her what did she think of her new daughter-in-law and mother only able to reply "What?" She accepted all he dished out, the scorn he displayed everyday, but still, she would rally around him eagerly, while he ignored her, and all I could wonder is, "Why won't she just forgive me, for simply being born?"

Rejected on a daily basis, my emotions endlessly trampled upon before abandoned, and even as a student, working, earning so little, supporting my way through college, and through love and a the sincerest desire to help her, from my savings I lent a tidy sum of money so she could buy another car, as my brother in accidents in a repeated pattern kept 'writing them off, ' my only proviso, guarding I believed her best interests, I begged of her, "Please please, don't let my brother drive it," 'it,' her new blue hatchback Chevalier, desiring so, for her to get the point, to not give in to all of his wants, "Please think about it mum, if he crashes this one too, which he's likely to do, what are you going to do then?" Then becoming testily short-tempered, snapping back, "All right then, stop going on, I wont let him drive it, satisfied!" Her assurance, and my money exchanged, but that was the last I was to see of that agreement, as true enough within a week, she had broken her word she gave to me, and my brother, was there driving her car and of at least no surprise to me, his behaviour and cavalier attitude toward, what didn't belong to him and what he didn't have to pay for, possibly not trying any harder, as almost immediately, he 'wrote off' that one too.

Not a penny did she hold him accountable for, and her, with her insurance void, unable to purchase a new car, stranded, complaining again, and I resisted to say, "See, told you so," or did I, at some point slip out, for I was so hurt, for she had gone against her absurdity to me, but from old, I guess I shouldn't have been surprised, as really, simply no change, my brother ignoring consequences or thought for another continued along with his behaviours, and my mother did the same. But what of the money I lent her, was that also gone too, almost, so close and very likely, for only bitter and severe arguments ensued over its recovery, then more recently, an older lady, in the wonderful community spirited street in Bolton where I used to live, shared what I have come to know as her wise words, as caring she unfolded her concept "Remember my dear, when you lend money, only do it if you can truly afford it. Anticipate getting it back but don't assume it. Be extremely careful, as many a good relationship between family and friends has been lost permanently, through doing that very thing."

True, "Why was I surprised when my mother didn't keep her word?" For really, evidentially, history had proven that her word could not be trusted. A month turned into a year, and a year to some more, and I began asking, for her to return my money, as not even a penny back had she given me, she, not caring not understanding, doing what she always did, snapping back briskly, "How do you expect me to give you that, I can't make it out of thin air? I have no car but still, I am paying- off a bank loan." "Perhaps insurance would have been a good idea, but hey, I knew far better than to make that retort. Through her actions I still felt huge betrayal and my words proclaimed, released, coated in a layer of pain, "Yes, but if you would have kept your word to me, you would still have your car and not be in this predicament." I spoke not designed to punish or rebuke, but forming a desperate emotional release, as so difficult knowing, my brother who she still doted on could do no-thing wrong, and I in-spite of all my might, could do no-right.

> *"It's not whether you got knocked down; it's whether you get back up."*
> *~ Vince Lombardi Jr*

So, at just 18, I was rapidly learning, that trust, honesty, and caring, was pretty much to be found no-where, and that it was not, only men who were untrustworthy, but women too, and in my limited deductions, I concluded, the closer the relationship, the less-likely it was to be happy, secure, or even safe, and that, no one was to be, honest or dependable within them, and the greater the closeness with anyone, the greater the emotional uncomfortable angst and hurt to endure, yet still, never was it worth complaining or expecting anything better, for never would it come, and "How did I know such?" Well that was the school I'd been indoctrinated into, as they settled as opinions and facts deep within my subconscious mind, and with the absence of anything to the contrary, and never did it even occur to me that there was such a thing, for I knew not, nor held a notion of any other kind, so into the crevices of my mind, forming my wall of defence and my natural default mechanisms, distrust, sank deep, and my firm belief that relationships = pain and hurt, and how enormously sadly, that turned out to be, far too many decades to prove to be, my reality.

Impossible to ignore those comparisons between me and my brother, where he, worthy of my mother's love and protection, but from her toward me, there flowed only babbling brooks of disgust, and certainly from days of old, brash and bold of her maternal deprivation. For sure, that was in abundance, and so frustrated, with hurt of scaring emotions causing aching pains, flourishing rampantly in my heart, wanting, desiring, even almost needing to know "Mum, why do you favour my brother so over me?" "Oh my" like a red rag to a bull, instantly, so utterly angry sternly shouting she pounced, "I do no such thing!" Really, so I was to wonder, "Why was it, I saw it, and felt it, deep within my deepest core?" For years, forever, she denoted it as my imagination and fervently denied such a thing, though what a beneficially surprise was to fall on me, for which I was so humongously grateful, as a friend of my brothers, and still, I don't know why he did it, or why to him it mattered to him, and he, not visiting our house too often or for too long, but even so, he noticed it, and following me inside to the kitchen one day, genuinely perplexed he asked me, "Why does your mother favour your brother above you?"

Surprised! Relieved! So thankful! At last, even though I knew not the concept back then, validation, another had seen what my mother was doing, as never once had she accepted even vaguely, my questions as I voiced my concerns with intense worry and sorrow, question or worry of the same, forever dismissing them as my fanciful notions, as she protested they were invalid and untrue. But, there, there was confirmation, from that young man of only 18 years, hip and trendy with a most congenial personality, he, had noticed it too. I had been right all along, my mother was lying to me like she so regularly used to, yet I was to give into mild emotional devastation for just a short while, at how sad the truth really was. My mother, from the past to the future, nothing was to change or improve her concepts or behaviour toward me, and still, as I watched her lavish love and more on my brother, her inconsistencies hurt tremendously so, for each gift to her, equated to portions of her love, and to me, she didn't give any!

My credibility and my own self-worth, were added to, for then I knew, I wasn't wrong, mad or even bad as she determined through my insistences and her denials that I was, for I had received from a most unexpected source, *validation*, and I was able to breath with unmeasurable relief, and of my mother, held a more fair, true, valid and appropriate insight of her intent. So obvious remained, by any other name, her favouritism, and her perpetual denials only served to hurt and cause me sorrow, and of her demands, of "Tell me who said that, I will put them right." Yet almost as if protecting his identity, never did I tell her of his name, but perhaps I should, because mother really quite liked him, and for her to know that he gave me, such clarification, well, certainly, minimally, that would have destabilized her conceit greatly.

Her actions, "If only" I hadn't needed to see them daily on display, as it only served to increase the torment of seemingly never-decreasing emotional anguish, of my troubles of hurt and sadness, that never seemed to cease, and perhaps on that day, it was seeing my lonely isolation, or a tone of desperation, just longing to be heard, that as I explained, how "Mum only gets really angry when I ask her 'Why?' does she discriminate between my brother and I, demanding that I give her examples of such, so of them, she can make excuses, deny or justify."

Then with a nod of her head and a disheartened expression of disappointment, with even sadness, shown upon, the usually warmth of her face, with eyebrows sympathetically raised, in a soft voice of empathy, after almost 2 decades I was to hear her say, "Yes, I know; I've seen it too." At her revelation, I was almost excited and in exclamation, "Really Grandma, really, you've seen it too?" My grandma, gently nodding, appearing forlorn that she had admitted such, out loud, but to me her words brought comfort and liberty, for I knew all along, I had been right, and then to have received 2 confirmations of the truth, above, my mothers deceit and lies, and right there, within my turbulent emotions, no-loner did I need to be confused, bemused, over my concerns or worries, because that information, had validated my accused, imagination, and somehow, to some degree, that had helped me to extinguish my plight, and from her, set me free.

"Comparison Conflicts Comfort"
~ Carole Jordan

Almost 3 and a half decades my mother was to trouble me, while she forever reminded me, that I 'was a thorn in her side' or often, 'a pain in her neck,' unwanted, a mistake and how she would have got rid of me 'if only' she could, that was until one morning, at the door came a rata-tat-tat, and I, already in work mode, as I answered it wearing my nurses uniform, only to find my mother standing there, already with daggers in her eyes, as she coldly looked at me, as it was not "Hello" or any other pleasantries she said, as she jolted her arm thrusting in my direction a hold-alls made from pigskin and embossed with a delicate pattern that I had bought from the Isle of Crete, with her splicing words like a double edged poisoned sword wafting with purpose through the air, "Here, you gave me these, and I don't want them anymore!" So taking the bag from her, my ex-fiancé, he who wouldn't leave my house, came to investigate what the raised voice was about, just in time to hear, my mother, who had barely paused to take a breath, with her eyes darting jerkily from side to side, probably, unleashing her well-rehearsed phrases, "I'm moving and I'm not telling you where I'm moving to!" Continuing, rolling in momentum, her un-fragmented words of rage flowing, "And I'm not going to be your mother until you decide you want one!"

"Oh my" considering, "What more could she possibly do?" and "What was she possibly talking about, 'this time'?" Yet hold up; she wasn't through, though really I was over her emotional manipulation she had, at last, eventually worn me down, and worn me out, she had chipped away at the block of our relationship one to many times, until 7 o'clock that morning, she had done her best, the stone crumbled into flimsy heap, nothingness, my patience, after 33 years had worn so thin, and no longer was I able to support or tolerate her self-indulgent and erratic moods, and bearing in mind, by that time, I was in 'work mode,' so my logical reply hurtled forthwith , "Well, if you don't tell me where you're moving to, how will I be able to inform you when I've decided whether I want one?" Well, "Vexed?" "Oh my" indeed she was so, in a partial miniscule, of one second. Most definitely! And as my ex stood beside me, inviting her to "Come on in, let's talk about this." Her reply holding, terrific significance, in our family history, a response, instantly recognizable, to depths unsurpassed, as a grossly huge insult, denoting absolute blatant offence and superiority, as "No! I will not step one foot over your threshold!" she spouted most deliberately.

True, I held absolutely no idea what formed the catalyst for her actions on that day, and I wondered, was it because I didn't travel with her in the family car at my granddads funeral, when she thought I should, as surely, another reason I could not think of, and individually I asked my brother and my mums sister, "Do you know what I've done to my mother, this time?" Then interestingly, although each one was asked separately, they gave the exact same response, "I don't know and I'm not prepared to get involved!" Amazing, as each also concluded the same way, "So don't, ask me again!" "Oh my" I wasn't asking them to intervene, I was only asking if they knew the answer, surely, it seems if nothing else, my family was surely consistent, and seemingly all indoctrinated into the same school of "Let's stick our head in the sand, and don't help Carole."

Though my Auntie, 6 years younger than my mother, did shed a little more insight, a notion that previously I wasn't privy to, "That's just your mother, we've always had to tip-toe around her, and obviously, you just did not tip-toe enough."

But really, I was over it, I was over her, as no-longer was I bewildered, by her begrudging motherhood, as I was weary, of a lifetime of trying to coax her out of her moods, to crawl on my belly on the floor, just to try and please her, nay appease her, and seriously, I'd had enough, I was tired of playing her relentless games, of just trying to get her to like me, of trying so hard, just to be 'good enough,' apologizing for being born, and forever subjected to her hate and scorn, yet not even being able to appease her, over again, all my attempts rendered unsuccessful and I held neither the inclination or commitment to pursue that seemingly evidentially, lost course anymore.

My mother really picked her times! As it was not off to school I was to go, with her meanness ringing true, it was my place of work, of 250 plus people who I was immediately responsible for their health and safety, of accident, injuries and emergencies, and all legal requirements of documentation to be precise and accurate, to ensure no litigation claims were filed against the company, and "How was I supposed to apply myself when my mother was to disown me that way?" Well funnily enough, from what I remember, with my mother forever displaying the same stuff on a different day, effortlessly, easily, undeterred I drove to work, for my decision, "What lay ahead of me, was of so much greater value, than that which was laid behind, and so simply, I took another step, and carried-on, as usual."

Then evening drew in, before I was to look inside the that bag that she'd rejected and given me back, "Oh my" I thought I have given her some pretty awesome stuff and to own it, really I'd be rather pleased so to look inside, I was hoping of treasures to find, but "What!" Hers was an empty gesture, as only little trinkets, not a one of any of those beautiful and elegant blouses I had given her or those hairstyling gadgets, which really, I could have made good use of. But to her, the gesture completely symbolic, which although unspoken she clearly expected me to understand, and true, of her vengeful intent, she got her wish, for I clearly did comprehend, but still, I considered her actions unworthy, and her spite the same, and true, I held not control over the choices she made on that day, though I believe that her behavior not random, but purposeful, again to start a battle, one she firmly fully intended to win. *BUT!* The tide of change had blown in.

She knew it not then, but she had transferred her power to me, as 'that time,' she'd misjudged it, or misjudged me, because there had been a shift and something had changed, that time, I chose to be, no longer mystified by my mothers actions, or pose as an unwilling recipient of her wrath, imparting relentless misery in my heart, and with her refusal to ease up, it ended up, in me not caring more, but caring less, and worse, through those turbulent emotions she tried tirelessly to impart on me, with a weight so heavy to push me forever down, well, eventually, she succeeded, in creating that terrible enemy, named 'apathy.' My emotions unable to proclaim affections for her anymore, as on route breaking free from her belittling ways, as I careered past caring, skidding into care-less, before sliding into interference, where that trio, settled and remained, as away from her demoralizing ways, my liberty I gained.

Away from my house that early morning, in such a temper, she turned and walked back to her car, where I imagined my lovely and kind stepdad, following his instructions, to keep the peace, was waiting for her, and true, I knew not then, that, was the very last time I was ever to see my mother, yet I knew, there was nothing good to miss, nor a sweet or wholesome memory to comfort me in that 'loss, for really, unwittingly, she had given me a gift, for she had dismissed me and though she did not know it, inadvertently, she had set the captive *free, me.* So I'd taken my first step to self-healing and self-discovery, where I was to grow, to know my own self-worth and my own personal value, then through it, I was to flourish, to blossom and become, more of me!

> *"Friendship with ones self is all important,*
> *because without it one cannot be friends with anyone else in the world."*
> *~ Eleanor Roosevelt*

Paris, it seemed so long ago, as my mind took a trip back in time, where I recalled the warnings, and not through poor judgment, but completely by mistake, I failed to heed, "Be careful where you settle, as some towns in France, will never accept you." And "Oh my" act in haste repent at leisure was certainly to be my cry, in that concept for contemplation. As too long surely I must have stayed in that French *ville*, as the people there continued to point and stare, and oddly, it seemed bizarre, to think of so many police TV dramas, depicting the excessive ease of obtaining camera surveillance footage, identified as being a most important tool for calling perpetrators to justice, and sited as the first and major task of each and every case they are to investigate, well, "What an irony that turned out to be, for surely, if it hadn't made me so sad, it would have made me mad."

But to 'build a bridge and get over it,' simply I seemed unable to do, as I, was brought up to respect policeman, and true had counted them as my close friends in both the UK and New Zealand, and on occasions when I needed the strength or safety of the police force, *always*, they were there to protect me, and in that situation, without help, I was lost, and adamant that I needed help support and answers, and to be able to significantly understand more of "Why I was ignored?" And of the injustice of it all, reassuring myself, that for the first time in my life, I was truly not to give-in or go-away, nor turn the other cheek, and when no one else would, I was to, "Stand up. Stand up for me!"

So advice and help from the necessary powers that be, outlining the bad thing that had happened, and the injustice, of all, which, had not been done, as

Officials from that country, were to discover, just what had gone on. And the outshot of it all, was that, at last, those 2 French girls were interviewed regarding the assault, and not surprisingly they denied it, sited in their defence, that all of us, had a street fight! Of cause untrue, but I found solace, that, their names regarding such an incident were on record and connected to it, after, I did receive a letter, inviting me, should I choose to take the matter further, to contact, a particular person, so carefully I deliberated and decided, to travel down that path any longer, was not worth my effort, for what was behind me, mattered least, to what lay before me, as that mattered the most, was what lay in front, and so, for my future, resolved, determined, I chose to let the matter go, as with reflection of my life, suddenly, the realization, looking forward to peace, held a significantly higher priority, than any vengeance I could cast behind me, and already with my new goal of nursing in Canada, I had already cast my new vision, and was looking forward to "Where I desired and deserved to be."

As emotionally I had changed, I had grown, and through that experience and was no-longer prepared to shut up and put up, and be quiet and not report it and let them 'get away with it,' like I had done with my ex-husband, ex-fiancé and the rapist, for that time, I chose to do something rather than nothing. For my character, my personality was changing, as I had no time or preference for looking in that rear view mirror for anything more than a quick glance, and so for my personal life to enhance, so for treats to come my way, as I ventured toward my future, I was to jollily skip over that bridge, to greet it happily and introduce myself delightfully with, *"Enchanté!"* Exclaiming, "I'm so extremely pleased and excited to meet you!"

Seldom, in some regards, are we different for each other, is in total, we are a product of the sum of our past experiences, and for some, who are fortunate, those with pleasure are good to replicate, while for others, perhaps those like me, away from them willingly we would fly, over the gate or over the moon, 'if only' we could get away, to find and receive, even a portion of rest or peace and it would, give us peace or rest, and my philosophy, to reach for the stars, and if I only get as far as the moon, well hey, I'm so very much further along my journey to safety and self-discovery than when I first began.

So hold tight to optimism and our dreams, for we never know quite when, a dream will come true, when negativity and inner-hostility, we will prove to ourselves only serves as our history and not our own self-fulfilling legacy. As so gladly I share with you, where I first began, as that child, living in that set of circumstances I held no control over, but now I am an adult, and the power is in my hands, power to make an overwhelming positive difference, for me, those I love and others, who perhaps like me have travelled through a set or a portion of particularly unfortunate experiences, and please, I petition you, take a light heart, be of the best cheer you can be, and in your mind take flight, until you emotionally and physically, until you arrive at your destination, that for you, is *SAFE & RIGHT!*

And *"No more,"* I declared, for I had learnt sufficiently, that I truly deserve so much better than what I was given, so from now on, I proclaim, and decree through inner-love, inner-strength, and inner-healing, in the immortal words of the late Bob Marley, I always will, "Get up, stand-up, stand-up for my rights!"

"To regret one's own experiences is to arrest one's own development. To deny one's own experiences is to put a lie into the lips of one's life.
It is no less than a denial of the soul."
~ Oscar Wild

Such a dark and injured specimen I used to be, for so long, living in the past, stuck, with no apparent way out, but "Why did I not look for a route out?" Because I knew not that I needed to, but the wind of change had started to blow in a different direction, and I was to implement a new strategy, not to resist its force or push against it, but, to harness its power to propel me into better functioning and improved-serving ways, to improve everyone of my forthcoming days, as mindfully after reading a book at a library, my new process began, to *'OBSERVE THYN OWN BEHAVIOUR FIRST'* and what a gift that proved to be, as I realized, that it was not on the outside, or to anyone else I needed to look for change, as it was on the inside of me where I needed first to look, and the power held within that succinct phrase, was to benefit me enormously, as that trick so often I practiced it, and in dong so, so many of those confusing emotions 'turned out' to have a reason behind them, and as I acknowledged them and dedicated myself to change them, I embraced that unraveling *process of progress,* and the benefit for me, my life, it improved quite astoundingly, as inner-growth and self-respect and that magnificent, self-worth, all, knew *MY* name!

And so it evolved, a situation so sublime, where I stopped hating those who hated me, as I realized, blame is basically, in effect, forever giving them who hurt us so, cart blanche, to carry on, doing exactly so, and that twisted rope of internalized bitterness that I used to hold onto so tightly, serving only to hold myself captive, as a prisoner to the past, so I made a decision, I decided, I chose to relinquish them, as I came up with a new and improved plan, as I choosing *to, accept it all and let it all go,* and from all those years, they had held me down, I was to dissolve, disperse and shattered their power. So wasting not even a moment of time for my recovery, delays stuck in traffic proved as benefits, for I utilized that time so well, listening to copious empowering CD's, and always my quite firm routine, while relaxing at café' partaking in the best latté, for my growth and education, a book was always in my hand, as my knowledge I did expand, learning, absorbing all I needed, of served me best, leaving behind, those diseased, contorted, unpleasant, unnecessary, 'I don't need them any-more memories,' as they, outdated, superfluous to requirements, as those emotions, I'd surpassed them all, and "Why?" Because I was a survivor and still am, and in this new life of mine, I am so very grateful to be, an *OVERCOMER!*

As I grew and knew, of those trials and tribulations that came my way, rather than recent them, tor begrudge them, I began to nurture myself through each one, as on my route to self-discovery, as I learnt, that when each was over and done, my life, was enhanced, better balanced and improved, achieving an even higher level of emotional health, and with each step I took, I moved increasingly away from that damaged person I used to be, as with hope for a future, longing to be better than I used to be, longing to be healed and whole, longing to be worthy, as old habits were gone and battles for progress, successfully won, and through that process, so gladly, I ploughed all I needed along my journey, heading toward the direction, where I was to meet, the *very* of *best ME*, that I was able and yet to be.

True, I learnt on that journey to discover the 'real me,' to value myself so very much more, as I was to leave behind all *their* hindering traits of captivity, as I realized my safety, it laid not bricks and mortar, for love cannot be found in those, and my fortress, of my bigger and better castles, well, experience revealed, while they made a prisoner of me, still, they remained unable to protect me, from *their* hurt and harm, and time, with its passing, allowing for space, proving to be a healer of significance, and I, embracing its attributes, wholesome and healthy, nurturing and kind, soulful and purposeful, as for my new life, those foundations, were built from the inside-out, with gentle and loving strength, welcoming me in, and through it all, I came to know, *finally*, in VICTORY...

I am free

free to be me!

Yet...

The End

This is not

*For it is,
Just the beginning!*

May my words, designed to bring you strength
& encouragement, for of them I know;
unequivocally, you deserve them so.

Conclusion

"I believe in pink. I believe that laughing is the best calorie burner. I believe in kissing, kissing a lot. I believe in being strong when everything seems to be going wrong. I believe that happy girls are the prettiest girls. I believe that tomorrow is another day, and I believe in miracles."
~ Audrey Hepburn

"Oh my oh my ~ I MADE IT!" I made it, through to Paris and beyond. And "Who would have believed it possible?" Perhaps not me, at least not before, I travelled along this journey, and Paris, I thought it was all about me leaning to speak French, but really, all along it may have been, that my whole purpose for going there, and the trials and tribulations, was all about getting to know, Me. As 'healing,' became my friend, as I, travelled from A to B, and onto C and D, and continued accelerating through the mythical alphabet, as I, was propelled by, everything, yet nothing, until I become, who I really am today.

And perhaps no one, is more surprised than I, to end up here, so far away from where I first began, from a place, deep in the dark, yet now, standing tall at the top of my mountain, bathed in bright warming light, with thankful memories of those evenings all alone in my living room, though not lonely, for I knew not how to be, for lonely was all I ever knew to be deep inside. But how wonderfully fortuitous, that CD, Soul Devotion, bought quite by chance at Boots, a quite historic UK store, and a track upon it, that after dancing around my living room, while filling my glass again, of a fine wine, such little amounts I drank, as I found my solace in something else, 'repeat' the button I would press again, as I would sing along loudly with her lyrics, "If you don't follow your dream you will never know what is at the top of the mountain, you will never know what is on the other side of the rainbow and you will never know where you would be at your journey's end."

And that, wonderfully sung by Melba Moore became my mantra, though way back then I didn't know it, as I focused with all my might of the spirit of hope and possibilities she portrayed, and I never had felt such intense emotions before, but something about it resonated with me deep within, and so it was, my great journey of self-discovery began.

And it's true, from small acorns great oak trees grow, and I was to wonder later, of my fortune that I had given me the opportunity for one to planted for my very own, and although I knew not, I was to nurture it, until it became transformed to nurture me, as was brave enough, to do what I had to do, as I faced my fears, to let go of what encapsulated me, of horrendous portions of low self-esteem, guilt, shame and hurt and pain, which in abundance accompanied me everyday.

For I, in my progress became a walking-taking mini-miracle, as I permitted through choice and determination, for all those negative non-attributes to dissolve and fade away, as gently slipping into my life, were peace, patience, kindness, gentleness, goodness with love and joy accompanying them, and as the crippling strife of my life disappearing, I was to continue along my journey's way with soft and gentle rejoicing.

So that 'job in progress' I remained for such a long time, was all worth the effort to it I relentlessly assigned, as persistence and resilience became my fortified, 'go-to's' as I was to get through, determined to be more healed, as I simply, sometimes, could achieve no more, than to simply get through another day, but that was one of the secrets you see to achieving my goal, to move from "Where I was, to where I deserved to be" as I grew and knew, all that I so desired was to come my way, just as long as I picked myself up, one more time than I fell, resounding to know, "I was worth, so much than they who harmed me, had told me so," as I permitted no longer, that caustic and toxic debris to fester, in those open wounds, damaging me, though concealed on the outside, as their effects, only felt inwardly.

Yet I, continually resided, to cast out their hostile emotions and teachings, castings them aside as "Null in void" and insufficient those curses they spoke over me, to any longer keep me a prisoner, as the shackles of their chains broke, corroded by the salty tears of recovery that spilt like concurrent waterfalls upon them, as they disintegrated, and I, through my own efforts and personal aptitude, I was most magnificently to rise from the pit they put me in, as my heart was to heal, and my soul to sing, as I, was to learn like an eagle to fly, on the wings of love.

And just perhaps, I needed to learn, I couldn't be apart of someone else until first, I could be apart of me, yet most importantly, through all the sorrowful struggles, I was never to give-up or give-in true, as I strived to climb out of that hurt place, as revelations along my journey, at first did not come easy, and mistakes, although hard to take, may be viewed of instruments of benefits, as invaluable they may prove to be, not to be missed or dismissed, as they help to move us from A to B, as we seek for the silver-linings to the clouds they elude.

For lessons learnt are indeed rewards to be received, can be seen strewn throughout history, with Alexander Fleming in his laboratory in 1928, discovered by mistake, that has since saved countless billions of lives, Penicillin. With Henry Ford's resounding success, through his ability to surpass stormy clouds and pick himself just one more time than he tumbled, as stumbling blocks posed a poor match for his tenacity and fortified efforts, and because of his application of time and commitment way back then, today we drive motorcars of his overriding invention.

So, with one tentative step, slowly but surely placed before the other along my journey to self-discovery and self-recovery, increasingly began to please me, as I pondered with each milestone surpassed, greater vigor I encompassed, so onto another, as eager I was for my progression to I became a master at recognizing whenever 'I got it wrong,' as I a connoisseur to view each, with specific significance, as they simply provided, one more opportunity, to 'get it right next time.' And that system I began to use as a guiding light, along my journey of personal progression, where I vowed to heal their wrongs, as with each step and learning curve climbed up, I absolutely knew, I deserved not to live with what they had done to me, as I vigorously resounded, to do better for me, than they had ever intended, as I developed a new concept, that "It matters *far less* from where we came, than where *we choose to go.*"

And true, how much better I would have benefitted, if-only I could have learnt these concepts so long ago, but the reality is, I did not, and better to learn the later than not ever, so I am content that I consider my age as just a factor, as I was able to travel, from, "Where I was to where I wanted to be." and how fortunately, that I learnt of libraries and a quest for knowledge, before it was too late, and the thirst for recovery the same, as I wandered so frequently to the library, for all those free recourses, and gain in my grasp, copious books and educational CD"S, as off to a café I would go, to sip on a latté, and then while driving my car, to maximize my recovery rate, of the most interesting topics, I would press, replay, and "Oh my" such empowerment was to come my way, as that light I began to see at the other end of the tunnel was I was hidden, was not the light of disaster heading toward me, but the fortuitous light, of hope, that was coming, wonderfully, to greet me.

For I nursed myself through the blisters and splinters, bruises and sprains, through the torrential storms, up hill and down dale, and through bad hair days, as I carried my own canoe, as the pain from which I desired, required to escape, propelled me forward, where, leaving tragedy behind, humbly in triumph, healing graciously I received my recovery, for I was able to smile, as success I recognized, for I had done the hard 9 yards, and paid the price for my progression, through my commitment to achieve steady progression, truly in my character, I had metamorphosed, for which I was enormously grateful, and such humongous amount of credit I should award to me, for when the 'going got tough' or life through me one of those often unpredicted curve balls, I clung tight to my newfound belief that I could effect what happened to me, as I simply picked up pace, forging ahead, preventing a slip away from my attributed place.

So a friendship I was to develop with myself, as my passion and purpose became to recover my power, from those who stole it, as I became a master at giving me, second chances, as I was able to create better opportunities for tomorrow by the choices I made each day, and such new concepts to consider for never before had I been able to even contemplate such an aim, yet with *Courage* as my new *best friend*, the idea to embrace and adore the thought of me, being worthy, of love from any source, well that idea, wonderfully grew, as I recommitted frequently, until I succeed to forgive their sins, enabling and gaining magnified power of inner-healing, where new and treasured emotions, of forgiveness, grace and peace were all mine to accomplish, as gratitude accompanied them, and the pain slipped away, and of the truly healthy kind, lust was replaced with love, healthy and kind, and restfulness replaced rage, and I no longer suffered tragic torment everyday, as peace in abundance, eventually was mine, and with me, to stay.

And my passion of "Where did I desire and dream to be" was quite simply it evolved, in a world, where I, leant to value that which could not be seen, but only felt, as I was able to grown to give and receive love, in my life, where poisonous fear was in my past, and my future, therein, held a heart that was whole and a soul that was free, where I was able to help, those that were longing and deserving to start or continue along their own journey.

"Was it easy?" Oh my how I would so like to say yes, but in reality, "Not really." But was it worth it? "Absolutely!" And that the significance, of the harmony and glee, wrapped up in a parcel of peace, of substantial increments added to most everyday, as we reach a place, comfortable inside to reside, as our delightful side effect, as we learn to like and love ourselves, others do to, and our life becomes, one not to dread but embrace, as we leave behind those old ill-serving habits, of being a human-doing and mellow into becoming a human-being, as we run our race, and win our war, that unfortunately was impossible to do before, and as another of those to-do-jobs as we work on us, now secure, with joy and delight, we may live triumphantly, knowing fully, that as woe-men we leave the past behind, and toward our future with continued hope, is ours to *enjoy* everyday, as we with *calm clarity*, magnificently *gently grasp*, that which *we are so worthy*, to *live* our *lives*.....

FREE in *Victory*!

 ☺

..........*And then*

5 Years Later On..........

Part Three

~~~ooOoo~~~

À Paris; Encore!

(To Paris; Again!)

Bonus Chapter

Step! One More Time! Because You Absolutely Can!

"It always seems impossible until it's done."
~ Nelson Mandela

"Oh a Paris," what a surprise I ended up back there, for at that time really, it had not been on my radar, and where had I been in the meantime? New Zealand was one place, and for the 9 months passed there, I lived out of a suitcase, and where in Auckland, many, serious accidents were to trouble me. A car accident at first, followed by a serious falls, and then amazingly my calf muscle was torn…my back twisted my knee adversely effected and my neck, don't get me started there, as a brace I had to wear, and all debilitating and adversely effecting my sleep and my writing as all were resulting in pain and incapacity and a regime of medical treatments, and without the companionship of a couple of lovely ladies I met from one little café I frequented, where through our daily catch-ups, we created our own mini-community, and without them, "Oh my" the time I stayed would have been extremely emotionally insane.

Then it was 2 planes to get to Jersey, a little island only 25 miles wide, sited 14 miles off the northern coast of France, where I was to spent a rather icy and snowy Christmas, but what a wonder there, for in my suitcase were only packed 3 inch high healed boots, so through the slush in them I was to tread, and as fortune would have it, another couple of lovely ladies I was to meet, and their kindness towards me, was really was quite a treat, and in my bargain accommodation I enjoyed a rather snazzy four poster bed and a most comfy latex mattress to curl up in, and a wardrobe; so all in all not too bad and made my 3 or so months stay there, really not that bad, an for my purpose of writing and ease of the same, I was really quite glad.

The Caribbean I wandered off to next, first an island, which from the British, in1962, it gained its independence, Dominic Republic I was also to visit, spending 3 months there, and as it happens, neither country turned out to be so good, as in the former I was to discover a maid 'standing guard' while another employee was looking through my room, and the latter, the air-con so bad, the bedding was wet with moisture and the holes in all the mosquito nets meant every night, I was served up as their banquet.

Etats-Unis d'Amerique, USA as the French call it, where from it's shores I needed to make a fairly quick exit from there, suddenly as my visa application had been positively extended, though it placed me in a major predicament, as the law that granted my stay immediately unbeknown to me became null and void, so leave there rapidly I must do, travelling to pastures new and what disharmony was to accompany me as I brought forward the date of my airline ticket to transport me to, "Wonderful wonderful Copenhagen."

But, "Really, should I have been surprised at its sudden eventuality?" Because true, I was still carrying my own canoe, but in excess of half a decade had passed by this point since I departed the shores of Melbourne and really, I was weary, yet still, I followed my inner star, my internal GPS, though really I would much preferred a detailed map, as 'trusting in what came next' resulted in a most nomadic lifestyle, which through longevity, emotionally and financially, was proving quite difficult, and I tried not to worry of all the uncertainty of "What was I to be doing?" and really, "Where was I to be tomorrow?" and the day after that, "Well, really, who would know?"

True, somewhere along the way of my journey to "Where?" I imagined that a door had been purposefully closed behind me, and there was not turning back, but the new door appeared not to have opened yet, as I seemed to linger in a never ending corridor, but surely as I did what I must, perhaps I was being 'prepared for something that was coming up, and I was in school taking my lessons and being prepared for what was coming up, and for sure even more, whatever that driving force was inside me was, I was to embrace it, value it, and took courage to examine what my dreams were at my very core; still properties, still renovating, yet writing, now that, I came to adore.

"Had dared to dream?" To have the courage to follow that ever-so softly, non tangible inner-guidance, trusting in something bigger than me, that although I did not totally understand it, embracing it, as it propelled me to move forward from A to B. And what a bonus, it took me to Paris, and then onward to smaller villages further down the country, but perhaps as no surprise, trials and tribulations revisited me, yet there was a gift wrapped within everyone of them, as they were served up to happily show me, how much further along my journey I was, than when I first began, as situations that may have caused me to react 'this way or that,' then I had progressed to responding in the format of the 'other.' And so absolutely wholesome it was to discover, absent, were those debilitating emotions of abandonment and judgment, as I stuck fast to my commitment, of sensible and wise rationales, as quite wonderfully and importantly, I learnt that those bygone tests which had come against me, I had received an astoundingly awesome prize, for I had discovered, of life, how well I fit in it.

"Starting point of all achievement is desire."
~ Napoleon Hill

At Paris's *Orly* airport, as I stepped from the plane such a wet and windy night greeted me at, yet nothing did it do to detract me of arriving in that city that I adored, even though by contrast, only a few hours earlier, it was a beautiful blue sky I left behind in the USA, and "Oh my" I thought of those enjoyable bike rides I went up on, so many and so long one almost rolled into the other, and not even those 98 degree days, plus humidity were able to deter me, for so they invigorated me, keeping me healthy and refreshing my soul, as the day was dawning each morning, I'd rise from my slumber, with only one destination in mind, and cycling past those beautiful painted wooden houses, until I reached my favorite and calming spot, where relaxing, I'd partake of a rather fine latté made with organic beans and grass fed cows milk, while perhaps chatting with some customers of the most congenial kind, before getting happily on with my business of writing.

Yet unfortunate were circumstances as on my way across the Atlantic on that fight, lasting not too long at 9 hours as I sped through the air to Denmark from Florida, as seated beside me, was a toddler, with its crying and screaming that kept me awake all night, so sleep deprivation slipped in, and nausea was giving way to sickness, so easily resulting, in one of 'those headaches' which placed me in bed for 4 days, so I decided to for-go my preplanned train trip to nip, on a brief and speedy train ride into that Danish city, and opting to save my money and avoid those high DDK exchange rates, plus my plan to place my hand luggage in storage, hit a hitch, when I was to learn those lockers had been relocated outside, and it overweight, I cared not to try and get it through customs once again, free from charge, so rest I did, to afford myself my best chance of recovery, as on that 6 hour layover, I awaited my ongoing flight to whisk me away, to my favorite city, the 'city of love.'

Foiled was my plan to visit Copenhagen, and suddenly, my plan to secure a last minute, Parisian airport hotel deal, didn't seem quite so ideal, so began the song and dance of trying to get internet access, to search for a place to stay in my favorite *arrondissement*, for my favorite price, that always being, 'as cheap as possible,' and with 24 hours and counting, since I'd left that bright sunny local in the USA, it was France, "Yeah" where I arrived, yet still no rest, as 10pm, and I had still not reached my destination. So a Shuttle Bus I hurriedly sought for, and with 2 suitcases in tow, for 15 minutes I raced around the airport, searching out the Information Kiosk, yet a hiccup, when I had used my best French, but thank goodness, he spoke excellent English, as when I requested such from that young man in his uniform who sat before, making my request for a bus to speed me off to central Paris, his uninspiring and worrying words, *"Désolé,"* "Sorry," you're too late. "The last one just left, 10 minutes ago."

"No. That can't be so." My stomach sank, at my money awaiting me to be spent, on a taxi driver that in my experiences have proven untrustworthy, and of cost, "Oh my" money, that would have gone flashing by, so I begged, so sorrowfully with despair rising from my heart upwards to be displayed on my face, as my pulse rapidly raced and mild panic set in at the risk of not getting communal transport. I protested, not through anger, but desperation, "That cannot be" as Shuttle Buses for me are the only way to go, they are safe and predictable with no variables, a set routes, a set price, they are clean and comfy, and through trials and errors, and all that criteria, fits perfectly into my priorities, then I pleased, "Please, can you help me? Is there anything that you can do?" then "Phew" thankfully, maybe he observing my despair, he uttered more encouraging words, "Just wait a minute, I will see what I can do."

"Oh thank you!" Yet a tense 5 minutes passed, as he talking in French, while I waited and contemplated "Oh why, didn't I stick with my original plan, to take an airport hotel room for the night?" As all this angst would have been avoided, and as I continued to wait, my body began to crumble with severe dehydration, as he discussed 'this and that' with a person on the other end of the phone line, and through that process, nothing I understood, and his facial expressions, I was unable to decipher, as they revealed not clue to whether I was to be fortunate in my pursuit, of avoiding taking a taxi, and with my anxiety increasing, under my breath I was praying, as true, until I was told 'no,' I was to hang-on to hope, then, as he replaced the receiver, with more than a little trepidation I posed the question, "Am I safe? Is the Shuttle Bus coming to take me to my hotel?" Then such sweet words, as I heard him speak, "Yes. It is on its way now, coming across from Terminal West." "Yeah!" Relief! Were my responses beside, "Thank you. Thank you. Thank you!"

What a relief! And what a treat to arrive in the street of my hotel destination, with hiccups some 40 minutes later, but heck, I was not complaining, yet out of the woods not quite, as the drivers GPS which indeed I had been watching, had sent him in the wrong direction down a one-way street, so the driver in his wisdom or not, on a sharp right angled corner parked his mini van, and leaving other tourists sat in it, he removed my bag and 2 suitcases, beckoning me to drag one, as he did the other, along the cobbled road and of that 8 minute jaunt, where my back was increasingly hurting, though in my mind I was refusing to accept it, trying my upmost to ignore it, but the noring ache was transferring to a sharpness of pain, yet still I wasn't to complain, as I was so immensely grateful, that in his bus, he had come across from whichever terminal he was at, to collect me, so although my slightly failing health could ill afford, what I was expecting it to do, I accepted it as a willing trade off, as so pleased I remained, that I was not stranded at the airport, for being safe & sound, in *arr, St Germain*.

"What to do?" All booked in, and my suitcases at last, for the first time in over 24 hours I was able not to have to drag, or keep them within my sight, and odd, but that gave me almost a new sense of freedom, and true I was exhausted and needed to go to bed, but I was in Paris once again, and the vibe of that fair city was calling me, or "Was I simply seduced by the sound of that clarinet, so soft, so soulful, effortlessly from the street below, wafting though my opened window?" So, from my 4th story room, to discover the player of those dulcet tones, on my tiptoes I stood tall, to see all I could, yet, unable to spy anything, and knowing it was almost midnight, still almost without a slither of hesitation, it was my hat and coat I reached for, seizing the value of that moment of opportunity, as I walked down the spiral staircase to discover the musician, on *rue de Bucci*.

"Oh my" I don't know how long I was gone for, but I do know I enjoyed basking in the vision of that architecture that never wearies me, and the humming of conversations from the flocks of customers all seated upon the terraces, at those multiple pavement café's, and so surprising, as the day was one in the middle of the week, but still not a spare seat on which to sit was to be found, and "Oh the sound", of those gentle Parisian dialects, far more easier for me to understand than in other regions, softly humming in unison, with English or American accents too, thrown into the mix, but after all that inspiring joviality, I returned to my most centrally located hotel, where it was a healing formula for my ailing back, that I needed to source and secure to fix it.

What amazing good fortune, as at hotel in Paris, for non of the others came anywhere close, had that shower with such power, which deluged tremendous hot and steamy water, that never ran out, as out of its jets that healing source flowed, and "Oh my" how I needed it so, to elevate those increasing spasms, so my neck so painful, the muscles tender and tight, I let the water massage it for the longest time, then first to the let and then the right, so grateful that the water force was so strong as I was able to direct it so specifically by moving the direction of my body, a bit of a science really, as beneath the stream I lingered, before bending forward, whilst most importantly, maintaining the *lordosis* in my back, as I lavished the passing of time, as the heat and the pressure of that water worked dispensing its magic, as my body released a deep and rejuvenating sigh.

"Oh my" firmly I knew it not a lie, that huge progress had indeed been made, for of my predicament, my normal, past go-to process was fear and panic, of how badly was it to deteriorate and how long was it to last for, "Wow!" they from my mind, had miraculously gone, as no longer was there a whirlpool of worries, wondering how much worse was it to get, before it got better. "No!" Turning over that new-leaf, I could hardly believe it myself, as I realized how miraculously those old defeating habits had gone, as I'd cast aside those self-defeating responses, affording significant and beneficial notification, positively for my progression, as indeed, for my inner-growth, as I opted not for a plan of discouragement, but one of action, for success, of my forthcoming, full recovery.

"A little more persistence, a little more effort,
and what seems hopeless failure may turn to glorious success."
~ Elbert Hubbard

So pleasingly, after so many hours of being awake and mainly sat up right, with sitting adding an extra 33% of pressure through the spine, so gladly I eased myself into bed, desiring the best nights rest I'd ever had, but that was hindered by that dreaded common cold, which from that other continent appeared to hitch a free ride, with its germs nestled inside me, yet the mattress to ease my discomfort, appeared to be made of latex, certainly almost my favorite kind, so I, more than a little contented, and with my back so in spasm, it could not have been better, as every minute indentation of my body was wonderfully supported, and what a brilliant bonus, as a rare occurrence, that for my precarious neck, the pillows were comfortable too, and white sheets of a heavy and luxurious thread count, cradling around me, then profiting from previous experience, as to optimize the possibility of a sound and restful nights *dormir*, sleep, I took 3mg of Melatonin, a double dose of magnesium, with a fortified 800mg dose of Ibuprofen, all geared to reduce that acute muscle spasm that was contorting and gripping my spine and muscles, then my arm, twisting it up high up my back, while using my knuckles, Vitamin E oil, I was able to gently massage-in, and to aid my recovery, with nothing else in my suitcase to hand, sips of water were to complete and complement, my formulated recipe, my well practiced plan, the very best I had done, and so it was off, to refreshing, adorable slumber land.

"Yet you know how it is," the very best nights sleep you can achieve in a hotel is only until, the first person in the rest of that place, gets up, as then, doors are a-slamming, suitcases are a-dragging and peoples voices are a-carrying, to right outside your door, and even as I did my best to catch up on sleep and substantially rest from those exacerbated twinges of nerve pains, from my back and my neck, that each time changed position or moved my body, even a little, as continually throughout the night my sleep was disturbed and "What?" "No!" as at 7a.m. it was not other guests, but workmen, a-drilling and a-hammering where from the adjoining room, noises were a-coming, and continuing-on for an hour or two, with the only thing left for me to do, was to utilize that awesome shower once again, "Oh" and hope, that following morning, I was not again to be disturbed by them from my slumber.

"Yet this was my life," and it needed to carry on, so *Carpe diem*, seize the day, became quickly, my engaged motto, as wasting no time I refused to permit it, as to see all the major sights, around Paris I needed to dash, as I, believing myself to be there, only for a few days, yet that did not quite work-out the same way, as one day turned into another and so they went on and on, as for my primary focus, transferred from all else, as I nurtured my slowly recovering back, to restore my good health, and with no other particular place to be, and with those suitcases in tow, not travelling too lightly, and armed, with what hindsight had taught me, I surmised, it was far wiser to rest in one place a little longer, to minimize those remaining sharp nerve pains, still interrupting my nights sleep, until my body, was more capable and stronger.

So content was I with my decision, that was right up until, I was to discover the price of my hotel where I was paying, 13% than I'd been quoted, unsatisfactory I thought yet when I queried the invoice, their response, so very French, as with a tilt of the head and raised eyebrows, their posture rising, standing taller, their shoulders pulled right back, and in my vision, conducive with an animal in the jungle about to strike, as their words which I paraphrase, "Too bad." Yet true, of that cost, I would not have prolonged my stay there, and as my health was much better, I considered it prime time to move on, though true, what a blessing in disguise, as I was soon to realize, a shower so excellent of that quality, in Paris, certainly within my budget range and experience, was impossible to find.

Yet still, onto the next, and though I didn't know it, I was going down hill, from there on in, as the next only had 1 Star above the door, and at only 10% cheaper, it proved and unwise swap, but not to complain, for the energy at that previous hotel seemed, so terribly wrong, and I simply had to get out of there. But "What of value at 83E?" Well that was to be non, in that consecutive hotel, as on entrance, from reception staff, courtesy was missing, and displaying overtly, their disgruntled dissatisfaction and opinion, that for my *valaise*, suitcases, with absence of an elevator, to take them up to the 1st floor, that I even dared to presume to request assistance, so it was, I was to surpass those encountered hazards, as *faire attention*, be careful, on that spiraling staircase, with loops of twine from the excessively worn carpet, were multiple and those loops of black rubber; I don't know what they were doing there, and metal trims coming loose and there sharpened edges sticking dangerously out, and every step posed a problem, and with the slightest miss-footing could cause to go tumbling, arriving in a heap injured at the bottom.

But the worst was yet to come, as it was a good nights sleep that I so desperately needed was not to be, on that mattress that sunk in the middle, by a good 8 inches, and that was before I even laid upon it, the pillows worse, with sharp jagged edges of foam poking right through them, as you can imagine, so terribly uncomfortable, the sheets certainly not hotel quality, with more in common with those placed on the floor, to protect carpets during house renovations, then in the shower I faired no better, indeed much worse, as in that evening there was not hot water, not even of a tepid temperature, for the pleasure to place the flow of healing water, for even just a few minutes, for my back's convalescence, well there was non of that, and to wash my hair impossible, and me, in Lilly Pulitzer dresses, only size 0, yet still, in that tiny cubical, a square of each side equaling not much longer than my forearm, with chunky mixer taps, dating back a couple of decades were jutting out, where on the white tiled wall, a disabled bar protruded into that diminishing space, and really, there was not room enough even for me, so a bigger person, I had no idea what they would do, and it became a bit of a masterful trick, as I raised my arms or turned around, without touching the concertina shower door, as it flipped wide open and water spread all over the floor.

Surely, "It couldn't get any worse?" "Not quite so," as unrefreshed I reached across for the deep brown and not so fluffy towel, how disappointing to have to use it, as the aroma was not fabric softener, but a smell of smoke, that oozed from it. "Yuk!" but with noting else to find, "Yep" I used it. Then foiled, my plan to enjoy a great nights sleep, was fraught and not to be, as my back muscles without support, those pillows pointy and harsh, with not even my face, as a tad painful, was I able to sleep on my side, yet still, that's what I needed to do, with that prolonged chest infection, with restful sleep, not to be my comforter, but a taunt, as discomfort was rife, as I tossed and turned all night, and as the dawn broke through and the light shone right through those faded and flimsy, pale blue floral curtains, hanging from a bold, chunky antique looking brass pole, singularly, the best thing in that room, and even that was broken, and relief there was to be known of my back condition that had deteriorated the night through, as of cause in the morning there was to be no relief from a good, nay even a mildly effective shower, for recouping or restoration.

Relieved to rise from that hugely unpleasant bed, where for the first time, I was able to absorb the aesthetics of that long and narrow room, which true, weren't half bad, where to one side lay a pale-stone, rough and old as the building, feature wall, and stood in front, the honey stained *armoire*, wardrobe, then the eyes were drawn to the excessively tall and slim French windows, where the warmth of oak and traditional antique fastenings, decorative in wrought iron, with the ornate Juliet balcony made of the same, all looking rather pretty, though for purpose totally unsatisfactory, as failed to close properly, and with its half inch round gap, enabled easily those cold, blustery, Parisian breezes, to blow right on in, yet that did not stop me, enjoying the vista of that petite café on the nearby corner, where back in the day, Hemingway with *copains*, friends, would write and discuss philosophy and more, all day.

"Mmmm," such a highly unpleasant 2 days I'd passed there, so really, it made no sense, actually equating to nonsense, that the night before my due departure, a bizarre decision, as I enquired of that man at the reception desk, "Do you have a room for a further couple of nights?" but "Why, did I think my worth so little, to prolong my stay there?" and of that perceived level I'd sunk to, that I'd accepted it, as though I deserved nothing more, "Why, of time, that so often underestimated and undervalued commodity, did I not utilize it to find something so much better for me, and 'trouble myself' to move there?"

For really, "Why, did I opt to stay at that, tremendously dreadful and quite dangerous hotel with reception staff that were most unhelpful hotel? Was I scared or were old habit butting back-in, for truly, I felt kind of desperate, unsteady in my emotions and where I was going, like a feather blowing in the wind, so very much, I was desiring, simply to not move-on so quickly again. Yet, seriously, should I not have paused and taken a pies, nay a portion of time for reflection, and tried so much harder to cast confusion away, and stop running around like a headless chicken, to have spent time to review, those 'old school' and outdated philosophies of 'putting-up and shutting-up, moving deliberately and masterfully away from, that ill serving foe?"

Indeed I knew, that I was further along my progression journey so "Why did poor judgment have me in its grasp?" As I pondered, "Was I stuck in a temporary rut, unable to have a quick fix?" or "Was I more vulnerable than that, temporarily, forgoing my newly gained wisdom?" For really, of it all, "When was I to recognize my personal value, and be proactive and not reactive of those, my unraveling predicaments, in the correct timings, to search for, to discover, appropriate solutions, and wisely, even implanting, that succinct old adage of 'a stitch in time saves 9,' as it, in format, as valuable today, as way back then, to be proactive and move forward with a plan, to reduce my stress and life's disruptions, through well rehearsed, good and constructed, preparation?"

Yet with no thoughts, of those concerns for calculations, "Why, in apparent emotional desperation, did I almost beg, for them to let me stay on?" where not even the internet I could access, so "Why did I allow that man at reception, who seemingly toyed with me for 20 minutes, as he went-on about this, that or the other, as my focus remained enact, to try and get a deal on one of the 3 vacant twin rooms, for the price I paid for the single?" "Oh my" I was polite and congenial, doing my very best to achieve my goal, indulging him in his copious and predominately one sided conversations, which to me, held little, to no merit, though a strategy I chose to employ, but really, on reflection, in reality, "I was not me manipulating him, as he held the power to my desire, so it was him manipulating me."

My goal remained unachieved, and in Paris, it was my 3rd hotel to find, so off down the *rue* I trundled, to seek advice, from my French friends, of "Where could I go for the best price?" A place suggested, the locations and price, good, 2 boxes ticked, but then, once bitten, twice shy, so before I booked the room I requested first to see it. My scan, the firmness of the mattress, the cleanliness of the sheets and the towels, though precariously above the bed, normally so adorable, a birdcage light fitting hanging from the ceiling, but "No" just one thread of the 3 coil wire was holding it there, with the other 2, loose, unattached and floating in the air, as perhaps too shabbily I contemplated, "Were those wires live?" Perhaps, but either way, for humor was to take photos. Yet "Yeah," no odors, so far, all appeared to pass muster, yet the shower I was less careful of checking that, but really, I should have paid far greater attention, as at only 78E nightly, I was so unwise, when that male receptionist enquired, "Do you want to pay for the full 3nights now in advance?" and irrationally, my response "Why not?" and right there, I was to breach my defense walls, of 'what not to do,' as I handed over my credit card, misguiding myself into believing, it to be '2 Star' award above the door, was not actually to be, 1.5 too many, yet 'too late' was my cry, as fraught the possibility, of getting any money returned to me, when I recognized, my huge *faux pas*.

On my arrival day, potentially, such a pretty spiral staircase I ascended, reaching to the 5th floor, where hiding behind that *chamber* door, a room, abundantly dirty, filthy, with a ripe aroma, that really, I never wanted to smell again, with sheets, stained, 'with who knew what' dragging across the 'oh so' grimy lino floor, then, in a flash I remembered, "They already have your money!" "Oops!" Yet I spoke with authority, "This will certainly not do! Take me to the room I was shown yesterday." Then after initial excuse, a tad surprising in that country, an apology came, before new keys found, to open that room on the 3rd floor, I'd been shown the previous day; so then, the 3 of us moved in, me, my grand *valaise,* suitcase, my hand luggage, and me, where for the 3 nights I was to stay, to gain some much needed rest, but 'watch this space' as a mini unraveling saga, was about to commence.

As a surprise awaited me, as the shower, transpiring to be not just tiny but so terribly grungy and unsuitable for purpose, as when I'd used it, I really needed another to clean myself off from it, and really, a better place, "Could I not afford it?" but perhaps not, a preserving what I'd got, as seemingly daily my exchange currency rate, was lowering, with my corresponding anxiety levels, of what I was spending, rising, as my actions unfolding in that cit of love Paris, trials and tribulations appeared as my constant companions, holding significant ramifications, while evolving, my forever unanswered questions, "What I was doing?" and more importantly, "Where I was going? Did I have a purpose or a plan?" or "Was I, uncomfortably, almost unwillingly, wandering quite aimlessly?" True, almost rhetorical, for I knew not, exactly where in the world to settle, not even in which country, in essence, "Was I lost, with fading hope?" or "Heading in the right direction?" and "Was I ever going to reach that distant of place, of my desired destination?" *Yet* true, even its name, I did not know, so the interim, though filled with frustration, I chose to concentrate on this publication, *yet* wondering, after all my preparations, "Why oh why, had it not *yet* come to fruition?"

Yet 'Relief!' as a pause for humor in that oh-so-old and so-outdated hotel situated on the corner, in my most favorite *arrondissement*, where, what looked to be a urinal, in entrance hall to the hotel must be passed, to reach the spiral staircase, where to lay, a threadbare dark blue carpet runner, laden with floral patterns, of a red and green bouquets, and the balustrade, as like the *Eiffel Tower*, hundreds of years of paint, had been applied, one on top of the other, and "Oh how I imagined" that beneath those layers, the warmth of oak or mahogany, would prevail and spindles too, were the same, as their delicate details difficult to see, almost lost through those centuries, but of any of it, not to worry, as during the entirety my 3 night stay, it was mostly concealed, by the hazards of high piles, of brightly colored, course nylon laundry bags, awaiting collection, as masterfully, it became my accomplished tick, for a firm footing to pick, with a good stride to place one foot over, safely to the other side, to ensure I didn't have a fall down the stairs , or worse, over the railing, and have to claim on my non existent, health insurance.

"Victory is always possible for the person who refuses to stop fighting."
~ Napoleon Hill

But "Were things to get worse or better?" As so keen was I to have a hot and revitalizing shower, but then the realization, you may have guessed it, there was no hot water, and the taps to touch, "Oh my" so greasy and slimy, but still failed by comparison to the depths of the dirt on the toilet, where even in that dim light, and without my spectacles, lingering there, easily visible, those multiple dried up drops of urine on the seat. "Oh my" my body cringed and my stomach turned, as I reached up on my tiptoes to opened the window but the catch, it slipped from my grasp, as they also, so grimy and grungy, but "What was I to do, complain?" "Certainly! Yes!" but, a cleaner room there was not, such an example, of acting in haste and repenting at leisure, as my credit card had gone before me and paved the way.

Yet a ray of hope was to glisten, as I so marveled at the simplest thing I'd done, as before I departed from those sunny shores of south west Florida, at the last minute, my pink-ribboned flip-flops, that had been on the 'leave behind pile' as unnecessary, to where I was going, quickly, in my case I threw them, and "Oh my" how they saved me, from walking barefoot across that sticky, yucky, white tiled floor, yet they were not so helpful to protect me from that rancid drain stench, encircling me, with its bad and vulgar aroma, impossible to escape as even in the middle of the night, it was to wake me, from my slumber.

In the far corner, in front of the old white painted radiator, blending with the ensemble of stark white walls and ceiling, there sat, a Louis XIV reproduction chair, that, in yeas so long ago, perhaps should have been put on the tip, or possibly, maybe it was taken from one, and "What a surprise" as not even the fabric of a green damask antique pattern, that normally would alight my senses and imagination, was even momentarily sufficient to spark my interest, but only reminisce, of the Big Bang Theory's red chair episode, as I was pretty convinced that creepy crawlies of those fibers and threads, were hidden within, surely I was never sit upon it, and such a wise choice, as even a plastic bag, I mistakenly placed there, when I removed 3 days later, it was extremely sticky and tacky.

Then faring not much better, the modern dust-drenched, velour mustard-striped curtains, encasing pretty much, my normally favored design of the traditional French window, of which there were 2, yet the most un-precarious, I'd ever seen, with only one opening, perhaps a good thing, as precariously dangerous that Juliet balcony, of only maybe between 1 to 2 feet high, "Oh my" such caution was necessary, to avoid a tumble down to the busy junction below, where people bustled, car horns tooted as with speed, and an apparent intent not to give-way to one another, at times, frequently barely missed colliding. Then 2nd window, just a few feet away, with a jaggedly cut piece of opaque Perspex, all scratched up was placed over the window as it was nailed shut, though shoddily done, as still insufficient to keep out that cold Parisian air, and certainly no barrier against noise, and perhaps not surprising, it too was adorned with the stock trade of that establishment, as usual, substantial dirt, grime and a decade of dust, bore its featuring accompaniments.

Amazed, perhaps a little stunned, as I looked around what I found myself in the middle of, as I began to contemplate, the revealing of all those mistakes that had gone before me, through choices in relationships and other, with a desire to strive to succeed, or as importantly for failure to be prevent, but still too often, I had travelled down a one way street, where men were taking substantial portions of money from me, and I had been too easily swayed, nay, fooled by those men and more, by the financial decisions I had made under my own cognizance, were really adversely beginning to effect me, and those missed opportunities, that un-seized, faded along my way, and "What of my errors of judgment of selling my houses as I left each country?" As with no grounding, no belonging, no strong financial investment, nothing tangibly profitable, of money-making substance, to fall back on, and with it all, the security in my mind, gone; and my perception, as I stood in that room, filled me with dread, how I really wanted to pick up my suitcases and leave, but there again, leave to, "Where?" Yet too long I stood peering in that rear view mirror, examining the errors of my judgments, that were accumulating in number, of all those past unwise choices, causing, present day realities, and seriously I was to wonder, right there, "Had I yet hit rock-bottom?" for surely if I had, at least then, I would have some leverage to push myself up from."

Yet still, trying to be more positive, I reflected in that moment, of "What I was doing and where I was going?" but most of all, really, "Where to from here?" For still I was without a plan, and "Why oh why, was it so terribly difficult to make a choice?" But was there any point whimsically pondering, when I could little afford that energy, when really, it all should have been redirected to being proactive, yet as a feather on a turbulent breeze I appeared to be, those revolving trials, seemed little able to improve my situations, or conditions of my mental confusion, though I did try, reflecting positively and desiring the best, but still the ability to be able to plan, appeared to evade me, rendering me, a voyeur in my own life, unable to establish direction, and with such torment, "Why, was I was putting-in so much and getting-out, such a minimal amount?"

But of it all "What was I to do? Get angry at myself like I used to do?" And as "Certainly not!" was my kneejerk retort to me, I was so very pleased to say, most definitely I recognized that, "I had come a long, long way." For real progress I'd made, as I no longer licked my wounds like I used to, then most amazingly, laughter flowed from my inside out, and that laughter didn't stop, and truly I made no effort to make it, as such a relief, as at last, 'to give myself a break,' and not 'beat up on myself' for those poor choices I made or those humongous indecisions I was unable to make, and again a huge triumph, as I was able for the very first time, to recognize what I'd done, and equally what I was unable to do, as everything that had gone before me, my mishaps and mistakes, and perhaps at the root of them, were possibly, likely, my limiting-beliefs, that through my abusive childhood, of those words and violence set against me, and without my permission, within me took up residence, as they closed the door behind them, put on their slippers and took up a good book, and calling my heart, my mind, my soul, their home, they hid, undetected, in the deepest corners. *BUT* then marvelously, quite miraculously, in my life, I was able to recognize *their* miss-carriage-of justice, so I was to revoke their squatter's rights, placing their book down, and removing their slippers, and firmly shutting the door behind *them*, for at last, from the inside out, I was finally leaning to be, loving, patient and kind, to *ME!*

"Oh" what progress I could not ignore, and for sure, I chose not too, for so many inner battles I had fought to get to that point, remembering the external ones too, of those of social isolation and financial deprivation, but most of all fear that used to hang around, like my very best friend, or a bad disease, one that I was unable to shake, and although I had decisions I still couldn't make, all, at least temporarily, fell far into insignificance, as I knew quite categorically and permanently, I was heading marvelously toward a healthier and happy future, and "Why?" because through that laughter I had realized I was free, I was optimistic, and all those wrongs that had gone before, over and above them, I was able to soar, and the power that derived from that revelation, filled me to overflowing with hope, and consumed me with an empowering desire to 'keep going on' and true, I didn't know exactly what I was heading to, but I knew absolutely with a consuming passion, that my improved future was, unconditionally, awaiting, to greet me.

As I looked around at what my money had bought me, still, I considered how, factually I was without a plan, but rapidly I refused to be in that confusing position again, for absolutely I was to keep a-hold of my progress, refusing any circumstances that were to come against me, to ever permit myself to regress, and "Oh my" spontaneously I began to chuckle, at those formulations in my brain, at just what my money had bought me in that Parisian hotel room, in that most visited city in the world, really, I needed a Plan B, as what Plan A had afforded me was not even, a hot steamy shower, or for that matter, insufficient seeped from the taps even for me to wash my face, but undeterred, Paris beckoned, so with a quick change of clothes, I totted off down the road, to that beloved sanctuary from 4 years earlier, where I was able to listen to the subtle and harmonious sounds of the jazz quartette, while my dear friend Flavien, exuded his charismatic charm, where I felt so welcome, and was to enjoy a pot of steamy *chochlate au chaude*, hot chocolate, so delightfully thick creamy, I could almost, stand my spoon up in it.

A delectable evening was spent, though fatigue was setting in, as so much sleep I needed to catch upon, then surmising "What were my chances?" and "What a better position I would be in, 'if' to spend more money was an easier option?" Then suddenly, my mind cast back to 2 nights earlier, where at that most amenable bar in *Hotel d'Aubuson* I sat, to hear 2 Americans couples chatting, as they sipped on Champagne, as they, who had just flown across, seated in business class, and of their journey to Paris, a discussion ensued, of what was good, or not, as not minimally but quite substantially, their pendulum fell on the side of 'not,' as their grumbling and complaining of 'this or that,' ensued, how in their airplane seats that stretch out into a bed, still afforded them, little sleep. "Oh my" how amazing I thought, that they could afford so much, and to stay somewhere so posh, in that wonderful hotel where I sat, where right then I could only dream of staying, and more, their comfort and convenience, no struggling with baggage, no making do as I need to, as private cars take them door to door, and it appeared with all they had, and all the did, it was first class all the way.

"Mmmm," a rapid reflection, as I couldn't help but consider, of all the ways that I 'see money' to be the solutions to my problems, yet really, how it appeared they had heaps of the stuff, perhaps more than enough, buying them all sorts of wonderful luxuries and conveniences, yet their attitudes, appeared almost to be a little poor, and not grateful, for their fortune at all, as in their appreciation for all they processed, they displayed not comfort or joy, only opting for unsettling complaints, and I could only think back, to when in NZ I booked my first 'around the world trip,' as I posed the travel agent my question, of my $2,900 ticket, "Does that award me any upgrades?" but his reply, un-inspiring, and in un-ingratiating tone, "Certainly not. You only get 'cattle class' for that!"

"Wow!" They, needed not to scramble to their destination, or wonder where their next hot shower was coming from, nor scrambling for money, as was my need, though I know looks can be deceiving, to appear to have no worries when you really do, and they could be viewed as a prime example how 'money can't bring you happiness," as they seemed certainly to have a lot of the former, but so little of the latter, as so disgruntled they appeared to be, and a far distance away from contentment. "Oh my" as my late night walk was taking me to that potentially flee infested pit, that, the best I could pay for, and all those struggles occurring, partially as a result of it, still I was to reassess, as "Was I looking at everything backwards?" as to their great financial fortune, by comparison, I held relevantly little, yet still, oddly somehow, on the inside of me, I appeared to be, so much more grateful and contented than them.

"Voila!" As true, we may guess, ponder or wonder, at the goodness which others possess, while in reality we don't know 'how it is,' for them and how so many may wear a mask of disguise, to conceal who they really are, or the distress that's hidden beneath their cloak of concealment, even though, *Haute Couture* maybe written on the label, and true, I'd rather be happy living in luxury, though sincerely, I have had such great 'stuff' before, my environment of location, and décor all to my choosing, a good and steady job that I immensely enjoyed, working hard and effectively, producing a fine income, all, extremely valuable, and I was doing, 'more than sufficiently all right' though worthy of note, as through my experiences, and inner-transformations, stemming from my heart, categorically I can explain, of my inner-healing, that true, has been slow in coming, though now, through now it is gathering momentum, and that tangible 'stuff' I once owned and enjoyed, pales in comparison, of the emotions of hope I now have, with a certainty that 'everything is always improving,' that quite marvelously, my inner-security and inner-growth have brought me.

In that late brisk cool Parisian night, as I made my way back down *rue Dauphine*, to my less than glamorous hotel, I was remising and reflecting on my good fortune, and how I must never loose sight of it, as increasingly grateful I became, that 'against the odds' I'd stuck at 'it' for what I had in my inner-spirit, was truly mine, and truly there to stay, though suddenly, it struck me, how easily people can be stray from their desired or even rightful path, the best one for them, the best for them to choose, the one in their vision, the one that their heart meditates on, the one they see for their future, and how all too easy, it is to be swayed from it, by a stranger, a parent, a sibling, a colleague or someone completely different, who may tell you, "*You* cant do that," or "That's never been done before," or "That's impossible," but be dis-swayed not, by any of them, because their words may effectively be concealing what they may actually mean, aka, "I cant do that, so you, will only embrace me, or make me feel bad about myself, when you succeed." or possibly, "It doesn't suit my agenda, if you do that, because my life will change, too much in a way I don't want it to, when you succeed." So "Pay head, and particular attention, to seek out good, rational and unbiased council, and certainly be mindful, not to be to mislead, by those who do not, have your best interests at heart." As you trust in your inner-GPS, and let not those in your history or genealogy, to separate you from something that is safe and good, and maybe absolutely, the *very best* thing *for you* to do.

True, such, I have received first hand, through a conversation I had with my brother, he and I, polar opposites, as he more like my mother, and dare I say it, I have more attributes of my father, as he did have some, but it was the 'other stuff' that he had which was the problem. And my brother never moving from maybe less than 30 miles from where he was born, yet I travelling the world, to see what comes, and when I telephoned him in England from New Zealand, during our 2 hour conversation, he told me all his woes, and voiced all his complaints, and just for a moment or two, I was able to tell him of my plans, I was selling my house, and to follow my career, I was moving to Australia.

But, instantly, unwanted, unrequested, came a barrage of doubts, bordering on criticisms, bombarding me, "How I mustn't do that; how it is unwise; how it is foolish; why don't I stay where I am; why move again; what's wrong with me that I want to keep moving; why are you never satisfied; all that trouble and all that hassle, why risky it; why bother; you're just making trouble for yourself?" He who was 15 months older than me, who I had not spoken to through a good portion of time, suddenly believed he had cart-blanch to tell me, what I could and should not do. How completely bizarre, for nothing gave him the right, and really, evidence had proven, it was not me, but himself, he was talking about.

"Oh my" I wasted no time reflecting on what he said, for I refused to loose my identity inside his, as I was to keep on carrying my own canoe, and would continue to do so, until I found a rather fine and well placed river to put it into. Because it was my decision, my stepping out of the box, that had got me that far, so I was to refuse categorically to let him put me back down init, with his seeming desire, to close its lid tightly, on it, on me, so never would I get back out there and live a fulfilling life again. But "No." I accepted it not, because the sum of all my decisions that had brought me to that point, my desires, my rationales, and to learn, of my life's journey, and to expand on it all, for me to be all I could be, continuing along, to blossom into the woman I was yet to be, so I was to continue to cast-aside, unwanted, unsolicited, obsolete opinions, and of my actions, for my growth, of my moves, I only wished I could have started them much sooner, and should anyone, ever invent a clock, where that is possible, I will hurry out and buy one a.s.a.p.

As should I have started my journey of discovery sooner, many more self-defeating opinions or options, or unraveling bad situations, most likely, would have already been eradicated, so I say as positively as possible, should that have been my blissfully fortunate case, through that seemingly endless duration of time, I may not have been surrounded by such unpleasantness, disharmony, destruction, or danger, with physical harm and emotions, cascading all over me, as I could have been benefiting, from a life, where I was enjoying a higher level of inner-healing, improved choices and a renewed mind.

"To thyn own self be true."
Shakespeare, Act 1, Hamlet.

Yuk! As that tiny space of perhaps only 4x5 ft, that they called a bathroom, I pulled open its plywood door, held shut by kitchen cupboard magnets, as my memory of relaxing and forgetting my troubles, while at *Café Laurent,* I tried to hold on to, so reluctantly I glanced in that little tiny space in the corner, hoping for the best, of what I did see, but darn it, nope, the vision hadn't changed. Yet, should I worry as I was being serenaded by an Opera singer and Pianist, those street entertainers from the street below, as their sound effortlessly wafted in through the one foot square, orange glassed window, of cause all scratched and dirty, but there hopefully, it was to allow those toxic drain fumes out, but that not an isolated barrier to inhibit a great nights sleep, as also from the street below, void of such great harmonies, were the nightly roadwork crew with their shouts and loud voices, which not even earplugs were able to drown out, and certainly, those high decibels of screeching and groaning from the crane, as it pounded metal against the tarmac, did nothing to help my slumber, as I waited for those darkened hours, to give way, to the busyness of another day.

So the morning dawned, and a second go I gave, as into that tiny room I made my way, where to greet me, from those taps, the most skinny flow of water, but "Yeah" small mercies, at least that time it was hot, and true to be pleased at such, my standards and expectations must surely be lowering, and for my long awaited shower, relaxing or refreshing, was not what it was to be, as the as mould and grime like an ameba on the wall, stretched out everywhere, and what a mistake as turned around, and my body touched those wall tiles, as instantly, automatically my body cringed, as "Who knew, whose grime and grease, from whose bodies, rested there?" "Oh my" in just about the smallest cubical I'd ever seen, the shower curtain too long for the space, and all bunching up on the cubicle floor, and to keep it away from my skin, that task, I would have received no medals for, as even without a breeze from the window, continually, as with static electricity, it clung to me, and worse, it only meant that I had to touch it again, to peel it away, and "Oh no" repugnant bacteria was lingering everywhere, as all the water that ran down the walls and landed in the shower-pan, with a blockage in the system, non of it was draining, and rising, to 2 or more deep around my feet, my skin crawled and it seemed, when I had finished that shower, I need another, just to get myself clean.

"Yeah!" Another day gone and soon I was to be out of there, but "Oh no" in the middle of the night I needed to use the toilet again, and "Oh my" what a tricky job that was, to tuck-up my pink silk pajamas, too loose and too big, but "Why that size?" for they were bought brand new, for a bargain price at a Thrift store, and "What to do to prevent them from dropping onto or dragging along that disgusting floor?" a very tricky and not too easy task, but still I mastered it, as I hovered and balanced above the toilet seat, yet worse, when I needed to do a number 2, with precision I prepared by placing tissue paper upon it, before gently lowering myself, as somehow, my body, my shoulder, just so I could sit the only way possible in that cramped and most oddly configured, germ pit extravaganza, as under the sink I needed it to tuck it, yet much worse, and how absolutely gross, that no matter how I tried, I remained completely unable, to prevent the upper lid from always falling down onto my back, "Yuk! and Yuk!"

"I am a slow walker, but I never walk back."
~ Abraham Lincoln

Yet hold-on; as *encore*, "Oh my" "Why had it come around again?" To hinder and trouble me, that old doubt and self-disparagement, perhaps I was simply remaining as 'a job in progress,' as I battled with what-was, and what I'd done as I left Australia, about what I'd bought and what I'd wasted, and really of selling my house in England before I left there, then the same as I departed the shores of New Zealand, 2 unwise calculations, indeed I perceived, my lack of security and income, would have been alleviated, should I have kept a-hold, of my beautiful, 3 bed-roomed bungalow with private sunny garden, and remembering my stunning 3 bed dethatched house, with views that I never got tired, of Sky City Tower, and across to the Gulf, and that was even before I thought of my most desirable antiques, and "Oh why did I let them all go? When was I to have them again?" and "When was I to stop asking myself such self-defeating questions?" Yet really, it would have served me amazingly far better, to apply my attentions, to forcing myself, even when it wasn't coming naturally, to think optimistically, making a firmer commitment, removing my eyes, from that rear view mirror, for clarity of vision, focusing for my future on the clearer windscreen in front of me, so at least then, I could see where I was going.

Yet, my temporary, unremarkable conclusions of it all, perhaps I had, hit rock-bottom, considering, "Why was I even in Paris?" and "Why had I made such apparently poorly perceived, bad choices?" and in reality "Hadn't I done, with the information I held, at the time, the very best I was able to?" and really "How much progress did I need to make, before categorically, I noted, absorbed and appreciated, within myself, those notions I deserved to reflect on, of how I survived, how I was learning to nurture me, as I was determined to overcome it all" True, in the matters of those big houses, they meant a lot to me, and indeed I mean to have them all again, but what matters the most, so amazingly so, are those emotions, on the inside of me, from a healing were increasingly, thriving.

True, nothing, was ultimately able to deter from my forthcoming recovery, for my emotions, in their healing capacity, had significantly made positive progress, as since I lived in those big houses, I have learnt that they were not my protection that I thought they'd be, as my emotions back then were murky and heavy, were healing from the inside out, and for the passing time, for longevity, what I had gained, was worth more than silver and gold, or precious stones, as jewels of treasure that live within me, for above all my insecurities of 'where I was going and what I was doing,' paled into insignificance, as above all I held within absolute truth, that I was to do and master through continued effort, all I could, to slay the dragons of discontent, and eradicate the lions of arduous labor, as I was to profoundly continue, adamantly knowing, that my-worst was behind me, as absolutely, *victory* lay *in* and around *me*.

So really, perhaps I should not even contemplate of exactly how far down I had fallen, and stopped complaining with regret of what I'd sold or let-go, for my security lay not in those possessions, but powerfully lay within me, and was always to remain there, so I made a decision, to stop my wailing and whining at what I no longer had, as I was to refrain from grumbling, groaning and complaining, as I grew to be grateful for my trials and troubles, as from that place at the bottom, there was, only one direction, and that was to look up, and so, with traction firmly beneath my feet, with a lions strength, I was to determine, that those debilitating emotions were to be long-gone, deliberately deciding, that with momentum I was to use to push myself all the way back to the top, viewing not my circumstances but the desires of my heart, with my destiny to revere, as with hope and thanks, as I was to look forward to, "Where to from here?"

"Oh my" what a revelation of my predicament, and how really over that past 5 years I had spent, being tossed around like a leaf in a storm, on a prevailing wind, yet through it all, good or bad, larger or less portions, certainly, mediocrity, fortunately was no friend of mine, and held no capacity, to prove as an enemy of my inner or outer desires, or personal growth, as all too often that unfortunate companion, quite substantially holding us back, in that middle place, luring us into a trap, only serving to keep us confined, bored or undisciplined, and in the absence of pain or pleasure or any other extremes to prompt me into action; and 'if only' my mother could have enjoyed the same, as she, experiencing lots or pain, remained, barren, helpless, restrictive to change in her own world, with her un-stimulating, confining words, trying so hard to hold me fast, to hold me trapped, *"Know your place!* and *"You can forget those fanciful notions of yours, because for you, nothing will ever change or get better; so stop dreaming, and get used to it!"*

BUT! Even though she was my mother, and my teachings came from no-other, still, somewhere on the inside, I must have disagreed with her, but possibly, her words spouted so frequently and with so many negative connotations, that I wasn't worthy of any thing more, must somehow have sank into my subconscious mind, dug its way in, for its free loading residency to begin, yet there again, between her and them, still, ultimately, neither posed as formidable opponents, to the desires of my heart, and the innate vibrations of my gut, as I was to strive for the very best, I possibly could in my life, and to ultimately win, as purely and simply, of her restraints of accusations, *"Adamantly, I was to refuse to settle, for just, whatsoever, came along!"*

As determined was I, to rise up on eagles wings, and fly to the amazing heights that I chose, to those rising above the storms, rejecting my mothers slim and confining categories, of that box, that she had no right, to slot me into. True, her words, her opinions, for that's all they were, may have been the very best she, could do for herself, because, was not her! She may have even spoken, or not, with her very best intentions, as she tried to pass on *her beliefs* to me, yet what a *faux pas,* as I so totally unlike her, as she forever lived in the past, where that child sat before the blackboard and getting her knuckles wrapped for something she had no control over, her poor eyesight.

"Oh my" that, some 50 years later, that story was rolled out weekly, and told with such viscosity, as though it happed just the previous day. So sad, she unable or unwilling to accept it, let it go or move on, her personality trait, perhaps to some degree I used to have, as after all, void of friends, she was my *only* influential teacher. Yet still, somehow, even from those bygone days, from my inner-GPS, quietly guiding and steering me to somewhere better, I never-ever permitted my circumstances to define exactly, *who I was,* but rather, *where I was,* as that was only a 'stopping point,' on my way to a new, better and brighter place, *passing* only *through* those portions of time, as now I am able to clearly reject, her premise of limitations for me, as purposefully, *my* beliefs, for *my* future, hers, I choose adamantly to decline.

Limiting-beliefs equate to our enemies, as without our permission, as we are unaware it happening, not obviously but so subtly, they perpetuate themselves, invading our minds, forming, self-defeating default mechanisms, where negative thoughts simply unchallenged can roll in, whizzing around our heads and maybe not leaving again. So throughout each day, be absolutely astute, deciphering between those that hinder or those that help us, along our way, as for each one, like iron filings to magnets, 7 more of the same will come to join it. Of cause, all jolly good when thoughts are positive and serve us most well, but not so, when the opposite is true, so be most mindful and willful, to avoid that scenario, to cast-out the bad ones, as each one bringing with it, their own, corresponding and matching-set, of emotional and body physical reactions, serving either to promote us onward or hold us back; so caution I suggest, and be not blasé of the benefits of a positive attitude, as we revoke pessimism, preferring to engage our optimism, helping ourselves in our endeavors, as our very best future to pursue, and with this new skill, as time goes by, we leave behind all that unpleasant demoralizing strife, as forward we move onward, to our very own, more wholesome, renewed and healthy life, and through our reward that eventuates, for ourselves, we are able to declare, we have, *a good job, well done.*

"Energy and persistence conquer all things."
~ Benjamin Franklin

Another day, and a little routine I carved-out for myself along the way, as strolling through my favorite *St Germain* to Paul's café, where not at first but eventually the staff warmed to me, as at 8a.m. my new *comme d'haitude*, usual habit, became my favored combo of a croissant and espresso, for just 2.50euros. True, never would I have thought I would drink such a strong coffee without milk, but with a desire not to get ripped off, with a café cream comprising of a cup only half full of tepid, warm milk, were the coffee beans must have bean hidden from it, and so un-enjoyable they continued to be, certainly not the standard I'd previously been used to in other countries I'd visited, and at the price of 5.50euros, I decided, to have non of that, as I wisely chose a new daily prescription, I settled into it quite well.

Then in the afternoon with nothing better to do, it was a steamy hot chocolate with its viscosity so dense, I could almost stand my spoon up in it, and the price of 3.45E, yet a whole 45c more than *dans la sud de la France in Nimme*, that post lunch, accompanied, my growing daily routine, dishing up comfort to me, and "Oh my" how pleased was I, that by chance on the street I noticed the delicious aroma of basting chickens, yet to purchase a hot and juicy piece, as I adored to do while visiting Florida, was not so, as my only options, to purchase a whole chicken, but without a fridge to put it in, the risk of catching Salmonella from leaving it out overnight and eating it the next day, posed as a little foolhardy, or to purchase a quarter piece, cold, tasteless and all dried up, trilled me not, but I convinced myself, to partake of such, at least several grams of protein I'd be getting, to promote my much needed tissue growth and repair, equally required, for my still, waning-back, and all for a non-princely sum, my wallet could spare.

As pretty soon, not another French baguette could I possibly consume, and the volume of nourishment within them often seemed rather sparse, as so often only a miniscule of filling there turned out to be, then my mind gave way to a whimsical query, "How do the French stay so slim when they eat so much *du pain*, bread?" But soon it became clear, as humorously with satire I say, "It must be all the tugging and chewing, at that bread that they ate," which burns up greater calories than those they're taking in. Yet, of all my observations, I had to be on my way, to burn-off those kilojoules from that bread and butter, more exercise I needed to take, and my preferred route, another exciting, sight seeing tour, to see me through the day.

"Be careful what you wish for," so often said, and sometimes it seems we can pass an enormous amount to time waiting, for our choices to come to fruition, yet, sometimes not, and how true that 'old adage' turned out to be, as with a happy heart in the 7eme *arrondissement*, I approached that almost burgundy painted imposing structure, that of the *Eiffel Tower*, then suddenly, how fascinating I thought and what a good financial opportunity, to allow tourists to climb it, rather than taking the lift to the top of it. And as I approached the large square with different queues here and there, breaking my routine, and instead of assessing which on was moving faster, I simply chose the closest one to me, and on checking the price for my assent, was quite surprised that the sum, was only 7euros. A bargain I thought and so with my *billet*, ticket bought, and passing through security I was looking forward to my assent, and as my feet started trampling onto the metal grid steps, then pounding a few more, but I didn't see it there, "Where was the elevator to transport me, up to the top, *la toisium etage?*"

Then, "Oh my" the realization, that I had inadvertently, though with amazing pleasure, had opted for the line, where indeed I was able to walk up, to the second level. "Wow!" For all to enjoy, the picturesque vista of all the surroundings, as I was able to pause and absorb, the benefits I was receiving, from taking that path, less-travelled, it was more effort, but, it was worth it, as I looked out into the distance, those visions, reflected in my emotions, and erupted in my heart, and it was liberty that I felt, as reminiscent almost symbolic, of just how far I had travelled along my life's journey.

Beautiful! A sense of empowerment was then my companion, as off to the largest museum in the world I ventured, situated on *rue de Rivoli*, that of *Musée du Louvre*, and what a fortunate time of the year to visit, for there was no wait in line to enter, only a swift 5 minutes before I was to snap my way through their doors that day, a quite amazing entrance, effectively an architecturally designed glass triangle box, generally known as the pyramid, yet such contrast it poses to the rest of the Palace, that was built in the 12th century for Philip II, and originally the seat of French Royalty, until in 1682, Louis XIV moved his state from Paris to the Palace of Versailles, some 18 miles away.

So encapsulated was my mind with wild creativity, as I was to observe and absorb all the finest details of what I saw, as my imagination of those centuries past, of the lives, the poverty, the extravagance, soared, so expansive in its areas and nooks and crannies, it was difficult to describe which held my most particular interest, perhaps the tapestries and mosaics traversing those centuries, all so intricate with the finest of embellishments, from furniture to the most exquisite jewelry, where even the Grandfather clocks and other pieces of furniture were studded with gems and pearls and from centuries past, artistic sculptures in marble, stone or bronze where the artisan with his skills, had captured and precisely defined muscles, feathers and lace, and the ceilings so amazingly ornate with their beauty to embrace, as too few words I have to describe their elegance, the expanse of the galleries which simply continued on and on and then I reached a hall maybe 7meters tall and painted in the darkest rich burgundy, with the Masters in oils, dense or delicate, so impeccable, looking more like photographs than paintings, stretching to the ceiling and their frames, in deepest of ebony or lavishly in guilt, carved and detailed telling their own story with pictures, and forming pieces of artwork in their own right.

"Oh my" how intensely captivating were such visions, but what captured and illuminated my inner-core, were the deliciously ornate ceilings, of plush and lavish cornices, their width and depth expansive, and centre point enormous chandleries of crystal, yet not even they could detract from the glory of the pristinely pained scenes in pastels, every time, so worth the tilt and contortion of my neck to examine every crevice and to meditate and absorb all I saw, then it was to be, but to find 'it,' I kept getting lost, but eventually there it was, noted in the world, as the most famous enigmatic smile, of the Mono Liza right in front of me, and after passing 7 marvelous hours away walking gladly all around that place, I was done and able to move on; and all had been absolutely delightful, yet true, on several occasions, I was to sincerely wonder, just "How many people died destitute, in poverty, while those few, lived in abundant luxury?"

Then on that unplanned vacation, another Exhibition, of *Madam Élisabeth Vigée Le Brun*, at the *Grand Palais* built for the *Universal Exhibition* of 1900, was to grab my attention, she, a French lady who around 1800's proactively did what was necessary, as because one of those historic European wars, to Belgium, she was to hail or escape, before venturing to where she needed, to do her best for her safety and her family, and everything I learnt of her, I so admired and resonated with, for her instinct for survival, doing what she must, what life determined was astute and best for her, as her strength of character and resourcefulness shone, and of cause to her obvious painting finesse, of her finest strokes of delicate brushwork of pristine lines of supreme expertise, with ribbons of silk, gowns of velvet and shawls of fur, all so elaborate and clearly identifiable, enabled her subjects to come to life, through her talents, that she exuded.

Like the Parisians, I quietly enjoyed all I perused, lingering for a lengthy time there, I was in no rush to move on, keen for another gallery, it was only a quick jaunt across Avenue Winston Churchill that saw me arrive at the *Petit Palais*, smaller, though no less grand than the other, and magnificent in its opulence, where more joy awaited me, but still when I was done, the day was still young so off to *Musée d'Orsay* of *Beaux-Arts* I went, to that building dating back to 1898, facing the river *Seine* on the Left Bank, where in that previously used railway station, the subtle, exuberant or extravagant statues of decadence I admired, and with camera in tow, as a truly wonderful time I spent there.

Another fun packed day ahead, as traversing a fine distance of maybe a couple of miles or more, from where, 'who knew which one of those hotels where I was staying,' as to the 8eme *arrondissement* I strolled, weaving my way in and out of the smaller streets, 'I wasn't lost of cause,' until I reached, that expansive and wide boulevard of *Avenue des Champs-Élysees*, iconic and lined on both sides with *magazines*, shops of that expensive location, and meandering on toward *Pont Alexandre III*, bridge, built in 1896, perhaps notably, one of the most ornately decorated bridges of which there are many, crossing over the river *Seine*, as lamps, laden with guilt in *Art Nouveau*, design, with cherubs and winged horses, to name just some of the statues detailed there, all to be seen, admired and enjoyed for free, and the same for *Jardin Luxemburg*, with its calming fountains and gravel promenades, surrounded by centuries old trees, for resting, wandering or exercising, sport or solace, relaxing or rejuvenating, to that peace, to escape the busyness of Paris, so many people gravitate, from the freshness, of early dawn, or following a days work, or in the evening when the sun goes down, so much it proves to be to so many, now that has to be a good thing.

Christmas was creeping up, and so to commence the constructing of those *petite chalets,* wooden in structure, all trimmed with lights, designed to be beautiful and make everything they sell look appealing to buy, an array of jolly *Noel* gifts or trinkets, items for enjoyment or those to keep you warm, all purposing to create fun for families and couples alike, candy canes and candy floss most popular, or to munch on traditional French *crêpes,* or partake of *cuisines,* foods from around the world, and with it's delicate aroma of spices and citrus fruit, a glass of fine hot *mulled wine,* to wrap my hands around to keep them warm, works like a charm and quite my favorite, and enhanced is that experience, when stood beside one of those impromptu ice skating rings, that during that festive season, pop-up in many a French *ville,* as I was to watch those little ones, as around and around they go, showing no fear and appearing without a care, if they were to stumble to the ground, as simply, as no one in life had yet put restraints on them, they simply got strait back up, believing, that they could do better next time, now then, I thought, surely, I could learn that trick from them.

"Hold fast to dreams, For if dreams die, Life is a broken-winged bird, That cannot fly."
~ Langston Hughes

Yet all in all, with the ambiance within me that evening, I was not to enjoy, for such a place to visit, full of families enjoying frivolity, or in big groups of friends, or maybe for those, romantically involved, which all made me a little sad, as still, I would have to visit on my own, but in reality, before those cabins and their *lumières,* lights were to be finally lit, I was to leave that city of love once again, and as I was to bid it 'farewell,' I was not to leave like 4 ago, as no longer was it a case of 'sweet sorrow', as it seemed, my love affair with 'gay Paris' had come to an end, so I declared not *à bientôt,* see you soon, but a more resounding, *au revoir.*

"Oh my" how transforming and revolutionary, my experiences in Paris were proving to be, with a whirlpool of emotions ever accompanying me, as those ongoing circumstances of obstacles, kept popping up daily, to unsettle me, though on reflection, realistically, many could have been avoided, but still, maybe it was it all forming apart of a subliminal learning process, which was leading me to situations where I was to face, challenges necessary to pass through, to prove that indeed, I had made it thus far, as eventually, through those weeks in Paris, such circumstances of uncertainty inducing regret over mast past decisions, wonderfully failed to come to fruition, as so many debilitating emotions and thought patterns, I'd overcome. And how marvelously true, that through each one, through that schooling, I learnt more about myself, and how on the inside, I'd grown, for tests I'd past, as no-longer was my 'go to' 'default mechanism' stuck in panic mode, for they had transposed, to a quiet and understated rational, for resolution, as I was able to seek remedies to those predicaments without unwelcomed and floundering emotions tearing up inside of me, for non proved as a sufficient adversary, to detract me from my elation, stemming from within, the renewing of my mind, and the healing in my heart, welcoming me in, to my brand new revelation, of progressive and recognition.

For I had begun to trust myself, and ditch those smoky-grey lenses that I had looked through for far too longer time, choosing instead to look trough my new asset of those of crystal clear kind, and "Oh what clarity" I was to receive as the circumstances of each predicament held not the power to influence me, tricking me into believing they were permanent or irreversible, for then I knew of them all, they were only temporary, so with *my new truth* that *empowered me*, I held fast, refusing to permit any adversity, to functionally or emotionally define me, as most determinedly, I vowed to confidently and positively move onwards and upwards, and to myself generously giving, full commitment, to forever enlarge my boundaries to what I was capable of, healing, the true and real, inner-me.

"Oh my goodness," what a huge favor I did for me, when I started trusting in *my instinct* to *guide me*, and true, a scholar in this field I remained for quite a long time, and even today, on every occasion I cannot claim I get it right, but forever I try, and try hard, to let my logical and rational thinking from me depart, as I permit those niggles to manifest deep from within my inner-core, and perhaps from there, an uncomfortable feeling or a notion that 'something just isn't quite right' may rise, as sincerely, what I have learnt to do, is not ignore those emotions or niggles, for likely it will prove to be to my peril, as so easily that possibility, may have transpired, that I have ended up in the wrong place, at the wrong time, doing the wrong thing, and "Oh my" 'if only' I would have learnt sooner not ignore those 'quandaries' and trusted my 'gut' for now I realize for astounding benefits I would receive, as I hold courage and trust in that process, and from here on in, as I trust in me, I will more frequently, be the victor.

So with invigorated hope I contemplated, in Paris, "Were all those adverse experiences of circumstances, no more than tools for confirmation, that 'Yes indeed,' I had learnt from the lessons previously that were set before me?" As perhaps, a fair assessment of those encountered episodes, of such verifications, fundamentally and certainly clarified that, indeed, that repetition, really had revealed itself to be a valuable teacher, as optimistically I surmised with vigor, through my fortified persistence and patience, proved themselves to be worthy as companions, and so for my troubles through that process, my latest reward, was a gift, so called because it's the present, of astoundingly beautiful inner-growth, and my treasure to behold, of a fulfilling and optimistic message to be shared and told, for all my future days, as I moved from A to B.

Perhaps a side-note, we need to remain astute, as caution we exhibit, as we perform our own and personal Risk Assessments, drawing on all the information and knowledge we hold in our armory, and when we think there may be gaps in it, we go and seek it, through examining, what we are good at or enjoy, and of cause, that gentle weapon in our armory, of due diligence, was we embrace all those transferable skills and talents, of those accumulations, of all of our previous experiences, drawing from our careers, hobbies, schooling or in certain circumstances, as it has been so for me, even TV as we engage discernment, doing our very best to be wise, as we surmise, as we contemplate, "Where to from here?" and really, from here on in, "What is best, for me to do?"

True, perhaps a cautionary not to add, to not 'rushing in,' ensuring, in your assessment you are not fooling, or being manipulated by another to do their bidding, of what 'they' think I the best for you, for perhaps be astute and remember their hidden agendas, and how they may better serve the person who is giving the advice and not the one who they are giving it to. And be not tricked by men as I was, remembering again, 'if' it is your Prince you are pursuing, consider the scenario of kissing a lot of frogs, then noting, how toads look so similar, and as one is harmless the other most certainly not. Then, 'if' it is an even more precarious game of 'cat and mouse' you venture upon, confuse this not with romance, but remain most astutely vigilant, not to "Fall under his spell," as reflecting on consequence, for your future, best to make sure, that you are not 'the one' who 'wins' the cheese, as that, hold no happy ending.

So ladies please, I urge you, don't do as I used to, through fear avoiding Mr. Right, trying so desperately with all my might, to find many Mr. Wrongs, as I used to, as true, in that arena of self-deception, I thought I was keeping myself safe, but sadly, with severe consequences, it turned out not to be, as that only formed as a self-deceitful falsehood, as I kidded myself that everything was alright, when really, mostly it was wrong, and I suggest for consideration, for you, the opposite to take place, as a notion I've since discarded from my mother, "You're too fussy you'll never get anyone that way. Why don't you just settle?"

But perhaps, that's what she said for that's what she did. Yet "Oh contraire" as a young lady, at a café, who I was speaking to, she was confident, popular and hailing from a happy family, so tremendously enlightening and refreshing her concept, to me absolutely proved to be, "Why not be fussy?" and certainly "Be patient?" Flabbergasted! I even had to ask her to repeat them, just to make sure I'd understood correctly, "Yep," I'd heard right, and after all those years of my mother, telling me I wasn't worthy of either, yet she in her 20's gave me a gift, as so oddly really, what she shared with me, set this captive free, *ME!* As my had been so wrong, as I, me, deserved to be fussy, and from then on in, when ever the time is to come, for choosing another man, that is exactly, what I will be.

> *"Ambition is the path to success, persistence is the vehicle you arrive in."*
> *~ William Eardley IV*

"Oh my" in that aspect of life, how much hugely better off I would have been, 'if' I'd learnt to trust that strategy so much faster, but so uncomfortably, it took so much longer, as so many decades had passed me by, before I recognized the practice of taking note when, perhaps, like the touch of snowflakes falling on my skin, or a flicker in my stomach, of 'I don't know quite what,' or even nausea or my racing heart, and of cause, that 'sense of dread,' all originating from my inner-core, manifesting as emotional sensations or physical symptoms, placed there to help, guide or direct our path, and never again will I ignore it, as I recognize its enormous value, those subliminal and free messages, all for our ease, to keep us safe and free from harm, as substantially, far fewer wrong turns I would have endured, and "So much" I wish I had been so aware back in the days, before senselessly, I made such poor decisions, most notably, selling my houses as I left those countries, or walking down the isle to meet my doom. Yet now, empowered with that most precious inner-instrument, as patiently I listen astutely, taking notice of all I experience, as so beneficially, I'm tuned into the right inner-frequency, with my heart healed and my mind restored, as so many more right turns I took with minimal detours, and fewer days spent in sorrow or regret, as greater safety and prosperity, became my travelling companions, as so frequently, from there on in, I headed, in the right direction.

Perhaps confirmation, that when we follow our inner-guidance, it helps us, but sometimes, through following it, we are able to benefit someone else, as oddly, when I was packing, leaving Florida, items certain unnecessary items I was guided to pack, all making no sense, especially when considering the extra weight, with extra money to have pay, for sure, a poor scenario, but still I simply had to include what I was led to, a pair of classic lined woolen shorts in dogtooth print, a designer cashmere jumper, delightful in cream, an A-line skirt of a most unusual faux denim texture, with perfect antique black velvet clutch-bag, including that precious mirror form yesteryear, with another, black suede with a strap, and how classic to match, strings of pearls and beads of glass all with decorative fastening clasps, all brand new and presented in small velvet pouches, true, fortunately non of it broke the bank, as all were purchased, you may have guessed it, during my frequent visits, to thrift stores.

Then, it occurred to me, "Was it all my imagination, or was I being tested?" Could I be trusted to firmly follow my inner-voice, and although I'd achieved success, was I to do it reluctantly or more easily, so to enable me to enjoy a simpler and better life, as true, I was forever improving, as in Australia, frequently so may garments I bought, a week or so later, 'something' within guided me to re-donate them to a different thrift store, a little odd for sure, but even when it was an item I wanted to keep, still, I always followed the leading, believing, that happiness, money and energy, attracts like to like and gathers momentum, so more of the same passes around, so through my weekends, contentedly with innate pleasure, in my little black convertible with rooftop down, to multiple suburbs I drove, dispensing those items, while choosing new, hoping that I was 'passing muster,' and through that process, I was learning and improving, to tune-in better, to my inner GPS, while gladly, helping others too.

Yet still, from France to Florida, I held no clue as to "Why must take them with me?" But clarity was to come, not at my 1st hotel but my 2nd the one with 1 Star above the door when really, 0.25 may have been more suitable, where on the 2nd floor, there *she* was, as if by an invisible magnetic source, instantly I knew her, her spirit soft and open, her face warm and kind, with eyes that seemed to reveal a gentle soul, that, throughout her life, may have carried more excess baggage than she ought, knowing, it was to her and no other that those extra items I brought, that amazingly, there was no need to pay an extra fee for, but true, I felt kind of wired, for a maid, I didn't know how to approach her, and of my gesture, to give her those things, would she be happy, angry or maybe insulted, I was a tad concerned, "How was she to respond?"

The following day I didn't see her, but from my inner-knowing, my inner-soft voice, before I left that hotel the following day, I simply knew, I was see her again, and I was proved right, as there she was working on the same landing, and tentatively, almost apologetically I approached her, and using my best French and trying particularly hard choosing my verbs, I asked if I could give her some items, that I'd brought across the Atlantic from the USA, then such relief as gladly she accepted, so I beckoned her into me to my *chamber*, and handed her the neatly packed paper bag, the type with the twine handles, that always I feel more special, when I have one, and as I handed it to her, her eyes were shining, as bountifully, she beamed a beautiful smile, my heart lifted when I saw her joy, so immensely pleased I was, that I'd had the courage to listen to my inner-guide, on a different continent, to happily benefit another persons life.

All seemed so pleasurable, and certainly not bizarre, as on a rainy day on *Blvd St Michael,* when above Paris, from heavy clouds rain was pouring down, and a homeless person, I was to pass, and not one of those who perhaps aren't really so, who hang-about the streets holding signs *'J'ai faim,'* I am hungry when really, their BMI, yet where had that truly homeless man gone, as every cell inside of me, was beckoning me to give him 10euros, but 2 things about those instructions troubled me, a) I didn't have that much money on me, in-fact I'd spent all my cash from my purse; and b) "Where did he go?" for there were 4 *Métro* entrances at that junction and into either one and onto any platform he could have disappeared to.

But I knew I had to obey, that inner-guidance nudging me so very well, so there it was, I turned back, not really knowing where to search first, and what to do when I found him, but I continued non the less, and success, as there he was, standing by the *Métro* kiosk, but unable to gain entry to the subway, then keeping an eye on his location, I checked my purse for the money, and truly, I could not believe it, by adding every cent and Euros coins, with not a penny to spare or a penny short, I had the exact sum of 10euros. Amazed! Gently I stepped forward and with my arm outstretched, quietly without ceremony, with my warm, soft and clean hands, I placed the coins into his, rough, torn, and callused, with his long fingernails, of odd colors from years of grime and all contorted in shape, and my heart reached out to his, and as I turned silently to walk away, quickly, I glanced back, and in that moment, he'd opened his palm and was looking at what I'd placed in his hand, and "Oh my" how wonderful to see" his smile to behold, his eyes illuminating his face that told a million stories, and his mouth smiled so big, it pushed-up into his cheekbones, and how so very grateful I was, that before I climbed the *Métro* steps, I caught a glimpse of that, as no longer did that air feel chilly or the rain feel cold, for his smile, warmed my spirit, and what a wondrous notion to know, that by doing something so small for another, I was able to gain such immense joy, so gladly to hold on to forever.

> *"Failure is only postponed success as long as courage 'coaches' ambition.*
> *The habit of persistence is the habit of victory"*
> *~ Herbert Kaufman*

"Yeah" my last night at that terrible hotel over, but still, I hadn't booked another, yet with logistics to take care of, as I struggled to work out, where to go and how to get there, and with issues surrounding internet access, and working out the SNCF site, it was around the corner I was to go, to venture to a decent hotel, where hopefully I would encounter a kind and knowledgeable receptionist, who might give me some good information, which sadly had been alluding me, and sure enough I was right, but only because she thought I was a guest there, but then again, you see, the good you do can certainly come back to you, for what I did, at that highly upgraded hotel, that never would I normally aspire to, was enquire with almost a throw away question, "Just how much would it cost to stay here tonight?" The price I was told, was at a good discount rate of just 119euros, though still in excess of my budget, though I listened to my quietly humming inner-voice, guiding me to take it, and with a healthy respect of the consequences should I not, as previous experience had taught me in just about the exact same way, when I had heard my inner-guidance, that 'knowing,' or that quiet voice, so soft, its almost un-audible, and way back then, when I ignored it, all sorts of s#*t hit the fan. So astutely, in my armory for my recall, and being a good scholar, I held onto that lesson, so only hesitating momentarily, before I agreed to pay the price.

Instantly as if by magic, to that wonderful establishment, at 11 in the morning those keys were handed to me, and instantly, "Phew!" At last I belonged! "Oh my" how subliminally such little things may hold the power to comfort us, so immediately I dragged my suitcases around, and then before me, "Yeah" an elevator, with no need to lift them, instantly easing the strain on my neck and back, then to my *chambre* where I swiped my key, and "Oh how lovely, the vision I saw before me," as I took some moments to gaze sublimely at the luxury and comfort, of what my money had bought me, the opulence of King Louis XIV style, in a collage of burgundy and deep cream, with a quilted bedspread with petit cushions resting on top, and the 2 French windows, overlooking a courtyard quad, were shaded by sheer nets and framed, by drapes of one of two-tone, lush shimmering damask fabric, perhaps quite Parisian with its padded walls, reminiscent, of those in that apartment where I rented a room at *Poissonniere*, from way back in my *la Sorbonne* days, though continuing my vista, the harshness of the striped print was mellowed by the gentle trestles of roses and ivy, and as my body, let out a great sigh, it made me realize, what unpleasantness in those other hotels I'd undergone, and really, exactly how significant, the atmosphere and décor of a room or house, can effect our psyche.

Then in the corner hidden behind the door, the elongated radiator that perhaps had sprung a bit of a leak, as the hot water had caused, a water stain from the top down to the bottom the dye of the darkest color, had damaged the fabric, then suddenly, how wonderfully as I recognized that all negative feelings on observing such, were no longer there, simply absent, that had marvelously disappeared, and it may sound all a little odd, but to me, absolutely so hugely significant, as literally, life-changing, as "Oh my" how I smiled and how the inner-me rose-up with glee, flying on eagles wings, and "Oh how I embraced it, recognizing exactly, the enormity of it, as how far along my epic journey of self-discovery and recovery I had successfully travelled, as for sure, in my pre-healed days, no-thing would have been the same, as I would have instigated a whole catalogue of self-defeating emotional responses, as a conspiracy, where immediately I would have felt judged and found myself lacking, surmising that I'd been given a substandard room, because 'they' who allocated it to me, thought I was 'worth-less' than others, as in my stomach knots and angst would have been substantially, tearing it up.

Whilst immediately, a whole bunch of other scenarios, planted by my mother and father, that previously slipped into my subconscious, through those decades of bombardment without resistance, would have jumped right onboard, with condemning judgments and complaints towards *them* of 'how stupid and incompetent *they* had been not make-a-mends for the problem,' but then again, 'had anyone been punished for letting it happen in the first place!' "But Hurray!" and "Oh My!". As on that day, as I stood so much taller, and how I wanted to *jump for joy*; and do you know, indeed I believe I did, as I threw my arms around triumphantly in the air, letting out, more than one or two tiny shrieks of pure delight, for the prove was in the pudding, as *a brand new day was dawning.*

Just, maybe, that sounds so little, but in my life, hugely it held for me such great significance, as the prove was in the pudding, and I had baked a perfect cake, as all those ingredients of those tentative yet tremendous steps I'd taken, one-by-one, held within them the perfect recipe to eradicate from my mind and soul, all *their* hindrance of confusion and manipulation, it was all gone, as *free, from* those angry thoughts of vicious vengeance, that twisted and contorted my body, each and every one, making it feel like it was in a vice as yet I was delivered from their evil, as I, no-longer, no-way, no-how, was I ever to passively hoard such venom, or curses pronounced over me ever again.

Such cruelty, to inflict such indoctrinations into your child, so young, who was always and forever, bombarded with hostile and aggressive notions of 'this and that,' harsh judgments, only the beginning of what was so cruelly inflicted, as in reality, never did I see her or he, doing the same sort of thing, in any sort of degree, to neighbors, colleagues, friends, or associates, as they seemed to reserve that type of behavior, especially, to bestow upon me, as passively, through that process of osmosis, their abominable actions, perpetuated and permeated, oozing into my brain and every tissue in my body, until I was a mess, filled with toxins and distress, and when their task was complete, absolutely I believed what they showed me, what they told me, that I was worth, no-thing better, and of all their badness of how they treated me, simply, I accepted their premise, that they were right, and I was wrong, and only deserving of more of the same.

As for sure, I held no other information to the contrary, and how extremely sad for a notion to ponder, of their twisted viewpoints, that in the school of my parents, they taught me, gave me, coached me, coaxed me, cast-down and indoctrinated within me, their wicked weapons of silent destruction, harmfully, noxiously, integrating within me, as I was stumbled and tumbled in the midst of my enemies storm, trapped and battered, with no escape, no hope, only misery and fear to accompany my days, and 'if only' I would have known how to wrap my arms around myself and with love, whisper gentle words, "Don't worry little girl, one day, the sun will shine and the birds will sing, and everything that is wrong, will be made right."

"If it were not for hopes, the heart would break."
~ Thomas Fuller

Yet suddenly! There in that hotel room, that truly, I had not even aspired to take, so dramatically that *breath of light* seemed to be so refreshing to my inner-sight, within my soul, rising up, with *joy* to *be-hold*, and "Oh my" instantly, vividly, it revealed how effective my inner GPS is, for the best for me to achieve, as there it was, I, was recalibrated, as a sense of wisdom flowed like shimmering snowflakes on a Christmas morning, that so gently, kindly wafted over me, with a mellow gusto of extreme thankfulness, as humbly my heart suddenly pumped with loving and inner-power, as so suddenly I was aware, of the enormity, of that Parisian trip I'd been on, as in so many ways, as I prayed and worked on myself, trying so very hard to use discernment in so many situations, drastically applying huge effort, to make *not* the same mistakes, twice, three times, one hundred or more, as so desperately I desired through my heart and with logic within my mind, of myself, to plead and petition, "Stay strong!" so all the trips that are yet to come, of my success and joy, to them, I will bountifully, build on.

"Oh my" I certainly don't mean to keep harping on, its just that I'm so immensely pleased and proud for myself, for a job well done, and the elation I feel I so wish for each one of you, that you can feel it too. And "How was it achieved?" well that was simply, by taking one more step every day, and what worked for me, a recipe, reading books and journals, cheap from thrift stores or free at the library, and watching specific TV shows geared to help me achieve my goal, then listening to the radio and audio CD's listed to on my computer or while driving my car, with internet searches of research studies, as most valuable information I drew from there, and what often I immersed myself in, were Preaching's on U-tube, that made the Bible come alive, relevant for life today, and then, like any good recipe, it was all mixed up exceedingly well, as step-by-step I added a little extra sprinkle of this or that as more information came to light, and baking conditions, just perfect, as my eagerness paid more dividends, as from inside out, I grew through all I perused, as I began to hear a hush of a whisper, I felt it in my soul, telling me, my *war was won*, as sublimely, to add to my life's armory, Triumph and Victory, for I am, more than a Conqueror.

"Oh what a reward!" and "What I prize!" and gaining so much, adamantly, I was never give it up, but continue along, striving more to add to it, so when those streams of adversity, come against me, resoundingly, I will push-on through, and those dark deep wells, where once I may have wallowed in self-pity, or bathed in bitterness, not knowing how, to try and get myself out of there, yet so gladly, that is behind me, and as with a harmonious smile and a twinkle in my eyes, so much so, that my petite crows feet, are increasingly clearly visible, but of those I worry not, as they significant, and a shining testimony displaying just how, *"I have made it thus far!"* so unconditionally I've learnt to appreciate them all, for I know the troubles and unraveling struggles, that I travelled through, and the victories and triumphs I have valuably gained, creating the length and density of each one, telling a meaningful story, of a milestone reached and a battle overcome, and to quote a favorite English colloquialism, I became so very *well-pleased*, for every step I trampled on that uneven and precarious pot-holed road, as miraculously it transposed, to one, level and even, and filled with safe and stable steppingstones.

Then quite odd, as something nudging, niggling me in my mind, of a comment the receptionist spoke, as I 'ummed and arred' about the price, "You won't even find a better price than this on booking.com." 'Something' guided me to check it out, and "Oh my oh my!" I couldn't believe what I found, all sorts of last minute deals, that several years earlier, when from Australia I tried to find them, never did they used to be around, but hang on a moment, hadn't I been racing around Paris like a headless chuck, a half-empty cup, worrying about every penny I was spending, and there, right in front of me for easy choosing, copious available hotels, all around including those in my preferred and favorite *arrondissement*, all delivering great deals. Astounded! "What!" I had absolutely no idea.

"Where had I been that last 5 years? And how could I have possibly known that?" but "Did other people not know it either?" as when so many people I asked, "Do you know a hotel that's good and cheap?" Not a person mentioned that website, or any other for that matter, and rather than be dismayed, I lit up as my fingers danced across the keyboard, and I scrolled through the lists of deals, so many rooms, in Paris at bargain prices, and "Oh my goodness," that dirty germ filled pit, that I paid x3 nights in advance at 78E, was advertized, with their top price of only 60E, and then, with a discount, it was brought down to only 50E. "What!" I mean, "What?"

Location is everything, and not one that I viewed on my adored Left Bank, some offering *graduit*, free breakfast, all of exceptional value and any I would have been to stay in, with some in the local of *la Lourvre*, looking pretty good, and by comparison, the realization of what a bit of extra money spent, would have bought me, but "Oh my" *how absolutely marvelous*, as my response to all I perused, no longer did self-hatred consume me or regret, for being so stupid, so irresponsible, as a septic mass would squeeze around my stomach and chest, as truly, marvelously, it was even a small hint of laugher, and a rhetorical question, "Oh my, why did I not know this before?" Astoundingly; an immense struggle was diverted, nay eradicated, as hugely positive progress, in this realm of, 'how far I'd come' was mine to claim, and *it wasn't a dream, it was all real*, and with such joy, as mildly ecstatic, I recognized, those old emotions, created by those old thought patterns, had disappeared and gone away, and shaking my head, as I could hardly believe so unnecessarily I'd gone through all that strife, but I'd gone through, but still most importantly, my mind, my body, my heart, my soul, all united, and with sincere gratitude, and in my memory, in the tissues in my body, with elation I was to solidify what I was experiencing, to secure, for thereon in, never would they stray, but always with me, stay.

"Wow!" I caught myself reminiscing on that enormous progress, as for sure, I wanted to ensure I was right, that truly, I was able to congratulate myself, as regarding those trouble I had gone though so needlessly, not an ounce of madness or anger did I attribute to me, as I viewed it all not as obstacles of inconvenience, but a 'test of progress,' as that process was moving me 'from where I wanted NOT to be, as marvelously I was on route, gladly heading to another destination; true, I didn't know where that place was to be, but what those experiences taught me, 'not knowing' or 'not being aware' were out-dated, obsolete concepts, distancing me from those previous emotional confines causing, nauseous, sickness, anger, with often a pinch of rage and a great big dollop of self disparagement thrown in, but in a flash, so thrilled I was, as I realized, all those tests in the school of trails and tribulations, coupled with the due diligence I'd done, through personal and self-education, equaling empowerment, all for a recipe to perfectly come together, I propose, a most magnificent gateau, as I had grown, I had overcome, I was stronger, I was wiser, my future was brighter, I was better healed and prepared, as I knew whatever was to come against me, to deal with it, I was more able, and of the silver lining of that passing of that perceived Parisian cloud, revelation and restoration, proving true and valuable inner-growth, and so with a grateful and humble heart to myself I was to declare, of *me*, "I'm really proud!"

My brand new day, just kept-a-rolling right along, like a good steam engine from back in the day, such wonderful proof, that nothing any longer held sufficient power to deter or detract me, form being all I wanted, desired, aimed and calculated myself to be to be, but not by chance, but by design, as I was preparing all I could and putting in all the necessary effort to achieve all for my life which I was choosing, as "At last!" I was free from my parents curses, as I was, tried and tested and found to be an A student, as no-longer were my parents, infestations of their bitter, hateful, debilitating words, to hinder, trap or confine me, as "Yeah" I had found the remedy, and for my future, I was consistently to stick with it, to live a brighter and better life, for then I knew, "Where to from here?" was forever going to be, a far greater place, than 'what I left, way back there!' For my hopes and my dreams, had sprung forth wings, and up to great heights, on the warmth of a summer breeze, always they were to fly, as deep down to my core, with my inner-values, renewed and restored, and I knew, of myself, quite marvelously, wonderfully, beautifully, I was, I am, worthy of loving.

And "Why?" Because, from my history, those 'trials and tribs,' as I now quaintly call them, previously, posing as problems, when detailed on a spreadsheet, calculating those short or long-term consequences or a pie chart to complete after analyzing comparability, with footnotes of emotional or physical reactions, including their longevity, the prognosis may not have been so good, but "What about our forthcoming legacy?" of a life to enjoy, so very much more valuable, as there to reach a place, where self-doubt is eliminated, as clarity is increasingly replicated, so fret not, about that 'schooling' of those tests, as for our benefit they needed to be passed, as we achieve our Honors and PhD's, so in such matters, casting aside our associated negative emotions, giving ourselves that opportunity to become an excellent scholar as we learn from each on them, examining and casting aside our rewinding and revolving negative behaviors and thought patterns, as positively we identify our progress, as our time and efforts we redirect as corresponding actions we make sure we take, for our rewards to come, attributes so right for a future most bright.

An 'anecdote' I truly wish to mention, for the sake of confirmation, really, of what we say, and the conviction we say it with, really does hold power to change 'things' and situations, an example in point, way back, or so it seems, when I lived in Australia, and a young man I met, while working at a factory, used to joke with me and make fun of the 'silver streaks just close by my face, always saying, "Look you've got grey hair." With me insisting, "No. No. You've got it wrong, they're blonde." And so, for the few months I worked there, that dance of the joke, continued, "Then would you believe it?" It actually happened, those silver streaks {he claimed were grey} became even brighter, changing color, to blonde, which wonderfully, they remain to this day, "Yeah!" So of all good things, dare to declare them and believe when you say it, that for you, it will come true, so caution, and be wary, for just think about it, 'if' I would have agreed with him, saying, "Oh yes you're right," by now, by now, prematurely, I could have been, totally grey.

And so many moons earlier, it was a new second-hand car I pursued, I knew the color, the make and the model, even the time of the year it was manufactured, as then I was guaranteed, to have the seats upholstered, in lush, plush air-force blue velour fabric, opposed to charcoal hessian, but my then fiancé dismissed my wish list, reciting over, "You'll never get all that, you're buying second-hand car so you'll have to take what you can get!" but "No!" I was adamant, I disagreed, which really with him wasn't my normal thing to do, yet categorically I knew, that I was to get what I wanted, and resoundingly, sure enough, as over and over I did confess, exactly what I meant to have, simply, with emotions of commitment, just explaining to everyone, "'this' is the car that I am buying," and sure enough, the Toyota garage who I gave my list of what I must have to, as my mind set, nothing else was worthy of my money, and within only 2-3 months, that most beautiful perfect car, was sat adorably in my driveway.

"The most beautiful things in life cannot be seen, not touched but are felt in the heart."
~ Helen Keller

For surely, I have learnt, it is not a smokescreen or my imagination, for so often I have made the study, of how the strength of a vibe may effect our lives, and aura's too, as energy exudes and holds power, to effect us quite dramatically, emotionally and physically, even the style of the décor, and everything we see and everything we touch, even the angels of furniture or the texture or prints of fabrics, with colors posing as significantly important, and the placement of the lights, of subtle or bright, with my preference, natural is best and for the rest, chandeliers are my favorite, and my bathroom, I prefer it t be serine, as that is where I set myself up for a great day or a great nights sleep, and my bedroom, soothing and harmonious that must always be, easing my mood for rejuvenating slumber, and visual comfort, a miniature plug-in nightlight, for me, is the way to go; and how grateful was I, that the 4th Parisian hotel I stayed in, confirmation of such was clearly demonstrated, and for the very first time, I was not huge regrets I was to have, at what I gave away, or wasted my money buying in the first place, it was so much more of a peaceful commitment, knowing, that of it all, that peace, joy and comfort, that a personal and precious environment can give you; as in my heart and in my soul, I simply knew, that I was, that I am, to have it all, again.

True, not an illusion I found that to be, as so often without any real rational, in some places I've visited, I discovered it impossible to write, as my mind, my spirit, was kind of stuck, and from it, nothing at all would flow, as not a word would stumbled out, though quite instantly, when I was to leave that environment, to alter and change the vibe, just to take a short walk, or even sit on a bus I'd take, and recurrently so, streams of thoughts, of recollections and imaginations, instantly, into my mind came-a-flowing, so when your trying to study or do some important thing, be not afraid to change your spot to try to get those inspirations-a-coming, and just for good measure, something else I highly value, is to sit serenely, or simply relaxing at a coffee shop, as surely from there, all good thoughts can come-a-tumbling-out, and true, when historically, home, had not been a safe or happy place for you, consider that it may be best to visit somewhere else, where the atmosphere is different, so simply in that space, you can think, or write your thoughts down, or whatever you choose to do, and remember, with your surroundings, if possible, you choose them, be detailed and specific in your choices, seriously, I have learnt not to underestimate the value of such, and I know when its good and conducive, as my heart, it really rejoices.

So hesitate not to change what you can, whilst remembering, perhaps to experiment in small or incremental ways, the seat you choose or its location in a room, or even which side of the bus you sit on, perhaps the direction you drive to work, or a different one you use for your return, all hold a degrees of possibilities, to either jump-start your day positively or alter it in a less favorable way, so by reviewing or possibly changing, a little bit of 'this or that,' in your heart or your psyche, of how you do what you do, may perhaps quite wonderfully, with such minimum effort, provide substantial different results, evidentially so, of those most valuable attributes, of swapping a little bit of this for a little bit of that, and of those succinct easy fixes, how highly significant and most successful they proved for me. "So maybe, try mixing it up, experimenting, until in your environment you feel, right, and be kind to you, and just keep seeking it, until you do."

Perhaps it is easier, to change our ways than we may think, as information new comes our way each day, and a tact I chose to implement was an innate skill I used everyday in my roll as an OH&S nurse, as perfect planning, methodically, with quickly changing priorities, where tenacity and prioritize, prioritize then prioritize some more, were winning streamlined and successful strategies I employed to do all that I needed, yet unfortunately, socially, I was to fall dramatically, as it was a strangers words, who perpetuated his notion forward, of placing, 'all my ducks in a row,' and somehow, quite subliminally, quite badly, my mind must have altered and accepted what he spoke as important, as my behaviors and positive habits were negatively hindered. Then again, whilst living in Melbourne, it was a health program on the car radio I was listening to, when the host spoke of a situation, of not habitually cleaning your teeth every night, which actually, I had done so all my life, yet somehow, effectively from that night, something in *my mind shifted*, my excellent spell was broken and from thereon in never have I been automatically able to do that thing again.

"Oh my" of those two examples, of which there are more, for us, for all we permit in our lives, as importantly for our futures, we need to be responsive and be prepared at a moments notice to say "Yes" or "No" to, as we reject or absorb the notions of others, so be discriminate, to recognize how what people say and the phrasing of their wording, as we really need to understand the possible power they hold within them, as for sure, so subliminally, instantly, they were able to alter my actions, dramatically so, so, *fair attention*, be careful, who you listen to, for when something is working well for you, its best to apply extreme discernment, and permit not another person's values or opinions, to detract you, from your proved and trusted commitment, of what already successfully works, for you.

But that was a decade earlier, and since my inner-growth has been significant, particularly, over the previous couple of months, and since my return to Paris, amazingly it appears, I have travelled full circle, as so much more so, I am responsive to my own needs, as I quite automatically, I am able to recognize what I need to do, to achieve my ease and comfort, so nowadays, leaving struggling behind, I opt for streamlined actions, especially for my writing, as now, when the notion grabs me in the middle of the night, to put pen to paper, instead of unnecessarily waking myself up, stretching for the light and scrabbling for my computer, I have progressed, to a purposeful stagey, with cable to the bedside light with the slightest of watts of soft pink hues, I hooked the light switch to the wall, so not even an arm stretch need I make, with only the most gentle pressure to turn it on, then my notebook how easy is that, as I leave it open at exactly the right page, with my pen poised in exactly the right direction, to pick up and start writing, yet not before, my purposefully placed glasses on top, I slipped on.

True, all may seem so simple, but at this juncture, worthy of remembering, my actions and the rational behind them, to make my life, more comfortable, even better, flew in complete opposition to what I was taught, nothing good or suitable, to bring me, any comfort or ease, indeed, previously in the UK, not even a nightlight did I believe I deserved to buy or use, and really, how terribly sad, as "Who wouldn't be worthy of that?" So truly, to be able to do all those little bits for me *now*, and *I believe I'm* actually *worthy*, for me is a milestone overcome, which gives to me, the most momentous, enormous and greatest pleasure, to know, that from where I first began, truly, I am, so much further along my journey of recovery, from where I first began.

Then to examine 'Maslow's Hierarchy of Needs' as so repetitively to his research from 100 years ago, with his conclusions still relevant today, and certainly with my blissfully transforming life, forever relevant to me, as I contemplate, his displayed scientific pyramid, with varying descriptions of what humans need for life he placed in order of significance, covering only 'shelter and food' where I, consistently resided at the bottom, perhaps symbolic as that was where my parents had always put me, and of cause, way-back-when I knew not that I needed to disagree them, but as 'healing' and 'growing' became my increasing companions, and I, freshly empowered, I knew that of those 2 basic levels of only 'food and shelter,' were insufficient for me, as my heart and my soul began to let me know, of so much more, I *was*, I *am truly* WORTHY.

So I set my sights, looking up, on my way to that top peak, where 'self-actualization' rests, meaning to me, "I'll get all I need as a human being desires, not just that ability to survive, but to thrive, to have a healed heart, and be comforting in nature, with a spirit that soars like an eagle, and feels gladness when they see another person smiling, giving encouraging support, to see your friends through difficult times, and where *love prevails*, and joy and peace and calmness, are fortified in your heart, and of any troubles that come against you, never do they abandon you or depart." Yet in my true reality, of all Maslow spoke, it posed only as a mirage, a mystery, of cause not logically but emotionally, as back then, in my days in my role as a Community Nurse, when 'all' was spoken of the importance of 'connectedness' my only concept, a person who needs such a thing, must be weak, and "Why?" Because my heart had not even begun to conceive, the healing I was to receive, or in absolute contrast, how, on the inside I was to feel, in 10 years time. "Oh my" with such relief and such pleasure now I am able to declare, what a different era I lived way back then, for these are different days, so with my healed heart and nurtured soul, afresh, anew and positive, I am ascending his 'scale of priorities,' and until I arrive at that peak, I will for my life, continue to seek.

"Oh my" so much I had to learn, so much growing I had to do, but really, "Was I up for the task, to put the effort in, when I sincerely believed, that was only for others, and never was it to be for me?" "Yes!" You better believe it! For I made a decision to leave behind the pain of my past, as onward, I was to embrace life, to live in a better place in my heart, as I was to let go of that heavy load I'd been carrying for too long, as purposefully, with a spring in my step to a better future I was moving toward, determined to climb that ladder, where *worthiness* and *self-esteem* knew my name, and to pursue that goal, consciously I noted, that through that process, of importance, was what-I-did or did-not-do, as they equally held power, to accelerate or hinder my achievements or success.

"The secret of getting ahead is getting started"
~ Mark Twain

My suitcases packed once again, full, with all I had brought from Florida, and that 50lbs sometimes heavy to move, but it was, black and serviceable, fit for purpose, as we say in the OH&S field, that was until the casters broke, and while strolling along a typical Parisian cobbled and narrow street, considering the possibility of buying another, there by the curbs edge in front of a typical tourist store, a matching luggage set, and looking quite lovely, as detailed in hues of charcoals, and pictured a silhouette of that most iconic landmark, my favorite, the *Eiffel Tower*, yet quickly I cast my eyes to the zip, instantly it only took a casual glance, as I surmised the 'drop test' it might not surpass, so to purchase such an item, at least on that occasion I was to pass, as *on y va*, carrying on, meandering and perusing all to see, in those multiple *artisan boutiques*, stores, on that particular *rue*, where sculptures and bronzes, with brightly colored large and imposing glass vases, and extensive paintings, extravagant in size from floor to ceiling, and clothes, in delicate fabrics, with designs elaborate, all most likely created, by the most imaginary minds, and of the diversity to view, I was most utterly pleased to do so.

Paris, such an artistic city, it appeared to be, perhaps most patriotic too, as even the cement mixers where painted the colors of the French flag, in stripes of red, white and blue, and what quite a surreal vision it depicted, as at the traffic lights it awaited to turn from *Pont Neuf* onto the boulevard running alongside the river *Seine*, and what a photographic opportunity, sparking the imagination, as laying in the background, by contrast, from dirty roads to modern cold metal, to *la Louvre*, an imposing sight, with the warmth of its stone, and as I cast my eyes in the other direction, *la Samaritaine*, that essentially quaint French department store, from yesteryear, with its opulence and artistic glamour, selling to the discerning Parisian shopper, from when it opened the 17th century, and quite famous too, for it was with a jump of glee that by chance I was to see a movie, James Bond possibly, where perhaps in the 1960's a chase was filmed inside, yet sadly, for quite some years it had been closed, as too costly to keep up to-date with health & safety regulations, but on that drizzly day those facts detracted me not, as the winter sunrays glistened and gently peered out from behind it, and so happy I was to stop and wallow, in those emotion it brought me, but all, for only a moment in time, as when the traffic lights changed, the vehicles moved on, and my vision of nostalgia meeting modern and enhanced by nature, was gone.

True, perhaps not quite so artistically quaint, but of a super idea, as while I was visiting that small isle of Jersey, one of the Channel Islands located in the English channel, located 14 miles above northern France, where their government garbage and recycling trucks, so insightfully impressive and sensibly so, where brightly and neatly painted, advertizing various topics of health promotion initiative slogans, including breast cancer prevention, healthcare checkups, with messages for protecting the environment included, and an array of many more, and how ingenious I mused to use such a vehicle, if you forgive the pun, that traveled the streets daily, to be seen by so many, and by immersion possibly, to not waste, {again no pun intended} but maximize, those most practical opportunities, to let those positive messages sink in.

> *" What progress, you ask, have I made? I have begun to be a friend to myself."*
> *~ Hecato*

"Oh my" at those almost euphoric moments, that seemed to happen quite frequently, perhaps like little gifts of beaming beacons just sent to encourage me on, as I continued travelling along my life's journey, repairing the past, and letting go of bitterness, and learning lessons and reflection on the same formed such a large part of that process, but learning to love myself was the greatest lesson of all, and one, that through the large number of the others I was contemplated was enabling me to quite marvelously do so, as through all those accumulating experiences, my self-worth, had risen enormously, and I had become a generous person, able to give and receive grace, not only to others but also to me, for I learnt to forgive others and of equal importance if not more so, to forgive myself.

As I was successfully leaving behind those revolving situations of beating myself up over the mishaps and mistakes I'd made, and more, I was quite marvelously and wonderfully, as it was on the inside of me, where the majority of my healing was benefitting me the most, as I relinquished the need to seek the approval of others, in order to feel better about me, and for sure, until I was able to do such a thing, never would I have been able to grasp the concept or believe the enormity, of the hugely beneficial and life-changing difference, that behavioral change could make, with the realization, that my best value for myself, above and beyond opinions of others, derived from within, as through my healing progress and accomplishments gained, I began and continued, to cease guessing or surmising, what other people thought of me, as it holds significantly greater and higher importance, of what I thought of myself, than what anyone else thought of me, and "Oh my" through that process, simply astonishing at how my self-esteem rose, as I began to soar like an eagle above the clouds, in my new, wholesome and developing soul-full self, as I was growing into a person, kind and loving, that really, I so wanted and always, deserved to be.

In other aspects, my life was changing too, as money, quickly with it, I needed to become more savvy, as at month end, no longer was an influx of it to arrive in my bank account, as my job I had left, with only had my savings to rely upon, and out of my control, 'post crash' my interest rate was slashed, and at the loss of that financial security, was suffering, as I had worked since the age of 13, a paper-round my first job, when my weakly allowance of a few pence my father used to give me, ceased coming, and since then, in the realms of money, I become completely independent, and so astute was I, to preserve all that I could, never adding to my credit card purchases, unless by month-end in full I knew I could pay it all off, for true, it is through those compounded interest rate payments where *they* 'get ya' trapped in a cycle, so difficult it is to break free from, creating a whirling of compounding debts, of that somehow quite innately I knew, so usually held quite sensible notions regarding spending, especially when considering the sacrifices I had to make to accumulate it, working at those 2 nursing jobs in Australia, where I was bullied by 2 different bosses, so enduring all that, I valued my income tremendously, and the last thing I was to do, was squander my revenue, on unnecessary ill-serving interest rate payments.

So most carefully, preservation of my financial recourses became the key for me, but not so for a roommate hailing from Granada, back in the day, who, instead of washing her clothes, which she claimed she had no time, yet time enough to go off to the store to buy some more, but at what cost, as again while she was spending her finances unnecessarily, equally refusing to act responsibly, paying her way, of half of the money for the monthly rent or quarterly bills. So caution I suggest of you 'flat' with, for should their values to money not be minimally adequate, you may find as I did, unpleasant and recurring unpleasant conversations, verging on arguments, just to get the money that rightfully to you is to be paid. And be not mislead into thinking, "Well her/his name is on the document to, as either way, if they default, unless you want a 'strike' against your name, the account will still be required to be paid, perhaps in full, by you.

Though, of my resounding awareness, there was my trip-up in Australia, where I had that 'blip,' that I needed to forgive myself for, as un-sensibly, as with no mortgage to pay, but only a rented apartment, with a second bedroom, with no flat mate in it, as bitten once, twice, third time I was shy, preferring to be responsible for just for me, and of my relatively high disposable income, well, I disposed of quite well, not on 'events' to capture my imagination or make memories to treasure, but a vintage clothing collection, where searching and purchasing, turned out to be the biggest part of my fun, as ultimately, non of it brought me any pleasure, in fact the opposite, as huge portions of regret it was to deliver to me, as those beautiful garments and matching accessories, hung in the wardrobe, or were neatly placed on shelves, or just one more, was squeezed into another draw, with pearls my favorite or jewelry from the 80's all neatly placed in boxes, and all were closed away, behind the spare-room closed door, and when it came my time to choose to depart, the world's largest island, dispensing of all those items that I had invested so much time into, as money was gone, with nothing purposeful to hold onto, and for resale, non of it turning out to be profitable, 'oh contraire' by contrast, only delivering, humongous portions of anxiety and regret, as it was all to be dispensed of, rendering my bank account unnecessarily lower, with no profits, at all to speak of.

Perhaps too slow was I to reflect on that valuable lesson, as in my finances through those for previous 5years I had missed out on a plan and a purpose for them, and needing to learn that lesson only once, as much more discerning I had grown, to become wiser and more astute once again, as I reflected on 'acting in haste repenting at leisure' once again, though positively, while I was leaning on that old rugged stonewall by the river *Seine*, a ray of hope, as to keep warm, I pulled my hat down over my ears, tucking my scarf up so I'd feel no cold draft of that blistery Parisian breeze, and my cream leather jacket with beautiful brass buttons, to keep snug, I wrapped it more firmly around my body, believing, "That I won't be making that mistake again." Then I smiled, as I looked across to the *Bateaux Mouches*, river boats, as I thought of all those layers I wearing and how with something I'd done was right thing, as budget mined consciousness, where I needed, 'to cut my pattern according to my cloth,' to prevent my fiancés from dwindling too much, thrift stores I began to frequent, buying a little bit of this or a little bit of that, when what I found was new and of exceptional value, and great dividends it proved to be, as I cast my mind to my daily accessories and apparel, as without exception, those purposeful treasures, I'd been able to purchase in various countries, had saved my more than a pretty penny, yet still, most pleasingly, I always to receive compliments on my style.

Then reminiscing over my delectable finds, my mind carrying itself along, remembering my preference of chosen fabrics, how I was drawn to purchase so many of natural fibers, perhaps cashmere my most favorite, abundantly warmth and so soft, while such little weight, for packing in your suitcase, with silks, definitely my second choice, so simple to launder and quick to dry, so light and perfect for multi-layering, creating thermal heat or cooling for the body, and I quite adore linen, that fabric defining its own style, easy and breezy, though hardly lightweight for packing, and it crinkles and creases easily, then leather and lace in exquisite chic and feminine designs, how completely sophisticated or terribly modern they can be, and true, not light to carry for baggage allowance, but all breathable to keep the chills of the cold or the winds at bay, or keep the heat of humidity away, in short, all 'so serviceable,' so for me that will do gladly.

So perhaps a point to ponder, be not seduced into passively accepting the spending patterns of our mothers or fathers, or even friends for that matter, especially when, it is them you have seen in debt, for if you follow in their footsteps, you may only progress to more of the same, missing your opportunity for a brighter financial future, that awaits you, as you form your own habits that serve you best, as you're astute in what your income can afford, so let that be your driving force, of what you spend and save, and perhaps equally important, as now I have firmly learnt my lesson, in the realms spending, if the money is not in my bank account, I have learnt to admire it without having to acquire it, and when I don't need it, happily, I leave it on the shelf, for that's best situation for me, and postpone that pleasure of purchasing some-thing, until another day.

> *"The great thing in the world is not so much where we stand,*
> *as in what direction we are moving."*
> *~ Oliver Wendell Holmes*

As for sure, with our recourses intact a more restful nights sleep we may enjoy, as experience has taught me, that can never be underestimated, as through trials and errors, a whole catalogue of tricks I have discovered and mastered, trying my very best to achieve great comfort, and a refreshing shower works best for me, just before I hit the sheets, to sooth my mind and my muscles, and to nourish my skin, lavish mellow fragranced moisturizing cream to gently rub in, and a scrub to apply twice weekly, to remove those dead cells, to make sure, it's easily absorbed, in total, a prescription to relax my thoughts and my body before my head hits the pillow, as within those fresh sheets with a spray of lavender aroma, I tuck myself up, as tiredness descends, and slumber comes my way, and in the morning, waking afresh I look forward to a healthy new day.

Yet I found it be of even more importance, of foods or beverages I partake of in the evening, as I have discovered they hold power of great significance, for a restful sleep to be my friend or foe, as when into the evening, I eat many cakes, cookies or sugary foods, or drink more than a couple of glasses of alcohol, consistently I will wake up throughout the night, tossing and turning as slumber evades me, with only frustration as my companion, and "Oh my" red food dyes, how desperately I need to avoid them, as their ingestion, day or evening renders me with not a wink of sleep that night will accompany me, so those trials and errors have proved great teachers, and I have mastered a great remedy, as a portion of protein proved to be the key, maybe turkey or a softly boiled egg, half and hour or so before bed, and I have to say, as a method of perfection, certainly it works for me, and 'ain't half bad.'

Even more, I was to profit from, as eventually I recognized even while we sleep what a positive difference natural fibers make, so to spend and invest good money in purchasing my bedding, in cottons, linens, duck down and wool, all I could afford I spent, buying where needs-be, and in sales, for under-blankets, and over-throws, as no longer were they only there just to look pretty, but they needed to be serviceable too, all in all, promoting that precious and no-longer elusive, great nights sleep, as those newly chosen fabrics, unlike manmade, are naturally able to breath, will keep us warm as well are cool, as all night, snuggly and cozy, and most comfy, all reducing the possibility, of waking up in the night in a sweat, perhaps of added benefit, when wrestling with the menopause.

For sure I have learnt never to underestimate the power of positive sleep patterns and what they provide, as I used to struggle with so little and now I receive a lot, with such huge differences noted in my day, with greater clarity to make decisions, and traversing each one, no-longer took up hill effort, as patience and wisdom were in more noticeable abundance, with the emotional dread of that night to be replicated, slipped away, with inspirational moments replacing them, and never more-so than during the alpha-stage, that lovely restful time, as we pass from awake to sleep, when such richness of thoughts visited me, and learning the hard way, quickly I learnt to disturb myself and with pen and paper make notes, as failing to hang around, or pop up again, each one of those wonderful and invigorating thoughts or ideas, of potential treasures of hidden opportunities, recurrently, in the morning, were completely gone.

So as a word of caution I mention, so you may avoid making the same errors as I used to, developing a format, to be prepared and poised with your writing equipment by your bed, so when in the middle of the night a striking idea springs into your mind, you may rejoice and say "Harrah!" "That will do nicely, thank you for that, million dollar idea." Foreboding the possibility in your almost slumber state, to say, "Yeah! Great! I'll write it down in the morning." but "No!" Hold-up, don't do that, lean by my previous mistakes, so you can avoid doing the same, as quickly you re-think your strategy, declaring, "Wow!" "That will do nicely. I'll get up right away and make a note of it." As still, while sleepy, seizing that opportunity, you grab your pen and paper, making notes of those notions that came so naturally, as maybe within them, a secret of transforming and redeeming power may linger, for an improved life, and a brighter and better future, for you to muster.

As, *Value, Value, Value!* It suddenly occurred to me, "Is that point of everything we try to achieve and do? The value of time spent with people, those we give a help in hand to, or those who add a little something extra to our lives and for each, to be grateful for?" As remember, the clock is always ticking, and of all our life choices, there are 3 commodities that once gone, they are impossible to retrieve. 1st the *spoken word*, so in anger before you speak, guard your words and be careful what we say. The 2nd is a *missed opportunity*, so in front of us, when that door or window opens, be ready, without delay to jump through it, for never do we know when it will close back up again. 3rd of cause, *time*, because as yet, they have not formulated a currency that can buy a ticket to get us back there, as once gone, time, has gone forever. So in the realms of all what we want, desire or choose to do, waste not time on people or relationships that pull us down, to detract us, from the goodness of our destinations, for inclusion, men, women, colleagues, or people in stores, as experience taught me, to permit them not to monopolize my time, as around them, I choose not to be, for that time, once gone, irretrievable, it will never come back around again.

"Mmmm!" Unfortunately, in that process, such a slow learner was I, so please learn by my mistakes, to waste not time, under the control of another, as all that I spent in bondage, non if it can I get back, so all those years while I was young, in my 20's and 30's wasted, impossible to retrieve, and through staying with them, I denied myself the opportunity, of moving forward and receiving in my life, something improved and better, so believe not, in that false concept, 'my whole life is before me,' when in fact, simply, those years you are stuck, doing something, or being somewhere, that displeases you, or is unhealthy for you, each and every day that passes, passes you by, as suddenly, 7 days easily gives way to a week, and 4 short weeks, and 'poof' a month, and as time speeds on, years rapidly give way to decades, and your 'whole life' that 'stretched out before you,' suddenly is not stretching quite so far, and with regret, that question asked all too often, "Where did all my time go?" As surely, 'it will go,' so for your best life, to live it well, to be safe with love in your heart, so carefully, diligently, remain astute, and let time serve you, and not you serve time, as onward to a life not wasted but embraced, as time transposes, not your unforgiving master, but your willing and embracing servant.

So it was from those relationships I escaped, from those men whose nature was consistently aggressive and hostile and true, like my father before them, with their tempers of rage and anger, their fists flew too, and everything I did and said, with *my* money I spent, all fell beneath their dark and evil umbrella of control, and so desperately sadly, it was almost too late, as it was my life that one of them, almost took from me, and *my time*, was absolutely stolen by those men, or maybe in reality, as I failed to do what was best for me, my lie and my safety, inadvertently, by mistake, so misgivingly, I gave it away, staying within those relationships, as *my life was passing me by*, as *they-told-me*, and true, way back when, my brain washed in their doctrine, I believed them, that I was worth noting more than what they were dishing out.

BUT no longer was I to be the their palatable entrée in their lair, as I was to get myself away from there, claiming, *"NO MORE"* as I refused to waste any more of *my precious time of my precious life* because inevitably, it amounted to *more* than what *they-told-me* it did. "Hurrah" for sure! *YET* the reality of those years that had *passed-me-by*, effectively passed away, as never was I ever able to claw, not even a one of them back, as in truth, none of us can, so "Please please, I beseech you, I beg you, please learn from my mistakes, and away from those, ill-serving, dangerous vicious, hostile or unsafe relationships or environments, you *make-haste* and flee.

Time passes, and slowly but surely I became right, as I discovered my own way of being of viewing my life, a jigsaw puzzle, I decided, where only part of it was completed, and for the rest, I could find all the pieces, to make-up the rest of the picture, and those that were placed init thus far, of dark and eerie colors, with shading, casting conspicuously unpleasant shadows, as so negatively with an almost spiteful aura, it seemed as if, tangibly it was to jump out at me, perhaps, even trying to get away from itself, but *"Was my life to get better?"* Surely! Was I to do my very best, to make sure the colors of the pieces that were left, were to be amazingly brighter and crisper, with better definition, that as my eye wandered over them were to be soothing to my soul.

Yet that did not come quite quick enough, as so badly, not before that time came to pass, when extra violence had risen up against me, but; *"I did wake up!"* Then to freedom, I clung by my fingernails as I scratched and scrambled away, from his exploiting and bewitching smokescreen, where within it he hid his deceitful armory of emotionally manipulating tools, to squash me deeper down, whilst simultaneously for his malicious pleasure, forever propelling himself up higher, though ultimately, he failed and proved as a grossly inferior adversary, to my inner-strength, that soundly lay, and so very thankfully, from me, never did stray far away.

So I say, as I wave my index finger triumphantly in the air, a new day was dawning, and I was to find brand new pieces to my jigsaw puzzle, as power within me rose, and I embraced my commencement, of being a person in recovery, and 'a job in progress,' for I was on the way up, and magnificently moved myself away from that position *they* confined me in, as no-longer, was I to be according to someone else's doctrine, 'what' *they* dictated I should be, nor through fear, do exactly what they decreed I should, as with great discernment, with my travelling companions, that discerning duo of patience and empowerment, as I began searching, *"WHAT WAS BEST FOR ME TO DO?"* as I gave myself permission, to move forward to a place of greater safety and peace, as was to leave behind me, my former life of hate and pain, and trouble and strife, as only dwindling traces remained, as I was to make my new picture puzzle as perfect as possible, of a scene most serene, of gentle hues of summer meadows, with spring flowers, where the warmth of shimmering sunrays, to embrace almost rose from the page to greeted me, and in my soul to absorb all the vision, representing, my gently invigorating and enlightening progress, and inside of me, "How did it feel?" Well, really, "It sure felt like love to me!"

So absolutely, marvelously I committed to be forever smarter, to master all I could possibly do, determined, and refusing to permit my yesterdays to impact my tomorrows, as no-longer was I prepared to suffer that sorrow, as definitely I was to continue along my way, to reclaim that which was rightfully mine, as I refused to believe *their* concepts anymore of "That is all I was worth" or "That will do for you," as behind, I was to banish all those troublesome roots of hostility, and the heavy burdens from them I was forced to carry, as forever onward, with my tenderly, purposeful steps I was to go, as I learnt to recognize, that it is far less important what *they* had done to me in my past, than the greater importance, of what *I* was doing for myself in my present, to regain *MY inner and personal power*, to propel me forward *to MY chosen future*, and with every piece of progress I made, through every tentative step, my gratitude rose, as they held treasure of prosperity, more precious gems or nuggets of gold, to blissfully hold.

Blowing in on a breeze of change, was my resilience to keep on trying, until I was to get 'so much more' within my life, right, as all those malicious behaviors from my past, were eradicated out my sight, almost by mistake, but actually on purpose, a quite amazing equation occurred, as from those past unpleasant episodes in Paris, 5 years earlier, as panic was eradicated and superimposed, with my new and emotional and inner and personal growth, as I had been able to move on, as then, I understood so much more, about me, about life, as the stresses that my parents placed in me, that were perpetuated by my husband and my ex-fiancé who I lived with, were resoundingly reducing stress, simultaneously creating a clearer mind with greater clarity, of 'who I was' and 'where I was going,' and odd little 'things' began to unfold, almost to give me subliminal messages, as I was able to recognize 'signs,' giving me insight, or words I read on billboards, or on commercial trucks passing by, and people who'd pass in the street, where just one word they spoke, audibly seemed so loud to me, and like a little child solving riddles, I began to make good sense of them all, with inspiration to carry on, so leaving behind that unpleasant and past time at *la Sorbonne*, as I was ready, willing and able to move on, away from that and other negative situations, as my present, the gift, and to my future, from thereon in, I welcoming in, peace and inner-improved, relaxation.

As in essence, truly my health was so much better, with all those emotional and physical ailments, that on my previous trip, so recurrently used to bombarded and burdened me, to a large degree had dissipated, and how wonderfully, through that time I had made progress, as I left behind the beating of *their* drum, loud and debilitating, no longer dancing to *their* tune, for I learnt to value my own orchestrator, creating melodies for my own life, with the tender taps on the tambourine, the dulcet tones from a grand piano, with gentle hues of the woodwind section, all to embrace, of a soothing harmony, strumming a cord into my soul, as innately I became the maestro, of my personal, smooth and resonating tune, then through the magnificence of it all, on a fine and beautiful day I knew, the dreams and desires that I held, were to flourish more so each day.

Yet right then, the cold was not the problem, yet the rising humidity was seeping into my bones, a little like in Manchester in northern England, so I needed to reach the warmth before it set securely in, so I ducked into the *Galleries La Fayette*, architecturally designed in the artistic *Art Nouveau* style and opened for business around 1912, and "Oh my" of it all how tremendously magnificent, with the grand extravagant dome of glass, curvaceous lines painted in pastels, with ornate scrolls crowned in gold, all so pristine and over a century old, so eagerly I continued up the escalator, as quickly my hand reached for my camera, to a snap shot here and another there, as what joy it brought me, such a vision invigorating my senses, reaching my heart and igniting my soul, for true, a landscape of hills, trees or mountains, to take a photo of those, unlikely I would be, but so seductive that architecture of that awe inspiring art and grace, serving to stimulate my imagination, as it drifted to a bygone time and place.

Then, surprise, who would have figured, of all those Parisian terrace's where I'd sat, and all those baguettes I'd consumed there, the best was to turn out to be, in a café, at the top of that *grand magazine*, department store, and as I partook in my *petite déjeuner*, breakfast with *du pain*, bread, soft and easily edible, with lashings of butter, *du fromage*, cheese and *jambon*, ham, whilst sipping on ever so healthy hot water, and keeping warm, at the top of that *bâtiment*, building, I chose to rest there awhile, then what an amazingly unexpected bonus, as I turned around, and right there clearly to see, posing perfectly as a picture postcard, dating back to 1669, *l'Opéra*, grand and opulent, magnificently construed, which once may have dominated that great Parisian skyline, before the *Eiffel Tower* changed it forever, yet in prime position, impressive and imposing, with its green dome and gilded horses, was a most delightful vision.

With my temporary respite done, I was to venture again into that bitingly cold Parisian day, my 10th and counting, and as one rolled into the other, I wondered, "Exactly what was I doing there?" and really, "Of my prolonged visit, "What was my intended purpose it?" as surely, in my practical calculations, "From that city, I should have already departed." Yet equally so, contemplating and pondering, really, right then, in my life, there was nothing I particularly must do, with the exception of my priority, to finish and prepare my book publication, and could that, "Somehow, form part of the reason, I was still there?"

Then quite unexpectedly, a notion sprang and expanded within my mind, "Was a scenario afoot, that I was unable to previously publish my book, I simply hadn't acquired, as all the information I needed to do so?" And permitting those thoughts to flourish, I passed each day with added patience, as increasingly it became clearer, that through those past 5 years, since I last rested in Paris for a while, how wonderfully splendidly, from all my past-life of deprivation and violence, causing all sorts of complications, physically and emotionally, and for progress, how far in my heart and my soul I had travelled, far outweighing those that on a plane, through the stratosphere I flew, and because as I moved on, most definitely and gloriously, with hope for a future, my attitudes and values were wholesomely renewed, as fun and love, for, *ME*, I was actually able to contemplate, that really, I was able to receive them all, and I say smiling, as I had grown sufficiently to know, that I, of it all, I was deserving too!

"How did I do it?" For sure, I believe the largest part of that process, was accepting what had gone-on, and learning to let-go, of all the anger and bitterness that though my child and adulthood, had wheedled like a pointed poisoned arrow, deep, so very deep down inside me, where that hurt and pain, so dense, almost impossible to dissolve or from my inner-core, to dig-it-out. Yet still, all proved as an insufficient challenge for me, as simply a recipe I was to find, a formula to create, of how to successfully get-the-lot-out-of-me.

And I so wish I could tell you, that I waved my wand and by magic it was all gone, but nay, not quite so easy, as it was those compatriots, of due diligence, first seeking, reading, listening, watching, asking, all posing for a specific purpose, to gain empowerment and education, as mindfully and deliberately, as I moved myself away from those people, who predominately served themselves, failing to have *my* best interests at heart, helping enormously to propel me forward, as their self-imposed jurisdiction over me, I, closed down, removing myself from their vicinity as I cast them aside, refuting the possibility to cause me, any more, emotional, mental, physical or financial harm, through their control and manipulation, disparagement or putting-me-down, their catalyst, succinctly put, for fear to be created. BUT, *I grew* to be *WISER*, and as I remained in that status of 'job in progress' I made it my job and my business, to align myself only with people, who no longer were to detract from who I was, but only adding to, who I was yet to become; and of it all, I was progressing along, rather quite well.

"Easy to do?" I so wish I could tell you, "Yes" but in truth, "Not necessarily," as old habits are the strongest, less easy to break, more easily rolling back in, yet still, I refused to permit that form as an excuse or pose as a stumbling block, for moving-on, moving forward, until I, succeeded, determined to put-down and cast-out, that revolving, seeping caustic mess that had been so prevalent in my life, **as** I had grown to know, such a scenario, really was for me, substandard, and from then on, I refused to bow to my mother's doctrine, 'that was my lot in life,' and how I needed to put-up and shut-up and simply 'get on with it,' then my resounding, *"Heck NO!"* As I chose not to settle as she had, as I began bypassing her inertia, setting myself upon a course of action to gain self-fulfillment, climbing up that ladder to Maslow's, 'self-actualization,' as each day, every task I was able to complete, or every tiny mindset thought, I was able to eradicate, change or alter, well, so-be-it, for I was on my way, I was, leaving my past behind, as my trotting, was progressing to a gallop, as those old routines, causing me pain, inconvenience or simply perpetuating the same old problems, I was to cancel out from my life, one small goal at a time, which I made SMART, i.e. Small, Measurable, Achievable, Realistic, in appropriate Timeframes, as I was on schedule to run my very best race, as one by one, I was to overcame.

"There are two ways of exerting ones strength; one is pushing and the other is pulling up"
~ Booker T. Washington

Perhaps there was a purpose why I stayed in Paris so long, but to discover it, I could not, and quite amazingly, as never did I think it possible, but I became, quite 'over Paris,' and quite happily, even eagerly, wanting to be out of there, true, since my last visit, the *Métro* had been cleaned up, no-longer were the homeless sleeping there, or found during the days, laying on the platform floor, or using it as a toilet, and it even seemed as though a mop had been splashed about, yet 5 years previously, never that had I noted, and those noises, those sirens giving customers a few seconds warning, before the grinding of the carriage doors, slamming shut, and while studying at *la Sorbonne*, "Oh my" how I would pick-up my pace as down the steps I race, just to catch it, and all used to seem so romantic somehow, or maybe new back then, or maybe, it was because way back then I was having a love affair with that fair city, yet on my latest trip, those rose tinted lenses, had been replaced with those for clear vision, and so it all transformed to be, well really, nothing special to me, all, even a little irritating, so I must confess, I withdrew for my previously held notion, that everyone should visit Paris before they die, as really, that concept had vanished into oblivion.

Yet still, I was not be distracted from sitting, at a street-side café, on one those quaint essentially Parisian terraces, with their whicker chairs, and usual ensemble, of a small circular table, where at my temporary favorite café, as I tucked into my croissant and espresso, the best deal around at 2.50euros, as only it contained, sufficient caffeine to jumpstart my day, as my experiences of drinking the Parisian lattés, not the same was able be said, and perhaps a bit of an acquired taste, as at first, it reminded me of drinking unpleasant medicine, and all so distant, from Naples in Florida, where for the price of $3.50, I could purchase a 12ounze latté, made from grass-fed cows milk and organic coffee beans, to drink not in the dampness of Paris, but beneath the shade of the summer trees in the café garden, as my invigorating ritual each morning, post my rejuvenating bicycle ride was to enjoy that beverage, while I made a plan, to be practical, and to move purposefully, forever-forward with my goals, "What was I to do, that day?"

But that so many moons ago, or at least it seemed so, where those happy memories resided, then as I reflected on so much, I was a little unsure, of my emotions, should they be of gladness or sadness, as quite remarkably it struck me, for the whole of my life thus far, happy memories, were not obvious, and my memory banks, and I would have had to do an in-depth search to find them, then for calculation, I wondered, how many, or few, fingers and toes would I need to count them, too sad to think about it really, so best not dwell on it, and no need to worry, as a new day was dawning, and the good news is, a fresh one consistently comes everyday, and within it, a new opportunity to pass-by what was behind me, embracing the opportunity for what lay ahead of me, to change my thought processes and resulting behaviors, changing for improvement, changing what I had always done, establishing new habits and life patterns, so in abundance, many joyful, peaceful and soothing memories, as with hope and anticipation, for my present, the gift, and future, I was to create, and as like attracts like, positivity for more, rolling around in my mind, will surely attract more of the same kind.

So quickly, seizing that philosophy, I recalled with such 'ease of pleasure,' those happier times while visiting Florida, how I'd sit and chat with many a different person, establishing, 'coffee house friendships,' to me, a quite common phenomenon, meaning, although we enjoy each others company and chat a lot while we're there, outside that environment, together, we really don't pass a care, yet still, they flooded in, those memories spent in that warmer climate, in that café I used to frequent, with joy, peace and comfort it brought me, and as I paused for a while and mused over them, with sincere gladness in my heart, I quite quickly surmised, how facing those pitfalls, and climbing those mountains and overcoming those torrents of storms, as relentlessly, step-by-step I'd trampled upon my path, and how magnificently, as I was so much further along my journey of recovery, than I had any notion I was, as in the distance behind me, lay those circumstances of adversity, as they proved no-longer to be my 'life as I knew it,' but only a fading and unfortunate start to it.

> *Learn from yesterday, live for today, hope for tomorrow.*
> *The important thing is not to stop questioning.*
> *~ Albert Einstein*

But right then, it was that narrow *petite rue*, which I was secretly convinced was cobbled on my previous visit, and there a collage to see, where tourists and Parisians, were so effortlessly interweaving, and with precision timing, mingling to and fro, as within only a matter of millimeters, mayhem and collisions were avoided, as cyclists raced about their business, not even seeming to apply their breaks as through the crowds, they darted in an out, as scooters swayed from side to side, not slowing down or even tooting their horns, as at substantial speed, as between those copious people they maneuvered skillfully around, and more astonishingly, the motorcycles did the same, as their speed was not even reduced or horns tooted, to alert pedestrians to be careful as they too sped into the crowd, but somehow, all made their way out safely, as not an accident or even a near-miss was I ever to have witnessed, as all appearing, with precision timing, delightful equaling the skilled choreography, of many a West-End show.

And what about *la femme*, the women, so gracious in their appearance, as if the last few hundred years, since the storming of the *Bastille* in 1789, where the working class took-over the city, holding little residue impact, in the realms of elegance, as the way they carried themselves, with a subtle demeanor, and rather regal, with more than a whispering hint of quite yet substantial grandeur from yesteryear, as there was no barrier for 'women of a certain age,' of how absolutely stunning was their appearance, as a pristine matching ensemble was readily guaranteed, as for many a Parisian woman, the temperature, never to low to display or show, their shapely legs covered by opaque *collants*, pantyhose, with their skirt lengths often settling slightly higher than the knee, maybe with ankle-boots, while for warmth of security, wrapping tightly around, a rather stylish tailored coat, often in classic camel or light brown, and of all to view, it was my own appearance I gave contemplation to, which in recent years, well "I'd let it go a little," so resoundingly, a note-to-self, once again, I was to 'up my game.'

Then, how lovely to observe those women of maturity, as each one exuded, a natural glow, appearing so healthy, with well-moisturized smooth skin, without a hint of a wrinkle, or a sign of a surgeon's knife, as their *maquillage,* make-up, so subtle and fresh, blended effortlessly as if on an artists canvas. And so easy to see, their hair, simply striking, as so well groomed, and always most flattering, often styled in gentle, loose soft curls, in length, sweeping past the shoulder, and in those brisk Parisian breezes, it flowed and twizzled behind them, and all for quick observation, as with a spring in their step, they hurried on by, perhaps with a purpose or a place they needed to be.

Lingering in Paris so long, well long for a tourist, as in those few days I'd got to know a few French people, who'd pass me by and bid a casual, "ça va?" "All right?" Or a more formal greeting, of "Bonne *journée,*" have a good day, and with increasing familiarity, *"Comment vas-tu?"* "How are you?" was spoken from a person I knew a little better, so enquiring after my well being, that gentleman, Parisian born and bread, a quite uncommon phenomenon, as is the case so often as in big cities, people are 'imports' from somewhere else, yet he, a man of a certain age, I knew him from way back in my *la Sorbonne*, days, and in the evenings when my studies were done, I'd escape to that wonderful place of *Café Laurent* at *Hotel d'Aubusson*, where at the end of the bar he'd stand, consumed several flutes of champagne, as he who understood nothing of what I said, with his younger friend who spoke exceptionally good English, most nightly, after a difficult day trying to learn French was done, to unwind, and immerse myself in relaxation, as with them, I was able to enjoy, plentiful, joviality and laughter.

There on the pavement we stood, as a conversation we pursued, and I so hoped to show him, that indeed, at last my French has improved, so as I spoke the best *langue française* I could muster, he listened intently, and "Oh how lovely," when an agreeable sigh was his response, and I 'think' he knew most of what I was talking about, yet when all else failed, I pleaded *"Exuze moi."* "Sorry," and true, exactly how much he understood of what I said, of my verbs, conjunctions, and perhaps worse, my under established pronunciation, as really, neither were guaranteed, but still, after the passing of those 5 years, it was so nice to see him and to enjoy a conversation, to check-out how he was, and if he was well and happy.

So void of that correct pronunciation for communication, a different tactic I'd observed and adopted, that when in doubt, to influx my words in all the right places, I tried, though still, not fail proof, so another tactic to employ, learning by what I saw, I engaged a further trick, which actually began to equal, in most circumstances, as my backup plan and default mechanism, and "Scientific?" certainly it was not, as simply it comprised, of what I had come to recognize, as a quaint essential *Gallic* shrug, accompanied by raised eyebrows and a frown, where the mouth, to pucker the lips, while somehow simultaneously contorting, that the corners dip down and the edges, then with a tilt of my head, before a pause, for effect, astonishingly, amusingly, "Yeah!" I don't know how, but agreeing, the French appeared to know exactly what I'd said.

Time was a-beckoning, time to begin my new daily ritual of taking a leisurely stroll *à côté de* along the banks, of the river *Seine*, all seeming quite jolly, as someone on-route caught my attention, a man at whom I did not want to stare, with his persona so relaxed and debonair, he sat with his companion at a café on *rue de Bucci*, at one of those petite, only big enough for 2 cups of coffee, round terrace tables, so unusually classic, I was seduced to observe a little more, as his appearance quite appealing as so casually he sat, understated, yet with an extravagant panache, leaning back in his chair, as one leg he crossed over the other, with his hand out-stretching holding his coffee cup, so distinctive in his *pantalon*, trousers, well actually, jeans in silver-grey, and detailed on the fabric, were subtle yet obvious patterns of poses and roses, in pinks and violets with pale crimson too, appearing to fit him quite well, as they tapered in at his ankle, where he sported, a stylish pair, of well polished, tan, laced-up shoes.

Then keeping him warm, his fawn tweed jacket, where under it, almost buttoned up to the neck, with only 3 buttons to spare, a pale blue checked shirt, trimmed on the inside collar, with a gentle red shade of gingham, with a scarf, looking like cashmere, well of cause, was strewn nonchalantly around his neck, while appearing precisely positioned, and in the absence of that quaint essential Parisian man's hat, in that mildly turbulent Parisian breeze, his light, lush, brown, soft locks, were left loose to flow and blow in the air, and "Oh my" in my vision, it only lasted for a few moments, yet in-design, so fine and appealing, the colors in harmony, the aesthetics of the way 'he put his ensemble together,' so pleasing to my eyes, and reminiscing of what I saw, significantly, it was resonating to my core, as so interestingly, it was the same satisfying emotion, of when in my own homes, I'd have my own preferred décor surrounding me, as I was able in quiet solace, to bath, absorb and enjoy it all, everyday.

Paris, thank goodness, still held an allure of something, that was to able to captivate me emotionally and intellectually, though true, I was most keen to leave, but there seemed to be an invisible force holding me there, but "What?" and perhaps I should have gave some thought to the concept, "Was I missing a subliminal message?" or possibly, "Was I waiting on synchronicity when synchronicity was waiting on me?" Questions, yet no answers forthcoming, and I tried so hard to work it all out, so with all else failing, at last, I made a choice to masterfully force the matter, deciding I was to move-on to something else, figuring that, having done all the tourist 'things,' though true, on my list of things to do, still I missed-out on taking a train ride, to visit the *Château de Versailles*, as my only daily adventures, evolved to be, wandering through those Parisian streets, apparently wasting money, then quite interesting, as quite oddly, it all came together, and I began to wonder, "When we take heart and make a decision, will it happen, that something or someone, situations that evaded us before, will come up and meet us?" As on the morning of my departure, a young lady at my preferred café, and previously, her and I had enjoyed light pleasantries, for some apparent reason, actually posed the question, "Daily, what is it you do here?"

Then smiling, I was as always proud to share, with her and everyone else, the purpose of my time spent relaxing, and as she spoke no English, in my very best French I was explaining, *"Avant que j'étais infirmière, maintenant je suis un écrivain,"* "Before I was a nurse, now I am a writer." Her ignited interest, clearly shown on by her facial expression, as quickly following, "On what subject are you writing?" Then with caution I preceded, as I have come to realize, sometimes, that with the genre, the topic, by their response, people seem to feel uncomfortable, so caution, and of cause, using my best possible verbs and key *mots*, words, explaining, *enfants parents et son mari*, children, parents and husband, *battre*, batter, with accompanying hand gestures, seemed to get the message clearly across, as she understood and was sympathetic too, and how extremely wonderful, swiftly, she offered me a pen and paper, requesting of my name, book title and "Where?" she was to buy it.

How amazing, as 'that' situation, appeared to unfold almost perfectly, almost subliminally, and somehow I knew that was somehow the moment I'd been awaiting, before I could get the heck out of Paris, of "Oh how fortunate am I?" that she like so many others, who have enquired of what I am doing, resonates extraordinarily, with those in her age group, of 20-something, as consistently they are so very keen to read a copy, and then that *jeune femme*, young lady, turned to her male colleague, he of a similar age, who stood behind preparing serves of coffee, he too on the topic showed significant enthusiasm, and how gladly I received such notification, that it was not just my imagination, but compounding knowledge, resonating deep in my soul and every tissue in my body, that certainly, it may not be by accident but on purpose that I, have travelled, around the world writing, making acquaintances and friends here and there, as such a positive 'buzz' of energy, on this serious genre, has encapsulated this work, it, designed to deliver a hugely important message, yet true, still holding snippets of humor, and so, reinvigorated, through all the uncertainly and 'trials and tribs' that were going before me, I was to carry-on, doing all I possibly could to publish this book: "Until I Flew… & On The Inside; Became Beautiful!" because with inner and loving power, it became my life's work, to enable others, to make positive changes and immense differences, in their lives, as they consider, "What to do?" and really, "Where to from here?"

Sincerely, I so hoped so, from her enthusiasm of all I spoke, that substantially so, she would pass that information onto others, to maximum the capacity, to try and help the most, and then following her request of exchanging of contact details I gladly assured her, "Soon, the book will be published." And then, in the oddest kind of way, a strange concept crept over me, that to make that connection with that particular waitress before I was to depart Paris, was somehow significant, though I knew not "Why?" and not contemplating it too much, as I chose to let it settle, where it fell, it was a cup of hot water in hand, I was to leave that café, bidding her a fond farewell, feeling perfectly peaceful, that somehow, my mission there was completed, so it was off to go to the *gare*, train station, that afternoon, to travel and discover, in the south west of France, "What was to greet me?"

So "Was I lucky?" or "Was it simple scenario, of preparation and opportunity gelling together?" or "Was it all because, of a much greater force than me in operation, enabling 'that,' all to happen?" as really, "Was it all for a plan and a purpose that gladly, simply and hopefully, or reluctantly I was following?" or "Perhaps by mistake or by design, I was the one who just happened to be in the right place at the right time?" as I was becoming increasingly able, to share with others the benefits of my experience, in the realms of insight, foresight and hindsight?" Really, as I had dared to follow my dream, and accomplished such huge leaps and bounds in my recovery, from "Where I was to where I deserved and desired to be," that I, could be so blessed, to make a resounding difference, to help others, who had not yet taken *their* first or tentative step, upon *their* journey, to discover, their own, personal, awaiting recovery.

Ladies and gentlemen, to you who are reading, I thank you so much for getting to the end of this book, as so truly I so desire for you, that through understanding my experiences, and from my stories, many lessons, you may be able to accrue, as a pinprick of light was pierced into that darkest deepest place, where previously, to examine it, you shunned from it; yet now I so sincerely hope, that at last, you have begun to recognize, with greater clarity, those hindering patterns of revolving cycles, perhaps identifying circumstances in your life, that may require mild or astute attention, for you to successfully move yourself away, from those hazards and risks, of thorns of distress, as boldly or subtly, you sever those suckers, draining your life's nutrients, as in your life, far less likely, that people will harm you financially, emotionally or physically, as you become, stronger and wiser, creating a bouquet of fragrant flowers of peace and happiness, with delightful aromas, of gentle inner-power of safety and security, for you to rest, relish, admire and enjoy your progress, day by day.

Please, please, be absolute, in your commitment, to not permitting your surroundings, past or present circumstances, or those people who so negatively impacted, so many of your yesterdays, to permit them to permeate or discouragingly, influence your today, or in the comings of all your tomorrows, to in any way prevent you from becoming, all that you are wonderfully made and able to be. As *triumphantly* you, *seize* upon *your* possibility, perpetuating permanent, *value to add to your life*, as your steps begin and your process unravels, as you learn to encourage yourself, enabling an ever *increasingly* permeating, into your life, pleasant and *prosperous*, for you to *pursue*, not by accident, but most definitely, and absolutely, *by purpose*.

Do this because, "You're worth it!" as through it, you'll hold your greatest inner-strength and inner-power you may ever possess, and never again will you 'refuse to settle for less' or 'digress from achieving the *your very best*.' So please, 'resist to permit' time to effortlessly pass you by, or suffer prolonged strife, as I, now healing more and growing better, as through clearer vision I chose no-longer to stare ineffectively into oblivion, and I beseech you, please for the benefits of the lessons or notions I have passed though, be speedier than I, of their uptake and application, to be integrated into your life, and "Please, please, seek until you find, and let no-other intimidate or control you, nor waste any more time trying to make yourself fit into life, when really, life should be fitting into you."

Way back when, this story first began, not a snippet of a notion did I hold that my life was ever going to get better, nor indeed did I hold any knowledge that there was even an other option, or more so, that I deserved to receive it, and certainly of what I have achieved thus far, was even actually possible; yet, away from that dangerous, dark and dismal place I removed myself, as I rejected the past and for a fine celebration, rejoiced with elation as *desire* and *anticipation* become my trusty companions, blossoming and flourishing, as on the softest of summer breezes, and luxurious shimmering sunbeams, *hope* was gently swirling, lavishingly nurturing, all that was necessary, for my glisteningly bright and abundantly wonderful future.

For that road I have trampled upon, where my footprints have now faded from, of that process to success, with those achievements to possess, a formula tried and tested, so "Please please let me encourage you, as what I have achieved, *YOU* can do too!"

And "Oh my" how wonderfully 'worth-it' this journey has been, as through the commitment of all my time and effort, I now am able to reap my rewards in full, as my heart soars and my soul is restored, as here I am, feeling so much better and so much further along my journey, as: *"WORTHY AM I"* of recovery.

May God Bless You abundantly for a brighter and improved future.

"Failure is the Master of Expertise."
~ Carole Jordan

"Let my pain be used for purpose"

Carole ☺

Notes

May they Bless Your Recovery

Acknowledgements

&

Thanks

To:

God, I give the glory, honor and praise, that 'I made it thus far!'
For now I may continue along my life's journey, with my soul renewed,
and with joy and peace in my heart.
&
Thank you again; for all I am, and all I am yet to be.

Grandma, who I believed loved me, who showed me affection, and
with whom I felt not judged.

Brent, my friend in New Zealand, who when I told him of this book I
so desired to write, I received encouragement: a completely new experience
for me, so enabling that seed to be nurtured as onto fertile ground it was
to fall; and perhaps, that is why right now,
that you are able to read this book:
My life's work, my life's call.

Bible References:
www.biblehub.com
www.biblegateway.com

Quotes Ref:
www.goodreads.com
www.brainyquote.com

Prelude/Paris Research:
www.enwikipedia.org

Google Tradition:
www.translate.google.com

Thesaurus:
Apple MacBook Air

www.ingramcontent.com/pod-product-compliance
Lightning Source LLC
Chambersburg PA
CBHW020631230426
43665CB00008B/125